# NEW YORK SPORTS

## Other Titles in This Series

*LA Sports: Play, Games, and Community in the City of Angels*

*Making March Madness:*
*The Early Years of the NCAA, NIT,*
*and College Basketball Championships, 1922–1951*

*San Francisco Bay Area Sports:*
*Golden Gate Athletics, Recreation, and Community*

*Separate Games:*
*African American Sport behind the Walls of Segregation*

*Baltimore Sports:*
*Stories from Charm City*

*Philly Sports: Teams, Games, and Athletes from Rocky's Town*

*DC Sports: The Nation's Capital at Play*

*Frank Merriwell and the Fiction of All-American Boyhood*

*Democratic Sports: Men's and Women's College Athletics*

*Sport and the Law: Historical and Cultural Intersections*

*Beyond C. L. R. James:*
*Shifting Boundaries of Race and Ethnicity in Sports*

*A Spectacular Leap:*
*Black Women Athletes in Twentieth-Century America*

*Hoop Crazy: The Lives of Clair Bee and Chip Hilton*

# NEW YORK SPORTS

## Glamour and Grit in the Empire City

Edited by Stephen H. Norwood

THE UNIVERSITY OF ARKANSAS PRESS
FAYETTEVILLE 2018

Manufactured in the United States of America

ISBN: 978-1-68226-059-3
eISBN: 978-1-61075-635-8

22 21 20 19 18 5 4 3 2 1

Designer: Jamie McKee

♾ The paper used in this publication meets the minimum requirements of the American National Standard for Permanence of Paper for Printed Library Materials Z39.48–1984.

Library of Congress Control Number: 2017954092

# Contents

# Series Editor's Preface

At its most fundamental level, sport has the power to bring people great joy and satisfy their competitive urges while at once allowing them to form bonds and a sense of community with others of diverse backgrounds and interests. Sport also makes clear, especially at the highest levels of competition, the lengths that people will go to achieve victory. Closely connected to business, education, politics, economics, religion, law, family, and other societal institutions, sport is partly about identity development and reveals how individuals and groups, irrespective of race, gender, ethnicity or socio-economic class, have sought to elevate their status and realize material success and social mobility.

*Sport, Culture, and Society* seeks to promote a greater understanding of the aforementioned issues and many others. Recognizing sport's powerful influence and ability to change people's lives in significant and important ways, the series focuses on topics ranging from urbanization and community development to biographies and intercollegiate athletics. It includes monographs and anthologies that are characterized by excellent scholarship, accessible to a wide audience, and thoughtful in design and interpretation. Singular features of the series are authors and editors representing a variety of disciplinary areas and who adopt different methodological approaches. The series also includes works by individuals at various stages of their careers, from sport studies scholars of outstanding talent just beginning to make their mark on the field to more experienced scholars of sport with established reputations.

*New York Sports: Glamour and Grit in the Empire City* provides important insights into the role and meaning of sport in one of the most influential and powerful cities in the world. Edited by Stephen H. Norwood—a well-known academician who has edited and authored a number of books and published many book chapters and scholarly articles on sport, Jewish history, Labor history, and an assortment of other topics—has put together a collection of fourteen essays by skilled writers that makes clear how important sport has always been in New York City. Careful to put their essays in proper historical context, and providing thoughtful and fresh interpretations, the authors cover topics that will hold interest for both academic and popular audiences along with those fascinated by sport in an urban setting or at various levels of competition. Among the topics addressed are the life and times of football icon Joe Namath, the New York Yankees and Brooklyn Dodgers rivalry, football's New York Giants, histories of the New York City Marathon and Belmont Stakes, the influence of Stillman's Gym, and the contributions of Jews and Italians to the city's sporting life. In all, the collection furnishes the story of sport in New York City that has never been told in such depth and with such obvious appreciation for the great athletes and teams that have graced the playing fields, hard courts, and tracks in the famous metropolis variously termed Gotham, the City That Never Sleeps, the Big Apple, and Empire City.

David K. Wiggins

# NEW YORK SPORTS

INTRODUCTION

# New York City

## Capital of Sports

*Stephen H. Norwood*

Following the 1976 Major League Baseball season, Reggie Jackson, the "most glamorous name" among the first players in the sport to become free agents, chose to sign with the New York Yankees, passing over offers from several other teams that were two to three million dollars higher. Jackson wanted to play in the city that he and nearly everybody else considered the pinnacle of the American sports world. "If I played in New York," he had presciently remarked, "they would name a candy bar for me." Not much more than a year later, after Jackson blasted three home runs off three Dodgers pitchers in the sixth and deciding World Series game, each of them on the first pitch, Standard Brands announced that it was bringing out a new *Reggie* bar.[1]

Although New York is America's leading cultural center, with theaters, concert halls, museums, art galleries, and film houses providing diversion and major social and learning opportunities, sports has held its own as a principal leisure pursuit. New York has had more championship teams than any other city, topped by the Yankees' forty pennants and twenty-seven World Series titles, far outdistancing the totals for any other major league club. New York teams faced each other in fourteen "subway" World Series. There have been only two other intracity World Series, one in St. Louis and the other in Chicago. For more than half a century, when baseball was America's national pastime, New York had three major league baseball teams, the only city ever to enjoy that distinction.[2] More important boxing matches have been staged in New York than in any other city. New York boasts one of the world's two leading marathon races. It has also been a major center for horse racing, and hosts the Belmont Stakes, the third event in the sport's Triple Crown. Since the nineteenth century, New York has been the capital of the nation's sporting press.

More of America's most storied sports arenas have been located in New York than in any other city. It was the home of three legendary baseball stadiums: Yankee Stadium, the Polo Grounds, and Ebbets Field. All three were also the home grounds of New York professional football teams, and the sites of major college football games. The former two hosted some of the most dramatic boxing matches in history, like Joe Louis's two bouts with Max Schmeling at Yankee Stadium in 1936 and 1938, and Jack Dempsey's slugfest with Luis Firpo at the Polo Grounds in 1923, the subject of a famous painting by George Bellows of the Ash Can school. When pugilism thrived it was every boxer's dream to fight in Madison Square Garden, America's leading site for indoor athletic contests.[3] The Garden hosted thirty-two title fights between 1925 and 1945, seven of them in the heavyweight division. Rocky Marciano's nationally televised bout against Joe Louis in 1951 that marked the end of the Brown Bomber's career was staged there, as was the first Muhammad Ali–Joe Frazier fight, in 1971. The Garden was the longtime "mecca" of college basketball (until the 1950s), and of indoor track and field contests. Teams from all over the country played double-headers against the New York colleges before sellout crowds. Professional basketball's New York Knickerbockers have played most of their home games at the Garden since the National Basketball Association was formed in 1949. The Garden also provided the home ice for New York's two National Hockey League entries, the Americans (1925–1942) and the Rangers (since 1926).[4]

More memorable events in sports have occurred in New York than in any other city. These include Bobby Thomson's pennant-winning "shot heard round the world" at the Polo Grounds, in the 1951 National League's deciding playoff game, arguably the most dramatic single play in baseball (and possibly American sports) history, and Johnny Unitas's guiding the Baltimore Colts on their "thirteen steps to glory" at Yankee Stadium to win the first National Football League (NFL) championship that ended in sudden death overtime. To this day, the NFL touts it as "The Greatest Game Ever Played." Many sports historians and journalists argue that the nationally televised game contributed more than any other single event to pro football's displacing major league baseball as the nation's most popular sport. New York Yankee Don Larsen pitched the only perfect game in World Series history, against the Brooklyn Dodgers at Yankee Stadium in 1956. Babe Ruth of the Yankees, more than any other individual, transformed baseball by making the home run a central offensive weapon. In 1961, two other Yankees, Roger Maris and Mickey Mantle, the "M & M Boys," captured national attention by challenging Ruth's single-season home run record of sixty, with Maris surpassing it at Yankee Stadium in the season's last game.

Perhaps the most historically significant athletic contest in American history, which transcended sports, occurred in New York: Joe Louis's first-round demolition of German heavyweight Max Schmeling in their rematch at Yankee Stadium in June 1938. For many, in both the United States and the Third Reich, the bout was a symbolic battle between democracy and Nazism, and dealt a stinging blow to Hitler's doctrine of Aryan supremacy. Louis's dramatic victory over Schmeling, who had received a hero's welcome from Hitler when he returned to the Reich after knocking Louis out in their first bout in 1936, electrified African Americans and Jewish communities on both sides of the Atlantic. In Paris's "Little Harlem" section, Jewish refugees who had managed to escape from Nazi Germany joined blacks in a "loud and merry celebration" that lasted two days. Many have referred to the fight as the first battle of World War II.[5] David Margolick noted that more people tuned in to the bout on the radio than heard any of President Franklin D. Roosevelt's fireside chats, and cited an estimate that more journalists were present at the fight than at the signing of the Versailles Peace Treaty.[6] New York antifascist activists were the driving force behind the movement to boycott the 1936 Berlin Olympic Games, which the Hitler regime turned into a propaganda festival for the Third Reich. Jackie Robinson broke major league baseball's longtime color line as a member of one of New York's teams, the Brooklyn Dodgers, in 1947, one of the most important civil rights achievements of the first half of the twentieth century.

More episodes allegedly causing players intense shame, but certainly deeply etched in fans' memory, have occurred in New York than anywhere else, although they merely involved an error, or what fans perceived to be a mistake or mental lapse, on the playing field. These included Fred Merkle's "bonehead" play in 1908, which contributed to the New York Giants' loss of the pennant to the Chicago Cubs; Mickey Owen's passed ball at Ebbets Field in the ninth inning of game four of the 1941 World Series against the Yankees, which undermined Brooklyn's momentum in the Series; Ralph Branca's home run pitch to Bobby Thomson in the 1951 National League playoffs; and Bill Buckner's tenth-inning error at Shea Stadium, when his Boston Red Sox were poised to win the 1986 World Series against the New York Mets.

New York was closely connected to what were probably the three most serious American sports betting scandals, involving basketball, baseball, and football. The 1950–1951 college basketball point-shaving scandal badly tarnished the programs at City College of New York, Manhattan College, New York University, and Long Island University, along with those of colleges far from New York: the University of Kentucky, the University of Toledo, and Bradley University. It is the second-most widely known American sports gambling scandal. Much of the preparation for the Black Sox Scandal, the most famous, took place in New York. The eight Chicago White Sox players participating in the effort to fix the 1919 World Series against the Cincinnati Reds made plans at Manhattan's Ansonia Hotel. New York gamblers were prominently involved in the conspiracy to throw the Series. The mastermind was likely Arnold Rothstein, one of New York's major organized crime figures. The only betting scandal involving a National Football League championship contest centered on New York. In 1946, a professional gambler offered two members of the New York Giants backfield, Frank Filchock and Merle Hapes, a bribe to make sure that their opponent, the Chicago Bears, won by at least ten points. Both players refused the bribe, but did not report it to the Giants coaches or front office, NFL authorities, or law enforcement.[7]

Yankee Stadium was the first sports arena to emphasize the importance of historical memory by establishing cemetery-style monuments in center field to commemorate its greatest deceased players, managers, and executives. The first one, placed in 1932, was for former manager Miller Huggins. It would be flanked by monuments for Lou Gehrig and Babe Ruth—the heart of "Murderers' Row"—immediately after their deaths, in 1941 and 1949, respectively. The widows of these two Yankee greats regularly attended games into the 1970s, and television cameras often focused on them seated in the stands, establishing a continuity going back to the 1920s. In 1969, the players considered the Yankees' greatest stars since Ruth and Gehrig, Joe DiMaggio and Mickey Mantle, presented each other with plaques that were attached to the outfield wall near the three monuments. In 1985, the monuments and plaques were shifted to a new Monument Park within the stadium, open to fans.[8] In the last few decades, other teams have copied the Yankees in placing the names of their former stars on the outfield fences. The Yankees also pioneered in staging Old Timers' games, another link to a glorious past.

The New York Mets, one of the two expansion teams added to the National League in 1962, also emphasized historic continuity by reviving the name of one of New York's late nineteenth-century teams, the Metropolitans, who played in the American Association, one of two major leagues at the time, from 1883 through 1887.[9] To further emphasize continuity, the Mets' uniforms merged the orange and royal-blue colors of New York's two departed National League franchises, the Giants and the Dodgers.

In a 1971 article entitled "The Year the Yankees Beat Lincoln Center," *New York Times* music critic Harold C. Schonberg commented that the needs of the city's major sports teams took precedence over those of its principal cultural and intellectual facilities. With New York in dire financial straits, "all but bankrupt," Mayor John Lindsay announced that the city would buy Yankee Stadium and refurbish it, at a cost of $24 million, in order to keep the Yankees (then owned by the Columbia Broadcasting System) and the NFL's Giants in town. Probably more than any other mayor, Lindsay had glamorized New York by highlighting Manhattan's cultural activities. Schonberg argued that Manhattan's Lincoln Center for the Performing Arts, home of the New York Philharmonic Orchestra, the Metropolitan Opera, and the New York City ballet, which was also badly in need of funds, dwarfed Yankee Stadium in importance. Lincoln Center was New York's second-largest tourist attraction after the United Nations, and had contributed more to the city's tax revenue than Yankee Stadium. Yet it did not receive similar consideration from the mayor. Schonberg also emphasized that unlike Yankee Stadium, the New York Public Library's research facilities had been shut down on weekends because of insufficient funds. An enormous sum of money was available to support big-time sports, while New York's subway and hospital systems were collapsing.[10]

New York has been America's center for sports journalism since its emergence. Its sports media has provided more publicity for athletic contests and achievement than has been available anywhere else. Most leading sports periodicals have been headquartered in New York, beginning with the *Spirit of the Times*, founded in 1831. The *New York Clipper*, established in 1853, was the first publication to carry box scores of baseball games, in the 1860s. Richard Kyle Fox's *National Police Gazette* was the premier sports magazine of the late nineteenth century.[11] Nat Fleischer's *The Ring*, founded in 1922, supplanted the *Police Gazette* as the nation's leading boxing magazine, a status it held for the next half century. The two most prominent sports magazines of the second half of the twentieth century, *Sport* and *Sports Illustrated*, founded in 1947 and 1954 respectively, were headquartered in New York.

New York's nineteenth-century sports periodicals, located in the nation's most important commercial and financial center, were in the forefront of introducing into athletic competition standard and precise measurements that were increasingly used in trade. Richard Kyle Fox introduced championship belts for six weight divisions, making bouts more intensely competitive. By providing opportunities for lighter fighters, the new weight divisions led to a greater focus on agility and counterpunching, resulting in an improved "product."[12] William B. Curtis, editor of the *Spirit of the Times*, pushed for the use of standard distances in track events, rather than adjusting distance to the peculiarities of each meet site. Curtis also lobbied for stopwatches that could measure time more exactly, down to the tenth of a second.[13]

The city is notable for its sportswriters' talent and influence, and many of its columnists have been nationally syndicated. Four of the six sportswriters awarded the Pulitzer Prize were *New York Times* columnists or writers.[14] One of them was Red Smith of the *New York Herald Tribune* (1945–1966), the *World Journal Tribune* (1966–1967), and the *New York Times* (1971–1982), whose writing Ernest Hemingway praised in his novel *Across the River and into the Trees*. Smith taught a weekly seminar at Yale University on "Sports in American Society." The University of Notre Dame awarded him an honorary doctorate.[15]

Smith left the *Philadelphia Record* for the *Herald Tribune* because New York "meant success and wonder"; writing for a newspaper there was like "Playing the Palace." Fred Russell, longtime sportswriter for the *Nashville Banner* and considered one of the South's best sports journalists, stated that Smith was so outstanding that newspapers throughout the country would purchase his syndicated column just to preempt competing newspapers in their cities from doing so. Smith believed that New York was the best place in America to write a sports column because there was always so much going on there in the sports world: "All you need is a good pair of legs—or taxi fare." Russell commented that New York "reeks with outstanding sports personalities, both resident and transient."[16]

Many of the New York sports journalists wrote about subjects that transcended sports. Stanley Woodward, sports editor of the *New York Herald Tribune* from 1930 to 1948, and again from 1959 to 1962, in May 1947 broke the story that the St. Louis Cardinals had planned to strike rather than play against a Brooklyn Dodgers team that included Jackie Robinson. Woodward's exclusive, entitled "One Strike Is Out," was unanimously selected for a major journalism prize by a panel of three distinguished writers: Franklin Pierce Adams, a member of the Algonquin Round Table, the famed literary set of the 1920s; John Chamberlain; and Quentin Reynolds.[17]

Woodward's approach as sports editor, consistent with that of the *Herald Tribune* in other realms, was to "cover sports on a national, even an international basis." At Amherst College Woodward had studied non-Shakespearean Elizabethan drama under Robert Frost. His staff at the *Herald Tribune* included the very talented Jesse Abramson, whom he considered the most versatile sports reporter and columnist he knew. Red Smith, who wrote Abramson's obituary, called him the nation's leading track and field writer, but noted that "many editors believed he was just as good writing about boxing and college football." Roger Kahn, who also wrote about major social issues including civil rights, began his career under Woodward at the *Herald Tribune*. Kahn later wrote what is arguably the most insightful book about baseball players, *The Boys of Summer*, on selected members of the Brooklyn Dodgers in the 1940s and 1950s and on their years after baseball. Kahn described his editor as "a scholar and innovator" who "assembled the finest sports staff in the country." Woodward pored over out-of-town newspapers, and set up files in which he placed sports stories that he considered particularly well written and perceptive. If the writer's work was "consistently excellent," Woodward hired him. In this manner he located a premier racing columnist, Joe H. Palmer, a PhD candidate.[18]

New York also produced a new breed of sportswriters in the 1960s and 1970s known as the Chipmunks, who introduced a much more irreverent view of athletes, and gave considerable attention to off-the-field issues, public and private. They explored how larger social, cultural, and political issues influenced sports. The Chipmunks' relationship with the sports establishment and with the athletes themselves was often contentious. Mostly Jewish, the Chipmunks included Leonard Shecter, Larry Merchant, and Maury Allen, all of the *New York Post*, and Stan Isaacs of *Newsday*, published on Long Island but with a sizable readership in the city of New York. Shecter collaborated with Jim Bouton on the 1970 best-seller *Ball Four*, which exposed players' immature behavior off the field, as well as racism and labor exploitation in the sport.[19]

The *Friday Night Fights*, broadcast live from Madison Square Garden, was at the time of its cancellation in September 1964, television's longest-running sports program. This was one of the major programs at the dawn of the television age. The television networks were centered in New York, and sporting events at the time were relatively inexpensive to broadcast. The first Friday night fight televised from the Garden, by NBC's New York station, pitted Willie Pep against Chalky Wright in September 1944. The telecasts were picked up by NBC's national network in 1946 and had a significant viewing audience by the late 1940s, considering the relatively small number of television sets to which people had access at the time. The appeal of *Friday Night Fights* undoubtedly spurred the sales of television sets. CBS in New York, impressed by NBC's success with *Friday Night Fights,* began televising a Wednesday night boxing series in 1949. Televised boxing contributed to the swift decline of neighborhood boxing clubs in all American cities. *Friday Night Fights* shifted from NBC to ABC in 1960. ABC's *Friday Night Fights* included the welterweight title bout between Emile Griffith and Benny Paret on March 24, 1962, one of the most famous fights of the postwar era, which resulted in Paret's death. ABC terminated the program in 1964, largely because of declining public interest in boxing and the proliferation of television shows, which provided viewers with a much wider choice of what to watch.[20]

During this period ABC-radio also broadcast nationally from New York two heavyweight title fights between Floyd Patterson, an American, and Ingemar Johansson, a Swede, staged in June 1959 and June 1960, with Les Keiter narrating blow-by-blow, and Howard Cosell doing the color commentary. The first bout, which took place at Yankee Stadium, was notable as the first heavyweight championship fight since 1933 won by a non-American, significant at a time when the title was a highly coveted symbol of national prestige. In the third round, Johansson knocked Patterson out with his "Hammer of Thor" right hand. The heavyweight title's departure from the United States at the height of the Cold War traumatized many Americans. Patterson won the rematch a year later with a fifth-round knockout at the Polo Grounds. He was the first fighter to regain the heavyweight crown, a goal that had eluded many previous boxers, including Jack Dempsey and Joe Louis.[21]

New York's media dominance caused considerable resentment outside the metropolitan area. Journalists claimed that this predominance resulted in insufficient attention to players in other cities while puffing up the reputations of players on New York teams. CBS-TV's 1960 documentary *The Violent World of Sam Huff,* for example, helped make the New York Giants middle linebacker the most famous defensive player in pro football. Nonetheless, the *Chicago Tribune* dismissed Huff as "Madison Avenue's idea of a linebacker."[22]

New York was distinctive in having the only team named for a borough, the Brooklyn Dodgers, a sign that baseball in the city enjoyed a particularly close bond with its followers. Brooklyn came across as raffish, irreverent, and sometimes zany. The team's nickname, "Dem Bums," suggested a close connection to ordinary working- and lower-middle-class urban Americans. Fans developed particularly strong attachments to players who often lived in close proximity to their neighborhoods and rode the subway to the ballpark. Red Barber, the Dodgers radio broadcaster from 1939 to 1953, declared: "I've never seen a community that was so attached to a team, or grieved so much when it left." Robert Creamer recalled that in the summer of 1941 you did not need to own a radio to hear Barber broadcast the Dodgers game: "You could walk up a street and hear the game through one open window after another and never miss a pitch."[23]

In a *Twilight Zone* script entitled "The Mighty Casey," aired nationally on CBS-TV on June 17, 1960, Rod Serling conveyed how the Dodgers' departure from Brooklyn in 1957 for "soulless" Southern California symbolized the disappearance of passion and authenticity from baseball. This was reflected in the sport's recent construction of symmetrical "cookie cutter" stadiums in bland suburban locales in cities like Los Angeles, remote and often inaccessible to working-class and lower-middle-class big-city residents. Serling has a scientist create a robot, whom he names Casey, who looks human and is a phenomenal pitcher. The robot becomes the ace of a team clearly modeled on the Brooklyn Dodgers. (In the short-story version Serling explicitly gives the team that name.) Casey racks up victory after victory, until well into the season a ball strikes him in the head, knocking him unconscious. It is discovered that he is a robot, and under the National League rules he is ineligible to play because he is not human. But the scientist implants a heart in Casey. Unfortunately, this makes him compassionate, and he is no longer willing to strike batters out.

The episode concluded with a statement meant to contrast Brooklyn's vitality and spontaneity in the 1950s with Southern California's sterility. Viewers were informed that the ball club moved to the West Coast, where it won "several pennants and a couple of world championships," led by a new staff of pitchers, robots made to look like men. None of them "smiled very much but . . . they pitched like nothing human." Viewers curious as to where these pitchers were from were invited to "check B for Baseball—in the Twilight Zone."[24]

*Los Angeles Times* staff reporter Josh Getlin found "noisy, scruffy and wonderfully intimate" Ebbets Field in Brooklyn far more appealing than Los Angeles's Dodger Stadium at Chavez Ravine, which he described as "beautiful but boring, a gorgeous dame with nothing upstairs." Getlin quoted a Brooklyn transplant living in Santa Monica, California, Ira Shepnick, who maintained that Los Angeles "fans are so boring, you could nap at Chavez Ravine, even with the bases loaded." Shepnick recalled that "the sheer noise of a game at Ebbets Field was unforgettable." The singer Carly Simon, an honorary Brooklyn

Dodgers bat girl in 1954, described Ebbets Field fans "hooting at enemy ballplayers and bickering in the bleachers over baseball strategy." It was a highly emotional atmosphere, "like a big Italian opera house." Tickets were priced much more cheaply in Brooklyn "so you didn't have to be a big shot to get good seats."[25] Frequent blaring of trumpets to prompt yells of "Charge!" from the stands underlined Los Angeles fans' lack of spontaneity, both at the Coliseum, where the Dodgers played from 1958 to 1961, and at Dodgers Stadium, where the practice was continued.[26]

New York played a central role in shaping the development of amateur and professional baseball and college and professional football. Baseball emerged as a distinct sport during the two decades preceding the Civil War, with competing versions played in New York and Massachusetts. The New York version proved more adaptable, although a few features of the Massachusetts game were incorporated into what came to be accepted as the standard version after the Civil War. The first bureaucratic organization formed to standardize, administer, and revise rules and promote the game nationally, the National Association of Base Ball Players, was established in New York. The participating clubs were mostly from New York and Brooklyn. William Cammeyer was the first entrepreneur to enclose a ballpark and charge admission when he opened the Union Grounds in Brooklyn in 1862, which was necessary if a club was to pay players.[27]

The first all-professional baseball team, the undefeated 1869 Cincinnati Red Stockings, several of whose players were recruited from New York–area clubs, faced its critical test early in the season when it visited New York and Brooklyn to play what were considered the top teams. Cincinnati's victories over them established the Red Stockings as the nation's best. One of the New York–area's top clubs, the Brooklyn Atlantics, handed the all-professional Red Stockings their first defeat in June 1870, 8–7, in a game decided in eleven innings. The game was played before what the *New York Times* estimated as a crowd of 20,000, enormous for that time. The *Times* described the fielding as "a model display on both sides." The intense passion Brooklynites felt for their teams was already evident, as the *Times* complained that "the only drawback was the miserable partisan character of the assemblage."[28]

New York's Intercollegiate Football Association's Thanksgiving Day game, matching that season's top two college teams, played eleven times from 1880 to 1893, was instrumental in spreading interest in football beyond the elite circles associated with the northeastern colleges where the sport originated. Football had emerged as a distinct sport only in the early 1880s. Several days of social activities surrounded the "big game," a practice strongly associated with college football to this day. Along with the Horse Show, the game ushered in the beginning of New York's winter social season. Parades up Fifth Avenue of colorful college floats, along with the sale of pennants, ribbons, college colors, and player pictures drew the attention of large numbers of persons not associated with the participating colleges. Numerous newspaper reporters attended the games, and telegraphists transmitted accounts to other cities, familiarizing many more people with football. Major nineteenth-century prizefights had provided precedents for the selling of colors, pictures, and other souvenirs, and for the days of anticipation of the event in the city. Most of the time the game pitted Yale against Princeton, the era's two major football powerhouses, but Harvard was sometimes also represented. Most of the games took place at the Polo Grounds or Manhattan Field in upper Manhattan.[29]

Women, who were almost entirely absent from baseball games and prizefights during the late nineteenth century, attended these Thanksgiving Day games in sizable numbers. Reporting on the 1889 Yale-Princeton game at Berkeley Oval in the Bronx, attended by 30,000 people, the *New York Times* noted that "the ladies were quite as enthusiastic as the gentlemen" as they cheered for the "Alma Mater of their respective husbands, fathers, brothers, or sweethearts." The *Times* observed that "nearly all the Yale girls wore bunches of violets, while on the breast of each Princeton maiden there blossomed a mighty yellow chrysanthemum." Some of the women also displayed ribbons bearing these colors, "left free to stream out on the November wind in a saucy challenge to the opposing college."[30]

The *Times* described the 1891 Yale-Princeton game, played at Manhattan Field in a torrential rain before 40,000 spectators, as "the greatest athletic contest that has ever been witnessed in this city from many standpoints," including the crowd's size and enthusiasm. The elevated stations on Manhattan's west side were crammed all morning with people headed for the game, and extra trains were put on to handle the crowds, "which seemed for a time to monopolize travel facilities." The "thousands of ladies" present, "arrayed in the bright-colored costumes always conspicuous at the intercollegiate contests, sat out on the 'bleachers,' cheering and waving their handkerchiefs as if it were no concern to them that their clothing was being ruined." The college boys and alumni present displayed a similar frenzy. The students "hurled their college cheers at each other until they grew hoarse, and still continued to yell." The "tin-horn brigade was there in full force." Some of the "peace-disturbing implements" they carried "were longer than the men who carried them, and gave forth sounds resembling those of Sandy Hook fog horns." Wooden rattles were shaken continuously.[31]

The *New York Times* underlined the prestige of the Yale–Princeton game in 1896, noting that New York society was "well represented." Many socially prominent persons sat with their parties in boxes in the grandstand, as though they were at the opera. Governor John W. Griggs of New Jersey "occupied a front box in the covered stand" and wore an enormous yellow chrysanthemum. He and his party cheered fiercely for Princeton.[32]

New York's west side Tenderloin "vice" district, whose brothels, saloons, and gambling dens attracted students and other middle- and upper-class male visitors to the city, "put on its gala dress" for the 1896 Yale–Princeton football game. The *New York Tribune* reported that "almost every shop in the Tenderloin showed in its windows the flags or symbolic flowers of the contesting colleges." Street fakirs hawked Yale and Princeton banners, buttons, and neckties. Students from the two colleges clogged the district, "wearing heavy tan shoes and smoking pipes." The *Tribune* stated that "it was impossible to walk a block without becoming aware of the game that was in prospect." The game was discussed "in every shop, in every hotel, in every café, on every corner. It was flung at you from every window." In the city's shopping districts, "two out of every three of the fashionably dressed and refined-looking women who passed wore a bunch of violets or a yellow chrysanthemum or a ribbon at the throat to indicate a preference."[33]

During the 1920s and 1930s, New York was a major center for college football, with Fordham, New York University, and Columbia giving the sport significant emphasis. In 1930, under alumni pressure, Columbia hired a very capable coach, Lou Little, for a high salary, and the next year doubled its football scholarships. Columbia won the 1934 Rose Bowl against Stanford, 7–0, using a hidden ball play Little devised in what many consider the biggest upset in the history of college football. One of the first sights for railroad travelers entering New York from the north was a striking billboard at Columbia's Baker Field on the Harlem River announcing the university's first football game of the season.[34]

During the 1920s, New York University (NYU) under coach Chick Meehan, similarly determined to develop excellent football teams, recruited "bull-necked icemen and truckmen," of whom there were a great many in New York. To highlight the football program's importance and give it greater visibility, NYU scheduled its games at the Polo Grounds and Yankee Stadium, and only infrequently at its own Ohio Field. NYU pioneered in developing several almost interchangeable units, a major advantage in the era before two-platoon football, when player endurance was critically important. NYU's opponents "shuddered when the three or four first-string NYU teams trotted on the field."[35]

Fordham during the 1930s also fielded premier teams, and boasted what is arguably the most famous line in football history, the Seven Blocks of Granite, who included Alex Wojciechowicz and Vince Lombardi. Wojciechowicz, who was perhaps the best center until that time, later played thirteen years for the Detroit Lions and the Philadelphia Eagles. He was elected to the College and Pro Football Halls of Fame. The Seven Blocks of Granite were coached by Frank Leahy, formerly assistant coach under Knute Rocke at Notre Dame, and later a very successful head coach at Boston College and Notre Dame. Fordham went undefeated in 1937 and played in the Cotton Bowl in 1941 and the Sugar Bowl in 1942.[36]

College football games in New York often drew enormous crowds. In November 1931, for example, a Fordham-NYU game at Yankee Stadium drew 78,000 spectators, with the country in the throes of the Great Depression. When Fordham routed NYU in 1935 at Yankee Stadium, ruining the Violets' prospects for a Rose Bowl invitation, 75,000 were in attendance. Another 50,000 saw unbeaten Fordham take on NYU in late November 1936.[37]

The biggest sustained college football draw in New York was the Army–Notre Dame game, first played there at Ebbets Field in 1923, at the Polo Grounds in 1924, and then for twenty-two consecutive years from 1925 through 1946. It was broadcast nationally over the radio. In part because of New York's sizable Catholic population this became the city's "Big Game." Since 1947, the Army–Notre Dame game has been played in New York only twice, at Shea Stadium in Queens in 1965, and at the new Yankee Stadium in 2010. Although the two schools had played each other since 1913, the 1924 Polo Grounds contest, which drew a crowd of 55,000, was the first to draw a very high attendance. The 1934 game attracted 81,000 spectators.[38] Grantland Rice opened his account of the 1924 game for the *New York Herald Tribune* with what is probably the most famous lead in sportswriting history: "Outlined against a blue-gray October sky, the Four Horsemen rode again. In dramatic lore they are known as Famine, Pestilence, Destruction, and Death. These are only aliases. Their real names are Stuhldreher, Miller, Crowley and Layden. They formed the crest of the South Bend cyclone before which another fighting Army football team was swept over the precipice at the Polo Grounds yesterday as 55,000 spectators peered down on the bewildering panorama spread on the green plain below."[39]

New York's reception for Red Grange, the nation's leading college football star, when his Chicago Bears came to the Polo Grounds to play the New York Giants, provided a tremendous boost for pro football and the fledgling NFL, just five years old. Grange had just left the University of Illinois two semesters short of graduating and was playing his first game as a professional. The game drew 70,000 spectators, the largest crowd that had ever seen a professional football game. Grange's biographer, John Carroll, noted: "After Grange demonstrated that pro football could potentially attract crowds of thirty, forty, and even seventy thousand to a single game, it was difficult to resist the process of transforming the NFL from an organization based on small franchises primarily surrounding the Ohio Valley to one grounded in larger cities." The *New York Times* reported that the crowd that "jammed" the Polo Grounds came "from every station in life . . . from society in the boxes to the newsboys in the bleachers." Many of them were watching football for the first time. The game was a major media event. Nearly one hundred reporters from the major northeastern and Middle Atlantic cities, Chicago, Cleveland, Cincinnati, Detroit, and from as far west as St. Louis, were present.[40]

Grange's New York encounter illustrated how the city could provide sports stars with huge financial rewards. Athletes would always consider New York to offer the best prospects of any city for receiving offers to endorse products, sign movie contracts, and make business connections. These opportunities could prove quite lucrative. The *New York Times* reported that Grange earned about $370,000 during the two days he spent in New York for the Bears-Giants game. He signed a $300,000 contract with the Arrow Picture Corporation to appear in just one movie. For endorsing a sweater, he was given $12,000; for a brand of shoes, $5,000; for a cap, $2,500; for a brand of ginger ale, $5,000. The *Times* estimated Grange's share of the gate receipts for the Bears-Giants game as at least $30,000. The *Chicago Tribune* stated a few days after the game: "Three weeks ago, Red Grange was a poor struggling student. Today his business is so great that it requires the services of four managers to handle it."[41]

Decades later, in 1960, the new commissioner, Pete Rozelle, contributed significantly to the NFL's growth in popularity during the decade pro football became America's most popular sport by transferring the league's headquarters from Philadelphia to New York, the nation's media capital. Unlike the previous commissioner, Bert Bell, a founder of the Philadelphia Eagles, and the leading owners, who had worked together since the 1920s and 1930s, Rozelle had a public relations background, a field the NFL's old guard knew little about. New York was the ideal city for him to apply dynamic new publicity and marketing techniques that helped to vastly expand pro football's audience.[42]

New York City was very important to both college and professional basketball's expanding popularity during the 1920s and 1930s. Basketball was especially suited to a crowded urban environment, where settlement houses, YM and YWCAs, YM and YWHAs, public schools, and playgrounds provided opportunities to participate. Dribbling and other ball-handling skills could be learned and practiced in the streets and back alleys. Steven Riess noted that before 1940 nearly one-third of professional basketball players came from New York City. The first professional basketball team to achieve renown, the Original Celtics, began at a settlement house on New York's Lower West Side. The barnstorming team that evolved from it, composed largely of New Yorkers, dominated professional basketball during the 1920s. In the 1930s, the African American Harlem Renaissance Five supplanted them as basketball's premier barnstorming basketball gate attraction.[43] The New York Knickerbockers franchise, located in the nation's leading metropolis, helped give the fledgling National Basketball Association credibility.

New York also boasted one of basketball's premier announcers, Marty Glickman, a native of the city, who broadcast the Knickerbockers games on the radio from the time the team was established in 1946 until 1967. He also broadcast the New York Giants and New York Jets football games for twenty-three and eleven years, respectively. For Jack Kerouac, Glickman's pro basketball broadcasts provided an example of the emotionally intense experience the Beat Generation savored. In his novel *On the Road*, Kerouac's main character Dean Moriarty, based on Neal Cassady, asks narrator Sal Paradise: "Man, have you dug that mad Marty Glickman announcing basketball games—up-to-midcourt-bounce-fake-set-shot, swish, two points. Absolutely the greatest announcer I ever heard."[44]

During the 1920s and 1930s, more highly ranked college basketball teams were concentrated in New York than in any other city. Basketball had become the second most popular college sport, after football. Robert Peterson stated that by the mid-1930s: "a bid to [play in] Madison Square Garden was the ticket to national prominence for college teams."[45] CCNY coach Nat Holman wrote the most authoritative manuals on how to play basketball during this period.

New York City was notable for its sports-oriented eating and drinking establishments that provided sportswriters and the public an opportunity to mingle with celebrity athletes. These establishments included Toots Shor's, Jack Dempsey's Restaurant, and Leone's. Dempsey, one of the greatest and most charismatic world heavyweight boxing champions, opened his restaurant in 1935 at the corner of Eighth Avenue and 50th Street, across from the previous Madison Square Garden. He was a mainstay in his corner booth, "with his back to Broadway," from the time he set up the restaurant at a new location between West 49th and West 50th Streets in 1947 until he closed it in 1974. Customers desiring to talk briefly about his fights and get their menus autographed found Dempsey easy to approach. James Montgomery Flagg's "heroic-size" painting of Dempsey "crouching and preparing to move in" on Jess Willard, whom he dethroned in 1919 in the "Massacre at Toledo," was displayed on a wall of the restaurant. The Smithsonian Institution acquired it after the restaurant shut down.[46]

Leone's Restaurant, located on West 48th Street "in the heart of the theater district" since 1917, hosted many notable sports banquets into the 1960s. The *New York Times* in 1952 referred to its owner and host, Gene Leone, as "caterer to the world's leading sports personalities." Sports-centered social events at Leone's included a 1934 testimonial dinner for newly elected National League president Ford Frick, attended by Major League Baseball commissioner Judge Kenesaw Mountain Landis, and sponsored by the New York chapter of the Baseball Writers Association. In 1956 a commemoration of legendary Notre Dame football coach Knute Rockne on the twenty-fifth anniversary of his death, was held at Leone's, at which two of the Four Horsemen were present.[47] The New York Jets in 1964 announced the signing of Joe Namath to an unprecedented $427,000 contract at Leone's.

No discussion of New York sports would be complete without mentioning stickball, a street game virtually unknown outside the nation's largest metropolis but played by many thousands of young people within it from the 1930s into the 1970s. Stickball was a form of baseball adapted to the cramped urban environment, played in narrow streets, usually with a broomstick for a bat and a spaldeen, a small rubber ball. Central Park was off limits for stickball, because families out enjoying the sunshine considered it disturbing and would call the police to stop the game. Unlike the other numerous street games played in New York, like punchball, stoop ball, ace-king-queen, skelly, or hopscotch, stickball was an organized team game and winning was taken more seriously.

It was played largely by males, unlike the other street games, in which females made up a sizable proportion of the participants, and in some cases all of them. Stickball rules were often flexible, adapted to the conditions of the block where the game was played. The number of players on each side varied, and was usually fewer than nine. Pitching was generally on one bounce, but often performed with some skill, with "hooks" aimed to the right or left, "drops," and "risers." The batter was given two swings, sometimes one. Infielders usually wore gloves with the padding removed. In the game's later decades, when it was played without running the bases, extra base hits were calculated by the number of sewers the ball passed on the fly. Hall of Fame center fielder Willie Mays, who enjoyed playing stickball with youth in the Harlem streets after his New York Giants finished a game at the Polo Grounds, may have been stickball's only five-sewer hitter. Games often ended when a batted ball broke a store or apartment window. Unfortunately, the proliferation of automobiles in New York's streets led to stickball's swift decline by the 1970s.[48]

# I

# Baseball
# The Era of the Subway Series

CHAPTER ONE

# The Yankees and Dodgers

## The Glory Years, 1947–1957

*Steven A. Riess*

The greatest era of one city dominating a professional sports championship were the years 1947–1957 when New York teams filled seventeen of twenty-two possible appearances in the World Series. New York in 1950 was the nation's largest city with 7,891,957 residents, and was the only city with three Major League teams. The Giants played twice, the Dodgers six times (and twice lost the pennant on the final day of the season) and the Yankees represented the American League (AL) nine times. Though the Dodgers and Yankees never played during the regular season, their postseason rivalry was probably the greatest in professional team sports. The two teams played six extremely competitive World Series that went seven games four times, although the Yankees won five of the six Fall Classics.[1]

During these years, the national pastime integrated, drew the best professional American athletes, though just a handful of Latino athletes, and had record attendances and profits. Yet the "New York era" ended in shocking suddenness, when the Dodgers, the most profitable team in the National League, and the struggling Giants, moved to the West Coast, changing the structure of Major League Baseball forever.

### The Yankees and Dodgers in Historical Perspective

The Yankees were the finest MLB team of the interwar years with nine pennants and seven world championships. They were first called the Bronx Bombers by sportswriter Dan Daniels of the *World Telegram* in July 1936, one month after heavyweight contender Joe Louis, the "Brown Bomber," lost to Max Schmeling at Yankee Stadium.[2] The Dodgers, on the other hand, were typically a second division team, whose only pennants between 1901 and 1946 were in 1916 and 1920. They were the second-rate National League franchise in Gotham after the Giants, who boasted thirteen pennants in those years.

The Dodgers were remembered for futile play, like the twenty-six-inning 1–1 tie game against the Boston Braves in 1920, and such daffy happenings like the 1926 game when three Dodgers ended up on third base on Babe Herman's double. In 1934, when queried about the Dodgers, Giants manager Bill Terry wondered "whether they were still in the league."[3] The Dodgers were a modest draw at the box office, even though Brooklyn's population was third largest in the NL, and did not lead the NL in attendance until 1941, just the second time they surpassed the 1 million mark.

The Dodgers were not competitive for most of the interwar era, finishing in the first division only five times from 1919 to 1939 when they came in third under President Larry MacPhail, who brought in quality players. The Dodgers rose to second in 1940 and first in 1941. The following year they had 104 wins, but fell to second place. The exciting play, bolstered by night baseball, radio broadcasts, and Ladies' Days substantially improved attendance. The Dodgers, from 1939 to 1942, drew one-third more than the other New York clubs, including a team record 1,214,910 in 1941. They led the NL in attendance from 1940 through 1947, except for 1944 when the team came in seventh. Yet fans still wondered about their franchise after the disastrous 1941 World Series. The Dodgers were down 2 games to 1 in game four, and led 4–3 in the ninth, with two out, none on. Reliever Hugh Carey struck out Tommy Henrich, but All-Star catcher Mickey Owen missed the ball, and Henrich made it to first. The Yankees went on to score four runs, and steal the game, effectively ending the Series. Still the fans were so proud of their boys that at least 500,000 fans paraded from Ebbets Field to Town Hall.[4] Then in 1946, the Dodgers tied the Cardinals with ninety-six victories for first place, only to lose the first postseason playoff in modern baseball history.

The Yankees, on the other hand, had fantastic teams in the interwar era. The *Baseball Almanac* rates the 1927 Yankees the best team ever, followed by the 1938 and 1932 Yankee teams. "Murderers' Row" in 1927 went 110–44, winning the pennant by nineteen games, and swept the Pittsburgh Pirates in the World Series. They were led by Babe Ruth whose record sixty homers surpassed every team in the American League. The 1938 team was part of one of the greatest all-time dynasties in sport history, capturing four straight World Series (1936–1939). From 1921 through 1943, they won fourteen pennants and eleven world championships. Spectators turned out to see the great play, and the Yankees led the AL in attendance nine times in the 1920s and 1930s.[5]

## The Local Press and New York Baseball

The popularity of New York baseball always owed a lot to the local daily press, and even after World War II, fans relied heavily on newspapers to keep them abreast of the latest baseball news. New York in the postwar era had the best sportswriters, especially columnists like Arthur Daley, Jimmy Cannon, and Red Smith, and the finest baseball beat writers. In 1946 at least ten newspapers sent reporters on the road to cover the sport, most of whom were underwritten by the local teams. The morning papers emphasized a detailed report of the previous day's game events, while afternoon papers were more oriented toward covering other baseball angles.[6]

The preeminent beat writer was Dick Young, who, beginning in 1947, covered the Dodgers for the *Daily News*, with New York's largest daily circulation (2.4 million). He was a quintessential New Yorker, known for his innovative, tough locker room interviews, hypercritical commentary and brassy style, employment of baseball jargon, and, in his early days, liberal social attitudes. Young's approach to sportswriting was "Tell people what's going on, and what you think is going on."[7]

One of Young's main contemporaries was Milt Gross, who reported on the Yankees for the *Post* (1938–1949), and then wrote its "Speaking Out" column until 1973. He was one of the first to write about the human aspects of athletics. Roger Kahn, author of the superb *Boys of Summer*, covered the Dodgers for the *Herald Tribune* in 1952 and 1953, replacing Harold Rosenthal, who went on to cover the Yankees. Rosenthal encountered so much antisemitism from Dodger manager Burt Shotton that he stopped naming him in his coverage. Kahn found that anti-Jewish feeling was "sustaining" the Dodgers, which he blamed on Walter O'Malley and Vice President Fresco Thompson.[8] Jack Lang covered the Dodgers for the Long Island Press (1947–1957). John Drebinger of the *Times* was an important old-timer who covered all three New York teams from 1924 to 1964. Finally there was Leonard Koppett, perhaps the most analytical of all baseball writers, who also covered all three New York teams, working for the *Herald Tribune* (1948–1954), the *Post* (1954–1963), and later, the *Times*. Most of them set the stage for the "chipmunk" journalists in the early 1960s, Stan Isaacs, Larry Merchant, and Leonard Shecter, who focused on criticizing the underbelly and foibles of sports. They were more concerned with sport's social significance than the game on the field.[9]

## The Dodgers and Brooklyn's Public Image

While Brooklyn fans did not turn out in great numbers until the late 1930s, the borough's working-class fandom became known for their loyalty to the Daffiness boys. The most famous baseball fan in America was probably Hilda Chester, an iron-willed woman, born in Brooklyn in 1897. She was a softball player and a fanatic fan who as a teenager stood outside the *Brooklyn Chronicle* to hear Dodger scores. She first attended games on sportswriters' passes, and in the 1920s got in by working as a peanut sacker. Hilda was a well-known bleacherite in the 1930s, identified by her booming voice, heard everywhere in the park. She stopped screaming after a heart attack, and instead banged a frying pan with an iron ladle. Dodger players gave Hilda brass cowbells to direct cheers, and she became a virtual team mascot. Manager Leo Durocher in the 1940s gave her a lifetime pass.[10]

In the mid-1930s, a cab driver asked Willard Mullins, the renowned cartoonist of the *World-Telegram*, "What did our bums do today?" He responded by drawing a caricature of an unshaven ballplayer dressed like a tramp, which became the team's unofficial symbol. As historian Carl Prince points out, the "bum" was "the pictorial incarnation of the Dodgers' scrappy reputation" and "an affirmation for many of the lower-class reputation of the borough," a symbol of working-class pride. In contrast, Mullins caricatured the Yankees as "clinical professionals in pinstripes" who represented Manhattan snobbery.[11]

American popular culture identified both the prewar Dodgers and Brooklynites with daffiness, ignorance, insularity, a working-class subculture and behavior, lack of sophistication, and incomprehensible speech patterns. During World War II, the new Society for the Prevention of Disparaging Remarks Against Brooklyn reported numerous media slurs against the borough. Back in the nineteenth century, Brooklynites were proud to live in a Major League city, but their self-confidence diminished following annexation into Greater New York in 1898. Subway riders traveling to Manhattan read a humiliating sign on north-bound platforms informing them they were "Going to the City." As Brooklyn-born editor Norman Podhoretz of *Commentary* pointed out, "One of the longest journeys in the world is the journey from Brooklyn to Manhattan."[12]

Brooklyn ethnic and working-class culture was consistently belittled in the cinema, even in war films. The prototypical Brooklyn GI in the movies was ironically Manhattanite William Bendix, a former Yankee batboy. In *Guadalcanal Diary* (1943), Bendix played Corporal Aloysius T. "Taxi" Potts, a fanatic Dodger fan, who gets shot by a Japanese sniper, and while dying, asks for the Dodgers' score.[13] Even Brooklyn bluebloods were silly and foolish. Historian Joseph Dorinson points to Joseph Kesselring's popular black comedy, *Arsenic and Old Lace*, a Broadway hit (1941–1944), and then a feature movie starring Cary Grant and his zany family, who embodied Brooklyn madness.[14]

Negative stereotyping of Brooklyn's working-class culture was reinforced on television by *The Honeymooners* (1951–1956), which followed the lives of Bensonhurst bus driver Ralph Kramden and his neighbor, sewer worker Ed Norton. They were uneducated, unsophisticated simpletons, overwhelmed by their daily struggles.[15]

Branch Rickey, who became Dodgers president and general manager at the end of 1942, admired the local folks' underdog mentality: "They have a real pride in their own and refuse to become parasitical. . . . When anything comes along distinctly Brooklyn, they rally behind it because it is an expression of themselves, even an entity as lowly as a baseball club."[16]

## Brooklyn Fans and Their Love of the Dodgers

New York fan affiliation was heavily based on geography (a relationship epitomized by Chicago's division between North Side Cubs supporters and South Side White Sox followers), as well as ethnicity, race, class, and social values. Dodger fans were overwhelmingly from Brooklyn, the city's most populous borough with 2,738,175 residents in 1950. They listened to Dodger games on radio, watched on TV, and read about the team in tabloids like the *Brooklyn Eagle, Daily News, Mirror*, and the *Post*, which made the sport very accessible and produced many new fans. According to one fan, "Everyone was interested in the Dodgers and everyone [was] talking about the baseball game." Bronxite and Giant fan Colin Powell felt "it was paranoia in Brooklyn that you had to be a Dodger fan." Dodger historian Peter Marquis was impressed by the widespread use of transistor radios to listen to games. He agrees with Dodger outfielder Cal Abrams's wife that postwar fans could follow a game just by walking down neighborhood streets, listening to radios blaring through open windows.[17]

However, all Brooklynites were not Dodger fans. Many fans whose parents were Giant fans who grew up in Manhattan, maintained their familial loyalties, but Yankee fans in Brooklyn were few and far between. Historian Stephen Norwood suggests that Yankee fans adrift in Brooklyn were probably upwardly mobile people who admired the Yankees' success and "class." Brooklyn fans outside the borough were numerous in Queens and Long Island, but were rare in the Bronx and Manhattan. Future film documentarians George Shapiro and Howard West, both Bronxites, were Dodger fans because they found the Yankees too dominant and felt the Dodger players were more colorful. Also, West's father was a Dodger fan who supported the underdog.[18]

The Dodgers, like many postwar era teams, drew a large ethnic working-class fandom, many second-generation immigrants who thought that supporting the Dodgers was part of becoming a real American. Attending games was inexpensive, with bleacher seats costing 60 cents (reduced to 50 cents in 1954), and general admission $1.25. The bus and subway in 1950 cost just 10 cents.[19]

Marquis examined the ethnic backgrounds of postwar Dodger fans based on evidence from the *Brooklyn Eagle*, and determined that most fans came from either Jewish/Italian Bensonhurst, or from heavily Jewish communities in eastern Brooklyn, sections of the borough who got to Ebbets Field by subway. Adults (twenty to sixty years old) comprised half of Dodger spectators, pretty equally divided by gender: male (53 percent) and female (47 percent).[20]

Dodger fans not only saw the "Bums" as their team, but also felt a strong personal affinity with individual players, whom they sat near to at intimate Ebbets Field and found them highly approachable. Kids like Manhattanite Robert A. Caro found Gil Hodges and other teammates very willing to sign autographs. Larry King, the famous TV interviewer, remembered, "You could walk players to their cars or the subway" and have a conversation with them. Dodger fans especially identified with Gil Hodges, who lived year-round in Brooklyn. They prayed on his behalf during the 1952 World Series when he could not buy a hit.[21]

Fans could easily identify with Dodger players who were not distant icons earning one hundred times as much as they made, but struggling family men who typically held off-season jobs to supplement their incomes, selling admirers insurance, clothing, or automobiles, like Hodges at Century Chrysler, or hosting them in their saloons. Carl Erskine, Gil Hodges, Pee Wee Reese, and Duke Snider all lived in nearby communities, where fans occasionally ran into them. Mary Walsh Heagney got Pee Wee's autograph by walking a few blocks to his apartment and ringing the doorbell. By contrast, historian Harvey Frommer found that changing neighborhoods, higher wages, and growing families pushed New York Giant and Yankee players to suburbia.[22]

## New York Giant Fans

New York Giant fans in the early 1900s were mainly Manhattanites from a wide variety of social backgrounds, ranging from poor Lower East Siders like young Harry Golden, who worked odd jobs at the ballpark to get in, to the Wall Street crowd because the team was very successful, the park was very close to the 155th Street subway station, and games started in the late afternoon after the stock market closed. Many well-known fans were local Democratic politicians who identified with the owners, who were prominent Tammanyites. In the 1920s, when the surrounding Washington Heights neighborhood became a predominantly Jewish locale, the Giants marketed to them by recruiting Jewish ballplayers. Giants fans in the 1950s were often sons of Giants supporters who, like Bronxite Colin Powell, was introduced to the game by his father. Colin's affiliation with the Giants was enhanced by the presence of black players, especially Willie Mays.[23]

A Giants survey of 1,500 New York spectators in 1955 found that 10 percent walked to the Polo Grounds, while 56 percent arrived by subway, 25 percent came by automobile (there was ample parking by the Polo Grounds), and the rest by bus. Overall, 60 percent of all fans, notably supporters from suburban Westchester County, and New Jersey (Jersey City was the home of their top minor league team from 1937 through 1950), arrived by car; and 25 percent by subway.[24]

Journalist Herbert Kupferberg, longtime music critic for the *Herald Tribune*, held the Giant faithful in high regard, and described them as polite, good sports, well versed in baseball knowledge (though they tended to disregard the junior circuit), and less likely to be hero worshippers, making them "the elite among baseball fans." On the other hand, he depicted Dodger loyalists as raucous spectators who were "nature's closest modern approximation to Neanderthal man." Kupferberg argues in 1949 that sportswriters incorrectly considered the Giant-Dodger relationship a "rivalry" since Giant fans did not hate Dodger fans, but "simply refused to acknowledge them." This attitude soon changed. According to Arnold Hano, author of the classic *A Day in the Bleachers*, Giant fans in the 1950s hated the Dodgers and the Yankees. Colin Powell remembers that such loathing "brought stability to our lives, knowing which team you supported and which one you hated."[25]

## Yankee Fandom

Yankees fans were mainly drawn from the 1,451,277 Bronx residents (45 percent Jewish and 91.3 percent white) or from Manhattan. Prewar Bronx had excellent housing and mass transit. After the war, the borough underwent important demographic changes. White South Bronx residents moved to private homes in the North Bronx, to other boroughs and to the suburbs, and about 170,000 poorer Manhattanites of color replaced them. The Yankee Stadium neighborhood, known as Highbridge (in the West Bronx), had a reputation as a safe area. Local fans walked to the field, and most other fans took buses or subway. The ballpark field was considered "the greatest attraction" in the Bronx.[26]

By the mid-1950s, increasing numbers of spectators drove to the stadium from New Jersey, whose Newark Bears had been the Yankees top farm team (1926–1949). The Bombers also drew fans from suburban Westchester and Connecticut, reflecting the migration of New Yorkers to the suburbs. Overall Yankee fans were probably more middle class than Dodger fans.[27]

Yankee fans were stereotyped as blasé spectators, who rooted for their "home town" team as a matter of course, and took for granted they would win—all the time. Yankee supporters did not need to wait for "next year" because every season was next year, especially the baby-boom era since the Bronx Bombers won fifteen pennants between 1947 and 1964. Sportswriter Al Laney of the *Tribune* posited that in 1951, Yankee fans were happy to see the nearby Giants, whose fans admired and respected the Yankees, beat the Dodgers, whom Yankee fans did not esteem, for the pennant.[28]

According to Marty Appel, longtime Yankees public relations expert, and team historian, the Dodgers and Yankees were not natural rivals: "The fans were very different. Dodger fans were the little guys the underdogs the working stiffs [who snuck into the box seats and] whose players lived in the neighborhood and seemed like regular guys. The Yankee fans were the Wall Street business crowd, better dressed, cockier" and did not sneak into box seats and did not expect to run into the ballplayers in their neighborhoods. Appel exaggerates, but not by too much. The Yankees catered to the well-heeled, opening the Yankee Stadium Club in 1946 with a lounge, bar, and restaurant facilities to encourage purchases of season tickets. A box with six seats cost $900, or $2.25

each per game, a 25 percent savings. The plan was to sell expensive reserved seating mainly to banks and other businesses that used the boxes to promote business. However, gamblers bought many of the high-priced seats. In 1950 the Yankees took in $850,000 in advance box sales, a scheme journalist Red Smith called "the biggest thing in baseball merchandising since invention of the rain check."[29]

Still, as New York baseball historian Henry Fetter points out, lots of working-class fans rooted for the Yankees. They followed the team in the press, on the radio, and on television. Furthermore, thousands attended home games, taking advantage of inexpensive mass transit (raised to 15 cents in 1953) and the large number of cheap seats (75 cent bleachers and $1.25 general admission). They got high-quality baseball at Yankee Stadium, accessible concessions, and clean restrooms. Yankee fans respected the created tradition that included the "Old Timers' Game" and the free-standing centerfield monuments dedicated to former Yankee heroes.[30]

The postwar Yankees were especially popular among second-generation Italian kids from ethnic enclaves like East Harlem (Manhattan) and Arthur Avenue (Bronx) who went to see ethnic heroes like Joe DiMaggio, Phil Rizzuto, and Yogi Berra who demonstrated that Italians were real Americans. There were also a lot of young Jewish fans from the Bronx who rooted for the Yankees. As actor Judd Hirsch remembers, "It was like an identification," even if they didn't wear a Yankee hat or uniform. He noted that "If there was somebody in your neighborhood that wasn't a Yankee fan that person was an outcast, and that was a dangerous individual. That person had to be confronted." He was not part of the "community." Bronx boy Ed Kranepool, one of the "Original Mets," agrees: "You were either a Yankee fan or you were the enemy." He and his pals identified with them because the Yankees were winners and exuded class, qualities Bronx boys sought, even if just vicariously.[31]

## Brooklyn and Its Special Relationship to the Dodgers

### Brooklyn Fanatics and Ebbets Field

Ebbets Field's capacity after the war was 34,219, just under the average for the NL. Yet despite the reputed support of the rabid fans, the seating limit was rarely tested except for postseason games, until 1945, when attendance rose by 43 percent to over 1 million, and then to nearly 1.8 million a year later. In 1947, Rickey returned $3 million to potential World Series ticket buyers because there were not enough seats. Ebbets Field was hardly a pleasure palace, beset by such problems as foul-smelling bathrooms, narrow aisles, growing vandalism, and interracial tensions. It was in such dire need of maintenance that the team spent $673,144.63 between 1944 and 1948 for repairs and improvements. The park did have its unique touches, like haberdasher Abe Stark's (city council president, 1954–1961) sign in the outfield that read "Hit sign, win suit."[32]

Management encouraged spectators to make the park their own. Fans came to games with handmade cloth or cardboard banners, and some were hung from the bleachers. They created their own amateur musical group, the "Sym-Phony Band" that performed in support of their team. In 1951, when the group got into a big dispute with the American Federation of Music, a professional union that felt the amateurs were taking potential jobs, team president Walter O'Malley responded by scheduling "Music Depreciation Night" on August 13, admitting for free 2,436 spectators who came with a musical instrument, including horns, trumpets, tubas, oboes, coronets, and one zither. Marquis argues that "By these gestures, the public took possession of Ebbets Field and also seemed to take over the club and its destiny."[33]

## The Dodgers as Philanthropist

The Dodgers were historically more effective than other teams in using humanitarianism to generate a positive public image to garner new fans. When Charles Ebbets opened his eponymous ballpark, he gave away tickets to local youth ostensibly to foster Americanization and civic pride, but also to create new fans. Thirty years later, the Dodgers supported around twenty baseball-oriented aid organizations to demonstrate concern with the welfare of white youth who belonged to neighborhood and religiously based organizations, while simultaneously promoting young people's interest in the franchise. Rickey and O'Malley believed that encouraging youth interest in sport helped to construct identity, create social balance in the borough, and form healthy bodies and minds. The team in the early 1940s did not reach out to black fans, just 4 percent of Brooklyn's population, until new team president Rickey added an African American group. The Dodgers focused most of their charity attention on the Brooklyn Amateur Baseball Foundation (BABF), founded in 1946 in conjunction with the *Brooklyn Eagle*, to stimulate interest in baseball, raise money for social organizations, and fight juvenile delinquency and Communism by promoting American values. By 1950, the BABF distributed $200,000 worth of sporting goods to sandlot groups.[34]

Jackie Robinson. Courtesy of the National Archives.

The Dodgers' most famous promotion was the Dodger Knot-Hole Club (DKHC), established in 1938 to create fans, provide role models, and strengthen family values and traditional morality, to prevent youth crime. The St. Louis Cardinals had originated the concept in 1917. During World War II, there was a lot of concern about juvenile delinquency since fathers were away at war and mothers were working. The concern grew in the 1950s, now blamed on the corrupting influence of movies, radio, TV, music, and comic books, along with street life and Communism. In 1951, the club distributed 100,000 free tickets to established charities, and 250,000 by 1955. Its annual highlight was a gala dinner attended by over 1,000 boys and girls who met various Dodger players.[35]

The Dodgers' support of traditional values was tested before the 1947 season after star manager Leo Durocher was taken to task for his marriage to starlet Laraine Day one day after her quickie Mexico divorce. Rev. Vincent J. Powell, director of the Brooklyn Catholic Youth Organization (CYO), called for a boycott of Durocher, claiming he was undermining Brooklyn youth, and got the CYO to drop support of the Knothole Gang. Durocher was also criticized for associating with known gamblers and other underworld figures. Commissioner Albert B. "Happy" Chandler suspended Durocher for the 1947 season for his dubious connections that harmed the reputation of MLB.[36]

## The Myth and Reality of the Dodgers as a Progressive Social Force

The Dodgers' postwar franchise had as forward looking a public image as any professional sports club. This contributed to its popularity, especially among non-sports fans. The key event was the hiring of Jackie Robinson in 1947 that broke the color line, and seemingly certified the Dodger's reform-minded identity. Brooklynites, especially African Americans, Jews, and political left-wingers, applauded Rickey and the Dodgers for hiring Robinson, and standing up for such fundamental American values as freedom, democracy, and opportunity. Most historians consider Robinson's achievement, in the face of widespread racist opposition by owners, ballplayers, and fans, the single most important event in American sport history and a key stage in the history of the civil rights movement, preceding the integration of the US Armed Forces in 1948 and *Brown v. Board of Education of Topeka* (1954) that overturned *Plessey v. Ferguson* (1896) that legitimized the concept of "separate but equal." The integration of baseball had enormous symbolic meaning because it showed the possibility for curtailing racism and segregation. Robinson was an ideal hero who broke the color line because of his abilities, performance, strength of character, and courage. His heroic story was retold in movies, biographies, autobiographies, and even an episode of the TV show *Brooklyn Bridge*. The Robinson story became a memory that demands retelling, like reciting the Exodus story on Passover.[37]

The public saw the roster of the "Boys of Summer" as evidence of the Dodgers' democratic treatment of their employees. The "people's team" included Italians, Poles, and Jews (three, if you count a coach). In 1950, it became the first team to have four African Americans (tied by the Giants in 1951). The Yankees, however, had no blacks until outfielder Elston Howard in 1955, but did have several players of Eastern and Southern European origins. The Dodgers were seen as the "team" of the underdog by political and social radicals. Tony Marzani, the only Dodger fan in my Manhattan elementary school class in the 1950s, was the son of a Communist intellectual. However, politics and baseball do not make perfect bedfellows, and Earl Browder, head of the American Communist Party, was a Yankee fan.[38]

Rickey provided important leadership in integrating the team, a choice influenced by his value system, which emphasized social justice and opportunity for all, though also motivated by business factors. Robinson's playing meant the team had a potential new star who could help the Dodgers win the pennant and make bigger profits without any financial costs, because the Dodgers paid no compensation to Robinson's prior employer, the Kansas City Monarchs.[39]

When it came to other political issues, like anti-Communism and patriotism, the team was probably more conservative than the average Brooklynite. In 1949, for instance, Rickey accused ballplayers who opposed the reserve clause of being Communist sympathizers. He also encouraged Robinson to appear before the House Committee on Un-American Activities to speak against African American activist Paul Robeson and African American support for Russia and Communism. President O'Malley became closely identified with General Douglas MacArthur after he was fired by President Harry Truman in 1951, and gave him free access to a box seat. O'Malley later supported him for the Republican nomination for president, and promoted him as baseball commissioner.[40]

Branch Rickey did not try to impose his own strict Methodist morals on other people, but he had his own prejudices. He was known to make anti-Catholic remarks at the dinner table, and exhibited antisemitic behavior. Former Washington Senator Bob Berman, who played in the majors in 1918, claimed that Rickey reneged on a contract offer when he found out that Berman was Jewish. A generation later, Rickey negatively characterized two potential Dodger buyers because they were "of Jewish extraction and characteristics."[41]

Although Brooklyn was one-third Jewish, the Dodgers had few Jewish players. In the 1940s they had Canadian Goody Rosen (1944–1946), an All-Star outfielder who batted .325, third highest in the NL, who was subsequently sold to the Giants; first base coach Jake Pitler (1947–1957); and Brooklyn-reared outfielder Cal Abrams (1949–1952), a left-handed batter, who had a stellar minor league career. In 1955 the team added bonus baby pitcher Sandy Koufax, a local boy, who seldom played his first two years and encountered prejudice in the locker room. Abrams and Koufax both felt their managers were antisemitic. Brooklyn star hurler Don Newcombe heard his teammates toss around phrases like "Jew son of a bitch," and he and other black Dodgers supported their Jewish teammates. In 1951, Abrams led the NL in batting early in the season, and got a hit in every game he started until May 25 (he peaked at .477), but manager Charley Dressen took him out of the lineup, even against right-handed pitchers, and failed to play him on "Cal Abrams Day," on July 12. He finished the season with a stellar .419 on-base percentage. Abrams later related to his son that there were occasions he was told to ride in a station wagon with the equipment manager because there was no room for him on the team bus. The discrimination was not limited to the players, as Abrams's wife also encountered prejudice from her fellow Dodger spouses.[42]

Jewish Major Leaguers were more likely to be Giants than Dodgers. The Giants began purposely recruiting Jewish ballplayers in the 1920s to encourage fellow Jews to attend games. On September 11, 1941, the Giants fielded a lineup with four Jews on the field: Sid Gordon, Morrie Arnovich, Harry Danning, and Harry Feldman. The Yankees, on the other hand, never singled out Jewish talent except for Hank Greenberg, a Bronx boy, but he signed with the Tigers, knowing he could never displace Lou Gehrig. The only Jewish Yankees in the 1930s and 1940s were outfielder Jimmie Reese (James Herman Solomon) in 1930–1931, batting .286, and pitcher Herb "Lefty" Karpel (two games in 1946). Reese played under a pseudonym to avoid antisemitism.[43]

## The Baseball Business, 1945–1957

### Attendance

The postwar economy was primed for an enormous boom given the pent-up demand for housing, consumer goods, and entertainment following the Depression and World War II. MLB took advantage of fan interest in seeing the return of their heroes to the diamond by holding night games that facilitated working-class attendance. Extensive press coverage and radio and TV broadcasts further enhanced interest. In addition, fans had a lot of discretionary

Table 1. Yankee and Dodger Attendance, 1945–1957

| | New York Yankees | | | Brooklyn Dodgers | | |
|---|---|---|---|---|---|---|
| *Year* | *Attendance* | *Daily Avg.* | *Rank AL* | *Attendance* | *Daily Avg.* | *Rank NL* |
| *1957* | 1,497,134 | 19,443 | 1 | 1,028,258 | 13,354 | 5 |
| *1956* | 1,491,784 | 19,374 | 1 | 1,213,562 | 15,761 | 2 |
| *1955* | 1,490,138 | 19,352 | 1 | 1,033,589 | 13,423 | 2 |
| *1954* | 1,475,171 | 18,912 | 1 | 1,020,531 | 13,254 | 4 |
| *1953* | 1,537,811 | 19,972 | 1 | 1,163,419 | 14,916 | 2 |
| *1952* | 1,629,665 | 21,164 | 1 | 1,088,704 | 13,609 | 1 |
| *1951* | 1,950,107 | 25,001 | 1 | 1,282,628 | 16,444 | 1 |
| *1950* | 2,081,380 | 27,031 | 1 | 1,185,896 | 15,204 | 2 |
| *1949* | 2,283,676 | 29,278 | 1 | 1,633,747 | 20,945 | 1 |
| *1948* | 2,373,901 | 30,830 | 2 | 1,398,967 | 17,935 | 4 |
| *1947* | 2,178,937 | 28,298 | 1 | 1,807,526 | 23,173 | 1 |
| *1946* | 2,265,512 | 29,422 | 1 | 1,796,824 | 22,745 | 1 |
| *1945* | 881,845 | 11,603 | 2 | 1,059,220 | 13,580 | 1 |

SOURCE: "New York Yankees Attendance, Stadiums, and Park Factors," http://www.baseball-reference.com/teams/NYY/attend.shtml; "Los Angeles Dodgers Attendance, Stadiums, and Park Factors," http://www.baseball-reference.com/teams/LAD/attend.shtml. Accessed May 18, 2015.

income, costs of attending games was very low, and there was not much competition from other professional team sports. MLB attendance rose by 71 percent in the first postwar season. Team attendance reflected its market size, the club's quality and success, the presence of star players, and ballpark ambiance.[44]

Total NL attendance rose from 5,261,000 in 1945 to 8,902,000 in 1946, and 10,388,000 in 1947. Thereafter, attendance dropped each year, bottoming at 7,244,062 in 1951. AL attendance was 5,580,420 in 1945, jumped to 8,621,182 in 1946, 9,486,089 in 1947, and peaked at 11,150,099 in 1948 (when MLB had a record 20.9 million admissions), and then dropped sharply. By 1952, Major League attendance was down to 14,663,055 (13,058 per game), and did not rise until 1954, one year after the Boston Braves moved to Milwaukee, the first franchise shift in fifty years. The decline has been attributed to the saturation of televised baseball games, the popularity of other entertainments including free network television, the aging of the first generation of modern ballparks, the decline of older eastern and midwestern cities, and the lack of competition, especially in the American League.

From 1945 through 1953, the Dodgers led the NL in attendance six times (see Table 1), and came in second four times, nearly always beating the rival Giants. Home attendance in 1946 (1,796,824) surpassed the Cubs Major League record

(1,485,166) set in 1929, which the Dodgers broke again in 1947 with 1,807,526 (23,173 daily average), which remained the team record until the club moved to Los Angeles. The addition of Jackie Robinson did not bring in much revenue at home, beating the prior year attendance by just 10,702. The Dodgers' share of total NL home attendance in 1947 actually dropped to 17.4 percent compared to 20 percent the previous two years, and further dropped to 14 percent in 1949 and 1950. Home attendance fell in 1948 by 22.6 percent when the team dropped to third place, and after 1950, never reached 1.3 million despite its excellent roster and pennant-winning seasons. When the Dodgers won their first World Series, in 1955, attendance was less than 60 percent of 1947. The Dodgers again won the pennant in 1956, but attendance was barely more than half of Milwaukee, which drew over 2 million.[45]

The "Boys of Summer" were a major attraction on the road, although in Robinson's rookie year, their crowds at the Polo Grounds and St. Louis's Sportsman's Park actually dropped from the previous year. The Dodgers were a crucial draw at the Polo Grounds, attracting 39.4 percent of the entire Giants attendance in 1953, and topped that with 39.7 percent in 1956.[46]

The Yankees were the top draw in the AL, setting a Major League record of 2,265,512 in 1947. The team had the largest attendance in the AL from 1946 through 1959 except for 1948, when it drew 2,373,901, a team record until 1979. In 1948 the World Champion Cleveland Indians surpassed the Yankees with 2,620,627 attendees. From 1946 through 1950 the Yankees drew over 21 percent of the AL attendance. Thereafter, despite the team's great success on the field, the average daily home attendance decreased from 27,031 a game in 1950 to 19,374 in 1956.[47]

## The Dodgers Front Office

Fans and journalists debate the relative roles of a team's organization and its players in creating winning teams. The Dodgers and Yankees both had outstanding ballplayers who produced successful pennant-winning teams, but they also had first-rate front office leadership to finance the business, scouts to discover talent, and managers to supervise the players on the diamond.[48]

Experts consider Branch Rickey the finest general manager of all time. Prior to coming to Brooklyn in late 1943, he helped the St. Louis Cardinals capture six pennants and four world championships (1926–1942). He replaced Dodger president MacPhail, who was off in the military, attracted by a financially stable team that won 204 games in two years, the promise of greater authority, and stock in the team. In 1944, Rickey, team attorney Walter O'Malley, and John L. Smith of Pfizer Chemical, each bought 25 percent of the team, and promised to work together. The remaining stock belonged to Marie McKeever Mulvey, daughter of the former Dodger partner, Steven McKeever, president of the team from 1932 until his death in 1938.[49]

Rickey brought in several outstanding prospects to overhaul an aging team, including pitchers Rex Barney and Ralph Branca, first baseman Gil Hodges, and future Hall of Famer Duke Snider. After the war Rickey spent over $100,000 on free agents, and by 1946, the Dodgers had over four hundred players and twenty-two minor league teams, creating the biggest and best farm system in baseball. Twenty-two of the twenty-five men on the 1949 World Series team were Dodger farm system products, an organization bolstered by the creation in 1947 of Dodgertown in Vero Beach, where the franchise housed, trained, and taught six hundred players at an annual cost of about $200,000.[50]

Rickey's greatest single accomplishment was breaking the color line in organized baseball when he signed Jackie Robinson in October 1945 to a contract with the Montreal Royals of the International League, and then promoted him to the Major Leagues in 1947. Integration had long been sought by Negro Leaguers and black journalists, and more recently by white journalists and northern big-city politicians, but was strongly opposed by many players fearful of losing their jobs, and baseball executives frightened of alienating fans. Yankee president Larry MacPhail wrote a secret 1946 report in favor of the color line. He argued that integration would doom the Negro Leagues with the loss of their stars, and injure Organized Baseball, since certain big league teams made a lot of money renting fields, like Yankee Stadium for $125,000, to black baseball entrepreneurs.[51]

In 1950, when Rickey's contract as chief executive expired, and was not renewed, he sold his share of the Dodgers to Walter O'Malley for $1,050,000. O'Malley then became the majority stockholder and team president. Rickey went on to run the hapless Pittsburgh Pirates. O'Malley was not a baseball man by profession, but got into baseball as the protégé of George V. McLaughlin, head of the Brooklyn Trust Company, who hired him to oversee the firm's financial interests in the Dodgers. When Rickey took over the job of running the club in late 1942, McLaughlin recommended O'Malley as the new team attorney.[52]

President O'Malley focused on legal and business affairs, dealing with media contracts, marketing, sponsorships, ballpark maintenance, and planning a new stadium. O'Malley put his baseball people, notably Emil J. "Buzzie" Bavasi, in charge of the farm system, and in 1951 Bavasi succeeded Rickey as general manager. Bavasi's Dodgers appeared in four of the next five World Series.[53]

O'Malley suspected his field was structurally unsound. It had bad plumbing, narrow aisles, small capacity, could not be expanded, and was located in a declining neighborhood. The borough seemed set for an economic downswing with the demise of major department stores, the closing of the *Eagle* in 1955, and the waning of the Navy Yard, the borough's biggest employer. Brooklyn lost 235,000 white residents from 1950 to 1957, while adding 100,000 less well-off nonwhites. O'Malley told Dick Young of the *Daily News* that "the area is getting full of blacks and spics." He worried that middle-class suburbanites would have to drive to Ebbets Field, which was not readily accessible by highway and had just seven hundred parking spaces.[54]

**The Dodger Managers**

Experts believe that a manager can win, or lose, 3 to 5 games a season. A capable manager had to have the respect of his players, and be skilled in communication, self-awareness, and prioritization. He must draw up the best lineups, wisely employ the pitching staff, use small-ball tactics where appropriate, and avoid strategic mistakes.[55]

The Dodgers started the "era" with the superb manager Leo Durocher (1939–1946, 1948), who won 56.6 percent of his games in Brooklyn. When Durocher was suspended in 1947, Burt Shotton, a former big league manager, and recent Dodger scout and minor league supervisor, took over. He wore a suit and a Dodger cap instead of a uniform, and consequently was not allowed on the playing field. The fans felt he was too low key, especially compared to the fiery and beloved Durocher, whose players respected him for his leadership and decision-making skills. The press was very critical of Shotton, who lacked Leo's panache, did not interview well, and was, according to Dick Young of the *Daily News*, "aloof," "indifferent to his players' problems," and "a vain, stubborn person." Despite Shotton's shortcomings, Dodger fans and players relished his results as the calm Shotton led the talented club to the 1947 pennant. Durocher returned the next season, but after the team started out 35-37, he moved on to the hated Giants. Shotton returned, and one year later led the Dodgers to another pennant. However, Burt was fired in 1950, in large part because he was closely identified with Rickey, who no longer ran the Dodgers organization.[56]

Shotton was replaced by Chuck Dressen, a former Reds skipper, Dodgers coach, and current manager of the Oakland Oaks of the Pacific Coast League. Dressen had a great roster in 1951, which squandered a 13½-game lead over the Giants, and then lost the playoffs on Bobby Thomson's ninth-inning home run. The Dodgers won the next two pennants, but when Dressen demanded a multiyear contract, he was replaced by Walter Alston, who had won three Class AAA championships with the Montreal Royals. In 1955, Alston became an all-time Dodger hero by beating the Yankees for the team's only championship in Brooklyn. He managed the Dodgers for twenty-three years during his Hall of Fame career, winning seven pennants and four World Series.[57]

### The Yankee Front Office

In late 1945 Jacob Ruppert's estate sold the Yankees for $2.89 million to former Dodgers president Larry MacPhail, Dan Topping, a wealthy sportsman and playboy, and Del Webb, a self-made man in the construction and real estate business. The syndicate struggled at first, going through three managers in 1946. Then in 1947, President MacPhail promoted farm system director George Weiss to general manager. The Yankees won the pennant and World Series, and after the season, MacPhail sold his share of the team to his partners for $2 million. Topping became president, and was in charge of daily operations, while Webb focused on league matters.[58]

Six years later, Topping and Webb sold Yankee Stadium, the land site, adjoining parking lots, and the ballpark of their top farm system, the Kansas City Blues, to business associate Arnold Johnson, a Chicago financier and industrialist, for $6.5 million. He then sold the stadium grounds to the Knights of Columbus for $2.5 million, and leased the property back to himself. Johnson sublet the land back to the Yankees for twenty-eight years at a cost of $11 million.[59]

Yankees general manager George Weiss is rated by baseball expert Daniel Levitt as the fifth best of all time. Weiss produced the rosters that enabled the Yankees to capture ten pennants and seven World Series. He helped amass a large pool of gifted players mainly through an outstanding farm system that excelled at developing position players. His farm system was less successful at producing pitchers, except for Whitey Ford and Vic Raschi. Consequently he built the team's pitching staff by trading surplus players and cash. Weiss was adroit at making late-season deals to acquire veterans to fill gaps in the lineup, starting in 1949 when slugger Johnny Mize was purchased for $40,000.[60]

Weiss's first contract was for $50,000 a year, plus 40 percent of whatever he saved below his budget. This arrangement propelled him to become an extremely tough negotiator in the 1950s when players earned modest salaries. Weiss regularly low balled players, even stars, explaining they would make up the difference, and more, from their annual World Series checks.[61]

Weiss did not support integration. He had no confidence in black players, did not diligently recruit black talent nor develop it in the minor leagues. Weiss worried about integrating the team and attracting black fans. He told Roger Kahn in 1954: "We don't want that sort of crowd. It would offend box holders from Westchester to have to sit with niggers." Furthermore, "We are not going to bow to pressure on this issue."[62]

The Yankees first legitimate black prospect was Puerto Rican first baseman Vic Power, who did not fit Weiss's image of a "proper" Yankee. Power was brash, flashy, and chased white women. He was traded to Kansas City, where he became an All-Star. The first black Yankee was catcher/outfielder Elston Howard in 1955, a tactful, nonthreatening family man. According to Larry MacPhail's son, AL president Lee MacPhail, "The Yankees were very anxious that the first black player they brought up would be somebody with the right type of character. Elston was ideal."[63]

## The Yankee Managers

The experienced Bucky Harris led the Yankees to the 1947 World Series, but after coming in third in 1948, Weiss replaced him with his old friend, fifty-nine-year-old Casey Stengel, manager of the champion Oakland Oaks of the Pacific Coast League. Stengel had previously managed nine years in the majors, never finishing in the first division. Fans and the press belittled the hiring, but Stengel proved them wrong, winning ten pennants and seven World Series in twelve years.[64]

Stengel was a sly old fox, an excellent judge of talent, who dealt with his players as individuals, and eventually became popular with the press, even if they did not always understand his patter. His main tactic was to platoon players, a long-forgotten maneuver going back to manager George Stallings of the Boston Braves, whose 1914 squad won the World Series. Stallings rotated eight outfielders based on their strengths and weaknesses. Stengel started out with a roster of aging veterans, and over time, mixed in highly talented youngsters to create a dominating team.[65]

**Business and Profits**

MLB thrived in the late 1940s. Operating income nearly doubled from 1945 to $27.5 million one year later, and surpassed $30 million the next four years. Profits in 1946 were up 17.8 percent, with a record profit of $4,886,931. The average team made about $250,000 annually through 1950, when franchises were worth an average of $2.5 million. But the tide turned in the early 1950s.[66]

The NL made $6,204,123 from 1947 to 1950, but then went through rough years. The eight clubs made just $184,611 for the period 1952–1956. Half of the teams lost money over those five years, ranging from $426,612 to over $1.9 million. The AL made out better from 1947 to 1956, making $6,085,735 from 1947 to 1950, and $2,583,156 from 1952 to 1956, for a combined total of $8,668,891. By 1956, MLB's gross income was $42,836,327, about a one-third increase from 1950 ($32,035,481).[67] Historian Robert Burk attributes the financial problems of the early 1950s to the saturation of baseball on TV, competitive imbalance in MLB, the rising popularity of other team sports, shifting demography, with the rise of the Sunbelt and suburbs, poor marketing, and paternalistic owners like P. K. Wrigley, who were not profit maximizers.[68]

**Dodgers and Yankees Profitability**

During the decade 1947–1956 (excepting 1951 for which we have no data), the Dodgers made $3,557,115, the most profitable team in the NL, and barely second behind the Yankees in all MLB. They did well at the box office and achieved superb returns from media and their farm system. In 1950, for instance, the St. Paul Saints of the American Association made $299,000. Nearly half of Dodger profits came between 1947 and 1950, when the Dodgers averaged $424,092 annually (despite losing $8,578 in 1950). This constituted 27.3 percent of NL profits, second to the Cardinals (38.0 percent), whose profits relied heavily on its farm system. The Dodgers at the start of the 1940s plowed most of its profits back into the team to retire its heavy debt, but under Rickey the team declared $173,250 in dividends between 1948 and 1950.[69]

The Dodgers led the NL in profits from 1952 to 1956, earning $1,860,744 (an average of $372,149), which was marginally greater than the Braves, who moved from Boston to Milwaukee in 1953. O'Malley became very jealous of the Braves' success there since they led the NL in profits in 1954 and 1955. The franchise made $2,027,508 ($506,877 per year) in its first four years in Milwaukee compared to the Dodgers' $1,385,969 ($346,492 per year) over the same period (see Table 2).[70]

Table 2. National League Clubs Consolidated Profit and Loss, 1945–1956

| Year | Boston/ Milw | Brooklyn | Chicago | Cincin | New York | Phila- delphia | Pittsburgh | St. Louis |
|---|---|---|---|---|---|---|---|---|
| 1945 | (137,142) | 252,721 | 45,554 | (33,224) | 339,079 | (202,923) | 43,942 | 94,826 |
| 1946 | 39,565 | 412,314 | 510,053 | 192,499 | (211,546) | 124,563 | 71,799 | 699,093 |
| 1947 | 229,153 | 519,143 | 278,918 | 207,685 | 529,827 | 64,163 | 39,497 | 630,978 |
| 1948 | 238,104 | 543,201 | 141,128 | 163,632 | (114,286) | (197,886) | 66,071 | 608,663 |
| 1949 | 147,934 | 642,614 | 211,523 | 73,162 | (88,103) | 46,757 | 194,899 | 857,553 |
| 1950 | (316,510) | (8,587) | (133,124) | (64,873) | (264,114) | 309,579 | 138,220 | 263,202 |
| 1951 | | | | | | | | |
| 1952 | (459,099) | 446,102 | 154,793 | (68,368) | (222,344) | (118,029) | (677,263) | (89,152) |
| 1953 | 637,718 | 290,006 | (418,363) | 15,518 | (63,307) | (10,688) | (421,422) | (702,193) |
| 1954 | 457,110 | 209,979 | (72,014) | 24,198 | 395,725 | (256,306) | (198,920) | (589,382) |
| 1955 | 807,395 | 427,195 | 68,684 | 53,145 | 151,113 | (270,671) | (601,846) | (43,142) |
| 1956 | 414,398 | 487,462 | (159,712) | 301,216 | 81,415 | (78,063) | (47,852) | 329,495 |

NOTE. Brooklyn Dodgers and Pittsburgh Pirates profits include associated real estate companies.
Boston moved to Milwaukee in 1953.
Parentheses indicate net loss.
There is no data available for 1951.
SOURCE: US Congress, House, Judiciary Committee, *Organized Baseball: Hearings before the Subcommittee on Study of Monopoly Power,* 82nd Cong., 1st sess., 1951, serial 1, part 6 (Washington, DC: Government Printing Office, 1952), 1600; US Senate, Committee on the Judiciary, *Organized Professional Team Sports: Hearings before the Subcommittee on Antitrust and Monopoly of the Committee of the Judiciary,* 85th Cong., 2nd Sess. (Washington, DC: Government Printing Office, 1957), 353.

The Yankees dominated AL bottom lines, making a remarkable 42.1 percent of all profits ($3,651,358) from 1947 to 1956, averaging $405,706 a year (see Table 3). The Cleveland Indians were second at 30.6 percent ($2,650,837). The Yankees led the AL in after-tax profits in 1946–1948 (a record $846,737 in 1947), 1950, 1952–1953, and 1956.[71]

It should be pointed out that MLB accounting procedures resulted in the under reporting of "actual" profits. Brooklyn congressman Emanuel Celler, chairman of the House Judiciary subcommittee investigating Organized Baseball in 1951, claimed the Dodgers underreported profits since their data did not reflect the income of certain club officials, notably Branch Rickey, whose bonuses surpassed $730,000. This amount appeared on the books as a debit, although it was actually part of the president's compensation. Rickey's base salary in 1943 was $25,000, raised to $50,000 after the war, while his partners made just $2,000. Rickey's contract included a 15 percent bonus of the team's pretax profit during the war and 10 percent thereafter. He earned more than $500,000 from 1945 through 1950 based on his salary, a $5,000 expense

Table 3. American League Clubs Consolidated Profit and Loss, 1945–1956

| *Year* | *Boston* | *Chicago* | *Cleveland* | *Detroit* | *New York* | *Philadelphia* | *St. Louis/ Baltimore* | *Washington* |
|---|---|---|---|---|---|---|---|---|
| *1945* | (30,287) | 102,237 | 108,737 | 191,755 | 200,959 | (17,026) | 30,452 | 222,473 |
| *1946* | 405,133 | 291,262 | 375,679 | 467,283 | 808,866 | 82,709 | 260,225 | 357,414 |
| *1947* | (95,109) | 209,264 | 318,801 | 196,750 | 846,737 | 129,809 | 303,170 | 457,195 |
| *1948* | (202,875) | 69,106 | 499,819 | 255,146 | 516,476 | 233,258 | 156,783 | 261,020 |
| *1949* | 21,257 | 102,554 | 506,218 | 33,229 | 346,806 | 90,306 | 83,482 | (18,323) |
| *1950* | (100,992) | 65,363 | 458,694 | 112,638 | 497,000 | (315,921) | 42,957 | 5,117 |
| *1952* | (342,014) | 65,052 | 204,088 | (26,265) | 223,943 | (51,437) | (329,637) | $58,471 |
| *1953* | (421,276) | 204,720 | 157,288 | 43,639 | 622,185 | (102,461) | (706,998) | 26,607 |
| *1954* | 3,086 | 202,897 | 583,283 | 86,465 | 174,876 | (217,936) | 643,407 | 48,800 |
| *1955* | 242,901 | 201,631 | 89,756 | 257,191 | 121,852 | 28,214 | (86,715) | 4,222 |
| *1956* | 122,032 | 141,089 | (167,110) | 81,591 | 301,483 | 1,657 | 69,307 | 23,218 |

Parentheses indicate loss.
There is no data available for 1951.
SOURCE: US Congress, House, Judiciary Committee, *Organized Baseball: Hearings before the Subcommittee on Study of Monopoly Power*, 82nd Cong., 1st sess., 1951, serial 1, part 6 (Washington, DC: Government Printing Office, 1952), 1601; United States, Congress, House, Committee on the Judiciary, Subcommittee on Study of Monopoly Power, *Organized Professional Team Sports: Hearings before the Antitrust Subcommittee*, 85th Cong., 1st sess., pt. 1, serial 8, June 17–August 8, 1957 (Washington, DC: Government Printing Office, 1957), 353.

account, $43,312.50 in dividends, and bonuses of at least $237,000 based on the team's pretax profits ($2,290,170.73). Rickey was baseball's most highly compensated executive.[72]

Another important tax consequence resulted from the team's purchase of the struggling Brooklyn Dodgers franchise in the All American Football Conference for $1 after the 1947 football season. The football team reported a loss of $400,000 in the 1948 season and nearly $350,000 in 1949 when the league dissolved. Accountants applied a $300,000 debt from the football club to the baseball team for tax purposes in 1948 and $167,000 in 1950. These legal deductions resulted in a reported profit that was far less than the baseball team actually earned.[73]

## Components of Profitability

Sources of revenue changed significantly in baseball's silver era. MLB's gross operating income (GOI) from ball games in 1950 was 74.1 percent (57.2 percent from home games; 14.1 percent from road games, and 2.8 percent from exhibitions), compared to 87.6 percent in 1929 and 82.5 percent in 1946 (see Table 4).[74]

Table 4. Sources of Major League Revenue (Percent of Gross)

| *Year* | *Home Games* | *Away Games* | *Exhibitions* | *Concessions* | *Other* | *Media* |
|---|---|---|---|---|---|---|
| 1929 | 62.4 | 21.1 | 4.2 | 5.5 | 6.9 | 0 |
| 1933 | 57.2 | 23.1 | 5.1 | 6.4 | 7.9 | 0.3 |
| 1939 | 55.9 | 19.2 | 4.6 | 7.0 | 6.0 | 7.3 |
| 1943 | 55.2 | 17.9 | 2.9 | 10.0 | 7.3 | 6.7 |
| 1946 | 60.5 | 17.5 | 4.5 | 8.7 | 5.8 | 8.7 |
| 1950 | 57.2 | 14.1 | 2.8 | 9.2 | 6.2 | 10.5 |

SOURCE: US Congress, House, Judiciary Committee, *Organized Baseball: Hearings before the Subcommittee on Study of Monopoly Power*, 82nd Cong., 1st sess., 1951, serial 1, part 6 (Washington, DC: Government Printing Office, 1952), 1610.

Concession sales rose only marginally from 7.9 percent of revenue in 1939 to 9.2 percent in 1950. However, media revenue grew dramatically, from merely 0.3 percent in 1933, 7.3 percent in 1939, and 3.0 percent in 1946, to 10.5 percent in 1950 and 17.0 percent in 1956. Major league media revenue of $4.16 million in 1952 rose to $7.3 million in 1956, more than a 70 percent appreciation.[75]

Sportswriter Joseph M. Sheehan of the *New York Times* estimated in 1957 that the average club in 1956 earned about $2.475 million in gross income, or a total of $39.6 million. The revenues consisted of $1.35 million (54.5 percent) in home receipts, $150,000 from park rentals, parking fees, and other related sources (6.1 percent), $275,000 in road receipts (11.1 percent), $400,000 in media revenues (16.2 percent), and $300,000 from concessions and advertising privileges (12.1 percent). He also estimated that the Dodgers and Yankees each made $300,000 by appearing in the World Series of 1956.[76]

The Dodgers in 1946 had the highest GOI in the NL ($2,679,869), with the Giants a distant second ($2,055,820), mainly because of lower ticket sales (see Table 5). Yet Dodger fans spent sparingly on concessions ($196,614), fourth in the NL, far below the champion Cardinals ($323,980). An average Brooklyn fan spent just 11 cents at the ballpark in 1946, compared to 31 cents in St. Louis. The Dodgers were fourth in concession income from 1952 to 1956 ($1,474,306), fifth highest in the NL.[77]

The Yankees in 1946 had a revenue of $3,455,173 (over $1.3 million more than the Tigers, who were second), and earnings of $808,866. The main source of revenue was home game ticket sales ($2,276,585). The team also made $327,204 from concessions (14 cents per attendee), double that of any other team in the league. From 1952 to 1956, the team made $2,242,749 (or $448,540 a year) from concessions, surpassed only by the Cardinals, and more than double the average of the other AL teams. The Yankee income per attendee of 0.29 was third in the

Table 5. Income, Expenses, and Profit, New York and Brooklyn, 1946, 1950, 1952–1956

| | Brooklyn | | | New York | | |
|---|---|---|---|---|---|---|
| *Year* | *Income ($)* | *Expenses* | *Consolid. profit* | *Income* | *Expenses* | *Consolid. profit* |
| 1946 | 2,679,869 | 1,682,566 | 412,314 | 3,455,173 | 2,141,279 | 808,806 |
| 1950 | 2,612,059 | 2,347,662 | -8,587 | 4,211,964 | 2,883,822 | 497,000 |
| 1952 | 2,833,963 | 1,859,273 | 446,102 | 3,996,665 | 3,066,181 | 223,943 |
| 1953 | 3,009,382 | 2,232,353 | 290,006 | 4,125,074 | 3,146,182 | 622,185 |
| 1954 | 2,816,589 | 2,040,184 | 209,979 | 4,504,836 | 3,750,175 | 174,876 |
| 1955 | 3,501,124 | 2,216,175 | 427,195 | 4,898,665 | 3,900,476 | 121,852 |
| 1956 | 3,880,824 | 2,384,311 | 487,462 | 5,017,094 | 3,913,183 | 301,483 |

SOURCE: US, Congress, House, Judiciary Committee, *Organized Baseball: Hearings before the Subcommittee on Study of Monopoly Power*, 82nd Cong., 1st sess., 1951, serial 1, part 6 (Washington, DC: Government Printing Office, 1952), 1604–5, 1608–9; US Congress, House, Committee on the Judiciary, Subcommittee on Study of Monopoly Power, *Organized Professional Team Sports: Hearings before the Antitrust Subcommittee*, 85th Cong., 1st sess., pt. 1, serial 8, June 17–August 8, 1957 (Washington, DC: Government Printing Office, 1957), 354–63.

majors behind the Cubs (0.36) and the Philadelphia/Kansas City A's (0.30).[78] The Yankees in 1946 also made about $250,000 from their farm system, and $100,000 from renting their ballparks in New York, Newark, Kansas City, and Norfolk to Negro League teams, $45,000 from radio, and $75,000 from local TV, making them the first ML team to make money from the new medium.[79]

## Media and Baseball

The first radio broadcasts of baseball occurred in 1921 when Pittsburgh's KDKA aired a game between the Pirates and the Phillies. KDKA and WJZ of Newark also broadcast the World Series, using reports sent to the station by telegraph transmissions. In 1925, the Chicago Cubs became the first team to permit regular airing of home games, but charged no fee, figuring it was good publicity. They attributed the 117 percent increase in attendance from 1925 to 1931 largely to radio. Other teams slowly followed, charging nominal amounts for the rights. However, the New York teams believed radio transmissions hurt them at the box office, and agreed in 1934 to bar broadcasts for five years. Then in December 1938, new Dodger president Larry MacPhail, formerly employed by the Cincinnati Reds, owned by Powel Crosley Jr., the world's leading radio manufacturer, announced the team would go on air. The Dodgers made money by selling rights to advertise during the game. General Mills, Socony-Vacuum (Mobil Oil), and Proctor and Gamble sponsored home and away games on 50,000-watt WHN (1050; renamed WMGM in 1948) for $1,000 a game. The

Yankees and Giants also went on air in 1939 with the same sponsors on WABC (the local CBS-owned station), and shared the same announcers. The Yankees expected to make $175,000–$200,000, while the Giants, who only ran games with the Dodgers, anticipated $150,000. Two years later the Yankees suspended broadcasts because they could not find a sponsor. The shared announcing format ended after 1946 because the Yankees wanted to send their sportscasters on the road to do live games instead of game re-creations.[80]

New York's first major baseball broadcaster was Mel Allen (b. Melvin A. Israel), an alumnus of the University of Alabama School of Law, who changed his name because CBS found it too ethnic. He joined the Yankees in June 1939, after doing the color commentary for the 1938 World Series, and became their primary broadcaster one year later. Allen reported Yankee games on WINS from 1942 to 1943, served in the military, and then returned after the war. He spoke from the perspective of a fan. Allen became almost synonymous with the team, renowned for such catch phrases as "How a-bout that?!" and "Three and two. What'll he do?" Allen called twenty-two World Series on radio and television.[81]

Brooklyn's primary announcer was Floridian Red Barber, who started with Cincinnati in 1934, and then followed MacPhail to Brooklyn. Barber re-created road games until 1948 as the news came in over the wire, using his imagination to fill in the details. By the late 1940s, some 300,000 people heard his Dodger broadcasts. Fans enjoyed his folksy manner, neutrality, and catchphrases like "They're tearin' up the pea patch"; "The bases are F.O.B." (Full of Brooklyns); and "Sittin' in the catbird seat." His most successful mentee was Vin Scully, who arrived in 1950, and replaced Barber in 1954.[82]

### TV and the Business of Baseball

In 1939, Red Barber broadcast the first televised Major League game on experimental station W2XBS. Seven years later, there were just nine commercial TV stations in the United States, serving 6,000 viewers, often watching in saloons. Eighteen Dodger games were televised on CBS on an experimental basis. CBS broadcast all 1947 Dodger homes games, sponsored by Ford Motor Company and General Foods. Barber worked the first six innings on TV and then switched to radio. Productions cost about $1,000–$2,000. So many women listened to games on radio that advertisers like General Foods became a sponsor in 1949. Schaefer Beer sponsored broadcasts on radio and TV by 1949, and two years later Schaefer signed a ten-year deal for Dodger radio and TV rights for nearly $5 million, joined by Lucky Strike one year later on radio.[83]

The Yankees signed in 1947 with Dumont (WABD, channel 5) to televise seventy-seven home games and eleven away games for $75,000, and NBC signed the Giants for $50,000. By June, televised baseball was so popular that nearly half of all TV shows were ball games. The World Series was televised by WCBS in New York, Philadelphia, Washington, DC, and Schenectady, sponsored by Gillette and Ford. TV rights went for $65,000, a fraction of the tried-and-true radio rights, which went for $175,000. In 1948, the single top show, and three of the five top-rated local broadcasts were Yankee games. The Bronx Bombers moved their night games to WPIX in 1951 because of conflicts with Dumont's network, and one year later all Yankee games were on WPIX, typically sponsored by Ballantine beer and Camel cigarettes.[84]

The penetration of TVs into homes was astonishingly rapid, and by 1950 New York alone had 2 million TVs, despite the hefty price. A 12-inch Philco console cost $499 ($5,084 in 2017 dollars), and a 17-inch GE table top cost $289 in 1951 ($2,729 in 2017 dollars). By 1952, one-third of all American homes had televisions. Barber broadcast the World Series from 1948 to 1952 over Mutual radio, and teamed on NBC-TV with Mel Allen. Refused a raise in 1953, and irate that O'Malley would not back him, Barber sat out the Series, resigned from the Dodgers, and moved over to the Yankees. By then 50 million people were watching the World Series.[85]

**Media Revenues**

Dodger media revenue in this era was always the highest in the NL, with the Giants second, reflecting the huge and valuable metropolitan New York radio and TV markets. Historian Henry Fetter credits the Dodgers and Giants in the 1950s with pioneering in the NL a new model of baseball economics heavily reliant on media revenue, which cushioned the decline in attendance. In 1946 Brooklyn made $150,000 in media revenue (essentially just radio), but that soon changed. From 1950 to 1956, the Dodgers averaged $624,425 from radio and TV, and the Giants $487,809. Media revenue made up about 30 percent of their GOI, compared to about 10 percent for the rest of the league. By 1955, New York teams had all their home games on TV and one-third of their road games. The Dodgers drew the largest TV audiences, double the Giants and 150 percent more than the Yankees. Media money enabled the Dodgers to earn a slightly larger profit in 1956 than the Braves, even though their attendance was 1 million less. That year the Dodgers made $888,270, at least double every NL team except for the Giants ($730,593). Milwaukee was last in media revenue among all MLB teams ($125,000).[86]

The Yankees barely outdid the Dodgers in media revenue from 1952 to 1956, averaging $636,042, and like the Dodgers, earned about double the average for all MLB. The Yankees led the AL every year in media revenue except 1956 when the Indians radio/TV revenue surpassed $1 million.[87]

### Team Expenses

Every year the Yankees had more income than the Dodgers, but also had larger expenditures. The Bronx Bombers led all MLB in expenses every year from 1952 to 1956, while the Dodgers were third in the NL in expenditures in 1952 and 1953, fourth in 1954, and third in 1955 and 1956. This was below what might have been expected given their outstanding lineup.[88] Team expenses included ballpark maintenance, operating the farm system, and salaries for players, coaches, and front office personnel. *Times* reporter Joseph Sheehan estimated in 1957 that the typical team spent $1.9 million each year for team payroll. He estimated the biggest expenditure was $600,000 (31.6 percent) for player procurement and development, and operating a farm system. Player compensation was about $400,000 (21.1 percent), the same as front office salaries and administrative costs.[89]

The other outlays were $250,000 (13.1 percent) for spring training, travel, and equipment, and another $250,000 for rent and ballpark maintenance. There are not a lot of data on the cost of operating a farm system or ballpark preservation. The Dodgers spent an average of 10.3 percent of their operating budget on its large farm system and $673,144.63 on park maintenance from 1944 to 1948, including $238,176.23 just in 1948.[90]

### Player Salaries

Player salaries were a significantly smaller part of team costs in the 1950s than in the past. Team salaries were about one-third of gross Major League expenditures from 1929 through 1939, falling to 28.9 percent in 1943. After the war, the players' share of expenses fell to one-fourth (24.8) and to one-fifth (21.6 percent) in 1950. The mean salary of $7,531 in 1929 dropped by 20 percent to $6,009 in 1933, the heart of the Depression, but was nearly recouped in 1939 ($7,306). Salaries dropped by 12.1 percent during the war due to declining attendance and second-rate players, but rose dramatically after the war to $11,294 in

1946, a 75.2 percent increase. Four years later the average salary reached $13,842 ($138,728 in 2016), with a median of about $11,000.[91]

Average MLB team salaries (which included players, coaches, and managers) rose from 1943 to 1946 by 75.6 percent. The Dodgers had been first in the NL in 1943, but fell to sixth three years later ($313,369) when the average NL was $321,625 ($4,179,800 in 2016), ranging from about $302,000 to $349,000. NL salaries continued to escalate, averaging $423,812 in 1950, and although the Dodgers won pennants in 1947 and 1949, the team's salaries barely kept pace at $420,259, good for fifth place. The league suffered a decline of 1,164,102 in attendance in 1950, and one result was a precipitous drop in salaries in 1951. Brooklyn fell to $357,500, yet moved up to second in team wages. The Bums were third in 1950, fourth in 1953, led the NL in 1954 at $441,500 (the average Dodger made $17,660), and third in 1955. Then following their only World Series title in Brooklyn, the team was again highest paid in the NL at $472,000 (average $18,880).[92]

Contrary to conventional wisdom, the Yankees were not always the highest-paid club in the early 1950s, although they were always higher than the Dodgers, except in 1955, and then just marginally. They were the highest-paid team in baseball in 1950 at $651,501 (the highest average MLB salary between 1950 and 1956), and 1951 (despite GM Weiss's niggardliness), but only fifth in MLB in 1952 and fourth in 1953. The Yankees led the AL in 1954, when its salaries rose from $438,250 to $510,000 (averaging $18,890), though still surpassed by the overpaid Chicago Cubs at $567,000, who came in seventh in the NL. The Yankees won 103 games in 1954, yet came in second to the Indians, who won 111 games. The Bombers had their salaries dropped by 19.3 percent, to an era low $411,500, only the seventh highest in MLB, and marginally lower than the Dodgers. After the Yankees lost the 1955 World Series to the Dodgers, they kicked up the team salaries for 1956 by nearly 20 percent to $492,000 (average $17,570), $47,480 more than the Indians, the second best-paid team.[93]

The outstanding players among the "Boys of Summer" did not receive outlandish salaries. In 1947, for instance, shortstop Pee Wee Reese was the highest paid at $23,500, and rookies Jackie Robinson and Duke Snider each made just $5,000. By 1950, Robinson moved up to $30,000, surpassed only by Reese at $35,000, and peaked two years later at $39,750. In the last pennant-winning campaign in 1956, Snider was the highest-paid Dodger, at $44,000, followed by star catcher Roy Campanella at $42,000.[94]

Yankee stars were generally better compensated than the Dodgers. The top-paid Yankee was superstar veteran Joe DiMaggio, who earned $100,000 in 1949 and 1950, and then $90,000 for his final year. Shortstop Phil Rizzuto made $55,000 in 1952, far more than any Dodger, and he was surpassed by Yogi Berra, who led MLB in 1956 at $58,000. That year Mickey Mantle, the young superstar who led all baseball in batting average, home runs, and RBIs, made just $30,000.[95]

## New York's Star Center Fielders, 1951–1957

A favorite topic of conversation among New York baseball fans was the comparative greatness of Mickey Mantle, Willie Mays, and Duke Snider. Mays was certainly the best over the course of his entire twenty-two-year career, eclipsing his rivals with 630 home runs, twelve Gold Gloves, and twenty-four All-Star appearances. *The Sporting News* in 1999 rated him the second-greatest player ever. However, during the 1951–1957 period, which encompassed the Mantle/Mays rookie season through the Giants last year in New York, he missed nearly two complete seasons due to military service (1952–1953), started only one All-Star game, and his prodigious offensive accomplishments lagged behind those of the other two stars. Snider was the most experienced center fielder, having played four more seasons. His batting statistics were awesome, and he was a great run producer. In these years, he averaged 36.7 home runs, 108 RBIs, and 111 runs scored. Snider hit 80 more home runs than Mays and drove in 109 more runs than Mantle, taking advantage of batter-friendly Ebbets Field. However, he started only two All-Star games and won no MVPs, which may have been more of a reflection on the many star players in the NL than any deficiency on his part.[96]

Mantle, an unassuming nineteen-year-old rookie from Oklahoma, was the American League's dominant offensive player from 1951 to 1957, when the Yankees won six pennants and four World Series. He was a switch-hitter, the fastest runner in baseball, and the sport's most powerful slugger. Mantle won the Triple Crown in 1956, leading not just the AL, but all of MLB in batting average, home runs, and RBIs. Through 1957, Mickey started on five All-Star teams, won two MVPs, two home run titles, and batted .316, with 195 home runs, 763 runs scored, 669 RBIs, and an incredible .424 on-base percentage, 35 points more than Snider and 38 points more than Mays (see Table 6).[97]

Table 6. Comparison of Mantle, Mays, and Snider, 1951–1957

| Player | All-Star Starts | MVP | B.A. (1) | Homers (1) | Runs (1) | RBIs (1) | Total Bases (1) | Slugging (1) | Player of Year (1) | WAR (1) | OPS (1) |
|---|---|---|---|---|---|---|---|---|---|---|---|
| *Mantle* | 5 | 2 | .316(1) | 207(2) | 763(3) | 669(1) | 1 | 2 | 1 | 3 | 3 |
| *Mays* | 1 | 1 | .311 | 187(1) | 531 | 509 | 1 | 3 | 1 | 3 | 2 |
| *Snider* | 2 | 0 | .305 | 257(1) | 757(3) | 778(1) | 2 | 2 | 1 | 1 | 2 |

Source: http://www.baseball-reference.com/players/.
Note: (1) = Number of times led league in a given season.
WAR = Wins Above Replace. A statistical summary of a player's total contributions to his team.
OPS = On base percentage plus slugging percentage.

## Dodgers vs. Yankees in the World Series

The New York-Brooklyn decade began with the 1947 World Series. In game four, at Ebbets Field, with the Yankees up 2 games to 1, Yankee pitcher Bill Bevens had a no-hitter going into the bottom of the ninth, with the Yanks ahead 2–1. With two out, and runners on first and second, Dodger pinch hitter Cookie Lavagetto drove the second pitch off the right field wall for a double, knocking in both runners to win the game. However, the Yankees won in seven games as reliever Joe Page came in during the fifth inning with the Yankees up a run, and pitched the rest of the way to win 5–2.

In the 1949 Series, the Boys of Summer won the pennant over the Cardinals by one game. They were led on the field by Robinson, Campanella, Reese, Hodges, Snider, Billy Cox, and Carl Furillo, and on the mound by Rookie of the Year Don Newcombe, Preacher Roe, Ralph Branca, and Joe Hatten. However, the Yankees, who won the pennant by one game over the Red Sox, captured the Series by four games to one.

The Dodgers lost the pennant in 1950 on the final day of the season to the Philadelphia Phillies. In the bottom of the ninth inning, with the game tied 1–1, nobody out, and runners at first and second, the Dodgers' Cal Abrams tried to score from second on a single, but was thrown out at home by center fielder Richie Ashburn. Third base coach Milt Stock did not notice Ashburn was playing close to the infield and failed to hold Abrams at third. The Phils won the game an inning later, only to be swept by the Yankees in the World Series.[98]

The following year was even more disappointing, as the Dodgers, led by NL MVP Roy Campanella, swooned late in the season, losing a 13 and a half game lead, setting up a 3-game playoff. The Dodgers lost in game three in the bottom of the ninth, when Bobby Thomson hit a dramatic 3-run homer off Ralph Branca, the "Shot Heard 'Round the World," to win the game 5–4. The Yanks then beat the Giants 4 games to 2.

In 1952, the Dodgers won the pennant by 4 and a half games over the Giants, placed seven players on the All-Star team, scored 775 runs, the most in the majors, and allowed just 603 runs. The Yankees took the AL pennant by 2 games over the Indians, led by seven All-Stars, including twenty-year-old Mickey Mantle. The Dodgers were up 3 games to 2, but lost the final two games at Ebbets Field. The big moment came in game seven with the Yankees up 4–2 when Brooklyn loaded the bases against Vic Raschi with one out. Reliever Bob Kuzava retired Snider, and then Robinson hit an infield pop fly. When no one took charge, second baseman Billy Martin rushed in to catch the ball off his shoe tops to end the inning. Kuzava shut out the Dodgers the rest of the way.

The Dodgers repeated as NL champions in 1953, going 105-49, best in team history. Player of the Year Campanella led the NL in RBIs (142), Furillo won the batting title (.344), and second baseman Jim Gilliam was Rookie of the Year. The Yankees took the AL pennant by 8 and a half games over the Indians. The Yankees won the first two games of the Series at home, and the Dodgers took the next two at home to even the Series. But the Yankees captured the next two to win their fifth straight World Series. Second baseman Billy Martin was Series MVP, with a .500 batting average, and a record 12 hits.

In 1954 rookie manager Walter Alston led the team to a 92-62 record, finishing five games behind the Giants, while the Yankees, with 103 wins, came in second to Cleveland's 111 victories. The following year, the Dodgers easily won the NL race (98-55) by 13 and a half games, leading in runs scored and fewest runs allowed, and Campanella won the MVP. The Yankees won the AL by 3 games over the always tough Indians, led by MVP Yogi Berra. The World Series went seven games. The Dodgers took a 2–0 lead in the deciding game with Johnny Podres on the mound. In the Yankees sixth, with runners on first and second, Berra hit a line drive near the left field line that looked like a sure hit, but it was caught by Sandy Amorós, and turned into a double play, killing the last Yankees rally. This was the first and only Dodger championship in Brooklyn, and the first Yankees World Series loss since 1942.

The Dodgers repeated as NL champions in 1956, finishing a game ahead of the Braves. Brooklyn was led by MVP and Cy Young award winner Don Newcombe (27–7). The Yankees beat Cleveland by 9 games, led by MVP Mantle, AP Athlete of the Year. The Dodgers and Yankees split the first four games. In game five, Yankee Don Larsen pitched the only perfect game in World Series history, but Dodger Clem Labine responded with a 1–0 shutout. The Yankees took the decisive final game by a resounding 9–0.

## The Dodgers Move West

In 1957, the Yankees again took the pennant, led by Mantle as MVP, but lost the World Series in seven to the Milwaukee Braves. On October 8, just before the end of the Series, the Dodger-Yankees era came to a resounding conclusion with the stunning announcement that the Dodgers were off to Los Angeles. O'Malley had tried for a few years to develop an alternative to the old Ebbets Field, with its small capacity and inadequate parking. He was also concerned about demographic changes in the neighborhood and the borough in general, as whites moved to Queens and the suburbs, and were replaced by lower-income people of color. O'Malley's preference was to remain in Brooklyn and build his own ballpark, provided that the city utilize the power of eminent domain under the Title I slum clearance program to help him secure a downtown location (at Atlantic and Flatbush Avenues). He also wanted the city to promise highway improvements to make his new park more accessible to Long Island residents. However, he could not convince the regional planning authorities, including master builder Robert Moses, the New York Board of Estimate, other leading city politicians, the local business community, or even the general public to support his plan. The consensus was that O'Malley's plan was not financially feasible, would require a misuse of public authority, and that O'Malley would not move his franchise. In addition, no top-tier Major League team had ever moved in the twentieth century. O'Malley rejected the offer of such alternative sites as Flushing Meadows, Queens, now the location of Citi Stadium, where the Mets play. He believed that any move out of Brooklyn would cost the team its identity.[99]

O'Malley did have a suitor in Los Angeles, where local boosters believed the time was ripe, especially with the growth of cross-country air travel, for a Major League team. In 1957, O'Malley made a deal with Los Angeles to heavily subsidize his move. He traded Los Angeles's minor league Wrigley Field for a downtown site known as Chavez Ravine, and the city and county agreed to grade the land and construct roads. The Giants joined the Dodgers in moving west, relocating to San Francisco. O'Malley made an astute business decision that was a godsend to Major League Baseball's national expansion, but it shattered the hearts of Brooklynites. Years later, when journalists Jack Newfield and Pete Hamill dined together, they each wrote down on napkins, in order, the three worst human beings who ever lived: "Hitler, Stalin, Walter O'Malley."[100]

## Conclusion

The Dodgers and Yankees dominated baseball after World War II because of strong leadership that spent heavily to build and promote their teams, taking advantage of the New York market and the quality of their players to draw well at the box office and earn large profits from radio and TV. The Dodgers under Branch Rickey led the way in integrating MLB, which, along with their farm system, helped them field outstanding lineups. The Yankees also assembled superb teams, relying on excellent scouts, a productive farm system, and trades. The Yankees were not, however, committed to recruiting African American prospects, and were the thirteenth team to integrate.

Dodger fans had a unique relationship with their team. They were primarily borough residents who strongly identified with the club and the players as representatives of their community and its presumed progressive beliefs. Fans idolized the star players, but did not put them on a pedestal, seeing them as members and residents of their society. Yankee fans were more middle class, with a smattering of the upper class. They mainly came from the Bronx and Manhattan, but with more support from the broader metropolitan area. They were less intense supporters, who enjoyed identifying with winners, and who took the team's success pretty much for granted. Yankee fans admired and respected their heroes, some of whom, like pitcher Whitey Ford and shortstop Phil Rizzuto, were local boys, but for the most part, considered the players remote demigods, especially the distant and reserved Joe DiMaggio and the shy Mickey Mantle.

Both teams' preeminence continued well beyond 1957. The Yankees won six pennants and four World Series between 1958 and 1964, while the Dodgers, ensconced in Los Angeles, won four NL pennants between 1959 and 1966 and three World Series titles.

The Dodgers left New York because city officials would not provide them the support O'Malley demanded. No one in New York expected the Dodgers or the Giants to flee the biggest sports market in the country. Before the Dodgers left New York, the only teams to move from their original host city, the Boston Braves, Philadelphia Athletics, and St. Louis Browns, were all second teams in a two-team city, and in no case did their municipality try to keep them home. The migration west by the Dodgers and Giants encouraged other NL teams to threaten to move, which pressured local governments in St. Louis, Cincinnati, Pittsburgh, and Philadelphia to cave into their demands and build publicly financed stadiums at sites served by multilane highways catering to suburban residents.[101]

The Dodgers left New York because O'Malley found a great opportunity to make more money in Los Angeles. The Dodgers were doing quite well in Brooklyn, and as late as 1954–1956, while decisions were being made about the franchise's future, the Dodgers made more money ($1,124,636) than the Yankees ($598,211), mainly because they had much smaller expenditures. However, O'Malley's attitudes were more influenced by the example of the new Milwaukee franchise, which thrived in spite of a meager TV contract. The migration westward was a great move for the Dodgers and MLB, but not for Brooklyn.

The loss of the team hurt Brooklyn financially, shattered the hearts of residents, and symbolized the area's economic decline and demographic changes. As Neil Sullivan, author of *The Dodgers Move West*, who supported the franchise shift, points out, "The Dodgers were more than a business. They represented a cultural totem, a tangible symbol of the community and its values."[102] The greatest cost to Brooklyn was to its collective psyche, demonstrating that Brooklyn was no longer a Major League city in any sense of that term.

The Dodger-Yankee era of the 1950s strongly resonates today in the memory of war babies and older baby boomers, marking the beginning of the end of their childhood and innocence. Baseball players, especially Jackie Robinson and Mickey Mantle, not generals or politicians, were the heroes of young boys. They played *the* American game, which was televised most afternoons. They remain icons. In 2016, a 1952 Topps Mantle baseball card sold for $525,000.[103]

Children who grew up in the 1950s may not have been raised in the best of times, in a world of racism, sexism, and the fear of atomic warfare, but compared to the youth of their parents, or the problems of their children in the postindustrial society and an international community of sectarian violence and brutality, the 1950s does not look so bad. While all children did not grow up in the middle-class white world of *Leave It to Beaver* or *Father Knows Best*, American families of all races and socioeconomic statuses were far more likely to have a "traditional family," in which they felt safe and secure. Kids growing up in metropolitan New York had relatively little sense of deprivation, especially compared to the twenty-first century. Working-class families like the Rileys and the Nortons were on TV (albeit typically with weak male characters and strong wives), and even Lucy and Desi lived modestly in Manhattan. Adults today remember growing up in the 1950s and feeling safe while walking to school, going to the movies, playing in the park, and even riding the subway. The rivalry between the boys in pinstripes and the boys of summer forms part of the positive remembrance of childhood in New York in the 1950s, with its well-ordered social system that included the World Series every fall. For youthful baseball fans in the 1950s, this comfortable world was torn asunder when the Dodgers and the Giants left New York.[104]

CHAPTER TWO

# The Team That Time Forgot

## The New York Giants of the 1950s in History and Memory

*Henry D. Fetter*

*Old men forget; yet all shall be forgot*
*But he'll remember, with advantages,*
*What feats he did that day.*

*Shakespeare, Henry V: Act 4, Scene 3*

By all rights, the New York Giants of the 1950s deserve a celebrated place in the annals of Major League Baseball. This was the team that fired Bobby Thomson's "shot heard 'round the world" to win the 1951 National League pennant playoff against the archrival Brooklyn Dodgers and cap the most dramatic stretch drive in baseball history. This was the team that, three years later, scored perhaps the greatest of all World Series upsets by sweeping the heavily favored Cleveland Indians—winner of a then record 111 games in the American League regular season—on the strength of "*the* Catch" in the Series' first game by Willie Mays and uncanny pinch slugging by journeyman Dusty Rhodes. This was the team that was led on the field by the greatest ballplayer of his era if not of all-time; that was managed by one of the few managers in the sport's annals who was a box office attraction in and of himself; that celebrated its 1954 pennant with a ticker-tape parade down Broadway before 1 million fans; that was cheered on by a glittering array of celebrities of stage and screen; that not only captured the imagination of an imposing array of literary talent but that inspired a pioneering effort in the then fallow field of stylish baseball book writing for adults.

The 1951 pennant and 1954 World Championship provide the hard evidence for the Giants as one of baseball's notable teams. But you have to look beyond

"The New York Giants' Last Hurrah": Dusty Rhodes homers in the second game of the 1954 World Series en route to a sweep of the Cleveland Indians. *Wikimedia Commons / Public Domain.*

the record book to capture the full dimensions of their rightful claim on the collective memory of the sport that still reigned as the uncontested "national pastime." Leo Durocher and Willie Mays were both the subjects of extraordinary acclaim and devotion. Durocher had such an avid following that a number of Dodger fans, even including Brooklyn's cowbell-ringing superfan Hilda

Chester, followed him across the East River when he traded the "B" on his cap for "NY" during the 1948 season, and swapped loyalties to an erstwhile most detested rival.[1] "No man in the game," a *Sports Illustrated* profile declared, "has inspired as much controversy and debate; no one has been more admired and feared and hated, often simultaneously."[2] Of center fielder Willie Mays, Murray Kempton would later write, "all of a sudden, you remembered all the promises the rich have made to the poor for the last thirteen years and the only one they kept was the promise about Willie Mays. They told us then that he would be the greatest baseball player we would ever see, and he was."[3]

And there was no lack of talent in Mays's supporting cast. Referring to second baseman Eddie Stanky aka "The Brat," Durocher once said, "he can't hit, he can't field, he can't run, all he can do is beat you"—which Stanky proved when he kicked the ball out of Yankee shortstop Phil Rizzuto's glove in the third game of the 1951 World Series to lead the Giants to a two games to one lead, only the second time since 1926 that the Bronx Bombers had been down after three games in a Series. Outfielder Monte Irvin was a Negro League star and future Hall of Famer. Pitcher Sal Maglie was feared by opposing batters as "the Barber" sure to give them a close shave at the plate. And the team as a whole displayed the kind of continuity that is now a casualty of free agency, with first baseman Whitey Lockman, shortstop Al Dark, catcher Wes Westrum, outfielders Irvin and Don Mueller, and pitcher Maglie joining Mays as teammates in both 1951 and 1954.

Star power off the field as well as on? Flamboyant actress and public personality Tallulah Bankhead backed the Giants with a brand of celebrity fandom that no other team could match. "My most violent enthusiasm?" Tallulah (for whom one name was enough of an identifier—just like "Leo") once confided. "Well, my dears, for all you've heard to the contrary, and I guess you've heard plenty, it's the New York Giants," lending the team a dollop of her own scandalous reputation by association.[4] She was known to be a "red-hot Giant fan" and a reporter interviewing her in advance of a return to Broadway in 1954 noted that "occasionally she would stop talking long enough to switch on the radio to check on the Giants-Phillies double-header . . . had it occurred in New York, it would have been on television, and Miss Bankhead couldn't have kept her eyes off it."[5] And as for Willie Mays, her appreciation exceeded even Kempton's. "There have been only two geniuses in the world, Willie Mays and Willie Shakespeare," she wrote, although admitting, "But, darling, I think you'd better put Shakespeare first."[6]

Hollywood may have made movies about the Dodgers but the Giants of the 1950s were actually married to the glamour capital. Laraine Day, manager Durocher's movie star wife, took on a novel role as the distaff public face of the Giants, hosting a pregame television show and becoming the first woman to perform at the otherwise all-male annual show of the New York Baseball Writers Association in 1951.[7] The next year, she published a chatty account of her experience with the team under the punning title *Day with the Giants.* "Every day is Ladies' Day for Laraine Day and she makes a good story of it," in the judgment of the *Times.*[8] The touch of star quality that Day brought to these unprecedented initiatives was not without sociological significance. Photographs of her embracing Willie Mays appeared in the New York press; publication of one of the latter on the cover of *Sports Illustrated* (Day in the center between Durocher and Mays with her arms around their shoulders) in April 1955 was unusual for a national magazine at the time and elicited a barrage of hate mail in a subsequent issue taking the magazine to task for "disgusting racial propaganda" that was "an insult to every decent white woman everywhere."[9]

Erudite support from the world of letters? The Giants inspired what may have been the first adult book of baseball reporting, Arnold Hano's pioneering account of the first game of the 1954 World Series.[10] The team fielded a literary support group second to none—Roger Angell, Murray Kempton, Paul Auster, and perhaps most devoted of all, the brilliant and troubled poet Delmore Schwartz, who left a trail of diary entries, story drafts, and letters attesting to his fandom that is likely unmatched among the intellectual set. As his journals reveal, Schwartz was a notably devoted fan, closely following their fortunes through the 1940s and 1950s, attending their 1942 road opener at Braves Field in Boston (while he was teaching at Harvard) under "a purple-black curtain of cloud,"[11] making notes in 1951 for a story in "lyrical prose" about a Dodgers-Giants game at the Polo Grounds, "gala and sunny and green and sparkling with activity," and the "flags on the grandstand snapped in the breeze,"[12] being "distressed by nightfall" after the Giants lost the second game of a double-header[13] and having a productive workday "spoiled" when the Cubs came from behind to beat the Giants on June 4, 1952.[14]

Exploits on the playing field aside, the postwar New York Giants wrote important pages in the social history of the sport and played a leading role in breaking the sport's color bar and making the "national pastime" live up to its pretensions. Following closely behind the Dodgers, they were the second team in the National League to integrate, signing three black ballplayers, including Negro League standout and future Hall of Famer Monte Irvin, in 1949. During the 1951 season, the Giants fielded four black ballplayers in a game "the first time any major league club had played so many non-white athletes at the same time."[15] For the opening game of that year's pennant playoff against the Dodgers, the Giants fielded an all-black outfield—Irvin, Willie Mays, and Hank Thompson—also a Major League first. In the playoff's decisive third game more blacks played for the Giants than the Dodgers.[16] "The Giants commitment to integration," Steve Treder has concluded, "sent a resounding signal to the rest of baseball and to the nation at large . . . and thereby integration was given a crucial push toward the unstoppable momentum it would eventually achieve."[17]

And when it came to another front in the fight against the all-white sport, the Giants did more than give "momentum" a push—they were the prime movers. If the New Yorkers had lagged behind the Dodgers when it came to racial integration, the Giants led all of baseball in reaching beyond the continental United States to tap baseball talent in Latin America. "I think we were the first club that signed players from that whole area," team owner Horace Stoneham recalled in 1973[18] and the New York Giants' pioneering efforts yielded a rich harvest of Major League talent, starting with Ruben Gomez, the first Puerto Rican to pitch in a World Series, in 1954, and Cuban catcher Ray Noble. Scouting in Puerto Rico yielded Orlando Cepeda and Jose Pagan. The Giants were especially ahead of the curve when it came to prospecting in the baseball hotbed of the Dominican Republic (which currently yields no less than 10 percent of all Major Leaguers), homeland of Manny Mota and Felipe and Matty Alou. Unfortunately for the team's Polo Grounds faithful, the most notable of the *New York* Giants's Caribbean acquisitions (including Cepeda and the Alous) made their mark only after the team had relocated to San Francisco.[19] Add to the (long) list of regrets about the Giants' move, the box office gold—not to mention community pride—that Puerto Rican Cepeda would have minted for the team (akin to that garnered by Joe DiMaggio two decades earlier among Italians for the Yankees) had the Giants not abandoned a New York City that was in the process of welcoming hundreds of thousands of his fellow islanders.

There is something else about that team and its time that is worth remembering: Mays was drafted into the army in the spring of 1952 and lost most of that season and all of the next season to his military obligation. "Speaking of Stalin," Delmore Schwartz wrote a friend in 1952, "they have just drafted Willie Mays, which is obviously the result of Stalin's lust for Korea, and the rest of the world, and though they have also drafted [Brooklyn pitcher] Don Newcombe, the Giants' pennant chances are seriously weakened."[20] That the Giants' pennants in 1951 and 1954 were separated by two less successful seasons was largely attributable to Mays's absence. Of course, Mays was hardly the only ballplayer whose career was interrupted by military service in the era of Korea and the Cold War—Dodger pitcher Don Newcombe missed the 1952 and 1953 seasons; the Phillies' Whiz Kid 1950 pennant winners had to play that year's World Series without pitcher Curt Simmons because of a late-season call-up; and Dodger 1955 World Series hero Johnny Podres went into the navy the next year. That a star ballplayer was a citizen first, subject to the obligations imposed across the board, is just as much a token of a vanished baseball era as a holiday double-header or road trips by train.

And for those with a taste for the macabre, a literal shot was fired during a game at the Polo Grounds in the summer of 1950 when a middle-aged baseball fan waiting for the start of the July 4 double-header with the Dodgers was killed by a bullet randomly fired by a teenage boy from a nearby rooftop.[21]

There's so much that should be remembered about the New York Giants in the 1950s who are indeed worthy of the title of a recent book about the 1951 team: *The Team That Time Won't Forget*: except for one thing—they moved to San Francisco in 1958 and are now largely forgotten. As one of the founders of a New York–based fan club for the Giants himself admits in his contribution to the overoptimistically titled "Time Won't Forget" book, "New Yorkers have mostly forgotten the Giants, but still worship the Brooklyn Dodgers."[22] Sportswriter Vic Ziegel, a fan from boyhood of the Giants—the "only team I would ever love"—observed in 2000 that, while New York City has memorialized Joe DiMaggio (a highway), Jackie Robinson (a parkway), and Gil Hodges (a bridge), "there is nothing in use today to remind anybody that the Giants . . . spent every baseball year until 1957 in New York."[23] "The New York Giants have disappeared," he wrote.[24]

Giant fans—at least those of a certain age—may be convinced that, as one wrote, "Bobby Thomson's home run that won the 1951 pennant for the New York Giants is quite possibly the most celebrated single play in the history of baseball,"[25] but Thomson's blast failed to win a place in a fan vote in 2002 of the sport's ten "most memorable moments,"[26] nor did Willie Mays's impossible catch—"*the* Catch"—off Vic Wertz's drive to the deepest portion of the Polo Grounds' 480-foot center field in the first game of the 1954 World Series. As for Thomson's blast, much of its aura may have been dimmed by the allegation that Thomson benefited from an elaborate sign-stealing ruse.[27] Arnold Hano's pioneering account of the first game of the 1954 World Series—"a splendid since-neglected piece of reporting" in Roger Kahn's accurate assessment three decades later—was quickly forgotten.[28] A Harvard professor's blog post in 2016 speculating about the ways in which that year's native New Yorker presidential candidates—Bernie Sanders and Donald Trump—reflect the images projected by the city's baseball teams (past and present) discusses the Yankees and the Dodgers as well as the Mets but ignores the Giants.[29] Mel Ott, the team's home run hero and one-time National League career home run king, makes most of his appearances in print these days as the answer to a crossword puzzle clue (thanks to his three letter last name), not in tallies of great sluggers.[30] "Do you know what used to be here?" a *New York Times* reporter pointing to the housing project that stands on the site of the Polo Grounds at 155th Street and Eighth Avenue in upper Manhattan asked a neighborhood resident. "Sure" she replied, "Yankee Stadium."[31] If you wear a black and orange New York Giants cap it will be mistaken for a blue and orange Mets hat.

And so, this great, colorful, pioneering—and successful—team has simply dropped off baseball's historical radar screen—the greatest lost chapter in the history of baseball. You don't have to be a card-carrying member of the "New York Baseball Giants Nostalgia Society" to believe that something is amiss.[32]

The question is why.

## "O'Malley's Willing Lackey"

The inquest can begin, logically enough, with the circumstances of the demise of the *New York* Giants and the move to San Francisco. As one still-resentful New York Giants fan complained a few years ago, "Stoneham was O'Malley's willing lackey" and that is a reasonable summation of what happened.[33] Even at the time, Horace Stoneham's readiness to leave New York with such alacrity—and so little advance planning—surprised observers. As one New York reporter wrote, "That Horace Stoneham would give up the ghost at the Polo Grounds at the mere crook of Walter O'Malley's finger seems inconceivable. Forsaking the traditions and background built by John McGraw and the rest of the Giant greats is coming easier than we would have thought for Stoneham. The past won't go west with Stoneham, only the shell of a once great franchise."[34] As Tallulah's "Willie" Shakespeare might have said, nothing in the New York Giants' life became it *less* than the leaving of it.

From the inception in August 1955 of his public campaign to win support for his plan to build a new stadium for the Dodgers in Brooklyn, Walter O'Malley warned that if the Dodgers moved, the Giants would also leave New York and that, of course, is what happened.[35] As O'Malley's battle against the united front of New York City officialdom—not, as the current received wisdom has it, only against planning czar Robert Moses[36]—opposed to his proposal, Stoneham watched from the sidelines, passively placing his team's fate in the hands of its archrival. Perhaps he—along with many of his fellow New Yorkers—did not believe that O'Malley would actually follow up on his threat. Stoneham's complacency was no doubt reinforced by the fact that, although their attendance at the Polo Grounds declined after the 1954 season, the team remained profitable due to their lucrative television and radio contract (second only to the Dodgers in the National League), and paid the highest executive salaries (including $70,000 to Stoneham himself while also carrying his son and nephew on the team payroll), together with regular dividends, in the league.[37] "He can remain in the historic Polo Grounds, thanks to TV receipts, without financial hardship for the next three years," one journalist correctly noted.[38]

The Giants' lease on the Polo Grounds at a favorable rental ran through the 1961 season, with the understanding that it could be renewed thereafter.[39] The ballpark's Harlem location had not deterred 1,155,067 fans from attending Giants games in 1954 (the team's highest attendance since 1949, more than 100,000 better than the Dodgers and trailing only the recently relocated Milwaukee Braves in the National League) and the drop-off in attendance in the years that followed is more readily attributable to the team's slide into the second division than to escalating concerns about safety in the neighborhood. To the extent Stoneham focused on a new home for the Giants, a readymade alternative was at hand just across the Harlem River—Yankee Stadium. From time to time Stoneham expressed interest in becoming a tenant of the Yankees, and a *New York Times* columnist agreed that this would be the "logical choice" for the Giants.[40] The upshot was that Stoneham apparently felt no urgency about moving out of the Polo Grounds—or out of New York—and his oft-stated position was that a decision about the Giants' future in New York did not depend on what O'Malley did or did not do and would be made independently.[41]

But by the spring of 1957, after O'Malley's negotiations with the city had come to a dead end and he clearly signaled his intention to move the Dodgers from Brooklyn to Los Angeles, Stoneham's complacency was put to the test—and he crumbled. As O'Malley had said back in August 1955, the Giants' *home* game attendance was heavily dependent on games with the Dodgers. By the mid-1950s, fully 30 to 40 percent of the Giants' total attendance was being derived from their eleven (one-seventh of their home dates) Polo Grounds games with the Dodgers.[42] In 1954, Stoneham had defused "talk" about the Giants moving to California by saying, "How could we possibly build up so strong a rivalry there as the one we enjoy here with the Dodgers? Why, one third of our season's crowds is attracted by the New York-Brooklyn series."[43] As O'Malley began edging his way out of town, Stoneham conceded that the move by Brooklyn would hurt Giant attendance.[44] The pundits agreed, asserting that the Dodgers were literally keeping the New York Giants alive as a going concern.[45]

And so, once the Dodgers announced their acquisition of the Los Angeles territory from the Cubs in February 1957, Stoneham was face to face with the fact that the Dodgers were really, truly and soon, going to be leaving town. "Horace Stoneham doesn't talk as much as Walter O'Malley," Robert Creamer observed that spring, "and he has no compulsion for forcing events, like O'Malley" and now the Dodger owner was indeed doing just that, leaving Stoneham to play catchup.[46]

Moving out of New York had not been an entirely ignored possibility amid the Giant's recent troubles. Stoneham had apparently thought, from time to time and without any deadline in mind, about transferring the franchise to Minneapolis, which was the home of the Giants' top farm club.

If the Giants were going to leave New York, Minneapolis appeared to be the logical destination. The Giants owned the city's Triple A minor league Millers, and as early as 1951 Stoneham had purchased a forty-acre parcel a few miles west of downtown that could serve as the site of a new home for the Millers—or the Giants should they move.[47] Late one sociable night in January 1954, Stoneham "lubricated by Scotch," had told the Millers' general manager that he was planning to move the Giants to that city, with the Cincinnati Reds taking the Giants' place in New York.[48] Two years later, Stoneham was quoted saying that "he was considering moving the New York Giants to Minneapolis";[49] Walter O'Malley privately recorded Stoneham as telling him in March 1957 that "he had made up his mind some time ago to move his franchise from New York to Minneapolis" and that "he is prepared to move for the 1958 season."[50]

But as of the spring of 1957 Stoneham had taken no concrete preliminary measures—engaging in serious negotiations with Minneapolis officials to lease the new Metropolitan Stadium, reaching an agreement to pay compensation for "invading" the territory of the St. Paul minor league franchise owned by the Dodgers (as well as with the American Association), securing the approval of National League team owners—to do so.[51] And at least for public consumption but consistent with his lack of initiative, Stoneham insisted that he was not giving a move to Minneapolis serious consideration.[52]

Robert Murphy, who has written the fullest account of the Giants' departure from New York, has attempted to "rescue" Horace Stoneham from what has generally been regarded as a reluctant secondary role in the tandem move of the Dodgers and Giants to California by claiming that Stoneham is "the real villain of New York baseball."[53] Murphy cites O'Malley's memo and vigorously argues that Stoneham had decided to move the Giants to Minneapolis whatever O'Malley did.

Although Murphy's novel twist on an oft-told tale properly restores Stoneham and the Giants to a prominent place in the story of New York baseball in the 1950s, his indictment of Stoneham pushes iconoclasm too far. Notwithstanding O'Malley's inference after his March 22 conversation with Stoneham that "Stoneham had made a commitment to the Minneapolis people at the time they built the new stadium," local Twin Cities officials don't seem to have been aware of any such pledge. When the Twin Cities Sports Area Commission met with Stoneham in New York on April 28, 1957, to discuss terms for a move, Stoneham palmed them off with a noncommittal expression of interest in the proposal. By the time the Sports Area Commission met in early June to discuss the meeting with Stoneham, the Giants had already joined the Dodgers in gaining National League approval for a move to California.[54] In fact, the terms for an acceptable agreement with the Giants were not reviewed with the Sports Area Commission by its chief negotiator until August 19, 1957, the day *after* the Giants formally announced their decision to move to San Francisco.[55]

Rather than pursue a Minneapolis option—or explore the prospect of occupying the city-built Flushing Meadows stadium in Queens that Robert Moses was proposing as a new home for the Dodgers—Stoneham stepped back and let the Dodgers determine the future of the Giants.[56] Stoneham appears to have been more of a "reluctant drag-in" than the "real villain."[57] Indeed it was O'Malley, not Stoneham, who then made the arrangements for the Giants' move to San Francisco. He brought Stoneham and San Francisco mayor George Christopher together in New York in early May a few days after his own return from Los Angeles.[58] The Dodgers' owner dispatched his own engineer Emil Praeger to San Francisco to survey stadium sites, something that Stoneham himself would not do until *after* he announced the team's move.[59] Under O'Malley's watchful eye the San Francisco mayor laid out the general terms under which the Giants could play in the stadium San Francisco would build for them on the tidelands between Hunters Point and Candlestick Point. As O'Malley recalled, "I sat him down with Stoneham. . . . Neither Stoneham nor Christopher was clear about what kind of agreement was necessary so I took an envelope out of my pocket, and on the back of it I wrote out the terms for what became Candlestick Park."[60]

At the end of May, the National League approved O'Malley's and Stoneham's joint application for permission to move to the West Coast after the 1957 season. By mid-July, Stoneham testified at a congressional baseball antitrust hearing that he was prepared to move the Giants to San Francisco, pending finalization of his agreement with the city. On August 6, San Francisco officials sent Stoneham a nine-point letter of intent, outlining the terms on which San Francisco would build a new ballpark and lease it to the Giants.[61] Two weeks later the Giants officially announced that they were leaving New York for the Golden Gate.

And so, Stoneham's Giants proved to be the tail wagged by Walter O'Malley's (Dodger) dog, an ignominious end that would undermine the legacy of the rich history that was abandoned. At the time, Stoneham escaped the opprobrium that trailed O'Malley out of town and endures to this day. No one has ever compared Stoneham—unfavorably—to Hitler or Stalin as a time-honored Brooklyn joke goes.[62] Most observers accepted the Giant owner's excuse for the move (although it hardly reflected the Giants' actual financial position): "Lack of attendance. I'm sorry to disappoint the kids of New York but we didn't see many of their parents out there at the Polo Grounds in recent years."[63] Nor had the Giants' fate been the subject of the two years of public debate and political controversy that accompanied the Dodgers decision to abandon Brooklyn. It was a quiet, anticlimactic leave-taking compared to the rhetorical fireworks that O'Malley triggered.

But it is not just Stoneham's passivity that has rendered the Giants' departure something of a footnote to the sad saga of the Dodgers' move out of Brooklyn. It also reflects the fact that there is virtually no firsthand documentary and archival material to chew over concerning Stoneham and the Giants compared to the massive amount of source material (unequaled with respect to business decision making in baseball) available when it comes to O'Malley and the Dodgers.[64] Reflecting on the failure of the Soviet Union to make its records available to scholars, English historian A. J. P. Taylor once mischievously asked, "have the Soviet government learnt the lesson of many past disputes over historical topics—that the only watertight way of sustaining a case is never to submit evidence in its support?"[65] Proving Taylor right, the wealth of material bearing on the Dodgers has given rise, not to consensus, but to a continuing debate, with no end in sight, over whether Walter O'Malley or New York planning czar Robert Moses should be arraigned in the dock of history.[66] But nothing comparable sheds light on Horace Stoneham and the decisions *he* made. Perhaps "there is no there there" (to quote a famous Bay Area native, albeit from the East Bay), but there is no way to know. And given the lack of material relating to Stoneham, the Giants are fated to remain shadowy supporting players in the ongoing controversy fueled by sources that relate to the Dodgers, but not the Giants.

## "You Can't Call Them the Giants"

If any trauma from the Giants' move has largely vanished in the wake of the passions still aroused by that of the Dodgers, so too did the New York Giants vanish quite literally almost immediately upon their departure for San Francisco, except in the lingering affections of the team's abandoned New York loyalists who made the pilgrimage to the Polo Grounds when National League baseball returned to that historic site in 1962 and accounted for one-quarter of the New York Mets' total home attendance that season (and one-fifth in the following seasons, including their first years at Shea Stadium in Queens). Old-line New York Giant loyalists had insisted, as the team's Hall of Fame second baseman of the 1920s Frankie Frisch put it when the move was announced, "You can't call them the Giants when they move to San Francisco. They can't be the Giants of John McGraw and Christy Mathewson." "They'll always be the New York Giants to me, even if they leave New York. . . . I guess all I have left now are memories," McGraw's widow said.[67]

Which suited San Francisco just fine. "The City" on the Bay didn't want anything to do with New York once they had hijacked the Giants. In his pioneering study of "collective memory," Maurice Halbwachs observed that "a remembrance is in very large measure a reconstruction of the past achieved with data borrowed from the present. . . . Collective memory . . . is a current of continuous thought whose continuity is not at all artificial, for it retains from the past only what still lives or is capable of living in the consciousness of the groups keeping the memory alive."[68] The Giants' first years in San Francisco did nothing to "keep the memory alive" of the team's last years in New York.

The team's break with their past in New York was more complete—and swift—than that of the similarly transplanted Dodgers. In their last years in New York, the Giants' championship team was already unraveling—unlike the Dodgers who after winning the World Series in 1955 again won the National League flag the next year and in their final season in Brooklyn were in first place as late as early June and remained in the pennant race until August en route to a third-place finish.[69] As for the Giants, sportswriter Milton Gross observed during the 1956 season, "you can dispute the proposition that any step in the right direction is better than no step at all, but when it is applied to the Giants the thought is indisputable. From October 1954 until yesterday, when they completed their eight-player deal with the Cardinals, the Giant front office had allowed a world championship team to disintegrate into a last place club."[70]

The Giants and the Dodgers introduced themselves to their new homes in radically different fashion. The transplanted Giants opened the 1958 season against the Dodgers at San Francisco's Seals Stadium with four new faces in their starting lineup while all but one of the Dodger starters had played in Brooklyn. When the Dodgers won the 1959 World Series the team featured familiar names from old scorecards at Ebbets Field: Gil Hodges, Charlie Neal, Don Zimmer, Duke Snider, and Johnny Roseboro along with pitchers Don Drysdale, Sandy Koufax, Johnny Podres, Roger Craig, Danny McDevitt (winner of the team's last game in Brooklyn), and Clem Labine. As late as 1963, the world champion Dodgers' pitching staff was still anchored by Brooklyn holdovers Koufax, Drysdale, and Podres. And Brooklyn Dodger manager Walter Alston would continue to pilot the team in Los Angeles until 1976.[71]

It was very different with the San Francisco Giants, who were a rebuilt outfit from the start. "The San Francisco Giants aren't much of a club," New York Giant fan Roger Angell wrote as the 1958 season got underway.[72] But the inaugural 1958 team with rookies Orlando Cepeda at first base, Jim Davenport at third, Willie Kirkland in right, Felipe Alou in left joining New York holdovers Mays and pitchers Johnny Antonelli and Ruben Gomez overcame Angell's doubts and featured enough new talent to propel the team to a third-place finish while Los Angeles's Dodgers collapsed to seventh. It was enough of a rebirth to make New York Giants' fans wish that the rebuilt team had hung on at the Polo Grounds long enough to reverse the decline that had marked the team's final seasons there. In 1959, Willie McCovey arrived on the scene and by 1962, when the Giants lost a seven-game World Series to the Yankees, Willie Mays was the last position player who could list the Polo Grounds as his one-time home.

Sadly, Mays would pay a price in San Francisco for his New York Giant roots. "I only hope," Angell wrote, "they cherish [Mays] in California, even when he pops up in the eighth inning" but it was not to be. Fans of the New York Giants retained their attachment to him as their loyalty to his team faded away. By 1962, Murray Kempton—who had previously thought that a little boy who had confessed to him "that he was only a Willie Mays fan and that if Mays left the Giants he would go to the team that Mays went" was "childishly irresponsible"—acknowledged that "the team is out of my system now; I am only a Willie Mays fan."[73] And Roger Angell would write that "with immense difficulty, I have sustained something of that affection for the San Francisco Giants, once my New York team, but I know that my attachment will not survive the eventual departure of Willie Mays."[74] But the Mays whom New Yorkers had taken to their collective heart, whether making impossible catches in the Polo Grounds' vast center field or playing stick ball in the streets of Harlem, met with a distinctly cool reception in the City by the Bay—while cold and foggy Candlestick Park, the "temple of the winds," posed a frustratingly difficult challenge for him at the plate.[75]

"Mays was the symbol of New York," his biographer Charles Einstein wrote, "being thrust down San Francisco's throat." In the team's new city, Mays would hear boos for the first time, and he would never receive the heartfelt devotion accorded "real" *San Francisco* Giants like Orlando Cepeda or Willie McCovey. In the Giants' first San Francisco season, Mays hit for his career-high batting average and led the team in home runs, hits, slugging average, total bases, stolen bases, and triples, but the fans chose National League Rookie of the Year Cepeda as the "Most Valuable Giant" in a newspaper poll.[76] After Soviet premier Khrushchev's 1959 visit to San Francisco, Hearst organization columnist Frank Coniff wrote, "It's the damndest city I ever saw. They cheer Khrushchev and boo Willie Mays."[77]

## "The Days of Mr. McGraw"

Then too, however accomplished they were, the New York Giants of the 1950s have inevitably been overshadowed by the team's even more notable past. For the Dodgers, their last decade in New York City represented the best years of the team's life, but that was not true of the Giants. When the history of the New York Giants was recalled thereafter, the Giants of the 1950s would inevitably be overshadowed by its forebears who had ruled the baseball world decades earlier. Halbwachs contended that "what stands in the foreground of group memory are remembrances of events and experiences of concern to the greatest number of its members,"[78] and it would be the Giants of the era of John McGraw who would claim the greatest attention from the community of baseball fans. No surprise that when *Sports Illustrated* compiled a list of the "100 best sports books of all time" the Dodgers and the Giants were each the subject of two of them. But those on the Dodgers revisited the era of Jackie Robinson and Duke Snider, those on the Giants that of John McGraw and Christy Mathewson.[79]

That the Giants of yesteryear cast a continuing shadow over their Polo Grounds successors was apparent at the time of the move: in response to Horace Stoneham's complaints about the loss of customers one newspaper replied that "the truth is the turnstiles clicked, long ago, because the product of John McGraw was the best in the business. For a long while, indeed, it looked as though they would be giants forever. . . . There were even cries—remember—that the Government or somebody ought to break up this serene and unshakeable monopoly."[80]

As time was running out for the team at the Polo Grounds the Giant management continued to cultivate and celebrate the legacy of greatness that extended back into the prehistory of Major League Baseball. When the Giants won the 1954 pennant, the team placed a full-page ad in the *Sporting News* thanking "all New York Giants fans for supporting and inspiring us to our 17th pennant" including those in 1888 and 1889 and illustrated with portraits of past field generals reaching back to nineteenth-century manager James J. Mutrie, as well as John McGraw, Bill Terry, and Mel Ott along with current manager Leo Durocher.[81] After all, the team owed its very nickname to the spontaneous exclamation by manager Mutrie in 1885—"My big fellows! My giants!"[82] Not surprisingly, "Departure Stirs Memory of Old Mighty Giants," the *Herald Tribune* reported when Stoneham announced the move: "Fans Recall the Dear Dead Days under Mutrie, McGraw and Terry."[83] Roger Angell bade "Farewell, My Giants" by recalling "that for the better part of two decades this team stood astride all baseball—well, like a giant."[84] But those decades of dominance had been more than thirty years earlier, the era of manager John McGraw.

Led by McGraw, soon dubbed the "Little Napoleon" by his growing band of chroniclers in the New York press corps, the Giants won the National League pennant in 1904, repeated in 1905, then won again in 1911, 1912, 1913, and 1917, before they hooked up against the Yankees in three straight Series beginning in 1921. No one in baseball was more widely known. He straddled the realms of Broadway, Wall Street, and Tammany Hall—no less a personage than George M. Cohan wrote the foreword for the memoir of *My Thirty Years in Baseball* that he published in 1923. In his history of the team, Joseph Durso wrote, "McGraw's circle of friends in this hippodrome atmosphere included the great and the small of the theater, the courts, the political clubs, the prize ring, the racetrack and the underworld, all somehow intertwined on Broadway as the demi-gods of public life." "There were two 'Misters' on the New York scene in the 1920's," columnist Gene Fowler wrote, men who were always so addressed, Charles F. Murphy, leader of Tammany Hall, and John J. McGraw of the New York Giants.[85]

Even the team's miscues earned long-remembered places in the sport's "hall of shame." Fred Merkle would forever be remembered as "Bonehead Merkle" for his failure to run the bases properly in a crucial 1908 game against Chicago, which wound up costing the Giants that year's pennant. Outfielder Fred Snodgrass's error on an easy fly ball—the "$30,000 muff" in those pre-inflationary times—in the 1912 World Series followed him to the grave: the headline on his obituary, six decades later, read "Fred Snodgrass, 86, Dead: Ball Player Muffed 1912 Fly."[86] No wonder that New York's jazz-era mayor and Giant fan Jimmy Walker once explained, "When the Dodgers lose a ball game, there usually is a laugh in it for somebody. When the Yankees lose, you just shrug it off, knowing full well they'll take good care of that defeat tomorrow. But when the Giants lose, it hurts all over."[87]

The impact of those early Giant teams was felt beyond the playing field itself. McGraw's Giants also made notable contributions to the lore of the game. The story goes that the sport's anthem "Take Me Out to the Ball Game" was inspired when the songwriter saw an ad for "Baseball Today-Polo Grounds" on a Manhattan subway or El train. Baseball's favorite ballpark fare, the hot dog, was supposedly christened by a cartoonist observing what the concessionaire called "dachsund sandwiches" at the Polo Grounds in 1901.[88] Whether or not the stories are true—and they have been disputed—is beside the point.

When Delmore Schwartz sat down in 1958 to reminisce at length about the team he loved, writing "Memoirs of a Metropolitan Child, Memoirs of a Giant Fan" (not published until 1986), it was the long-gone Giants of the 1920s, not the more recent editions of the recently departed team, that was his subject.[89] Recalling his childhood in Washington Heights, "near Coogan's

Bluff and thus near the Polo Grounds," the young Schwartz (the adult Schwartz remembered) linked his own childhood optimism with the fortunes of his team and accumulated a number of life lessons in the process. Those were the years when the Giants won four pennants in a row between 1921 and 1924 and "it seemed entirely obvious . . . that everything was getting better and better in every way, day by day, especially if one lived in Manhattan and was a Giant fan." But "these joyous speculations about an abundant and triumphant future as a Giant fan proved quite untrue," Schwartz remembered: "The Giants did not win the pennant in 1927, the Yankees won the World Series in four straight games, much to my disgust, and Ruth broke the home run record he had previously set." Looking back on his blasted expectations for the Giants' "abundant and triumphant future," Schwartz wrote, "Then, as now, reality was very often astonishing and unpredictable. . . . It is now years since I first became aware that the reality of the future was very likely to be different than any present image or expectation."

"I'm getting tired of living on memories," Tallulah Bankhead wrote in the late 1940s. "They say a man named Christopher Mathewson once pitched three shut-outs against the Athletics in a World Series. Could it be that I was born a generation too late?"[90] The triumphs of the 1950s could not match the glories of those long-gone times.

The McGraw era cast another shadow over the team's 1950s incarnation. In the final years at the Polo Grounds, the Giants were living off the capital accrued in earlier decades but the changing population mix of New York City had swept away the spatial and ethnic environment in which that team had flourished. Giant loyalties forged in the "days of Mr. McGraw" were challenged by a demographic tide that was running against the team. The team's home borough Manhattan's share of New York City's total population fell from half in 1900 to about one-fifth in the 1950s, and Manhattan's population had declined in absolute numbers as well.[91] The predominant place in the early twentieth-century city held by the Irish and the Germans had been swept away by the ensuing tidal wave of immigration from southern and eastern Europe.[92] "New York used to be an Irish town," Daniel Patrick Moynihan wrote a few years after the Giants moved to California, "but it is no more."[93] Meanwhile, the black composition of Manhattan's population increased from 2 percent to 25 percent, and it is likely that the loyalties of the baseball fans among them had been secured, for a time at least, by the Dodgers in homage to Brooklyn's pioneering role in breaking the color line in Major League Baseball.

Identifying who the Giant fans were has eluded the grasp of baseball historians who have tried to map the landscape of New York's baseball allegiances. Writers who have confidently pontificated (whether rightly or wrongly)[94] about the composition of the fan bases of the Dodgers or the Yankees have drawn a blank when it comes to the Giants, and none has delineated the connections between the Giants and the community with the careful attention that Carl E. Prince and Peter Marquis have lavished on the Dodgers and Brooklyn.[95] Perhaps the Giant fan base that had been nurtured by McGraw and Terry and Ott was collateral damage to that demographic shift.

And so the postwar New York Giants, the team of Mays and Thomson and Durocher and Rhodes, have fallen into the sport's collective memory hole. If you look in a library or search on Amazon you will find a *Dodgers Reader* and a *Yankees Reader*; you won't find a "Giants Reader."[96] Prolific baseball historian Peter Golenbock has written lengthy books about the Dodgers and the Yankees—as well as the Red Sox, the Cubs, the Mets, the Cardinals, and even the Browns—but not about the Giants.[97] "The members of the New York Giant Nostalgia Society know this: Their team's history is just as rich as that of the Brooklyn Dodgers," Richard Sandomir wrote after attending a meeting of "60 or 70 Ottophiles" fifty years after the team's move, but "they cannot alter this irrefutable fact: They long ago lost the nostalgia battle to Pee Wee Reese and the Duke as well as Jackie Robinson's civil rights breakthrough."[98] It may be unfair but it is undeniable.

But the near total eclipse of the Eisenhower-era Giants was actually set in motion as long ago as spring training in 1952, while the cheers still echoed for Bobby Thomson's pennant-winning homer. That March the *Herald Tribune* assigned a twenty-four-year-old reporter to Florida—"younger than every later day Hall of Famer and indeed younger than any regular on the squad"—as the beat writer for the Brooklyn Dodgers.[99] Some years later, when the idea of writing a retrospective book about that team and its players "had developed to embryo and I exposed it to an editor, I found myself being put down. . . .'Those Dodgers are no more special than say the Boston Red Sox of 1948. You only think they're special because you covered them. They're only special to you.'"[100] But the editor was wrong. The young reporter was Roger Kahn and when he published *The Boys of Summer* in 1972 it was not only a runaway bestseller—the first sports book to lead the *New York Times* list—but would come to be considered the "most influential work of sports literature in the Twentieth Century."[101]

The book's appearance was bad news for the Giants. The year that Kahn's book appeared a Gallup Poll reported that football had overtaken baseball as the country's favorite sport—by a margin that has steadily increased in the years since.[102] Thereafter, baseball would increasingly rely on the playing fields of memory to shore up its once unquestioned status as the "national pastime." As Kahn rather sourly reflected some years later, his book launched a flood of writing by others on the Brooklyn Dodgers—as well as multiepisode television documentaries on ESPN and HBO.[103] The storage capacity of collective memory is limited. "In order to remember some things, other things must be forgotten," a scholar of memory has written recently.[104] *The Boys of Summer* and its offshoots preempted the sport's growing nostalgia market for that Dodger team. "Roger Kahn made sure that . . . people who weren't alive when the Dodgers were choking in October are walking the streets of this city wearing the words 'Brooklyn Dodgers,'" Vic Ziegel wrote.[105] And the Hall of Fame gift shop, Ziegel found, is overflowing with Dodger, but not Giant, memorabilia.

If only, the dwindling ranks of aging New York Giant fans must think, the *Herald Tribune* had assigned Roger Kahn to cover the Giants, not the Dodgers, in the spring of 1952.[106]

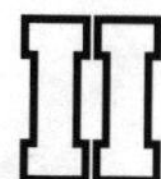

# Football
# The Glamour and the Gore

CHAPTER THREE

# The New York Giants and Cold War Manhood

## Pro Football in the Age of the Marlboro Man and the ICBM

*Stephen H. Norwood*

Playing on a frozen field that resembled "a concrete landing strip," the New York Giants on December 30, 1956, staged "one of the greatest displays of power and pulverizing line play" in a professional football championship game, as they clobbered the Chicago Bears 47–7. Boasting probably the greatest defense in the sport's history until then, the Giants completely stymied the National Football League's (NFL) leading rushing offense. Red Smith of the *New York Herald Tribune*, one of the nation's premier sportswriters, described the Giants "driving the Bears into the frozen ground like tacks." Smith stated that the Giants' defense rushed Bears quarterback Ed Brown "like a blonde in a logging camp."[1] Brown completed only eight of nineteen passes. Meanwhile, the Giants' "terrific trio" of running backs—Frank Gifford, Alex Webster, and Mel Triplett—"were tearing the Bears' vaunted line to shreds." New York quarterback Charlie Conerly, a World War II marine combat veteran of Iwo Jima, Guam, and Taraway, completed seven of ten passes for 195 yards. *New York Times* sports editor Arthur Daley noted that the Giants "never eased off for an instant . . . in the brutal way they pushed the [Bears] around." Every time the Giants scored, the Yankee Stadium crowd of 56,836 howled, "We want more!" *Chicago Defender* columnist Leslie Matthews commented that the Bears appeared frightened of the Giants: "afraid to pass, afraid to run, afraid to buck the huge Giants' line."[2]

The New York Giants thoroughly intimidated a Bears team that only two weeks before had thrashed the defending NFL champion Detroit Lions in a contest to determine the Western Division title, in what Arthur Daley described as arguably the season's roughest game. On that game's second play, television announcer Chris Schenkel gasped at the viciousness of the hitting on the field. The *New York Times* declared that the Bears and the Lions had "appeared intent on maiming one another," throwing punches and "kneeing, kicking, and elbowing." Lions quarterback Bobby Layne was "flattened and hospitalized" after Bears defensive end Ed Meadows blindsided him only seventeen minutes into the game.[3]

Like most other NFL championship games of this period in which the Giants participated, the 1956 contest was played in frigid late December weather. *New York Herald Tribune* sportswriter Harold Rosenthal wondered whether the spectators "would die of cold on the premises." Arthur Daley reported that the cold was "so paralyzing that it froze the mimeographing machine in the press box." The gridiron resembled a Siberian "steppe just north of Vladivostok." Many Americans considered a football team's ability to prevail in such forbidding wintry conditions a true test of manhood. The *Chicago Tribune* reported that New Yorkers along Broadway hours after the Giants' victory were calling the Bears overrated: "the best hot weather team in football," rendered impotent in the cold.[4]

Professional football, a sport built around violent confrontation and intimidation, appealed to the sizable number of Americans determined to see their country vigorously respond to Cold War Soviet and Communist Chinese probing actions along the boundaries of the West's sphere of influence. They believed that such probes were designed to measure America's resolve in standing up to Communist expansionism. Failure to respond firmly and quickly to such provocations communicated weakness. Unlike America's other major sports, like baseball, basketball, track and field, golf, and tennis, football was played outdoors in any kind of weather. A significant proportion of the male population in the United States consisted of World War II and Korean War veterans, many of whom had fought in bitter cold, snow, and mud.

America's rapid and well-publicized construction during the 1950s of an early warning system to protect the nation against a sudden Soviet nuclear missile or atomic bomb attack influenced the new fascination with defense in football and with explosive, pass-oriented offenses. This new protective network consisted of radar stations stretching "across the Arctic from Alaska to Greenland," radar-equipped Constellation aircraft to patrol the Atlantic and Pacific Coasts, and naval picket ships to detect the approach of "enemy planes or submarines." The *New York Times*, reporting on the construction of this "far-flung system of radar warning lines [and] interceptor bases," proclaimed 1954 to be the "Year of Defense." The press also devoted considerable attention to America's construction of underground nuclear missile silos to house intercontinental ballistic missiles (ICBMs) and long-range bombers that could quickly penetrate deep into Soviet territory and inflict nuclear devastation. The ICBMs carried names like Thor, Atlas, Titan, and Jupiter, communicating their enormous destructive power.[5] During the 1950s, sportswriters, broadcasters, and football fans began referring to the long pass, rapidly becoming a primary offensive weapon that could instantly move a team a vast distance forward, often with devastating impact, as the "long bomb."

President Dwight D. Eisenhower himself, in a 1958 address at the National Football Foundation's Football Hall of Fame banquet, declared that football would play a significant role in America's struggle against the "persistent [and] deadly" threat of "international Communism," which "is out to win by whatever means and at whatever cost." Eisenhower, a former West Point halfback who had played football against Jim Thorpe, called the sport an important morale booster that would help develop "healthy bodies and alert minds among American youth." The football coach was therefore as critical in the nation's competition against Communism "as the most respected professor."[6]

Pro football's surging popularity after the mid-1950s can also be attributed to the widespread postwar American anxiety that affluence, consumer abundance, desire for immediate gratification, and dependence on automobile transportation and labor-saving devices had softened the United States, undermining the toughness and self-denial necessary to combat a seemingly more disciplined and aggressive Soviet enemy single-mindedly focused on victory. Pro football teams insisted that their players undergo rigorous training and physical conditioning, often in Spartan, military-type settings. Marine Corps veterans who played for the New York Giants during the 1950s compared the team's training methods to those of Marine Corps boot camps. Giants star defensive end Andy Robustelli recalled that Jim Lee Howell, the team's head coach from 1954 to 1960, a World War II Marine Corps combat veteran, treated the players "as if we were all members of his [military] unit."[7] Pro football emphasized strength, endurance, and the ability to withstand pain. The sport thus provided an important alternative model for American males during the Cold War to the paunchy middle-class suburbanite and indolent, overindulged teenager.

At the same time, pro football had come by the 1950s to incorporate major features of postwar bureaucracy: well-defined hierarchies, group-based work, synchronization of parts, and specialization of tasks. In 1954, sociologist David Riesman noted that football coaches had come to resemble "group-dynamics leaders rather than old-line straw bosses."[8] As a result pro football drew many fans from the rapidly expanding white-collar salariat. Watching pro football games allowed men employed in sedentary office work to vicariously express anger and violent impulses they had to suppress in the office as disruptive to the harmony of the work team. Pro football was considerably more violent than the college version. In 1955, *Life* magazine, in an article revealingly entitled "Savagery on Sunday," quoted an NFL quarterback's statement that the pro game "is getting rougher every year. It's war rather than sport."[9] Consigned to office drudgery, white-collar men in managerial, clerical, and many professional positions witnessed on the gridiron, and fantasized about, heroic physical exploits that they themselves could never perform.

Pro football players resembled another object of 1950s male fantasy, the hero of western films, in their determination to stand firm when challenged by an adversary and to solve problems with violence. The western film attained its highest level of popularity ever during the 1950s. Although football required a considerable amount of coordination among players, particularly on offense, it also involved direct one-on-one matchups, particularly on the line and with pass receivers and defensive backs. Much of a player's pregame preparation involved studying films of the man who would be his primary opponent in the upcoming game. The grizzled western hero, courting danger and living outside of settled society, provided an important counterpoint to bureaucratic man and dramatized men's rejection of women's influence. As Jane Tompkins noted, "the most salient fact about the Western [is] that it is a narrative of male violence" and "a genre pervaded by death and the threat of death." It is "obsessed with pain and celebrate[s] the suppression of feeling."[10] These are central features of football, in which hard physical contact occurs on every play, injuries are frequent, and players learn not to worry about inflicting pain on opponents. Although pro football players do not die on the gridiron, there is the risk of severe injury on every play, and many suffer serious lifelong physical damage.

Charlie Conerly, New York Giants quarterback from 1948 until 1961, was the original Marlboro Man, appearing on billboards, and in television commercials and magazines, in "one of the major advertising triumphs of the era."[11] During the 1950s, the Philip Morris Company decided to transform what it had marketed as a women's cigarette, using the slogan "Mild as May," into a man's product. Philip Morris drew on the premier symbol of traditional American masculinity, the rugged frontier cowboy, for its new Marlboro Man. Giants halfback Frank Gifford introduced Conerly, his on-the-road roommate, to his friend Jack Landry, the Philip Morris executive who had charge of advertising the brand. Gifford recalled that "Jack took one look at Charlie and hired him" as the Marlboro Man. Conerly resembled the western hero in being a man of action but very few words, his press interviews often limited to answering, "Yep" and "Nope." Conerly's teammate, Giants linebacker Cliff Livingston, succeeded him as a Marlboro Man.[12]

Pro football was played before predominantly male audiences and lacked the pageantry and partying of college football weekends, which attracted sizable numbers of women and drew attention away from the games themselves. Newspapers during the 1950s and early 1960s published fashion advice for women planning to attend college football games. The *New York Times* in 1959 reported that women in Baton Rouge were having difficulty getting appointments at beauty parlors because so many wanted to look chic for Louisiana State University's nationally televised season opener.[13] By contrast, pro football crowds were overwhelmingly male and focused much more on the game action.

Pro football, more violent than college football in any period, was probably rougher during the 1950s and early 1960s than at any previous time. This reinforced its image as a man's sport. The Giants, with the NFL's best defense for much of the 1950s, had a reputation as a very hard-hitting team. Y. A. Tittle, a pro football quarterback from 1948 until 1964, recalled that referees during the 1950s called few penalties and let the defense "get away with murder." Half the time the hitting did not stop after a play was whistled dead: "It was the era of hitting, hitting, and late hitting." The NFL's leading middle linebackers—New York's Sam Huff, Philadelphia's Chuck Bednarik, Detroit's Joe Schmidt, and Chicago's Bill George—"stepped on hands [and] gouged eyes." Tittle emphasized that "they delighted in hitting quarterbacks, smashing them to pieces." Bednarik explained that "the pro linebacker's prime weapon is his right forearm, aimed to spoil the assault (and the profile) of the blocker." Detroit head coach Buddy Parker claimed in 1956 that pro football was becoming "a slugging match."[14]

Concerned about "the increasing evidence of intent to maim" in pro football, *Sport* magazine in December 1955 ran an article entitled "Confessions of a Dirty Football Player" by "a hard-bitten" (NFL) veteran. This eight-year veteran mocked NFL commissioner Bert Bell's claim that players did not use dirty tactics: "Excuse me while I laugh through the gap in my mouth where eight of my front teeth were knocked out" as a result of opponents' elbowing, kicking, and head-butting him in the face. The NFL, to be sure, had introduced face masks earlier that year to reduce the number of broken cheekbones caused by forearm blows, but the author of "Confessions" considered this "a grisly joke." He argued that face masks actually made football a rougher sport, because they encouraged head butts: "we've been given a set of brass knuckles to wear on our faces." *Sport*'s editors commented that pro football players would soon need suits of armor to remain safe in a pileup.[15]

Cleveland's Hall of Fame running back Jim Brown in his 1964 autobiography accused the New York Giants defense of deliberately damaging his vision in a game the previous year as they attempted to tackle him and in pileups. Brown maintained that the Giants "pounded my eyes mercilessly with forearms and elbows," digging through the face bar of his helmet at least seven times. As a result, he suffered blurred vision for most of the game. Brown became alarmed when the blurring persisted into the next week's game against the Philadelphia Eagles. In the autobiography he warned the Giants that he would violently retaliate if they ever took shots at his eyes again: "A broken bone is one thing but blindness is another. Jeopardize my sight and I'll kick your teeth in."[16]

Pro football's violence and military-style hierarchy and organization led the press during the 1950s and 1960s to repeatedly employ war combat imagery, drawn from the army, navy, and air force, in describing gridiron action. The modern T-formation, the offensive alignment every NFL team used by 1953, provided a better balance between a "ground attack" (rushing) and an "aerial attack" (passing), than the heavily run-oriented single wing. Coaches discussed their "battle plans" with players. By the 1950s most professional players were divided into offensive and defensive "platoons." Quarterbacks, who called the offensive plays, were known as "field generals." Newspapers referred to injured players as "casualties." *Look* magazine reported in 1960 that veteran Giants quarterback Charlie Conerly "has known the blast of the rush line," comparing opposing defenses' overwhelming blockers to enemy cannon fire blowing holes through troop concentrations.[17]

Journalists covering pro football during the 1950s and early 1960s drew parallels between the passing game and aerial warfare, increasingly emphasized in American military strategy. *Sport* magazine in 1953 described Los Angeles Rams passing ace Norm Van Brocklin as the NFL's "deadliest bombardier." Arthur Daley in 1962 reported that Giants fullback Alex Webster had all season been "slugging away in old-fashioned battleship fashion," plowing up the middle for sizable gains. In the most recent game, Webster "went modern and employed [aircraft] carrier tactics" to haul in ten passes. Sportswriters compared the defensive secondary in pro football to the nation's antiaircraft warning system and antimissile shield. The *Washington Post*, for example, in its article on the 1961 NFL championship game between New York and Green Bay, commented on the Giants quarterbacks' efforts to "pierce the curtain thrown up by the Packers' air raid wardens."[18]

The New York Giants played a significant part in pro football's emergence as America's most popular sport after 1956, surpassing Major League Baseball, long the national pastime, and college football. As the pro football team based in the nation's largest metropolis and media capital, the Giants provided enormous publicity for the sport by playing in the nationally televised NFL championship games of 1956, 1958, 1959, 1961, 1962, and 1963. This was the period in which television became America's most popular entertainment medium. In 1954, nearly two-thirds of the nation's households already had television sets, and by 1960, 90 percent did. CBS began regular season telecasts of NFL games in 1956, and that same year NBC signed a contract to televise the championship contest. This occurred right on the eve of the Giants' emergence as one of pro football's greatest teams.[19] The Giants introduced modern managerial techniques to pro football, with head coach Jim Lee Howell delegating authority to an offensive coordinator, Vince Lombardi, and a defensive coordinator, Tom Landry. Both men, after leaving the Giants a few years later, established reputations as among the best head coaches in pro football history.

The Giants made another very important contribution to enhancing pro football's popularity by devoting more emphasis to defense during the 1950s than any other NFL team except for the Philadelphia Eagles. Philadelphia's legendary head coach Greasy Neale (1941–1950) had been the first to make significant defensive innovations to counter the T-formation that most NFL offenses adopted in the 1940s. During the 1950s, the Eagles "Suicide Seven"—two linebackers positioned just behind the defensive ends in a five-man forward wall, an alignment Neale had developed—enjoyed a reputation for ferocity.[20] But under Tom Landry, the Giants introduced the 4-3 defense with three linebackers stationed behind a "front four," which proved more effective and soon became standard in the NFL. Landry also developed many new and sophisticated defensive formations and plays.

In 1956, the Giants signified the prestige they accorded to defense by becoming the first NFL team to introduce the starting defense rather than the starting offense in the pregame ceremonies. Defensive players' machismo appealed to fans who during the workday felt emasculated in office cubicles, wearing gray flannel suits. Unbridled anger, which can easily undermine an offensive player's performance, often enhances a defensive player's.[21] Hitting is more spectacular on defense.

The Giants' role in what many have called the greatest football game of all time, the 1958 NFL championship contest against the Baltimore Colts, also greatly stimulated interest in pro football. The Giants hosted the game in storied Yankee Stadium, "the Home of Champions." The Colts' offense was considered the NFL's best; the Giants had the league's premier defense. Viewed on television coast-to-coast in nearly 11 million households, it was the first pro football title game decided in sudden death overtime.[22] The Giants' rivalry with the Cleveland Browns during the 1950s, one of the most intense in pro football history, generated considerable excitement in the sport as well.

Sam Huff, Giants middle linebacker from 1956 to 1963, glamorized defense in a CBS television documentary entitled *The Violent World of Sam Huff*, which aired nationally in October 1960 and was introduced by Walter Cronkite. Huff had already appeared on the cover of the November 30, 1959, issue of *Time* magazine. The middle linebacker position was critically important in the 4-3 defense that Tom Landry created for the Giants, and which all NFL teams later adopted. The middle linebacker was described as "an agile and ferocious stand-up predator."[23] Longtime NFL quarterback Y. A. Tittle, who played his last four years, 1961 to 1964, with the Giants, called the middle linebacker "the fastest gun in the West" and football's "number one killer." Huff was wired with a tiny microphone during training camp and in an exhibition game, transmitting to viewers the sounds of violent contact on the field. *Sport* magazine stated that the sounds of players colliding "resounded across living rooms like an invasion soundtrack from *Victory at Sea*," a television series about World War II naval combat. Huff declared in the documentary that there was "no place for nice guys" in pro football: "it's either kill or be killed." He told viewers: "you have to be tough. . . . I always feel real good when I hit someone." *Sport* commented that when Huff hit a running back or receiver head-on, he was "as neat and complete as a guillotine." During the late 1950s and early 1960s, Giants fans repeatedly rocked Yankee Stadium with chants of "HUFF-HUFF-HUFF."[24]

During the 1950s, the Giants linebacker corps, led by Huff, helped to introduce the most-dramatic and well-publicized defensive maneuver yet seen in pro football, the "red dog," a term drawn from the imagery of the hunt. It also came to be known by the military term "blitz." Red-dogging linebackers rushed quickly forward at the snap of the ball, determined to penetrate the offensive line and sack the quarterback "the way a pack of redbone hounds might pull down a deer."[25]

The New York Giants victory over the Chicago Bears in the 1956 NFL championship game provided a major boost for pro football, whose following expanded significantly every year from that time. Gifford noted that when he entered the NFL with the Giants in 1952, pro football was "the ugly duckling of sports." When Gifford returned home to California after each of his first few seasons, his friends asked him where he had been. Some Giants home games during the early 1950s drew fewer than 10,000 people. Gifford recalled that if you tore your game jersey or pants during a game then, you wore it the next week patched. Marty Glickman, who broadcast the football Giants play-by-play on radio from 1948 well into the 1960s, noted that around 1950 the major national networks, CBS, NBC, and ABC, were carrying only college football; pro football was available only on local stations.[26]

Giants attendance benefited from the team's move for the 1956 season from the decaying Polo Grounds, where they had played since the franchise's founding in 1925, to Yankee Stadium, the nation's most prestigious sports arena, which had a larger seating capacity and was located in a safer neighborhood with better parking facilities. The Giants signaled that the move to Yankee Stadium had heightened their status by discarding their solid red jerseys, some of which dated to the 1940s and had numbers of varying size, for navy-blue uniforms, the color sported by the baseball Yankees, with their long winning tradition. The Giants also added a stylish (some said "snooty") "NY" to their helmets.[27]

The Giants firing of head coach Steve Owen in 1953, who had held that position for twenty years, opened the way for a significant improvement in the team's public image, as well as its on-the-field performance. The Giants had won only three games that year. Frank Gifford described Owen as personally very crude, and possessing little or no knowledge of, or interest in, the offensive game. Perian Conerly, wife of Charlie Conerly and a football columnist for the *New York Times* during the 1950s and early 1960s, similarly described Owen as having very little grasp of the modern game of football. Gifford described Owen as "a fat, snarly Oklahoman who dipped snuff—the juice would dribble down his dirty rubber jacket." He "stuck rigidly to his 'old ways' of doing things." Owen had no grasp of modern methods of personnel management, using only intimidation and insult to motivate players. Perian Conerly commented that she did not believe Owen ever "convinced himself that the forward pass was fair," and noted that the Giants offense had not scrapped the single wing for the modern T-formation until 1949, the next to last NFL team to do so. Gifford stated that Owen refused to fly in an airplane, forcing the Giants to travel by train to all of their games, including those on the Pacific Coast.[28]

The New York Giants also benefited from the sharp decline of college football in New York City. Columbia, which had won the 1934 Rose Bowl, no longer gave football serious attention. New York University closed down its intercollegiate football program in 1953. City College of New York, Manhattan College, Long Island University, and St. John's University had already done so. Fordham, which played in the Cotton Bowl in 1941 and the Sugar Bowl in 1942, abolished football in 1954. It had drawn fewer than 50,000 spectators to its four home football games that year. There had been no college football played in Yankee Stadium since the Army–Southern California contest in 1951.[29]

Frank Gifford, the NFL's Most Valuable Player in 1956, added glamour to the New York offense, enhancing the team's appeal in a city considered one of the world's leading cultural centers, with a glittering night life. Gifford, the Giants' number-one draft choice in 1952, was a very talented running back and Charlie Conerly's favorite receiver. Gifford's teammates, along with the news media, considered him a Southern California "Golden Boy," a "man about town" with "movie star good looks," as Sam Huff put it. Gifford's wife at the time he played for the Giants had been Queen of the 1949 Rose Bowl, as well as a Vargas model. She appeared in an *Argosy* centerfold. Universal, Twentieth Century Fox, and Warner Brothers all gave Gifford screen tests, and he appeared in several films in bit parts and as a stuntman. These movies featured major stars like Tony Curtis, Jerry Lewis, John Derek, James Garner, and Jack Palance. Gifford read for the lead for the film *Battle Cry*, based on Leon Uris's novel about US Marines in World War II, a part given to Tab Hunter.[30]

Gifford's movie roles and the numerous offers he received to model clothes and to endorse consumer products caused resentment among some defensive players, on both the Giants and opposing teams. In their rougher, more traditional conception of masculinity, good looks and modeling were suspect. Opposing defensive back Johnny Sample would warn Gifford to "watch out there, Pretty Boy. You get that face messed up and you won't be able to go back to Hollywood." Gifford appeared in sweater ads in the *New Yorker* and *Sports Illustrated* wearing "a V-necked Jantzen pullover" and "a tartan cap tilted rakishly to one side of his head." He endorsed sherry, shaving cream, aftershave lotion, and Vitalis, and posed for bathing suit ads in the Bahamas. His teammates began to call him, with a touch of mockery, "the male Betty Furness." Gifford knew that some Giants saw him as "a media-made glamour boy, all glitz and no substance." The *New York Herald Tribune* in 1961 reported that when Gifford posed for a Lucky Strike ad on the Fordham football field, "the big football hero" was the subject of "some pointed remarks from the kids on the sidelines" for "having makeup applied to his face."[31]

The Giants defense tended to resent the team's offensive players and sometimes impugned their masculinity, although it did hold some key members of that unit in high esteem. The offensive backfield and the pass receivers generally received higher pay and greater media attention. Giants quarterback Charlie Conerly and his successor Y. A. Tittle, however, conveyed a traditional masculine image of toughness that the defense, and large numbers of fans, appreciated. Modern T-formation quarterbacks were viewed with some suspicion in the 1950s because their role involved almost entirely passing and handing off the ball. Unlike tailbacks in the single wing, they almost never ran or blocked, much less played defense. Benny Friedman, who had been a single wing tailback for the Giants in the 1920s, published an article in *Sport* magazine in 1953 in which he stated that the modern T-quarterback had a "rocking-chair job." It was rare to see one in a dirty uniform. Red Smith remarked in 1960 that NFL quarterbacks would as soon "carry a cobra in their arms than a football."[32]

Yet during the 1950s, NFL quarterbacks were often at great physical risk when passing the football. Mammoth defensive linemen and red-dogging linebackers zeroed in on quarterbacks, often severely pummeling them as they dropped back to pass.[33] T-formation quarterbacks to succeed had to display "coolness under fire," a quality much valued in military combat.[34]

Conerly and Tittle had both played tailback in the single wing, and earned defensive players' respect for their courage and fortitude. Both played without complaint when seriously injured and in pain, as Tittle did in the 1963 NFL championship game. Conerly had been in the thick of combat in the Pacific; his rifle was shot out of his hands by a Japanese sniper on Guam. Frank Gifford recalled that in 1957 Conerly quarterbacked the Giants for half a season with a separated shoulder in his passing arm, "probably the most painful injury you can get." In his first game with the Giants he was hit in the face and suffered what the team physician called "a severe cheekbone depression," which fourteen years later was still noticeable.[35]

The Giants defense also viewed running back Alex Webster, recruited from the Canadian Football League in 1955, as very different from "Hollywood types" like Gifford or Los Angeles Rams quarterback "Beautiful Bob" Waterfield, who was married to movie star Jane Russell. Giants defensive captain Andy Robustelli stated that "no physically tougher player has ever worked in the NFL than Alex Webster." Robustelli recalled that Sam Huff once said that Webster "belonged with the defense because he was so tough." Webster earned the Giants defensemen's respect because in training camp and practices he "gave as good as he got."[36]

Defensive players could not consider offensive linemen's masculinity suspect because they were repeatedly on the receiving end of their bruising blocks, both at the line of scrimmage and downfield. Offensive linemen labored in even more obscurity than most defensive players, depriving them of the opportunity for commercial endorsements, and their salaries were often even lower. The New York Giants offensive line from the mid-1950s through 1963 was respected around the NFL as very talented and physically intimidating. Roosevelt Brown (1953–1965), the third African American to become a regular starter for the Giants, was one of the NFL's best offensive tackles, an eight-time All-Pro. Brown was one of the six Giants from the division champion teams of the 1956–1963 period selected for the Pro Football Hall of Fame, along with Huff, Gifford, Tittle, Robustelli, and defensive back Emlen Tunnell. He was proud that he "hit on every play," unlike the running backs, who "on many occasions merely run a pass route or a fake without any physical contact." Brown missed only three regular season games in his thirteen-year Giants career, one of them because of a fractured cheekbone, which caused a "big hole" in his face. But he was back in action two weeks later. The 6'3", 255-pound Brown joined the defense on goal line stands. He had the assignment in the 1956 championship game of blocking Bears defensive end Ed Meadows, who had shortly before sent Lions quarterback Bobby Layne to the hospital. Meadows had a reputation around the NFL for "hatchet jobs"—efforts to deliberately injure opponents. Brown rendered him ineffective.[37]

The *New York Times* stated that 240-pound guard Darrell Dess, who played for the Giants from 1959 through 1964 (and again from 1966 through 1969), "gives and takes as much punishment as anyone in football week after week." The *Times* reported that Dess loved the contact, blocking defensive tackles who were usually fifteen to fifty-five pounds heavier. But because guards were taught to block with their heads, Dess broke helmets and was "woozy a lot." He had a headache after every game and confessed that sometimes "everything goes black."[38]

The 1958 NFL sudden-death championship game is considered the single most important event giving credibility to pro football's challenge to Major League Baseball's status as the nation's most popular sport. However, the Giants' two victories over the powerful Cleveland Browns at the end of that season, immediately preceding the championship game, also contributed significantly to pro football's advancing to that position. Both of the closely contested games were played in subfreezing weather, the first in a snowstorm. Sam Huff claimed that there was "no greater rivalry in all of sports" than that between the Giants and the Browns during the 1950s: "We had the great defense, and Cleveland had the great offense." Andy Robustelli described the rivalry as "the most intense in the NFL" and stated that it "only grew hotter" during the decade. The Browns offense in 1958 was powered by fullback Jim Brown, who in his second year already held the NFL record for most yards gained rushing in a season, and halfback Bobby Mitchell, arguably the league's best outside running threat. Robustelli noted that there was "also the specter of Paul Brown coaching against you," a man considered one of the greatest head coaches in pro football history. The rivalry began in 1950, when the Browns, champions in each of the four years of the All-America Conference's existence, joined the NFL. They proceeded to win the NFL championship or the Eastern Division title every year until 1956 and added another division title in 1957. The Giants handed the Browns their only two defeats in 1950, inflicting on them the first shutout in the franchise's history. No other team had ever defeated the Browns twice in one season.[39]

On December 14, 1958, the Giants needed to defeat the Browns at Yankee Stadium in their last regularly scheduled game to force a playoff with them to determine the Eastern Division champion. A tie would give the conference title to the Browns. The Giants and the Browns, evenly matched, had each placed seven men on the Eastern Division Pro Bowl team. Jim Brown put Cleveland ahead with a spectacular sixty-five-yard touchdown run on the Browns' first possession. Behind 10–3 going into the fourth quarter and "seemingly on the road to defeat," the Giants tied the game when Frank Gifford hurled a long halfback option pass to Kyle Rote that brought the Giants to the Browns' six-yard line. Shortly afterward, on third down and goal, Gifford connected with end Bob Schnelker on another option pass for the tying touchdown.

With only two minutes and seven seconds in the game, the Giants appeared doomed as they lined up on frozen turf on fourth down for what appeared to be a forty-nine-yard field goal attempt in blizzard-like conditions. The snow had obliterated the yard markers. Hobbled by a bruised and swollen kicking leg, Giants placekicker Pat Summerall had been unable to practice all week, and he had missed a thirty-three-yard attempt a few minutes before. The 63,192 spectators had trouble seeing the ball, which Summerall propelled through the goalpost to provide the Giants with a 13–10 victory. Giants president Wellington Mara, son of team founder Tim Mara, called Summerall's field goal the "greatest single play in Giants' history."[40] Red Smith maintained that in all of sports history only Bobby Thomson's "Shot Heard Round the World," that won the 1951 National League playoff for the New York baseball Giants, compared with it in dramatic impact.[41]

The next week before 61,274 fans "dressed as if ready for admission to the Arctic," the Giants clinched the division title at Yankee Stadium by beating the Browns 10–0. The Browns had not been shut out since 1950. Jim Lee Howell stated that the Giants had put in "the best defensive effort against a top team I've ever seen in pro football." The *Los Angeles Times* declared that "it would have been much safer for an errant pedestrian to amble down the middle of the Hollywood Freeway yesterday than to be caught in Cleveland's backfield." The Giants "mayhem minded monsters," including Sam Huff; defensive linemen Rosey Grier, Andy Robustelli, and Jim Katcavage; and other "tigers turned loose by Jim Lee Howell," held the Browns to only twenty-four yards rushing. Jim Brown gained only eight yards in seven carries.[42] Paul Brown admitted that his club had been "soundly defeated." The Cleveland head coach praised thirty-seven-year-old "grey-haired" Charlie Conerly's steely performance as a major factor in the Giants victory: "An experienced quarterback means a great deal in a game like this. Conerly has been through the mill." By contrast, Paul Brown believed that Cleveland quarterback Milt Plum, his starter from 1957 to 1961, lacked "the ability to play under stress."[43]

Officials ejected Giants fullback Mel Triplett from the game when he threw punches at Browns players after being gang-tackled in the second quarter. The Giants charged that the Browns 240-pound defensive end Paul Wiggin had kicked Triplett in the back and 260-pound defensive tackle Don Colo had grabbed Triplett by his face mask and wrenched it. The *Washington Post* reported that Triplett went "berserk" and "threaten[ed] to clean up the whole Cleveland defensive team." He was so angry that Giants center Ray Wietecha had to tackle him twice to keep him away from the Browns players. New York head coach Jim Lee Howell unsuccessfully protested Triplett's ejection. He complained that "the Browns were throwing a lot of elbows."[44]

New Yorkers' enthusiasm for the football Giants was palpable in the days immediately preceding the championship game with the Colts, as huge lines of persons who hoped to purchase tickets snarled traffic at Grand Central Station. At Yankee Stadium, "police details kept order . . . far into the night" as the prospective ticket buyers "inched toward ticket windows."[45] Tom Landry recalled that after New York won the 1956 NFL championship, the Giants "became instant heroes" in the city, and the players all "basked in the unaccustomed glory." The football Giants faced less competition from Major League Baseball than ever before, because both of New York's National League franchises, the New York baseball Giants and the Brooklyn Dodgers, had relocated to the Pacific Coast after the 1957 season. About 17,000 fans were expected to travel to the game from Baltimore. More would have come, but the railroad companies were able to provide only three excursion trains from Baltimore, with a capacity of 3,000. Every available bus in the Baltimore area was chartered to bring fans to Yankee Stadium for the game. Oddsmakers listed the Colts as a slight favorite, although the Giants had beaten them earlier in the season in New York, 24–21, before 71,174 spectators.[46]

The 1958 championship game featured twelve players—six from each team—and three coaches (the Colts' head coach Weeb Ewbank, and the Giants' Lombardi and Landry) who would later be voted into the Pro Football Hall of Fame. The *New York Times* reported that "the excitement generated by football's longest game left most of the 64,185 spectators" at Yankee Stadium "limp." New York trailed 14–3 at the half, but its defense staged a dramatic goal line stand early in the third quarter, just when it appeared "that Cinderella [the Giants] was about to be chased out of the park." When the New York defense hurled Baltimore fullback Alan Ameche for a loss on fourth down, it "seemed to ignite a fire" under the Giants offense, which proceeded to stage "an almost incredible comeback." The seemingly nerveless Charlie Conerly moved New York ahead early in the fourth quarter, 17–14, on a fifteen-yard touchdown pass to Frank Gifford.[47] From that point, "the game degenerated into a jungle war of fists and knees and elbows."[48] With about two minutes to play, Baltimore quarterback Johnny Unitas engineered a drive that ended with a tying field goal with seven seconds left, sending the game into sudden-death overtime. The first team to score would win.

When the Giants, having won the coin toss, failed by inches to make a first down they punted, and Unitas moved the Colts from their fourteen-yard line to the Giants' one in twelve plays. Alan Ameche then bulled over for a touchdown after eight minutes and fifteen seconds of overtime, the culmination of what came to be known as "the thirteen steps to glory."[49]

The *New York Times* reported that many people were calling the game "the greatest they'd ever seen," among them NFL commissioner Bert Bell. *Sports Illustrated* in its January 5, 1959, issue called it "The Best Football Game Ever Played." Arthur Daley noted that the widespread public enthusiasm over the game "shows how completely pro football has arrived." Wellington Mara recalled that new requests for season tickets poured in to the Giants office during the weeks after the game. The next season, 1959, proved to be the first in which the Giants sold out every one of their home games. Alan Ameche appeared that evening on the *Ed Sullivan Show*, one of the nation's most-watched television programs. In Baltimore, 30,000 people crowded Friendship International Airport to greet the victorious Colts upon their return from New York. Traffic was jammed up for four miles beyond the airport.[50]

More than 45 million people saw the game on television, although the NFL required that it be blacked out in a seventy-five-mile radius around New York City. However, many of the city's residents were able to pick up the game broadcast from Philadelphia's WRCA Channel 3. The picture they received was "badly speckled and streaked," but the *New York Times* noted that "even with the visual handicaps the game was the sports spectacle of the TV year."[51]

Frank Gifford recalled that during the late 1950s, the football Giants "owned New York." Defensive coordinator Tom Landry commented that when he and his wife accompanied Giants players and their wives to the city's premier nightclubs, they "received celebrity status." At Toots Shor's, New York's sports-oriented "celebrity hot spot," where famous baseball players like Joe DiMaggio and top prizefighters mingled with movie stars and world-renowned writers, the football Giants, who previously had not excited much interest there, were "shown to the best tables." Gifford described Shor himself in the late 1950s as "a passionate [football] Giants fan who knew everything we were doing." Shor "was so fascinated by Charlie [Conerly] that he never let him leave the place."[52]

The Giants (10-2) and Colts (9-3) met again in the 1959 NFL championship game in Baltimore. Red Smith wrote that "this was the rematch that every palpitating pro fan in the Western Hemisphere had been waiting for."[53] Again, the press promoted the game as a battle between Baltimore's "unstoppable" offense and New York's "impregnable" defense. The Colts, however, boasted one of the NFL's best defensive lines, with Gino Marchetti, Art Donovan, and Gene "Big Daddy" Lipscomb. The Colts also led the NFL in pass interceptions.

And Giants quarterback Charlie Conerly had enjoyed one of his best seasons, completing 58.2 percent of his passes, with only four interceptions. His 1,706 yards passing led the NFL.[54] Expecting crowd noise in Memorial Stadium to be deafening, both the Giants and the Colts introduced sets of visible hand signals in case automatic calls were drowned out at the line of scrimmage. The *New York Times* noted that many Baltimoreans preferred to call the Colts by the more macho name of "Hosses" (or "Steeds").[55]

Game day witnessed what the *Chicago Tribune* called "the biggest exodus" from Baltimore since British troops pillaged it during the War of 1812, as an estimated 200,000 people headed outside the blackout area to watch the nationwide telecast in motels or taverns. Television salespeople were advertising outside antennae throughout Baltimore and its immediate environs, which made it possible for local television sets to receive the game broadcast from outside the blackout area.[56]

The championship game, played before a sellout crowd of 57,557, remained tight for three quarters, with the Giants ahead 9–7 going into the final period. But in the fourth quarter the Colts outscored the Giants by a significant margin to win 31–16. Another sign of pro football's growing status was the presence in the stands of Vice President Richard Nixon, who attended with Attorney-General William Rogers. Robert F. Kennedy was seated nearby, identified as former counsel of the US Senate rackets-investigating committee and brother of Senator John F. Kennedy, a potential Democratic presidential nominee.[57]

Vice President Nixon visited the team locker rooms after the game to congratulate the Colts and offer condolences to the Giants, shaking hands "with as many players as he could reach." He quickly recognized the "gray-haired" Conerly, and told him: "It was a great game for three quarters, Charlie, and for a short while there I thought you fellows were going to pull it off. I don't think you have a bit to be ashamed of."[58]

In 1960, the Giants were "belted out" of contention by Philadelphia linebacker Chuck Bednarik's bone-crushing open-field tackle of Frank Gifford that forced a fumble and knocked New York's most versatile offensive back out of commission until 1962.[59] At the time the Giants were 5-1-1 and the Eagles 6-1. Gifford had caught a pass from substitute quarterback George Shaw around the Eagles' thirty-yard line and was driving for a tying fourth-quarter touchdown. Bednarik's hit ended the Giants' chances of victory. Frederick Exley recalled his horror at Yankee Stadium watching Bednarik zero in on the unsuspecting Gifford "like some fierce animal gone berserk." It was like "watching a tractor

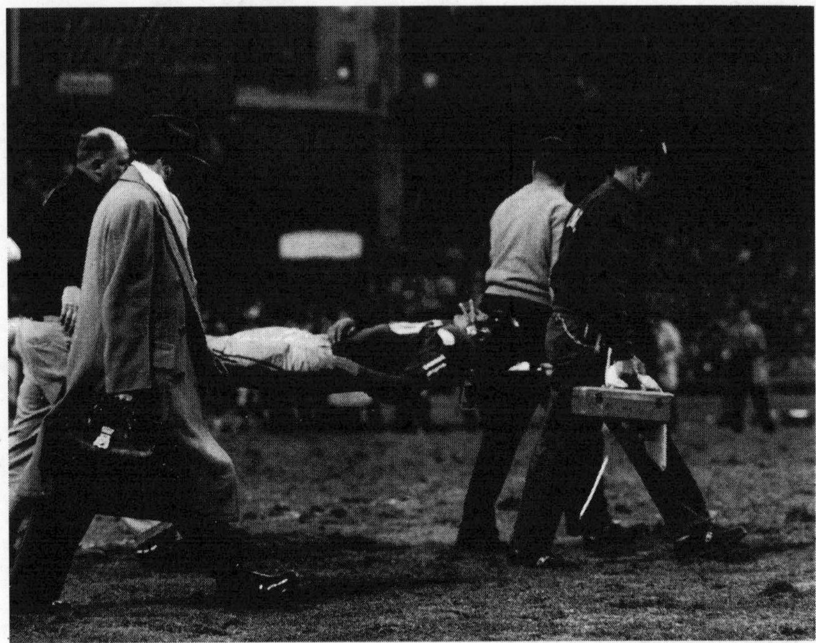

Frank Gifford is carried off the field at Yankee Stadium on a stretcher after taking a hit from Philadelphia Eagles linebacker Chuck Bednarik, November 20, 1960. *Courtesy of the Associated Press.*

trailer bear down on a blind man." Gifford was knocked unconscious before he fell to the turf and had to be carried off the field on a stretcher. He did not regain consciousness for several hours. Gifford was hospitalized for two and a half weeks. The *New York Times* reported two days later that Gifford had suffered an acute deep brain concussion and a contusion of the occipital region of the skull and neck.[60] The Giants loss to the Eagles the next week for all intents and purposes ended their chances of winning the division.

Giants fans at the stadium were angered when Bednarik, in Arthur Daley's words "impulsively . . . danced with joy" beside the unconscious Gifford, although a great many football players and fans expressed open admiration for Bednarik's hit. Bednarik explained that he had not been aware when he was celebrating that he had knocked Gifford senseless; he was just excited that the fumble ensured an Eagles victory. The *New York Times* carried a photograph of a Giants cheerleader weeping inconsolably about the severe injury the rough-hewn Bednarik had inflicted on Gifford, whom Daley, in a column entitled "The Matinee Idol Type," referred to as "the Dream Boat from Southern Cal."

Charlie Conerly, who had witnessed Bednarik's hit from the sidelines, "profanely accus[ed] him of making an illegal tackle." But Giants head coach Jim Lee Howell and Sam Huff considered Bednarik's tackle "clean." Huff later joined Bednarik on the speaker's rostrum at a Touchdown Club dinner in Columbus, Ohio, and expressed admiration for his tackle of Gifford: "Goddamn! We linebackers dream about making those kind of tackles—a good, clean whack that knocks the other team's big gun out of the game."[61] The photograph of Bednarik standing over the fallen Gifford hung in many Philadelphia homes and taverns for decades.

The Giants for the 1961 season made three personnel changes that significantly transformed their offense, acquiring another quarterback for the 1961 season, Y. A. Tittle, to spell their forty-year-old longtime starter Charlie Conerly, and split end Del Shofner in trades with the San Francisco 49ers and Los Angeles Rams, respectively. The Giants hired a new head coach, the offensively minded Allie Sherman, to replace Jim Lee Howell, who had retired after the 1960 season. Vince Lombardi had left to become head coach of the Green Bay Packers in 1959, and Tom Landry assumed the head coaching position for the expansion Dallas Cowboys in 1960. Sherman alternated Conerly and Tittle at quarterback in 1961. Tittle, who turned thirty-five during the season, was a thirteen-year veteran of pro football with the All-America Conference Baltimore Colts and the NFL's 49ers. He was an adept ball handler, one of the NFL's best long passers, and a master of the screen pass. Tittle was so proficient at deceiving defenses with fakes after taking the snap from center that the *Chicago Tribune* commented: "Merlin, the magician, would have been run out of court if Tittle had turned up in King Arthur's time."[62] Conerly retired after the 1961 season, and Tittle was the Giants starting quarterback for the next three years.

Tittle had a reputation for playing through injuries dating back to his college years at Louisiana State University (LSU). He played both offense and defense at LSU and won the team's trophy for "most minutes played." A 1947 *Sport* magazine profile on Tittle reported that he had been badly hurt making a head-on tackle of a Vanderbilt ball carrier and was taken to the sidelines to inhale ammonia. The team physician informed LSU's coach Red Swanson that Tittle was through for the evening because he was barely breathing. Swanson pleaded with the physician to "*Make* him breathe" so he could return to action. Tittle, according to *Sport*, "solved the problem" by rising from the bench, returning to the game, "and promptly completing three straight passes." Star NFL running back Hugh McElhenny, who played in the backfield with Tittle on the 49ers and Giants, recalled his breaking a cheekbone in a game and continuing to play, ending the day with twenty-nine pass completions. McElhenny had also watched Tittle play with a broken left hand. Tittle endured searing pain whenever he took the snap from center.[63]

Del Shofner emerged as one of the NFL's premier pass receivers in the early 1960s and provided the Giants with the deep pass threat their offense had lacked. A top-level college sprinter who ran a 9.8 hundred-yard dash, Shofner almost immediately became Tittle's favorite target. He fit the model of the western hero, a silent and expressionless counterpoint to the other-directed organization man. *Sport* commented that one of the pleasures of pro football was that "unlike many other highly competitive, complex businesses, it does not demand that you effect an effervescent personality, make small talk . . . or even smile when you don't feel like smiling." The pro football player's focus was only on "hitting harder, kicking farther, throwing better, or scoring more than anybody else" at his position.[64]

Pass-oriented Allie Sherman, a backup quarterback for the Philadelphia Eagles under legendary coach Greasy Neale from 1943 to 1947, had during the mid-1950s taken the Winnipeg Blue Bombers to the playoffs three years in a row in the Canadian Football League, which played a more wide-open style of offense than the NFL. While with Philadelphia, Sherman helped Neale install the modern T-formation. In 1949 Steve Owen, on Neale's recommendation, hired Sherman to convert Charlie Conerly from a single wing tailback into a T-formation quarterback. When Vince Lombardi left the Giants to become Green Bay's head coach, Sherman replaced him as the Giants' offensive coordinator.[65]

In his first three years as Giants' head coach, Sherman took the team to the NFL championship game, each one played in unusually fierce winter cold. In 1961, the "pass-minded" Giants led by Tittle played Lombardi's Packers, known for their "powerful running game," in Green Bay. NBC paid a record $615,000 for the rights to broadcast the game over a network of more than two hundred stations across the nation. The local newspaper "facetiously referred to the twenty-degree weather" on game day as a "heat wave," because the previous week temperatures in Green Bay had dipped to fifteen degrees below zero. Workers had to shovel nine feet of snow from the paved areas of the stadium parking lot the morning of the game. Before a sellout crowd that "resembled a convention of Eskimos," assembled in the "roofless igloo known as City Stadium," the Packers crushed the Giants, 37–0. Poor footing on the "rock-hard" field hampered the Giants pass receivers, who had trouble holding on to the ball in the bitter cold.[66]

During a regular season 49–34 victory over the Washington Redskins the next year, Tittle put on one of the most spectacular displays of passing in football history before a crowd of 62,844 at Yankee Stadium. He completed twenty-seven of thirty-nine passes for 505 yards, including seven for touchdowns, tying an NFL record. Del Shofner caught eleven of Tittle's passes for 269 yards, tying Frank Gifford's club record for receptions. The Redskins at the time were on top of the Eastern Division, undefeated in six contests. The game drew enormous national interest, and both Tittle and Washington quarterback Norm Snead, who himself threw four touchdown passes, were invited guests on the *Ed Sullivan Show* that evening. Greasy Neale called Tittle's performance "the finest exhibition of pin-point passing I've ever seen." Arthur Daley acknowledged that football "fundamentalists" wedded to the ground game shuddered at the lopsided emphasis on the aerial attack in this contest. Fans by the early 1960s, however, were unlikely to consider the aerial game less macho than running, partly because they appreciated the importance of long-range strategic bombers and intercontinental ballistic missiles in Cold War military planning. Moreover, Daley emphasized that "this was no effete ball-flipping contest [like] basketball." He explained that the game had become a "passing duel" because "the two huge defensive lines smothered the ball carriers." Wellington Mara stated that "a runner took his life in his hands every time he carried the ball."[67]

In 1962, the Giants (12-2) and Packers (13-1) met again in the championship game, playing before a capacity crowd of 64,892 in New York in weather even more frigid than the previous year in Green Bay. Vince Lombardi called the conditions more forbidding than he could ever remember for a football game.[68] The problem was not just the temperature, which hovered between 17 and 20 degrees, but the "frigid, swirling gusts of wind that frequently reached thirty miles an hour." Arthur Daley described the wind as "blasting . . . into Yankee Stadium . . . with all the venom of one refrigerated on the Siberian steppes." These conditions made accurate medium- and long-range passing almost impossible, placing the Giants at "a singular disadvantage." Tittle, who had set an NFL record with thirty-three touchdown passes that season, "overthrew or underthrew open targets far down the field." The wind blew passes back at the quarterbacks.

Daley reported that the game became "a battle of brute strength, a savage throwback to the more primitive days of football." It was a slugfest on the lines and in pileups. Green Bay's hard-running fullback Jim Taylor charged that Sam Huff had tried to cripple him, using his knees and elbows when Taylor was down. Giants defensive tackle Dick Modzelewski accused Taylor of biting him.[69] The Giants lost 16–7, scoring their only touchdown by blocking a punt into the end zone. The victorious Packers were greeted at the Green Bay airport upon their return from New York by 10,000 "shrieking" fans. Some of them hanged Sam Huff in effigy.[70]

Huff after the game had no apologies. He denied hitting Taylor when he was down, but conceded that the Packers fullback was a special target of the Giants defense. Huff explained: "If you try to pussyfoot with them good backs, they'll run all over you." *Los Angeles Times* columnist Jim Murray wrote that Huff had played a "brass-knuckle game" that would frighten any children who watched the reruns. Huff's comment was: "We hit each other as hard as we can. This is a man's game." The *New York Times* in September 1963 reported that Huff's bruising and punitive style of play had proved highly popular across the United States, noting that during the previous winter and spring "he was in more demand than ever as a dinner speaker at good prices."[71]

The 1963 NFL championship between the New York Giants (11-3) and the Chicago Bears (11-1-2) was a similarly fiercely contested game played on frozen ground in temperatures that fluctuated between eight and eleven degrees. The Bears "granite-like" defense surrendered only 144 points all season, the NFL's lowest since 1950, when teams played only twelve, rather than fourteen games. The Giants combined their usual solid defense with the league's most spectacular offense, averaging 32 points a game. Tittle had the best year of his career, breaking his season touchdown pass record with thirty-six, and leading the NFL in completion percentage and average yards gained per pass. The *New York Herald Tribune*, however, warned that passing against the Bears was "like tossing a chunk of meat into a pool of piranhas." The Bears not only expected to intercept the pass, but fought "over who's got first dibs." Chicago played a "drab" and "deliberate" ball-control offense, with some short passing. The *Herald Tribune* called the Bears offense "as exciting as twin beds."[72]

An estimated 50 million people watched the championship game on television, which was played in Chicago's Wrigley Field, filled to capacity with 46,901 "shivering" spectators. Many Chicago-area residents moved outside what Red Smith called the NFL's "iron curtain" to watch the game on motel and bar televisions beyond the blackout zone. For the first time, the title game was shown on closed-circuit pay television, to 26,000 people at three sites in Chicago.[73]

The bitter cold undermined the Giants' passing offense as it had in the previous year's championship, turning the game into another bruising defensive struggle. Tittle put the Giants ahead 7–0 in the first quarter with a touchdown strike to Frank Gifford, but twisted his left leg when blitzing Bears linebacker Larry Morris slammed into him as he threw. In the second quarter, Morris, blitzing again, "shot at" Tittle's leg and badly injured the quarterback's knee. With the Giants ahead, 10–7, Tittle hobbled off the field leaning on Hugh McElhenny and was out of commission for the rest of the half. Tittle recalled: "This time the pain shot clear up my leg. It was like someone had stuck a knife in the knee joint. . . . This time I knew it was bad."[74] The *New York Herald Tribune* reported that "9 out of 10" of the Wrigley Field spectators, out for blood, responded by joyfully shouting: "They got Tittle!" Andy Robustelli denounced as despicable the Chicago crowd's cheering as Tittle limped off the field. He recalled that some of the Giants players were on the verge of charging into the stands to retaliate. Rookie Glynn Griffing, who replaced Tittle at quarterback for the remainder of the first half, was confused and ineffective.[75]

Determined to get Tittle back onto the field, the Giants' physician at halftime shot his knee with Novocain and cortisone to kill the searing pain. Tittle returned after the half, but he was not able to plant his foot properly, and was too slow on the drop back. Passing on one leg, with yards of adhesive tape wrapped around his knee, he had his worst day of the season. Tittle completed only eleven of twenty-nine passes and suffered five interceptions, four of them in the second half. Interceptions set up both of the Bears' touchdowns. Hampered by the cold, Del Shofner dropped what appeared to be Tittle's certain touchdown pass in the first quarter, and Aaron Thomas dropped another one in the second quarter after he got behind the Bears' secondary.[76]

When the game ended, with the Bears victorious, 14–10, the Giants left the field "like Napoleon's troops retreating from Moscow," in the *Chicago Tribune*'s military analogy. But the *Tribune* praised the Giants for taking the defeat like champions. Red Smith noted in his *New York Herald Tribune* column that "Tittle took ferocious punishment" from the Bears defense throughout the game. But the Giants defense was equally rough. The *Chicago Tribune* stated that Sam Huff and Giants defensive back Erich Barnes had "played as though they had been locked out of a saloon."[77]

The aging Giants suddenly fell apart in 1964, finishing with a 2-10-2 record, the worst in the franchise's history, as Tittle experienced one of the poorest seasons of his career. Many of the Giants were now well past their peak. Allie Sherman had traded Rosey Grier (in 1962) and Dick Modzelewski (in 1963), longtime mainstays of the defensive line, and sent Sam Huff to the Washington Redskins for two mediocre players after the 1963 season. Tittle, Frank Gifford, Andy Robustelli, Alex Webster, and thirteen-year veteran guard Jack Stroud retired after the 1964 season. William Phillips, cofounder of the literary magazine *Partisan Review,* noted in 1969 that the Giants owners, the Mara family, had not spent enough on signing players to compete effectively with more ambitious NFL franchises or with teams in the upstart American Football League. They had failed to develop a modern scouting apparatus. Phillips maintained that the Maras permitted the Giants' decline because New York City had become so passionately committed to pro football that its residents would fill up the stadium "week after week with almost any kind of team."[78]

The Giants' collapse was symbolized by a photograph of Y. A. Tittle taken in Pittsburgh during the second game of the 1964 season, after 270-pound Steeler defensive end John Baker crashed through inexperienced Giants offensive tackle Lane Howell and drove Tittle into the ground, badly injuring him. The picture was snapped by Morris Berman of the *Pittsburgh Post-Gazette,* a prominent World War II army combat photographer. Berman was known for his photograph of "the bullet-ridden corpses of Mussolini and his mistress" after they were killed by antifascist partisans in 1945. His Pittsburgh photograph showed Tittle on his knees, dazed, with his helmet knocked off and blood trickling down his bald head. In addition to head lacerations, he suffered broken ribs and chest bruises.[79]

The New York Giants in the period from 1956 to 1963 assumed a leading role in pro football's displacement of Major League Baseball as the nation's premier sport. Fear that American men had grown too soft to meet the challenges of the Cold War led large numbers of US citizens to embrace pro football as a means of reinvigorating American manhood. William Phillips noted that pro football owes "much of its popularity . . . to the fact that it makes respectable the most primitive feelings about violence, patriotism, [and] manhood."[80] Pro football's strikingly high level of violence had become the subject of much mass media comment by the mid-1950s, when the Giants began their ascent. As one of the first two teams widely publicized for emphasizing defense, the Giants were consistently associated with the use of force and intimidation to resist enemy conquest of territory. The Giants also pioneered in elaborating sophisticated defensive strategies and tactics. The Giants in the late 1950s, as a result, drew many people to pro football who related the team's defensive prowess to America's effort to contain Communist expansion.

The Giants benefited from television's emergence as the nation's prime entertainment medium. Based in New York City, America's media capital, the Giants received considerably more exposure than other pro teams. Violence was a feature of many television programs, but it was antiseptic; pro football provided a much more graphic view of its impact.

Moreover, the New York Giants' charismatic offensive stars greatly enhanced pro football's appeal, notably Frank Gifford, Charlie Conerly, and Y. A. Tittle. They were highly publicized by the New York–based television networks, mass circulation magazines, and newspapers, and in Gifford's case, the Hollywood film industry. They also received many commercial endorsement offers, which were almost unheard of for pro football players in the early 1950s.[81]

Gifford and Conerly presented different, but equally glamorous male images, both of which the mass media avidly promoted: the Southern California movie actor and bathing suit model and the rugged Marlboro Man, respectively. Both appealed to the vast numbers of men consigned to the anonymity and dependency of modern office work. Tittle, whom many considered the best long passer of his era, dramatized pro football's new emphasis on a quick-strike offense, which fascinated an American public fixated on new methods of warfare emphasizing intercontinental ballistic missiles and long-range strategic bombers.

The Giants, of marginal interest to New Yorkers only a decade before, had by the late 1950s and early 1960s become a central part of Manhattan's glittering social life, deeply admired by celebrities in a wide range of fields. Frank Gifford recalled that on Sunday nights during that period, he and Charlie Conerly would host cocktail parties at their Grand Concourse apartments across from Yankee Stadium, attended every week by "a movie star or two, a hot singer, some TV personalities, a couple of Pulitzer Prize winners" and sometimes the vice president of the United States, Richard Nixon. Frederick Exley noted that the Giants had acquired such prestige in the city by that time that the sellout crowds every week were full of "Chesterfield-coated corporation executives and their elegant-legged mink-draped wives."[82]

Within the sports world, New York was considered the most glamorous football city, where players could find themselves showered with a glittering array of goods that masses of American men of that era coveted. George Plimpton, editor of the *Paris Review,* who trained with the Detroit Lions in the summer of 1963, described the Lions players' envy and disbelief at pregame ceremonies at Yankee Stadium, when one of the Giants was honored: "gift after gift" was "wheeled out," including "golf clubs, a red convertible (driven out by a Miss Rheingold), a Hammond organ, hundreds of dollars' worth of fishing equipment, a television console, a camping outfit with a barbecue stand . . . and a . . . yacht." The Lions "stood watching . . . like country cousins."[83]

CHAPTER FOUR

# Joe Namath

## Player on and off the Field

*Eunice G. Pollack*

### A Star Is Born

On January 2, 1965, the New York Jets of the American Football League (AFL) held a cocktail party at Toots Shor's to introduce the newly signed $427,000-quarterback Joe Namath to the press. By far the highest-paid player in football, the closest was the Heisman trophy winner, Notre Dame quarterback John Huarte, just signed by the Jets for $200,000, who would become "expendable" as soon as Namath failed his physical and his draft board classified him 4-F. The contract included a $7,000 Lincoln Continental in green, the team color, chosen by the Jets president, who had been born on St. Patrick's Day. The Jets had outbid the St. Louis Cardinals of the National Football League (NFL), who had also drafted Namath in the first round, but dropped out of the running at $389,000. Other players' resentment of the massive payload was palpable. The Jets erstwhile quarterback Dick Wood protested, "If a kid who's never played a single pro game is worth $400,000, I must be worth about $2 million."

Sportswriters warned what would happen when "some mammoth, sadistic AFL lineman, who gets one tenth his pay for taking quarterbacks apart, combines his envy, anger and muscle to see if he can break Joe into itty, bitty pieces." But Namath only shrugged, "You've got to expect it. If I wanted a no-contact sport, I'd have tried out for swimming." When a reporter at the party challenged him, "Suppose you don't make it, Joe. Do you still get all the money?" the quarterback responded flatly, in "a tone much more confident than arrogant," "I'll make it." When another inquired cheekily, "And what do you think about the fuss being made about you?" the twenty-two-year-old replied equably, "You think I should answer that? If I say I like it, I'm a glory hound. If

I say I don't care, I'm a smart-aleck. So I won't say." In fact, even after his first year in the pros, when he had thrown eighteen touchdown passes, was named Rookie of the Year "by a landslide in every poll," and was the Most Valuable Player of the AFL's All-Star game against the league champion Buffalo Bills—as well as being "the most-fined of all the Jets"—it appeared that Namath was "worth every penny of his pay check." By 1973, in the assessment of many, "the $400,000 rookie [had] turned out to be a bargain. . . . He had become a legend in his own time."[1]

It was David "Sonny" Werblin—pronounced, *Variety* underscored, "Sonny, Just Like in Money"—who recognized Namath's star power, and in signing him, made what the columnist Jimmy Breslin characterized as "clearly . . . the best move . . . in sports in my time." Werblin and his cronies at the Monmouth Park and Bowie race tracks had purchased the bankrupt Titans in 1963 for $1 million and Werblin announced that he was determined to make the team—now modernized as "the Jets"—"like the Yankees in the 1920s." All he needed was "a Babe Ruth, a star." Two years after he acquired Namath, he explained to a reporter why he needed a Bambino: "Stars sell tickets. That's why you're here doing a story on Joe and not on someone else. When the Yankees had stars, they accounted for 45 percent of all American League attendance. If they had those stars today, you don't think they'd be drawing 500 people to a game, do you?"

Werblin often recounted his search for a star that culminated in the signing of Namath. "I knew he was a star the minute I saw him," he recalled. "We'd been going around looking at all-American quarterbacks. They had one at Tulsa"—the record-setting Jerry Rhome. "He came into the room, a little introverted guy. I said, nah, I don't want him. Never mind how good he is, I need to build a franchise with somebody who can do more than play. So we went down to Birmingham [Namath was playing for the University of Alabama] and the minute Joe walked into the room, I know. I said, 'Here we go.'" Werblin retained "vivid memories of the first time he saw the young folk hero in action," in the Orange Bowl between the undefeated Crimson Tide and the Texas Longhorns on New Year's Day, 1965. "The moment he came on the field, I knew he was a leader. I knew I had to have him." The Jets publicist Frank Ramos had watched the action on television, the first bowl game shown in prime time. Although Namath had been injured and was not slated to play, Ramos could still picture him "pacing the sideline, . . . glaring out onto the field," as Texas led 14–0. At last, the coach, Bear Bryant, summoned the wounded warrior. As the crowd roared, Namath came out "limping, in his white shoes, [and] was absolutely electrifying." With Texas leading 21–17, only seconds remaining, and the ball on the one-foot line, the hero was thrown back, and for "the first time . . . millions of people felt sorry for someone with $400,000."

Recognizing the quarterback's "star-quality," Werblin commented at the signing, "I don't know whether you'll play on our team or make a picture for Universal." Whatever his trajectory, Werblin now took "the greatest" under his wing—running interference for him—some accusing him of "spoiling Joe by being so close to him." Werblin brought "everyone's darling in the pro-football draft" home with him and took him along on the Triple Crown racing circuit, making "a well-publicized stop in Louisville for the Kentucky Derby." Indeed, Namath would share his New York penthouse with Joe Hirsch, "a member of [Werblin's] racing crowd and a columnist for the *Morning Telegraph* and *Daily Racing Form*."[2]

Before Werblin bought the Titans, he had "worked and schemed and planned and plotted" for almost thirty years for the Music Corporation of America (MCA), "the biggest talent agency ever known to show business." Retiring in January 1965 as vice president of MCA Inc. and president of MCA-TV, he was widely considered "broadcasting's . . . greatest promoter and salesman." Although viewed as a mysterious figure who "never gave interviews," Werblin was "reputed to be the most powerful man in television." Among the stars he "personally handled" were Ed Sullivan, Jackie Gleason, Abbott and Costello, Alfred Hitchcock, Jack Paar, Jack Benny, Eddie Fisher, the Nelson family, Burns and Allen, and several others of equal stature. Werblin's friend Toots Shor recognized that he would "handle the sports game like show business, getting it to the public. He knows the value of publicity." A vice president of MCA concluded, "Sonny is the great judge of talent. . . . He can spot talent in any area. He has a nose for greatness."[3]

Drawing on his MCA playbook, Werblin staged the contest for quarterback, having given Huarte and Namath each "a pot of gold." Covering the competition for *Sports Illustrated*, Robert Boyle observed: "A few years ago, when the Jets were the hapless Titans, most football fans could not have told you if the team even had a quarterback. . . . Now . . . the competition for quarterback has achieved all the super-colossal proportions of the casting of Scarlett O'Hara in *Gone with the Wind*." Where the Jets had only sold 11,000 season tickets by July 1964, as "a result of the brouhaha," a year later they had sold over three times as many. Still, given Werblin's determination to feature a quarterback who would occupy "the throne room," it wasn't much of a contest. Unlike

Namath, described from the beginning as a magnetic personality, "a swingin' cat with dark good looks who sleeps till noon," "relishes the limelight," and whose "major interests are 'girls and golf, girls and golf,'" Huarte was "ramrod straight, . . . reserved, . . . wore conservative suits and rep ties, . . . reads the *Wall Street Journal*," planned to attend graduate school in business in the off-season, and was considering "a career on the Street."

Before long, Werblin's (along with other AFL owners') "purse-draining price war for top draft choices" like Namath and Huarte had not only generated massive public interest, but led to the merger of the American Football League and the National Football League. At the time of the signings, Werblin had denounced the NFL's condescension and "immature attitude" toward the AFL, complaining that they "won't talk to us." Their "whole attitude . . . is that they found it, it's theirs and no one else can get in it." "I think a lot of this stuff about the National League being so far superior is a lot of bunk." Expressing his own contempt, Werblin was dismissive of the owners of the supposedly "richer, older league," which consists only of "a bunch of jaded old guys" who "couldn't buy shoe polish from most of the owners in the AFL." In June 1966, the jaded old guys yielded, and announced that the leagues would officially merge in 1970, forming one league, to be called the NFL. The new league would be composed of two conferences, bringing about the Super Bowl, slated to begin in 1967.[4]

## Pro Football's Only Superstar

Werblin's well-honed instincts about Namath's "star-quality" on the gridiron and at the box office quickly proved true. Even in 1966, Billy Sullivan, owner of the Boston Patriots (1960–1988), deemed Namath "the biggest thing in New York since Babe Ruth." The same year the sportswriter Dan Jenkins noted the difference between Namath and "all of the sports celebrities who came before him in New York"—including Babe Ruth, Joe DiMaggio, and Sugar Ray Robinson—observing that "they were grown men when they achieved the status he now enjoys. . . . Their fame came more slowly—with the years of earning it." By contrast, "Joe Willie Namath was a happening" from the moment he arrived, and unlike the others, who remained "more or less aloof from the crowd, Joe thrusts himself into the middle of it." The sportswriter John Devaney observed that after only two years as a pro, Joe Namath was already "more famous than anyone . . . in pro football today," with the exception of Johnny Unitas and Bart Starr—adding that "not even Unitas became a superstar at the box office so quickly." Namath's own comparison was even more pointed. When asked in 1968 if he "ever thought about some day succeeding Unitas as the best quarterback," he responded, "No, . . . because I feel that way now."

From the moment of his arrival in the city, Namath attracted and electrified New York's fans. In 1967, when the players were introduced before a game at Shea Stadium, the "crowd of more than 60,000 reserved its loudest roar for Joe Willie." And while the *New York Times* reporter was disdainful that Namath acted as if he had "sold every one of those tickets," he conceded, "The fact is that he was responsible for selling a lot of them." *Time* magazine fully acknowledged Namath's impact: "Before Joe, the Jets might as well have been the Pottstown Firebirds for all anyone cared about them; their only fans were grumpy football buffs who could not afford to pay scalpers' prices for scarce New York Giants tickets." After all, between 1956 and 1963 the Giants had won six Eastern Division titles. But in 1964 the Giants record had suddenly become 2-10-2 and in 1966 they won "but a single game and lost 12," evoking mainly "derisive laughter." Worse, Namath was now drawing and thrilling New York fans, and the Giants felt the pressure keenly. Hence they made "an expensive trade," giving up their "top two draft choices for 1968 [and] their No. 1 choice for the following season" to acquire the "crowd-pleasing" quarterback Fran Tarkenton from the Minnesota Vikings—in the hope of competing with "the James Bondish legends of Joe Namath."[5]

By 1972, pro football had captured more interest than baseball. As *Time* put it, "Baseball may be the national pastime, but pro football has become the national obsession." The previous year, the NFL's regular attendance had "surpassed 10 million for the first time" and the commissioner, Alvin "Pete" Rozelle, was considering "expanding to . . . Honolulu and Mexico City." Central to the appeal was Namath, whom *Sport* magazine labeled "this most charismatic of all athletes." *Time* noted, "Win or lose, Namath generates more high-voltage excitement than any other player in the game." ABC-TV sports commentator Howard Cosell designated Namath "pro football's only superstar": "You'll never make a superstar out of Roger Staubach, no way," he explained. "He is a fine quarterback, but you are talking about more than athletic prowess. You are talking about a personality that . . . mass communicates."

Indeed, it was Namath who had the greatest impact both on ticket sales and television ratings. Cosell observed, "When you do a promotion for pro football, you use Joe Namath." Not surprisingly, ABC featured him on its first Monday night football game, "Joe and the Jets" vs. the Browns (1970). The network's publicist, Beano Cook, summed it up best: "Having Joe on one of our Monday-night games is like having the Pope say your mass." Ramos, the Jets publicist, commented, from the moment Namath signed with the team he "immediately" became "an identity, even to people who didn't know a touchback from a touchdown." In fact, the fans he drew to football extended well beyond them. Buffalo Bills publicist Jack Horrigan observed that many "women and elder men [had] become interested in football"—attending the games or watching on television—only because "they had heard of Namath" and "he excites them." Other commentators, recognizing that Namath was "unquestionably pro football's No. 1 attraction, [that] there is no one else close to him in popularity," worried "What happens without him to pro football's sky-high TV ratings?"[6]

## Celebrity in a Celebrity-Conscious Town

The interest in Namath of both the fans and the press extended far beyond the goalposts. Even before Super Bowl III, when he became Super Joe, a sportswriter for the *Baltimore Sun* predicted that "the 42nd Street library [in Manhattan] will soon have to construct an annex just to stock the stories about the new darling of pro football"; he suggested that the stories be filed under "American folklore." Namath was a celebrity and the press corps found "his extracurricular activities far more intriguing than his exploits on the playing field." The journalist remarked sardonically, "You have to read between the lines to discover he also has a rare talent for throwing a football and finding someone to catch it." Even by 1967, Namath's name was appearing "in the gossip columns almost as frequently as on the sports pages." Later, Jets safety Jim Hudson recalled that traveling with Namath was like being with a rock star. When Namath's teammate, the offensive guard Pete Perreault, was traded to the Vikings in 1971, he "suddenly realized, this is what it's like for all the teams who don't have Joe." Although the Vikings also had "real stars, . . . when we travel to a city there's no big excitement at the airport, no TV cameras waiting at the hotel, no crowds around the bus screaming for autographs. . . . Without him, you're just another team."

Hudson, who roomed with Joe on the road, elaborated on the impact of stardom. Joe had to "eat dinner at midnight," he explained, "just to get a little peace and quiet." "We couldn't eat at normal times because so many people wanted his autograph." And as soon as they checked into the team's hotel, they would "take the phone off the hook or it'd be ringing all the time." On the day of the game, the Jets always had to "devise secret ways to get Namath in and out of the stadium." In one case, he was "shuttled . . . out in an armored Brinks truck"; other times, he arrived and left in "a laundry cart, buried under dirty jocks and socks." In San Diego, he made his getaway in "an equipment truck, and the team picked him up on the freeway two miles from the stadium." Even in 1977, Namath's last year in football, when he played for the Los Angeles Rams—and contributed little on the field—Namath could avoid the excited hordes only by climbing into a golf cart that pulled up to the locker room door and sped across the Coliseum floor to the press exit tunnel, where a limousine awaited, his date inside, his road manager "riding shotgun."[7]

By the end of the sixties Namath had become a "cult hero"—certainly in part because, as the *New York Times* columnist James Reston gushed, he embodied "Hemingway's definition of courage: grace under pressure." "He could wait until the uttermost split-second, while his receivers were driving and faking . . . and then throw with geometric accuracy, long or short, bullet or lob, to the primary or secondary target, just before he was buried by the charging front four of the opposition." But Namath had also become "a big celebrity in a celebrity-conscious town" because he was recognized as a "libertine . . . a rogue," the media showcasing him as New York's first "bona fide rake hell hero since Babe Ruth," and endlessly spinning "wild tales of girls and booze, of riotous predawn odysseys through Manhattan saloons." In *Playboy*'s felicitous portrait, he became "[Jean-Paul] Belmondo with a jock strap." Fittingly, the director Federico Fellini wanted Namath to star in his film *Casanova,* but after Jimmy Walsh, the quarterback's business manager, had arranged a dinner for the three of them in New York, Namath complained, "That's a 35-mile drive into the city. I don't think I'll come." In 2014, almost fifty years after he had landed as a Jet in New York, when Namath was being interviewed on *CBS Morning,* the reporter summed up his impact: "Men wanted to be like you and women wanted to be with you." She then added, tilting her head flirtatiously, "I grew up in that era—I think that was pretty true." Ever the responsive "player," Namath rejoined, "I wish I had known that at the time."[8]

Initially, (male) sports reporters seemed puzzled by women's response to Namath. One recalled his impression when he interviewed him in 1965: "He is not handsome. There is the bird-beak of a nose, the hooded sleepy eyes, a swarthy face . . . and that frog-like back." At best, another conceded, "it is . . . an unusual face—ugly-handsome—and you don't forget it." By contrast, from their first meeting, Werblin recognized "that animal sex appeal," those "bedroom eyes"—identifying him with "Sinatra . . . [and] Cary Grant." To the *New York Times* sportswriter, who was of the same cohort, he was the "sweatsuit Sinatra." A (female) journalist, who had conducted a survey, concurred—though the quarterback's appeal was more overt and raw, and he never voiced someone else's lines. Indeed, 90 percent of her respondents considered Namath "the sexiest sports personality ever"—and were certain he would continue "to be until he abdicates." *Time* magazine adjudged that "No American beauty could regard her career as complete without a date with [him]."

Far more than "American beauties" were attracted by "his dark, rugged good looks and his flashy tailoring." It was clear that sizable "chunks of the female population" hoped "to get to know" Namath—"yes, in the Biblical sense," a reporter observed. Even in his first year with the Jets, as soon as he completed a two-session, 10 a.m.–5 p.m. workout in Peekskill, a man rushed over to inform him, "I got these two girls here who want to meet you"—one blonde; the other, brunette. A reporter with an appointment for an interview "never did get to see" Namath, "but the blonde did." As the quarterback repeatedly and openly confessed, "My weaknesses are clothes and blondes." At times, he elaborated: "A filly with brown hair is all right, so is one with black hair. But blondes, they come first." Nor was it different when the Jets were on the road, where "in every city," the team's hotel had "to post a guard—sometimes a guard plus a ferocious dog"—in front of Namath's room, "to protect him from avid females."

In January 1969, after Namath accepted *Sport* magazine's award as the Most Valuable Player in Super Bowl III, he was only able to reach the awaiting Lincoln Continental provided by the mayor through the strenuous efforts of the NYPD. "Mini-skirted admirers held up traffic on 48th Street as they surrounded the limo, climbed onto the hood for a peek at his shaggy mane, brushed-forward bangs and mutton-chop sideburns," and finally "chased the car down the street." Al Silverman, the editor of the magazine and toastmaster of the event, commented that this was "the largest crowd . . . we have ever had for the award luncheon," adding, "I notice there are more women here than there ever has been. Even more than there were for [Paul] Hornung," the Packer halfback, when he won the award. As others observed, it appeared that pro football had its "very own Beatle."[9]

Wherever he went, women "ferreted him out." Even when a journalist and her husband had dinner with Namath and his girlfriend, the (blonde) model, Randi Oakes, at the staid 21 Club, she found, when she and Oakes returned from the powder room, a "line of well-dressed females . . . impatiently waiting to speak with the politely standing quarterback." Oakes commented resignedly, "It happens every time." Nor had the crush of women diminished by 1977, Namath's last year in football, when, as a free agent, he signed with the Rams. The "resentment" of other stars on the team of his "notoriety and . . . independent life-style" was quickly dissipated when they found they "had never seen so many fine-looking women hanging around [training] camp and in the local taverns." Apparently, "the leftovers kept everybody happy." Even the next year, after Namath had left the gridiron, women's attraction to him had not dimmed. As he ate "his favorite '600-year-old chicken'" at a Chinese restaurant in LA, a steady procession of women wound their way to his table. One "bent over and whispered in his ear. The next left a card with her phone number. Another breathed, 'Hi Joe, remember me?'" Still gracious, perhaps still interested, Namath responded, "No, but I'd like to"—although now he would leave alone, hurrying home to catch the reruns of the Rams game on TV.[10]

## Did the Big City Corrupt the Quarterback?

*New York Times* columnist James Reston characterized Namath as "a familiar American type—the poor boy out of the Pennsylvania hills via the University of Alabama who conquered the big city and was corrupted by it," adding, "When he came to New York a few years ago, he was a story straight out of Victorian melodrama." Reston alleged that now, five years later, it was clear that he was simply "repeating the Thomas Wolfe theme of the Southern boy who takes over the big town and is defeated by success."

In fact, success in the Big Apple could not fully account for the trajectory of the "boy bachelor's" life-and-carousing in the pros. After conducting a long interview with Namath for *Playboy*, the associate editor Lawrence Linderman described admiringly how in his senior year in college the superstar "completed 64 percent of his passes on the gridiron—and probably even more than that with Alabama's comely contingent of Southern belles." There, the "heroic stature [Namath] had achieved throughout the state" had only been enhanced by the "whispered adventures" of the young Lothario. To be sure, in the North, the whispers would become screaming headlines. Above all, Linderman wanted to determine if the current "legend" of him as "one of the great womanizers of our time . . . is merited." Namath assured him that "it's merited. . . . I do all right with the ladies." But the interviewer wanted to know more, and pressed him for figures—"estimates" would do. Trying to be helpful, Namath recalled, "with a great big smile," "When I was in boring classes at Alabama, I used to start making out lists to see how well I was doing, and I guess I was pretty close to 300 by the time I graduated"—or, more accurately, when he left for the pros, 21 credits short of graduating.

Responding openly and volubly to the follow-up query if those were "fond memories," Namath volunteered that at the time he had understood that "the aim of making love was simply to . . . achieve your own satisfaction and not even worry about your partner's." But as he "grew up," he "started" to recognize "that sex is a two-way street and it's much better for both of you to be sexually satisfied. Once you realize this," he concluded, "you should really go all out and make a sincere effort to make 'em happy." In short, far from being corrupted by his move to "the big city," the hero's life—and, it appeared, the lives of his "conquests"—had been enriched by the move. These were, after all, the early years of the second wave of feminism, with its condemnation of sexual asymmetries, along with direct discussions—and oft-quoted empirical studies—of female orgasm.[11]

Namath's admissions, however, only elicited *Playboy*'s further probes: "There are thousands of guys—some of them fairly glamorous celebrities—who feel the same way about giving as well as getting sexual satisfaction. But they don't make out like you do. What's your secret?" Namath responded guilelessly, "I really like women." In later conversations with *Inside Sports*, Namath elaborated. When the journalist Tony Kornheiser observed, "You seem so good with women . . . you seem better with women than men," Namath agreed: "It's a gift. And an effort also. . . . I may put in more of an effort with women. . . . I'm more sensitive to the female definitely. And I will take more time with a female than a man to get them more comfortable." Others added that he had "cultivated a shy, Southern politeness with women that borders on the courtly." But *Playboy* also wanted information on the "types of girls that especially attract" him, given that he had "sampled" so many. And here one could see the enduring influence of his pre-big-city days, as he explained his strong preference for "a quiet girl . . . a soft-spoken girl." In short, he continued, "I like Southern girls. . . . They seem sweeter, gentler. They're not as hard as New York girls." Still, he added quickly, "I want to thank the broads in New York for all they did for me last season"—the season the Jets won the Super Bowl. "They really helped build my morale."[12]

## The Traditionalist's Nightmare

To the consternation of many traditionalists—journalists and fans—Namath combined football, sex—and scotch—and openly praised the mix. When *Playboy* inquired if he honored "sport's great tradition . . . that the night before the big game, the athlete goes to bed early—and by himself," the magazine—and everyone else—already knew the response: "No . . . most of the nights before games, I'll be with a girl." In fact, Namath claimed to have found a doctor who "told me that it's a good idea to have sexual relations before a game, because it gets rid of the kind of nervous tension an athlete doesn't need."

Namath expanded upon his routine to the columnist Jimmy Breslin, with whom he felt particularly comfortable: "The night before the Oakland game [in December 1968, for the AFL championship], I got the whole family in town and there's people all over my apartment and the phone keeps ringing. I wanted to get away from everything. . . . So I went to the Bachelors III [the club he co-owned briefly in 1968–1969] and grabbed a girl and a bottle of Johnnie Walker Red and went to the Summit Hotel and stayed in bed all night with the girl and the bottle." By contrast, Breslin explained, the next morning, the Raiders, "fresh-eyed from an early bed check and a night's sleep, uniform-neat in their team blazers, filed into a private dining room in the Waldorf-Astoria for the pre-game meal," while "just across the street in the Summit Hotel, . . . Namath was patting the broad goodbye, putting an empty whiskey bottle in the waste basket, dressing up in his mink coat and leaving for the ballgame, . . . [where] late in the afternoon Namath threw one 50 yards to Don Maynard and the Jets were the league champions." Namath added that he had done the "same thing before the Super Bowl. I went out and got a bottle and grabbed this girl and brought her back to the hotel in Ft. Lauderdale and we had a good time the whole night."[13]

Unlike his renowned attraction to women, however, Namath explained that "I didn't learn how to drink, really, until I got to New York." In fact, the new attachment began in Boston when "I got hit on a safety blitz, got a real deep bruise. . . . When I got home that night I hurt so bad I could hardly get out of the car. I didn't have any pain pills . . . so I got some scotch. . . . Johnny Walker Red really kicked my ass."

A number of traditionalist sportswriters strongly disapproved of Namath's off-the-field play. Typical was Al Hirshberg, who snarled in *Esquire*, "[Does] he [ever] say to himself, 'I must live right tonight so I can play right tomorrow . . . ?'"

"Why won't he admit that his flamboyant waste of energy and money is going to catch up with him. . .? That, not his knees, will shorten his career." Indeed, whenever the Jets performed poorly the naysayers suspected the quarterback's nighttime activities were at fault. Namath recalled that once, when the Jets lost to Houston 24–0, and a writer asked "why the team had looked so bad," he responded, "putting him on," "Booze and broads, what else?" which became the headline in newspapers "all across the country" the next day. In fact, Namath stated, "We came ready to play. We just got beat." And when *Playboy* asked, "In line with your much-reported fondness for Johnnie Walker Red, . . . has drinking ever taken anything away from your performance on the field?" Namath was adamant: "I know my drinking limits." Just as was true of his habits with women, he explained, "Look, I'm a football player and that's my number one thing. . . . I've been playing football for a long time, and by now, I know what I should and shouldn't do to stay ready at all times." "I'm not about to take a chance on how I perform."

Once, Namath had famously announced, "I like my Johnnie Walker red and my women blonde," but a few years after leaving the gridiron, he found, "Like any whiskey, it'll beat you. . . . So I quit drinking scotch. . . . I mostly drink vodka now." He quickly qualified this, however, explaining that he meant "Smirnoff and Wolfschmidt," and definitely not Stolichnaya. "I'm honest-to-God pro-American and I boycott every damn Russian thing. . . . I don't like 'em."[14]

## The Appeal of Sex, Money, and the Quarterback

Namath benefited from—but also hastened—the most recent transition in American women's "sexual fixation . . . from Broadway stars to movie stars to rock stars" and now, to the "professional athlete." This was attributable, in part, to women's tendency to follow the money. The columnist Kay Gilman found that women are now "turned on by the pros . . . . They can't read enough about the . . . private lives of the best-looking athletes, who in many cases are almost as wealthy as Robert Redford and Mick Jagger."

But it was not just the glow of the lucre that attracted women to athletes—and notably, their gaze was focused, above all, on the men on the gridiron. Even in the mid-1950s, the social scientist David Riesman commented on "the high percentage of women in the American football audience, compared with that of any other country," and observed that "the presence of these women heightens the sexual impact of everything in and around the game." He noted that in college, unlike in the case of football, women were "not expected to attend baseball games," and when they did, they were supposed to understand the action on the field "on a basis of [near] equality with their male escorts." By contrast, it was assumed that the women in the football stands could not follow the plays—the military strategies enacted on the field—but were focused instead on the exaggerated shoulder pads, the raw muscularity and power so clearly on display. Riesman was concentrating on middle-class women at the college game, but their erotic gaze persisted when their attention shifted to the pros.[15]

And then television magnified the quarterback's appeal. In 1963, television introduced multiple cameras, slow-motion shots, and instant replay. Formerly, whether from the stands or the sofa, the focus on the quarterback generally lasted only seconds and, as Adam Gopnik, who was covering the game for the *New Yorker*, observed, fans only saw "offensive and defensive lines meeting in a pit . . . a kind of black hole of heaving, battling bodies—who knew exactly what's going on in there?" The new technology, however, heightened the drama and made the game appear "quarterback-centered," each play a clear portrait in "courage and determination"—the camera lingering on the arch of his body, tracing the arc of the throw, now delivered again and again. From the vantage point of the press box, Gopnik explained, the quarterback has only "a series of forced choices," but in the replays, he has "free will," becomes the "gallant general peering out," in control.[16] But the last half of the sixties was also the time of the antiwar movement, when middle-class women now said "yes" to men who said "no"—to the draft and the war. And football featured manly combat—the quarterback in command—of a battlefield where the gore was limited and the wounded didn't die.

## The Swinger at Night

The public—not just those who followed football—wanted to know about Namath at night. After all, he proudly identified himself as "a swinger." "I swing. If it's good or bad, I don't know, but . . . it's what I like. . . . Why hide it? It's what the fuck we are." His "caterwauling" led to the enduring nickname, attached to him by his teammate, offensive tackle Sherman Plunkett, upon seeing him on the cover of *Sports Illustrated* (July 19, 1965), surrounded by the lights of Broadway, a marquee flashing "Football Goes Show Biz." But Broadway Joe was, *Time* pointed out, a "geographical misnomer," because Namath's "favorite haunts . . . were many blocks and light years away from Broadway." As Jimmy Breslin explained, "Broadway as a street has been a busted out whorehouse with orange juice stands for as long as I can recall. . . . And it certainly represents nothing to Namath's people," who inhabit the world of the singles bars on First and Second Avenues—the Upper East Side—with Namath's own Bachelors III located at 62nd and Lex.

"Whirling around the city in his . . . Lincoln Continental, the radio blaring, parking by fireplugs whenever possible," "Swinging Joe" makes the scene. Having "closed the sports celebrity gap," Namath was seen by sportswriter Dan Jenkins "crawling into the Pussy Cat during the late hours when the Copa girls and the bunnies are there having their after-work snacks, even though the line at the door . . . stretches from Second Avenue to the Triborough Bridge." He easily entered two of "his other predawn haunts, Mister Laffs and Dudes 'n Dolls, places long ago ruled impenetrable by earth people, or nonmembers of the Youth Cult." Breslin, who accompanied Namath one night, depicted the bars—that proliferated in New York in the last half of the sixties—as a "world made of long hair and tape cartridges and swirling color and [stylish] military overcoats, [where] the girls go home with guys or the guys with girls and nobody is too worried about any of it." "It is out of these bars and the [nearby] apartment buildings and the life of them that . . . Namath comes . . . with a scotch in his hand at night and a football in the daytime."[17]

Inside, Breslin compared Namath's prowess at the bar with that of the Bambino: he had "never met anybody who could drink like [Ruth] . . . [but] it is the same thing when you stand at the bar with Joe Namath." Still, he was quick to add, "Don't try to tell Namath's people . . . about Babe Ruth because they don't even know the name. . . . In fact, with the young," he lamented, "you can forget all of baseball. The sport is gone." Namath's world featured a barmaid with "long black hair, . . . sitting on top of the bar with her chest coming out of her dress and her skirt useless against the amount of leg she was showing." Here he witnessed Namath "at play . . . nighttiming . . . studying the defensive tendencies of New York's off-duty secretaries, stewardesses, dancers, nurses, bunnies, actresses, shopgirls." Journalist Dan Jenkins also closely followed Namath's moves, describing him as "stoop-shouldered and sinisterly handsome, . . . slouching against the wall, a filter cigarette in his teeth, collar open, . . . self-assured, gazing through the uneven darkness to sort out the winners from the losers. As the girls come by wearing their miniskirts, net stockings, big false eyelashes, long pressed hair and soulless expressions, he grins approvingly,

. . . 'Hey, hold it, man—foxes.'" *Playboy*, on first meeting Broadway Joe, a few minutes before midnight in Bachelors III, conveyed his presence, as he "cuts one hell of a striking figure . . . [with] his boxer's build—slim at the waist, broad through the torso. . . . This night, in a white lace body-shirt and broadly striped bell-bottom slacks, he was Errol Flynn, swashbuckling his way into the hearts of every girl in the club. They really come on with him and vice versa."

Divulging his pattern of play on the late-night field, Namath explained, "I don't like to date so much as I just like to kind of, you know, run into somethin', man." Later, his teammate, defensive back Steve Tannen, elaborated on his methods: "We would be sitting in Bachelors III and when it came time to go, Joe would walk to the front room, tap a woman on the shoulder and say, 'Let's go.'" The other players were generally impressed. But one night at a singles bar, when Namath "was preparing to go home with a woman who was not, to be kind, a drop-dead beauty," Jets running back Ed Marinaro objected: "Joe, you were my idol. . . . I just can't imagine you leaving . . . with anything less than a 10. And to be honest, . . . this woman, even on her best nights, is a 6." But Namath was more familiar with the field: "Eddie, it's three in the morning, and Miss America ain't coming." Here was the beginning of the modern hook-up culture.[18]

The "superbachelor" brought the fox, filly, or "broad"—adding defensively, "to me, broad is not a detrimental term . . . it's simply another word for female"—whom he "flushed in the hip saloon" back to his pad at 76th Street and First Avenue, a penthouse over which sportswriters—as well as other journalists—lavished considerable attention—and unadulterated praise. As the (now well-to-do) son of a steelworker, Namath had spent $25,000 refurbishing it, proud that "I had the same decorator that Sinatra had for his pad." *Time* was convinced that "some of the unholiest debaucheries since Petronius' last house party" were taking place there. The central feature of the bacchanalian lair was—as every fan knew—a wall-to-wall six-inch high, wispy white llama carpet, which accounted for a "hefty chunk" of the twenty-five grand, but which, Namath complained, was "rough to dance on, and the next day you just can't get it clean." Described by a teammate as "one of the most fantastic dancers I've ever seen," Namath had once done the frug on the sidelines of the field when the Alabama band began to play—much to the displeasure of Bear Bryant. In addition to the carpet, reporters wrote endlessly—and enviously—of the brown suede sofas, the cheetah-skin bench, the "miniature Spanish galleon" encased in a French provincial cabinet, the hi-fi "in every room," and enough closet space to house "the biggest collection of shoes anyone's ever seen." And then there was the bedroom with "an immense oval bed," and everything, including the satin sheets, in the team's color, green. When asked about women's response to the décor, Namath responded defensively, "It's meant to appeal to me. I don't care if women like it or not."

This was a center of the sybaritic life "filled with booze and broads and bread" so admired by the frustrated fan who "has trouble getting a plumber when he needs one, can't talk to his own son [anymore], and feels as impotent in his office as at the polls." For many, Namath validated a new form of manhood—a new style of manliness—a strong contrast with Fran Tarkenton, the Giants' "non-drinking, non-smoking, non-swearing . . . soft-spoken" quarterback, who rented an "English Tudor home in New Rochelle" and spent his evenings with his wife and daughter, reading, or watching *The High Chaparral* on television. Where Namath invested in Bachelors III, Tarkenton owned two Shoney's restaurants, known for middle-American family fare. A preacher's son, member of the Fellowship of Christian Athletes, and pillar of his hometown's Methodist church, he identified as "a Christian soldier" and felt it necessary to justify his "playing games for money on the Lord's Day": "In my way, I'm preaching a sermon when I play on Sunday."[19]

## Singles Bars vs. Playboy Clubs

By the late sixties the singles bars, the venue of choice of the "No. 1 sex symbol in sports," had fully eclipsed the Playboy clubs, which had been considered risqué in the early years of the decade, but whose earnings were now in "a steady . . . decline." After all, unlike the singles bars—which were proliferating by the early seventies—and where "any presentable fellow" could now "find amiable companionship for the night," the Playboy bunnies remained untouchable, "tightly encased in their rigid corsets," forbidden to "sit down with a customer, much less make a date with him."

Remarking on the long line of young people waiting in the cold to get into a nearby singles bar, J. Anthony Lukas, who was doing a story for the *New York Times*, asked a "high-ranking Playboy executive" if he had considered introducing a singles bar, in an effort to "revive the clubs." The official recognized that it would "bring in some of those swingers," but pointed out the impact this would have on "our crowd in here"—"Look at them," he explained. "They're not in here after girls. They're quite happy to have a meal and a brew and ogle the bunnies. . . . If you brought all those swingers in here, these guys would have to start wondering: could I really pick up that girl? . . . and if I actually got her home, could I perform in bed? It is a threat they don't want," he concluded, "and I don't think we're ever going to give it to them." Indeed, the reporter found that despite all the "Gouda breasts overlapping those bunny corsets," he "rarely saw anyone so much as kissed," even at Playboy parties. Apparently, the singles understood how staid the clubs were, and when the clubs made "a half-hearted attempt to capture a bit of [their] trade by handing out thousands of free Playmate keys to airline stewardesses," few responded.

Nor did Namath find the clubs—where the bunnies embodied Hugh Hefner's (adolescent) fantasies—the now "outmoded" "well-scrubbed" "virginal cheerleader look"—of much interest. As a worker at the Baltimore Playboy club recalled, the one time Namath came, "he treated us like younger sisters." The bunnies, in turn, wanted his autograph, but even more, they all "kept running to" the cloak room, where they wanted to try on—and fondle—his "white mink coat."[20]

## The Transformation of Manhood and the Fear of Namath's Furs

Although "bunnies" loved the fur he wore to the club—he also had a black mink coat—many male football fans and sportswriters were far less pleased to have the sybaritic male in their midst. At a time when American "advisors" appeared to be losing the war in Vietnam; when young men resisting the draft were portrayed in the media as preferring to toss Frisbees and smoke grass than to fight; when women were demanding entry into heretofore manly realms and roles, traditionalists viewed the warriors on the gridiron as the last line of resistance to the feared "feminization" of the culture and the American male.

George Bugbee, covering an exhibition game in the *Memphis Press-Scimitar*, was clearly threatened: "The name of Joe Namath . . . is a household word in any football family. It may be an uncomplimentary word with some, for there are . . . a few things which tend to keep him from being exactly exemplary and a model for youth. For one thing," he complained, "he wears his hair in that mode so attractive to burrowing insects and so much deplored by parents and barbers, and . . . I find his newest penchant for wearing mink coats less tolerable, and if he succeeds in making this a universal fashion for males, I hope the wobble in his knees becomes an utter hobble." The television ads Namath appeared in only intensified the traditionalists' fears of the blurring of the lines of gender identity. Unlike the Yankee pitcher, Catfish Hunter, who boasted that he promoted "Purina dog food, Sulfodene dog shampoo, Dodge trucks," Namath shaved his legs and "slipped into pantyhose" for Beauty Mist; displayed his typing skills, "ten fingers and all," as a secretary for Olivetti, while his boss, "a woman, kept making passes at him," and was featured as the poster boy for Faberge—although, to be sure, for Brut cologne.[21]

Namath's furs caused much ink to be spilled on the sports pages and evoked considerable consternation—and condemnation—among fans. It was bad enough that young men had donned floral ties—the symbol of male power now betokening flower power, that they sported earrings and carried handbags, and that women had turned to pantsuits and floppy ties. But it was even more unsettling that the quarterback of America's own battlefield had swathed himself in mink. Many found it destabilizing that instead of the asceticism of American male garb, the rough-hewn leather jacket of the frontiersman, or the epaulets of the military officer, the embodiment of American manliness preferred the softness and sensuality of mink.

To be sure, the New York furrier George Kaplan was elated, and took out an ad legitimizing Namath's choice: "It started with the man of the Stone Age. Man met beast. Man killed beast and wore its skin." Elsewhere, Kaplan assured Americans that "furs are guaranteed to revive a man's 'primitive' instincts"—increasingly at risk in the feminized office and home—and reminded them that "furs were once a male prerogative . . . restricted by laws to the backs of kings, nobility, prelates of the church." In short, Americans need not fear that Namath's minks heralded the triumph of the androgynous male. Still, after seeing "that photograph of Joe Namath wearing a mink coat," a seasoned sportswriter gave him no chance of winning the AFL championship, much less Super Bowl III.[22]

## Manhood and Hair

Adding to the public's discomfort was the cost of the coats. As one writer noted, "fur coats, as you may have heard, are not cheap," and each of Namath's minks was "tagged at $5,000."[23] Instead of spending his earnings on a swing set, remodeling the kitchen, even the den, or on a new four-door sedan, the athlete—the last great hope of American manhood—had chosen to expend a sizable sum on self-indulgence—not on a motorcycle or a Mustang, but on items of personal adornment. Still, the unease over the length of Namath's hair was even more palpable. Surely this foretold the end of American manhood—and for some, the end of the American "empire" as well.

What did it portend that Namath—and increasingly many American men—were forsaking the barbershop for the stylist at the hair salon? Widely quoted, a lead article in the magazine of the Texas High School Coaches Association, quickly reprinted in *The Intellectual Digest*—along with a piece on "Sexual Adequacy in America"—warned coaches against fielding teams of males that "look like females." The author, Tony Simpson, reminded readers that "only in the animal world is the male designed to be most attractive or the prettiest. . . . This is normal in the animal world only."

The problem was that the "athletes' grooming standards" were being influenced—really "set—by females with warped norms." These were the years of the second wave of feminism, and Simpson explained that a woman who preferred a man with long locks was not "a real woman in her soul," and he expressed his contempt for the males who apparently "wear their hair long because they know the female will like it." He informed his fellow coaches, athletes, and countrymen that in encouraging the men to grow and style their hair, the women were creating "mousy husbands, . . . pantywaist boyfriends, . . . feminine sons." The athletes and other men bent on pleasing the women were developing "a nation of men with women's souls, looking for someone or something to submit to."

This was the era of the Cold War, and Simpson sounded the alarm: "What will our present-day cute, sweet and pretty boys do when it comes their turn to fight in battle, as every generation of Americans has had to do?" He pointed out to coaches who are training these men that "the only reason males are free to look like females . . . is because we had real men that were not cute, not sweet and not pretty, with courage and sense enough to kill our enemies on battlefields all over the globe." Disaster now loomed, however, because of the trend set in motion by Broadway Joe and other pioneers who legitimized long hair for real men. It appeared that the prediction of one writer at the time—that Namath was "the only man in the country who can induce cops to grow their hair long"—had now come true. Still, Simpson and some others continued to hope for the return of the era of Johnny U, when "you could always tell an athlete by his [military-style] crew cut, . . . bone-close shave" and his manly black high-topped shoes.[24]

When Namath was asked to assess the avalanche of condemnations of his long hair—even by fans who admired his "booze and broads approach to life," and by coaches who alleged that it interfered with his play—his response was dismissive—and unequivocal. "I wear my hair the way I like to wear my hair. What does that possibly have to do with how well I throw a football?" As he told a reporter in his first year in the pros, and always maintained, "I can't see why, just because I'm a football player that I have to wear my hair a certain way." A few years later, he elaborated: "Look, I've dedicated myself to football; I've played the game for a long time now and I am absolutely positive . . . my hair does not slow me down. But I've read so many times that you can't play football . . . with hair that is the least bit long. . . . I think if [coaches] just concentrate on the sport and forget a guy's hairstyle or clothes, everybody will be better off, man. Too many times, we judge a person by the way he dresses or cuts his hair." And he denounced all the "parents—they're the ones at fault"—who tell their children that "long hair is only worn by freaks. Where else does a kid get the idea . . . that a man can't have more than a crew cut? As soon as that child . . . sees all that hair on our forefathers, he's gonna wonder what the hell kind of history we've had."[25]

Increasingly, from 1970 to 1975, the "cries of outrage" evoked by Namath's mane and football's other "longhair pioneers" were dimmed or became a low grumble. Many coaches, sports executives and even fans became resigned to defeat, and even the signs in the stands that screamed "Joe #12, Get a Haircut!" disappeared. Still, this was the era in which the boundaries between blacks and whites, gays and straights, males and females, singles and married, were crumbling, and some tried to make a last stand. When Ed Khayat became coach of the Philadelphia Eagles in 1971, he found that the locker room resembled Woodstock, and he immediately "ordered an end to long hair." A reporter dismissed this effort to turn the clock back by pointing out that Khayat, after all, "speaks in a drawl and wears a tiny American flag in his lapel"—the reporter and the coach forgetting that the Confederate officers who spoke with a drawl went into battle sporting long locks. Still, Khayat—and the current South—were trying to preserve the old bifurcations, which were dissolving. Similarly, when the Kansas City Chiefs won the Super Bowl in 1970 with "players who wore their hair short," and Hank Stram, the coach, was asked how "this miracle came about," he responded, "Oh, it's pretty easy. I don't like long hair. And it's $500 if they don't keep it short."[26]

Still, many now retreated from the affray. The general manager of the New England Patriots, Upton Bell, explained that Steve Kiner, "a linebacker with shoulder-length hair," had "great football talent. . . . I don't care if a guy's hair is down to his behind. If he's a good football player, we can use him." College football coaches also recognized, and moved to accommodate, the new order. Responding to the query of Jack Curtice, the former Stanford coach, John Ralston, who succeeded him, confided, "You can do certain things to maintain discipline on the field. You can make the players run to every drill. You can make them bounce off the ground. . . . Now, if you can carry that discipline over to what they do off the field, all the more power to you. But it's getting tougher and tougher." When it was later remarked that Stanford had "won two consecutive Rose Bowl games, upsetting unbeaten Big 10 teams each time," with players "with hair straight out of the Gay Nineties," Ralston sighed, "I can't do anything about long hair." Even on the tennis courts of Haverford College, where modern warfare was certainly not simulated, a coach who continued to "bar long hair" was "bade . . . good-bye after 41 years."

Perhaps the last desperate line of defense—as the hair war neared its end—was that of Tony Simpson, who translated Revelation 1:14 from the original Greek to reveal that Jesus himself had "short hair." "Therefore, any . . . image of Christ showing him to be a skinny, weak, long-haired hippie is totally wrong, anti-Biblical, anti-Christian." He concluded that it was "time that American coaches realized that a male's hair is not just an American tradition, but an issue involving Biblical principles."[27]

## Namath as Rebel: Rejecting the Breakfast of Champions

Namath—and the counterculture generally—were staging a many-pronged assault on the hallowed rites of the Temple to American manhood, for which Revelation provided no guidance. Most fans, journalists, and the sports establishment hoped to preserve football as they knew it, and manhood as they imagined it. Many sought to protect—or restore—patriarchy, deference to authority, self-denial, self-control, the humility of youth. But the Beatles had landed in New York in 1964 and the "mod quarterback" arrived the next year, and football, like music, would never be the same.

Above all, Namath insisted that the team's rules could not apply to his life off the field or to his personal grooming preferences, if they did not affect his play. When *Playboy* observed that "the league frowns on ballplayers who drink in public," Namath dismissed its position as "childish. . . . The owners may worry about the public's reaction on seeing a player out drinking, but I sure as hell don't." He added definitively, "Rules like that are really hypocritical and outdated," and he would not comply. Unlike Babe Ruth, "who tried to conceal [his] alcoholic adventures," Namath, as the sportswriter Arnold Hano put it, had "made Johnny Walker the most famous Red since Stalin." Namath went on to characterize the proviso that "players must at all times wear coats and ties while in a hotel lobby" as another "fool rule." Indeed, Sonny Werblin had fined Namath when, photographed backstage with Barbra Streisand, then starring in *Funny Girl,* he was not wearing a tie!

When, in 1968, Namath flouted convention and grew a Fu Manchu mustache, he was deluged with letters informing him that "it's bad for the image, or it's bad for children, to see a ballplayer" with facial hair. Frank Navarro, the "vigorous new football coach at Columbia" at the time, was certain that the combination of facial hair and flowing locks "lead[s] to other things, to lying under trees and singing songs." At Alabama, Namath had sported a goatee, but shaved it when he learned that Coach Bryant disapproved. Now an adult, Namath refused to heed the dire warnings from "sports administrators" and fans, and shed his "Mandarin mustache" only after he had powered his team to the AFL's Eastern Division championship—and Gillette paid him $10,000 to remove it—on camera, of course.[28]

Notably, Namath was rejecting the right of coaches and owners to act *in loco parentis* a few years before the infamous Linda LeClair case at Barnard College that challenged the school's right to regulate students' lives outside the classroom. Indeed, before similar uprisings on campuses across the country, Namath had openly defied football's curfews.[29]

Youth were waging a war of independence and Namath was on the front lines of the conflict. As James Reston put it, Namath "is not only in tune with the rebellious attitude of the young, but he doubles it." In August 1967, on the night before the Jets opening exhibition game in Bridgeport, Connecticut, Namath defied Coach Weeb Ewbank's denial of permission to leave the training camp in Peekskill, New York, drove to Manhattan, and spent the night drinking at the Open End, one of his haunts on the Upper East Side. Namath repeatedly explained, "If [something is] not right for me, then I can't go along with it." In June 1969, Namath dramatically and tearfully retired from football—temporarily, it turned out—rather than submit to the commissioner of pro football Pete Rozelle's "edict" that he immediately sell his half-share in Bachelors III, where bookies were allegedly using the phones to place bets. Notably, Philip Iselin, the Jets president, received the call, informing him of the superstar's decision, at the Monmouth Park race track, of which he was president and chairman of the board.

The next year, in August 1970, in what one sportswriter dubbed "the latest cause célèbre of Namath's career of causes célèbres," the quarterback failed to appear at the Jets training camp after the players' strike ended, and newspapers photographed him "taking the sun" in a boat off Miami Beach. Jets middle linebacker Al Atkinson, member of the Fellowship of Christian Athletes, retired—briefly—in disgust. Other teammates derided the missing quarterback as "the extreme hedonist," and questioned "how a man can devote himself so totally to a life of pleasure." Upon Namath's return, the fullback Matt Snell sneered, "Hooray, hooray, he's back" from what he termed "the annual stunt. Now we all rejoice, and the TV people come and record it all." The deep and enduring resentment of many of the Jets of what defensive end Gerry Philbin characterized as the club's "double standard" had been exposed. Indeed, while five players who had been late for a team meeting had just been fined within two days of their offense, Ewbank explained that he would not take any action against Namath "till I hear his side of it." "The truth," however, was that "as of October, he still hadn't been fined." Still, whatever the—limited—consequences, Namath was determined to play by his own rules.[30]

To James Reston, Namath had become the "anti-hero of the sports world." Unlike players in the past, Namath—and a few others—were refusing to play the part of "the humble athlete creeping on his belly to his coach for a fond pat on the head like a good doggie," as the sportswriter Arnold Hano observed. They formed a vanguard of football players who understood that it was "their sport"—not Ewbank's or the commissioner's or the TV networks'—and were overthrowing the traditional system of "athletic feudalism." Moreover, Namath—like Holden Caulfield—detested "phonies"—insisting on "killing the phony public-relations image" of the "modest, clean-living" athlete, "gleefully grateful" for the chance to play a "boy's game." He refused to fit into the long-revered "Jack Armstrong mold," the athlete as all-American boy. He did not owe his strength to eating a breakfast of champions, and openly admitted that he often spent mornings nursing a hangover instead.[31]

Many commentators expressed their strong disapproval of "the new breed of sports hero" that Namath portended. Pat Horne, spokesperson of the Patriots, derided the "Namath mystique" as: "Have a good time, live your own life, the hell with everything [else]; here I am, you lucky people."

In a long, strident interview in *Esquire,* the sportswriter Al Hirshberg condemned Namath as uncoachable: "Ewbank can't have much use for Namath, who had a disciplinary problem from the start. How can Ewbank control a whole team when his biggest star does what he pleases . . . ? I doubt if Ewbank could ever tell Namath anything, for Namath makes his own rules and ignores everyone else's." Responding to the quarterback's complaints about Ewbank, Hirshberg applauded the coach: "If Ewbank ever gave Namath mental abuse, I would say, 'Hooray for Ewbank!' The guy must be up to here with Namath." Hirshberg concluded that "Namath probably hates Ewbank's guts, for Ewbank has tried—unsuccessfully . . . —to keep Namath in line." In short, traditionalists would not countenance the athlete who rejected the old image of superstar as "Boy Scout," who refused simply to defer to authority, and would not conform.[32]

## From Mouthy Quarterback to Super Joe: Super Bowl III

To the chagrin of his innumerable detractors, the young quarterback, committed to absolute candor, would not exhibit "the false modesty so long expected of champions." Instead of "hanging his head shyly" and muttering, "Shucks, anybody coulda done it," Namath openly—the critics said arrogantly—acknowledged his prowess, although he was also openly self-critical of any ineffective play. It was only the rare journalist who recognized that humility was "swell for Trappist monks, but not for trapping guards." Then came Super Bowl III and many adults and much of the press predicted—even hoped—that Namath would fail spectacularly, would get his comeuppance at last. Jimmy the Greek, "America's bookmaker," set the odds at "the Colts by 17," noting that the Colts even had Unitas—reputedly the game's best quarterback—"available as a backup." Tex Maule, who covered football for *Sports Illustrated,* foretold that the Colts would shut out the Jets 43–0. This was not unreasonable as the Colts, with a season record of 15-1, "had allowed the fewest points of any team in the annals of the game."[33]

Namath, by contrast, was not only certain that the smug forecasters were dead wrong, but true to form, openly—"brazenly"—guaranteed the Colts defeat. Indeed, after the Jets had beaten the Raiders for the American Football Conference (AFC) championship, Namath commented that Daryle Lamonica, the Raiders quarterback—and "at least three other guys"—were better than Earl Morrall, quarterback of the Colts—Namath assuring his

Joe Namath on the eve of Super Bowl III. *Courtesy of the Associated Press.*

listeners that it was not the scotch talking. In addition to the querulous response of the beat reporters—and the din of disapproval for his rejection of what most still considered proper form—the comment elicited Morrall's and his teammates' vows of revenge. Incensed, the Colts quarterback told his placekicker, "I want to beat these guys by 40. I want to beat them bad." Billy Ray Smith, the Colts defensive tackle, warned, "There's nothing I like to hit more than quarterbacks, and when you get a mouthy one, it makes it that much better." In fact, Morrall had been named UPI's Player of the Year, having led the NFL in passing, with "eleven more touchdowns and two fewer interceptions" than Namath.[34]

But the mouthy quarterback was not done. Even before the Jets left for Fort Lauderdale, where they would spend the ten days leading up to the Super Bowl, Namath advised the owner of a bar he frequented near the team's training facility at Hofstra University—one of his longtime "medicine men"—to "Bet the ranch" on the Jets. When the barman hesitated, "You sure?" Namath was adamant, "Positive." A few days before the game, on the phone with the top executive of Liberty Records, Namath was again insistent: "Listen to me. You got nothing to worry about. Bet ten grand if you want. We will beat this team." And then, three days before the Super Bowl, at a banquet at which the Miami Touchdown Club was honoring him as pro football's Player of the Year, when a heckler—another in the endless stream of smug naysayers—interrupted his speech, Namath responded definitively: "The Jets will win Sunday. I guarantee it." To be sure, Namath—and many others—would "remember" the circumstances of "the guarantee" differently over the years.[35]

Although the guarantee would become "the most famous prediction since Babe Ruth's 'Called Shot' . . . in the 1932 World Series," sportswriter Mark Kriegel found that few papers deemed it newsworthy at the time. Still, the guarantee was not simply bluster. Namath had been studying films of the Colts games and had identified many vulnerable patterns in their defensive plays. Dismissing journalists' praise of the Colts defense, he informed them, "I'm going to go with what the one-eyed monster shows me. The one-eyed monster doesn't lie." As his teammates now began to review the films of the "rapidly aging [Colt] sonsabitches," they too were unimpressed. To wide receiver George Sauer Jr., the Colts "looked slow, less inventive, both offensively and defensively." To tight end Pete Lammons, "They couldn't pass for shit. On defense, they all played zone. We could kill a zone. And they loved to blitz. Blitzing? Hell . . . our backs could pick up anybody." It was not just journalists who discounted what they saw only as the arrogance, the swagger of the long-haired, mink-clad quarterback and his team. Hall of Fame quarterback Norm Van Brocklin scoffed, "On Sunday, Joe Namath will play his first professional football game." Even Johnny Unitas shrugged, "They haven't really been put under that much pressure. Our pass rush will be something . . . Namath will remember a long time."[36]

But, as it came to pass on January 12, 1969, the sports world would be turned upside down and it was the sportswriters and the oddsmakers—not Namath—who would be forced to eat crow. Before a sellout crowd of 75,000, some of whom had paid $150 for a $12 seat, Namath guided the Jets to what the announcer Curt Gowdy called "one of sport's greatest upsets in history." The sign in the stands—held by a man in a cowboy hat emblazoned with the Colts insignia—read: "Earl the Pearl Will Make Joe the Mouth Eat his Words." But when the "baffled Morrall" was chased out of the game after three of his passes had been intercepted and with four minutes remaining in the third quarter, Baltimore still had not managed to put any points on the board. When Unitas replaced him, it quickly became clear that the earlier view of Unitas, now thirty-five, as "heroic javelin thrower was merely a memory, something to be mourned."

The Jets had won 16–7 and Broadway Joe was the MVP. Namath—who "defied all the old-fashioned rules," who was renowned for his "cocksure demeanor and bacchanalian lifestyle," the "maverick" who didn't show up for the team's photo shoot a few days before—"If they want pictures of me, they're going to have to take 'em later than ten o'clock"—who spent the night before the game with a woman he had met at a local club a few hours before—the "Cool Kid" and his team were now, as he indicated, waving his index finger at all the erstwhile doubters, the disbelievers, Number 1. For Spiro Agnew—former governor of Maryland and forlorn Baltimore fan, who witnessed the team's humiliation while seated with Bob Hope—at least there was the consolation of the inauguration eight days away.[37]

Most writers had eagerly anticipated that the Super Bowl would force Namath to "eat his words." Instead, in the postgame interview, the vindicated quarterback turned the tables on the journalists, announcing, "I hope they will all eat their pencils and pads. We Won!" Although many adults retained their "anti-hero image" of Namath, Dave Anderson, "always Joe's favorite writer," observed, the "mod quarterback [had become] the king of the kids." Jimmy Breslin, watching the postgame interview with fourteen-year-old twin boys, reported their elated response as they "burst out of the chairs," shouting, "Yeah, Joe Willie! Outasight!" Translation: "Screw the adults." Breslin reflected, "I knew [then] that Joe Namath was going to mean a lot more than merely the best football player of his time." When New York celebrated the victory at city hall, it was estimated that 90 percent of the crowd of 5,000 were "youngsters," who yelled for Super Joe to return for a second speech. Dressed in "an Edwardian double-breasted glen plaid outercoat, with a broad sword tie peeking out, and silver-buckled loafers," Namath proclaimed, "We're the new faces for the new generation!" The *Washington Post* reporter recognized, "He owned them."

Tex Maule, the dean of football writing, finally acknowledged that Namath had "proved that his talent is as big as his mouth—which makes it a very big talent indeed." He was impressed that Namath "read the puzzling Colt defenses as easily as if they had been printed in comic books, and the Colt blitz, a fearsome thing during the regular NFL season, only provided Namath with the opportunity to complete his passes." At last, Maule understood that "John is crew cut and quiet and Joe has long hair and a big mouth, but haircuts and gab obviously have nothing to do with the efficiency of quarterbacks."[38]

## The Playboy as Genius on the Football Field

Unlike the Colts, who had been sure they would expose Namath as "just an over-publicized playboy in a second-rate league," there were those who recognized that "the funlovin' Bon Vivant" had a surfeit of talent and was "deadly serious once he stepped onto the football field." Contrary to his image, Namath "practiced throwing, . . . reading defenses, ball handling and footwork" every day and was a devoted student of the game. As he wistfully asked his interviewer Larry King, "Why can't they judge me on my performance on the field?" Indeed, Paul Brown, considered the "Einstein of the coaching profession"—who once "had a pretty good quarterback named Otto Graham"—had warned before the Super Bowl that "because of Namath, the Jets have an equal chance against any team in football. That goes for any team in the AFL and . . . the NFL, including the Colts." He had concluded, "Any club which has a man who can throw a football like Namath can best anybody."

After the historic upset, most coaches concurred. In a survey of NFL coaches in 1971 that asked, "With your own quarterback excluded," which pro quarterback "would you most want to have?" nine chose Namath, and one chose Unitas. One longtime American Conference coach commented, "That's a stupid question, which quarterback I'd like to have. Joe Namath's got more talent than anybody in life." In the assessment of assistant coach Ken Meyer, "Joe's football intelligence must be in the genius range." Almost all the football commentators agreed that "Namath has no peer in analyzing the situation during the crucial 2.5 to 3.5 seconds between the time he takes the snap from the center, . . . drops back into the defensive pocket and cocks to fire." An American Conference coach explained: in "preparing for him and playing him, Joe Namath scares you both times. When you play the Jets, . . . you're so conscious of him that it disrupts your planning, moreso than against any other quarterback. And in the game, no matter what the down or distance, he's capable of hitting a big play on you." Not surprisingly, then, defensive linemen and blitzing linebackers "charge at Joe Namath with a half-ton of padded bone and muscle," bent on getting "a good shot at him." As one Charger explained, "Get him out of the game and the Jets are no threat." But the palace guard surrounding him included the tackle Winston Hill, who, "deadly earnest," cautioned, "I protect Namath like I protect my wife."[39]

In enumerating Namath's skills, virtually all paid tribute to his "bazooka arm." Even in his sophomore year at Alabama, pro scouts were "so excited over his passing ability that he was marked 'blue chip'" in their reports. Indeed, in the first play of his first varsity game, during his sophomore year, he threw "a perfect 52-yard touchdown pass," which helped mitigate the fans' resentment of the Yankee—the "swarthy" "Penn-syl-vania kid"—who had taken the quarterback position that should have gone to a southern lad. By 1972, Miami coach Don Shula concluded that Namath was simply "without equal as a passer." The same year, *Time* waxed lyrical when it described the first time the Jets played "in Baltimore's cavernous Memorial Stadium, [where] Namath put on the most spectacular aerial circus this side of the Lafayette Escadrille." Although in the entire regular 1971 season, the Colts had only yielded nine touchdown passes, in this game, Namath "completed 15 of 28 passes for 6 touchdowns and 496 yards in the air, the third highest in league history." Redskin cornerback Mike Bass commented resignedly, "If he has the slightest amount of time, there is no real defense against him. He'll get off a perfect pass." Moreover, Ewbank, who coached both Unitas and Namath, observed, unlike John, who "always followed through with the back of his hand pointed inward, like a pitcher throwing a screwball," and thus has an arm "as tender as lettuce," "Joe's motion is straightaway" and he will likely "avoid having arm trouble."[40]

Almost all football commentators—including coaches and opposing players—also expressed awe at Namath's "trigger-quick release." From the time he arrived in the pros, many noted that his was "the quickest release anyone had ever seen—and he got back into the Jets' exceedingly secure passing pocket . . . of 'body guards' so fast" that, Kansas City's All-AFL lineman complained, "He makes the rush obsolete." Jim Hunt, the Patriots defensive tackle, observed that "Joe gets rid of the ball so quickly it's almost impossible to get him unless he is throwing the long bomb." When asked how he developed the fast release, Namath explained, "Strictly out of fear. When you see those sonsabitches coming at you, you get rid of it."[41]

Namath was also widely acclaimed for his "almost supernatural ability to read complex defenses in a matter of microseconds." The press reported that in the 1972 game against Baltimore, he "dissected one of the two or three best defensive units in pro football" "with deadly skill." *Time* advised prospective quarterbacks to observe Namath's performance in the game "with the same solemn intensity that surgical residents devote to watching a kidney transplant." The Jets quarterback acknowledged, "Unless I have some sort of mental lapse, I know what they're doing on the defense every time." He noted that "the public thinks it's a big deal if a quarterback can switch plays a lot at the scrimmage line. They think it makes him brainy. Man, most of the time it means he's stupid." You should know, he explained, "what the defense will be when you're in the huddle," adding that he "only calls five or six audibles a game now." Still, sometimes, as in his rookie year, when the Patriots were "using a stunt defense" and "their linebackers and some of their linemen would shift around, making it necessary to change most of the plays at the line of scrimmage," he was able to "figure out their defenses and react to them on the spot." It was then that he knew "I was a real pro quarterback."[42]

Along with those who praised Namath were those who dwelled on his high number (215) and percentage (5.9 percent) of interceptions over the course of twelve years with the Jets. In each of five years, his passes had been intercepted over twenty times. Still, in 1967, for example, when he endured twenty-eight interceptions, he made twenty-six touchdown passes and passed for a record 4,007 yards. And although Ewbank had fined him for throwing twenty-seven interceptions the previous year, the coach understood, "Young quarterbacks are proud of the way they can sling that ball to a receiver in a crowd. But they try slinging it in there once too often and they get intercepted." Ewbank recalled that "John [Unitas] had an interception problem, too. The thing about both of them is that they're so good, they thought they could complete anything."

When Namath was asked about interceptions, he shrugged. Reading from a magazine he kept on hand, Namath quoted Unitas in 1958: "You don't get intercepted if you know what you are doing." Then, citing another passage, he added, "Two years later Unitas threw 378 passes. He had 24 intercepted, a 6.3 percentage," concluding, "When *he* has 24 of them intercepted you know it can happen to anyone." Still, by 1968, Namath had learned how to reduce the odds, and had only seventeen passes intercepted as opposed to twenty-eight the year before—and "10 came in two games." Knowing that the Jets "defense was so strong stopped me from worrying about scoring early and often . . . [and] so, if my first receiver was covered and if my second also hadn't gotten free, instead of going to the third or fourth, and taking a big chance on having the pass intercepted, I'd just throw it away or keep it." Still, Namath was stunned when he read "a couple of years ago . . . that Johnny Unitas once said, 'When you know what you're doing, you don't get intercepted.' That year, he just about led the league in interceptions. I remember thinking that was a pretty stupid thing for him to say." After all, there are "always [good] reasons for interceptions."[43]

Although "off the record" several Jets expressed their disdain for Namath's "doing his own thing" and "going his own way," given his talents and dominance as a quarterback, most were said to "look on him with almost religious awe." They recognized he was their "meal ticket, the No. 1 breadwinner" for the team. Dave Herman, the 255-pound offensive guard, explained, "I . . . like him because I like what he means to us on the field. He means success. A lot of the guys who knock him would be a hell of a lot poorer if Joe weren't around." Even the defensive end Gerry Philbin, who complained bitterly and at length to the press that "there's been a double standard on this club ever since he came here"—leading OJ Simpson of Buffalo to protest that Philbin should have shown "more class" (!)—acknowledged Namath's literal value to his teammates. Philbin admitted, "We can't do anything without him. He makes us a 50 to 75 percent better football team. . . . We need him more than he needs us."[44]

## Achilles on the Gridiron

Namath's record is particularly striking because he played his entire pro career with "glass knees." His right knee was injured for the first time in his senior year at Alabama in a game against North Carolina State, resulting in surgery on the knee even before he played his first pro game. Namath recalled that the surgeon told him that "everything went well and I had four years. . . . I was elated because there were some doubts I could play at all." Namath explained that it was because he "understood that I might not be able to work very long" that he had had an "intense drive" to reach the Super Bowl early in his career.

When playing for Alabama, he had done "a lot of running, because our most effective play was . . . the run-pass option" and he could "cover 40 yards in 4.7 seconds, which is pretty fast for a quarterback in uniform." Fortunately, given his "surgical knee," the Jets "don't even have a play where I carry the ball." The sportswriter John Lake commented dryly, "Joe Willie would rather snuggle up to Phyllis Diller . . . than abandon his wall of protective blockers, a mountain of muscle which most AFL coaches regard as the best in the league." Even at twenty-five in 1968, Namath's "career was in constant jeopardy." Dave Anderson recognized, "Another whack on . . . his knees and he might hobble off the field, never to return." To be sure, even currently, "most players are [only] a snapped knee ligament away from street clothes." But for Namath, "every step . . . away from his pass protection was an invitation to disaster."[45]

Over the course of his first five years in the pros, Namath had four operations on his knees. "Running differently to favor the right knee," he had damaged the left knee as well, which "exploded in pain." Then in a "meaningless exhibition game" against the Lions, when he tried to tackle linebacker Mike Lucci, who had intercepted his pass, his knee "collapsed under him" and he was forced to miss over half the 1971 season. Often Namath would play with his knees "girded . . . in steel and rubber, like radial tires." "Fluid is always collecting in my knees," he explained, "so when they hurt too much or the flexion is decreased, I get the fluid drained," often at halftime. "Before a game, I usually get shots of cortizone and butazolidin." Namath observed, "Lots of us couldn't play at all without various medications. I know I couldn't play at times without the shots." After the game, when "the adrenalin is [no longer] pumping," he added, "that's when you feel the aches and pains and discover all the bruises," and that's when he downs "a few stiff drinks—alcohol helps as a painkiller." Still, the toll on his legs is palpable, and he "can't practice very much during the week" because after the game his knees "swell up and get sore for a few days" and "practicing just puts too much strain and pressure" on them. "Once the season is underway," he elaborated, "going up and down stairs is a problem for me . . . and even walking bothers me. But it's something you just accept." "Shit, that's the way it is. You're lucky if you have legs at all, and if they hurt, they hurt."[46]

Although Namath remarked, "during a game, it's all pain," he made it clear that "I'm not looking for any sympathy." The offensive lineman Sam DeLuca, whose own career would end with a severe knee injury in a preseason game, commented, "I'll say this for Joe and I admire him for it. Not once did I ever hear him complain about the pain or use the knees as a crutch when he had a bad day." Jets trainer Jeff Snedeker, who shared this view, observed that in the 1966 season "none of the press ever realized that Namath's knee hurt so badly most of [the] year he could barely hobble for two or three days after a game," because "nobody ever came out to watch practice." One day, however, an assistant to Howard Cosell "came out to watch them work out . . . and noticed that Joe couldn't even walk without pain." "On the air that night [Cosell] predicted Namath would miss the next game entirely." In fact, Snedeker continued, "Joe played, naturally. It's just the same thing he went through every week all season." Within a few years, journalists came to recognize this and in June 1969 at the Waldorf-Astoria the Pro Football Writers Association honored Namath as the "most courageous" player of 1968. Namath stated flatly, "Learning to put up with pain is part of becoming a pro."[47] Many traditional football fans had been discomfited by Namath's long locks, ultra-fashionable clothes, his mink coats, his closets of shoes, his manicures—the 4-F classification by his draft board—but all this was eclipsed by the wounded warrior's ability to withstand so much pain. This was the true test of manhood.

The intense drama that always followed Namath on the field was because, "if the truth were told," sportswriter John Devaney attested, the defensive linemen and blitzing linebackers "come with the kill-kill instinct of savages, their primitive fierceness" released in the "hope to hurt him so badly he has to leave the game." The Bills defensive tackle Bob Tatarek, who collided with Namath, stated flatly, "Get the quarterback, that's the story of this game." From Namath's position on the field, "it's really something else to see such big guys . . . coming at you. A lot of pro linemen are 6'6" and 6'7", run just as fast as the little guys, are very, very agile, weigh close to 300 pounds—and can really slam you."

With Namath balanced "on those vulnerable knees," this created "unbelievable pressure" on the Jets offensive linemen. The center John Schmitt recalled the line coach telling the team at their first meeting in Namath's rookie year: "If your man gets to Joe and hurts those $400,000 knees, don't bother to walk back to the huddle. Just keep right on walking out of the park." The guard Randy Rasmussen added, "Those are the most expensive knees in football we are guarding." Fullback Matt Snell, though openly resentful of the, in effect, preferred sibling, was committed to keeping blitzing linebackers and defensive ends off Namath "like a guy chasing thieves away from a valuable necklace." Virtually all who guarded him agreed that "if their man slashed Joe's . . . knees for the last time, they would never . . . forgive themselves." Tackle Winston Hill commented, "I'll tell you what it feels like when your man hits Joe. It's just like if someone were to walk up to your wife and punch her right in the face."[48]

On the other side of the line of scrimmage, the players were equally determined to "eliminate" Namath—to "get him and . . . get him good." Most of the opposing players queried by Devaney appeared to agree with San Diego defensive tackle Steve DeLong, who shrugged, "When I go after [Namath] I hit him high or I hit him in the knees, wherever I can get a good shot at him. Out there you don't have time to pick spots. This is a rough game, a violent game, and you got to expect that people will be hurt." Or, as Boston linebacker John Bramlett openly stated: "I would only hit him in the knees if I had to—like if it was a case of hitting him in the knees or missing him." Still, Ron Mix, the San Diego defensive tackle with a law degree, observed that Namath's "notoriety has made him a target of cheap-shot artists, who see in maiming [him] a chance to get the notoriety he has gotten." As a result, "he gets hit late more often than any other quarterback"—even when "walking back to the huddle."

In the Jets first game of the '69 season, Bob Tatarek, the Bills 255-pound defensive tackle, smashed into blocker Winston Hill, spinning him backward. Devaney described how "the 280-pound Hill fell against Namath, toppling him. As Namath fell, his right knee bent under him at a grotesque angle. Namath screamed." Convinced he had disabled the quarterback, the "exultant" Tatarek "leaped into the air," pumping his fist, and "the big Buffalo crowd roared in delight." But Namath was a player, and at the end of the game, he complimented the man who had just "danced happily over his body"—"Good game, Bob," he said. In the second game of the season, Bronco defensive end Richard Jackson slammed into Namath, "wrestling him to the ground." Before long, 265-pound defensive tackle Dave Costa plowed full-force into Namath's chest, "hurling him five feet through the air." When Namath returned to earth, "his legs were jerking convulsively." Devaney commented wryly, "The mating season had begun."[49]

A few years later, in 1972, the sportswriter Jack Horrigan related how, in a game against Buffalo, Namath, hit hard, "crumpled to the grass, the right leg bent grotesquely underneath him. In pain, he grabbed his helmet and dashed it onto the ground"—and for a moment both Horrigan and everyone there thought Namath's career had come to the abrupt, long-feared, bone-crushing end. But, Horrigan continued, "After checking whether he had two legs," he got up. "On the next play you'd expect he'd hand off to Matt Snell and get out of the way. Instead he sets up, stands there in the teeth of a pass rush, and throws a bomb to Don Maynard for a touchdown." In an interview with Larry King, Namath once explained why he persisted, playing with so much pain and always in the face of imminent danger: "The thing that makes this game so damn great is that winning is all that matters, which is why we [he and the other players] take chances." Unlike on the battlefields of Southeast Asia, where winning was proving increasingly elusive, on the gridiron—in what Vikings running back Ed Marinaro called "the ultimate macho sport"[50]—men could still be tested, could still exhibit endurance, achieve decisive victories and personal glory—whatever the cost to their bodies.

## The Bitter End—East and West

Namath played for the Jets for twelve seasons, belying the sportswriters' oft-repeated—almost annual—refrain that "Namath may be on his way to an early *finis*"—if not this year, surely next. Still, in all those years—indeed, in the almost fifty years since Namath's triumph in Miami—the Jets had not been in another

Bowl game. In 1975 and 1976, Namath's last two years with the team, the Jets' record was 3-11 each year. Despite hiring Lou Holtz as the new head coach for the 1976 season, the Jets only managed to defeat Tampa Bay (who were 0-14) and Buffalo (2-12) twice. In 1975, at a 37–6 loss to the Cardinals, a banner in the stands read: "For Sale—1 Coach, 1 Q'back," and after the coach was let go, fans insisted, "They fired the wrong guy! They should fire Namath." Dave Anderson defended him: the quarterback "is not a boxer or a golfer, or even a baseball player, who essentially do solos. . . . Like any quarterback, he needs a defensive unit that will get him the ball in decent field position occasionally." Though his "poise is always there," Anderson reminded Namath's erstwhile fans, "with his knees, . . . without protection, he is virtually helpless."[51]

Namath's last game in New York was played against the Bengals in the rain at Shea, with over a third of the seats empty. Jimmy Breslin was there, watching as "his legs betrayed him and his receivers were slow and his passes were off." Breslin described Namath "dropping back slowly, his legs dragging across the wet ground, and when he turned to pass he had time to consider only one receiver." The massive Cincinnati linemen, "grunting, smacking helmets, . . . wrenching, [were] pushing to get at him." Namath threw, and while "his arm still was extended," a lineman "whacked him." And so it went—on and on—"the field was wet, the receivers sluggish, the blocking poor"—the final score, a humiliating 42–3. Namath's "passes gained [only] 20 yards," and although he left the field after the first half, they had been intercepted four times. Later in the day, Namath defended himself: "I got hit 70 percent of the time," but Richard Todd, the Jets quarterback for the second half, "was hit 90 percent of the time." Namath explained, "There's no way you can have a passing game if the quarterback's always getting hit. They talk about my mobility. It all starts in the line. . . . The receivers just weren't beatin' anybody."

Still, at halftime, when Joe Willie Namath left the field for the last time, "the crowd booed him." Once, New Yorkers "loved him. . . . They saw him as a populist, one of their own. [When] they saw him on the street, they called to him. They stopped their cars for him." And now they disowned him, wanted the once-beloved "fearless cripple" gone.[52]

An hour after the game, Namath was at LaGuardia airport, tossing back "blackberry brandy on the rocks, . . . a large beer for a chaser," leaving the city where he had become Broadway Joe, now almost alone. A teammate remarked on the young dark-haired beauty he had seen Namath chatting up earlier in the day. That was Karen, Namath responded, "Isn't that some body! Worst part about her is her face and, damn, that's one of the best faces you'll ever see." She had told him "how she followed me when she was in junior high school." Namath was asked, "Do you have to do homework with her?" "Almost," he replied, as the quarterback left the New York limelight at thirty-three.[53]

Hoping to escape from the "deteriorating situation in New York," for several years Namath had urged the Jets to trade him to a team "with Super Bowl potential," but no team expressed interest in a $450,000-a-year quarterback with "damaged knees." As a result, Namath became a free agent, and the Rams acquired him "without surrendering players or draft choices," signing him in 1977 for about a third of what he was paid in New York. The Rams not only had the strong offensive line that could provide the protection he needed, but for the past four years they had been in the playoffs—the last year coming "within a blocked field goal of the Super Bowl." With "knees of wet Kleenex," Namath could not run, but built up his stamina by swimming sixty-six laps a day, and when, after training, practicing, and receiving treatments from 8 a.m. to 10 p.m., he and his new teammates went to a bar, they found he had become—what they dubbed—"Chablis Joe."

Yet, despite Namath's discipline and exertions, he led the Rams to "an underwhelming 2–2 start, . . . managing three touchdowns," and passing for only 606 yards. What proved to be his final bow took place on a rain-soaked Soldier Field, where, as Rams guard Dennis Harrah complained, after being ejected from the game, "all the Bears wanted to take cheap shots at Joe." Broadcast on *Monday Night Football*, and leaving "the mouths of the country agape," Namath threw four interceptions, was sacked twice, hit in the mouth, the eye, in the Adam's apple, as Chicago played, he observed, "like they were trying to start a war out there." Knocked out of the game with 1:55 left, Namath spent the remaining ten games of the season on the bench.[54]

******

Shortly after Namath had signed with the Jets, and while he was still at the University of Alabama, a sportswriter, spending a few days with him, accompanied him to class. The topic was the poems of T. S. Eliot. Now, as Namath limped away from football, after the last inglorious years, he may have recalled the lines: "This is the way the world ends / Not with a bang but a whimper." Still in his thirties, Namath hobbled on "80-year-old knees . . . can't flex his right knee . . . can't straighten his left leg . . . can't run three strides at full speed . . . is in pain every day." Decades later, in a televised interview, the reporter inquired, "You know, today a lot of the talk is focused on . . . head injuries. You had some concussions yourself. Do you think you had any long-term effects . . . ?" Namath responded pensively, "I've seen some things on my brain, but I've had treatment and I've improved." Then, shaking his head, he added, "*None* of the body was designed to play football. Excuse me. We're just not designed for . . . ," he trailed off.

After Namath left the football arena, he turned to performing for a time on the stage and small screen. He was Li'l Abner, then Shoeless Joe from Hannibal, Mo., in *Damn Yankees*; he made appearances on *The Brady Bunch, Married with Children, The Flip Wilson Show,* and was featured on *Waverly Wonders,* where he was jeered by the critics as "a wooden soldier" and "a walking chalk talk"—the show panned as "'vacuous' and worse." But surely the ache exceeded the old pain in the knees when the quarterback promoted the Joe Namath Rapid Cooker, guaranteed to make you "the MVP of your next bar-b-cue."

Still, as his football fans (along with J. Alfred Prufrock) "grow old . . . grow old . . . wear the bottoms of [their] trousers rolled," as sportswriters whom Namath once dismissed as "sick bastards" now confront only players who are "guarded," "boring," offering little "that has not been pasteurized first by the agents and the league," and who recognize that "the reporter is on nobody's side but his own," they—much like the owner of Rick's Café—will always have Broadway Joe.[55]

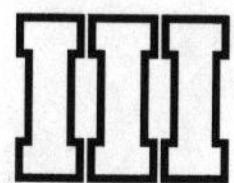

# III
# Basketball
# The Ultimate Urban Sport

CHAPTER FIVE

# From Basket Ball to Hoop Heroics

## The City Game, 1891 to the Present

*Dennis Gildea*

It is a hackneyed expression now, two decades into the twenty-first century, but when Pete Axthelm used it to begin his book in 1970, the statement was valid, hardly overused, and as direct and to the point as a slam dunk: "Basketball is the city game."[1] Axthelm was writing about basketball in New York City—on the courts during the season, on the playground courts throughout the year. "Basketball has always been something special to the kids of New York's bustling streets," he wrote, noting that over the decades the city's immigrant groups—Irish, Italians, Eastern European Jews as well as African Americans—learned the game on "strips of asphalt between tattered wire fences or crumbling buildings," and have gone with the game to individual athletic greatness for a few or a lifelong love of the sport for all.[2]

Basketball began its journey in New York City as early as 1892, just a year after James Naismith convinced eighteen robust students at the International Young Men's Christian Association (YMCA) Training School in Springfield, Massachusetts, that his creation would be more fun to play than doing gymnastics. YMCA instructors who had played or at the least experienced the game under Naismith in Springfield helped spread the popularity of the new sport in incredibly rapid fashion. For the winter of 1892–1893, YMCA branches in Manhattan and Brooklyn had teams playing in regulated leagues.[3] Early newspaper accounts referred to the game with two words—basket ball. Stylistic peculiarities aside, even before the dawn of the twentieth century, the American sport and the city of New York were beginning a whirlwind romance. At no other point was the glow greater than in March 1950 when five New York City players ruled the world of college basketball. At no other point was the glow darkened so considerably than in February 1951 when the word "court" came to suggest legal problems, not basketball courts.

## Midcentury—The Best of Times, the Worst of Times

The December 4, 1950, edition of *Newsweek* magazine included what amounted to a celebration of New York City basketball. Nat Holman, the coach of the College of the City of New York's (CCNY) team that won both the National Invitation Tournament (NIT) and the National Collegiate Athletic Association (NCAA) championship the previous March appeared in full color on the cover, his hand draped over a basketball as he gazed confidently into the future.[4] And on the cusp of the 1950–1951 season, Holman had every reason to be confident. A good nucleus was returning from his double-championship team, the only college team to win both the NIT and the NCAA in the same year; topflight basketball talent from everywhere in the metropolitan area and around the country wanted to play for New York City colleges; and the double-headers in Madison Square Garden, widely and accurately acclaimed as the mecca of college basketball, were as popular as ever.

What most magazine readers could not have foreseen as they perused the story on Holman and CCNY is that before the season was over, the gilded creation that was metropolitan New York basketball would crumble mightily. It would crumble under the oppressive weight of the college basketball point-shaving scandal, a scandal that had its origin in the city but soon spread to other college teams throughout the land. In New York, CCNY, Manhattan College, Long Island University (LIU) in Brooklyn, and New York University (NYU) would be ensnared. Elsewhere, Bradley University, Toledo University, and even coach Adolph Rupp's Kentucky team would have players found guilty of cooperating with gamblers to control the points of games.[5] If the point spread, the product of a mathematically inclined individual named Leo Hirschfield, who ran the Minneapolis Clearinghouse, established a team as a five-point favorite in an upcoming game, gamblers would pay certain players to make sure their team won by less than five. Or more than five, if that was how the "smart" money was bet.[6] "You don't have to lose," was the pitch one of the leading gamblers, Salvatore Sollazzo, used to involve the players, "just don't win by more than the spread." For the players, the money was good; the temptation was hard to resist.[7]

But all of this came to light in February 1951 in the space of two days with the arrest of three CCNY players; four from LIU, including Sollazzo's contact man Eddie Gard; and one from NYU. When the LIU players, the most celebrated of whom was the *Sporting News* player of the year Sherman White, were booked,

Coach Clair Bee and his excellent 1950–1951 Long Island University team before the gambling scandal ended their season and Bee's LIU coaching career. LeRoy Smith (*front row left*), Adolph Bigos (*front row center*), and the Sporting News Player of the Year Sherman White (*back row right, above Bee*) all were arrested and charged with point shaving. *Courtesy of LIU Athletics.*

the *New York Journal-American* ran a front-page photo of White, LeRoy Smith, and Adolph Bigos flanked by the arresting detectives. The caption, demonstrating the layout editor's nasty sense of irony, read: "Line-up for Today's Game."[8]

In December when the *Newsweek* edition hit the newsstands, there was no bite to the journalistic treatment. The city game was still untarnished. More than untarnished, in fact. The magazine story glorified basketball, CCNY, and Holman. The piece, unsigned but headlined "Drive, Drive, Drive!" began by referencing Holman's inadequate and even dingy office, a space that served as the "headquarters of [the college's] best-known personality: the handsome, complex, 54-year-old Nat Holman, a self-winding marvel known far beyond New York City as 'Mr. Basketball.'" Moreover, the marvelous coach Holman had put together a team comprised of genuine students, the piece contended, students who felt that "a free education at City was better than the free-plus offers from out-of-town colleges." The *Newsweek* writer made special note of Holman's returning stars, Ed Roman, Al (Fats) Roth, Ed Warner, and Floyd Lane, all of whom would eventually admit to shaving points even in the double-championship season. Roman was photographed working with test tubes in a laboratory, while Lane was posed by a bus stop, a pile of books under his arm. Academics and athletics were in perfect balance at CCNY, the article argued. Holman could not "get his hands on" a scholastic prospect unless the talented young man had at least "an 82 high school average" in his courses and "could pass a proper entrance exam."[9]

Reality, though, was far different from journalistic puff. In the wake of the gambling scandal, one of Holman's former players acknowledged that forging transcripts and arranging for passing grades was a tradition at CCNY: "All Nat wanted was ballplayers. He didn't care how he got them."[10] Roman, pictured in the magazine as he worked in a laboratory class, "had to be made to see that laboratory courses conflicted with basketball practice" and that basketball took precedence.[11] The New York Board of Higher Education and a committee of CCNY faculty investigated the academic practices of the basketball program and reached the conclusion that the scholastic records of key CCNY players were "tampered and falsified" in order to make them eligible for admission to the university.[12]

Sprinkled among the journalistic fluff in the *Newsweek* article, though, was one comment that proved sadly true. The writer observed that the latest CCNY team entered the season as the leading college team in the country, "pending 1950–51 developments."[13] As early as mid-January, before the arrests occurred, Holman had a definite inkling of tragic developments. During a Madison Square Garden game involving other teams, not CCNY, Holman took Seton Hall coach Honey Russell to a remote location in the upper reaches of the arena and told him that he believed his players were in league with the gamblers.[14] Of course, he was right. And he did nothing about it.

An unfortunate bit of collateral damage resulting from the point-shaving scandal was that the summer basketball league based around the Catskill Mountain resorts was declared off-limits by the athletic administrations of most of the vaunted basketball institutions. Sollazzo and Gard, in particular, prowled the Catskills in the summer where topflight college players picked up a fair amount of money by playing in and fixing games or manipulating final scores between hotel teams. The Catskills, little more than a hundred miles north of New York City, had long been the summer vacation destination for metropolitan area Jews, and the basketball games provided great entertainment for the hotel guests, as well as an opportunity to place a wager. As reports of the scandal's wide reach proliferated in the media, accusing fingers were pointed at the Catskill resorts as providing near occasions of gambling sin, a theme that Judge Saul Streit emphasized in his lengthy sentencing statement when the players accused of cooperating with the gamblers appeared before him in November 1951. The players who accepted money to play in the Catskills in the summer, he argued, were not true amateurs. Moreover, Streit blamed the coaches for either ignoring or even encouraging a culture of corruption.[15] Sherman White said that he would see Gard and Sollazzo at the resort games, and that one or the other, or both, would slip him fifty dollars, "just to keep me on the string."[16]

The collegiate basketball seasons of 1950 and 1951 were pivotal ones in which the blurring between top-of-the-heap glory and inescapable disgrace ran together like so many Madison Square Garden double-headers. By the start of the 1952–1953 season, Holman was replaced as coach at CCNY by Dave Polansky, although Holman would eventually appeal his dismissal and win his case.[17] At LIU, the board of trustees immediately abolished the university's entire athletic program, a decision it amended to target only basketball. LIU did not play intercollegiate basketball again until the 1957–1958 season, and by that time highly successful coach Clair Bee was gone. When the basketball program was not reinstated on any competitive level, Bee resigned. A year later, he became coach of the Baltimore Bullets in the National Basketball Association (NBA).[18]

From 1943 through 1950, the NCAA tournament was held in Madison Square Garden seven times. The 1951 NCAA tournament was again scheduled to be played in the Garden in March, but as details of the scandal appeared in the press and the Garden became tainted, the NCAA moved the tournament to Williams Arena on the campus of the University of Minnesota, where Kentucky, yet to be ensnared in the point-shaving investigation, won the title by beating Kansas State, 68–58. Madison Square Garden, an arena that basketball promoter Ned Irish never tired of referring to as the mecca of basketball, was shunned. From the Chicago headquarters of the NCAA came the word that member schools should hold their competitions on campus fields and campus field houses and "avoid playing in huge public arenas like Madison Square Garden."[19] The NIT, however, was contested as usual in the Garden that March, but the attendance was down almost 50 percent from the previous year. "There is no question that the scandal hurt the basketball gate," the *Journal-American* observed.[20] In its preseason 1957–1958 magazine, Dell Sports publications featured a piece headlined "Gone But Not Forgotten" that argued that on-campus arenas had taken over in prominence and profitability from "large commercial arenas." The article was accompanied by a photo of a sparse crowd at Madison Square Garden to watch the CCNY-Lafayette game.[21]

As if to emphasize the magazine's point, the same edition included a story on "McGuire's Miracle," a reference to former St. John's coach Frank McGuire, who made the post-scandal jump to the University of North Carolina where his team won the 1957 NCAA championship in triple overtime over Kansas. It was a victory hard earned by McGuire's "transplanted Yankees" over a Kansas team led by Philadelphia expatriate Wilt Chamberlain. McGuire, a native New Yorker, specialized in recruiting New York City players. Ten players with New York City backgrounds were on the 1957 Tar Heel roster. Tommy Kearns, UNC's All-America guard, played his scholastic basketball at St. Ann's Academy in New York City where he was coached by Lou Carnesecca before he became head coach at St. John's University. Lennie Rosenbluth, a Bronx native, was also a starter on the North Carolina team. The 1950s was a period when it proved difficult to keep a city prospect in the city.[22]

It would only get worse. The 1961 collegiate season had hardly concluded when another gambling scandal broke involving more teams than the 1951 scandal. When the legal dust settled, thirty-one players from twenty-two college teams admitted to fixing games. The historian Albert J. Figone estimates that at least "nine players received money from fixers or gamblers but were never convicted of crimes."[23] Some players with New York City backgrounds were involved, but Fred Portnoy of Columbia and Ray Paprocky of NYU were the players representing city colleges who gained infamy. Art Hicks and Hank Gunter from Seton Hall in Orange, New Jersey, were also involved in the fixes.[24] Former Columbia star and Bronx native Jack Molinas was believed to be one of the "master fixers" in 1961. Moreover, simply as a consequence of his playground association with Molinas, Connie Hawkins, who had left the city to play for the University of Iowa, was caught in the dumping arrests, as was another New York City standout, Roger Brown, who was forced out of Dayton University. Hawkins was expelled from Iowa at the end of his freshman year, but he eventually got his chance to play in the NBA.[25] Molinas was convicted, served a prison sentence in Attica, and was eventually murdered in Los Angeles in 1975.[26]

An image Ned Irish and the NIT organizers liked to use as an easily recognizable brand for the event was a cartoon basketball character wearing a king's crown emblazoned with the letters "NIT." The iconographic message was clear—the tournament, the Garden arena, and New York City were the kings of college basketball.[27] As the 1950s drew to a close, enough had happened to depose the king. Basketball, even college basketball, was far from dead in the city. It just wasn't what it used to be.

## The Early Days: "Basket Ball and Its Success"

It was just two weeks before Thanksgiving in 1893—a time when most New Yorkers and certainly the city's sports editors were focusing their attention on the annual Princeton-Yale football game on Thanksgiving afternoon—when the *New York Times* published a story headlined "Basket Ball and Its Success."[28] Basketball was less than two years old, yet, as the story reported, its "devotees are numbered by the thousands" and many of them were located in metropolitan New York. Because of the sport's newness and unfamiliarity to many readers, the reporter went out of his way to explain what the game was all about. An indoor, wintertime sport, the story asserted, basketball could be recognized as a "modified kind of football with every element of roughness eliminated." The opening paragraphs of the story explained the basic rules of the game before going on to highlight its popularity in New York City. "The baskets are the goals, and the aim of the teams is to throw the ball into its opponent's goal. . . . Any ordinary basket large enough for the ball to enter will answer the purpose."[29]

What accounted for basketball's burst of popularity? "The great stronghold of the game lies at the present in the gymnasiums of the various Young Men's Christian Associations in the city," and it was gaining favor as a sport suitable for participation by women and men in numerous colleges. The reporter marveled at the fact that the 23rd Street Y had "eight or nine teams playing the game," while Y gymnasiums at three other locations in Manhattan had active teams. In addition, Y branches in Brooklyn were forming teams so that a city championship game could be played at the end of the season.[30] By 1894, the New York City champion played against other championship teams throughout the state for a true state championship title.[31] By no means was the sport's popularity confined to the YMCA teams. Young Jewish men at New York's Clark House and University Settlement House "dominated the intersettlement tournaments."[32]

A major factor in the rapid increase in the sport's popularity in New York City was the matter of urban space, or to be more precise, the lack of space for many outdoor sports. "Because [basketball] did not require much space or costly equipment . . . it fit in well with the inner-city environment. The spatial factor was a clear advantage for basketball over baseball, for as Basketball Hall of Famer Barney Sedran remembered, 'It was difficult for an East Side youngster like myself to play baseball because there were no diamonds nearby.'"[33] As early as 1892, however, there were 348 YMCA gymnasiums in cities throughout the nation, and they were staffed by 144 full-time physical directors serving an estimated 250,000 members.[34] Moreover, even the architectural design of YMCA buildings—a design that did not vary from city to city—contributed to attracting basketball enthusiasts to the buildings. The gymnasiums, for example, were always located on the level below the main hall, thus providing a degree of welcoming familiarity for the men who would use them.[35]

The man responsible for spreading the gospel of the game in New York was J. H. McCurdy, physical director of the 23rd Street Y and a man who learned the rudiments of the game under Naismith at Springfield. McCurdy was "the first to introduce" the sport to the city, and young men flocked to it with great enthusiasm.[36] Ironically, based on his subsequent research, McCurdy would later attack basketball as being too strenuous a game, an assertion that James Naismith would debunk. McCurdy was a professor at Springfield College, as the International YMCA Training School became known, when in the years immediately following World War I he undertook experiments that led him to conclude that the game was too "strenuous." Naismith, then at the University of Kansas, conducted and published the results of his own experiments defending the physical benefits of basketball as well as the nonphysical benefits, not the least of which were benefits dear to Naismith's view of sports. Basketball played in the proper spirit, Naismith argued, benefited the athlete's emotional and moral character.[37]

The metaphysical benefits of basketball, though prized by Naismith, proved insignificant in the game played by New York City's early professional teams. In 1912, a group of Irish young men formed a professional team they named the Celtics, a team that by the 1920s became the most celebrated and successful outfit in the nation.[38] The Original Celtics, as the team became known, boasted many fine players, but the player regarded as the best of the lot was Nat Holman. Holman played collegiately at NYU, and like numerous other basketball standouts for city colleges, he earned a few extra dollars—typically six dollars a game—by playing for professional teams under an assumed name.[39] By 1919, Holman was playing professional basketball and coaching at CCNY. His first professional team, however, was the New York Whirlwinds rather than the Irish-dominated Celtics. For the 1922 season, Holman and a Whirlwind teammate, Chris Leonard, joined the Celtics largely because the Celtics, funded by Manhattan businessman Jim Furey, could afford to pay the players a bit more.[40]

Holman teamed with Joe Lapchick, who would go on to coach St. John's University and the New York Knicks, and Dutch Dehnert to make the squad virtually unbeatable. The Original Celtics barnstormed the country, often playing a hundred games a year. To a great extent, the players made most of their money on bets on the outcome. Holman, though, was said to have been paid $12,500 annually, an astronomical figure in the 1920s.[41] From 1920 through 1928, the Original Celtics compiled a record of 720-75.[42]

Holman was retired as a player in 1933 when the Original Celtics scored their last major victory, a win over another outstanding New York team, Bob Douglas's Harlem Renaissance Big Five. "Basketball fans who journey to the Washington Auditorium Wednesday night to see the Renaissance team, colored champions, do battle with the Original Celtics, will focus their glimmers on a team that has established what is believed to be a record for winning games."[43] The *Washington Post* reporter's urging basketball fans to "focus their glimmers" on the Rens was justified. The report claimed that the Rens had won seventy-seven straight games to that point; other more reliable accounts put the number at eighty-eight victories compiled over an eighty-six-day stretch.[44] The discrepancy likely reflects the rag-tag nature of professional basketball at the time. Regardless, the Rens could play at the highest level. In the twenty-six years of their existence, the Rens won 85 percent of their games playing a style characterized by "lightning fast passes, quickness on the floor, and tremendous ball handling."[45]

Douglas started the professional team in 1923 when opportunities for African Americans in organized sports were limited. Douglas named his team after the legendary Renaissance Casino Ballroom in Harlem, which is where they played their home games. The court was temporary, located on the casino's dance floor. "They set up a basketball post on each end of the floor," William "Pop" Gates, a Ren star in later years, remembered. Couples would use the floor to dance immediately before the games, at halftime, and after the games.[46] Interestingly, the Rens' games, if not the dances, were attended by a large number of white spectators.[47]

By 1928, Douglas took his team on the road more frequently, touring the Midwest and even the South. Except for their trips to the Jim Crow South, the Rens played against more white teams than all-black teams. In the South, they would play against black college and club teams.[48] The 1931 Ren team was nicknamed the "Magnificent Seven" because of the skill of players such as Charles "Tarzan" Cooper, Clarence "Fat" Jenkins, John "Casey" Holt, and William "Wee Willie" Smith, to name just a few. Hall of Famer "Pop" Gates began his career with the Rens in 1938, and he led the Rens to the championship of the World Professional Basketball Tournament with a 34–25 win over the Oshkosh All-Stars, champions of the National Basketball League.[49] The tournament was held in Chicago, and it was covered extensively by many mainstream newspapers. For the most part, though, sports-page coverage of the Rens appeared in the black weeklies. Romeo Dougherty of the *Amsterdam News* in Harlem covered the Rens. In addition, Sam Lacy at the *Baltimore Afro-American* devoted columns to the Ren players, as did reporters from the *Pittsburgh Courier* and the *Chicago Defender*.[50]

In addition to the Rens' "Magnificent Seven," New York in that period could boast another excellent team with an equally flashy name, the "Wonder Five" of St. John's University, whose four-year record at the Queens institution was 86-8. Moreover, coach Buck Freeman's squad all came from the metropolitan area. The "Wonder Five" had a six-feet, five center, Matty Begovitch, who could control the tap, which in those days occurred after every successful basket. If need be, given the ebb and flow of the game, Mac Kinsbrunner could take the tap from Begovitch and dribble circles around the opposition, preventing them from getting a scoring opportunity. Immediately after the 1936 season, the National Basketball Coaches Association voted to do away with the mandated jump ball following every score. The vote was hardly unanimous. Clair Bee, coach of the LIU team that went undefeated in 1936, opposed the change, fearing that it would diminish the role of the big man in the game. Of course, that fear proved groundless. Dominant big men such as George Mikan at DePaul University were on the sport's horizon.[51]

The "Wonder Five" so overwhelmed foes that it once kept City College scoreless for thirty-eight consecutive minutes and held Manhattan College scoreless from the field for the entire game. "It is virtually impossible to think of the immortals without thinking of the Redmen of the late 1920s," John D. McCallum wrote in *College Basketball, U.S.A.* The St. John's players were so good that they "graduated intact from St. John's to the pros and more than held their own against tough American Basketball League competition."[52]

To a great extent, that St. John's team represented a segment of the city's population that enthusiastically adopted basketball as a special sport and dominated the city game in the years prior to and immediately after World War II. Begovitch was the only non-Jew on the "Wonder Five." Kinsbrunner, Max Posnack, Rip Gerson, and Allie Schuckman made up the heart of the team. A check of the boxscores of games involving city teams in those years would reveal a number of Jewish players on all New York teams, especially St. John's, LIU, CCNY, NYU, and Brooklyn College.

Events following the 1936 season proved to be especially challenging for the Jews on the more successful city teams. Basketball was to be included in the Olympic Games scheduled for that summer in Berlin, and the players on Bee's powerhouse LIU team were figured to have a solid chance of qualifying for the United States squad heading to Germany. The final tryouts were to take place in April in Madison Square Garden, virtually the home court for Bee's Blackbirds.[53]

However, many Americans felt the nation should boycott the Berlin Games to protest Adolf Hitler's treatment of Jews, especially German Jewish athletes who were excluded from participating with the German teams. The debate was especially intense in New York City, and the boycott movement received support from former New York governor and presidential candidate Al Smith and Mayor Fiorello LaGuardia, a man whose opposition to Nazi Germany led one American member of the International Olympic Committee (IOC) to denounce him as "the Jew LaGuardia." LaGuardia's mother was, in fact, Jewish; his father was Italian.[54]

After some internal debate, CCNY, NYU, and LIU declined invitations to participate in the Olympic tournament. Leo Merson was one of four Jewish players on the LIU team that may well have qualified for the Games. Prior to the decision to boycott, Merson's grandfather would come home from synagogue and urge him not to go to Germany. On March 3, 1936, Bee assembled his team to vote on the question of participation, and the result was unanimous—LIU would boycott the trials as a protest to Hitler's stance on Jews. The LIU players gave up their chance to win gold medals. In April 2009, the entire 1935–1936 LIU squad and Bee were inducted into the National Jewish Sports Hall of Fame in Commack, New York. "In their own way, the LIU team stood up for what they knew to be right," Hall of Fame chair Lynne Kramer said.[55]

It would be impossible to write the history of basketball in New York City without mentioning prominently a man who never played the game but was, nevertheless, hugely instrumental in making it popular. Ned Irish, a sportswriter-turned-basketball-promoter and later president of Madison Square Garden, had a key role in organizing in 1934 the first of what would become legendary Garden double-headers. "Irish was farsighted enough to take basketball out of college gymnasiums and put it into Madison Square Garden," Roger Kahn wrote.[56] Operating with the idea that fans would turn out to watch a local team play a team from elsewhere in the nation, Irish matched NYU against Notre Dame and St. John's against Westminster College of Pennsylvania. The games attracted 16,188 fans, and, "Suddenly, Irish's future was as big as basketball's."[57] The Garden double-headers became so successful, in fact, that in ensuing years teams from every league in the land would clamor for a chance to play in the city. Significantly, their athletic departments would also covet the payday a Garden game provided.

The story of how the Garden double-headers were conceived is dramatic, amusing, and most likely apocryphal. In a version popularized by radio sportscaster Bill Stern, a man infamous for his on-air play-by-play apocrypha, Irish, then writing sports for the *New York World-Telegram*, had to crawl through a basement window to gain entrance to the Manhattan College gym to cover a sold-out game. In doing so, he tore his pants, a sartorial casualty that prompted him to yearn for games in Madison Square Garden, games promoted by him. In later years, Irish insisted that he "ripped his trousers," but another reporter, Lou Black, who covered the same game, "is not sure that anyone's clothing was torn, or that Irish's subsequent thoughts advanced beyond the usual newspaperman's complaint: 'Something ought to be done about this mess.'"[58]

The actual genesis of the double-headers came in 1933 when Mayor James J. Walker, looking for a way to raise funds to help the unemployed during the Great Depression, organized a committee of New York sportswriters, a group that included Irish, to promote "a marathon seven-game orgy" of college basketball in the Garden that drew 20,000 people.[59] It didn't take long for the city's sporting press to devote columns of coverage to college basketball. Noteworthy college basketball beat writers in the early days of the sport's growing popularity included David Eisenberg of the *Journal-American*, Ben Gould of the *Brooklyn Eagle*, Tom Meany of the *Telegram*, Arthur Daley and Francis J. O'Riley of the *Times*, and Stanley Frank, who wrote for city newspapers and for national magazines such as *Collier's*. The

Metropolitan Basketball Writers Association held luncheons and news conferences with the city's coaches every Monday during the season at Mama Leone's restaurant.[60]

In 1938, Irish, who later would become the owner of the New York Knicks National Basketball Association franchise, and the Metropolitan Basketball Writers Association put together a six-team field for the first National Invitation Tournament. Temple won the initial tournament; LIU won in 1939, giving New Yorkers a reason to celebrate.[61] The NCAA tournament began in 1939, but the NIT received more acclaim for many years. The NIT would flourish in Madison Square Garden until increasing television revenue made it possible for the NCAA tournament to squeeze the NIT into secondary status in the 1970s.[62] The NCAA's efforts to diminish the importance of the NIT, though, began as early as 1954 when the collegiate athletic governing body enacted restrictive rules calculated to frighten university athletic directors from accepting NIT bids. Beyond that, the NCAA expanded its bracket to twenty-four teams in 1954.[63] In recent years, only the semifinals and the final game of the NIT are held at Madison Square Garden. The early round games are contested on the home courts of selected college teams.

Basketball historians point to the featured nightcap of a December 30, 1936, Garden double-header as a revolutionary moment in the sport's history. Clair Bee's Long Island University Blackbirds, winners of forty-three straight, were up against John Bunn's Stanford Indians. Bee's team thrived on the Eastern game, a style of play that favored two-hand set shots. Stanford, and especially its star Angelo "Hank" Luisetti, preferred one-handed shots, including the unheard of jump shot. The final was Stanford 45, LIU 31. "Overnight, and with a suddenness as startling as Stanford's unorthodox tactics, it had become apparent today that New York's fundamental concept of basketball will have to be radically changed if Greater New York is to remain among the progressive centers of court culture in this country," Stanley Frank wrote in his game story. "Every one of the amiable, clean-cut Coast kids fired away with leaping, one-handed shots which were impossible to stop."[64]

As early as the 1920s when the game was gaining popularity in colleges, Eastern players were taught the alleged surety of the two-handed set shot. Even in the immediate wake of Luisetti's and Stanford's success in Madison Square Garden, Nat Holman bristled at the notion of abandoning the two-handed set shot. "I'll quit coaching if I have to teach one-handed shots to win," Holman said. "They'll have to show me plenty to convince me that a shot predicated on a prayer is smart basketball. There's only one way to shoot, and that's the way we do it in the East—with two hands."[65]

Holman, of course, was behind the basketball times with his pronouncement. The one-handed jumper was already being employed by West Coast players, but because the New York media were on hand to publicize the technique that night in the Garden, Luisetti was credited with leading the revolution. "Getting all that publicity in New York changed my life, my whole life," Luisetti said later. "It made me a national figure."[66] And Luisetti's shooting style most definitely helped usher in the modern era of basketball.

## Kareem, the Goat, and the Rise of the Women's Game

Throughout the 1960s and 1970s New York City produced more than its fair share of "can't miss" basketball prospects and its tragic assortment of playground legends who had the talent to succeed on a larger stage but never did. The story of Lew Alcindor—Kareem Abdul-Jabbar—and his playground workout partner Earl "The Goat" Manigault serves as a classic example of the extremes of possibilities looming before gifted city players.

Physically, the teenagers were as different as their eventual outcomes. Alcindor stood seven feet tall; Manigault was six feet-one. Despite their obvious physical difference, Kareem called Manigault "the best basketball player his size in the history of New York City."[67] The problem was that except for basketball insiders and the fans who attended the games of the annual Rucker Tournament held on a Harlem playground every summer, nobody knew what The Goat could do on a court.

As the 1965 basketball season was concluding, virtually every media outlet and every fan in the country acknowledged that Alcindor was, as the *Sporting News* called him, "quite possibly the greatest schoolboy basketball prospect in history."[68] Alcindor was making headlines and winning games for Power Memorial High School in Manhattan. He combined remarkable quickness and agility to go along with his height and a stellar academic record, making him the proverbial can't miss prospect.

Manigault was a star at Benjamin Franklin High School, where he outclassed his opponents in the New York Public School Athletic League. "Earl and I would get together on certain Saturday mornings and play a lot of three-on-three basketball in the park or wherever the real good games were being played," Abdul-Jabbar remembered. "Earl was more of a street player than

I was, so he never really got the same type of mainstream recognition that I got in high school. But people who really knew the game knew that Earl could play."[69]

Manigault flashed his talent on the playground courts, especially in the Rucker League games that drew players from scholastic, collegiate, and professional basketball. Holcombe Rucker, a Harlem native and a director in the New York City parks department, started teaching basketball and organizing games in 1946 on the playground courts on 138th Street between Lenox and Fifth Avenues as a way to draw the interest of Harlem youths. "On warm days, his classroom was a park bench or a basketball court."[70] The inaugural summer tournament that eventually featured the play of some of the best basketball talent in the city and beyond came in 1950.[71] One veteran Rucker fan noted, "That brand of hard-nosed basketball, combined with high-flying, artistic moves to the basket created during years of one-on-one and full-scale battles on the asphalt, became in essence the true identity of the city game, separating it from the way the game was being played in places like Indiana, where country boys were perfecting their long-range shooting in driveways or local gyms."[72]

Not many, if any, were playing the city game better than Earl "The Goat" Manigault. He could dunk; he could fly; he could handle the ball like a magician. But unlike his friend Alcindor, he was the quintessential street kid, and that was his tragic flaw. Holcombe Rucker arranged for Manigault to go to Laurinburg Institute in North Carolina, where he earned his high school diploma. The next year he dropped out of Johnson C. Smith University in Charlotte, North Carolina, and he drifted back to the Harlem streets. Alcindor was at UCLA where he led John Wooden's Bruins to three NCAA titles from 1967 through 1969. The Goat was in Harlem where he began using heroin. "That's when I went right to the bottom," Manigault told author Vincent M. Mallozzi.[73]

The tale of the two divergent New York talents reached a tragic climax as the 1969–1970 basketball season was starting. Alcindor won the NBA Rookie of the Year award that season as he led the Milwaukee Bucks to the Eastern Conference finals where they lost to the New York Knicks. Manigault was arrested for possession of drugs and sentenced to five years in prison. He served sixteen months before being paroled, but his chance at basketball glory was lost. About his lost opportunity and his relationship with Kareem, Manigault observed, "Growing up, Kareem and I were very close. We both had talent, and we both ended up taking separate roads in life. He chose his road, and I chose mine, and I paid for it."[74]

It is impossible to do justice to the wealth of talent that graced the Rucker playground courts over the decades.[75] Ed Warner and Floyd Lane, both disgraced in the dumping scandal of 1951, received second chances to play courtesy of Holcombe Rucker.[76] A short list of stars who played on the playground court reads like a Hall of Fame roll call: Wilt Chamberlain, Connie Hawkins, Julius Erving, Nate Archibald, Walt Frazier, Earl Monroe, Willis Reed, and Kareem Abdul-Jabbar. And then there are genuinely gifted players such as Earl Manigault; Jumpin' Jackie Jackson; Richard "Pee-Wee" Kirkland, who ended up playing some of his best basketball for the Lewisburg (Pennsylvania) Federal Prison team; and Joe "The Destroyer" Hammond. A Lou Carnesecca comment on Hammond could well apply to all of the players in the latter group: "The guy was from the streets. He was their guy, their local hero, who never left them."[77] Even if some of them tried but failed.

The New York Knicks had been operating in the NBA since its inception in 1949, and in 1970 Ned Irish's franchise won its first championship. Never a league power prior to that season, the Knicks were, nevertheless, considered a valuable professional basketball property. Irish owned the team; Irish controlled the Garden schedule; and the NBA desperately wanted to maintain a presence in New York City.[78] That triumph in 1970 came courtesy of a four-games-to-three margin over the Los Angeles Lakers in the NBA finals. To advance to the finals, though, the Knicks beat Alcindor's Milwaukee Bucks by a decisive four games to one. The Knicks compiled a 60-22 regular-season record that year. It was a Knicks team loaded with talent, such as Willis Reed, Walt Frazier, Dave DeBusschere, Bill Bradley, and Cazzie Russell.

The events of the fifth game of the 1970 NBA finals became instantly the stuff of basketball legend. The series with the Lakers was tied at two games apiece as 19,500 people flocked to the new Garden above Penn Station. Virtually all of them were hoping and praying for a Knicks win. The date was May 4, 1970, and earlier that afternoon news had broken of the killing at Kent State University of students protesting the United States' involvement in the Vietnam War.

On the court, the battle was largely between Wilt Chamberlain of the Lakers and Reed of the Knicks. The Lakers were ahead 25–15 early in the game when Reed took a pass from Bill Bradley and drove to the basket for what appeared to be an easy two. But he never got off the shot. Instead, he crumpled to the floor with what later was diagnosed as a torn tensor muscle in his right leg. Reed was out of the game, and for all intents and purposes the Knicks appeared to be out of luck in the series.[79]

"We thought it was over," Walt Frazier said years later.[80] Red Holzman was coaching the Knicks, but it was Bradley who suggested the strategy that would pull out a crucial, almost miraculous 107–100 victory. With Reed out, he said, the Knicks should spread the floor with five players who could shoot from the outside and even drive inside. The strategy would force Chamberlain away from the basket; it would take him out of his comfort zone and force him to guard a quicker shooter. "It was Bradley's idea all the way," Reed remembered. Decades later, as he was watching the game on tape, Reed telephoned Bradley, who by that time was a United States senator from New Jersey. "Senator," Reed said, "You know what, you guys did a hell of a job that night without me."[81]

In the seventh game of that series—another Garden meeting—Reed came off the bench to play through pain and help the Knicks win both the game, 113–99, and the NBA championship. The Knicks would lose in the finals to the Lakers the following year, but in 1972 they would repeat their title-winning effort. Of those Knicks teams and those glorious seasons, film director and basketball fan extraordinaire Spike Lee observed, "Of all the sports teams in New York, they may be the most beloved, the one we can be most proud of . . . [I]t wasn't just how they played; it was who they were, all the things they went on to do."[82]

New York City gained another NBA team when the Nets of the defunct American Basketball Association evolved into the Brooklyn Nets and played their home games at the new Barclay's Center in Brooklyn. As for the Knicks in the seasons following their championship years, the wins and the glory have been harder to come by. In *Tabloid City*, novelist/journalist Pete Hamill writes of a fictitious New York newspaper that succumbs to the financial reality of dwindling readership and advertising revenue in the beginning of the twenty-first century. The editors and reporters combine to print a mock edition of the paper to celebrate its demise. The lead headline on the sports page reads: "UCONN WOMEN BEAT KNICKS BY 23."[83]

Hamill may have been writing fiction, but women's basketball was rising to the fore. The 1960s saw considerable change and progress for women on many fronts, and that included basketball. In 1969, the Division of Girls and Women in Sports of the American Association for Health, Physical Education, and Recreation (AAPHER) did away with the six-player version of the game that women played for many years. Instead, the five-player game, a version identical to the men's game, was instituted along with a thirty-second clock.[84] The Association for Intercollegiate Athletics for Women (AIAW) held its first national championship tournament in March 1969, the last time the women played the six-player game. West Chester State from Pennsylvania, the tournament host, beat Western Carolina for the title.[85]

Six years later, the women were hitting the big time. College basketball attractions in Madison Square Garden always drew sizable crowds, but on February 22, 1975, more than 7,000 people left the arena before the second game of a double-header, a game pitting the men's teams of Fairfield University against the University of Massachusetts. The reason—most people were in the stands to witness a historic first, a women's game between three-time national AIAW champion Immaculata College and New York City power Queen's College. Immaculata, a small women's college in suburban Philadelphia, prevailed, 65–61. The caliber of play exhibited by both teams "generally dazzled the 11,969 spectators," a *New York Times* game story noted.[86]

It was the salad days of women's basketball, a time when absolutely nobody could imagine a professional women's team such as the New York Liberty of the Women's National Basketball Association (WNBA) playing in the Garden. The WNBA's first season of play came in the summer of 1997.[87] Most of the people who attended the Immaculata-Queens game were curious and most likely dubious about the talent they were about to witness. "I thought they would play like girls," Miguel Gaston told a reporter. "But they're really hustling out there." A Queens guard, Debbie "The Pearl" Mason, Gaston remarked, "moves like Earl Monroe."[88]

Thirty-five years later, reporter Harvey Araton interviewed the coaches and some of the players in that pioneering game. "I don't think everyone understood at the moment what that game meant," said Immaculata coach Cathy Rush, who has been inducted into the Naismith Memorial Hall of Fame. As the teams took the court for warm-ups, the arena's sound system launched into Helen Reddy's iconic anthem, "I Am Woman." Donna Chait Orender, a freshman guard for Queens, said, "I heard the music, and tears started streaming down my face." She was the high scorer for Queens that day with 14 points, and as an adult she became president of the WNBA.[89]

Immaculata's Marianne Crawford Stanley, who had seven points in the game, told Araton that she went through her customary pregame ritual before the magnitude of where she was hit her. "I got to midcourt, looked up, and then it set in. We're in Madison Square Garden. I'm from Philly, so I have a fondness for the Palestra, but it hit me that what was happening that day was groundbreaking."[90]

And the game was instrumental in helping shape the future of women's basketball. High in the Garden stands, transfixed by what she was watching, sixteen-year-old Nancy Lieberman, a future Hall of Famer, saw the possibilities unfold. "For a girl who'd grown up in New York being called a tomboy, that day changed my life, how I felt about myself," she told Araton.[91] Lieberman went on to earn an athletic grant-in-aid to Old Dominion University, an accomplishment that in the pre–Title IX period a few years earlier would have been unheard of.

Just as women were getting greater opportunities to play collegiately in the final decades of the twentieth century, so, too, was the men's game gaining popularity and profitability, due in no small part to an influx of television contract money. The 1979 NCAA championship game that pitted Michigan State and Earvin "Magic" Johnson against Indiana State and Larry Bird is regarded as the event that lifted college basketball into the prosperous big-time. That and the entrance that year of ESPN to the cable television market.[92] The seasons when New York teams such as CCNY, LIU, and NYU were national powers were remnants of a bygone era. Basketball talent in the city was as abundant as ever, but that talent was leaving the city and its colleges for better scholarship deals elsewhere. In the final decades of the twentieth century, only Lou Carnesecca's St. John's teams figured prominently on the national scene. The Hall of Famer coached at St. John's for twenty-four seasons, interrupted by a short stint coaching in the professional ranks. Carnesecca retired after the 1992 season, but his St. John's teams qualified for postseason tournaments in all of his twenty-four years as head coach. His 1985 team made the NCAA Final Four, and Carnesecca was selected as National Coach of the Year in 1983 and 1985.[93]

On February 12, 1995, Nat Holman died at the age of ninety-eight. His obituary in the *New York Times* cited his 1950 double NIT and NCAA champion CCNY team, his overall coaching record of 421-190 compiled during a thirty-seven-year career, and his pioneering role as a star for the Original Celtics. The obituary writer also noted that Holman used a "street-smart style" in his playing and coaching, a style he developed when he "began his basketball career on the Lower East Side of New York. His teachers were players in the streets and schoolyards, where he learned the strategies and rhythms of an early brand of playground basketball."[94] In that respect, Holman's introduction to basketball was exactly like the introduction that many who followed him—boys and girls of the city streets—experienced and cherished.

# IV

# Racing On the Track and in the Streets

CHAPTER SIX

# The New York City Marathon

## Celebration of a City and the Back of the Pack

*Maureen M. Smith*

### Introduction

"The scene seems culled from a space movie," wrote Neil Amdur, "a herd of humans penned in by the imposing towers and rows of metal on the Verrazano-Narrows Bridge. But in reality, it is the start of the New York City Marathon."[1] Amdur's description in 1977, when 4,823 runners participated, could hardly have imagined almost forty years later, over 50,000 runners "penned in" ready to start the annual ritual. This renowned image of the race's start, thousands of runners making their way over the Verrazano-Narrows Bridge, is one of the most iconic images of the city, as runners head hopefully over the bridge into Brooklyn. The 2013 version of the event came after a one-year hiatus due to Hurricane Sandy and as a result, included 50,740 participants, a far cry from the 127 entered in 1970. A year later, marathon entries broke the one-year record with 50,896 entrants and 50,530 finishers. Over 1,000,000 runners have crossed the Central Park finish line and can proudly claim the title of New York City marathon finisher.[2]

The New York City Marathon has been hailed as the world's greatest footrace, a celebration of the city. This chapter examines the history of the New York City Marathon, from its early days as a looped run around Central Park in 1970, to the five-borough version that began in 1976 and continues today as the world's largest marathon. Attention will be paid to race director Fred Lebow, who cofounded the event and nurtured the race into a global phenomenon with his innovative marketing strategies and single-purpose devotion. The New York City Marathon is routinely cited as the impetus behind the growth of the marathon around the world; this chapter will examine the relationship between the New York City Marathon and its influence on the sport. Developments in the event, such as television, race money, and notable performances, will also be included in this chapter. Finally, in considering the New York City Marathon as an iconic "New York" event, attention must be given to the unique ways the annual event showcases the city, its five boroughs, and diverse inhabitants who run the race, but also serve as its volunteer force and cheer squads every first Sunday in November.

## The First New York City Marathon, September 13, 1970

On September 13, 1970, a Sunday morning, 127 runners paid a $1 entry fee for the privilege to participate in the inaugural New York City Marathon. Sponsored by the New York Road Runners, the race was hosted in Central Park, with the participants running the small 1.7-mile loop and then four rounds of the larger 5.9-mile loop. Leading up to the event, co-race director Fred Lebow proclaimed, "It's going to be more exciting than a marathon on a regular course because spectators will be able to keep track of the runners." He also boasted of the "big hill from East 72d Street up to 84th." Joseph W. Halper, commissioner of the city's Department of Recreation, explained the race as the result of "the efforts and enthusiasm of New Yorkers who participated in physical fitness programs and jogging."[3] The race was sanctioned by the Amateur Athletic Union, which meant that women who participated in the event would not be "official" competitors. The morning of the event, the *New York Times* reported that two husband-wife duos would compete, Richard and Nina Kuscsik and George and Patricia Tarnewsky. Both couples had previously competed in the Boston Marathon. The newspaper also noted the entry of three male runners, Ted Corbitt, a physical therapist and champion of the American 100-mile; Gary Muhrcke, a fireman and winner of the 1969 Yonkers Marathon; and Jim McDonough, the winner of the 1967 Yonkers Marathon, among the expected crowd of 200 runners.[4]

Of those 127 runners who started the race, 55 finished, with Muhrcke winning the first New York City Marathon in 2 hours 31 minutes and 38.2 seconds, four minutes ahead of his nearest competitor, second-place finisher Tom Fleming. Corbitt finished in fifth place. Nina Kuscsik, who had run the Boston Marathon in 3 hours and 11 minutes, did not finish the race. Murhcke, Fleming, Corbitt, along with the other runners finishing in the top ten, received wristwatches, while the next 35 finishers received clocks. Each finisher received a commemorative trophy.[5] Among those finishers was one of the race cofounders, Fred Lebow, who finished the Central Park course in 4 hours 12 minutes and 9 seconds.

## Fred Lebow, Founder of the Marathon

Central to the story of the New York City Marathon is Fred Lebow. Lebow was born Ephraim Fishl Lebowitz in Arad, Romania, in 1932, the sixth of his parents' seven children. The family, devout in their Orthodox Judaism, survived the Holocaust by working in labor camps and then escaping through various means. Fishl and a brother first went to Czechoslovakia. He arrived alone in New York City in 1949 for a brief stay before heading to the Midwest and at some point changed his name to Fred Lebow. Lebow returned to New York City in the 1960s and found success in fashion and garment manufacturing. He also enjoyed playing tennis, though eventually he turned to jogging as his preferred form of exercise. As a result of his new interest in running, Lebow was encouraged to enter his first race event, a five-mile race consisting of eleven laps around Yankee Stadium, sponsored by the Road Runners Club of America, New York Association, the first iteration of the current New York Road Runners Club (NYRR).[6]

Soon after the event, in which he ran quite slowly and showed little acumen as a distance runner, Lebow joined the Road Runners Club for three dollars. Motivated by fitness and health, Lebow did not feel a kinship with the other Road Runners, who were fueled by their love of running and competition. Instead of giving up, Lebow began training for the 1970 Cherry Tree Marathon, held in the Bronx and considered "the mother of the New York City Marathon."[7] With two hundred other runners, Lebow plodded his way through the race course, which was up and down Sedgwick Avenue four times. He finished in 4 hours and 9 minutes, but was disgruntled with the entire experience.

Lebow approached Vince Chiapetta, president of the Road Runners, proposing the event should be relocated to Central Park, which Lebow viewed as a more scenic setting with wider roads, trees above, and no cars. Though the Road Runners were not convinced to sponsor the event, Lebow and Chiapetta joined forces to cohost the event. The pair were given permission from the parks department, with Lebow chipping in his own monies to cover the costs of "soft drinks, safety pins and cheap watches for the winners."[8] With that, the event was set for September 13, 1970. The relative success of the first running of the

New York City Marathon was enough to convince Lebow to continue—not only marathon running, he ran thirteen in 1970—but the second annual New York City Marathon.

## The Early Years

The first iterations of the New York City Marathon, the looped run through Central Park, were run in relative obscurity, though the number of participants increased each year. In 1971, the number of entries doubled to 246, this time with 164 finishers. Among those finishers were Beth Bonner and Nina Kuscsik, who became the first women to complete a marathon in under three hours. Bonner finished in 2 hours 55 minutes and 22 seconds, with Kuscsik just 42 seconds behind. Lebow was supportive of women running the event, despite the opposition from the Amateur Athletic Union (AAU). Norman Higgins won the event on the men's side.

The next year, the issue of gender was at the forefront. The AAU insisted on the women having a separate starting time ten minutes prior to the men; they had actually preferred a separate race entirely. Six women had registered for the third running of the Central Park event, and the October 2, 1972, edition of the *New York Times* included a photograph of the six women seated at the start of the race, protesting their separate starting time. When the gun went off for their male counterparts, the women joined the race. Kuscsik, who earlier in the year had won the Boston Marathon, was the top woman and finished sixty-third among all the competitors. Sheldon Karlin won on the men's side. Robert Reinertsen commented on the mindset of the participants, admitting, "Sometimes I wonder why we do it. Every race I have I say will be the last one. But when you're running out there, every marathon runner thinks he's the best in the world. We're all nutty individualists."[9]

By this time, Lebow was president of the NYRR. In the first year of his presidency, Lebow grew the club membership to 800 members, and it no longer operated out of anyone's apartment. For the 1973 marathon, he was able to secure sponsorship in the amount of $5,000 from Olympic Airways to help defray the costs of the fourth running of the New York City Marathon. Four hundred and six runners started the race, including 12 women, and 287 finished the race—the highest total in the race's short history. Tom Fleming, who had finished second in the inaugural marathon, finally found his way to the victory stand, winning the event. Nina Kucscik won the women's marathon in 2:57, with Kathrine Switzer finishing second in 3:16, shy of her goal of breaking the three-hour mark. The New York City Marathon was central to the development of women in long-distance running and marathon events, with Switzer hailed as a model for other women interested in running. Cooper explains that "women's marathoning became a part of a feminist attitude toward health care," as well as an "opportunity for women to explore their own physical limits of endurance and speed."[10] Lebow even created a "mini marathon" event for women only, and by 1976, the event attracted over 400 runners, sponsorship, and national media attention. The growth of the mini-marathon helped grow the number of women in long-distance running and the New York City Marathon.[11]

Olympic Airways upped their sponsorship to $8,000 for the 1974 marathon and marathons were becoming more popular, with over one hundred marathons hosted across the country that year. The 1974 marathon attracted 501 runners to the starting line, the second-largest marathon behind Boston. Winning the New York City Marathon in 1974 was Norbert Sander, a Bronx internist. Switzer returned to the event and this time won, though falling short in the hot and humid weather, with a time of 3:07:29. Bill Rodgers, who would stake his claim in the event in the next several years, finished in fifth place. Both Sander and Switzer won trips to Greece from Olympic Airways as part of their winnings.[12]

In 1975, without sponsors, Lebow scrambled to raise funds from the NYRR members to cover the costs of the event. Though the event lost money, it did gain some new respect and notoriety. The AAU sanctioned the event as the National AAU Women's Championship (nine years before the event would be held in the Olympic Games). It also landed on the front page of the *New York Times*, marking its arrival; Ron Rubin suggests the "publicity breakthrough transformed the Big Apple's impression of the race from a small run-of-the-mill marathon to one of flamboyance."[13] The 1975 New York City Marathon was the last time, though it was unknown at the time, the event would be held exclusively in Central Park.[14]

## Celebrating America's Bicentennial with a Five-Borough Marathon

In early summer of 1976, it was announced that the New York City Marathon would alter its course and run the event through all five of the city's boroughs, as a means to celebrate the nation's two-hundredth birthday, and "making it a spectacle for the entire city."[15] Thought to be a logistical nightmare, with security issues, road closures, and maintaining the safety of the runners, while allowing the city to function, it appeared to be quite a challenge for Lebow, the NYRR, and the city. George Spitz is credited with the "celebratory five-borough marathon," an idea Lebow initially did not think logistically feasible. Once convinced, Lebow "threw all his energy and know-how into the race," at that point, "the biggest challenge of his career." Manhattan Borough president Percy Sutton proposed the five-borough event would "draw together and unite [in] common purpose many of the different neighborhoods and communities that make up the City of New York."[16]

The entry of two top-class marathon runners helped to promote the event—Frank Shorter, the gold medalist in the event in Munich in 1972, and the recent silver medalist in that summer's Montreal Games, and Bill Rodgers, who had also run in Montreal, and had won the previous Boston Marathon. Initially, Lebow and his organizers expected over 1,000 entrants. There were just over 2,000 runners at the starting line, an almost unimaginable number in 1975, when just a quarter of that amount ran the Central Park event. Runners from thirty-five states and ten countries were among the runners, half of whom had never run a marathon. George Hirsch was among the runners, whom he remembered as "ecstatic about the crowd reception and the news media attention." Hirsch contends the success of the five-borough, initially a one-year plan, gave Lebow "his life's work." Organizers from around the United States and Europe used the five-borough model for their own marathon events.[17]

Writing about the first citywide marathon, the *New York Times*'s Neil Amdur opined, "The race embodied the city's character, good and bad. Spectators cheered all competitors, carried signs and flags for some, snapped pictures and lined much of the route, particularly a six-mile stretch along Fourth Avenue in Brooklyn and the final three miles in Central Park. The police had no official crowd estimates, but as many as 500,000 people could have caught a glimpse of the runners at one time or another during the midday journey. Some spectators watched out of curiosity, unfamiliar with the mystique of long-distance running. Others enjoyed the controlled confines of Central Park."[18] This was just the first of many Amdur articles about the New York event in the years to follow. From this first description of the initial five-borough marathon, it's clear that the event was a citywide celebration not only of the runners, but of the neighborhoods that cheered them along and the volunteers who helped the event run smoothly. The five-borough route became a model used by other cities in the planning of their marathon events at a critical time of development in the sport.[19] The inclusion of Shorter and Rodgers was a great success, as Rodgers won his first New York City Marathon in 2:10:10, with Shorter coming in second three minutes later. Fleming, who had won the last Central Park marathon, finished in sixth place. Californian Miki Gorman finished first among women with a time of 2:39:11.[20]

The five-borough event became the norm, with the event moving outside of Central Park permanently. The race numbers more than doubled the next year, with 4,823 runners in 1977, the largest marathon in the world. The ability to attract elite runners helped promote the event as a top marathon, but the inclusion of recreational runners making their way through the world's unofficial capital was an equally lucrative draw. By the mid-1970s, marathon running attracted elite runners and recreational runners alike, so much so that Cooper asserts a marathon event was actually two races, an "elite race" with selected runners competing for prize money and a "mass race" for those running for "more personal goals."[21] New York's marathon event, according to Cooper, offered a "wide variety of reasons" for participating in the race—good health most certainly, but New York also "provided a festival atmosphere and symbols," such as t-shirts and finisher medals that increased the prestige and value of the event for the recreational runner.[22]

Shorter, on the 1977 event, proclaimed, "This marathon is going to be better than the Montreal Olympics. Besides the great field, you've got the unbelievable course and all the publicity that will be generated." His competitor, Tom Fleming, crowed, "New York has a different kind of drama from Boston. You've got the start, the five bridges, the streets, the whole neighborhood flavor."[23] Others felt the same. Boston and New York, rival cities with two distinct marathon events, seemed to recognize that each offered something unique. Boston was a much more exclusive event, only inviting runners who had met a qualifying time, while New York's emergence with their five-borough marathon and the masses soon became the largest marathon event. In 1978, New York welcomed 9,875 runners and went over 10,000 the next year with 11,533 runners. By 1980, and a decade of marathons, there were 14,012 runners at the starting line. There would be no looking back at the small pack of runners in Central Park.[24]

## Overview of the Five-Borough 26.2-Mile Run through New York City

Since the first five-borough marathon through New York in 1976, the route has been altered only slightly. The prerace village is Fort Wadsworth on Staten Island. Many runners are bussed to Fort Wadsworth from a pick-up at the New York Public Library in Manhattan, while many others arrive on the Staten Island Ferry, across the New York Harbor, passing the Statue of Liberty on their way. Liz Robbins writes of the prerace Fort Wadsworth, "For the better part of five hours, the grounds will turn into a self-sustaining village of approximately 50,000 people—an intricately planned operational marvel populated not only by the runners, but also volunteers."[25] With the exponential growth of the marathon, there are actually three different areas—color-coded blue, orange, and green, to help divide up the runners and their various starting times, with the groups of runners leaving the start in waves, professionals early in the morning and then wave after wave until the last group of runners leave Fort Wadsworth and Staten Island. Each start begins with the firing of a cannon and Frank Sinatra's "New York, New York," for a memorable beginning.

The race begins on one side of the Verrazano-Narrows Bridge, using both the upper and lower decks (although early iterations used the upper deck only). The first mile is up and over the bridge, the sixth New York bridge designed by Othmar Ammann and erected in 1964 as the longest suspended span of the time period. It is currently the eleventh-longest span in the world and the longest in the United States. Closed to cars for the event, the bridge typically hosts over 190,000 cars daily.[26] Runners on the lower deck are warned about runners on the upper deck urinating, though runners on the upper deck are also threatened to not urinate while on the bridge. The image of thousands of runners making their way across the Verrazano-Narrows Bridge is recognizable around the world, for runners and nonrunners alike. Tom Fleming, who ran in the first New York City Marathon in 1970, has said of the start, "To look out there and see the skyline and that feeling of space it's enough to take your breath away even before you take your first step."[27] Jim Fortunato, who served as the general manager of the bridge for twelve years, claimed, "The Bridge *is* the Marathon. It's the shot seen 'round the world."[28] Grete Waitz, of Norway, and a nine-time winner of the event, found the starting line to be a "virtual sea of people, an overwhelming sight for someone used to standing with a handful of runners on the track."[29] Bill Rodgers, who won the events four years in a row beginning in the bicentennial, has called the starting line a "kind of a giant time bomb behind you about to go off. It is the most spectacular start in sport."[30] Of the start on the Verrazano-Narrows Bridge, Lebow offered his own assessment, claiming "there is nothing like it in sports. The start of the New York City marathon is in a class by itself."[31]

What lies ahead for the runners is, according to New York's mayor Bill DiBlasio, "an unforgettable journey through the world's most diverse city, right in the heart of iconic neighborhoods, public spaces, and urban landscapes that encompass all five of our dynamic boroughs."[32] Similarly, Joe Cody hailed the urban settings, noting the "Bay Ridge spirit, Spanish *salsa,* Greenpoint *gemütlichkeit,* and Harlem soul are highlights marathoners will long remember."[33] The first mile over the bridge is the longest and steepest hill, while mile 2 is all downhill. Miles 2 through 4 take the runners down Fourth Avenue in the Bay Ridge neighborhood in Brooklyn. Miles 4 through 6, runners are still heading along Fourth Avenue making their way through Sunset Park before Miles 6 through 8, which takes them by the last remnant of Ebbets Field, its left-field wall, and nearby newly erected Barclays Center, home to the Brooklyn Nets and New York Islanders. At mile 8, the three color-coded groups converge and continue through Brooklyn through Fort Greene for mile 9. Miles 10 through 12 take runners through the Hassidic neighborhood of Williamsburg. In the first version of the five-borough event, Lebow was intent on including this neighborhood, despite his own straying from his Orthodox roots.[34] On the urban marathon's route through Brooklyn, Fowler wrote, "The marathon as a distinctive New York experience was nowhere better displayed than along Bedford Avenue in Williamsburg section of Brooklyn, where the world's 'melting pot' on this warm day took on dual meaning. In a neighborhood populated by sizeable numbers of Hassidic Jews, blacks and Hispanics, the seemingly endless flow of runners got encouragement and sustenance from the residents who lined the route."[35]

Miles 12 and 13 go through Greenpoint where runners are met with the Pulaski Bridge, the second bridge of the race, and the halfway point of the race. The Pulaski Bridge delivers the runners into their third borough, Queens and the Long Island City neighborhood, where they will run miles 13 to 15. Mile 16 is the Queensboro Bridge, the third bridge of the route and the one leading runners into their first jaunt into the borough of Manhattan. The Queensboro Bridge is a thoughtful deliberation of running, as runners anticipate the turn onto Manhattan's First Avenue and throngs of cheering crowds. Runners are warned to not get carried away in the excitement and speed up too soon, as there is too much of the race left to pick up the pace at this point.

First Avenue hosts runners for miles 16 through 20, with the last half of the run going through East Harlem, before their fourth bridge, the Willis Avenue Bridge, and fifth borough, the Bronx. The neighborhood of Mott Haven in the Bronx cheer runners along miles 20 and 21, before they head over their last bridge of the day, the Madison Avenue bridge over the Harlem River and back to Manhattan. Runners go around Marcus Garvey Park, and at mile 23 are running along Fifth Avenue and the outer perimeter of Central Park at mile 24. Continuing along Fifth Avenue and Central Park, runners turn onto Central Park South and then Columbus Circle with less than a mile remaining. The finish line is inside the confines of Central Park, where runners are greeted with cheers, a finisher's medal, and a poncho to keep them warm as they weave and wander wearily finding their exit out of the park, sometimes adding another mile to their already lengthy trek around the city.

## Grete Waitz, Queen of the Marathon

One of the greatest performers in the history of the New York City Marathon is Grete Waitz of Norway. Waitz entered her first marathon—the New York City Marathon—in 1978. Her longest run prior to the marathon was a 20-kilometer training run. Waitz was initially rejected from entering the event; there was some misunderstanding around the cost of her attendance and if her coach/husband would be funded. Lebow, however, recognized her accomplishments on the track in shorter distances and hoped that by including her in the women's field (which was now up to 938), Waitz would take the group out and help someone achieve a faster time. Waitz surprised Lebow and herself by winning her first marathon in 2 hours 32 minutes and 30 seconds, taking two minutes off the world record. Her victory in 1978 changed the direction of her running career and was the first of her nine victories in New York City.

Waitz's success in New York had a tremendous impact on the growth of the marathon for women, both elite and women interested in running for fun and personal challenge. She came back the next year to repeat her title and returned in 1980 for her third consecutive title.[36] Waitz won the event every year from 1982 to 1988, her last victory. By 1992, the last year she ran the event, there were almost 29,000 runners, including 5,609 women. Waitz's success in New York contributed to the growing voices working to convince the conservative

International Olympic Committee to finally relent and offer the event at the Olympic Games for women in 1984.[37]

## The Marathon in the 1980s: Television, Drugs, and Money

As the New York City Marathon grew in size with more runners every year and was able to attract some of the sport's top talents, Lebow and the NYRR found new ways to promote the event. There was a significant influx of monies during the 1980s, moving in both directions, from the race to runners and from sponsors to the organizers. The 1980s was a decade of structural changes in the event as it continued to move from an "amateurish" type event to a highly organized and branded global event.

In the first years of the 1980s, Cooper contends the race organizers were spending in excess of $150,000 to top runners, and $200,000 by 1983. However these payments were paid in cash in secret arrangements, creating some dissension among runners who didn't receive funds, as well as offending the amateur sensibilities of some members of the running community and politicians.[38] Some of the sordid details of the secret payments were made public by Lebow in his 1984 book *Inside the World of Big-Time Marathoning*. These revelations then led to a showdown with New York mayor Ed Koch. The mayor wondered why the city should cover the costs of the event if the race had enough sponsorship to pay athletes, forcing an agreement between the city and the NYRR.[39]

By 1984, top athletes were openly provided with financial prize money as well as incentives to appear in the event. That year, NYRR paid the city over $300,000 to contribute to the cost of hosting the event. That amount was agreed upon in part based on the amount of prize money awarded to runners and the ABC television contract, which paid the NYRR $100,000.[40] Koch had initially resisted the idea of awarding prize money, admitting to holding a "Victorian point of view" on the issue, but also conceding that prize money attracted top runners, which helped promote the event. One area in which Koch's views were not Victorian, his insistence on paying the top male and female finishers equal prize money. In all, the 1984 event costs $610,000 to operate with the costs shared by the NYRR and the city.[41]

In an assessment of Lebow's business acumen, the *New York Times*'s Jane Gross considered Lebow to be the equal of New York Yankee owner George Steinbrenner (though worth much less; Lebow earned $35,000 annually for his NYRR position). The organizer of the Los Angeles Olympic Games in

1984, Peter Ueberroth, commended Lebow's marathon as the model for the Olympic event that year.

When Waitz won the 1985 NYCM, she earned $25,000 in cash, was given a $30,000 Mercedes-Benz, and received $70,000 in appearance fees. Compare that to the $14,000 she was reportedly given for her win in 1982, and this shift toward transparent payments certainly provided elite runners with adequate financial incentives. It also marked the event as one of the most lucrative races in the country.

Drug testing was introduced at the 1986 NYCM. This marked the first time drug testing was administered at a road race in the United States that was not the Olympic Games, Olympic Trials, or world championships. Lebow was in support of the new measures, telling the *New York Times,* "years ago, runners cheated and that was before there was money. Now, the value of winning New York can add up to a half million dollars."[42] Koch himself said of Lebow at the time, "As it related to organizational ability and stick-to-iveness, Fred Lebow deserves all the credit in the world." And while many NYRR members lamented, according to Gross, their "lost power," they also recognize that he "has mounted the most elaborate and popular marathon in the world." His lawyer, Harold Rubenstein, who helped negotiate the settlement between Lebow and Koch after the secret cash revelations, admitted to Gross, "O.K., so they don't like how he talks, how he negotiates, or that he's fast on his feet. But he managed to turn this into a world-class event. That's a big trick and he did it."[43]

## The Growth of the NYCM

Despite the infusion of financial rewards for elite runners, the increase in the number of participants was the result of a running boom in the United States and around the world. Marathons and road races of varying lengths, such as 5k, 10k, and half marathons, were enjoying an increase in the number of runners. Many critiques of the growth in the marathon include a discussion of the social class of marathon runners, and this certainly holds true for the first two decades of the NYCM. The amount of time needed to train for a marathon, in addition to the costs of footwear, race fees, as well as traveling to and from the event, make marathons, including NYCM, out of the price range for many avid runners. Marathoner Kenny Moore, writing for *Sports Illustrated,* noted that of the close to 10,000 participants in the 1978 marathon, "Eighty-five percent had college degrees. Half had *graduate* degrees. There were 767 lawyers, 547 doctors, 977 teachers. There were 98 company presidents."[44] Over the event's forty-year history, the participation numbers have continued to grow, causing organizers to debate the ideal size of what had become the largest running of the marathon on an annual basis. The location of the event—the five boroughs—really became one of the unique features that attracted growing numbers of runners, most of them recreational. Tanser, in his guide to running the event, proclaimed, "New York is the unofficial capital of the world, a city where millions of people's paths cross, and for many runners, the ultimate experience in marathoning is the New York City marathon."[45] Taking his argument further, Tanser credited New York with "giving birth to marathon racing for the populace. One of the toughest disciplines on the Olympic agenda has been made popular for the masses. More than a half-million people have finished the marathon in Manhattan's Central Park."[46] Since its inception, the number of participants has grown, providing Tanser with plenty of evidence. In the days following the 1986 marathon, the first time the event had over 20,000 runners, 20,502 to be exact, Lebow admitted that the event "may have gotten too big." He claimed, "Our success has created a problem. We've reached our limit." One of the major concerns of the increased numbers is congestion at the starting line, what Lebow called "marathon gridlock," explaining that "there were people backed into the toll booths and beyond. When the lead pack was at the one-mile point, many runners were still trying to reach the starting line." Lebow offered one solution: capping the number of participants at 20,000 or even reducing the size. An alternative, proposed by Lebow and Allan Steinfeld, the race coordinator, was to use the upper and the lower deck of the Verrazano-Narrows Bridge, an idea they had previously proposed to the city, which had been rejected. Peter Alfano, writing for the *New York Times*, lamented that the NYRR lost money on the annual event despite the race being "an artistic success, portraying enthusiastic New Yorkers in a favorable light."[47]

Clearly, the solution has been to find ways to increase the capacity of the event, allowing for more runners to be a part of the festivities. By 1990, there were 25,012 runners, and four years later the number reached 31,129, the first time exceeding 30,000 entries. By 2005, runners numbered 37,597, and four years later, reached 44,177, the first time the event exceeded 40,000 runners. Hurricane Sandy led to the cancellation of the event in 2012, amid much controversy. Runners were guaranteed entry into future events, making the 2013 NYCM the largest ever, at the time, with 50,740, the first time the race reached 50,000 runners. The next year, the event broke its own record, with 50,896 runners and a record number of finishers at 50,530. The most men to ever run in the marathon was in 2013, with 30,699, and the most women in one marathon was 20,422 in 2014.

Among these 50,000 runners are elite athletes, athletes in wheelchairs, slow runners, fast runners, recreational runners, New Yorkers, Americans, and world citizens—including participants who take over twice as long as the winners. The roster includes anonymous runners cheered on by friends, family, and strangers, and more recognizable faces from Hollywood and the world of professional athletics, most recently Ryan Reynolds, Pamela Anderson, Uzo Aduba, Sean Combs, Katie Holmes, James Blake, Carolina Wozniacki, Alicia Keys, and Ethan Hawke. It also includes retired music teacher Dave Obelkevich, who in 2015, ran his fortieth NYCM, completing it in just under five hours.[48]

## Winning the Lottery—or—Getting to the Starting Line

Before the race even begins, there is fierce competition simply for a spot at the starting line. With over 50,000 participants in the New York City Marathon, there have been a number of methods to grant access while also paying attention to the diversity of the field, including international runners, qualified runners, wheelchair athletes, committed NYRR members, runners raising monies for charities, and those lucky lottery winners. In 2015, there were 80,080 lottery entrants—with 14,326 winners.[49] Automatic entry goes to runners who meet qualifying times; in 2015, this number was 3,541, up from 1,750 the year before. Automatic entry for runners with qualifying times is one aspect that the NYRR continues to monitor and modify in efforts to make the race more accessible to a broader range of marathon runners. Ahead of the 2016 event, the time standards were modified to be more inclusive. In their statement, the NYRR claimed that the event "is known for being an extremely diverse race . . . we pride ourselves on offering many methods by which runners can gain entry." As one means of continuing such diversity, their new time standards will "increase the number of runners who will be able to earn guaranteed entry by meeting time standards. To celebrate our most competitive athletes, we have also decided to relax those standards."[50] In addition to the lottery and qualifying times, runners gain guaranteed entry if they are members of the NYRR and complete nine NYRR race events in the preceding year *and* volunteer at one additional race event. A new feature of this 9+1 is the 9+$1K, where instead of volunteering, the runner can donate $1,000 to the NYRR's Youth and Community Services programs. Runners who have completed fifteen or more New York City marathons are also granted guaranteed entry into the event. International runners are able to have guaranteed entry through a number of tour operators, giving the event an international spirit that adds to the diversity of the participants. The other group of runners, in addition to the elite runners who finish the race sometimes before the last wave of runners has started, are runners who gain entry to the race through a charity. Runners raise thousands of dollars for their selected charity for the privilege to run, jog, walk, or slog 26.2 miles through the five boroughs. In fact, in 2014, more than $34.5 million was raised for three hundred charities, including $5 million for NYRR Team for Kids runners. While some marathon purists are opposed to offering such entries into the event, it is through such entries that many runners are able to achieve a dream, while also raising monies for good causes.

## The Finish Line

Lebow was diagnosed with brain cancer in the summer of 1990 and boldly announced his goal of running the marathon. Though he had run the Central Park event, he had never run the five-borough marathon. He stated, "I have run 68 marathons in 35 countries, but I've never run the five-borough New York City Marathon. That's my goal: to run one marathon. I don't care how slow it is. I want to finish a New York City Marathon."[51]

When Lebow's cancer went into remission, he announced he would run the 1992 NYCM.[52] His longtime friend, and nine-time winner of the event, Grete Waitz agreed to run with him. The pair took five hours 32 minutes and 35 seconds to finish the 26.2 trek, Lebow's hello and goodbye to his adopted home. Longtime *New York Times* sport columnist George Vecsey cheered, "this New York City Marathon was all about him, all about Fred Lebow and Grete Waitz running together, to celebrate his 60th birthday earlier this year and his defiance of brain cancer."[53] Lebow's NYRR colleague George Hirsch recalled, "Their long, slow run, which was cheered by millions of spectators, remains to this day the emotional high point of the race's history."[54] Richard Finn, spokesman for the NYRR, agreed, adding, "The image of the two of them coming across the finish line—hands raised—is one of the emotional moments in the history of this race, and an iconic image of New York sports."[55]

When Lebow died two years later, only weeks before the 1994 NYCM, Vecsey penned a tribute to the race organizer, suggesting the city find a way to honor their longtime civic booster. "The New York City Marathon will go on. The city should name something after him, maybe one street in each of the five boroughs he united one Sunday every November. But definitely the final stretch in Central Park should be named Fred Lebow Boulevard."[56] In Lebow's obituary, Michael Janofsky celebrated his contributions to the city, specifically his role in the development of the marathon "into not only the largest such race in the world but also a citywide celebration."[57] Henry Stern, former commissioner of parks and recreation, once said of Lebow, Janofsky reminded his readers, "People devoted to a single cause are usually a little crazy. That's what you expect and you don't judge them by normal standards . . . But, Lebow delivers and Lebow performs. If you're asking me if New York City is better off because Fred Lebow is around, the answer is yes."[58] Vecsey shared his remembrances of Lebow, praising him for the "charming hustler that he was," bringing "big-time appearance and prize money" to the marathon. But, he suggested, "the reason so many of us enjoyed him was that he turned this giant city into a playland one Sunday every November."[59]

Weeks after Lebow's death, the 1994 NYCM was a celebration of the race's founder. Unveiled at the event was a statue of Lebow, posed as if he were standing at the finish line looking at a timer. The idea of a Lebow statue was hatched after Daniel S. Mitrovich ran the 1990 NYCM. He experienced the marathon as "one of the greatest events I'd ever been in" and was "so impressed" with the event, he felt its founder merited a statue. Mitrovich almost singlehandedly led a campaign to raise funds and work with city officials to make it happen. Initially Henry Stern had expressed his doubt about a statue, but relented, concluding, "here was a guy, Fred Lebow, who really brought about a new sport."[60] For most of the year, Lebow welcomes runners to Central Park near 90th Street and Fifth Avenue. But every November, Lebow's statue is relocated to the finish line inside Central Park, welcoming the finishers of his great race.[61]

The 2015 NYCM, officially called the TCS New York City Marathon to recognize the sponsorship of Tata Consulting Services (their second year sponsoring the event, after many years of ING's sponsorship of the event). Only five years earlier, George Hirsch, chairman of the NYRR and publisher of *Runner's World,* fondly remembered his friend and fellow runner in the days leading up to the 2010 NYCM, forty years after the first event through Central Park, claiming, "If Fred Lebow, founder of the New York City Marathon, could see the 43,000 runners crowding together on the Verrazano-Narrows Bridge on Sunday morning, he would surely allow himself a slight smile. He would not be satisfied, however. He would want to see even more. Lebow was a dreamer and a schemer who combined a deep passion for running with a genius for promotion. Without him, marathoning in New York and around the world would never have reached its current mass appeal."[62]

Spike Lee served as the grand marshal in 2015, only the third time in the event's history a grand marshal was named. Largely a symbolic title, but one meant to acknowledge one of the city's notable residents, Lee and the city welcomed 50,000-plus runners, from over one hundred countries, to the Marathon Expo and the related race events. Ten thousand volunteers and over 1 million spectators along the race course contributed their necessary service. When Lebow and Chiapetta paired to sponsor their Central Park version in 1970, the event was a two-man show. Decades later, the NYRR now has 175 year-round full-time staff working on the annual event. Nine hundred and fifteen buses delivered runners to Fort Wadsworth, with 24,100 runners arriving on the Staten Island Ferry. At Fort Wadsworth and along the race course, runners left 207,000 pounds of clothing, all donated to Goodwill, in eight UPS trucks. Along the course, 1,952 portable toilets line the course, available at every mile, serving runners who will drink 62,370 gallons of water and 32,040 gallons of Gatorade along the way.[63] Friends and families can follow their runner with a mobile app, checking on their progress every mile of the race.

## Conclusion

The New York City Marathon is the world's largest marathon event, as well as one of the most beloved by the runners and volunteers alike. Certainly there are many top-quality marathon events around the world; Chicago, London, Berlin, and other cities working to enter the top tier. Boston, still very exclusive, though now also offering invitations to runners who raise money for charity, is held every April and its history and exclusivity make it one of the world's most prestigious marathons. New York's marathon, run in November (allowing runners the possibility to run both Boston and New York), is not simply the largest marathon in the world, it is one of the most recognizable with iconic photos of the starting line heading over the Verrazano-Narrows Bridge, as well as images from around the five boroughs. The New York City Marathon was also instrumental in stimulating the growing number of women in marathon running, from the early female entrants like Nina Kuscsik and Kathrine Switzer, to the mini-marathons, to the star power of Grete Waitz. These early female pioneers led the way for the thousands of women who participate every year in the New York City Marathon. The tremendous size alone however does not adequately explain its cultural significance. The decision to modify the race course to include running through the entirety of New York's five boroughs was ingenious and makes it a quintessential New York event. The city, streets, bridges, neighborhoods, and its residents are what "make" the New York City Marathon so special.

The New York City Marathon is an "internationally recognized institution." With over 50,000 runners annually, the event has achieved Lebow's fundamental goal. As stated by the city's parks and recreation website, the city's marathon pioneer "envisioned the New York City Marathon as a race for everyone—men and women of every color, creed and country, regardless of ability. Each runner seeks his or her own goal—whether to win, to achieve a personal best, or simply to finish."[64] Or as Lebow biographer Ron Rubin would say, "Anything for a T-shirt!"

CHAPTER SEVEN

# "This Isn't the Sixth Race. This Is the Belmont"

## The Belmont Stakes and the Rise and Fall of the "Sidewalks of New York"

*Bennett Liebman and Henry D. Fetter*

*East Side, West Side, all around the town*
*The tots sang "ring-a-rosie," "London Bridge is falling down"*
*Boys and girls together, me and Mamie O'Rourke*
*Tripped the light fantastic on the sidewalks of New York.*

*"The Sidewalks of New York" by James W. Blake and Charles B. Lawlor (1894)*

New York horse racing has the longest lineage of any organized American sport—horses were racing on the Hempstead Plains on Long Island in the seventeenth century, and Saratoga Race Course has been operating since the Civil War—and it is quite easy to believe that its traditions are timeless. So it was only natural for those of us who first became aware of the sport in the 1960s to believe that it was a time-hallowed ritual to accompany the horses to the post for the running of the Belmont Stakes at Belmont Park with the playing of "The Sidewalks of New York," just as it was during the post parade for the other two legs of the Triple Crown with a rendition of "My Old Kentucky Home" at the Kentucky Derby and "Maryland, My Maryland" at the Preakness. In 2014, a racing reporter wrote that "Sidewalks" had been "sung during the Belmont Stakes post parade from misty times."[1] But as is often the case, "'traditions' which appear or claim to be old are often quite recent in origin and sometimes invented."[2] And therein hangs our tale.

The ink was barely dry on Lee's surrender at Appomattox when the horses went to the post for the first running of the Belmont Stakes in 1867 at Jerome Race Track in the Bronx. The race was named in honor of financier August Belmont Sr., one of the founders of the American Jockey Club. Beginning in 1905, the race was contested at Belmont Park (named for his son, August Belmont II, who played a key role in building the track) on the border of New York City and Elmont in Nassau County. The Belmont is the oldest of the races that constitute the sport's Triple Crown for three-year-olds—its first running had been six years before the inauguration of the Preakness and eight years before that of the Kentucky Derby. It boasts a roster of winners—"Ruthless, Harry Bassett, Duke of Magenta, Spendthrift, Grenada, Hanover, Commando . . . the names are like plucked strings," as Joe Palmer, the acclaimed horse racing columnist of the *New York Herald Tribune*, wrote, recalling some of its early champions[3]—that was second to none. It was at the fourteenth running of the Belmont in 1880 that the long-since customary post parade made its first appearance at an American race track. And at the "classic" English distance of one mile and a half (the Derby distance is 1 1/4 miles, the Preakness 1 and 3/16) it proudly claims to be the true "test of the champion."

But as the concept of a "Triple Crown" became part of the sport's vernacular in the 1930s,[4] the Belmont Stakes, the final leg of the quest for that honor found itself something of an afterthought to the races that preceded it in that triumvirate. Unlike the Derby and the Preakness, the Belmont simply did not enjoy the recognition—or the respect—it deserved from either the organizers of the race or the racing public. The Derby and the Preakness were highlights on the political and social calendars of their host states. That was much less true for the Belmont. New York did not legalize pari-mutuel wagering until 1940, and its politicos were often wary of too close an association with the sport. Additionally, bucolic upstate Saratoga (the "Spa") offered a more refined alternative gathering place for society plus, until 1950, the opportunity to partake of high-class entertainment offered at casinos that were tolerated by the local law enforcement authorities.

A private entity, the Westchester Racing Association had operated Belmont Park since its opening. The membership of the patrician and self-consciously exclusive association was largely drawn from the elite (and elitist) Jockey Club. Its leaders maintained stud farms and were devoted to horse racing as a sport—to "improving the breed" so to speak. Unlike the entrepreneurial promoter of the Kentucky Derby, Colonel Matt Winn, the association shunned anything that smacked of hoopla or ballyhoo. According to Red Smith, George Widener, head of the Racing Association from 1942 to 1955, and his colleagues in Belmont's Field and Turf Club thought that "catering to the public was undignified if not downright vulgar."[5] And the public got the message—the horse racing fans who made it out to Belmont Park tended to be more upper crust than those at aging and decrepit Aqueduct and Jamaica race tracks (both in Queens), which were (or were perceived to be) more welcoming to the $2 bettor than suburban Belmont. "Jamaica's horse players are to some extent oppressed and downtrodden," Joe Palmer once wrote. According to Arthur Daley of the *New York Times,* the Jamaica track "has less comfort than a Bronx Express at rush hour."[6]

From the vantage point of the Racing Association, there was no need for showmanship or ostentation before any horse race, most definitely including the Belmont Stakes. As the 1948 renewal of the Belmont approached, Joe Palmer was troubled. That year Citation, winner of the Derby and the Preakness, was vying to become the sport's fourth Triple Crown winner of the decade (Whirlaway had done it in 1941, Count Fleet in 1943, and Assault in 1946) and seventh of all time, but something was amiss. "I like Belmont," Palmer wrote, "maybe better than any track I know," quite an admission coming from an otherwise proudly loyal son of Kentucky. "It has not the homey charm of, say, Keeneland, or the intimacy of Pimlico, or the nostalgic somnolence of Saratoga. You don't get those in areas served by the L.I.R.R. [Long Island Rail Road], but taking it all around, Belmont is the top year after year. It puts up the most money and it draws the best horses. Go out to Belmont and you get the best there is."

The Belmont Stakes "will be the sixth race, June 12, at Belmont," Palmer continued. "In May, this tourist saw divers citizens . . . cry into their third julep . . . as the horses filed from under the stands at Churchill Downs to a very inadequate rendition of 'My Old Kentucky Home.' . . . And you could see ancient Maryland turf writers try to pull in their—ah, stomachs—as 'Maryland, My Maryland' rose on the afternoon air before the Preakness. Well, curse it, the Belmont is a better race than either of them."

But at the Belmont Stakes, there was silence. What the Belmont needed to claim its rightful status in the horse racing hierarchy, Palmer decided, was a song. "So, while I'm probably not going to get it, I want a band. . . . I don't care if it plays 'The Sidewalks of New York' or 'Camptown Races,' when the Belmont field comes out, but I want it to play something that says to the assembled multitude holding the return half of L.I.R.R. tickets, "Look, chums, this isn't the sixth race. This is the Belmont."[7]

It would certainly be an uphill struggle to place New York's premier racing event on a par with that of the Bluegrass State. "The authentic romance of America!—You have more of it packed into a tighter space in Kentucky than in any other state," those New York horse players who took their eyes off the past performances were reading that spring in the pages of John Gunther 's recently published bestselling "Inside U.S.A."[8] How could a race that was run at the urban edge of New York City compete with the down-home charms of "mint juleps, Churchill Downs, the Derby" which Gunther celebrated? Moreover, New York horse racing's powers that be had no interest in doing what Palmer yearned for. "What do you think we're running here?" George Widener had once responded to a suggestion that the Belmont Stakes have a musical calling card, "a race track or a circus?"[9]

But *New York Times* sports columnist Arthur Daley picked up the cause—and some of Palmer's verbiage two days before the 1948 race. "The Belmont Stakes, oldest and best of the hoss races which combine to form turfdom's fabled Triple Crown will be staged at beautiful Belmont on Saturday. . . . There will be no blare of trumpets, no rendition of some nostalgic tune, no brush, no lather, no rub-in, no nothin'. . . . It's just the sixth race of the same approximate importance as a maiden claiming race for 2-year-olds. . . . The stuffed shirts at Belmont prefer that it be treated most casually." Yet "the Belmont," Daley continued, "has more than the Derby ever could hope to have . . . it has everything but promotion. . . . The austere and unbending folk who conduct the Belmont . . . have no theme song. They could use 'The Sidewalks of New York' or they could even use 'Nature Boy.' But, for heaven's sake, they should use something. This is much more than the sixth race. This is the Belmont!" "Every schoolboy has heard of the Kentucky Derby," Daley summed up. "Not one in a hundred thousand has heard of the Belmont except as the tag end of the Triple Crown . . . the race shouldn't be kept such a state secret. It's much too great for that." The response from the hidebound Westchester Racing Association was surprisingly immediate—if incomplete. For the 1948 race, a band was placed by the walking ring at the back of the track, and played "Sidewalks of New York" as the horses entered the ring. The song was not played as the horses went on the track to parade to the post. It was not carried on the public address system and could only be heard by the fans who were standing close to the walking ring.

Nevertheless, Joe Palmer considered it a victory. The day after the race (which Citation won to clinch the Triple Crown), he wrote, "Belmont broke down and got a band. It didn't get on the track, but was stationed modestly in the big paddock behind the stand, where it attracted considerable crowds between races and got an encouraging reception. And when the Belmont field came into the ring, it played 'The Sidewalks of New York.' An era had ended."[10]

The plaudits for the appearance of the band at the Belmont went to Palmer. His colleagues at the *Herald Tribune* saluted his effort. Sportswriter Bill Lauder reported that in the walking ring "the band struck up 'The Sidewalks of New York,' (thanks to Joe Palmer's insistence) and the horses went out to the track."[11] Palmer's close friend and fellow columnist Red Smith wrote, "Due to what must, reluctantly, be described as nagging by a horse author whose initials are Joe H. Palmer, the Westchester Racing Association loosened one button of its checkered waistcoat and going hog-wild, produced a band to class up America's greatest horse race. It had, naturally a band redolent of austere dignity, being composed mostly of white-haired gentlemen bowed down by braid and epaulettes. Still somewhat shame-faced about this concession to the vulgar taste, the management tucked the musicians away behind an administration building under the trees beyond the walking ring."[12]

But that was as far as the racing authorities were prepared to go, for the time being at least. When Joe Palmer suddenly died of a heart attack at the age of forty-eight in October 1952, the Belmont would still lack a musical accompaniment for the horses when they come onto the track itself to parade to the starting post, to provide the race with a theme song comparable to "My Old Kentucky Home" and "Maryland, My Maryland."[13]

In 1951, there had been a rumor that "Sidewalks" would be played by a band in front of the crowds. The *New York Times*'s James Roach in his account of the Belmont noted, "A startling report was received in the press box early in the afternoon. It was to the effect that the band was going to come out in front of the stands before the running of the Belmont Stakes and play 'Sidewalks of New York.' The report was untrue. The band stayed in the paddock. Let Churchill Downs and Pimlico have their infield bands. Not Belmont."[14] Red Smith similarly reported "that early in the day a rumor swept the grounds causing wider excitement than a $2,500 daily double or the disqualification of a favorite. The report was that Miss Adelaide Lander's band which Belmont ordinarily conceals in the shrubbery beyond the paddock, would be permitted to appear in public and play 'The Sidewalks of New York' as the horses paraded for the main event."[15] Smith added, "It is difficult to describe the sensation this rumor created in informed circles, where it is unthinkable that the Westchester Racing Association would offend its patrons with anything smacking of a circus parade. In the Turf and Field Club, strong men blanched and women swooned when the ugly whisper was heard."[16]

Before the 1952 Belmont—Palmer's last—*Newsday*'s horse racing columnist Art Kennedy joined the press box chorus complaining about the lack of pomp at the Belmont. He stated, "The Belmont is completely lacking in the 'schmaltz' department. It's only a horse race about which no rhymes have been written or songs been sung. . . . But no brass band gives out with a 'dolce con expresso' rendition of 'Sidewalks of New York' or even 'Take Me Back to Old Broadway' (and not a bad idea if it did) as the field comes on the track for post parade."[17] Three years later, nothing had changed. "It is a deeply moving moment when the band plays 'My Old Kentucky Home' at the Derby," Red Smith wrote in 1955. "At the Preakness, red-jacketed tuba toters blast away at 'Dixie' and 'Maryland, My Maryland!' According to rumor, 'The Sidewalks of New York' is played at the Belmont Stakes, but this is strictly hearsay, for Belmont hides its musicians away off the paddock area, out of sight and out of earshot, like a maiden aunt who has brought shame to the family name."[18]

The breakthrough finally came in 1956, a time when tradition—whether renewed or invented—was in fashion in the counsels of New York horse racing. Two years earlier, thoroughbred races on a grass (turf) course returned to New York as a regular feature for the first time since 1910.[19] As the date for the 1956 Belmont Stakes approached that June, one observer could still lament that "it does not seem very likely that any man, woman or child could be anywhere within the limits of Jefferson County, Kentucky, on May 5th and not know it was Derby Day for it's in the very air. Nor could one travel far in the Free State of Maryland on Preakness day and long remain ignorant of the fact. But it is conceivable that a not too observant turf fan could spend June 16th at Belmont Park and come home not realizing that he had seen the running of the third, and certainly the brightest, jewel in the Triple Crown. No band plays 'My Old Kentucky Home,' 'Maryland, My Maryland' or even 'The Sidewalks of New York.'"[20]

Even as that lament was being voiced, that was about to change, less due perhaps to the pleas of sportswriters than to a shake-up in the organizational structure of horse racing in New York. By the early 1950s, New York thoroughbred racing, based in antiquated facilities that dated from the turn of the century—and even earlier in the case of Saratoga—faced intensified pressure from new tracks in neighboring New Jersey as well as the explosive growth of nighttime harness racing. "Race-track patrons across the nation could usually expect to be served with as many of the luxuries of life as they would come upon within the confines of a state penitentiary," *Sports Illustrated*'s racing correspondent Whitney Tower observed in 1956. There had come "a gradual awareness on the part of management that a horse player, rich or poor, a regular or a once-a-year bettor, is not a mysterious creature running around (with blinkers on) seeking only to place a bet and a view of the finish. He was, it emerged, at least as appreciative of the joys of living as anyone else."[21]

But the New York tracks lacked cash for such badly needed and long-overdue upgrades. In 1955, adopting a plan proposed by the Jockey Club, New York State placed all of the state's thoroughbred race tracks under the control of the newly formed nonprofit Greater New York Association (renamed the New York Racing Association in 1958) with a mandate to modernize the tracks.[22] The tradition-encrusted and innovation-averse Westchester Racing Association went out of existence. George Widener no longer was the president at Belmont. Industrialist and investment banker John Hanes served as the president of the Greater New York Association.[23] In his initial plea in 1948 to provide the Belmont with some pomp, Joe Palmer had "diffidently moved . . . that Belmont Park recognize the twentieth century," although "to be sure, it will not be accomplished fact for fifty-two more years, but let's get in ahead of this one." By the spring of 1956, the Greater New York Association was ready to do that, with only forty-four years to spare.

And so days before the running of the 1956 Belmont on June 16, the association bowed to Joe Palmer's almost decade-old wishes and announced that "The Sidewalks of New York" would be played in front of the crowd and on the public address system as the horses for the race entered the track to parade to the post. This was a major news story. The *Associated Press* noted that the leading horses in the Belmont would have company "when the band swings out with the 'Sidewalks of New York.'"[24] In a separate article, the wire agency focused on the musical change and wondered how the past proprietors of the track would have reacted. "Shades of old August Belmont, and his Jockey Club companions. They opposed such carnival atmosphere so strenuously that bands at Belmont were not to be seen or heard, unless one forsook his seat and strolled into the gardens near the Turf and Field Club."[25]

Credit was given to the Greater New York Association "for this contribution to music loving horseplayers at Belmont."[26] The article added that "Tin

Pan Alley, and Petrillo will be pleased. Sutherland's Band always has been well camouflaged in the trees and deep shrubbery behind the grandstand on other Belmont Stakes days. This time they'll be smack dab out in front, for all to see and hear. What's more, when Needles, Fabius and others, in the probable field of eight parade postward for the $100,000-added gallop, the strains of 'The Sidewalks of New York' will be heard."[27]

Red Smith, who had edited a posthumous collection of Palmer's racing columns, was delighted. In a column published the day before the race, focusing on old-time jockeys and trainers attending the Belmont, he wrote, "They have seen the elephant and heard the owl, and tomorrow, they'll hear something else—a band playing 'The Sidewalks of New York' over loudspeakers."[28] Come Belmont Stakes Day 1956 "a strange sound disturbed the air as eight colts paraded to the post for the 88th running of the Stakes inaugurated in 1867. . . . The sound was band music, and if the tune the instrumentalists tootled forth sounded like 'The Sidewalks of New York' that was because it was that very composition, characteristic of the world's largest city."[29] The appearance of the band playing "Sidewalks of New York" in front of the crowd went off without a hitch. Racing industry journal *Blood-Horse* reported that the horses were "accompanied by an introduction over the public address system and a band played 'Sidewalks of New York.' The concession was a reversal for management which before had run the Belmont as the sixth race of an 8-race card."[30]

James Roach, the racing reporter for the *New York Times* was complimentary. "Belmont used some showmanship in introducing its great race for 3-year-olds. The announcer Jack O'Hara introduced the horses and their riders during the post parade, and Major Francis W. Sutherland's band played 'Sidewalks of New York.'"[31] The new departure was also noted in the coverage of the race in *Sports Illustrated*, which recorded that "during the parade to the post the audience was treated to the 7th Regiment Band's eastern version of 'My Old Kentucky Home,' which for this occasion, turned out to be 'The Sidewalks of New York.'"[32] But it may have been an annoying distraction to at least one especially prominent presence at the track that day, albeit not in the press box: "during the post parade, Needles bolted and had to be pulled along by the head towards the starting gate by an outrider."[33] Not that it stopped Needles, the heavy favorite at 13–20 odds, from winning the race.

And so Joe Palmer had finally prevailed, albeit posthumously, over Belmont's anachronistically stuffy self-image as the band played a "lively, happy tune . . . more identifiable . . . with political hullabaloo than with the hallowed environs

The belatedly adopted and unceremoniously abandoned theme song for the Belmont Stakes. *DeVincent Collection, Lilly Library at Indiana University.*

of stately and ancient Belmont Park."[34] The choice of "The Sidewalks of New York" as the post parade accompaniment was an appropriate tip of the hat to the turn-of-the-century environment within which Belmont Park had opened its doors. The song, written in the 1890s, is suggestive of a simpler and more innocent time when children played street games all around New York City. When the song, without any prearrangement, was played at the 1920 National Democratic Convention when New York governor Al Smith's name was placed in nomination, "the crowd caught the significance of the words as embodying perfectly the Smith nomination and caught the lilt of the music and the demonstration began."[35] "As the band finally dropped into a repetition of 'On the Sidewalks of New York,' milling crowds on the convention floor would not let it stop and the strains were taken up and repeated over and over again."[36] The song became an indelible part of Al Smith's legendary career and became associated with the immigrant's rise from the shanties and tenements to a position of the highest honors.[37] It is a story of urban mobility accompanied by the personal humility garnered from honoring one's roots in the mosaic of New York City. It is *the* New York song.

"Sidewalks" also had one big thing in its favor compared to its rival Triple Crown anthems which, although similarly representative of their homes, highlighted some of their *least* attractive traditions. "The Sidewalks of New York" gives us a London Bridge, Casey's stoop, and the light fantastic. "Sidewalks" offers simple pleasures that the other anthems do not. It is no surprise that numerous artists as diverse as Duke Ellington, Mel Tormé, and the Grateful Dead have covered it.[38] Its lyrics are timeless and beyond reproach. By contrast, although the world is supposed to well up in tears when "My Old Kentucky Home" is played before the Kentucky Derby, the lyrics have had to be repeatedly bowdlerized. In order not to constitute a racial slur, the words "the darkies are gay" were changed to "the people are gay" in the early 1970s. Nor was this a recent example of political correctness. Broadcast networks in the 1950s started taking out the racially offensive language from songs like "My Old Kentucky Home."[39]

The Preakness's "Maryland, My Maryland" may be even more offensive. It was written in 1861 by James R. Randall as a poem in support of Maryland's secession from the Union after the Sixth Massachusetts Regiment fired on secessionist sympathizers who attacked them as they marched through Baltimore.[40] "Randall's poem did not just record what happened; it gave voice to the state's secessionists when it called on them to 'Avenge the patriotic gore / That flecked the streets of Baltimore.'"[41] "The song . . . contains a plea for Maryland, a border state, to secede from the Union and join the Confederacy. In some verses rarely performed these days, President Abraham Lincoln is referred to as 'the despot' and 'the tyrant,' while the Union is called 'Northern scum.'"[42]

However, whatever the virtues of "The Sidewalks of New York," the crusade to vest the Belmont, via a post parade theme song, with the trappings of tradition that the Kentucky Derby and the Preakness commanded was something of a quixotic one from the get-go. For one thing, it was founded on a misreading of history. When Joe Palmer launched the campaign in 1948, the post parade musical "traditions" of the Derby and the Preakness were anything but long-standing. Rather than extending back to those races' nineteenth-century origins, they were most likely no more than about twenty years old themselves at the time Palmer first pressed the case for a Belmont song. The facts are as hazy as a mint julep hangover, but the Derby's official history acknowledges that "tradition is an integral part of the Kentucky Derby and its history. . . . No question about it, the tradition that is most likely to make spectators misty-eyed is the playing of Stephen Foster's song 'My Old Kentucky Home'. . . . No one is certain when this particular tradition started. Some historians say 1921, the 47th running of the classic. . . . Famous scribe Damon Runyon pegged it as 1929; a report in the *Philadelphia Public Ledger* has it in 1930. It is known for sure, though, that since 1936, with only a few exceptions, the song has been performed by the University of Louisville Marching Band."[43]

A historian of the Derby found that "the first published reports of the playing of 'My Old Kentucky Home' at the Kentucky Derby appeared in 1921."[44] According to the *New York Herald Tribune,* the song was not performed that year during the post parade but only after the race as part of the victory celebration for Derby winner Behave Yourself. It was only around 1930 that "My Old Kentucky Home" replaced "The Star Spangled Banner" as "the song to be played as the Derby contestants made their way onto the racetrack."[45] It did not take long, however, before "journalists covering the race were conveying an incorrect assumption that the song had been a part of Derby tradition since the very beginning."[46] By 1939, New York sports columnist Frank Graham could write, "There is something about it that clutches at the emotions as no other race does. Maybe it is the setting. Maybe it is the moment when the horses come out and the band plays 'My Old Kentucky Home.'"[47]

The same fog of memory—and myth—envelops the origins of the playing of "Maryland, My Maryland" at the Preakness. The Preakness media guide gives a date of 1909 as the date when "Maryland, My Maryland" was first heard on Preakness Day, but it may not have been until the late 1920s when it was actually played by a band before the race.[48] Whatever the Belmont lacked in 1948 by way of a theme song compared to the other allegedly more-tradition-endowed legs of the Triple Crown races, it was a fairly recent, not a long-standing, deficit.

But as it turned out it would take more than a song to make the Belmont Stakes a special event on the racing calendar, even perhaps the "brightest jewel in the Triple Crown," and not just "the sixth race." In its coverage of the 1956 race at which "Sidewalks" made its debut as the post parade theme, *Sports Illustrated* acknowledged that "Belmont has retained its atmosphere of grand austerity, and on this traditional afternoon you can sense everywhere an alert and keen awareness of the importance of this championship test" but cautioned that "there is something first to be said about Belmont Day as a national spectacle. It is not at all, you know, like Derby Day in Louisville, and there is absolutely nothing about this great old race track which might confuse even the most absent-minded patron into thinking he was at Pimlico on Preakness Day."[49] Almost a decade later, a *New York Times* headline read "The Belmont? Oh Sure, That's the Seventh Race."[50] "Once again," the *Times* reported, "the oldest, longest and most demanding of the Triple Crown classics—'The test of the Champion'—was to many in the crowd of 58,027 merely the seventh race at Aqueduct. . . . As one handicapper remarked from behind a stubble of beard: 'I don't care who's running. I'm only here for one thing—to make money. I don't even like these stakes races. You can never get a price.'"[51]

Ten years after the New York Racing Association had wrested control of the Belmont from the Westchester Racing Association, and nine years after the debut of "Sidewalks," "the atmosphere was anything but festive," according to the decidedly downbeat report in the *Times*. "For this lack of Belmont enthusiasm, the New York Racing Association has only itself to blame. At the Belmont, the approach is strictly soft sell which is how the N.Y.R.A. wants it. There are no prancing majorettes, no waving banners, no misty eyes as at the Kentucky derby and the Preakness. At the Belmont, nobody cries unless maybe his horse is disqualified. Yesterday, the message that greeted horseplayers entering the track consisted of seven conservative words on a sign the size of a giant postage stamp: 'Welcome to the Belmont Stakes, $125,000 added.'"[52]

Some fifteen years later, in a feature article published before the 1979 renewal with the defensively insistent title "Why the Belmont Is a Great Race," Stan Isaacs, the longtime sports columnist for the Long Island newspaper

*Newsday*, took notice of the backhanded way the Belmont was often reported in the press. Isaacs recalled that "at Riva Ridge's Belmont in 1972 . . . a reporter did a story on people who were leaving Belmont Park *before* the start of the Belmont Stakes."[53] Such negative reporting, Isaacs suggested, reflected an unfairly selective bias against according the Belmont its proper stature: "It is inevitable that in a metropolis like New York, where so many people go to the track for different reasons that some would leave early—and it's not unlikely a loser or two might be found departing Churchill Downs before the derby if somebody bothered to take notice."

And yet Isaacs had to acknowledge—over thirty years after Joe Palmer had sounded the call for more pomp at the Derby, and almost a quarter century after "Sidewalks" had made its way from the back of the track walking ring to the parade to the post—that Belmont officialdom was still struggling to showcase properly the "Test of the Champion." "If the races have made the Belmont of late," Isaacs wrote, "the officials in New York have helped by taking a 20th-Century approach to the event. What people called a dignified reserve in not following the promotional hijinks that helped make the Kentucky Derby, was more of a case of blueblood laziness."[54] According to a racing official quoted by Isaacs, "in the last few years we have tried to market the Belmont and our other races better than before. We have tried to make it an event that New Yorkers would come out to see. We are putting our best foot forward so people will come out for the race and then come back again." But Isaacs had to admit "it may take 10 more Belmonts like the recent ones [in which Secretariat, Seattle Slew, and Affirmed had each captured the race to win the Triple Crown in 1973, 1977, and 1978] to bury the old feeling that the Belmont Stakes is not much more than the eighth race at Belmont on a Saturday afternoon in June."

So why had Joe Palmer's hopes for the Belmont fallen short over the ensuing decades? Perhaps for two reasons, in addition to lackluster promotion. In the quarter century after Palmer wrote his column on the Belmont's need for pomp and Citation won the race to complete the Triple Crown, no horse had been able to match that feat. The Belmont was billed as the "brightest jewel in the Triple Crown," but it was a "jewel" that was going unclaimed year after year and necessarily losing some of its sparkle.

The Belmont as stand-out spectacle may also have been a counterintuitive victim of the tremendous popularity of the sport in New York during the postwar years and into the 1960s. During that golden age for the sport, coverage of the sport dominated the sports pages in the afternoon papers whose successive editions provided updated results for the afternoon's races—and also provided lead stories and banner headlines in the morning "quality" press as well. "There was a time," *New York Times* reporter William Grimes has written, "when names like Man o' War, Citation, Kelso and East Goer were as familiar to New Yorkers as Mickey Mantle or Joe Namath. . . . The top horses were famous athletes, and the culture of the racetrack was familiar to everyone. Fans looked forward not only to the Belmont . . . but also to important handicap races like the Suburban, the Brooklyn and the Jerome." In the late 1940s, even the Communist *Daily Worker* printed the entries and results from New York's tracks, along with the selections of its own (not bad) handicapper, in response to requests from its comrade readers.[55]

Massive crowds, rivaling and indeed often exceeding those coming out for the Belmont Stakes, turned out for other top fixtures on the New York racing calendar (see figure 1). If you look up a key date in New York baseball history—Jackie Robinson's debut at Ebbets Field in 1947, for example—chances are that you will find that more people were at the race track that day, even when no major races were being run, than at the ballpark. "Horse racing, which used to be called the sport of kings," the *New York Times* reported in 1953, "is threatening to become the king of sports."[56] Attendance at the Wood Memorial, the state's premier Kentucky Derby prep race for three-year-olds, and the Suburban Handicap, regularly run on Memorial Day by the Westchester Racing Association (after the Greater New Association took control of racing, it moved the Suburban to July 4), often outpaced that for the Belmont Stakes. Crowds of over 50,000 regularly turned out for those races.

Joe Palmer himself had recognized the outstanding merits of such other highlights of the New York racing season. While bemoaning the Belmont Stakes's status as just the "sixth race" on June 12, 1948, he saluted the Suburban as "the pearl of the handicaps. . . . There's no owner with money enough to stay in the game but would rather have the Suburban Trophy than a handful of richer races."[57] In 1948, in fact, while 48,669 fans passed through the turnstiles for the Belmont, 63,499 showed up for the Suburban. Derby Day at Churchill Downs or Preakness Day at Pimlico had no rival as a gate attraction at those tracks. But the Belmont Stakes did, "Sidewalks" or no "Sidewalks."

And so the "Sidewalks" band played on, into the 1970s, the 1980s, and the 1990s, providing the Belmont Stakes with the signature tune that joined those of the Derby and the Preakness to provide each Triple Crown event with a distinctive musical soundtrack. But all was not well with horse racing in New

**Figure 1: Attendance at Major New York Horse Races, 1946–2016**[58]

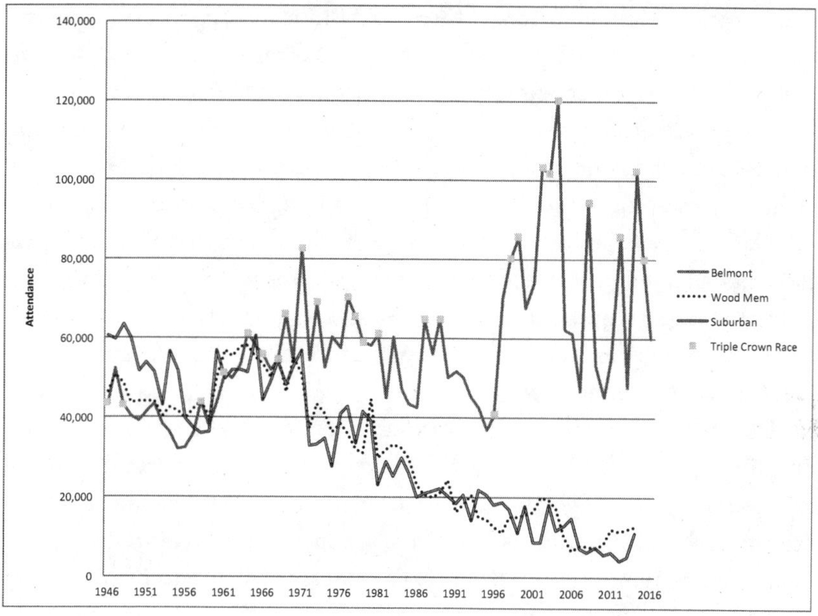

York as those decades unfolded. As William Grimes recently observed, "today most New Yorkers would need footnotes to understand the opening number of 'Guys and Dolls,' with its arcane references to the 'Morning line,' 'the horse likes mud,' 'The Telegraph,' and 'five to nine.' Is there one New Yorker in a hundred who knows what the morning line is?"[59] (It must be added that any presumed failure by contemporary audiences to understand these references has not dented the popularity of this frequently revived show.) In time, "Sidewalks" itself would become collateral damage in a largely futile effort to restore the sport to health.

Some of what afflicted the sport was beyond the control of the racing authorities. The afternoon dailies that had competed with one another to rush papers with the latest racing results (and more importantly to many, the payoffs) to sidewalk kiosks and subway station barkers dwindled to one by the mid-1960s (the *New York Post*), about the time that Joe Palmer's old paper, the *Herald Tribune,* also shut down. The *New York Times,* of course, survived, but by 1982 had stopped printing the daily entries at the track; a few years later it discontinued daily reports of the racing results as well. The generation of sports columnists who wrote frequently about horse racing and its personalities (both equine and human) passed from the scene (Arthur Daley died in 1974, Red Smith in 1982). The 1960s fashion for long hair depleted the ranks of the barbers who once flocked to the track on Mondays, their day off. The decline of itinerant employment on the docks and aboard ships also cut into the potential audience for weekday afternoon horse racing. The growing numbers of professionals and college graduates, who as a group had never been avid track goers, posed a long-term demographic challenge to racing's popularity.[60] Perhaps the rise of feminism made traditional "masculine" pastimes like attending horse races, as well as boxing, seem "out of it." But without doubt the major blow to horse racing as a spectator sport in New York came from within the sport and from the top: the introduction of off-track betting in New York City in 1971.

It's not often that real life provides the opportunity to run a controlled experiment, but the fate of horse racing as a spectator sport thereafter did just that. Since time immemorial, there had been room to debate whether the large crowds flocking to race tracks were there to experience the colorful spectacle of the "sport of kings" or just there for the more mundane purpose of placing (and, on occasion, cashing) a bet at a time when other forms of gambling were unlawful. Were the habitués of the turf dedicated to—as the saying goes, "improving the breed"—or simply looking for some easy and blessedly legal money without working (although it has been said that you have to work like a sandhog to pick out winners from the "past performances" in the *Racing Form*). But the advent of off-track betting left little room for further argument.

In the decades after 1971, live attendance at New York's downstate race tracks collapsed. This was true for day-in, day-out nonstakes races that make up most of the racing programs, but it was also true for headline attractions like the Wood Memorial and the Suburban Handicap, which were once attended by as many, and often more, patrons as the Belmont Stakes itself (see Table 1). A quarter century after the advent of off-track betting, only 12,866 fans showed up at Aqueduct for the running of the Wood in 1996, and 18,166 at Belmont for that year's Suburban. In 2015, the New York Racing Association simply stopped counting daily attendance at Aqueduct and Belmont, a creative solution to the problem of declining turnout. Across the board, the *New York Times* reported in 2010, "despite repeated government efforts to prop it up, horse racing has lost much of its appeal. The racing association says that total attendance at its three tracks [Aqueduct, Belmont, and Saratoga] last year was 1.6 million, about one-third what it was two decades ago."[61] The threat to attendance at New York's

Table 1: Attendance at Major New York Horse Races

| *Year* | *Belmont Stakes* | *Wood Memorial* | *Suburban Handicap* |
|---|---|---|---|
| **1946** | **43,599** | **46,695** | **60,631** |
| 1947 | 52,344 | 50,840 | 59,745 |
| **1948** | **43,046** | **48,711** | **63,499** |
| 1949 | 40,421 | 43,669 | 60,095 |
| 1950 | 39,152 | 44,111 | 51,864 |
| 1951 | 41,253 | 44,230 | 53,824 |
| 1952 | 43,598 | 44,250 | 51,337 |
| 1953 | 38,335 | 40,352 | 43,122 |
| 1954 | 36,482 | 42,670 | 56,736 |
| 1955 | 32,097 | 41,721 | 51,732 |
| 1956 | 32,441 | 39,673 | 39,658 |
| 1957 | 36,094 | 42,122 | 37,474 |
| **1958** | **44,025** | **44,078** | **36,048** |
| 1959 | 38,105 | 40,063 | 36,488 |
| 1960 | 43,338 | 50,055 | 57,141 |
| **1961** | **51,186** | **57,109** | **50,071** |
| 1962 | 50,032 | 55,458 | 52,154 |
| 1963 | 53,281 | 58,064 | 52,136 |
| **1964** | **61,215** | **58,132** | **51,390** |
| 1965 | 58,027 | 55,189 | 60,603 |
| **1966** | **56,011** | **53,764** | **44,425** |
| 1967 | 52,120 | 50,251 | 49,282 |
| **1968** | **54,654** | **55,716** | **54,336** |
| **1969** | **66,115** | **46,709** | **48,288** |
| 1970 | 54,299 | 55,074 | 53,124 |
| **1971** | **82,694** | **51,103** | **56,900** |
| 1972 | 54,635 | 37,451 | 33,071 |
| **1973** | **69,138** | **43,416** | **33,329** |
| 1974 | 52,564 | 41,156 | 34,832 |
| 1975 | 60,321 | 36,379 | 27,957 |
| 1976 | 57,519 | 38,446 | 41,172 |
| **1977** | **70,229** | **36,178** | **42,869** |
| **1978** | **65,417** | **32,056** | **33,697** |
| **1979** | **59,073** | **31,327** | **41,688** |
| 1980 | 58,090 | 44,814 | 39,032 |
| **1981** | **61,106** | **30,020** | **23,149** |
| 1982 | 45,128 | 32,213 | 29,170 |
| 1983 | 60,397 | 33,212 | 25,214 |
| 1984 | 47,369 | 32,410 | 30,020 |
| 1985 | 43,446 | 30,022 | 26,188 |

Attendance at Major New York Horse Races, *continued*

| *Year* | *Belmont Stakes* | *Wood Memorial* | *Suburban Handicap* |
|---|---|---|---|
| 1986 | 42,555 | 23,240 | 20,210 |
| **1987** | **64,772** | **20,856** | **21,145** |
| 1988 | 56,223 | 20,149 | 21,700 |
| **1989** | **64,959** | **21,170** | **22,283** |
| 1990 | 50,123 | 24,468 | 20,358 |
| 1991 | 51,766 | 16,421 | 18,664 |
| 1992 | 50,204 | 18,325 | 20,628 |
| 1993 | 45,037 | 20,743 | 14,434 |
| 1994 | 42,695 | 15,287 | 22,075 |
| 1995 | 37,171 | 14,528 | 20,770 |
| **1996** | **40,797** | **12,866** | **18,166** |
| 1997 | 70,682 | 11,151 | 18,977 |
| **1998** | **80,162** | **15,293** | **17,019** |
| **1999** | **85,818** | **15,104** | **11,364** |
| 2000 | 67,810 | 15,684 | 17,907 |
| 2001 | 73,857 | 16,568 | 8,776 |
| **2002** | **103,222** | **20,103** | **8,611** |
| **2003** | **101,864** | **19,392** | **18,326** |
| **2004** | **120,139** | **17,354** | **11,707** |
| 2005 | 62,274 | 9,944 | 13,184 |
| 2006 | 61,168 | 6,636 | 14,829 |
| 2007 | 46,870 | 7,848 | 7,116 |
| **2008** | **94,476** | **7,698** | **6,184** |
| 2009 | 52,861 | 7,209 | 7,667 |
| 2010 | 45,243 | 8,553 | 5,745 |
| 2011 | 55,779 | 12,144 | 6,441 |
| **2012** | **85,811** | **11,514** | **4,166** |
| 2013 | 47,652 | 12,119 | 5,047 |
| **2014** | **102,199** | **12,719** | **11,184** |
| **2015** | **80,000** | **N/A** | **N/A** |
| **2016** | 60,114 | N/A | N/A |

Bold text denotes a Triple Crown year.

racetracks posed by off-track betting was compounded by a plethora of other gambling options, whether state lotteries or nearby casinos.

Something had to be done—and the fall guy turned out to be "Sidewalks." For the renewal of the Belmont in 1997, racing officials abruptly scratched "Sidewalks" from the post parade after its forty-one-year run and substituted a performance of Kander and Ebb's theme from "New York, New York" by

Broadway and recording star Linda Eder. The switch was made without any official explanation in an apparent attempt to attract younger fans to the track, a perennially coveted, and perennially elusive, target audience.[62] And so while "My Old Kentucky Home" continued to sound at Churchill Downs and "Maryland, My Maryland" at Pimlico, "The Sidewalks of New York" was put out to pasture at the Belmont forty-nine years after Joe Palmer had first argued for it and forty-one years after its debut at the post parade.

The shift reflected an ongoing effort by the New York Racing Association "to give the race the ballyhoo it merited. Just as New Yorkers have sprouted a Big Apple boosterism about Gotham in this time of extremis, the NYRA no longer takes the appeal of the race for granted. It has restored the Belmont Ball. It has been courting the press. It puts on popular musical entertainments on Belmont Day that add to the festive spirit of the day. It is *reaching out*."[63] "In recent years," one commentator observed, "as an attempt to lure in a younger crowd, more contemporary acts have been performing on Belmont Stakes Day. In 2014 it was LL Cool J, which didn't go over very well with the racing crowd."[64] The high quality of the racing itself—what Joe Palmer insisted on as the reason to care about the event—had become extraneous to the "ballyhoo."

Thereafter, "New York, New York" provided the post parade musical accompaniment (frequently by way of a recording of Frank Sinatra's celebrated rendition) until 2010 when it was pushed aside as too old hat in favor of rapper Jay-Z's "Empire State of Mind." According to the marketing director of the New York Racing Association, Jay-Z's song was the "quintessential 21st century theme song for New York City."[65] Fan reaction to that bombastic anthem was negative—the song's performance by Jay Z and Alicia Keys was booed at the track—and the next year Sinatra's recorded voice was brought back to "start spreading the news" at the Belmont post parade. And "New York, New York"—including a live performance by Frank Sinatra Jr. in 2014—has been the Belmont's answer to "My Old Kentucky Home" and "Maryland, My Maryland" ever since.[66]

Many lamented consigning "Sidewalks" to the memory hole after 1997. For a time, campaigners to bring "Sidewalks" back to the post parade could cite "the curse of Mamie O'Rourke" (in honor of Ms. O'Rourke, who tripped "the light fantastic" on New York's sidewalks) as the years passed and bids for the Triple Crown by horse after horse—Silver Charm (1997), Real Quiet (1998), Charismatic (1999), War Emblem (2002), Funny Cide (2003), Smarty Jones (2004), Big Brown (2008), I'll Have Another (2012), and California Chrome

(2014)—were turned back in the Test of the Champion.[67] How could that be a mere coincidence?

But then in 2015, with the Frank Sinatra version of "The Theme from New York, New York" playing over the public address system as the horses paraded to the post, the "curse" was reversed by American Pharoah, who became the first Triple Crown winner since Affirmed in 1978. The "curse" was hardly the best, or even a rational, reason to bring "Sidewalks" back. Its own charming evocation of an earlier New York when Belmont Park itself was built, as well as its reminder of the post–World War II era in which horse racing was at the center of New York's sports world and the song was added to the race's repertoire, were better arguments on the merits. But with the "curse" shattered, the odds that "Sidewalks" will ever return as the Belmont's theme song became even longer than those on American Pharoah's ownership winning a spelling bee.

These days the Belmont Stakes has gone from strength to strength (attendance topped 100,000 when Triple Crowns were at stake in 2002, 2003, 2004, and 2014 before problems of crowd control led to an attendance ceiling of 90,000 for the 2015 race)—"the only race on the New York schedule that most of the city's residents even recognize today"[68]—while the rest of New York's once-celebrated races have lost their box office appeal and slipped out of the consciousness of sports fans. "Part of the city's soul" is "disappearing" as the sport has lost its place "as a vital part of the city's culture and identity," William Grimes has written.[69] It might even be said that the Belmont Stakes today has fulfilled Joe Palmer's ambition that it command the attention of the public as something more notable than just another race on a Saturday racing card. But it has achieved that status less for its own sake as the "test of the Champion" than as the third leg of a potential Triple Crown. As the attendance figures attest, the crowds have been far larger in those years when a horse is vying for a Triple Crown (in recent years, 2002, 2003, 2004, 2008, 2012, 2014, and 2015) compared to those when not (see Table 1).[70] And some of the Belmont's claim on the public has come about by default—there is simply nothing else on the New York racing scene that attracts much notice at all, which is hardly what Joe Palmer had in mind when he launched his campaign to celebrate the Belmont Stakes with a song.

# V

# Sporting Spaces
# Play in the Crowded City

CHAPTER EIGHT

# New York City's First Ballparks

## From the Origins of Paid Admissions to the Emergence of Yankee Stadium

*Robert C. Trumpbour*

New York was an early leader in commercializing sport, and was, arguably, the most influential in prompting professionalism in athletics. Lending credibility to such an assertion, historian Steven Riess confidently argues that New York "has historically been the center of organized sport in America."[1]

In a similar vein, New York served as a national leader in finance and communications, too, factors that intensified the Big Apple's role as a major force in shaping the direction of professional sports in America. The penny press emerged from New York with Benjamin Day's founding of the *New York Sun* in 1833, and the popular press that rose to prominence in the decades that followed did so, in part, as a result of local sports coverage that served to boost newspaper circulation. As technology advanced, sports became immensely popular on the radio and, later, on television, with New York entrenched as the center of the commercial media empires that fed, and continues to feed, a seemingly insatiable consumer demand for sports-related content.

Before such full-blown commercialism could occur, sports, most notably baseball, needed to develop and mature. A key part of that process was the development of a credible and respectable infrastructure. As the nineteenth century unfolded, sports gradually became sufficiently mature to sustain itself as a viable and successful commercial product. In turn, sports was able to rise to a level where notable sports venues could house popular events. That evolution would take time, however.

As the industrial revolution gained momentum, leisure for the masses was not a priority for the captains of industry whose largesse convinced immigrants and native-born citizens to abandon their agrarian roots to work in urban factories. Over time, more structured leisure options did begin to take shape in America's cities, particularly as automation and technology increased leisure time for working citizens. However, the advancement of such leisure options was often a messy and haphazard process.[2]

Evidence of baseball's origins in America came from eighteenth-century Massachusetts, though substantial evidence of the game's European roots might be uncovered elsewhere.[3] The first indications that grown men were attracted to this recreational pastime in the New World emerged in New York City. Despite assertions that baseball's roots took hold in Hoboken, New Jersey, the move to the storied Elysian Fields in 1846 took place at least a year after competitive games unfolded in Manhattan and Brooklyn.[4]

The earliest history of baseball fields is riddled with uncertainties, but historian Michael Benson suggests that the move to a New Jersey location was prompted by real estate development, which in 1846 rendered a ball field near the current site of Madison Square Park unusable.[5] Baseball also expanded to Staten Island and Brooklyn, with a team called the Washington Club playing at the Staten Island Cricket Club in 1853. The team was later renamed the Gotham Club.[6] The decision to organize clubs as part of early baseball's structure likely resulted in some exclusionary practices, whether class based, skill based, or a combination of the two.[7] The Brooklyn-based Atlantics, one of the nation's top teams in baseball's early development, was comprised of dockworkers and day laborers, suggesting that exclusionary patterns, in some instances, may have been unrelated to class.[8]

The conversion of cricket fields to baseball venues occurred elsewhere nationally, and as baseball's popularity rose, top players began to be paid by entrepreneurs who hoped to field winning teams. During the nineteenth century, cricket and baseball coexisted, but, over time, baseball emerged as a more desirable option. Historian George B. Kirsch offers a range of factors that contributed to baseball's emerging popularity. Among the most compelling were the typically shorter duration of baseball competition and the ongoing assertions from the sporting press, though dubious, that baseball was a sport with uniquely American roots. From a practical perspective, Kirsch indicates that one of baseball's key advantages over cricket was that "baseball diamonds did not have to be as well manicured as cricket surfaces, which were supposed to be rolled frequently to keep them level."[9]

The 1869 Cincinnati Red Stockings are universally cited as the first fully professional baseball team and professional football owed its origins to paid players in the Pittsburgh area, but New York led the nation in profound ways regarding the overall development of professional sports, including advancing its commercial underpinnings.[10] In one tangible example, the New York metropolitan area is where the first paid admission for baseball spectators took place.

Since the emergence of commercialism in sport, New York has been a coveted market for sports entrepreneurs, largely because of its strong population base and its role as the nation's most powerful financial center. In 1890, even before Brooklyn was absorbed by New York City, Gotham's total population was 1,515,301, with Brooklyn containing an additional 826,555 residents. As Brooklyn was considering annexation in 1894, it was the nation's fourth-largest city, with New York as the largest by a wide margin. By 1900, with Brooklyn integrated into New York City and an influx of immigrants to the region, the city's total population was a robust 3,437,202, making the market a highly desired prize for numerous sports entrepreneurs.[11]

In 1898, as Brooklyn became part the nation's largest city, the promise of improved transportation, water system, and other infrastructure upgrades provided a set of conditions that enhanced potential profitability for team sports in Brooklyn and elsewhere in the city. With improved travel infrastructure throughout all boroughs, investing in New York City sports became even more appealing, though the firm hand of machine politicians might temper the overarching value of such sports-related investments. Nevertheless, any league that wanted to establish long-term, national-level success set its sights on bringing a strong team to New York.

However, before teams such as the Yankees, Giants, and Dodgers could thrive commercially in Gotham, a system for paid spectator admission needed to be instituted and popularized. The move to paid admission for baseball competition first occurred on the Fashion Race Course on July 20, 1858. This facility was located in what is now Corona, Queens, just slightly west of Flushing where the New York Mets currently play their home games. The race course's grandstand was used to seat some spectators, while the larger venue was closed off, to the degree that was possible, with movable barricades that would let individuals with horse-drawn carriages as well as pedestrians into the area to watch the game from the field level. Those without carriages were able to stand or sit on the periphery of the field, while carriages were parked closely together slightly farther away, allowing much larger crowds to enjoy the game than would have been possible if restricted to available grandstand seating alone. Patrons were charged an admission fee of ten cents, with a fee of twenty cents per horse levied for those riding their carriages into the venue. After expenses were covered, the event yielded a profit of $71.10. That sum was then split and donated to the Fire Department's widows and orphans funds in Brooklyn and Manhattan, respectively, a move which provided compelling evidence that the profit imperative in organized athletics had not taken full root yet.[12]

The contest was an all-star game that featured athletes from various top New York and Brooklyn teams. The New York squad was represented by the Knickerbocker, Gotham, Empire, Eagle, and Union Clubs, while Brooklyn was comprised of players from the Putnam, Excelsior, Atlantic, and Eckford Clubs. Although attendance figures offered for the game vary, with some reporting as many as 10,000 in attendance, the *New York Times* estimated the crowd to be in excess of 8,000, suggesting the highest estimates may have been exaggerated. The New York squad won by a 22 to 18 margin, and after the game, players were invited to the venue's Committee Room where polite toasts were offered and refreshments were served. The *New York Times* stated that "the Base Ball match between the Brooklyn and New York nines will be long remembered with pleasure by all lovers of this noble and invigorating game." The game coverage provided elaborate details of the transit options available to spectators, which included railroad, horse-drawn carriages, and ferries. The Flushing Railroad reportedly added cars to accommodate the anticipated traffic. Despite that, the coaches were still extremely crowded, while ferry trips were densely packed with patrons, too.[13] Although the crowd was described as well behaved, with the presence of numerous women emphasized, perhaps to suggest achieving a civil atmosphere, a large number of pickpockets were in attendance, too. They were reported to be "ready to exercise their peculiar talents upon the people who had assembled there." The local police took immense pride in apprehending and detaining a "notorious English 'knuck,'" whose attempt to rob a respected lawyer was thwarted.[14]

This first game was part of a series that unfolded at the Fashion Race Course, with over 6,000 spectators attending the second game on August 17, with transportation, once again, included as a key part of the coverage. According to the *New York Times,* "Railroad trains and omnibuses and almost every other vehicle which could be pressed into service were loaded with passengers." A sumptuous meal was served for players and dignitaries in the venue's clubhouse following the game, where polite pleasantries were once again exchanged. The 20 to 8 victory for Brooklyn prompted a third game in September that would determine the series victor.[15]

Entrance to Hilltop Park. *Courtesy of the Library of Congress, LC-DIG-ggbain-50292.*

The final game, scheduled on September 10, received enthusiastic newspaper previews. The *New York Times*, for example, indicated "the match no doubt will excite the highest interest, and draw immense crowds of persons to witness it, for whom, as in the previous occasions, every accommodation will be given to allow them to enjoy the exciting contest." Injury reports and other team-based information were offered, too, providing clear evidence of intense fan interest.[16] The final game resulted in a 29 to 18 victory for the New York nine, with the outcome described as a "glorious victory" for New York. For this heavily publicized event, *New York Times* game coverage was moved to the front page. However, the coverage failed to indicate attendance or transit issues, as had occurred in the prior games, focusing most prominently on the game itself. In contrast, the *Brooklyn Daily Eagle* provided a brief game preview, but, perhaps as a result of the Brooklyn's defeat, failed to cover the game's outcome entirely.[17]

As the 1860s approached, the infrastructure for baseball was haphazard and uneven, with games taking place in numerous venues with the most rudimentary of amenities, largely because the profit imperative was yet to be woven into the fabric of organized athletic competition. A desire for increased outdoor physical activity in the 1850s, particularly among an increasing number of indoor-bound, white-collar urban workers also contributed to baseball's rising popularity, with Adelman offering evidence that from 1850 to 1855 more than three out of four ballplayers came from the ranks of white-collar laborers.[18]

In addition, for top-tier teams, the emergence of the penny press, and the potential for the telegraph to transmit information rapidly over long distances, allowed average citizens to follow the most talented local ball club, even when unable to attend games. Yet for those who wished to attend ballgames, mass transit was gradually improving, with rail, ferry, and coach transportation available to those willing to travel to games. In fact, ferry service had become so popular, that at its peak, ferry departures between Manhattan and Brooklyn would unfold in seven-minute intervals.[19] While the typical nickel fare for mass transit might be difficult for most unskilled laborers to afford, for many in the emerging middle class, such an expense was not a problem.[20] The rising popularity of outdoor physical activity among adults, particularly for white-collar workers, contributed to a broad public passion for organized athletics that, over time, made team sports increasingly popular, and, in turn, as top-tier teams attracted more spectators, the growing crowds at their games led to the construction of new and more impressive venues.[21]

In 1862, approximately four years after the Fashion Race Course was used as baseball's first commercial venue, William Cammeyer, a politically connected heir to a leatherwork business, converted a Brooklyn skating rink into the nation's first commercial ballpark. Cammeyer bought land at Marcy and Rutledge Streets in 1861, then opened his skating rink, and took careful charge of its daily operation. His managerial abilities were respected locally. He developed a positive reputation as a result of his success with the skating facility.[22] One article dubbed him the "Skating Pond Barnum," a compliment at the time, while praising his ability to integrate numerous amenities such as a steam-powered calliope, a "refreshment saloon," a cloak room, and comfortable spectator seating for nonskaters. The facility he created was described as "far superior to the one found in Central Park."[23] Nevertheless, a seasonal enterprise had limited money-making potential, so Cammeyer looked for an alternative enterprise for spring and summer months.

The ballpark venture was not entirely supported and controlled by Cammeyer. The conversion was also supervised by an organization initially called the Union Club, later to be renamed the Rutledge Club. This club's president was William J. Pease, an entrepreneur tied to Fulton Iron Works and ship production in Brooklyn, though Cammeyer was the hands-on proprietor of the project. Plans to move forward on the enclosed ballpark were announced in April, with an early indication that the facility could serve as the home to three local teams. According to the *Brooklyn Daily Eagle*, "club houses and accommodations for spectators will be erected," and, instead of each team being charged a rental fee, as was customary elsewhere, "a small fee will be charged for admission" on game days. Nevertheless, Cammeyer and his colleagues made it clear that their construction plans had an exclusionary dimension. The proprietors cautioned potential tenants that they did not want second-tier teams involved, noting "none but first class clubs need apply."[24]

At the time, what is now known as Brooklyn had a mix of agricultural and urban settings, with farms dotting the landscape through 1900, though the extent of rural living diminished with each decade. In 1860, 96 percent of Kings County's 279,112 residents lived in the city of Brooklyn, with the remaining inhabiting agricultural outposts outside of what was then Brooklyn. These sparsely inhabited farmlands often maintained a Dutch character, while providing food products to Brooklyn and Manhattan residents. The surrounding towns of varying names were subsequently absorbed by Brooklyn, whose population was more mixed in overall ethnicity.[25] As such, it was not automatic that Brooklyn would serve as a pioneer in baseball facility construction, though its subsequent growth, proximity to Manhattan, and deep passion for baseball made it an ideal testing ground for the transition to for-profit athletic competition.

The Union Grounds were first unveiled on May 15, 1862, in a game between "McKenstry's side" and "Manolt's side," with approximately 3,000 spectators on hand. The teams were comprised of players from the Putnam, Eckford, and Constellation Clubs, the three teams who called the Union Grounds home in the ballpark's inaugural year. Manolt's side won the contest by a 17 to 15 score. The game coverage offered indications that the admission fee, set at ten cents, as well as the enclosure of the grounds, would "provide a suitable place for ball playing, where ladies can witness the game without being annoyed by the indecorous behavior of some of the rowdies who attend the first-class matches." If the focus on decorum was not sufficiently emphasized, later, the *Brooklyn Daily Eagle* asserted "indecorous proceedings will cause the offenders to be instantly expelled from the grounds." As was common for the time, the game festivities began at 3:00 p.m., though, with technology unavailable for night competition, some games would begin slightly earlier or slightly later. This inaugural event opened with the playing of the "Star Spangled Banner," likely the first time the now-common ritual unfolded at a ballpark, and music was offered at various intervals as the game commenced. A large clubhouse was erected to serve the three teams that would be the venue's primary tenants, while the infrastructure for the skating facility was repurposed to serve baseball fans. The opening was clearly determined to be important to the baseball community, as "there were representatives [in attendance] from almost every club in the city, besides several from New York."[26]

Eventually Cammeyer was coaxed into sharing some of the gate revenue with teams. In addition, this enclosed ballpark included seating, gradually conditioning fans to willingly watch the game while in seating areas. In a precursor to the Polo Grounds design configuration, Benson described the Union Grounds as having "a horseshoe-shaped, single-decked grandstand, [that was] roofed behind the plate." Prior to the construction of this fully enclosed ballpark, men would typically stand along the field's periphery and outfield, with available seating reserved for female spectators.[27] Fans continued to stand on field-level in the years that followed with coaches occasionally on the periphery as well, yet, over time, seating options became increasingly popular and spectators were less frequently segregated by gender.

The Union Grounds, located in Brooklyn's Williamsburg section, prompted a conceptual shift that, over time, inspired future ballpark construction and, subsequently, the introduction of significantly more substantial commerce within the ballpark itself. In an 1867 championship-clinching game attended by more than 10,000 fans, reported to be a record for the time, "Lewis, the famous chowder-maker" received prominent mention in the *Brooklyn Daily Eagle* for "an immense business in his line." The Brooklyn Atlantics 28 to 16 victory over the Philadelphia Athletics was the most emphasized information in the story, but the fact that a specific vendor was identified and highlighted in a reporter's coverage suggests an emerging consumer dimension in baseball culture not unlike today's highly specialized ballpark food vendors.[28]

Additionally, Cammeyer was among the first to recognize that satisfying the press was more likely to ensure profitability, as he established a media area that made newspaper writers comfortable. In coverage of a July 12, 1867, game, a reporter confidently asserted, "the Union Grounds is the best place in Brooklyn where members of the press are sure of having any decent accommodations. Here, Mr. Cammeyer has erected a large and comfortable desk, with seats attached, covered over with an awning to protect those seated there from the sun."[29] Marketing and press relations were clearly emphasized by Cammeyer in Union Grounds management.

Brooklyn fans were extraordinarily passionate about baseball, with many feeling that their community provided the best-quality baseball in the nation. However, many Brooklyn fans were intimidating to visiting fans, including nearby Manhattan residents. Baseball historian Dan Stout asserts that as baseball evolved, many Manhattan visitors made the trip to Brooklyn, but may have done so with "trepidation" because "Brooklyn's feisty partisans soon earned a reputation as the most rabid and unruly in the country."[30]

The shift to paid admission fostered conditions in which professional athletics could grow, but before professionalism could fully flourish, the infrastructure of sport needed to mature in a number of significant ways. Although New York was an acknowledged leader in bringing commerce to sport, its role as a leader in sports-related construction was often challenged, and in numerous instances superseded, by other locales. Still, Gotham frequently served as a benchmark for other cities, and, early on, one could see that in several instances New York was looked upon as a reference point for others to follow.

As an example, emulating Cammeyer's model, in 1867, the Cincinnati Red Stockings constructed their own ballpark, also called the Union Grounds. It became the first venue in Cincinnati to charge admission for baseball games and likely inspired the Queen City to pursue a fully professional model for its baseball team. The main seating area of this Ohio venue, which included some covered areas that shaded patrons, was sufficiently substantial to earn the nickname "the Grand Dutchess." In 1870, on the heels of an undefeated 1869 season, the Cincinnati Red Stockings, a fully professional team with an 81-game streak of undefeated play, disbanded after losing to the Brooklyn Atlantics, with several of the star players, most notably Harry Wright, heading to Boston to establish a team that became known as the Red Sox.[31]

Though Cincinnati continued its baseball tradition, with meatpackers George and Josiah Keck establishing another team after 1870, its role as a leader in professionalizing baseball had waned. Cities with bigger populations and greater commercial opportunities stepped ahead of Cincinnati, despite its early leadership in establishing a professional model in sports.

New York, as a vast population center, fielded several well-known and highly talented baseball teams, many with paid athletes. The Atlantics, the Brooklyn-based team that defeated Cincinnati in 1870, was a leader in this regard. To ensure commercial viability of these teams, ballparks needed to be constructed and maintained. As with other cities, swaths of land that may have been used for other leisure activities were converted to baseball fields. In several major cities, including New York, cricket fields were used for baseball. In Gotham, similar patterns unfolded, while land previously used for polo became a popular baseball facility in Manhattan. During the late 1870s, top-quality baseball was played in Brooklyn at the Union Grounds and at the Capitoline Grounds.

The Brooklyn Bridge was not completed until 1883, so any ballpark trips away from Manhattan, whether in New Jersey, Brooklyn, or Staten Island, typically unfolded after somewhat inconvenient ferry excursions. That situation would change with the conversion of Manhattan's Polo Grounds to baseball use in 1880. The Polo Grounds was initially used by James Gordon Bennett Jr. and his wealthy friends for polo matches, but the son of the *New York Herald Tribune*'s founder was coaxed into letting baseball games take place on the idyllic Manhattan real estate located between 110th and 112th Streets.

The first game unfolded on September 29, 1880, between the New York Metropolitans and the Washington Nationals, two independent teams, but the site remained a venue for polo long after that first contest. Author Noel Hynd indicates that Metropolitans owner John B. Day, a youthful tobacco entrepreneur, grew tired of traveling to Brooklyn and elsewhere with his team. At the recommendation of a bootblack who was perplexed that Day's team, the Metropolitans, did not play in Manhattan, Day was convinced to approach Bennett to use his facility for baseball competition. Prior to the contact, Day was unaware of the Manhattan property that is currently located just north of New York's Central Park.[32]

The facility was just two blocks from a Harlem Railroad stop and horse carriages could travel through Central Park to bring some patrons to the site. As such, this new location became highly attractive for Manhattan's baseball fans. Day bought another team, the Gothams, later to be renamed the Giants, and the two teams shared the location from 1883 onward, with polo matches subsequently moving to the Bronx by 1892. The Polo Grounds name remained, with two baseball fields being constructed that were separated by nothing more than a simple canvas barrier.

The southeast field featured an impressive two-tiered grandstand with a capacity that could accommodate 15,000 fans. However, as with earlier ballparks, those attendance numbers included patrons who might stand deep in the outfield or along the periphery of the field, so the venue would have been less impressive than a typical minor league park today. The stands were shaded with a combination of a wooden structure and striped canvas awnings. In addition, the venue was decorated with patriotic bunting. The field that the Metropolitans more frequently called their home was built over garbage that was hastily used as landfill. Not surprisingly, the odors emanating from that field made the southwest park immensely less attractive to fans. The less desirable and more pungent field prompted pitcher Jack Lynch to mockingly assert that in this ballpark "a player may go down for a grounder and come up with six months of malaria."[33]

Needless to say, by 1885, after second-tier treatment by Day, the Metropolitans were sold to Erasmus Wiman, who chose to move his team to Staten Island where a two-tiered facility on the St. George Cricket Grounds was constructed with design flourishes that included six spires that were nicknamed "witches caps." Because of these features, the venue looked more like an ancient theater than a conventional ballpark. It seated 5,000 patrons and could be used for nonsports events, too. It was part of an amusement park that was owned by Wiman. Some sections of the seating overlooked New York Harbor, allowing fans a panoramic view of Manhattan as well as the Statue of Liberty as it was being constructed in 1886. Wiman was chief proprietor of the Staten Island Ferry, so his amusement park venture was based on a business model that was intended to directly benefit from luring Manhattan traffic to his ferry line. With a Manhattan ballpark as a viable option and bridge transportation to Brooklyn made more convenient as a result of the Brooklyn Bridge's unveiling, recreational trips to Staten Island became less appealing. As a result, Wiman's baseball team ceased to exist after the 1887 season.[34]

From a commercial standpoint, Day did well with the team he chose not to sell, the Giants, but once he gained full control over the Polo Grounds property, he had to generously bribe local alderman with game tickets to prevent them from cutting a road through his ballpark, as was proposed several times. In an era when politicians were frequently motivated by graft, Day's inability to placate Tammany Hall's political insiders cost him dearly in 1889. Some leaders were irritated that Day did not offer them enough complimentary game tickets in the year prior. In response, they made good on plans to construct a road directly through the ballpark land, a move which would connect 111th Street on the east and west sides of Manhattan. Day attempted to undo those plans in February 1889 with an offer to "donate" $10,000 to city charities, as specified by those who were angered, but several politicians were intent on demonstrating their political muscle, so his efforts were in vain. The Giants were forced to vacate the venue as heavy equipment for road construction was moved in abruptly to eliminate the ballpark.[35]

Although a facility named the Polo Grounds would be later moved further north and rebuilt several times, a suitable Manhattan site was not ready as the 1889 season approached. The Giants had no choice but to move, so they chose the Staten Island ballpark built by Wiman as their temporary home. Although impossible to know at the time, the Staten Island location was a less-than-ideal choice. Eastern rainfall was sufficiently heavy that Johnstown, Pennsylvania's tragic and infamous flood occurred in May, while, approximately 300 miles east, New York got its share of heavy rains, too. The field, located in low-lying property in Staten Island's St. George neighborhood, was inundated with rain so often that wooden planks were placed in the rain-soaked outfield to allow for improved traction when fielding balls. The Staten Island relocation was not a success by any measure, and an attendance drop-off clearly challenged the team's bottom line. To limit the damage, Day tried to move some games to Jersey City, but until he was able to move the team closer to his Manhattan fan base, the Giants would continue to struggle at the gate.[36]

Knowing the perils of inconvenience for game-day revenue, Day worked hard to establish a ballpark in Manhattan. He found an area that was largely farmland in one of the northernmost corners of Manhattan, and he set out to build a ballpark there. Unlike other parts of New York's most populous borough, upper Manhattan had swaths of land that remained unused. The property Day isolated was located on undeveloped land near 155th Street, just feet away from the Eighth Avenue elevated station, making rail transportation reasonably convenient for his Manhattan fans. As a bonus, the venue was near a Macombs Dam Bridge construction project that would connect Manhattan and the Bronx, offering Day's team convenient access to fans from that borough, too. Day hoped the team's return to Manhattan would improve his bottom line.

He called the facility "the New Polo Grounds," even though the site would never be used for polo matches. Ballpark construction was a far cry from the carefully planned process that would emerge in the twentieth century. Construction started on June 21 and the facility was ready to open on July 8. In time, the Polo Grounds would evolve into the most influential open-air sports facility in New York City and perhaps the nation, but one more move would unfold before the Giants would settle at its final Coogan's Bluff location. The New Polo Grounds was a pear-shaped facility with a steep incline in the outfield. It had seating for about 5,000 patrons, but by placing fans on the field's periphery and in the outfield, as occurred frequently during that era, the venue could accommodate as many as 15,000 patrons and often did.[37]

The National League Giants were a top-tier team, and at the conclusion of the 1889 season, advanced to the playoffs to face the American Association's Brooklyn Bridegrooms, a team that was also known as the Superbas, and also the Trolley Dodgers. With several on the team getting married late in the season, to appease the players, the "Bridegrooms" name was applied until the more popular Dodgers moniker became permanent. The Bridegrooms were playing their last season in the American Association before shifting to the National League, yet the New York versus Brooklyn rivalry was palpable. In an opening game preview, the *New York Times* called the rivalry "unparalleled in the history of the game." The Brooklyn team tried to delay and stonewall when they held leads, forcing games to end early because of darkness. After losing one series game under such circumstances, Giants manager Jim Mutrie complained that "such methods are disgusting and do not tend to elevate the national pastime." Despite these underhanded tactics, the Giants ended the season with a championship after beating Brooklyn in five out of nine games.[38]

Team names and ballparks were in an odd flux during this era. Some team names carried tradition forward, but others were malleable and could be rapidly changed based on owner, team, fan, or media preference. New leagues were also being proposed and tried, with failure involved at times. Clearly, the institutions that shaped competitive sports were not fully established. In a similar way, ballparks were often hastily constructed with very little thought going into developing a permanent structure. Such an attitude may have been the result of the same political vagaries that caused the Giants to be forcibly moved from their original Polo Grounds site by agitated and greedy politicians. Asking players to assist in construction or ballpark operations was not unheard of, either, though as the twentieth century approached, construction methods began to move in a more professional and permanent direction.[39]

After the 1889 season championship over Brooklyn, Giants fans reacted with euphoria. However, as soon as the season concluded, a rival league was being formed that threatened the team's future. As the National League attempted to implement a salary cap, popular players broke away to form the Brotherhood of Professional Base Ball Players. The rival player-inspired league would undermine the National League and baseball's overall commercial viability, but Day was popular with the players, so they invited him to join their enterprise.[40] Out of loyalty to the National League, Day declined. The Players' League, as it was popularly called, would be a thorn in the side of the Giants, draining Day's roster of the most popular players and causing him dramatic financial woes.

To intensify the war between the leagues, the Players' League financial backers Edward McAlpin and Edward Talcott chose to locate the New York team's home field right next to the site that Day selected for his team. The new ballpark, called Brotherhood Park, consistently outdrew the Giants, and with team defections, the former championship team, a shell of its previous capabilities, struggled to attract fans.[41] Fans flocked to see the most popular players, most of whom were on a Players' League team, also called the Giants, in a ballpark that was similar in look and design to the ballpark constructed by Day a mere one year earlier. To further confuse matters, the games often started at the same time, and both teams raised championship pennants while each featured similar live music.[42]

Following the 1890 season, the two leagues brokered a peace agreement that led to the dissolution of the Players' League. However, the drain on attendance did considerable damage to popular Giants owner John B. Day, who was pushed to the brink of financial ruin. After selling off numerous assets to keep his team afloat, he was forced to relinquish control of the team. The new group of owners moved the National League's Giants into Brotherhood Park, and shortly thereafter began to make improvements to the newer ballpark.[43] The location was slightly north of Day's ballpark, on Coogan's Bluff.

The facility's grandstands were torn down and the renovated ballpark took on its famous horseshoe shape. New paint and new sod were also added as the 1891 season opener approached.[44] Not surprisingly, it was renamed the Polo Grounds and was New York City's most popular baseball destination for more than three decades. Despite subsequent renovations and rebuilding, the Coogan's Bluff site remained the permanent home of the Giants until they moved to California after the 1957 season.

The Giants were not the only team to shift into a former Players' League park in 1891. In Brooklyn, George Chauncey, the principal stockholder of their Players' League team, agreed to take over the Bridegrooms, but insisted that the team move from Washington Park to Eastern Park, formerly home to the Players' League team. Eastern Park featured greater capacity, accommodating up to 12,000 fans.[45] It also featured cool ocean breezes and a double-decked grandstand with several imperial cone-shaped spires. The ambiance prompted *Brooklyn Eagle* columnist Albert Osterland to assert that the ballpark was a major factor in "making Brooklyn a major baseball city." Despite its idyllic charm, Eastern Park's location, on Brooklyn's southeastern edge, was more difficult to access than the older ballpark. Ballpark scholar Michael Benson asserted that "it was considered a hardship for the majority of fans to reach," an issue that led to subsequent attendance declines.[46]

The Bridegrooms shift to the National League in time for the 1890 season was fortunate because the American Association, considerably weakened by brief Players' League and ongoing National League competition, folded after 1891, leaving the National League with a monopoly on Major League quality play until Ban Johnson established the American League a decade later.

Charles Ebbets took over as president of the Bridegrooms in 1898, though at the time he was a minority owner. He had served as team secretary the prior two years, and before that did everything from ticket taking, to laundry, to janitorial duty.[47] Although he was not principal owner yet, one of his first moves was to shift the team back to Brooklyn's inner core, close to where the original Washington Park was located. Not surprisingly, the new ballpark was also named Washington Park. Ebbets dedicated $60,000 to its construction, but instead of having the team pay the full cost, he cleverly arranged to share the costs with two streetcar lines, who were presumably excited at the prospect of increased ridership on game days.[48]

The numerous streetcars had Brooklyn's team informally renamed the "Trolley Dodgers," which was later shortened to Dodgers, but before that, reporters assigned the name Superbas to the team in 1899. The odd name unfolded in 1899, when a popular vaudeville play entitled "Hanlon's Superbas" gained extensive publicity as Ned Hanlon was being introduced as the new manager of the Brooklyn team. After co-owner Charles Byrne passed away in 1898, Baltimore beer entrepreneur Harry Von der Horst invested in the Brooklyn club, transferring Baltimore Orioles manager Hanlon to Brooklyn, sensing far greater profits could be earned with a strong team in Gotham. As the 1899 season approached Von der Horst owned 40 percent of the team, Byrne's partner, Ferdinand Abell, owned 40 percent, while Hanlon and Ebbets each owned 10 percent. In addition to shifting Hanlon to Brooklyn, Von der Horst cleverly orchestrated lopsided trades that brought Brooklyn most of the Orioles best players. The move made Brooklyn a first-rate team, creating enthusiasm that boosted ballpark attendance from a disappointing 1898 season.[49]

Washington Park had what Benson described as "a small and tasteful front entrance, which was always done up with bunting for opening day." The inner-city location created a haphazard, eclectic environment in which some onlookers watched the games from nearby building rooftops. The frivolity was fueled by profiteering local pubs. The owners gladly encouraged employees to fill buckets of beer for rooftop onlookers, even providing rope for hoisting the libations upward via the fire escape platforms. However, opposing outfielders faced the possibility of being hit with projectiles launched from rooftop locations, too.[50]

When Brooklyn had a championship-caliber team, as they did in 1899 and 1900, enthusiasm and attendance held up, despite the unpaid onlookers. However, competition from Ban Johnson's fledgling American League, eventually in the form of the New York Highlanders, and Hanlon's enigmatic personality caused some of Brooklyn's players to jump to rival teams. Hanlon could be a difficult taskmaster, so despite being a creative and well-respected on-field tactician, the Superbas faced defections and became a losing team as a result.[51] Management tired of the out-of-control, freeloading rooftop fans, too, while ballpark attendance dwindled. As other owners soured on the investment and liquidated their team shares, Charles Ebbets continued to buy up stock, eventually emerging as the Brooklyn's principal owner.

By 1908 Ebbets had control of the team, and he invested $22,000 in enlarging and improving Washington Park while quietly and without fanfare trying to acquire land to build a new and more lavish ballpark elsewhere. Box seats were installed in Washington Park to give more comfortable seating to select spectators, while Ebbets installed "dugouts" for the players, lowering the location where the players would sit in order to give an unobstructed view to as many spectators as possible. With the renovation, the owner squeezed so many new seats into the ballpark that box seats were located a mere fifteen feet away from home plate.[52] As a result, players rarely caught foul balls, though the strategy allowed Ebbets to increase gate revenue, something he would later need to acquire property to build a new ballpark.

While the Brooklyn squad settled into Washington Park, a new team, initially to be called the Highlanders, settled into a wooden structure named Hilltop Park. The team was part of the new American League, a professional league formed by Ban Johnson to challenge the Major League Baseball monopoly then held by the National League. Two years after its initial formation in 1901, Johnson was finally ready to install a team in the nation's largest city, despite being thwarted in a variety of ways. Before the 1903 season, he orchestrated a shift of players from a Baltimore franchise to New York, predictably in search of higher profits. Nevertheless, establishing a foothold in the nation's largest city was an even more important goal if the new league was to succeed. Unlike the more established National League, the new league aggressively clamped down on foul language and disruptive behavior, something that helped solidify its reputation among fans as more family friendly than the National League.[53]

New York Giants owner Andrew Freedman, a Tammany Hall insider with a vindictive demeanor, kept Johnson's league out of Gotham with a variety of actions, but Freedman sold his National League team to John Brush late in 1902. However, the sale did not end Johnson's problems. In a game of real estate chess, before liquidating his team, Freedman had bought or leased land in places throughout Manhattan, making it difficult for anyone to build a venue anywhere that could compete with the Giants. Despite stepping away from the Giants, Freedman was still involved with real estate and city politics. He had a mean streak that made him a force with which to reckon, and his distaste for Ban Johnson was evident.[54]

As a result, to make the new American League franchise a success in New York, Johnson needed ownership with political insight and abundant connections. He found some of those qualities in Frank Farrell a saloonkeeper, stable owner, and gambling house proprietor, and Bill Devery, a former New York police official with a reputation for successful real estate speculation. The two bought the Baltimore Americans, and without hesitation, shifted the team to New York. With the Giants entrenched in Manhattan, the new owners needed a venue of their own, and they promptly worked to isolate land to build a new ballpark.

Despite making a strong case to build on a 142nd Street site that would have convenient access to a subway line, then under construction, the proposal was blocked when it reached the desk of the Interborough Rapid Transit (IRT) Company's director, despite lining up influential political support elsewhere. The IRT director was Andrew Freedman.[55] They were pushed farther north to an area that was less developed, with much less convenient public transit access. The single line serving the site required a fifty-minute commute from city hall, a disadvantage that was not alleviated until a new line was completed in 1906, then cutting travel time in half.[56]

To counter Freedman's ongoing political ire, Ban Johnson astutely lined up Tammany Hall insider Joseph Gordon to partner with Farrell and Devery in a move that would ensure that the deal eventually went through. Gordon became the front man for the team's management while Farrell and Devery stayed in the background.[57]

The land for what was to become Hilltop Park was located on 165th Street and Broadway and was leased from the New York Institute for the Blind for $10,000 per year. The terrain was rocky, full of weeds, uneven, and very difficult to develop, but it was, nonetheless, available to lease and develop a mere two months before the 1903 season was set to start. Community activists, expressing concern that construction might bring unsavory saloons and unwanted visitors, unsuccessfully petitioned to stop the construction, with some residents continuing their hostility even after construction was complete.[58] Baseball was marketed by team owners as a wholesome form of entertainment, but this community opposition to ballpark construction, which appeared to be independent of Freedman's influence, suggested less ideal real-world outcomes.

Despite initial community opposition and Freedman's efforts to sabotage its construction, the land soon became the site of Hilltop Park.[59] The team invested $75,000 to construct the single-decked, wooden structure, but $200,000 was poured into excavation costs alone, with dynamite and hard labor from Irish, Italian, and Polish workers required to make the field sufficiently level for competition.[60]

Though it was described as "half-finished" when it was first unveiled on April 30, 1903, the new ballpark still attracted 16,243 spectators for its home opener. "The Greater New York Club of the American League," as they were described in the *New York Times* coverage, showcased a 6–2 victory over Washington on that day. According to reporters, even with partial construction, "the occupants . . . seemed perfectly happy with the seating arrangements." The quality of the infield was praised, but the outfield was described as "rough and uneven" with a section of right field "that has yet to be filled in."[61] To ensure that the initial game was memorable, Ban Johnson had arranged for each fan to receive an American flag upon entrance, while introducing the Sixty-Ninth Regiment Band to play the "Star Spangled Banner" before that was established as a baseball tradition.[62]

This ballpark, though a clear second in stature to the famed Polo Grounds, was one of the largest ballparks of its time. With Gordon serving as the front man for management, the team was popularly known as the "Highlanders," in part, because Gordon's Highlanders was the name of a well-known British army regiment. The ballpark's location on Manhattan's high ground may have been a secondary rationale for retaining the Highlander name. Despite Freedman's ongoing attempts to sabotage the team as well as various predictions that their first season would "prove to be a financial disaster," Gordon reported a modest profit as the first season concluded.[63]

Still, Hilltop Park was described as a "flimsy edifice" on land "that never lost its slum like appearance" and was not regarded as a good ballpark.[64] Nevertheless, it attracted large crowds and served to establish the American League in the nation's financial capital and its most populous metropolitan area. Although the Giants had long hoped that the Highlanders would become a financial failure, they remained a New York City fixture, eventually to be renamed the Yankees.

The Polo Grounds was considered New York's premium sports venue, and its commercial underpinnings made it a national leader in how sports was marketed elsewhere. In the 1890s, the Seeley and Rappelyea Café offered patrons fine wines, liquors, and cigars.[65] Later in that decade, Harry M. Stevens, a New York–based vending entrepreneur, established the sale of scorecards and hot dogs in the Polo Grounds. Although Stevens began his entrepreneurial career in Ohio, his career took off after moving to New York, where his scorecard concept offered opportunities for both advertising and sales revenues. Later his son Frank convinced him to offer German sausages on a fresh bun. The product was hawked by vendors as "a red-hot dachshund sausage on a roll." In 1905 the product was renamed the "hot-dog," a term coined by Hearst cartoonist Thomas Dorgan. With the popularity of the scorecard, the hot dog, and other ballpark products, Stevens's concession business was expanded to venues throughout the nation, with concessionaire contracts in place throughout most of the twentieth century.

Stevens's concession operation increased its profits after John McGraw took over as manager of the Giants in 1902. The team's success at the Polo Grounds from 1903 onward improved attendance significantly, with National League pennants earned in 1904, 1905, and 1911. However, on April 14, 1911, fire decimated the Polo Grounds, forcing the team to temporarily play in Hilltop Park while the charred debris was removed and extensive renovation and rebuilding took place. Although no one was ever able to confirm the cause of the blaze, the *New York Tribune* speculated that a cigarette might have ignited peanut shells following an April 13 game.[66] Less rational theories blamed American League president Ban Johnson, Cubs manager Frank Chance, and a Bolshevik plot.[67]

Giants manager John McGraw was one of the first to be contacted after the fire erupted, as he was in a nearby pool hall that he owned when reports came in shortly after midnight. Not understanding the severity of the incident,

McGraw believed that the charred debris could be quickly removed and play could continue without incident later that same day. The team quickly made arrangements to play at Hilltop Park instead. Although the fire was severe, in coverage of the Giants next game, a *New York Times* reporter quipped "maybe it is a good thing that the fire at the Polo Grounds burned up the Giants' bats" since the team was not hitting well at the time.[68] That coverage and McGraw's initial response suggested the limited significance and value attributed to a team's ballpark during the era.

As the twentieth century unfolded, a venue could be erected in a few short months with limited and haphazard planning. However, that dynamic was shifting as rickety wooden ballparks were being phased out. Safety, with the popularity of tobacco products raising fire liability concerns, and a quest for greater profits drove a desire to fund such construction. Fire had decimated other ballparks, with at least five fires unfolding in 1894 alone. A fire took place in Washington Park when the Bridegrooms were on the road, but others in Baltimore, Boston, Chicago, and Philadelphia that year suggested that alternatives to wooden ballparks needed to be sought.[69] At least a half-dozen fires in urban ballparks between 1900 and 1911 intensified safety concerns. By the early twentieth century, city officials had less tolerance for archaic wooden fire traps. In response, numerous baseball teams planned to construct elaborate concrete and steel ballparks, a trend that began with the unveiling of Philadelphia's Shibe Park and Pittsburgh's Forbes Field in 1909.[70] A year later Charles Comiskey opened a grand edifice in Chicago, with a fire at the White Sox venue in 1909 as a possible motivating factor for its construction.

Political pressure mounted to build more fireproof venues. For example, perhaps in response to Comiskey's recent ballpark fire, Chicago building codes were revised to enhance ballpark safety in 1910.[71] After the Polo Grounds fire a year later, Gotham officials increasingly pressured team owners to begin building facilities that would not endanger fans. Specifically, New York's Board of Coroners argued that fireproof materials needed to be used in future ballpark construction, bluntly stating "we, the Coroners say the public must be protected."[72] In response, Giants owner John Brush made plans to use concrete and steel in the Polo Grounds renovations, but he hoped to do much more than that.

Historian Stew Thornley explained that the Giants owner, despite struggling with severe health issues at the time, "had ambitions for a stadium that would surpass all others in terms of size, structure and design."[73] The project moved forward at a brisk pace, and although the venue was not fully completed, it was opened and unveiled to fans on June 28, less than two and a half months after its initial destruction. Construction continued during the season, with workmen on site during off days and road trips. The still haphazard nature of construction timetables provided clear evidence that sports infrastructure was evolving, yet not fully developed.

Before the fire, the Polo Grounds could serve 30,000 patrons, the highest capacity of any major sports facility at that time with the exception of Harvard Stadium, which upon completion in 1903 was the first fully concrete and steel outdoor sports venue to be built in North America. Polo Grounds capacity was just 16,000 when it initially reopened, but by season's end it could seat 34,000 spectators. It was New York's first concrete and steel ballpark.

*Baseball Magazine's* John Foster described the new venue's "majestic beauty," asserting that it contained "everything . . . that can be found in a first-class theatre," while Allan Sangree, also writing for *Baseball Magazine,* called it "the mightiest temple ever erected to the goddess of sport and the crowning achievement among notable structures devoted to baseball."[74] The new facility featured luxurious touches including boxed seating areas that were described as similar to "the royal boxes of the Coliseum in Rome," intricate friezes, and artistic shields of all eight National League teams that were displayed above the upper deck.[75] Instead of settling for stock, manufactured seating, a decorative "NY" was custom designed into the outside of seats to add an extra feel of luxury. Modern amenities such as telephones were added, too.

Despite the posh upgrades, historian Glenn Stout indicated that passionate Giants fans made the new environment "easily the most intimidating place to play in the major leagues," asserting that those in attendance responded to Giants manager John McGraw's aggressive and pugnacious on-field tactics "like a lynch mob."[76] The Giants were a good enough team to play in the World Series in 1911, 1912, and 1913, but lost to the American League champion in each of those three seasons.

As the National League champion Giants received accolades for their new ballpark and solid on-field performances, their crosstown rivals, formally known as the Brooklyn Baseball Club, struggled to stay out of last place. Still, Charles Ebbets was able to consolidate his ownership of a team that was now interchangeably called the Superbas and the Trolley Dodgers, though in 1914, as Wilbert Robinson took over as manager, the "Robins" moniker would add an additional level of confusion.

While gaining team control, Ebbets worked diligently to acquire the land necessary to build a new ballpark for his team. It took him four years to acquire all the necessary property to build the new ballpark. To do so, he needed to keep his purchases secret since the use of eminent domain for private projects such as a ballpark was not an option in early twentieth-century America, and leaked news of Ebbets's intentions would cause land prices to skyrocket as purchases moved forward.

Ebbets was aided by Barney York, a political and personal friend. York solicited New York realtor H. C. Pyle to acquire the necessary parcels, though George Gray and Charles Brown, Pyle's assigned agents, did not know they were working for Ebbets, nor did Pyle. After paying almost $200,000 to get all the necessary land under contract, one detail eluded Ebbets. The final plot, an insignificant 20-by-50-foot parcel, was among the most difficult to acquire. Agents tried to track down the absentee owner, first looking in Europe, then in California, eventually finding him in Montclair, New Jersey. Although the small piece of land was estimated to be worth a mere $100, once the owner sensed he was dealing with a desperate buyer, Ebbets was forced to pay a premium, reportedly $2,000, though some historic accounts list $500 as the final agreed-upon price.[77]

Ebbets managed to keep such a tight lid on real estate acquisition that not one New York journalist was even close to guessing where the new ballpark would be built.[78] Yet to move construction ahead, Ebbets had to make considerable financial commitments, forcing him to sell a sizable share of his team ownership to move forward. Edward and Stephen McKeever, local contractors with strong political connections, bought half the team, while Ebbets kept the remaining half.[79] Nevertheless, the McKeever brothers were happy to allow Ebbets to remain in control of the team's day-to-day operations. By the time construction was complete, $750,000 had been dedicated to the project, approximately $18.5 million today.

The ballpark offered a number of unique and luxurious flourishes. Among the most memorable was a marble-floored rotunda with ornate marble accents along the walls. A large, custom-made chandelier that, instead of displaying crystal and glass, featured baseball-shaped lighting that was suspended from chains connected to a circular cluster of baseball bats. From the exterior, arched windows adorned the first and third levels, with a series of rectangular windows in between. The words Ebbets Field were boldly emblazoned at the top of the structure's main entryway, with a welcoming awning greeting fans below.

Dodgers historian William McNeil asserted that in 1913 it was "the most modern and the most beautiful stadium in the country."[80]

Yet the facility was not without its issues. On opening day, one deficiency became embarrassingly apparent; a press box was not in the original plans, forcing sportswriters to use the first few rows of the upper deck until a formal press area was installed in the 1920s. Although the area around the ballpark was somewhat undeveloped when the ballpark was built, nine different trolley lines and subway service made Ebbets Field easily accessible to 90 percent of Brooklyn residents, while it was a reasonably convenient trip for visitors from Manhattan. A vibrant neighborhood developed around the ballpark in subsequent years. As was the case with Washington Park, seating was extremely close to the field, allowing fans to see the action as well as the players' facial expressions, but also subjecting opposing players to taunts as well as projectiles that might be tossed by the most rabid patrons.[81]

The Highlanders were the last New York team to play in an all-wooden ballpark, but in 1913, they moved out of Hilltop Park and into the Polo Grounds, paying rent to the rival Giants. Giants manager John McGraw never liked the American League franchise, and his animosity intensified as the team, now named the Yankees, welcomed Babe Ruth and began to feature teams that consistently performed well on the field. McGraw's Giants beat the Yankees in the 1921 and 1922 World Series, and as the 1922 season began, the American League rivals were told it would be the last season in which they could play their home games inside the Polo Grounds. Their rental agreement with the Giants would not be renewed.

At the time, McGraw and his Giants appeared to be on top of the world, with a level of popularity that no other manager or team could match. McGraw believed that if the Yankees could not find a home in Manhattan, the team would struggle and might, over time, be forced to cease operations. However, McGraw did not count on Yankees owner Jacob Rupert building a grand edifice in the Bronx, one that would be close enough to overlook his Polo Grounds. The Yankees owner, who plied his trade as a brewer, had affluence, but building a massive and opulent ballpark when Prohibition was in full force seemed unlikely. Yet Ruppert pushed forward with construction, nonetheless.

The unveiling of Yankee Stadium in 1923 contributed to dramatic changes in the sports power structure. McGraw lost to the Yankees in the 1923 World Series and, in doing so, lost two games inside a shiny new ballpark that he had to detest as much as he disliked the rival team. Not only did he face those defeats within eyeshot of the less-lavish Polo Grounds, but the Yankees outdrew the Giants during the World Series, with substantially higher attendance at every game in Yankee Stadium than at any game played within the Polo Grounds. After 1922, the same year that the Giants decided to force the Yankees out of their Manhattan venue, McGraw never won another World Series crown.

In contrast, the Yankees won numerous championships after earning their first-ever World Series victory in 1923, fittingly over McGraw's Giants. Beyond that, the impressive venue in the Bronx attracted prominent dignitaries and average citizens alike, bringing with it substantial revenues that gave the Yankees the ability to lure, attract, and retain high-profile stars such as Babe Ruth, Lou Gehrig, and Joe DiMaggio, just three in a long line of nationally recognized sports luminaries who plied their trade in Yankee Stadium.

The emergence and establishment of the New York Yankees as a top-tier team that played in a top-tier venue prompted changes in New York City fan preferences. Their ongoing success challenged the hegemony of the Giants, while it diminished the stature of the Dodgers. A first-class stadium in the Bronx was one key variable, among many, in the shifting power of sports teams in New York City. Furthermore, Yankee Stadium's construction prompted the production of numerous books and articles, making it one of the most analyzed and researched sports structures ever built.

Eventually, both the Giants and the Dodgers left Gotham for lucrative deals in California after completion of the 1957 season. By 1962, an expansion team, the New York Mets, began to play in the Polo Grounds, before 1964 when the team moved into a shiny new facility in Flushing, Queens, not far from the location where the Fashion Race Course once stood. Before the Dodgers and Giants left Gotham, ballparks like the Union Grounds, Washington Park, Hilltop Park, the Polo Grounds, and Ebbets Field were the center of the sports world to those individuals who were part of New York City's vast population during the late nineteenth and early twentieth centuries. These old ballparks, though forgotten by many, contributed much to the foundation and evolution of New York sports history.

CHAPTER NINE

# Municipal Golf in New York City since the 1960s

## Courses for All Social Classes

*George B. Kirsch*

New York City was the birthplace of municipal golf, and the advent of public courses was the most critical factor in the democratization of golf. This essay will begin with a review of the first sixty-five years of the history of golf in the United States and the city's public links, and then present a more detailed description and analysis of the subject over the past six and a half decades. In 1960 Gotham had thirteen links. Four were in the Bronx (Van Cortlandt, Mosholu, Split Rock, and Pelham). Four were in Queens (Clearview, Douglaston, Kissena, and Forest Park). Two were in Brooklyn (Marine Park and Dyker Beach). Three were in Staten Island (Silver Lake, LaTourette, and South Shore).[1]

The movement to build golf courses open to all the citizens grew out of the crusade to construct public parks in American cities, which began with the planning and opening of Central Park in New York in the 1850s. After the Civil War, officials in Boston, Philadelphia, Chicago, and numerous other metropolises followed New York's example and dedicated space for parks. Initially upper- and middle-class reformers persuaded government leaders to support and develop parks, but by the late 1800s representatives for workers and immigrants were clamoring for facilities that would also serve the needs of the poor. Those who first lobbied for public parks believed that they would improve the urban landscape and metropolitan society, which was fragmented and plagued with social problems; would alleviate class conflict by bringing residents from different social strata together; and bring badly needed open space and a rural environment to urban residents. Acting as the "lungs of the city," they would bring innumerable health benefits to congested disease-ridden communities, and elevate public morality by providing the urban masses with the opportunity to participate in wholesome recreational activities in a setting more conducive to virtue than the saloons, brothels, theaters, and other centers of vice downtown. Finally, they wished to protect precious public land for the benefit of future generations, stimulate the local economy, boost real estate values, and raise the prestige of their town by building a first-class park for its people.[2]

During the late 1800s and early 1900s upscale reformers, public officials (especially park commissioners), and advocates for the interests of workers, immigrants, and other groups (including golfers) debated three main issues: the location of the first municipal parks; the classes that would benefit the most from their construction; and activities that park officials deemed appropriate for these new municipal facilities. These topics raised issues of fairness of access when private golf associations requested privileges to use public parks. During the early 1900s many commissioners were still enforcing the restrictions implemented by Frederick Law Olmsted for Central Park and widely copied after the Civil War. Olmsted had decreed that public parks were suitable only for quiet, "receptive" recreation, not "exertive" active amusements. His park designs featured pedestrian paths and carriage roads where visitors could view beautiful landscapes and scenic vistas. He frowned upon active sports in parks, limiting ball play to children. "Keep off the grass" signs sprouted on lawns that were provided for observation and perhaps for picnics but were off limits for baseball, cricket, or other athletic pastimes.

The pioneers of early American golf had to persuade park commissioners and managers that some of their precious real estate should be reserved for courses. Thomas Bendelow was a Scottish immigrant and early designer and promoter of public golf links who encountered initial resistance to his cause. He recalled that some commissioners opposed the use of parks for golf, "believing that golfers had no right there whatever, that golf was a rich man's game." He explained: "the keep-off-the-grass signs forever barred them from utilizing the great open spaces in public parks for recreation and should a poor man with his family come into a park and the children attempt to play ball, the brave defender of park rule, if true to his oath of office, would have to stop them." He knew that the first requirement for municipal golf was to persuade the officials that it was acceptable to play on the lawns. Once they conceded that point, he and others would convince the more liberal commissioners that all classes would benefit from golf courses built on public land. Prior to World War I daily newspapers and golfing periodicals actively supported their construction.[3]

Bendelow also pioneered golf landscape architecture for public purposes. He believed that they should "secure the greatest good for the greatest number." Accordingly, they should not include "water hazards of the lagoon type," because they "impeded play and caused congestion." That in turn led to conflicts among the players that were unfamiliar with golf etiquette. By the same logic he reasoned that "the fewer short holes there are in a public course the better, and they ought not to be of such a hazardous nature as to cause congestion." He also thought that to spread out the golfers, municipal golf courses should be at least 6,500 yards long, built on "slightly undulating" ground, with few trees or shrubbery. Finally, to accommodate the maximum number of players he argued that the first hole should be at least 440 yards and the ninth hole should be at the greatest distance from the starting point and not near the clubhouse.[4]

New York City built the first public golf course of nine holes at Van Cortlandt Park in the Bronx, and its founding and early history illustrate many issues that public officials would grapple with in creating other municipal links that opened in the United States prior to World War I. The first was the question of private use of public land, for the original impetus for the creation of the Van Cortlandt grounds came from a group of affluent residents of suburban Riverdale in the northwest Bronx. They had searched the surrounding region in vain for a suitable site available at a modest rental fee, and then as a last resort petitioned New York City parks commissioner James Roosevelt to include golf in his plans for developing Van Cortlandt Park. Roosevelt also favored the idea of public links in general "if they will make the new parks known to the public and bring crowds to them on holidays," but he denied their request to have a private club play on public land. The petitioners then organized themselves into the Mosholu Golf Club and played two or three afternoons a week on the Van Cortlandt links until the crowds forced them to relocate. In 1896 the superintendent of New York City's parks announced that the use of the course by private clubs would be regulated and that "No club is going to have a monopoly of the Van Cortlandt Park links for any special day or days." An exception was made for an amateur public golf tournament sponsored by the St. Andrews Golf Club in late November 1896.[5]

Roosevelt wasted no time in getting the nine-hole course ready for at least rough play during the late summer of 1895, at a cost of about $624.80. The nine-hole layout featured a par five 700-yard "monster" finishing hole. Golfers,

Van Cortlandt Park Golf Course, Bronx, New York. "Second Round Match Play for the Herald Cup." *Courtesy of USGA Archives.*

hitting gutta percha balls (which covered much less distance than the modern ones) had to clear two stone walls and a brook before reaching the green. (The wall and brook are long gone but the course still has the longest hole in New York City—602 yards.)[6]

The city's policy of free admission no doubt partly explains its popularity, to the point where the *New York Times* suggested that the park commission should institute a modest fee which "might happily serve to keep away all the pestilential dubbers who block the limits and chop the turf with borrowed clubs."[7] Play was open to all who obtained $1.00 permits at Central Park. The Van Cortlandt facility was an immediate success, attracting large crowds of golfers on holidays and Saturdays, despite the price gouging by caddies, poor greens, and chaotic, even dangerous, playing conditions. Although there was no greens fee, at first caddies charged the highest price they could get. A new rule entitled them to twenty-five cents for carrying a bag for nine holes—as compared to fifteen cents at private clubs. Players who took the train from Manhattan to Van Cortlandt Park in the Bronx encountered a "small army of yelling, howling caddies," and "many a scrap ensued between the rival caddies as to who should secure the opportunity of chasing the ball over the links."[8] In 1899 a new regulation forced the caddies to wear badges and to go out on the course in order. But the new rules apparently did little good, for in 1900 the *New York Times* reported: "those urchins roam unrestricted, intent upon fleecing every strange golfer, out of as much money as can be extorted, while cases have occurred where balls were purposely not found that have been driven into high grass or into a woody section. An unemployed confederate keeps his eye on the spot, however, and when the player has passed from sight the ball is picked up, and perhaps sold for a dime to the very man who lost it."[9] The presence of so many women on Saturday afternoons prompted complaints from more proficient players. City officials designated Thursday afternoons as "Ladies days," but did not ban women on weekends.[10]

Although golf clubs could be very expensive for members of country clubs, for those who patronized municipal courses the cost could be less than twenty dollars, with golf balls going for between fifty and sixty cents each.[11] A major part of golf's appeal was the opportunity to take a long walk of several hours duration throughout a scenic piece of countryside. William Garrot Brown viewed the game as one method of returning to nature, a "means of awakening a sense of the beauty of wild flowers, and many another delicate loveliness in nature." He believed that golf "permits and induces moods scarcely conceivable in other athletic competitions," adding that "it permits one to be contemplative." For him, it was the ideal pastime for businessmen, for "serenity and tranquillity are in truth the very moods which Americans of the classes who play golf need."[12]

Three hundred members of the New York Athletic Club, who had a summer facility at Travers Island, requested that New York City build a new municipal course at nearby Pelham Bay Park. Construction problems delayed its opening until the spring of 1901, and the course initially was in very rough condition. During the early 1900s New York City's golfers could also play at a course in Forest Hills, Queens, and in the spring of 1914 construction began on the Mosholu links in the Bronx, which added eighteen more holes to Van Cortlandt Park.[13] In 1922 New York City's public golfers founded the Municipal Golf Association, which was designed to serve the same function for public golf as the Metropolitan Golf Association did for the private country clubs. Its officers administered tournaments and pressed the city officials to invest greens fees into course improvements rather than deposit them into a general city sinking fund.[14]

The interest of German Jews dates from the late 1890s and early 1900s. Excluded from the leading upper-class clubs, they founded their own in the suburbs of New York City. Among the first were the Century Club, founded in 1898 in the Throgs Neck section of the Bronx; the Inwood Club, founded in

1901 in Inwood, New York; the Progress Club of Purchase, New York (1925); and the Metropolis Country Club (1922) of White Plains, New York. New York State had twenty Jewish country clubs—the most in the nation. White Christian country clubs barred Jews and set fees limiting their membership by social class and financial status, and Jewish clubs followed their example. They restricted their membership to American Jews of German descent. Their goals were clear: to distance themselves from waves of East European Jewish immigrants who lived and worked in urban ghettoes. According to Peter Levine: "If wealthy German Jews eager for assimilation and acceptance found in the country club movement an opportunity to distinguish themselves from 'de trop' Jews, they also hoped it would ease their admission into an elite Protestant culture familiar for its utility for social distancing and social acceptance."[15] According to an editorial in the *American Hebrew*: "The participation of wealthy German Jews in elite sport would demonstrate that they were no different than their gentile counterparts, either as Americans or as elites, thus doing away with any logical reason for their exclusion."[16] Women were also active in Jewish country clubs. Levine noted: "The wives and daughters of wealthy Jews took up games and sport denied most American women by sexual and class distinctions . . . More than any other sport in which these women engaged, golf was clearly their favorite."[17]

The earliest evidence of African Americans playing golf was cited in 1915 by E. L. Renip, golf editor of the *Chicago Defender*, when he described an outstanding round of golf played by Laurie Ayton at a course at Evanston. In 1921, a sportswriter for the *Chicago Defender* reported: "George Aaron and Arthur Gibbs of the New York Colored Golf Club have finished a successful season at the Van Cortlandt links."[18] In 1926, Dr. J. R. Anderson was one of the founders of New York City's St. Nicholas Golf Club. Four years later, Charles Thoroughgood and his wife, Laura, with a few other players created the New Amsterdam Golf Club.[19]

During the Great Depression of the 1930s golf lovers who refused to be deterred by the hard times flocked to public courses. But as the economy worsened between 1932 and 1936, patronage at municipal grounds fell 25 percent nationwide and as much as 40 percent in some cities. New York City's experience proved an exception to the downward trend. In 1934 Gotham's eight public courses recorded a total of 370,580 rounds, with over 500,000 projected for 1935. By the late 1930s the number on ten public links had swelled to over 600,000. In June of 1935, A. B. Britton, writing for the *New York Times*, divided Gotham's public golfers into three categories. The first included "the old timers—the doctors, dentists, small businessmen, brokers and merchants, who have been playing a particular course for years." The second were "recent graduates from the ranks of caddies," who "play a pretty sound game, affect a careless disorder of dress and seem frequently to make a point of going around with as few clubs as possible, perhaps in studied contrast to less spectacular elders." The third group constituted the novices, both men and women, whose ranks included many bookkeepers and secretaries. Their play featured "wild swings and flying divots"; some had "only the haziest conception of the difference between a golf club and say, a hockey stick."[20]

New York City was a prime beneficiary of government funds invested in the expansion and improvement of its ten public courses. In 1934 *Golf Illustrated* printed a brief editorial on "The Disgrace of Gotham's Public Courses,"[21] but three months later it praised the work of Robert Moses as the city's new parks commissioner and John R. Van Kleek as supervisor of golf course renovations. Although the federal government's aid to municipal golf courses began in 1932 at the end of Herbert Hoover's presidency, the major boost to public golf came from Franklin D. Roosevelt's New Deal. The Civil Works Administration (CWA, 1933) and the Works Progress Administration (WPA, 1935) financed the building or improvement of six hundred courses nationwide. In the spring of 1936 the famous golfer Bob Jones visited several New York City facilities and singled out the new Split Rock course for special commendation.[22] In 1936 the *New York Times* affirmed: "When the economic recession has receded it will not be quite the same America that rises above the waves. Among other things, it will be studded with golf courses." Citing the new highways, bridges, dams, and land reclamation, it reported: "There will be golf links to play on [in] a nation in the mood to play."[23]

After World War II, in the New York City metropolitan area the supply of golf courses fell far short of the demand. In 1953 *Golf Digest* estimated that within sixty miles of Times Square about 350,000 active golfers (out of a total population of 14 million) had access to about fifty public courses and two hundred private clubs. Real estate developers had bought out most of the semiprivate daily fee courses in suburban counties, with the exception of New Jersey. In New York patronage of the ten municipal courses rebounded strongly after World War II, during which the total number of rounds per year declined about 25 percent to 445,000 in 1944. In 1948 the figure reached 685,423, despite an increase in permit fees from five to ten dollars plus a nominal greens fee of twenty-five cents per round on weekdays and fifty cents on holidays and weekends. About 3,500 of Gotham's municipal employees were avid golfers during these years, including large contingents from the police, fire, sanitation, and other departments. Thanks in part to assistance provided by the Metropolitan Golf Association, the New York City Police Golf Association was especially active, sponsoring monthly tournaments and competing against teams representing organizations from neighboring states.[24]

As city governments struggled to balance the budgets of municipal golf courses and justify keeping them open and in good condition in times of fiscal distress, they faced another challenge. This one came not from angry taxpayers who were not golfers, but rather from militant environmentalists who charged that munys wasted precious water, poured dangerous pesticides into the ground, and threatened endangered species. City officials countered by claiming that the courses provided all of the people with precious wildlife preserves in an age of urban sprawl. Many were sensitive to environmental concerns, and worked toward the "greening" of their grounds by conserving water, staking preservation areas adjacent to several holes, and requiring all golfers to stay on cart paths to keep them off of breeding grounds of endangered species.

In December 1948, bird lovers from the Audubon Society, biology teachers and students, representatives from the American Museum of Natural History, and other nature groups opposed a proposal by New York City's park department to redesign the Van Cortlandt Park Golf Course in the Bronx. They objected to filling in thirty-two acres of a swamp at the northern end of Van Cortlandt Lake as the only freshwater wildlife sanctuary in New York City. The park department plan, prompted by the construction of the Major Deegan Expressway, relocated the final four holes over the landfill. On December 10, Arthur S. Hodgkiss, executive officer of the park department, announced that it would fill in only seven acres of the marshland for two holes. The naturalists were not satisfied with that ruling, arguing that those seven acres constituted the only part of the swamp suitable for nature study and observation of birds and other wildlife. They demanded that Robert Moses, New York City park commissioner, halt the trucks that had been dumping landfill into the marsh. Mrs. C. N. Edge, chair of the Emergency Conservation Committee, stated: "There will still be a golf course in Van Cortlandt Park... but in our democracy our children must come first." John Kieran, author and amateur naturalist, wrote: "Here we have within sight of the subway and within reach of millions of people of moderate means, a wonderful wild-life refuge, an outdoor museum that has been a valuable adjunct to our city school programs in science . . . As a city possession for cultural and educational purposes the Van Cortlandt swamp is unique and priceless."[25]

During the 1950s, golf celebrated its second golden age. President Dwight D. Eisenhower's obsession with the sport was one of several factors that contributed to its growing popularity. (The others were the prosperity of the period that generated a rising standard of living for blue- and white-collar workers, new rounds of suburbanization and the extension of resort communities, the promotion of golf by media celebrities, the advent of golf carts, popular heroes, and the rise of television.) On October 15, 1958, Eisenhower named golf as his favorite recreation. (The other two were fishing and bird shooting.) According to the *New York Times,* he stated: "First, they take you into the fields. There is mild exercise—kind that an older individual should have." A few hours later President Eisenhower was on the Burning Tree Club golf course. He said that his chief motivation as a golfer was that it took him away from the cares of office and official routine.[26] On June 28, 1960, he advised the winner of a national youth leadership contest, eighteen-year-old Stephen K. Smith, to take up golf as a way of remaining healthy. "He told me 'I had better get into athletics, and said it would keep me healthy. And he suggested that golf would be a good game.'"[27]

In April 1963, Barry Gottehrer, writing for *Golf* magazine, quoted Lou Strong, president of the PGA: "It's not difficult to understand why golf is doing so well on television . . . Golf has always been a great game, but television showed that golfers were a lot more interesting than just names in the newspapers. That's how TV has helped golf. But golf has helped TV by providing the drama and the personalities. Today, Arnold Palmer is as much of a TV hero as any baseball or football star. There are thousands of people who've never had a club in their hands who'll be watching TV this year just to see if Palmer can keep coming from behind."[28]

In June 1963, Paul Gardner, writing for *Golf Digest,* remarked: "No audience is more alert to view shortcomings and strong points of golfers who watch the game on television."[29] He continued: "Suggestions and criticism notwithstanding, there is little doubt that golf on television has broadened the game's general popularity. Ten years ago, there appeared to be little future in presenting a game, which is played over about 150 acres, on a 21-inch screen. Miracles of technical improvement, principally in the mobility of cameras, have given golf its boost via the cathode tube."[30] Gardner concluded his essay by quoting Walter Schwimmer: "It is important to concentrate on the technical mastery of a small number of holes, rather than try to cover too much of the course . . . The producer of a live show, especially, has to have the same judgment as an artillery officer, in that he must station his best 'guns' to saturate a limited amount of territory."[31]

In 1963 New York City opened two new municipal golf courses—Douglaston Park in Queens and Marine Park in Brooklyn. Gotham's golfers had waited impatiently twenty-eight years since the creation of Dyker Beach Golf Course. The Douglaston facility was formerly the private North Hills Golf Club. Robert Moses explained that private clubs were moving out of New York City because of its growth and taxation. He stated: "You simply have to ride the parkways to reach the divots. It's the middle-income man's game now, and pretty soon the municipal courses will shrink from a full eighteen holes to pitch-or-putt or ride out to Suffolk." He was correct on the democratization of the sport but dead wrong on the future prospects of municipal golf in New York City.[32] When the course opened in late April of 1963, the first to tee off was Julius Goroff, a truck driver from Flushing, Queens. He claimed the honor by arriving at 3:20 a.m. His foursome included Sheldon Wecker (a Queens College sophomore), Tony Litterrelo (assistant clerk in New York City's criminal court) and Jack Kunkle (a lithographer).[33]

The Marine Park layout was literally built on garbage—land reclaimed from the New York Harbor and filled with waste. While Brooklyn's golfers complained that the course should have been completed much earlier, city officials responded that it took thirty years to collect the garbage, which saved the city millions of dollars of land costs. Like Dyker Beach, Marine Park is close to the ocean. Although traffic jams on the Belt Parkway and screaming jets taking off and landing at Floyd Bennett Naval Station detracted from the golfers' fun, they were glad to have an alternative to Dyker Beach.[34]

Playing conditions on the most crowded public courses worsened during the late 1950s and early 1960s. Steven Schlossman, professor of history at Carnegie Mellon University, recalls that when he was twelve he lived in a garden apartment in Douglaston, Queens, a few blocks from the Clearview Golf Course. With a few borrowed clubs he snuck onto the course during the winter when it was not crowded. As he improved his game he found that Clearview was packed during the summer, with eight-hour waits to tee off on holidays. He and his close friend, Robert Weintraub, would go to the course as early as 3:00 a.m. to sign up for a starting time, return home to sleep and go back at daybreak. Eighteen-hole rounds sometimes took up to six and a half hours. At

Clearview the tees lacked grass, and the ground was so hard that he needed a hammer to place his tee. In the spring the fairways were fine and there was not much rough. The sand traps were not raked and the greens were slow. Clearview had food and bathrooms only at the clubhouse.[35] Schlossman recalled that there were a few black players at Clearview, and a few more at Split Rock in the Bronx. Weintraub remembered no black golfers at Clearview but stated that there are more now.[36]

While public golf remained in a relatively healthy state in the greater metropolitan New York City region during the late 1970s, the situation was far bleaker (and even sometimes frightening) within the five boroughs. More than 130 public golf facilities served suburban residents of northern New Jersey, adjacent New York State counties, and southwestern Connecticut. City dwellers had to contend with deteriorating conditions on thirteen municipal courses. Perhaps the only good news was that waiting times to tee off decreased as patronage plummeted from 756,000 patrons in 1970–1971 to 476,000 in 1977–1978. Part of this decline was no doubt due to a mass exodus of golfers to suburban enclaves, but a good deal of it was a result of poor maintenance caused by slashed spending due to New York City's bankruptcy and mismanagement. In 1981 *Golf Digest* called the four-hour wait on weekends on New York City links "a thing of the past." It described grim, poorly maintained clubhouses; flagsticks constructed out of broomsticks, bamboo poles, and tree branches; listless employees; and broken-down, useless machinery. The following year, the *New York Times* reported that when a golfer on the par three 140-yard fifth hole at Douglaston, Queens, struck his tee shot, "his eyes are cast on a forbidden, dried-out gully replete with carcasses of shopping carts, automobile tires and other golf course anachronisms that makes his heart yearn for the tranquility of a water trap." "Just as frightening, if not frustrating," the reporter continued, "is the putting surface of the green which sometimes looks like the German Luftwaffe recently passed for a post-war retaliatory strafing . . . Putting on a city golf course becomes a three-step process: putting, praying, and profanity." Other disturbing sights included "stalled, broken-down and beat-up golf carts haphazardly left abandoned in the middle of fairways, green pins that are skinny branches adorned with a handkerchief, water fountains that sprout genuine New York rust, green-to-tee walk paths that could be utilized for training grounds for jungle guerillas . . . strewn rubble."[37]

Other accounts of conditions on New York City's public golf links highlight youths building campfires and drinking beer at night, stealing flagsticks and bunker rakes. Thieves stole and stripped automobiles and abandoned them in sand traps. Patrons littered fairways with trash; rats and graffiti were everywhere.[38] Even scarier stories described armed robberies, golf cart thefts, and the occasional dead body left on the grounds. In his July 2013 posting on Golfdigest.com, David Owen interviewed Lou Carducci, tour director of the Shore View Golf Club, based at Brooklyn's Dyker Beach Golf Course. Carducci recalled that decades earlier as he arrived at the course on a June morning he learned that the police had closed the grounds because "somebody took two in the back on the 14th green." Carducci persuaded the detective to cordon off only the thirteenth and fourteenth holes so that eighty or ninety golfers could compete in the scheduled Father's Day event.[39]

Facing inflation, soaring labor costs, and increasing budget deficits, during the 1980s New York City, Philadelphia, Los Angeles County, and many other large communities chose the strategy of "privatization," contracting out the operation of golf courses to management corporations. Faced with losses running about $2 million a year, in 1983 New York City leased six of its thirteen grounds to the American Golf Corporation and sublet three others to two former golf professionals. In 1986 the chief of the Revenue Division of New York City's Department of Parks and Recreation claimed that the city was "netting between $50,000 and $75,000 on the leased American Golf Courses, against a former loss of about $200,000 a course. That year the National Golf Foundation counted about 150 courses that were privately managed, with only a modest increase in players' fees. American Golf, Kemper Sports Management, Pope Golf, Morton Golf, Trump Golf, and other companies reduced costs by hiring nonunion workers, employing experts to supervise several facilities instead of just one, and utilizing more efficient purchasing and decision-making procedures. But some writers criticized the trend toward privatization. Golf club professionals who lost pro shop revenue and labor officials who lost jobs were upset with the shift toward management companies. In several cities officials thought that their operations could do just as well financially without leasing their courses. The city of Los Angeles rejected the leasing option favored by Los Angeles County and instead concentrated on better hiring and management procedures. Yet over the next decade the nationwide trend was clearly in favor of outsourcing golf management. In 1995 a survey of 120 communities found that between 1987 and 1995 the percentage of local governments that contracted out management of their golf courses grew from 16 to 24 percent. That year the American Golf Corporation alone operated more than 163 public and 37 resort and country club courses in twenty-two states and England.[40]

During the final decades of the twentieth century, municipal and semi-private courses continued to be the primary venues for the democratization of American golf, whether they were operated by public officials, individual owners, or corporations. In the largest cities, there were frequently long waits at the first tee and crowded fairways. There and elsewhere on suburban and rural grounds a wide diversity of social classes and ethnic groups gathered to enjoy a pastime first popularized by Scottish and English immigrants. As they hacked their way across the courses men, women, and children shared a camaraderie that was a primary benefit of belonging to the golfing community of the nation.

New York City was the birthplace of public golf in the United States, and from the 1960s through the 1990s, before and after privatization, its courses sustained its time-honored tradition of attracting enthusiasts from a startling array of classes and communities. In 1966 *Golf Digest* featured Brooklyn's Dyker Beach Golf Course, where visitors encountered "Priests, ministers and rabbis . . . police officers of every calibre [sic], nurses and school teachers, bankers, judges, doctors, truck and taxi drivers, sailors and ships' officers from remote Oriental seas, United Nations attendants of every description, actors, actresses, and ballet dancers."[41] In June Larry Sheehan of *Golf Digest* reported lengthy waiting times on weekdays and weekends. Golfers killed time napping (and snoring) on benches, chatting idly about "firemen's pensions, the price of coffee, and Medicare." Others played chess on the clubhouse flagstone terrace, putted on the bumpy practice green, or socialized in the dingy snack bar. A few made better use of the time between sign-up and tee-off by leaving the course to do errands, or to attend church services if the day is Sunday.[42] For nearly a half-century, Greg Midland, writing for the *New York Times,* reported that Dyker Beach remained popular among Gotham's golfers. They took the R subway train and carried their clubs four blocks along 86th Street in Brooklyn, lured by its new clubhouse and greatly improved grounds. Midland described the "morning scene" at Dyker Beach as "uplifting," with "the dew-covered fairways, chirping birds and lively cross section of humanity." He added: "Then you realize that the sun has barely risen, there are already dozens of people waiting to be called to the tee, and it's taking about 40 minutes to play the first two holes."[43]

Driving ranges also contributed to the democratization of golf. Chelsea Piers, built on formerly dilapidated Hudson River docks, opened in 1995 with athletic facilities that included fifty-two heated and covered stalls on four levels.

According to Douglas Martin, reporting for the *New York Times*: "you stick a card in a slot. Immediately, the little plastic in front of you disappears into the ground. A second later, it emerges with a ball on top. You don't even have to bend over to tee up."[44]

During the 1960s golfers who could not afford to join country clubs or buy expensive equipment had the option of playing on municipal or daily-fee courses. The National Golf Foundation estimated that a round on public courses cost between $1 and $5. According to William Barry Furlong, reporting for the *New York Times*: "The beginner can seek bargains in bags and clubs; one enterprising pro in Peoria, Ill, sells a 'beginner's set'—seven club and an inexpensive canvas bag—for $39.95."[45]

Gambling and "hustling" remained common on both private and public courses. According to Furlong, "The special attraction of golf for gamblers is that it is one of the few enterprises of modern man in which he can bet on his own physical achievement. In football, baseball, and horse racing he must bet on other men or animals; in golf he can bet on himself—and his own delusions of grandeur."[46] "Hustling" also was endemic on all courses—especially in a "Calcutta," in which competitors in a tournament are "auctioned off" to members of a club. The money went into a pool and those "owning" the golfers who finish high in the tournament are paid out of the pool. Members were likely to bet more for the more-accomplished golfers, and to bid low for the lesser-known players. The return on the investment is much greater if an unknown competitor—acquired at a low "bid"—wins the tournament. According to Furlong, "a few cunning men made a living out of 'fixing' Calcuttas. Exceptional good golfers, playing under phony names and phony records, were entered in tournaments, usually local affairs that attracted good bidding but not much newspaper attention. The 'fix' was arranged so that a few club members in on the deal would acquire the unknown 'phenoms' at a low price in the Calcutta, then split the take all around when the unknown suddenly beat everybody."[47]

In 1995 the *New York Times* reported a resurgence of play at the nation's first municipal course, Van Cortlandt Park in the north Bronx, which celebrated its centennial that year. Its patrons included Koreans, Hispanics, and African Americans. That paper described its tournaments as "frequent and maniacal," explaining that "outings sponsored by nearby Irish bars are outdone only by the police and firefighters get-togethers, which sometimes degenerate into games of bumper carts." Retired bankers, transit workers, newspaper deliverymen, and countless others packed the grounds despite the highways that cut through the course and the occasional discovery of corpses.[48]

Although playing conditions at the historic course had greatly improved since the 1970s, there were a few reminders of its darker days. In August 1999 the *New York Daily News* reported the discovery of a "badly decomposed body that had disintegrated into three parts in the woods about fifty yards from the seventh hole." Its grisly account added: "His head and neck were dangling from a tree branch inside the hood of a sweatshirt. The torso was found on the ground, and the jean-clad legs were found nearby." When the police arrived they surmised that he hanged himself, and barred golfers from playing past the third hole while they conducted their investigation.[49] In late August 2004, the *New York Times* reported that vandals hacked up fairways and spray painted antiwar political messages on greens at the Van Cortlandt course. Newspaper accounts of the incident suggested that their motive was to disrupt golf outings of delegates to the Republican National Convention held in Manhattan.[50]

In 2001 *Golf Digest* reported that on a weekday morning in May a solitary "walk-on" at Van Cortlandt Park paid $25, waited thirty-two minutes to tee off, and finished eighteen holes in three hours seventeen minutes. He could also look forward to $18 million in renovations that would make the course "Big Apple's gem." Six years later the restoration fund had shrunk to $5 million from Forest Park Golf Corporation and William Larkin became the course's general manager. He told Andrew Boryga, a reporter from the *New York Times*, that the historic course had become "a dump," with "unkempt fairways and a proliferation of prostitutes and drug dealers operating much too close for comfort." He added: "If this were a regular golf course, I would be bored to death. It is such an underdog that you have to be creative to make it work." In 2012 Midland still trekked to "Vanny," taking the Number 1 line to its last stop at 242nd Street, "and making a pleasant if circuitous walk through the park to reach the landmark clubhouse."[51] In the late spring of 2014, under Larkin's management, the improvements finally were completed, including the construction of seven new greens, a new drainage system, and a redecorated clubhouse with a larger deck overlooking Van Cortlandt Lake.[52]

In 1998 New York City's mayor, Rudolph Giuliani, announced with great fanfare that 222 acres of blighted Bronx parkland would soon be the site of the city's first championship course, a driving range, a clubhouse, two playgrounds, a banquet hall, and a restaurant. Situated on top of a former landfill at Ferry Point Park on the banks of the East River, the Ferry Point course would be a first-class facility that would qualify to host the US Open. Designed by Jack Nicklaus and John Sanford, it would feature a tree-less, Irish-style layout with dunes and tall grasses. Its elevated tees would provide scenic views of the Manhattan skyline, eight miles to the south. The path was breathtaking, even magical: converting a desolate garbage dumping ground into an elite country-club-quality golf course. In 2000 the city signed a thirty-five-year lease with Ferry Point Partners, a land developing company that would finance the project and also pay the city at least $1.25 million in annual licensing fees. The initial cost of the Ferry Point course was estimated to be $22.4 million; its grand opening was scheduled for 2001.[53]

But nothing is easy in the Big Apple, especially grandiose golf course schemes. Multiple issues delayed construction. Residents and environmental groups filed lawsuits, claiming inadequate impact studies, and the discovery of toxic substances in the soil, including methane gas created by rotting garbage in the ground. In 2012 the *Daily News* reported that MFM, a contracting company the city had hired to build the course, had ties to a troubled corporation, Felix Associates. MFM's owners had a passive financial interest in Felix Associates, one of whose principals pleaded guilty to bribery charges two years before. Although the city's Department of Investigation did not charge MFM with any wrongdoing, it recommended that the Department of Parks and Recreation audit the company, which it declined to do. By 2006 the cost had ballooned to about $100 million, with completion set for 2009. The city's park department then voided the contract with Ferry Point Partners and searched for a new developer. In 2008 Mayor Michael Bloomberg decided to build the course at NYC's expense, and hired one of Donald Trump's companies, Trump National and International Golf Clubs, to manage the course after its completion. Trump agreed to pay $10 million to build a clubhouse with no licensing fees for the first four years of the twenty-year deal. For the fifth year and thereafter, Trump's company would pay more fees. By 2009 the projected cost had swelled to $123 million, surpassing by far the record for the most expensive municipal golf course, previously set by Crossings at Carlsbad in California. Three years later the cost had reached $180 million and opening day was pushed back to the spring of 2014.[54]

Critics charged that Trump had trumped New York City by signing a sweetheart deal, noting that the greens fee would be about $125 for city residents and higher for others—three times more than the price to play the other thirteen New York City municipal courses. After paying all expenses, Trump was likely to net $2 million annually before he had to pay the city in the fifth year. In September 2012 Ginia Bellafante of the *New York Times* asked: "Were we to commit ourselves to making a master list of what New York City needs more of, it is fair to say that many of us would wear a third or fourth pencil down to the nub before settling on a 18-hole golf course and the increased presence of Donald J. Trump." Bradley Klein, a golf architecture writer who grew up playing public courses in Queens and other New York City boroughs, was skeptical of the Ferry Point project. For him, municipal courses were for kids and the masses. He explained: "If you were a city kid or an everyday wage earner or schoolteacher or firefighter or retiree, then golf was a blessing for the freedom it afforded you." The upscale Ferry Point didn't seem "quite right." He wrote: "I am in the end made uneasy by the scale and ambition of this place, by the cost, by the deliberate effort to be grandiose and theatrical. Ferry Point has nothing to do with golf and everything to do with pretending to showcase the city and the ego of its master builders." He conceded that Ferry Point might host a major championship and look great on television. But he concluded: "It's not on a scale that relates to the everyday lives of the people who will be playing it week after week . . . It's the kind of monumental project that overawes you but that does not cultivate neighborhood intimacy.[55]

Bellafante was even more emphatic in questioning the justifications for building a golf course at Ferry Point. She doubted golf's value and cited figures to prove its declining popularity in New York City. Mostly she stressed the Ferry Point course's social class consequences. She noted that more than 30 percent of the Bronx's people live below the poverty line, but sarcastically reported that they would soon get a welcome opportunity to improve their handicaps at greens fees higher than those at most municipal courses. Bellafante believed that the course at Ferry Point was "one of the more egregious symbols of class division in a city already so famously replete with them." She explained: "On the eastern side of the park, which will house the golf course, the city has committed tens of millions of dollars to a playground and a waterfront esplanade, among other things. The vast expanse of the park on the other side of the Whitestone Bridge is a poorly maintained stretch where immigrants commune on weekends, lampposts are broken and dust swirls up from worn soccer fields. Garbage cans are little in evidence; litter is strewn everywhere." A young mother who visited the park regularly told Bellafante that maintenance personnel have handed her trash bags so that she might clean up the park herself. She added that visitors relieved themselves in the woods because the bathrooms were not yet completed. She concluded: "Someday though, those who come may be able to point binoculars toward the golf champion Phil Mickelson." A Trump executive volunteered: "We anticipate having world-class P.G.A. events, or even a U.S. Open."[56]

David Owen, writing for GolfDigest.com, believed that the course was "terrific," but his only criticism was that "even though walking is supposedly encouraged, pushcarts and pullcarts are not allowed." When Owen called Trump he praised the course but complained about the pushcart ban. Trump replied: "Yeah, that's because they don't look proper on a course like that . . . You know we're doing a very high-level job, and we don't like the look of a pushcart." He added that he didn't like golf carts, either; he preferred that golfers take caddies. Owen remarked: "Ferry Point has a limited number, and besides, they're $115 per bag. And golf caddies can be very slow."[57]

Several of New York City's municipal golf courses remained open during the winter months, when diehards braved frigid temperatures and snow and ice to play golf. In January 2004 a *New York Times* reporter followed a half dozen Shore View golfers around the Dyker Beach grounds on a morning when the temperature was eight degrees. He explained that Dyker Beach attracted winter golfers because putting greens remained open all year long and because less snow accumulated in its location near New York Harbor. But conditions still could be trying. He wrote: "Golf balls were frozen solid and had all the zip of a rock. Any shot not hit cleanly off the ground sent stinging shock waves up the men's arms . . . Golfers smoked cigars and wore gloves between shots." In 2005, David Owen of the *New Yorker* described New York as "an appealing winter golf destination, like Hilton Head or Myrtle Beach but easier to get to." Owen recounted a mid-February outing at the Dyker Beach course in Brooklyn, home of the Shore View Golf Club. Its membership of 140 men included carpenters, cops, lawyers, firefighters, accountants, masons, and city employees, which Owen believed was "typical for a New York City course."[58]

During the late 1900s men, women, and children from a variety of social class, ethnic, and racial groups patronized New York City public golf courses. The game was becoming more middle class and multicultural. In the mid-1980s one-third of the nation's golfers had an annual household income of less than $30,000; during the late 1900s the household income of the average golfer was just under $60,000. Participation by Irish, Italians, and Jews continued a trend begun during the early decades of the century, but joining them were increasing numbers of Hispanic Americans, Asian Americans, and African Americans.

During these years, golfers throughout the United States, including New York City, gained new role models. Among the most popular was Lee Trevino. Al Barkow, writing for *Golf* magazine, explained: "Lee Buck Trevino has made a shambles of the Hoganistic school of golf course concentration, that severely tight-lipped and expressionless manner that turned almost all of an entire generation into walking mummies."[59] He continued: "Lee Trevino's mouth is his relief valve—the escape hatch from which all of his fear, doubt, downright anxiety, and his confidence and sheer love of what he is doing, gushes forth. He wears his emotions on his sleeve. If he didn't talk all the time he'd explode like a steam engine with its exhaust pipe stuffed with steel."[60] Barkow concluded: "But if you like your folk heroes bigger than life don't look to Lee Trevino. Right down from his foreign name to his over-sized cap to the sometimes raunchy joke lines to his wide open stance and awkward swing that is straight out of the public golf course, Lee Trevino is the stuff of the American proletariat. Lee Trevino is the people's pro—pure."[61]

In the neighborhoods of Flushing, Bayside, and Douglaston, Queens, Korean immigrants were regulars at both municipal courses and driving ranges, such as the Alley Pond Golf Center. According to the *New York Times,* that facility "dispenses the American dream by the bucketful." Koreans were attracted to the game because of its affordability compared to the astronomical prices charged in their homeland. But some also liked golf because it gave them an opportunity to display their newly acquired affluence in their adopted country. According to Johnny Mun, a Korean immigrant from Flushing, most Koreans took up golf "as a status thing, to show off," citing the spending of thousands of dollars on lessons and clubs. David Long, a computer consultant who is part Korean, believed that golf provided Korean American immigrants with a challenge to succeed at a game that required inner discipline and a meditative, repetitive approach. Nationwide the 2003 National Golf Foundation study counted 1,520,000 Asian American golfers, with the majority of them of Japanese or Korean ancestry.[62]

Since the mid-1990s the most important factor in boosting golf has been the enormous success and popularity of Tiger Woods, who has generated great enthusiasm for golf among minority youth and adults. The success of Woods has not made much of a difference on the hiring of blacks or other minority members as head professionals at private and public golf clubs. In 1967 Harold Dunovant became the first black professional golfer at New York City's thirteen municipal courses, when he was hired to manage the pro shop and give lessons at the Kissena Park course in Flushing, Queens. As an eight-year-old growing up in Winston-Salem, North Carolina, Dunovant knew that he wanted to be a golf teacher. His family moved to New York City when he was a teenager. He achieved his childhood dream when he became a professional in 1954. In 1965 he became a pro at the Winston Lakes Golf Club, a Negro public course in Winston-Salem. He quit after three months because he did not think that the club could afford a pro. For the next two and a half years he competed on the tour of the United Professional Golf Association, which was mostly Negro. But he could not earn enough from the weekly purses of $3,000. So he applied for the job at the Kissena Park course.[63]

The hiring of Dunovant was highly unusual for the 1960s. A recent study revealed that while 21 percent of active golfers are members of minority groups, they constitute less than 2 percent of the Professional Golfers' Association. In 2011 there were only eighty-five African American club professionals—less than half of one percent of the nation's 28,000 pros. (Hispanics held 263 of them; Asians were 196). Half of that total of 544 pros worked at large city municipal courses. Al Green, a former PGA member and uncle of Rodney Green, director of golf at Innisbrook Resort in Tampa, Florida, stated: "If it wasn't for public golf courses, black PGA members, wouldn't have the opportunity to work in the industry because the private clubs simply aren't going to hire them."[64]

Women's involvement in golf in the United States began in 1894 when the *Ladies Home Journal* urged them to take up the game. An article by John Gilmore Speed stated that men and women could easily learn to play the game "in middle life." He continued: "With golf links in every neighborhood there is no reason why a middle-aged woman should fasten herself in a rocking chair and consent to be regarded by the youngsters as antiquated and forty-five. Instead of that, she can, with her golfing club, follow her ball, from link to link, renewing her beauty and her youth by exercise in the open air."[65]

In 1937 Helen Webb Harris, an African American woman, founded the Wake Robin Golf Club in Washington, DC. On April 22, 1937, a dozen of them proclaimed their creed: "To perpetuate golf among Negro women, to make potential players into champions, and to make a permanent place for women in the world of golf."[66] In 1939, when Franklin D. Roosevelt was president and Harold Ickes was secretary of the interior, Ickes decided to build a public nine-hole golf course on an old city dump—the Langston Golf Course. Two years later, in 1941, Secretary Ickes ordered that the public golf courses be desegregated. At one course, the East Potomac Golf Course, some of the Wake Robin members were stoned when they tried to use it. Ethel Williams, the only surviving member of the club, recalled: "White men and their children would come onto the course after we hit the ball, and they would pick it up and run with it. They kept taking our balls. Their dogs would run with them on the course. And the stones would come flying. But we kept on. We were taxpayers too."[67]

In 1995 Marcia Chambers recalled feeling hostility on public golf courses. Starters and rangers (sometimes called marshals) were usually unfriendly. She explained: "Many starters need an education in courtesy and respect for women players." She quoted Rachel Shuster, a sports columnist for *USA Today*: "I joined a threesome of women at a public course this summer and found them unnerved by what the starter said: 'You ladies are standing too near the first tee, and you're talking too loud.' Thing is, they weren't that loud, and they were a decent distance back off the tee. They weren't angry, though. 'That's the way we're always treated,' the ladies said."[68] Chambers also complained about how rangers treated women, who often assumed that they were slow players. She quoted Becky Powell, a marketing and public-relations executive from Houston, Texas: "Marshalls assume we play slowly. Last July 4th our foursome—we were the only women on a daily-fee course—had an encounter with a marshal. Somebody hit the ball into the rough; a marshal came over and got all over us. We shoot all in the nineties and got done in the right amount of time. That sort of thing angers me. Just like any other discrimination, this has to do with preconceived ideas without any validity to them."[69] Chambers also complained about how difficult it was for a woman to get an early morning tee time. She quoted Sylvia Garlowich, of Deer Park, Texas, who described her experience in a letter to the *Houston Chronicle* in the summer of 1994: "I am an executive in a major retail firm and have found discrimination toward females at several public golf courses. I have golfed with several men in the past few years and have tried to call and place tee times for us. On several occasions I have been given tee times in the afternoon. Later in the same day, my husband would call and be given a tee time hours earlier."[70]

Women have also struggled to achieve equal opportunity on municipal golf courses. In April 1971 Helen Finn became the first female golf professional in New York City when she accepted an offer from the parks department for the Douglaston Park Golf Course in Queens. A former teacher and fifty-three-year-old grandmother, she learned to play the game as a teenager at a Manhattan Beach golf range. In her first month in her new job, Finn hoped to bring minority and disadvantaged youth "into the mainstream of life through golf." She outlined plans to launch free group lessons in the summer when she will show National Golf Foundation instructional films to "teach the etiquette and joys of golf." She also planned for her twenty-two-year-old son and her husband to manage the golf shop while she gave lessons.[71]

Municipal golf has played a critical role in the democratization of the sport in the United States. These city courses host the most rounds at the lowest cost to the golfer and have provided learning environments to novices. Since much of the industry's future growth will be among minority and lower-income households with traditionally low golf participation rates, maintaining affordable municipal golf is very important. New York City was the birthplace of municipal golf in 1895 and benefited the most from the New Deal programs during the 1930s. During the 1960s and the 1970s, its thirteen courses struggled, but after privatization they recovered and prospered since the 1990s. The luxurious and pricey Trump Golf Links at Ferry Point, which opened on Wednesday, April 1, 2015, provided golfers with an upscale and challenging experience.[72]

# VI

# Sport in the Multiethnic City
# Jews and Italians

CHAPTER TEN

# During the Heyday of Jewish Sports in Gotham

## The Case of CCNY, 1900–1970

*Jeffrey S. Gurock*

For most of the twentieth century, New York City was the site of an efflorescence of athleticism that was unparalleled in the long history of the Jewish people. In ancient times, some Jews participated in Greek and Roman games, much to the chagrin of religious leaders. After a medieval time-out from sports, in modern times, men and women of that minority faith and culture attempted to prove their mettle as citizens of Western and Central Europe by gaining admission as respected competitors with, and against, all-gentile comers in host societies. And, in Eastern Europe, radicals and Zionists alike used their clubs to strike blows against endemic Jewish passivity toward hostile foes. Zionist ideologue Max Nordau articulated a forceful game plan in 1898 when he rose at the Second Zionist Congress to champion "muscular Judaism": the creation of cadres of proud, athletic Jews who would help their nation take its respected place within the modern world. He wanted young Jews to emulate the ancient Maccabees and to become again a "warrior" people who would be prepared to take on all antagonists, whether on the athletic field of honor or, if need be, on the military battlefield. Jewish socialists contended that for "the worker-sportsman struggle for the liberation of the working class, sport is . . . not a goal in itself, but a means by which to educate a physically developed and class-conscious member of the international family of workers." But it was only in America—and most certainly in Gotham, the country's largest Jewish settlement by far—that athleticism became a mass movement among the boys and girls of newcomers, producing hundreds of champions in scores of sports. In the period 1910–1940, for example, twenty-five Jewish boxers held world titles in seven different weight classifications. New York–born Barney Ross wore three different championship belts. He was one of ten titleholders who first learned the art of pugilism through numerous street fights in the city's immigrant tenement districts.[1]

In fact, by the 1930s, Jewish success on the city's courts, squared circles, base paths, pools, and gridirons was so apparent that it moved one jaundiced Christian journalist to opine that there was something inbred in the Jews that contributed to their predominance in the sport most closely identified with the metropolis—the city game of basketball. Paul Gallico's oft-quoted remark was: "I suspect, that basketball's appeal to the Hebrew, with his Oriental background is that the game places a premium on an alert, scheming mind, flashy trickiness, artful dodging and general smart-aleckness." Of course, nothing could be further from the truth about the background and nature of the Jew. The views of Gallico, a sports editor for the *Daily News,* were infused with the falsehoods of the scientific racism of the day. Rather, American Jewish athleticism constituted both a bodily and mental change for a people that historically honored only the scholar, the person of intellect and not of the physical.[2]

From the turn of the twentieth century to the 1970s, this new intersection for Jews of the body and the mind is readily apparent in their athletic experience at the most Jewish of Gotham's institutions of secular higher education, the City College of New York (CCNY). For almost seven decades, the student body at this school for young males—women became full-fledged students only in 1951—that was referred to adoringly in the 1920s as "the cheder [Jewish schoolhouse] on the Hill" [St. Nicholas Heights, west of Harlem], and by its detractors as the "College of Circumcised New Yorkers"—was made up overwhelmingly of Jews of East European heritage. As a point of comparison, from 1920 to 1930, the percentage of Jews at Gotham's most elite school of higher education, Columbia University, dropped from approximately 30 to 20 percent due to a quota system.[3]

In their Jewish space on St. Nicholas Heights, CCNY undergraduates contributed not only to the intellectual vitality of the institution but to its robust athletic profile as well. A proud alumnus and erstwhile track team member Stanley Frank—the author of one of the earliest tracts on Jewish athletics in America—is unquestionably correct: "City's" sportsmen transposed "the characteristics inherent in the Jew . . . mental agility, perception . . . imagination and subtlety"—ingrained in them over the centuries in halls of study—to the basketball court and arguably to other realms of competitive athletic action as well.[4]

Although one particular group of collegiate Jewish sportsmen—the school's hoopsters—were destined for approbation, renown and ultimately vilification, they were not the only athletes on campus whose exploits evidence the wide embrace of sports among second-generation immigrant Jews in New York. Beyond their affinity for competition, these "sturdy sons of City College"—as its school anthem describes them—did much to create a positive self-image within the student body during the school's—and Gotham Jewry's—athletic heyday. Sports were a way for participants and spectators alike to make prideful statements about how they belonged in America, and often athleticism was also a unique means of affirming their Jewishness.

Until the turn of the twentieth century, during the first fifty years of the school's existence—it was founded in 1849 as the Free Academy of the City of New York—the institution kept a very low profile in the sports arena within its concrete campus on Manhattan's 23rd Street. While there was a City College Athletic Association (CCAA) up and running by the early 1870s, and in 1882 it joined the Intercollegiate Athletic Association—which linked CCNY on paper with the sports powerhouses of the day like Yale and Harvard—reportedly it "took no positive steps to send contestants to intercollegiate activities." Forced to rely on the student body for funding, since the faculty and administration showed no interest in collegiate competitions, the CCAA's efforts to assist the sports-minded were roundly and routinely judged as failures. While in the early annals of CCNY athletics, there were some notable victories over other schools—in 1866, for example, the CCNY Reliance Base Ball Club upset Columbia's "college nine by the one-sided score of 45 to 8" (the metrics of scoring back then were different from today) in front of adoring fans who traveled to then remote Morrisania in the Bronx to cheer on "City"—but "athletics were not the chief glory of the City College campus or the main pursuit of the students." One student pundit of the day suggested, perhaps somewhat facetiously, that "the superstition held that college students came to college to study." On balance, it seems that "City College boys were much more successful in their literary and oratorical activities than they were in athletics." In 1876, the school was proud when two of its rhetoricians won prizes in the Intercollegiate Debate competition.

More popular among students of that day were the informal and intramural games and activities; usually low-budget items that they initiated themselves. When the young men found time—and their days at the school were closely regimented—CCNY students could be found "running foot races" and roughhousing around Gramercy Park, located just a few blocks from their school. In winter, they skated in Central Park or played ice hockey on Beckman's Pond on 60th Street. Over the early years, there were several rowing and yachting clubs that used the Harlem River as their base of operations. Still, according to a chronicler of the college's history, until the twentieth century "in spite of regattas, meets and games, it was obvious that City College athletic activity was in a woefully dormant state."[5]

Several factors conspired to produce the observable "feebleness of its athletic activity, the inadequacy of its Athletic Association and the inferiority of its teams." To begin with, the athletic devotees did not have the funding that more fortunate institutions possessed to construct the sports facilities and to hire the coaches necessary to compete on a level playing field. Second, CCNY was—to use a contemporary term—a "commuter school." Students were at 23rd Street for just a few hours a day, before returning home to live and work "off campus." The students' travels and the closely regulated hours in class—often with but fifteen minutes for recess—left relatively little time for extracurricular activities of all sorts, including sports. Even when sports became important later in CCNY's history, the complaints in the locker rooms remained that as a nonresidential school, its athletes had less time for training than their opponents. But, arguably, the school provided neither the monies nor the time for full-fledged athletics because its mission was different from that of the nation's elite institutions.[6]

Elsewhere, athletic activity played a major role in American campus life because the core of their mission was to produce generations of well-rounded gentlemen—the future elites of society. It was deemed necessary that the student not only hit the books but also be a rough-and-ready participant on the sports field. The expectation was that while exposure to the classics of a liberal arts education and training for the professions was a desirable goal, the model student was a fellow who did not tarry too long in the stacks if a match was in the offing on university grounds. Within that collegiate culture, significantly, the few Jews on campus were stereotyped as the consummate "grinds"—bespectacled, callow fellows who could be found only in the library when extracurricular activities beckoned their gentile counterparts. At Yale University, for example, at the beginning of the new century, the campus slogan was: "we toil not, neither do we agitate, but we play football." Such was the atmosphere where "the professional spirit prevails in . . . athletics [while] the amateur spirit prevails in Yale scholarship." Indeed, at that Ivy institution and elsewhere, the often ultraviolent early incarnation of football was considered the consummate character builder for the muscular future leaders of the nation. For the projected complete man, football "embodied so many factors that are typically American . . . virile, intensive, aggressive energy that marks progress is the root which upholds and feeds American supremacy."[7]

By contrast, at the Free Academy and later at CCNY, though the school's leaders spoke hopefully that its graduates would be "profession[al] . . . cultivated gentlemen," little effort was expended toward shaping that well-rounded man who was the pride of the aristocratic colleges and universities. This omission in mission, evidenced through the absence of any physical education courses until the start of the twentieth century, was public knowledge. Robert Maclay, president of the city's board of education, criticized CCNY's disinterest in the athleticism of its students when, after attending commencement in 1896, he complained to a reporter from the *New York Tribune* about graduates who "with a few conspicuous exceptions, were narrow chested, round shouldered, stooped men, and in exceedingly imperfect condition physically."

CCNY president Alexander Webb's rejoinder opened with a tongue-in-cheek invitation to Maclay to work out with the football club members and ended with a serious critique of his interlocutor's board of education and the city's board of estimate. For Webb, if there were indeed "puny" students on the campus, it was because the government did not view that part of their education as important. Notwithstanding this exchange in defense of his athletic program, there is no record of Webb doing much to promote sports during his thirty-three years as head of the college. On occasion, however, the school had a few top-notch football players. In 1896, a quarterback named Smith and a halfback named Kelly were stars in the "great football match of the year." But these "old CCNY men" had transferred out of the Manhattan school and participated in the Yale-Princeton game. Back at CCNY, a student scribe opined: "we can feel a little glow of pride on our own account." That year, City's football club played against teams like the Fanwood Athletic Club.[8]

During the first decade of the twentieth century, a combination of circumstances spiked the growth of athletics at CCNY. First, a new president, John H. Finley, who came aboard in 1903, brought to the campus a background and interest in sport. As a student at Knox College and Johns Hopkins University, he had played football and he wanted his students to be physically fit and the best of them to compete against students of other colleges. He believed that the college had a mission to provide his "boys . . . intelligent care of their bodies for the first time." Early in his tenure, he arranged for the use of the Sixty-Ninth Regiment Armory in midtown Manhattan for physical training under the watchful eye of an instructor. In 1907, when the college moved to a commodious campus in St. Nicholas Heights, he made sure that a gymnasium would be part of the complex. And in 1910, he listed the construction of a stadium as his first priority in his "to-do" diary. This was realized in 1915, when, right before Finley left office, Lewisohn Stadium opened.[9]

Even more important in elevating the sports profile of the college was the arrival along with Finley of new a group of students who soon became predominant. Significantly, many of these Jewish students from immigrant east European homes did not have to be convinced of the value of physical training. In this arena, as in so many other cultural and social venues, they were very different from their newcomer parents. By the time they arrived on Convent Avenue, physical education and an affinity for sports had become second nature to them. In other words, these undergraduates were products not only of the public schools, where they acquired the intellectual tools and earned the grades to gain admission to that free school, but also of the settlement houses, where they had become quite proficient in sports. In the latter arena, they also learned that to be considered true Americans, they had to demonstrate an acumen for athletic achievement. Sports success became a subtle yet powerful answer to those who stereotyped their people as puny and unmanly. Although their academic abilities were lauded almost immediately by professors who characterized the Jewish students as "studious, keen and forthright [and who] analyze any subject to its fundamentals regardless of tradition or age," those who were sportsmen were also praised for bringing a new "spirit" to campus. And the sport that they brought uptown, which engendered immense school pride, was basketball. It was a game that, like the student-athletes themselves, was a newcomer to university settings.[10]

It was only in 1891 that Dr. James Naismith had invented this game at a YMCA school. And while initially the game spread primarily among small midwestern colleges, New York's settlement houses also picked it up quickly and taught their charges well. From these afternoon and weekend community centers, the best athletes went on to public school varsities in the city—the prime focus of informal recruitment for CCNY. In 1907, the fifth year that CCNY fielded a team, that squad—that had at least eight Jews on its twelve-man team—won eight of its nine games.[11] A year later, in 1908, CCNY knocked off both Yale and Princeton—to the delight of its newly acquired fans. At that early point, the student newspaper praised the team for bringing the college community together: "The games," it editorialized, "are giving expression to the stifled social instinct of the students. It has been said a hundred times that the College gives its young men no opportunity to be together, to feel and to cheer and to sing together. . . . The basketball team gives us practically the only chance of seeing concretely the spirit of the college."[12]

These early successes on the hardwood were harbingers of decades of future victories. From 1910 to 1950, CCNY roundballers suffered through but three losing seasons, even as they confronted a schedule that included many of the top squads from all over the country. During the 1937–1938 campaign, for example, where CCNY went 13-3, the opponents included local elite squads like St. John's and Manhattan and national powerhouses from Pennsylvania, Illinois, Rhode Island, and California's Stanford. Through all of these years, the overwhelming majority of the players and most of the stars were Jews.[13] From 1919 on, Nat Holman—one of the most recognized Jewish athletes of the twentieth century—coached his charges to appreciative student crowds. Besides his own athletic pedigree as a member of the Original Celtics—one of the first barnstorming professional basketball teams—and his acumen as a tactician, the nattily dressed, well-spoken, professorial Holman, a Jew of immigrant parents, added a large measure of style and class to the program. Unquestionably, with the basketball varsity's cachet and competitiveness, this flagship sport fulfilled a mission of unifying the student body, at least during game time, even if the student newspaper occasionally took rowdy fans to task for turning Wingate Gym into what we would call today a "snake pit" for opposing players. Ritually, on a "Saturday night in December and across the cement campus . . . one hears the Allegaroo (the fame cheer baffling to etymologists) urging on the basketball team to another triumph."[14]

But as a "Jewish" school—to its critics and fans alike—there were additional elements in play when the CCNY team took the court. Through what was called this "serious" business of sports, these second-generation New York Jews countered some of the antisemitic canards of their day. They said, in athletic rebuttal to so-called scientific racists of the day, who perceived in the coming to America of racial inferiors the decline of civilization, to take a look "at the dizzy weavings, at the City College gym, of five dark, gargoylesque figures triumphing over the blond and sunny frankness of their opponents." Victories in Wingate Gymnasium placed "another nail in [Oswald] Spengler's coffin of the declining West." And to those who would characterize Jews as interlopers, standing outside American life, "our victories," wrote one memoirist, "over famous colleges and universities . . . were important beyond the actuality of the score; immigrants or (mostly) sons of immigrants, we triumphed over the original settlers, retrospectively hacked out for ourselves . . . a place in the aboriginal wilderness." For this writer, even more than what he and his fellows did in the classroom, it was through sports that "we came out of the settlement houses, off the streets, into what seemed the mainstream of American life."[15]

This prideful feeling that through athletics, the Jews of CCNY belonged in America peaked in 1950 when the college upset a series of top-notch, nationally ranked opponents and captured both the National Invitational Tournament and the National College Athletic Association championships. For observers of sports, this was a remarkable achievement. And given the way future competitions would be structured, it was a double championship that would not be duplicated. Among the college's partisans, it was a far more transcendent victory. The personal identification with the team was so profound that the sense on the streets around Convent Avenue was that the ballplayers "did not do it for us, it was us that did it." There was an aura of "reflected glory and a vindication of our way of life." These were the fellows from the "hardscrabble" Jewish neighborhoods whom their classmates knew from their daily encounters at the local candy store and from the schoolyards—fully approachable athletes. And they—and we—had defeated all comers. There was also a satisfaction that it had been done with the able assistance of some outstanding African American athletes who belonged in this uniquely integrated campus. In no small measure, they had demonstrated what a successful multicultural America might become.

Indeed, along the way, as an important backstory to their on-the-court accomplishment, they had struck a blow against racism. The story was told and retold on the campus about how they had gone out and routed Adolph Rupp's Kentucky Wildcats after the southern hoopsters had refused to shake the hands of CCNY's black players before the opening tip-off. It was not lost on the school's loyalists that just five years after the fall of Nazism, Jews and blacks had defeated a man named Adolph. That particular game has been recalled as "cultural war, as a religious war." In the aftermath of the victories in the two tournaments, Nat Holman received national attention, including an appearance on the *Ed Sullivan Show*. More important to the Jewish students on St. Nicholas Heights, there was a palpable joy about their achieved status as equal to all others in the country, through an American pastime.[16]

Though not nearly as successful in their athletic achievements—and certainly not as widely lionized off campus—the exploits of Jewish sportsmen on "City's" other teams also received extensive coverage in the college newspaper. Reports on what they called the "minor sports"—that ranged from swimming to water polo to wrestling to tennis to lacrosse to handball—often garnered front-page placement in the biweekly or triweekly, the *Campus*, next to weighty articles on efforts "To Raise Funds for European Students" or on how "Freudian Theory of Dreams Is Explained to Psychology Club." And these athletes, in turn, were on occasion seen as making their own emphatic statements about who they were and from where they came.[17]

For example, the "modern" era of football on the dirt-and-stone-filled field of Lewisohn Stadium began with a freshman team in 1921. A varsity had been organized a year earlier. Like other early sports on the campus, gridiron squads had come and gone since the game had first arrived at CCNY as a club in 1872. The tragic death of a player during a game in 1893 was one reason that the school suspended the sport for a number of years. It remained for the 1920s—when there was considerable student interest in the game—for CCNY to field a varsity each year. In 1921, CCNY's president Sidney E. Mezes blessed the program as "a potent force for unifying an institution, inculcating genuine manliness . . . and a modest and well-based pride in the students, alumni and friends of an institution." From that point on, the gridders had eleven winning seasons. Their best streak was the five years in the 1930s (1934–1938), although their triumphs were primarily against local opponents like Manhattan College, Brooklyn College, St. Francis, and St. John's. During this high point for football at the college, another Jewish sports legend, Benny Friedman—late of All-American status at the University of Michigan and stardom for the New York Giants—coached the team. Victories certainly contributed to the turnouts of fans who packed Lewisohn Stadium when the team did well. But even before the winning streak started, during a down year on the scoreboard, in 1933 it has been estimated that "upwards of 50,000" students and alumni sat in the stone bleachers for the five home games. The enthusiastic fan of the team who reported these attendance figures may have inflated the numbers at least a tad as the outdoor arena held but 8,000 seats.[18]

In all events, as with basketball, arguably what spiked interest among devoted fans—beyond mere school spirit—were the statements made by and about Jewish athletes when the team took the field. Notably, after the 1928 season, when the team lost only one of its seven games, it was said: "the success . . .

is perhaps, a sign of Americanization." A "competent eleven" had "exploded . . . the hallowed dogma that Jews could not play the game." That was the year when reportedly the "best efforts [were] made . . . in the quest to make the gridiron game the outstanding course in the sports curriculum of CCNY." During that campaign, at least eight of the eleven starters for the college team were Jews. For one admiring sportswriter, the victory over a highly ranked Drexel club in front of "four thousand undergrads and alumni" who sang the alma mater after the win, this triumph was a case of their players "outfranking Merriwell." Frank Merriwell was a fictional Yale-educated character who appeared in many late nineteenth-century dime novels where he consistently showed off his combination of mental and physical prowess—"the perfect union of brains and brawn." For "City" fans, halfbacks like Morty Targum, whose performance in Lewisohn "equals anything seen in the stadium for a long time," were their stars to be emulated.[19]

Also indicative of their college's celebration of its combination of brains and brawn was the juxtaposition of two front-page articles that appeared in the *Campus* before the Norwich tussle several weeks later. One lead story reported on philosopher Morris Raphael Cohen's lecture on the "Jews' Thinking Traits." In front of three hundred devotees, he argued that "the greatness of individual men [was] not a product of race." Next to the Cohen piece was a box with the lineup, which listed Rosner, Timlinsky, Targum, and Bienstock as among the gridiron starters.[20]

For another backer of CCNY sports achievements, there was an even more explicit Jewish element in football triumphs. For this observer—who sounded much like Stanley Frank, and not totally different from Paul Gallico—the CCNY group did not rely primarily on brute strength—what was then called "Yale football," Frank Merriwell notwithstanding. Instead, they "did little heavy line-plunging." They "were light, fast and cynically deceitful." In fact, it was observed, "sometimes it was uncertain whether its plays were within the rules." Nonetheless, when push came to shove, the CCNY team "could anchor in the shadow of the goal posts and hold its line." The ultimate source of that resiliency on the one-yard line, it was argued, emanated from "a viciously stubborn strength that the condemned transmute from their very weakness." In other words, Jewish athletes drew upon a reservoir of inner strength to succeed.[21]

In the fall of 1935, the CCAA tied itself to Jewishness more than ever before when its all-Jewish, seven-man board positioned itself at the forefront of a campus-wide movement to deny Hitler a major propaganda coup through the use of sports. The issue that galvanized this most Jewish of college communities was the crusade to move the US Olympic Committee (USOC) to boycott the Berlin games scheduled for 1936. The rank-and-file of students needed little convincing of the correctness of this cause, for it intersected with two fundamental values that they held dear. They were worried about the fate of their co-religionist under the heel of the Third Reich. And politically speaking, so many of them—who harbored left-leaning feelings to begin with—were opposed to fascism of any sort worldwide. Fittingly, the same Great Hall—CCNY's major auditorium—which was the site of a "Boycott Olympics" rally in October 1935, was only three weeks later the venue for a "Mobilize for Peace Assembly."[22]

Just two years earlier, Jewish varsity men had differed fundamentally from the majority of their classmates on another political issue that came to the fore. In 1933, a move was afoot to drive the Reserve Officers Training Corps (ROTC) off campus. For student radicals, who opposed participation in any future capitalist—or fascist—inspired war, the presence of ROTC at CCNY was a major provocation. They frequently disrupted military reviews, turning them into antiwar demonstrations. Their position was consistently supported by more moderate elements on campus, such as the student editors of the *Campus*. In May 1933, this political push attracted city-wide attention when a "Jingo Day" protest ended in a melee involving the police. The street struggle included President Frederick Robinson, who waded in with his umbrella as a weapon. It is not known whether any college athletes fought on the streets of Convent Avenue. But in the aftermath, the CCAA and the Varsity Club made known that its sympathies lay with the administration. At a sports dinner a month after the battle, two hundred lettermen—including baseball player Lou Trupin and Arthur Koenigsberg and lacrosse stars named Cohen, Gottfried, and Rosenberg—vigorously applauded the proposal of Major Herbert M. Holton, associate professor of hygiene, that "City College athletes organize a vigilance committee to eradicate 'rowdyism'" on campus. If at that moment, CCNY sportsmen set themselves apart from the antimilitarism spirit around them, two years later, with Nazism becoming an ever-increasing threat to peace and to Jews, this ideologically diverse campus came almost completely together.[23]

Almost all City College men gave unquestioned support to one of their own who led the boycott movement nationwide. Judge Jeremiah T. Mahoney, class of 1895—and a former Olympic hopeful in the high jump before the Athens games of 1906—was the president of the Amateur Athletic Union. From that perch he took on Avery Brundage, head of the USOC, who consistently asserted that politics of this sort should not interfere with what he deemed to be pristine, international games. Predictably, the *Campus* was full-throated in support of its distinguished alumnus' position as it asserted, "we will refuse to add America's 'Heil' to the Hitler madness." So positioned, it also upbraided the editors of the *Yale News* for characterizing the boycott as "patently absurd." The view from St. Nicholas Heights was that their Ivy League counterparts had "forsake[n] every ideal of the furtherance of humanity which is, in the final analysis, the end of all education." Proactively, student activists—CCAA leaders and others—solicited thousands of signatures on petitions at CCNY, attempted to take the cause to other campuses, and garnered statements of support from most of the school's coaches, who decried "race discrimination." Nat Holman hoped that in "fairness to other athletes and athletes of all other countries" a more fitting location be found for the games. But if "the games are held in Berlin, we certainly should not participate." Lacrosse coach Leon "Chief" Miller—a Native American who had played at the Carlisle School with the legendary Jim Thorpe and who faced much discrimination in his own life—empathized strongly with "the restrictions and inhibitions" placed "on so-called non-Aryans athletes" in the Reich. Thus, he asserted that Germany was no place for American sportsmen. In the end, as is well known, these efforts and statements both within and without the halls of City College did not dissuade the USOC from participating in Hitler's Olympics. The Fuehrer achieved his propaganda goal of projecting an image to the world of a revitalized and powerful Germany, even if the achievements of African American sprinter Jesse Owens dispelled Nazi myths about Aryan racial superiority.[24]

Though a number of great Jewish athletes from other schools went to Berlin to show how wrong the Nazi ideology was—and for their efforts, sprinters Marty Glickman and Sam Stoller were humiliated when the USOC kept them from competing in a signature event in the Olympic Stadium—back at CCNY its best Jewish athletes paid a heavy personal price when they supported the boycott. The CCAA understood the sacrifice these elite performers were making in being part of a college community that bore "the distinction of being one of the few institutions of higher learning which officially subordinated its selfish desires for a possible Olympic winner to the moral principle of what it believes right and wrong." The 1936 Olympics was the first time that basketball was included as a medal-bearing sport and the hope was that some of CCNY's outstanding hoopsters—deemed on campus to be "athletes of Olympic caliber"—might be selected to play on the team. Though President

Robinson did not directly address the dilemma his Jewish athletes faced, he differed from the CCAA when he asserted, "it would be better for America to send a powerful team to the Olympics including its best Jewish athletes and gain greater glory for our own country and for the Jewish people world-wide."[25]

Elite CCNY trackman Benny Zlatnick was among the athletes who were convinced by the boycott campaign to forego the chance to try out for the Berlin games. This "erstwhile 200 meters sprint star," the *Campus* reported proudly, "has turned the other way." However, not everyone on campus fell into line. An outstanding fencer, S. Thompson Stewart—arguably a Christian student—was totally unmoved by the protests. This tenth-ranked national sabre man—who after graduation was employed in the college's recorder's office—let the school paper know that for him "politics should [not] be permitted to interfere with athletics." Four days after Stewart's assertion, a student reporter took the athlete's coach, Joseph Vince, to task for his "non-compliance" with all requests to "clarify his views on American participation in the Olympics." First, Vince refused to comment on his disciple's decision and when asked whether as a coach, he would "go to Berlin . . . if you happen to be chosen [to coach]," Vince would only "smile" and say to a jaundiced correspondent—who lampooned the coach's accented English—"that I cannot answer."[26]

Twelve years later, in 1948, at the London Olympic games—the first such competition after World War II—CCNY's wrestler Henry Wittenberg brought home the school's first gold medal when he triumphed in the light-heavyweight free-style classification. Wittenberg, who was lauded as the "pride . . . of Gotham in general and the college in particular," learned the sport at CCNY—he had been a mediocre high school swimmer—and legendarily trained for his bouts by running up the steps of Lewisohn Stadium. He returned to coach at the college in 1967 and a year later led the US Greco-Roman wrestling squad at the 1968 Mexico City games. Wittenberg's other connection to the Olympics occurred as a sidebar to the tragedy at the 1972 games in Munich. A day before eleven Israeli athletes were murdered by Palestinian terrorists, he and his wife, Edith, spent time with Israeli wrestling referee Yosef Gutfreund, who was killed in the massacre.[27]

The long-enduring palpable bond between the students on this overwhelmingly Jewish campus and its predominantly Jewish athletes ended in the early 1950s. The most traumatic fissure took place in 1951 when seven star players, five Jews and two blacks—who just a season earlier had together stunned the basketball world—were arrested for "shaving points." It was the first of several basketball scandals, which rocked the American sports world in that decade. These players were implicated for intentionally missing makeable shots to reduce the margin of victory, to the benefit of gamblers who controlled the betting line on contests. *Newsweek* magazine characterized the nefarious goings-on as "the most sickening scandal in the history of American sports."

On campus, students were first stunned by their classmates' betrayal. They were soon outraged, as it was revealed that these athletes had made it to St. Nicholas Heights with the help of altered admission documents and had remained eligible to compete through corrupted transcripts. A *New York Times* editorial assessment early on in the investigation, that "somehow the home, the neighborhood, the campus, the college fostered a crooked, distorted sense of values and produced moral shipwreck," contributed to the gloom. At CCNY, the home, neighborhood, and school always had been closely connected as a source of community pride. For so many, "it was a moral breakdown, a humiliation for Jews," because CCNY "represented Jewish culture." Fortunately, the scandal did not morph into blatant antisemitic canards against this Jewish school and its students, even if Adolph Rupp did opine that New York gamblers—perhaps intimating Jewish gamblers in Gotham—"could not reach my boys with a ten foot pole." As it turned out, soon some of his own stars were brought to law courts for comparable chicanery on the hardwood courts. Still, it has been argued that "CCNY would never have the same place in the hearts of New York Jews as it did before February 1951" when the scandal broke.[28]

In the two decades that followed the debacle, sports lost much of their cachet among CCNY students. As far as the flagship sport of basketball was concerned, to keep gamblers away, the New York City Board of Higher Education decreed that the team would no longer play its key games in Madison Square Garden. But CCNY was no longer an attraction for promoters at this mecca of New York sports, since the team was not successful in recruiting top-notch players and the school had downgraded its schedule. Though Holman was reinstated for the 1953–1954 season as coach—much of the enduring blame on and off campus focused on his assistant Harry "Bobby" Sand, who had recruited the questionable student-athletes—the legendary court eminence was now directing his charges against teams like Rider, Montclair State, Kings Point. And for an out-of-town trip, they played a new Jewish school, Brandeis of Waltham, Massachusetts. In the glory days, two years before the scandal, the team had traveled over an inter-session to California for a three-game stint. They traveled by airplane at a time when few teams, college or professional, made such expensive transcontinental trips. In Los Angeles, excited CCNY alumni—including film star and former student Edward G. Robinson—feted them. But now, the thrill of getting up close and personal with boys from the old neighborhood was over. As a sign of declining times, in December 1959—two games before an aging Holman turned over the coaching reins to his former player and assistant coach, Dave Polansky—the past national-power CCNY was matched up against, and lost to, the most religiously Jewish of Gotham's colleges, Yeshiva University.[29]

Yeshiva, which, as early as the 1930s, had maintained a low-key program, had begun to move up in hoop talent, beginning, ironically, when a player from the CCNY freshman squad of 1948–1949—which included the players who would two years later gain fame and then suffer ignominy—transferred uptown to the Washington Heights campus. Now, in the 1950s, sportsmen at that Orthodox school felt that they could compete against CCNY for the lower- and middle-level varsity players from New York's public schools whom "City" also hoped to bring in. The best Jewish basketball players that Gotham produced—and there still was a considerable number—were recruited by schools all over the country and neither CCNY nor Yeshiva had a chance of getting them to enroll. A more likely destination for those collegians that knew the city game best was south of the Mason-Dixon Line. In the mid-1950s, former St. John's University coach Frank McGuire moved to the University of North Carolina and created what was called his "underground railroad." He built the Tar Heel program with, in his own words, "Jewish players and Italian players . . . boys from the city," tough competitors who brought an aggressive, urban attitude to Tobacco Road. McGuire's prize passenger was Lenny Rosenbluth, who garnered first team All-American honors and was voted National Player of the Year in 1957. Meanwhile, as McGuire and others rose in basketball stature, back at CCNY, given the constraints imposed upon him, Holman's club won only 49 of 103 games during his last five years at the helm.[30]

Although just two months after the scandal broke, the football program was suspended "until such time as adequate game facilities and appropriate finances are provided," and that team then ended its half-century run, some of the minor sports did quite well in the 1950s. Most notably, for a number of years in the mid-1950s, the soccer team, a club that formed as a varsity only in the late 1940s, picked up the basketball team's fallen standard, and became a national power. Its impressive record included a seven-year skein as Metropolitan Conference champions. Even more remarkable, in 1957, CCNY and Springfield College of

CCNY soccer team in Lewisohn Stadium, 1952. *Courtesy CCNY archives.*

Massachusetts were voted co-national champions by the college coaches. Two years later, in 1959, when a national tournament was held, the booters made it to the semifinals of the NCAAs before bowing out to St. Louis on their opponent's home turf. Overall, from 1954 to 1959, the team compiled a compelling 71-9-7 record and went undefeated in fifty league matches from 1953 to 1959.[31]

The key to this success was the arrival on campus of postwar refugees who had extensive experience with soccer either in Europe or in competition on the streets and fields of the ethnic neighborhoods where they settled in Gotham. They chose CCNY for its free education—as had immigrants and children of newcomers for a century—but also because many other local colleges did not have teams. They were part of a multiethnic squad "of diverse . . . backgrounds and nationalities" that included men with names like Schlisser, Manfredi, Riviere, Wolke, and Paranoson, along with teammates named Saul Fein and Eric Bienstock. Star defenseman Lester Solney's saga intrigued one student scribe, who chronicled how this Budapest-born Jewish refugee had survived because he was "lucky" to have "had many kind Christian friends who hid us in their roofs." Effectively, Solney and his teammates brought the game to the school and taught the sport to those who turned out at Lewisohn Stadium.[32]

One of their pupils was the CCNY soccer coach, Harry "Doc" Karlin, who was the beneficiary of a talented crew from many countries who presented themselves at try-outs. Karlin reported that more than half of his 1957 team came from foreign nations. During practices, "the air was repeatedly shattered with strange utterances known only to those who play the game." Karlin readily admitted that he "knew less about the strategy of the game" than most of his players. A professor of hygiene at the college since the 1920s, his sport of choice was baseball, but he had been tapped over the years to coach swimming, water polo, tennis, and handball before he was asked to lead what his charges called a "football" team. To learn more about the sport, he would attend German-American League games in the city. Youth contests were a good place to recruit athletes; at that point, New York public schools did not have soccer teams. He saw that his job was to "weld these players, unfriendly at best, into a unified team." One crucial point of deliberations and contentions, which led to a "free exchange of ideas," was whether the "European style of 'long' passes" as opposed to the "tight passing game of the U.S." should be the team's style.[33]

But on the field success did not galvanize the campus as basketball had once done or completely erase the "depression" wrought by enduring "thoughts of the scandal." Students of the 1950s, it was said, lacked "the college spirit" that had once been so noticeable. They no longer possessed "the great gusto" of the past "when the basketball team was in its heyday." Enrolled in "a very large . . . college in the middle of a very large city," the men—and now the women too—of CCNY more often than not went their separate ways when classes were over. They evinced little interest in taking part in extracurricular activities. There was no unifying agenda that would bring them to athletic events. And those who grew up on the sidewalks of New York and who played games with their hands and not their feet did not immediately comprehend the new flagship sport or feel a natural, organic connection to what was a strange athletic endeavor. Sensing this apathy and lack of connection, in October 1957, after this varsity had won sixteen games in a row, the *Observation Post*—the school's second undergraduate newspaper—commented critically that "on a nice, clear Friday . . . more students could be found sprawling on the South Campus lawn than at Lewisohn Stadium." For these editorialists, it was a shame that not enough support was forthcoming for athletes who "come up with fine clubs without shouts of 'commercialism' ringing in their ears."[34]

Several weeks later, angling to increase student interest in what was clearly a very successful team, the newspaper itself sponsored a "Beat Army" rally on campus featuring "gab jockey" Jean Shepard—today he would be called a "talk show host." This celebrity attracted some five hundred students to the Finley Student Center Ballroom, where they heard him pitch this away game as a contest between "the guys of a city college and those whose fathers know a senator." To gain admission to the United States Military Academy, of course, required a congressional nomination. Whether because their guest had evoked the image of what was termed "underdogism"—that had previously dogged CCNY students when they thought of elites of all kinds—or simply because the club was so good, several busloads of hard-core and rowdy fans made the trek to West Point and made their sentiments known to their hosts. But this call to arms did not move the vast majority of students.[35]

"Grown accustomed to playing before empty seats," the team was reportedly most "gratified" in November 1959 when one thousand fans turned out for its first-round NCAA tournament victory against Williams College at Lewisohn. They were touched when moments after scoring the winning and only goal of the contest with but twenty-seven seconds left on the clock, supporters ran onto the field and carried their heroes on their shoulders. CCNY star fullback Claude Spinosa was moved to say, "the whole thing looked like a college for a day." Several years later it would be recalled how "our notorious apathy was shed for some time in proud, pensive, jubilation," even if, at that memorable athletic moment, more than seven thousand seats had been empty. And this "temporary push" toward national sports prominence did not last beyond the graduation of this elite corps of soccer players. In the 1960s, the club had to be satisfied with being competitive in the Metropolitan Conference League. It won its last local championship in 1961.[36]

Ultimately, beyond the trauma of the scandal and the ensuing limitations placed on the profile of sports at CCNY, an even more powerful dynamic undermined the commitment and enthusiasm of the student rank-and-file for its teams. Campus critics hinted at the roots of this palpable apathetic attitude when they upbraided their fellow students' lack of engagement with soccer success. After all, it was a brief, shining, moment of national recognition for athletic prowess at the college. But the triumph lacked a crucial compelling component, because the ethnic and religious defensive drive that had unified the campus and underscored competitors' achievements in prior decades was gone.

In the 1950s and 1960s, the institution persisted as predominantly Jewish—as of 1962, at least six of ten students at the school were Jewish—and Jews still found spots on all the varsities that represented CCNY. These third- and fourth-generation young men continued to play the city game and all the minor sports at the college. In the 1966–1967 athletic campaigns, six of the ten basketball players were Jews. Among the college's twenty soccer players there were five Jews. And of the twenty-four lacrosse players who together led CCNY to its best season in decades, there were fourteen Jews on the squad. Some of these competitors were star performers on what were now increasingly multinational, multiethnic, and multiracial teams. Of the fifty-six former Jewish athletes who had competed for CCNY in the 1960s, twenty-two were eventually elected to the school's athletic hall of fame. (By comparison, Jews constituted close to 75 percent of the athletes honored for on the court and in the field achievements in the 1930s.) But the more recent individual and squad accomplishments were not that important on Convent Avenue. At this point Jewish athletes were no longer seen as proving important points about their people's place and status in the United States. Unlike in previous eras, the Jewish athletes at CCNY in the early postwar period in no way played for the Jewish people.[37]

This creative tension to succeed for that higher cause ended in the first decades after World War II as American Jews began to find ever-increasing acceptance among their fellow citizens. Though social antisemitism—the form of prejudice that previously had stymied their integration—had its final heyday during wartime, in the decade that followed, anti-Jewish animus and negative stereotyping declined. For example, though some locales retained restrictive covenants against Jewish residents into the 1960s, wide expanses of suburbia were open for these former city dwellers who had lived in their own ethnic enclaves. To some extent, this change was due to Americans' revulsion over what Hitlerism had wrought. Jews had also garnered street credibility from their fine efforts when the Allied Democracies had been existentially challenged. But perhaps, most important, they benefited from the beginnings of a growing respect for cultural differences. A more egalitarian-minded America in the making opened many doors for Jews.[38]

Amid the milieu of growing acceptance, elite colleges and universities that were previously restrictive became increasingly receptive to Jewish students. Now, those who were dedicated to cultural pluralism—at least as it applied to white applicants—preached, and acted upon the belief in, the importance of building a diversified campus community. As important, as good Cold Warriors, academic officials subscribed to a national ethos that asserted—in an era of *Sputnik* and the battle of political and economic systems—that America had to educate the best and the brightest to serve the country. And Jews—in so many cases—did extremely well on entrance examinations.[39]

At CCNY, undergraduates did not feel as if they were up against an unfriendly elite when they thought of their former high school classmates, whose secondary school GPAs had been a bit higher than theirs and who were doing quite nicely at Ivy League colleges. After all, CCNY continued to be ranked very high as an academic institution. It was still the place of rarified learning that in the generation that preceded these students' arrival had produced seven future Nobel Laureates—"the most of any public university in the United States." And this education remained tuition-free. Accordingly, in this calm environment—where there was much less to prove to others—in the 1950s and 1960s, if and when a CCNY player competed against a man from Yale, he did not see himself as a disadvantaged underdog. Nor was he making a point through his athleticism about his background and his community's position in America. CCNY's unique form of pride in Jewishness, moreover, would not be in play in the stadium, natatorium, or in the arena because, in many instances, opponents on the lacrosse field or soccer pitch or in the pool or on the wrestling mats also might be Jews.[40]

By the 1960s, Jews were no longer seen as predominant in basketball. It had become the African American sport. For the record, while in 1963, Oceanside, Long Island–born Art Heyman of Duke University—following in the footsteps of Lenny Rosenbluth—was named the Associated Press's college hoopster of the year, in the fifty years that followed only two Jews would be elected members of NCAA Division I All-American teams.[41] Still, American Jews remained college athletes and could be found on many of the once called "minor sport" varsities at CCNY and elsewhere. All told, when the Jewish athlete at CCNY of the 1950s and 1960s played his game, his goals were just the same as those of his opposition. When as a sportsman he stood arm-in-arm with his non-Jewish teammates—as CCNY too had become more ethnically and racially diversified—he saw himself, at most, as competing for the honor of alma mater. He was neither pursuing, nor was he seen by others to be striving toward, a higher Jewish cause.

Meanwhile, on Convent Avenue, members of the student body read about their teams' successes and failures in the two student newspapers—although sports reports now were rarely front-page news. During the 1969–1970 academic year, only one of some twenty-five numbers of the *Campus,* featured a page-one sports headline. And the two articles that appeared under the headline noted both that the basketball team's fortunes had fallen on hard times and that fan support at the school had sunk to a low ebb. A columnist commented: "the sad saga of the poorest back-to-back seasons in CCNY cage annals (5-13 and 3-17) coupled with almost total student disinterest have brought the sport to its current nadir." Two months later, as the team suffered the end of another losing campaign in Wingate Gymnasium, a student editorialist allowed that the some two hundred fans who regularly attended home games were perhaps among the minority on campus who had a "hereditary pride" in the team's efforts, even if that "hardy band" of followers recognized that "City College basketball is just a step above the intramural level."[42]

The end of significant numbers of Jews playing sports at City College began in the early 1970s, concomitant with the school's losing its attractiveness as an academic institution to local Jews. Their enrollment percentages dropped precipitously from almost 75 percent of the student body in 1969, including those enrolled at the main St. Nicholas Heights campus and at its Baruch business school branch in Murray Hill, to only 20 percent of the uptown student population ten years later. These declines are attributable, in part, to a perception that the school no longer stood for academic excellence. In the spring of 1969, a city university system-wide fight over "Open Admissions" focused on CCNY. This policy granted a place in any unit to all New York high school graduates, regardless of grades. Those who objected to the plan argued that it meant bringing young men and women unprepared for higher education into advanced academic environments. Simply put, with the pool of Jewish students dropping, Jewish student athletes were no longer on campus to be recruited—as had often been done with its minor sports—from gym classes and from intramural reputations. In the 1973–1974 athletic year, there were two Jews on an overwhelmingly African American basketball team, two Jewish lacrosse players and one Jew on the always multinational soccer squad. In the decades to come, the next generations of New York–born Jewish athletes would make their marks on numerous college campuses, but not at CCNY.

CHAPTER ELEVEN

# Italians and Sport in New York City

## The Road to Americanization

*Gerald R. Gems*

In the summer of 1877 Cesare Orsini expected to gain a measure of wealth and celebrity as a sporting entrepreneur in New York. He transported fourteen professional athletes from Italy to introduce its "national game" of pallone, similar to jai alai, to American audiences. His timing and his judgment proved deficient. Americans showed little interest and spectators proved sparse, leaving the players destitute. New York had long been a hotbed of America's national game, baseball. As early as 1858, twenty-two New York clubs formed the presumptuously titled National Association of Base Ball Players. At their 1870 convention disagreements over the use of paid players led to the establishment of the National Association of Professional Base Ball Players a year later. A National League of professional teams representing cities in the East and Midwest ensued in 1876.[1]

In addition to the American indifference to such foreign influence, Italians had little sense of any national identity despite Orsini's proclamations. Italy's history was one of warring city-states subjugated by foreign occupiers after 1494, and alternately ruled by France, Spain, and Austria. Not until 1861 did Giuseppe Garibaldi succeed in liberating Sicily and the peninsula from foreign rule. Nominally united under the king of Piedmont, a northwestern region, the process of consolidation continued over the remainder of the decade. Residents of the new country remained fragmented by the economy (centered in the North), social class (southern poverty), culture (localized), geography (varied), and language (local dialects). The Mezzogiorno, the overpopulated territory south of Rome, was afflicted with poor soil and hungry peasants. The island of Sicily served as the crossroads of the Mediterranean, alternately ruled by Greeks, Romans, Arabs, Normans, Germans, French, Spanish, and

Austrians. Lacking a national language, local dialects prevailed, unintelligible to others. Primary allegiances rested with family and friends rather than any national state. Northern Italians considered southerners a blight on the new republic and even regarded Sicilians as racially inferior. Karl Marx claimed that "in all human history no country or no people have suffered such terrible slavery, conquest and foreign oppression . . . as Sicily."[2] Nor did conditions improve after unification. Booker T. Washington traveled to Italy in 1910 and drew a comparison with the American South, stating that "the Negro is not the man farthest down. The condition of the colored farmer in the most backward parts of the Southern States in America, even where he has the least education and the least encouragement, is incomparably better than the condition and opportunities of the agricultural population of Sicily."[3]

Italians, mostly illiterate peasants, had already begun a mass migration to America by 1880. New York served as the primary port of entry. By 1900 some 220,000 Italians took up residence in the city and only a decade later they numbered 500,000.[4] There they settled in communal colonies known as Little Italies with Neapolitans on Mulberry Street, Genoese residing on Baxter Street, and Sicilians between Houston and Spring Streets. Conflicts between the immigrants and other ethnic groups were frequent. A 1903 report on residents of Greenwich Village stated that "the racial feeling is very strong. The Irish hate the Italians ('dagoes') and the negroes ('niggers'); and the North Italians hate the Sicilians ('sic')."[5] With such animosity Italians preferred living in a community where the merchants and neighbors spoke their dialect and understood their customs; but that only inhibited their integration in the mainstream American culture. In 1903 the *Boston Globe* claimed that Italians are "the most clannish of all the nationalities that emigrate to the United States," and the hardest to assimilate.[6]

Italian men provided much of the labor for ongoing construction projects in the city, but they were often regarded and treated as less than white. In 1896 Italian laborers received the lowest wages, less than blacks or those considered to be white. Among the subway workers Italians received between $1.75 and $3 per day, while Irish laborers got $3–$5 per day. By 1916 more than half of Italian men in the city were employed as laborers.[7]

The Italian peasant emphasis on physicality rather than education hindered their socioeconomic mobility, but transferred well in the sphere of sport. In 1903 Luther Gulick, the director of physical training for the New York schools, instituted a comprehensive athletic program that included interscholastic championships in the city. Girls were provided with intramural competition by 1905. Gulick's efforts coincided with those of other social activists to assimilate the hordes of European immigrants that arrived in the city each year. After the turn of the twentieth century, Progressive reformers campaigned for legislation banning child labor and introducing mandatory education laws. Italian families often resisted such efforts and employed their children as soon as possible in order to meet basic sustenance needs. Nevertheless, the diligence of truant officers and local authorities resulted in an increasing number of Italian children in the New York school system and their exposure to American sports and games.[8]

The rise in school attendance coincided with the development of an Italian national identity among the disparate groups of immigrants. Sport figured prominently in that transition, led by early Italian boxers. Paolo Vaccarelli migrated from Sicily to New York and assumed the alias of Paul Kelly, fighting in Brooklyn and throughout the Northeast before assuming leadership of the Five Points gang in the city and organizing labor unions on the New York docks. Ugo Micheli adopted the moniker of Hugo Kelly as a nationally prominent middleweight from 1899 to 1912; but Casper Leon (Gaspare Leoni), born in Palermo and known as the Sicilian Swordfish, proved to be a contender for the bantamweight crown in a long career from 1891 to 1904. Leon resided in the city and provided a sense of ethnic pride to other Italians.[9]

As Leon's career declined, another Italian arrived from Europe to bring some unity to the regional factions. Dorando Pietri had to concede his Olympic marathon victory to American Johnny Hayes in a controversial finish in 1908; but Pietri then voyaged to New York to challenge Hayes in an indoor showdown in Madison Square Garden. The *New York Times* described the unified effort to fete the Italian hero. "The Italians were received by deputations from the numerous societies in this city representing their native land and frantically embraced. On behalf of the Italian newspaper *Il Progresso*, it was stated that Dorando would get a silver cup and a purse containing $200 if he succeeded in defeating Hayes."[10] Pietri did not disappoint, not only beating the American, but also setting a new world record before ten thousand wildly cheering spectators, who carried their champion off on their shoulders. Pietri had vindicated Italian honor in a Social Darwinian competition that temporarily assuaged the ethnic insults hurled at Italians.[11] Pietri's victory resulted in a national tour over the next nine months competing against a host of other ethnic runners, including Hayes. Pietri experienced mixed results, but the disparate groups of

Italians throughout the United States, many of whom came out to support his efforts, began to coalesce in a greater national identity.[12]

Gaston Strobino, who migrated from Europe as a young boy, settled in Paterson, New Jersey, where he found work as a machinist's apprentice and started running for a local athletic club. Strobino chose an American identity and became a naturalized citizen, and in 1912 he qualified for the US Olympic team at a race in New York. At the Stockholm Games he won a bronze medal for his adopted country in the marathon, and upon his return to the New York docks a throng of supporters cheered his accomplishment.[13]

Johnny Dundee (Giuseppe Carrora), born in Sicily, learned to fight on the streets of New York, where he turned pro in 1910. Known as "the Scotch Wop" due to his alias, his ring career lasted for twenty-two years and more than three hundred bouts in which he held the junior lightweight championship from 1921 to 1923 and the featherweight title in 1923–1924.[14] Frankie Genaro (Di Gennara), a native New Yorker, won the Olympic flyweight gold medal in 1920 and also turned pro, holding the American title at that weight class until 1925, when he lost it to another Italian, Fidel LaBarba. Genaro gained the world flyweight championship in 1928 and held the crown until 1931. He retired in 1934.[15]

Italian fighters proliferated throughout the interwar years, considerably raising Italians' visibility and identity in interethnic battles; but a more complete acceptance within the American society required success in the national game of baseball. While not the first Italian to engage in the sport, Willie Garoni, the son of immigrant parents, made a brief appearance at the end of the 1899 season with the New York Giants as a pitcher. Frank La Porte had a decade-long career as an infielder starting in New York in 1905.[16]

The first Italian to attain baseball stardom in New York had already achieved considerable celebrity before his arrival in the nation's largest city. Ping Bodie (Francesco Pizzolo), the son of Italian immigrants in San Francisco, quit school to begin his baseball career. In 1910 he slugged thirty home runs for the hometown team in the Pacific League, three times as many as any Major League player, and the Chicago White Sox quickly offered him a contract. Bodie's slugging and clowning attracted fans to the ballpark, but sportswriters still denigrated him as an ape, due to his short, squat frame, despite his 112 runs batted in the 1911 season. After a stint with Philadelphia, the Yankees acquired Bodie in 1918 for a three-year stint in New York, where he was the roommate of Babe Ruth and a favorite of the growing Italian fan base in the city. Fans honored him with Ping Bodie Day at the Polo Grounds in 1920. He was not as popular with his father, however, who disowned him for Anglicizing his name and denigrating his Italian heritage.[17]

San Francisco proved to be a center of Major League talent and the Yankees signed a succession of Italian players from the West Coast city. Tony Lazzeri, born to immigrant parents in 1903, followed in Ping Bodie's steps by quitting school and pursuing an athletic career, first as a boxer, but ultimately in baseball. In 1925 he hit an amazing 60 home runs and drove in 222 in a 197-game season at Salt Lake City. The Yankees brought him to New York the following year, and he remained a mainstay as a second baseman until 1937, finishing his career with the Brooklyn Dodgers and New York Giants in 1939. One New York sportswriter claimed that "he was almost as big a drawing card as Ruth. Italian societies in New York, Boston, Detroit, almost everywhere the Yankees played, held banquets in his honor and showered him with gifts." More than a thousand attended a banquet sponsored by Italian Americans in his honor in 1927. Despite such recognition by Italians, Lazzeri still faced disparagement and ethnic slurs. The media often referred to him as a "dago" and a "wop," as Italians had not yet gained full acceptance in the mainstream society.[18]

Frank Crosetti, another San Francisco Italian, followed Lazzeri to the Yankees' infield in 1932. While both displayed a taciturn demeanor off the field, Crosetti served as a sparkplug at shortstop and third base. While not the offensive threat of Lazzeri, he proved to be a defensive stalwart, playing with the team until 1948 and then continuing as a coach for another two decades.[19] On the other side of town Tony Cuccinello, a native New Yorker, had begun his baseball career on a semipro team, but by 1929 he had reached the Major Leagues with Cincinnati and became the darling of Brooklyn fans when he was traded to the Dodgers in 1932. His brother, Al, had a brief appearance with the Giants in 1935.[20]

During the same era Gus Mancuso appeared as an all-star catcher and captain of the Giants. His prowess on a Texas industrial team earned him a minor league contract, and a trip to the Major League Cardinals in 1928. By 1933 he had been traded to the Giants, where he was considered to be one of the best catchers in the game. Mancuso would eventually enjoy a forty-year career in baseball as a player, coach, manager, and television announcer, but during his playing days he was often referred to as "Blackie" a reference to his skin color and his Sicilian immigrant father.[21]

Throughout the interwar period Italians continued to face discrimination and prejudice. When Luis Angel Firpo, an Italian Argentinian heavyweight, traveled to the United States in 1922, he amassed a string of victories before meeting Jack Dempsey for the championship the following year at the Polo Grounds. American sportswriters characterized him as a "wild man . . . the progeny of Italian vendettists" and "absolutely cold blooded."[22] Journalists described the slugfest in primitive characterizations as follows:

> Luis sat in his corner as watchful as a beast in the jungle. . . . From the first the fighters flew at one another like savages . . . Firpo's mouth gushed blood. . . . In a frenzy of anger and desperation . . . Firpo pounded Dempsey on the jaw with a sledgehammer right . . . (but) under short left and right hooks to the jaw and right hands that threatened to tear the heart out of his side, Firpo went down seven times in that first round. He came up each time, not covered in defense, but lashing like a wild beast in a jungle fury.[23]

Firpo had knocked Dempsey through the ropes where he landed on the sportswriters who helped him back into the ring before he could be counted out, and the fight continued into the second round with eleven knockdowns between the two combatants before Firpo suffered a knockout. Despite his power and courage American sportswriters reasoned that "If Luis Angel Firpo had the brain power in proportion to his tremendous strength, there is no denying that he and not Jack Dempsey would be world's heavyweight champion this morning. . . . But Firpo with all his great strength to give and take punishment, lacked that one essential—a fighting brain."[24]

Sport provided opportunities to overcome such stereotypes and extol an American identity in the latter part of the decade as Italian youth earned spots on the 1928 US Olympic team. Eleanor Garatti set national swimming records and won a gold medal at the Amsterdam Games. The following year she set a world record in the 100-meter freestyle event. Ray Barbuti, born in Brooklyn in 1905, earned accolades as a football and track star in high school, and then took his talents to Syracuse University. He too made the 1928 Olympic team, where he "saved the United States team from humiliation of a shutout on the track by a stirring triumph in the 400-metre final," as the squad had failed to win a single individual event up to that time. Barbuti returned two days later to anchor the 1600-meter relay team that won another gold medal and set a world record. He later affirmed his American identity as a veteran of World War II, serving with the US Army Air Corps.[25]

Still, the Italian quest to obtain whiteness and full acceptance in the mainstream society remained incomplete and was further complicated by the arrival of Primo Carnera in the United States. The Italian giant, 6′7″ and weighing as much as 270 pounds, was portrayed as Mussolini's fascist superman. Carnera made his first trip to the United States in 1930 amassing twenty-four wins with twenty knockouts, but often under suspicious circumstances. Carnera returned in 1932 for a more triumphant tour, followed by throngs of Italian Americans for whom he represented Italian strength and a newfound respect under the throes of Mussolini's dictatorship. In 1933 Carnera knocked out Ernie Schaaf in a bout at Madison Square Garden. Schaaf died a few days afterward. Later that year Carnera knocked out Jack Sharkey before 40,000 fans in Queens to gain the heavyweight championship. For many Italian Americans, Carnera and Mussolini became heroes. Many American transplants even sent their wedding rings to finance Mussolini's invasion of Ethiopia; another $700,000 in funding was sent from New York alone. Young Italian Americans even embarked from the New York docks to join the military campaign. When Joe Louis knocked out Carnera in Yankee Stadium before sixty thousand onlookers in 1935, a series of clashes ensued in Jersey City, Harlem, and Brooklyn between Italians and blacks, who viewed Ethiopia as part of their ancestral homeland in Africa.[26] Such attachments to Italy led other Americans to question the loyalty of the Italians.

That sense of limited Americanization began to change with the rise of Joe DiMaggio, the son of Sicilian immigrants in San Francisco. DiMaggio dropped out of high school, but eschewed the life of his fisherman father to pursue baseball. As a nineteen-year-old in 1933 he hit in sixty-one straight games for the San Francisco Seals in the Pacific Coast League. By 1935 he was named the Most Valuable Player in the league, and a year later he joined the Yankees in New York. Twenty-five thousand Italians attended his debut, and his stellar play attracted thousands more to Yankee Stadium, where they waved Italian flags and bombarded him with fan mail. Their attraction to the American game provided a counterbalance to Italian Americans' embrace of Mussolini's fascism. By 1939 DiMaggio was named the Most Valuable Player in the American League, and the Yankees had garnered four World Series titles. Still, a writer for the popular *Life* magazine characterized him as a freak with genetic advantages, asserting that he was lazy, shiftless, and inarticulate. The author granted him a limited measure of assimilation by stating that he combed his hair with water

Joe DiMaggio, ca. 1939.
*Courtesy Wikimedia Commons.*

rather than "olive oil or smelly bear grease" and that he did not "reek of garlic."[27] Despite the continuing negative connotations DiMaggio's greatness could not be denied. In 1941 he produced a fifty-six-game hitting streak, still the Major League Baseball record. He also patrolled center field with consummate grace and was acknowledged as a five-tool superstar who could hit, hit for power, run, catch, and throw with ultimate skill. He became the most famous player in the game until his retirement in 1951. Over the course of his career DiMaggio led the Yankees to ten World Series, won the Most Valuable Player award three times (1939, 1941, 1947), and appeared in thirteen All-Star games, having been selected each year that he played.

Teammate Lefty Gomez claimed that "All the Italians in America adopted him. Just about every day at home and on the road there would be an invitation from some Italian-American club."[28] Italian American youth as well as many non-Italians idolized him. Actor Ben Gazzara stated that "he was our god, the god of all Italian Americans."[29] George Pataki, later to become the governor of New York, claimed that "he was every American boy's hero, including mine."[30] For many second-generation ethnic youth caught in a liminal existence and living in two cultures, caught between the ancestral language and customs of their parents' homeland and their own birthplace and the American culture fostered by their schooling, DiMaggio represented a bridge and future promise.

In 1941 Dolph Camilli, a first baseman for the Brooklyn Dodgers, won the National League Most Valuable Player award, while DiMaggio claimed the same honor in the American League, further enhancing the stature of Italians in the national game. Despite their prominence and growing significance, when World War II erupted Italian Americans, including DiMaggio's parents, were considered to be "enemy aliens" and removed from their coastal home in California. In New York City, Italians who had not yet obtained citizenship were fingerprinted, photographed, and registered with the Federal Bureau of Investigation, subject to limited travel, nightly curfews, and domestic raids.[31]

Italian American men, however, left little doubt about their loyalty when they joined the American military forces in massive numbers during the war. Those numbers included Joe DiMaggio and Phil Rizzuto, another native New Yorker who had established himself as the Yankees' shortstop in 1941. Both players gave three years in the prime of their careers to the war effort. Many more gave their lives to the American cause, ending any doubt as to the allegiance of Italian Americans. Historian Dick Crepeau assessed DiMaggio's role in the Americanization process. He "played out a mythic ideal for them (Italians) about American dreams and American promise. . . . He was a hero to later generations because some came to believe that he embodied some lost ideal. . . . He was a successful non-WASP in the WASP world."[32]

DiMaggio's ascendance coincided with the rise of other Italians in the popular culture, such as Frank Sinatra, and a resurgence of Italian boxers. Rocky Graziano (Thomas Rocco Barbella), a product of New York's mean streets on the Lower East Side, had only a fifth-grade education. After three trips to and six years in reform school for stealing and a dishonorable discharge from the army, he used his boxing skills to escape his youthful past. His brawling style won a legion of fans, especially after taking the middleweight championship from Tony Zale in 1947, honored as the Fight of the Year, in which Graziano earned $70,000. Graziano continued to fight through 1952 and then parlayed his celebrity into a variety of roles as an author, actor, comedian, and television personality, widely beloved by middle America.[33]

Jake LaMotta, a contemporary of Graziano and his reform school acquaintance, did not fare quite as well. The son of an Italian immigrant peddler, he too learned to fight on the New York streets at an early age. By the age of nineteen he had turned professional in 1941. Two years later he ended Sugar Ray

Robinson's consecutive professional win streak at 40-0 in the first of their six brutal encounters, and the only one that LaMotta would win. LaMotta held the middleweight championship from 1949 to 1951 and retired after his last fight in 1954, but never enjoyed the celebrity of Graziano, although he, too, turned to comedy, wrote books, and managed nightclubs. He was jailed on a morals charge involving procurement of an underaged female, but the 1980 movie, *Raging Bull*, proved a critical success in its brutal portrayal of his tormented life and restored a measure of fame. LaMotta also made numerous films and appeared on television, but lacked the lovable persona of Graziano. Still, he enjoyed a long life, engaging in his seventh marriage in 2013.[34]

The career of Joey Giardello (Carmine Tilelli) paralleled that of LaMotta in some respects. Born in the Bedford-Stuyvesant community in Brooklyn in 1930 as Carmine Tilelli, he learned to fight in the street gangs of the city. Like LaMotta, both would spend some time in prisons. At the age of fifteen he borrowed cousin Joe Giardello's identification to join the army in 1945 and became a paratrooper with the Eighty-Second Airborne Division, where he honed his boxing skills. The war ended before he saw any combat experience outside the ring, and his parents exposed his ruse in order to gain a discharge. Still using his alias he began his professional boxing career in Philadelphia, often fighting other Italians on the eastern circuit. By the 1950s he had become a nationally ranked contender in the middleweight division, but could not get a title fight. Jake LaMotta had faced the same dilemma. During the 1940s a syndicate of gangsters led by Frankie Carbo and Frank "Blinky" Palermo had taken control of boxing and dictated title bouts and venues in conjunction with promoters known as the International Boxing Club (IBC). In 1947 LaMotta had to throw a fight to Billy Fox in order to get a chance at the title, but did not report the subterfuge to the authorities. LaMotta explained, "Besides coming from the neighborhood I came from, I could never be a screw. You know, a stool pigeon or a rat. You could never do that in my business. Because of your ego, your manhood, your pride, whatever, you could never do anything like that. Even if you were being hurt and it was all wrong. You had to fight your own battle. The mob was on the other side, and I was on my own side, so I had to take it on the chin."[35]

Rocky Graziano had been offered a $100,000 bribe to throw a fight, but feigned an injury to avoid the bout. Joey Giardello turned down $12,000, but failed to report it. He claimed that "the code of ethics he learned in the streets of Brooklyn prohibited any form of squealing, about fixes or anything else."

Each of the boxers subscribed to a sense of honor instilled in their ancestral homeland over centuries and continued in America, but at odds with WASP notions of rectitude. Both Giardello and LaMotta lost their boxing licenses before eventual reinstatement. The federal government finally investigated the IBC in 1960–1961 and sent Carbo and Palermo to prison. Giardello finally got a title fight in 1960, but did not gain the middleweight crown until he defeated a Nigerian boxer, Dick Tiger, in 1963. Like LaMotta, a portion of his boxing career was portrayed, but inaccurately and in a disparaging manner, in the 1999 movie *Hurricane*, for which he filed suit and received financial compensation.[36]

By that time, numerous Italian ballplayers had succeeded Joe DiMaggio as local stars on the New York teams. In fact, the Yankees, Dodgers, and Giants largely monopolized baseball laurels in the postwar era with a bevy of Italian players. In the 1947 World Series the Yankees faced the Dodgers, and Italians figured prominently in the outcome. The Dodgers gained the National League championship on the strength of all-star pitcher Ralph Branca. In game four of the series the Dodgers' Cookie Lavagetto broke up a no-hitter in the ninth inning with a game-winning double. In game six, Dodgers' outfielder Al Gionfriddo robbed Joe DiMaggio with a spectacular catch of a long game-tying drive, eliciting a disgusted kick at the infield dirt from the usually stoic Yankee star. Other Italians, including Phil Rizzuto and Yogi Berra, contributed to the Yankees win in the deciding game seven.

The Yankees would dominate the series over the next decade, winning ten titles from 1947 to 1962, fielding such Italians as Frank Crosetti, Johnny Lucadello, Vic Raschi, Ken Silvestri, Charlie Silvera, Zeke Bella, Bobby Del Greco, Billy Martin (Italian mother), as well as the hall of famers, DiMaggio, Berra, and Rizzuto over that span. In the 1954 World Series the New York Giants captured the crown with Sal Maglie, Mario Picone, and Johnny Antonelli on their pitching staff, while Joe Garagiola served as a backup catcher, and Joey Amalfitano patrolled the infield. The following year the Yankees faced the Brooklyn Dodgers in the World Series, as the latter included Carl Furillo, Tom Lasorda, and Roy Campanella (Sicilian father), as Brooklyn prevailed. The Yankees reversed the outcome the following year as the same two teams captured league flags in 1956. The Yankees would appear in nine of the ten World Series from 1955 to 1964. The emergence of so many second-generation Italians in the American national game in the media capital of the United States demonstrated a clear level of assimilation and DiMaggio's brief marriage to Hollywood icon Marilyn Monroe in 1954 solidified Italians' claim to whiteness and acceptance.

The status of baseball as the national game waned as football assumed greater popularity throughout the midcentury. The nationally televised 1958 NFL championship game between the New York Giants and the Baltimore Colts was played in Yankee Stadium, which ended in a dramatic sudden-death overtime victory for the latter, and is often credited as the transitional event in the rise of professional football. The Giants' defensive line was anchored by Andy Robustelli, while Gino Marchetti served as his Colts' counterpart. Vince Lombardi served as the Giants' offensive coordinator. All three would gain entry to the football Hall of Fame. Lombardi would become an American icon as a football coach, and his name would be bestowed upon the national championship trophy. But Italians were once thought to be incapable of playing the sport. Elmer Mitchell, a professor at the University of Michigan, published an article entitled "Racial Traits in Athletics" in 1922, in which he claimed that "the Italian was better fitted for games of quickness, dexterity, and skill, rather than of rugged strength. He lacked self-discipline and was too fiery and impulsive of feeling for contact sports. . . . Italians' tendency to the extreme of elation, or to the opposite extreme of despondency, made them fearless, daring, and reckless but also more easily stampeded into a rout if beaten."[37]

Lou Little (Luigi Piccolo) contradicted such assertions as a veteran of World War I and an early professional player. In 1924 he became the head football coach at Georgetown before assuming the same role at Columbia University in 1930. Four years later he led the university to a Rose Bowl victory. Little's coaching abilities earned him a spot in the College Football Hall of Fame.[38] As Little progressed in his career, Vince Lombardi, born in Brooklyn in 1913, was enduring ethnic slurs that led to fights on high school gridirons. Lombardi attended Fordham University, where he won renown as one of the "seven blocks of granite" on its offensive line. He began his coaching career in the local high school ranks, where he languished from 1939 to 1947 before his alma mater hired him to coach its freshman team. By 1954 he graduated to the professional ranks as the offensive coordinator of the New York Giants, but feared that he would never get a head coaching position due to his ethnicity. In 1959 the forlorn Green Bay Packers took a chance on him, and he rewarded them with five NFL championships and two Super Bowl titles.[39] Lombardi dispelled the stereotypes of Italians' inabilities regarding executive qualities with his adherence to discipline, order, precision, and organization, while reinforcing his ethnic cultural values of religious devotion and family life.[40]

Joe Paterno, another product of Brooklyn, born in 1926, gained admittance to the prestigious Brown University, but despite his skill on the football field, he also endured ethnic slurs and rejection by some of the school fraternities. His perseverance and football acumen landed him a position on the football staff at Penn State in 1950, where he would eventually amass more victories than any other coach in major college football history.[41]

While New York playgrounds are well known for producing basketball talent, Italian players have been relatively scarce among the top echelons of the sport. Gene Melchiorre, though not a native New Yorker, made a name for himself at Madison Square Garden in the National Invitational Tournament (NIT) of 1950. An All-American guard for Bradley University, Melchiorre's team made it to the championship game, where it lost to the City College of New York (CCNY). CCNY would go on to capture the NCAA championship as well. Melchiorre was the number-one pick in the following NBA draft, but both schools were implicated in a point-shaving scandal involving thirty-two teams, and Melchiorre was banned from the NBA ranks.[42]

Al Bianchi, born in Queens, did graduate to the NBA ranks as a guard for the Syracuse Nationals from 1956 to 1963, and Rudy LaRusso proved to be a prolific scorer for the Minneapolis Lakers and an NBA all-star during his tenure in the league (1959–1967). Tom Gugliotta, another product of the New York high schools, enjoyed a stellar collegiate career and was a first-round pick of the Washington Bullets in 1992, playing for seven NBA teams from 1992 to 2005.

The number of basketball coaches emanating from New York, however, is quite impressive. Jim Valvano recruited Gugliotta to play at North Carolina State. Valvano, born in Queens, gained his acumen in the New York area and became a college coach in 1967, winning the national championship at North Carolina State in 1983. Lou Carnesecca, a contemporary of Valvano, enjoyed a storied career at St. John's University, where he was twice named the national Coach of the Year (1983, 1985), and elected to the Basketball Hall of Fame. The university acknowledged his service by naming the basketball arena after him in 2004. P. J. Carlesimo also got his coaching start in New York at Fordham in 1971 with additional stints at Wagner College and nearby Seton Hall before joining the ranks of NBA coaches, including the Brooklyn Nets.

Italians also added to the city's football glory in the waning decades of the twentieth century, as Bill Parcells (Italian mother) led the New York Giants to two Super Bowl victories (XXI and XXV). One of the team stars, Mark Bavaro at tight end, earned All-Pro honors in 1986 and 1987. Parcells would return to New York as head coach and general manager of the New York Jets from 1997 to 2000, and Eric Mangini served as his assistant from 1997 to 1999 before assuming the role of Jets head coach from 2006 to 2008.

At the turn of the twenty-first century, New York buttressed its athletic honor under the tutelage of a native son, Joe Torre, born in Brooklyn in 1940. Torre played baseball for three National League teams, including the New York Mets (1975–1977), earning all-star recognition on nine occasions. He was named the National League's Most Valuable Player in 1971. From 1996 to 2007 he managed the New York Yankees, bringing four World Series titles to the city. Another Italian, Joe Girardi, assumed managerial duties for the Yankees in 2008, and added the 2009 World Series title to the Yankees' fabled history.

New York served as the primary port of entry for most Italians migrating to the United States, and the metropolitan area still serves as the primary residence for those claiming Italian ancestry in the United States. Several "Little Italies" continue to exist as ethnic enclaves within the city's boroughs, where the Italian language, foods, and religious festivals mark visible differences with the mainstream WASP culture of America. Among Italian youth a vibrant resurgence of Italian pride is evident in the guido culture featured on popular television shows, New York radio stations, online chat rooms, and in particular urban dance clubs. Italian studies prosper at Queens College as students embrace their ancestral past. Some sociologists have asserted that such developments amount to a limited or segmented assimilation in the American society in which the ethnic group picks and chooses between alternatives in adopting and adapting cultural norms, values, and standards.[43] It is quite clear, however, that in sport Italians found a means to express their physicality, gain a measure of respect and acceptance, and prosper in their adopted land.

CHAPTER TWELVE

# Jewish Institutions and Women's Sport

## New York City in the Late Nineteenth and Early Twentieth Centuries

*Linda J. Borish*

### Introduction

In the late nineteenth and early twentieth centuries, first at Jewish settlement houses and then at Young Men's–Young Women's Hebrew Associations, middle- and upper-class reformers promoted immigrant Jewish women's physical health and sport as part of their Americanization program within Jewish social and religious contexts. Jewish immigrant aid associations included vocational, religious, and educational training as well as physical training, exercise, and sport in their mission in New York City. Why did these programs of the Hebrew Technical School for Girls, the Clara de Hirsch Home, and the New York City Young Women's Hebrew Association emphasize physical culture and sporting activities as important for Jewish immigrant young women? This chapter examines how sporting experiences fostered a community and ethnic identity for young Jewish women and the ways gender and ethnicity shaped the types of sports deemed appropriate for them. Some American Jewish women and girls engaged in sport and promoted their physical health. At times young Jewish women and girls competed with Jewish and non-Jewish women to display their athletic skill and ethnic pride.

Many images portrayed Jewish women as lacking in physical energy and sporting ability; the historical evidence I have uncovered, however, shatters this stereotype as well as the claim of their failure to participate in American sport. In 1914, in the American Jewish paper, the *Sentinel,* journalist Bertha A.

Loeb described the stereotype of the Jewish woman as a lower-class feeble and weary immigrant without bodily verve. Although she articulated the prevailing conception about sport and physical health of Jews of both sexes in the early twentieth century, she foresaw that: "The undersized, anaemic 'Jewish weakling' will soon be a recollection of by-gone days." Some Jewish institutions were building gymnasiums "for the youth of both sexes."[1] Another stereotype depicted the Jewish woman as mother, wife, and childrearer, with exceptional domestic and cooking skills, but no ability or interest in sport and physical fitness. The ample and hefty Jewish woman stood in sharp contrast to the slender and energetic American woman championed by several health and sport commentators in the early twentieth century.[2] Unlike "ladies," Jewish women, like the Jewish mother, or "Yiddishe mama," cooked in Kosher homes, ate too much, neglected physical exercise, and insisted on "cooking, cleaning, and caring for children."[3]

The historical record of Jewish women in immigrant aid associations organized by middle- and upper-class German Jews in American society demonstrates the ways these women at times advocated for greater access to sports for females within a Jewish context. Like Jewish men in immigrant associations, Jewish women's exposure to sport occurred largely at urban Jewish institutions. Historian of sport Steven Riess explains that when the influx of Eastern European Jews occurred in the 1880s, "athletically minded German Jews formed their own ethnic (non-Zionist) sport clubs where they could display their prowess among people of similar background and class. Second-generation, working-class Eastern European Jews were introduced to sports that fit in well with their environment in streets, public parks, settlement houses, and boxing gymnasiums."[4] Moreover, German Jews had brought with them to the United States their physical culture, especially their German gymnastics, the Turner societies. The German Jews "were active participants in competitive sport, which supplanted the old interest in fencing and gymnastics."[5] The National Jewish Welfare Board (founded in 1917), which in 1921 became the national parent organization of the YMHAs, YWHAs, and JCCs (Jewish Community Centers), emphasized serving Jews of both sexes in new programs, including sport programs. The National Jewish Welfare Board reported on the long interest in physical culture of the Jewish people it served: "Historically health and physical education programming has played an important role in YM-YWHAs and Jewish Community Centers of this country for a great many years." The German Turnverein Society stimulated interest in keeping physically fit "through formal calisthenics and apparatus programs." "In addition," the report continued, "a sports program was beginning to develop in colleges and schools throughout the United States."[6]

Historians of American sport have investigated immigrant groups such as the German American Turners, and research has been conducted on the "Lady Turners." They have explored women in sport in such groups as the Czech Sokols or Polish Falcons.[7] The subject of Jewish immigrant women in sport, however, remains little explored. This study of the organizations in New York City that included sport for young Jewish women in their programming and plans helps to meet the need for scholarship in this field.

Jewish immigrant women were exposed to American life and sporting forms at settlement houses and immigrant aid associations in the last decades of the nineteenth century and then at Young Men's–Young Women's Hebrew Associations. Eastern European Jewish immigrants settled in large cities like New York, Boston, Philadelphia, Chicago, and Detroit. I found that "Progressive Era, middle-class social reformers like Jane Addams and Jewish American Lillian Wald, alarmed at the vice and danger they perceived in the city culture and street life of lower-class eastern European Jewish immigrants, sought to inculcate youth into middle-class gender roles and cultural values, and they believed women needed physical stamina to fulfill their domestic roles."[8] Recreational and sporting pursuits became part of the program to promote the well-being of young Jewish women and girls. German Jews, who by the last decades of the nineteenth century had become wealthier and oriented to American culture and institutions, sought to aid the newest Jewish immigrants to adjust to American life. German Jews opted to promote assimilation rather than nurturing the ethnic identities and religiosity of these new Jewish immigrants.

In particular, middle- and upper-class reformers promoted immigrant Jewish women's physical health and sport as part of their Americanization within Jewish social and religious contexts. During the late nineteenth century, young Jewish immigrant women from Eastern Europe faced urban conditions that threatened their well-being, and social reform efforts of German-Jewish Americans focused on securing their physical and moral health. Sport historian Benjamin G. Rader argued that "a quest for subcommunities in the nineteenth century furnishes an important key to understanding the rise of American sport." Rader explored what he termed two types of subcommunities: "ethnic and status," explaining, "The ethnic community usually arose from contradictory forces of acceptance and rejection of the immigrant by the majority society." This concept of sport as part of the forging of ethnic communal identity is manifested in this study of Jewish women, sporting activities, and ethnic organizations. Young Jewish women's participation supported the Jewish women reformers' conviction "that sport . . . was useful in socializing youth."[9] Rader did not focus on Jewish immigrants and ethnic communities; nor did he focus in depth on women.[10] Yet most studies that address Jewish men and sports support historian Donna Gabaccia's contention that "most histories of immigrants in the United States begin with the experiences of migratory men disguised as genderless human beings."[11] Historical studies of sport that focus on Jewish men explore how Jewish immigrant males from the 1880s to the 1920s found that "through sport . . . [they] could be more American and not any less Jewish," especially when they engaged in these activities in urban areas with large Jewish populations.[12] I seek to add to the historical understanding of sport in American culture and to contribute to American Jewish and gender history, by focusing a spotlight on some of the American Jewish women's institutions in New York City, illuminating how they promoted Jewish women's sporting activities in the late nineteenth and early twentieth centuries.

## The Hebrew Technical School for Girls

At the Hebrew Technical School for Girls in New York City, organized in 1881, classes prepared Jewish girls in domestic education and physical education. Jewish girls learned hand sewing, machine sewing, drawing, millinery, dressmaking, cooking, stenography, typewriting and bookkeeping, arithmetic, English, literature, and physical culture. In 1900, Emily M. Opper, superintendent of the school located on Henry Street, reported on "Our Gymnasium": "Two gymnasium classes, one for the Commercial, one for the Manual course, have just been started." Although the school lacked its own gymnasium, "we have again, through the courtesy of Miss Wald [founder of Henry Street Settlement], secured the use of the large gymnasium room" at the Children's Aid Society. Opper emphasized, "Physical Culture is necessary to the development of moral and mental culture," adding that the gymnasium classes "were immensely popular." The enthusiasm for girls' physical training generated efforts to secure expanded space. In the 1902 *Annual Report of the Hebrew Technical School for Girls,* the president of the school remarked on the work in physical culture and surmised, "The girls love this work; but the pity is that our facilities are ridiculously limited." In fact, for the Jewish girls, "We want a swimming pool, shower baths and a fine gymnasium, in which not only the physical well-being of our girls will be promoted, but, at least of equal importance, in which also will be instilled a love of athletics."[13]

Moving to expanded quarters, the Hebrew Technical School for Girls maintained its focus on mental and physical activities. Mrs. Grover Cleveland, wife of President Cleveland, laid the cornerstone of the new building in November 1904, with President Cleveland attending, too. The Hebrew Technical School for Girls moved to a larger building, dedicated in May 1906, located at 15th Street and Second Avenue in New York City, where physical education continued to play a prominent role in the girls' activities. The Jewish girls stayed at the school for eighteen months, and in the summer focused more on "wholesome physical exercise." In reflecting on the new quarters, President Nathaniel Myers stressed that the girls now "have fresh air, clean surroundings, medical attention, nourishment, roof garden, Gymnasium and Swimming Pool."[14]

The *American Hebrew* in 1908 highlighted the place of the sporting activities for the Jewish females at the Hebrew Technical School. "In addition to the roof-garden and gymnasium, which are used to the limit during the summer, next year the girls will enjoy a splendid swimming pool which is being erected at a cost of $23,000, for which excavations are now being made under the sidewalk immediately in front of the building." This pool "will be connected with shower baths, will be supplied with constantly running water, and will be in charge of a teacher and a physician, to insure all sanitary precautions."[15]

The girls' swimming pool opened in 1909 at the Hebrew Technical School for Girls. The excellent facilities for vocational work and physical training gained praise from the school's leader. President Nathaniel Myers claimed in the 1909 *Annual Report* that the swimming pool "is now among our best utilities. Nearly every girl in the school can to-day dive and swim." Myers explained that the swimming pool gave these Jewish girls other benefits, as it "is not alone a great boon to their health; it fosters a love of cleanliness, and it also tends to overcome an inherited undue timidity," and "in its place to substitute wholesome self-confidence and a love of beneficial exercise and sport." Not only did the young women enjoy using the swimming pool and gymnasium at the Hebrew Technical School for Girls, but they played "Basket Ball on the Roof."[16]

The gymnasium and the swimming pool became a popular athletic site of both girls and boys in American Jewish life. The Hebrew Technical Institute for Boys in New York lacked an adequate gymnasium, and the president acknowledged in 1909 that the boys used the gym "supplied by the courtesy of our neighbor, the Hebrew Technical School for Girls, which has continued to allow our boys to make use of its gymnasium at periods when it was not otherwise needed," and expressed thanks to the girls' school for its hospitality. Given the popularity of swimming for Jewish youth of both sexes, the pool received much use for aquatic activities. In the girls' programs, the *American Hebrew* reported in February 1909, "its directorate was almost totally Jewish and it was based upon Jewish ideals."[17]

This Jewish institution continued to aid girls in New York, and athletics became an integral part of its successful programs of education and recreation. Indeed, in 1919 the *American Hebrew* highlighted that the Hebrew Technical School for Girls provided "Training for Womanhood": on the East Side, "there is an institution which has dedicated its powers to the training of girls for the important job—of being women. Mind and body, fingers and brain share alike in the educational program." Specifically, pupils learned skills in "'womanly' arts, and "hygiene, swimming and gymnastics." The philosophy underlying the training of these Jewish girls rested on the Greeks and physical culturists who taught "a sound mind in a sound body and they add, too, the future of the women and of all society depends upon the foundation of good health which is laid during the formative years of girlhood." To safeguard the health of the five hundred Jewish females, this institution had "a completely equipped medical department" with two proficient physicians. Physical culture formed a significant component of the Jewish girls' activities. "In the gymnasium, pupils enjoy beneficial exercises, folk dancing, and basketball, and in the pool are taught to swim. A roof garden is used for gymnastic work in the spring, summer and fall."[18] The image of the Jewish girls engaging in dumbbell exercise in their proper gym indicates their active participation in sporting pursuits. An image in the *American Hebrew* (1919) of the Jewish girls engaging in dumbbell exercise in their proper gym costume indicates their active participation in sporting pursuits.

Indeed, in the early 1920s, the new president of the Hebrew Technical School for Girls, Adolph Lewisohn, announced the significance of physical culture and sporting activities there: "Through the exercises in the gymnasium and the swimming pool and the other facilities," Jewish girls "are built up to be stronger and physically better than when they entered the school, and by the general instruction they receive and the example that is set them they are greatly improved in knowledge and character."[19]

Other Jewish immigrant aid organizations believed physical training ought to be part of the immigrant's adjustment to American culture. The Educational Alliance, founded in 1889, evolved from the merger of three social welfare agencies led by German Jews. The Educational Alliance proclaimed as its mission to help the throng of Eastern European immigrants in the Lower East Side of New York in the transition to American society. New York City's Educational Alliance considered physical training and sporting experiences for immigrant Jews to be part of its Americanization mission. In 1895 the alliance stated in its "Physical Work" that "Competent instructors have been engaged both for the male and female classes, and now both young men and young women and children receive the benefits of well-regulated physical exercise."[20]

The women's section of the Educational Alliance played a dynamic role in shaping the physical culture training for working-class Jewish women. Female gymnasium activities consisted of bodily exercises, marching, fancy steps, and work with dumbbells, wands, clubs, balls, hoops, horse rings, rope, and jumping. Physical culture teachers emphasized health-building activities rather than competitive contests, in keeping with gender conventions of middle-class women. Yet young women desired active sport and recreations. A female social worker reported that an athletic meet of the girls was "a great success." In 1911 Julia Richman, Jewish philanthropist, argued that the gym ought to be opened on certain afternoons for "girls between the ages of eleven and fifteen, who are wandering aimlessly about the streets and who might be attracted to amusement halls and other places of doubtful influence." As a counterpoint to the dance halls, saloons, and street life for Jewish girls, the alliance's physical culture promoters wanted women to participate in sport and exercise. Women physical culture instructors endorsed "The Walking Club" with the purpose of "arousing girls' interest in city history and at the same time stimulating in them a desire for healthful outdoor exercise." The director of Girls' Clubs in 1916 remarked that the "Athletic Club" had done "excellent work."[21] This New York Educational Alliance served as the model for the Jewish Educational Alliances established in other cities with immigrant Jews such as in Baltimore, St. Louis, and Atlanta.[22]

## The Clara De Hirsch Home for Working Girls

To serve Jewish working-class immigrant girls in New York City, in 1897, Baroness Clara de Hirsch endowed and founded the Clara De Hirsch Home for Working Girls. Baroness de Hirsch was the wife of prominent philanthropist and wealthy financier Baron Maurice de Hirsch of the Baron de Hirsch Fund, which had been established in 1892. She drew on the fund's mission to promote the Americanization of Jewish immigrants from Russia, Romania, and Austria-Hungary. This fund "at the outset of its career . . . fostered various local enterprises for the education of Jewish immigrants" and donated money to local organizations to assist Eastern European Jewish immigrants.[23] Oscar and Sarah Straus, German Jewish benevolent leaders in New York, along with the Baroness de Hirsch, launched the Clara de Hirsch Home for Working Girls, with the baroness initially contributing $200,000 and then an additional $175,000 for building costs. When the baron died in April 1896 in Hungary, the Baroness de Hirsch continued the generous philanthropy. The *New York World* reported, "on the authority of the Baroness Hirsch herself that she has decided to spend $1,500,000.00 in this city." Oscar Straus, trustee of the Baron de Hirsch Fund, stated that the baroness "has also informed me that she will put up a working girls' home on plans which have been considered by her and similar to other homes she has had built in cities abroad."[24]

At the Clara de Hirsch Home for Working Girls in New York City, the baroness planned "to establish a trade training school for girls, with a boarding department for those who went to work." The founder expressed that the home should be "'a Jewish nonsectarian institution'" while the institutional control was to always be Jewish. Sarah Straus served as the first president of the Clara de Hirsch Home and the board of directors consisted of wealthy New York German Jews; of the thirteen directors on the original board only two were men—Oscar Straus and Treasurer Edmund E. Wise.[25] The Baroness de Hirsch declared the purpose of the home was to enable the working girls to achieve self-support and "also to improve the mental, moral, and physical condition of the girls, by providing a good home, and also to train them for such occupations as may be practical and for which they are best qualified." In addition to training in domestic service, cooking, and sewing, they could also receive instruction in millinery, "stenography, typewriting, and other useful arts" for the girls to be "placed in suitable wage-earning positions."[26] The girls at this home ranged in age from fourteen to twenty-one. After a two-year period of renting space, in 1899 the Clara de Hirsh Home opened on East 63rd Street, with a five-story building housing 25 girls, and space to serve 75 to 100 girls. Later, at one point it cared for 160 girls.[27]

Early on, the physical health of the girls received attention from the directress of the house, and "a roof garden" provided a place for them to engage in some outdoor exercise, as appropriate recreational and sporting activities became part of the schedule of Jewish girls. On May 23, 1899, on the opening of the Clara de Hirsch Home, the *New York Times* reported on the board's goal: "Later in the year a gymnasium will be fitted up."[28] The type of physical culture and sport for these girls reveals gender and ethnic concerns as the Jewish girls' participation was initially to improve their physical health to fit them for their role in American society, rather than for athletic competition. The Clara de Hirsch Home provided recreational and vocational training for immigrant girls through its affiliation with organizations like the National Council of Jewish Women and the Educational Alliance. These groups ardently desired Jewish girls to partake of the physical recreation and sports they sponsored, as a way to counter the evils of city life, such as the lure of prostitution, vices of drinking and gambling, and commercial amusements.[29]

In the 1901 *Report of the Resident Directress* of the Clara de Hirsch Home, Rose Summerfield, a Jewish settlement house worker, detailed the disciplined schedule for the young women of the home. The schedule integrated exercise even though the gymnasium was not complete. Summerfield stated that the "daily routine of the trainees" included English instruction as well as vocational and physical education: "One hour each afternoon is devoted to outdoor exercise, and each trainee has an hour in the English class." President of the Clara de Hirsch Home, Mrs. Oscar S. Straus, explained in her report of 1900–1901 that "One of the features of the Home is the newly organized club which is open to both boarders and trainees." The purpose of this club "is to provide the members with instruction in cooking, millinery, physical culture, English, and German" for a fee of 10 cents a month.[30] These classes took place within a Reform Judaism context, with Jewish holidays and the Sabbath being observed in the first years of the home; in 1911 the home maintained kosher dietary practices. Physical culture, consisting of gymnastics, calisthenics, and outdoor exercise like walking, involved health-enhancing activities and sport, as health reformers and sports advocates used the term at the turn of the twentieth century. In 1914 the Clara de Hirsch Home, known as the "'Welcome House Settlement,'" reported a "Physical Culture" class instructed by Miss Kottek.[31]

Due to lack of space at the Clara de Hirsch Home, the staff facilitated outdoor boating and swimming at properties sponsored by other Jewish settlements. For example, in a report of June 10, 1910, assistant superintendent Viola Eckstein wrote, "At present through the kindness of Miss Wald and the Nurses' Settlement, five of the trainees are enjoying two weeks' vacation at the Rest, Grand View on the Hudson." She noted that during the summer months activities like outdoor exercise, conducive to physical health, available at the outdoor camp, seemed preferable. "The girls like to be on the streets and it is hard to attract them elsewhere" with the "picture show and the ice-cream parlor" offering more enticing diversion, than the roof of the home.[32] The quest for outdoor sports like swimming for these girls at the home remained an important summer activity. The minutes of the Clara de Hirsch Home in 1911 recorded that the home's camp facility in New Jersey, the "Welcome House Vacation Home," had opened July to September: "The Gals had [a] most enjoyable time—the bathhouses were rented—which included also bathing in the pool, if the lake was too rough." A concerted fund-raising effort was undertaken so that Jewish working-class girls could enjoy access to outdoor sports especially in the hot summers in the city. Rose Summerfield reported in March 1916 that she "would like to send" the seventy-nine trainees, "all of whom were Jewesses," "to the various camps this summer." "No one can form an idea unless they see the girls, what even one week in the country means to them."[33]

The emphasis on gender-appropriate physical activities within a Jewish environment continued at the home. In her November 1919 report, Summerfield documented, "The Gymnasium class which was organized in October is attended by 30 boarders, who seem to like it very well." The Clara de Hirsch Home girls' interest in physical exercise and sport prompted the superintendent to announce additional programs. Summerfield explained in 1922, "Mrs. Wilcox is to have two evenings a week for physical training, dividing the work as it is too heavy for one night."[34] The girls and trustees continued funding efforts for sporting activities and equipment, such as "to pay partly for the mats they use in the physical training classes." By 1920 sports increased for the Jewish girls of the home. In the summer of 1922 Jewish girls from the Clara de Hirsch Home participated in an array of sports at the Young Women's Hebrew Association's Ray Hill Camp at Mount Kisco, New York, opened in May 1922. Sports at the camp included swimming and boating, but also basketball, tennis, baseball, and archery. The superintendent of the home in 1925, Bessie B. Spanner, commented on the expanded sports program for Jewish young women under the direction of Miss Mann. The use of the "Julia Richmond High School gymnasium every Monday afternoon" proved popular and the "Beth el girls have already challenged ours to a Basket Ball game."[35] In fact, basketball has a strong link with Jewish young women and girls, as it became popular at Jewish Ys as well.

The commitments of the Clara de Hirsch Home for Working Girls served as precedents for the emphasis on physical activities and sport for Jewish women at Young Women's Hebrew Associations. In an interview about the Clara de Hirsch Home for Working Girls, Bessie N. Rothschild, who joined the home in 1946, stressed that it was under Jewish auspices to serve Jewish girls. She remarked that she was born "The year that Clara Hirsch [Home] was born. Eighteen ninety-seven. That's why I always remember the date." Rothschild stated that the residence always consisted mostly of Jewish girls, "Oh, yes, I think that the contract from the Baroness said that there should always be some percentage of non-Jewish girls . . . 6% or 8%." Rothschild noted that in her activities on the board of the home, "I remember giving a lot of thought to getting somebody who would be sympathetic in a Jewish way and would not be overwhelming to the ones that weren't so orthodox."[36] In 1962 Clara de Hirsch Home's directors decided to merge with the 92nd Street Young Men's–Young Women's Hebrew Association. Rothschild recalled, "The Y had been trying to negotiate with us to do something to build a building with them on a wonderful piece of property that extended from the middle of the block on 92nd and 91st on Lexington Avenue, which had been given to the Y by one of the 'Warburgs,'" referring to Felix Warburg, past president of YMHA, and his wife, past president of the YWHA. She remarked, "We realized we couldn't really put the old residence at 63rd Street into order properly." Thus in 1962 the Clara de Hirsch Home services consolidated with the YM-YWHA of New York City.[37]

## The Young Women's Hebrew Association of New York City

It is clear then that Jewish young women in the early twentieth century often learned about American sport at Jewish institutions, such as Young Men's and Young Women's Hebrew Associations, and later at JCCs. The YMHAs and JCCs typically catered to men interested in sport, much like the athletic clubs, working-class teams, and YMCAs for ethnic and Gentile men in early twentieth-century America. Yet, Jewish women sought access to the sport programs and facilities at Jewish institutions designed to aid immigrant newcomers and at Jewish communal centers in urban areas with large Jewish populations. Jewish women and girls often demonstrated leadership in pressing for sporting activities and for time to practice and compete in sports both against Jewish sportswomen at Jewish Ys and against sportswomen at Christian Ys.

The Young Women's Hebrew Association of New York City, founded by Bella Unterberg (Mrs. Israel Unterberg) in 1902, became a major institution for Jewish women immigrants, providing opportunities in education, vocational training, and sport within Jewish environs. The first building, at 1584 Lexington Avenue, was dedicated on February 1, 1903. The need for larger quarters led to a new home at 1578–1582 Lexington Avenue in 1906. In 1908 the YWHA reiterated its purpose: "We are striving to raise the standard of Jewish Womanhood," and in addition to classes in dressmaking, stenography, typewriting, Hebrew, and Bible, the YWHA supervised "a gymnasium with average attendance of twenty-four."[38]

In the 1911 class report, the chairwoman stated that the girls devoted time to "apparatus work, jumping, and folk dancing, and Thursday evening to basket ball, athletic games and drills."[39] For upholding their Jewish identity, the YWHA declared that on the "question of the observance of the Sabbath in the building" staff and teachers "create . . . an atmosphere in the association which distinguishes it from any other social or communal activity and which justifies the existence and makes of your work a Young Women's *Hebrew* Association."[40]

The increasing numbers of Jewish young women and girls using the facilities, rising from 30,000 in 1906 to 102,000 in 1913, prompted the board of directors to undertake a campaign for a third YWHA. The fine new building at 31 West 110th Street opened on November 22, 1914.[41] This larger YWHA fostered Jewish identity, as the building "contained a synagogue" as well as a "gymnasium, swimming pool, class and club rooms, dining room, and residence quarters for more than 170 girls."[42] As Mrs. Unterberg explained to women workers at YWHAs, in carrying out "suggestions for social and athletic work that I have intimated" they should understand that "the organizers felt the need of establishing some center where Jewish ideas and Jewish ideals will be developed."[43] Over the years this impressive YWHA "served the spiritual, education, recreational and housing needs of Jewish girls in New York City."[44]

Sport, under the auspices of this Jewish Y for women, helped to uphold the spiritual and religious identity of women and girls as members of a Jewish team, association, or club, yet at the same time prepared them to participate in the growing sporting culture for women in white Anglo Saxon Protestant American society. The new gymnasium featured facilities that encouraged sporting activities:

> The large gymnasium, connecting lockers and the shower baths in the basement, will hold a class of 200, in, say, Swedish floor work. We are planning regular gymnasium classes under competent instructors, and there will be organized sports, activities that were not possible in our former crowded quarters.[45]

The New York City YWHA was an autonomous organization distinct from the YMHA of New York City, and the female directors of the YWHA maintained their policy of providing sport and physical culture programs appropriate for Jewish young women. A separate association, this YWHA remained the oldest organization for Jewish girls and women that sustained "religious work, gymnasium, social work and educational work" in the effort to promote the social and physical welfare of Jewish females. (The Ladies Auxiliary of the New York YMHA, organized by Jewish philanthropist Julia Richman in 1888, was the forerunner to the YWHA.) In the early twentieth century, the YWHAs in New York, Baltimore, Louisville, Philadelphia, Pittsburgh, Nashville, and other cities existed as Ladies Auxiliaries to YMHAS, assisting immigrant and working-class girls and women. Their Americanization efforts emphasized domestic skills, English, and citizenship classes, as well as physical education to help Jewish females adjust to American life. As Mrs. Bella Unterberg later reminded her fellow YWHA workers, "it is the finest thing a Young Women's Society can start with, with the gymnasium and the basket-ball teams for your recreational work." At most YWHAs affiliated with YMHAs, women secured only limited access to the gymnasiums and swimming pools, and suffered from a lack of female physical training instructors. This New York City YWHA remained the exception, not the rule, in its athletic facilities and sport and physical education for Jewish women. Housed in a new building, in 1914 the female president of this pioneering YWHA declared, "We have made ample provision for the physical welfare and recreation needs of girls," with a large gymnasium for classes and organized sports. In 1916, an indoor swimming pool opened that later hosted national championship swimming meets.[46]

Most YWHAs at this time experienced inadequate women's sport programs. This went along with women's limited authority and political sway in the male-dominated structure of the Jewish Ys. The Nashville, Tennessee, YMHA illustrates how Jewish women played a vital role in the growth of this association, but at first remained on the margins of its sporting activities. Jewish women, however, pressed for their right to participate in the physical education and sports activities at the Nashville YMHA and formed a YWHA to promote their efforts. Organized first as the Ladies' Auxiliary of the YMHA, founded in 1902, it assisted with fund-raising for the first building, which was erected in 1907. In 1915 the YWHA was organized, with Mrs. Harry Weintrub elected as its first president. In 1916, the name of the auxiliary was officially changed to the YWHA of Nashville. The year before, the *Nashville Y.M.H.A. News* had printed "An Appeal to the Ladies," who had expressed their desire to use the sporting spaces: "The Athletic Committee has set a night aside for the benefit for the ladies and girls exclusively." It pointed to its health advantages: "A good night's exercise in the old Gym will benefit you more than all the medicine a doctor could prescribe and will make you healthier, stronger," adding that it will provide the ladies with "a better complexion." The athletic department also noted the interest of the girls and women in basketball and indoor baseball. The YWHA secured the services of Miss Madeline Schwartzman for the gymnasium class, and swimming and basketball were made part of the classes." In May 1917 in an article in the "Y.W.H.A. Notes" of the YMHA newsletter, a YWHA leader reported, "At last the superintendent has promised to allow us the use of the pool at least one night a week." She urged, "So please get your suits and caps ready for the first call." The Monday night swimming for YWHA girls "attracted large crowds," and the YWHA boasted "the girls have the strongest lungs in Nashville as is proved when they first hit the cold water."[47] Still, women held little sway at many of the YMHAs and encountered resistance to the effort to merge YMHAs with YWHAs so women could play sports. For example, when the St. Louis, Missouri, YMHA moved to a new location in the early 1920s, men remained in control of the athletic spaces. An anniversary bulletin of the YMHA-YWHA stated, "The 'W' part of the 'Y' had little or no activity with the Physical Department being strictly male territory."[48]

At the New York City YWHA the women leaders exercised their authority to make sporting activities a key part of the programs offered to young women. In the *Annual Report* for 1916, President Unterberg underlined the special qualities of the YWHA in New York City. "The Young Women's Hebrew Association is unique. It is the largest if not the only association of its kind that is devoting itself exclusively to the religious, mental and physical life of the Jewish young women of our city."[49] Unterberg reminded fellow YWHA workers at a meeting of the Council of YMH and Kindred Associations in 1916 that "it is the finest thing a Young Women's Society can start with, with the gymnasium and the basket-ball teams for your recreational work."[50] The sports facilities of the YWHA's new home featured "a swimming pool, 20 feet by 60 feet, a

Young Women's Hebrew Association swimming pool, used for recreational and competitive events, early 1920s. *Courtesy of the 92nd Street YM-YWHA Archives.*

gymnasium" and "a roof garden with tennis courts." In fact, in describing the new building, President Bella Unterberg emphasized the importance of physical culture: "there will be organized sports, activities that were not possible in our former crowded quarters."[51] This YWHA housed what one New York newspaper hailed as "the most comprehensive program of physical education in the country for Jewish women and girls."[52] The indoor swimming pool opened in October 1916 and girls enjoyed contests in water sports.[53]

In marking its twenty-fifth anniversary in 1927 the YWHA declared, "Our classes in physical education and swimming are a great stimulus and give an opportunity for wholesome and refreshing relaxation after a hard day at work." A New York YWHA *Bulletin of Classes* for the 1920s called on women, "Maintain your physical fitness by joining our class in Gymnastics. Play Basket Ball! Use our Swimming Pool!"[54]

The YWHA's indoor swimming pool, opened in October 1916 at 31 West 110th Street, became a popular site for Jewish American women to enjoy sport and physical recreation. The YWHA boasted that swimming promoted "Health-Sport-Safety."[55] This swimming pool drew "large crowds for instruction and for the refreshing and stimulating opportunity it gives for exercise." The pool held a prominent place in the physical training of both the novice and the more-advanced swimmer. A 1920s YWHA brochure stated, "'Meets' are planned and contests in water sports and individual supremacy test are held, all of which call forth a lively interest."[56]

The director of the swimming pool clearly expressed the need to ensure that the females did not suffer from health problems before being allowed to swim. Concerns that too much physical exertion might harm the women led to the requirement that they have medical clearance before using the swimming pool. A 1916–1917 *Bulletin of Classes* indicated that a "Physician's certificate is required of all those using the pool"; the examination cost 25 cents. Moreover, girls had to wear suitable clothing for the pool. Each swimmer "must bring a plain, rubber bathing cap. Silk and fancy caps are not permitted . . . suits may be purchased for 50 cents at the Association Building." The swimming pool rules made it clear that only appropriate bathing suits must be used ("only gray Annette Kellermans are permitted"), and "all suits must be left at the building to be sterilized." Wearing the fashionable and comfortable Kellerman bathing suits, the one-piece bathing suit showing shoulders and legs, made popular by Australian swimming star Annette Kellerman, by 1910, Jewish females participated in an extensive swimming program that included everything from swimming lessons and "plunges" (dives) to competitions held at the pool. The Young Women's Hebrew Athletic League hosted its swimming meets at this YWHA pool.[57]

In the 1920s the excellent pool of the New York City YWHA hosted not only swimming classes but also national competitive swimming championships featuring such outstanding national and Olympic champions as Aileen Riggin, Gertrude Ederle, and Helen Meaney. Riggin, gold medal diving and swimming champion at the 1920 Antwerp Olympics, recalled how, as a member of the Women's Swimming Association (WSA) of New York, she swam at the YWHA. Jewish American Charlotte Epstein and other businesswomen interested in swimming for exercise and in promoting competition for female swimmers founded the WSA in 1917. Epstein, who had previously headed the Athletic Branch of the National Women's Life-Saving League, had developed swimming competitions for team members, including Jewish American swimmers Rita Greenfield, Lucy Freeman, and others. Epstein and a few of her colleagues resigned from the National Women's Life-Saving League to form the WSA because, as she explained, "the members felt thereby they could best further the interest of all women desiring to learn how to swim and those of the competitors as well."[58] Epstein was elected president of the WSA, and fellow Jewish American Frances Ricker, a former member of the Women's Life-Saving League, served as a secretary.[59]

Charlotte Epstein became prominent as the WSA club manager and gained acclaim as the 1920 and 1924 Olympic women's swimming team manager. Epstein petitioned the male Olympic officials to allow women swimmers to compete for medals in the 1920 Olympics for the first time. Eppie, as her teammates called her, needed a pool to host national championship events. In fact, as chair of the Committee on Sports of the WSA, Epstein worked with Jewish organizations with suitable swimming pools. Aileen Riggin recalled that WSA team members "went to the Young Women's Hebrew Association and had meets there—they had a standard pool." In 1921 the WSA acknowledged "a debt of gratitude to the officers of the Y.W.H.A. for their generosity in allowing us the use of their handsome natatorium for our swimming meet of March 12th."[60] In the early 1920s, the WSA held National Swimming Championships that were governed by the Amateur Athletic Union rules at the YWHA pool. This was a highly competitive swimming meet that included prizes for the champions. In December 1924, at the meet the WSA held at this New York YWHA, "for the first time in the history of women's athletics in this country, a full corps of women officials was in charge." Some men worried that WSA member and former Olympian Alice Lord, who acted as a starter, might have difficulty firing a pistol to start the race![61]

Basketball also proved to be an enjoyable sport for the girls at this Jewish Y in New York City. Basketball held wide appeal for girls at Jewish Ys, and its popularity in the Northeast extended to immigrant Jews, women and men. In intramural and team competition in the excellent gym of the New York City YWHA, or in the YMHA gyms when women's play was scheduled, or in community gyms, young Jewish women in numerous communities played basketball. Jewish young women who played in basketball games in the early twentieth century exhibited ethnic pride.[62] Jewish men's basketball became extremely popular during the first half of the twentieth century. In his study of Jewish male sporting experiences, sport historian Peter Levine stated:

> Both as spectators and as participants, Jewish involvement in basketball, especially between 1900 and 1950, was greater than in any other sport. A rich part of second generation community life, both as experience and symbol, it served

> as a middle ground in which the children of immigrants took advantage of opportunities provided by themselves and by others to determine their own identities as Americans and as Jews.[63]

Some commentators saw basketball as a "Jewish" sport. Levine explained that "in Jewish communities large and small, scattered throughout the United States, the children of East European immigrants, as players and as spectators, took up this American game and made it their own."[64]

The women's basketball game differed from the men's version in order to accommodate concerns of women's physical educators, male athletic directors, and doctors about basketball being too physically rough on a woman's constitution. Lithuanian Jewish immigrant Senda Berenson, born in 1868, immigrated to America with her father in 1874. Known as the "Mother of Women's Basketball," Berenson became a leading woman physical educator. In 1892 she became the director of physical training at Smith College, Northampton, Massachusetts, at the new Alumnae Gymnasium. Having observed Dr. James Naismith's new game of basketball at Springfield College, Berenson then organized the first women's basketball game in 1892 at Smith College. She adapted the rules for women: dividing the court into zones, prohibiting snatching the ball from another player, allowing five to ten players on a team, and emphasizing teamwork. Berenson explained that the women's game avoided the physical contact and physical exertion of the men's game. Berenson's version of basketball gained popularity at colleges, high schools, YWHAs and YWCAs, and in leagues for working-class women.[65] To honor her important role in basketball, Berenson was the first woman inducted into the Basketball Hall of Fame.

## The New York City YWHA Promoted Basketball for Its Members

The New York YWHA bulletin for girls' physical education classes stated, "Basketball—Enjoy a weekly work-out playing the greatest of all indoor games."[66] In keeping with the rhetoric of female physical educators, the YWHA hoped to promote Jewish womanhood and the spirit of play rather than a male competitive ethic on the basketball court. So the New York YWHA president remarked, "We have several Basket Ball teams which are making excellent records in inter-association games," but added, "We teach them that the game is the thing—not the victory."[67] The Young Women's Hebrew Association Athletic League included basketball in its sporting events, and contests took place against other Jewish Y teams and non-Jewish teams. Sporting forms remained part of the YWHAs mission. In "How We Serve the Community," published in 1922, the twentieth anniversary of the New York City Young Women's Hebrew Association, the president reiterated, "Physical Education" and "Dormitory," "Religious Work," "Education, Commercial School, Trade and Domestic Arts" are among the association's aims.[68] Basketball for Jewish women remained an important component of the sports program at the YWHA.

Jewish young women at the New York YWHA also participated in tennis and track and field. These Jewish sportswomen competed against other Jewish women's teams in the city area in the YWHA League. Whether pursuing the sports for health or vying for trophies to demonstrate athletic success, many young Jewish women in the YWHA desired to participate in sporting activities. Some of these women continued their involvement with the physical education and sport programs of this Jewish Y by becoming leaders in the sport programs and teaching sporting skills to other Jewish young women.

## Conclusion

In the late nineteenth and early twentieth centuries Jewish women affirmed their rights to practice sport and took action to enhance their participation in sport in America. From immigrant aid associations and Jewish educational institutions to the YWHAs, sport formed an important part of programs offered Jewish young women in New York City. The New York City YWHA, as well as the Hebrew Technical School for Girls and the Clara de Hirsch Home for Working Girls, provided sporting opportunities and physical culture classes for New York City's young Jewish women and laid the foundation for Jewish young girls to participate in expanded sport programs in later decades in American society.

# VII

# Hangouts
# Sporting Culture by Day and Night

CHAPTER THIRTEEN

# Boxing in Olde New York

## Unforgettable Stillman's Gym

*Mike Silver*

Once in a while, when a nostalgic mood strikes me, I walk over to the west side of Eighth Avenue between 54th and 55th Streets and stare wistfully at the space now occupied by an apartment building. Perhaps you are thinking I am reminiscing about some long-ago love affair. Well, in a sense I am. You see, for many years I was in love with the sport of boxing and one of the major objects of my affection stood on this very site. I can still remember the address: 919 Eighth Avenue. If you are a boxing fan of a certain age you will recognize that address right away and know that I am referring to the legendary Stillman's Gym—the most fabled and colorful gym in boxing's history.

If you wanted to see some of the best professional boxers in the world up close and personal Stillman's was the place to go. If you wanted to understand firsthand the attraction that boxing held for so many of us you would get more than a taste of it at Stillman's. Whether you were a boxing fan or not, the place made an indelible impression. The gym had an international reputation. Many tourists to the city considered it as important an attraction as the Empire State Building, Radio City Music Hall, or the Statue of Liberty. But don't bother trying to find anything like it today because you will search in vain. The unique confluence of circumstances that created and nurtured Stillman's Gym from the 1920s to the 1950s—a veritable golden age for the sport—no longer exists.

### Background

For some forty years, from 1921 to 1961, Stillman's Gym was an iconic presence in New York City. It is no coincidence that the life span of the world's most famous gymnasium coincided with boxing's golden age of talent and activity.

Entrance to Stillman's Gym, 1954. *Courtesy of the Stanley Weston Collection.*

Stillman's history, like that of New York City, was a product of the seismic social and economic changes that occurred when millions of mostly poor and uneducated immigrants from Eastern and Southern Europe came to America between 1881 and 1924.

At the turn of the last century, rapidly industrializing American cities presented the best opportunity for employment so that is where a majority of the immigrants and their families settled. Of immediate concern was the need to find work. Although menial low-paying jobs were available, having one was no guarantee of financial security. Four of every ten immigrant workers did not earn enough to support a family. By 1914 at least half the populations of major cities in the United States lived in poverty. Not surprisingly, the majority of these people were immigrants.[1]

There weren't many alternatives to working in a sweatshop or behind a pushcart. One alternative was to enter the world of show business. The flourishing vaudeville circuit employed thousands of people, many of whom were first- or second-generation immigrants. Another thriving industry with close ties to show business was professional boxing. Both show business and boxing were open to anyone regardless of race, religion, or ethnicity.

The first great wave of immigration (some 3 million strong) came to America from Ireland between 1846 and 1870. The Irish brought with them an athletic tradition that included boxing. They dominated the sport in America from the latter half of the nineteenth century to the 1910s.

Nudging and eventually replacing the Irish American boxers from their dominant position were Jewish and Italian boxers who derived from the second and much larger wave of 24 million immigrants mentioned earlier (a figure that included 4 million Italians and 2 million Jews). This change in boxing's hierarchy was due not only to increased competition but also to improving employment opportunities for Irish American youth. As noted by historian Steven A. Riess, "The ethnic succession in the ring reflected the changing racial and ethnic complexion of the inner city as older ethnic groups who were doing better economically moved out and were replaced by the new urban poor."[2]

At the time there were only three professional sports of any significance in America—baseball, boxing, and horse racing. For the aspiring athlete, boxing was not only the most accessible professional sport; it also offered the best opportunity to earn quick money. As a result, thousands of young men hardened by poverty and possessing street smarts and physical strength were motivated to test their mettle in the prize ring.

It was common knowledge that successful boxers were the highest-paid athletes in the world. In the 1920s superstar boxers Mickey Walker, Benny Leonard, and Harry Greb were each taking in well over $100,000 in annual income—the equivalent of several million dollars in today's currency. In 1924 the highest-paid African American boxer in the sport was the popular heavyweight Harry Wills, who received $150,000 for his bout against the Argentine contender Luis Angel Firpo. The $80,000 annual salary paid to baseball great Babe Ruth in 1927 paled in comparison to the $1 million heavyweight champion

Gene Tunney received for his title bout with Jack Dempsey that same year. Of course not everyone could be a world champion or top contender, but even an ordinary preliminary boxer could make more money in one 4-round bout than a sweatshop laborer made for an entire week.[3]

Yet the benefits to both the boxers and the ghetto communities that spawned them went beyond monetary rewards. Champions and title contenders, virtually all of whom came from ethnic minorities, were heroes in poor urban neighborhoods. They were a source of inspiration, pride, and hope to a population struggling to break free of poverty and gain acceptance into the social and economic mainstream. More than any other sport or activity, boxing became a symbol of the immigrants' struggle for status, assimilation, and a path to Americanization.

In the 1920s New York City, along with being the hub for commerce, communications, media, and theater, was also the world capital of boxing. Other cities could boast of great fighters and bustling competition, but New York had more of everything: fighters, trainers, promoters, managers, arenas, and gymnasiums. It was not only home to the sport's most famous gymnasium; it was also home to boxing's holy of holies—Madison Square Garden.

Boxing activity in New York State reached record levels during "the roaring twenties." In 1925 the New York State Athletic Commission's annual report stated that 1,890 licensed professional boxers resided in the state—up from 1,654 the year before. Two years later, in 1927, that number had climbed to 2,000 licensed professionals with over half the boxers either Italian or Jewish.[4] (In 2016 only 107 licensed professional boxers resided in the state.)

It was into this environment that Stillman's Gym was born. Prior to its existence, the most widely known training facility in the city was Grupp's Gymnasium and Athletic Club, located at 116th Street and Eighth Avenue. An ex-fighter named Billy Grupp started the gym in 1915. Most of the city's top professional boxers trained there, including the great Jewish lightweight champion Benny Leonard.

Unfortunately, Billy Grupp had a drinking problem and when plastered would often launch into an antisemitic tirade blaming the Jews for World War I. This was not exactly good for business as many of the boxers who worked out in his gym happened to be Jewish. Fed up with the lush's behavior, Benny Leonard led a mass exodus of all the Jewish fighters to a new gym located a few blocks away that was operated by the Marshall Stillman movement. Two millionaire philanthropists had established the movement in 1919 to rehabilitate juvenile delinquents. The gymnasium was managed by a thirty-two-year-old former police officer named Louis Ingber, who was thrilled to have a famous world champion training in his facility. The fighters agreed to work out in the evenings (the juvenile delinquents used the gym in the afternoons).

When word got out that Benny Leonard was no longer training at Grupp's, the new gymnasium became a magnet for other boxers and trainers. Fans of Leonard began crowding into the gym to watch him train. Ingber saw a business opportunity, and he began charging admission to the spectators. But the small gym would accommodate only a limited number of people. So, two years later, in 1921, he moved to much larger quarters at 919 Eighth Avenue.

The new facility would be for the exclusive use of professional and amateur boxers. Unlike the previous location, they would be able to use it in the afternoons. The patrons at the new gym continued to call the manager "Mr. Stillman," thinking that was his name. Lou Ingber eventually tired of correcting everyone so he had his name legally changed to Lou Stillman.[5]

The Eighth Avenue location was perfect. It was in an exciting part of the city, near the Broadway theater district, and only four blocks north of Madison Square Garden. Of course Stillman's was not the only boxing gym in the city. The Pioneer Gym on West 44th Street was competitive with Stillman's for a time, but it closed its doors in 1943. Gleason's Gym opened in the Bronx in 1935. It was a fine facility, but most of its membership was confined to fighters who lived in that borough. Uptown, Grupp's was still around, but it had neither the charm nor charisma of Stillman's. There were other gyms as well, such as the Seward Gym on Hester Street, the St. Nicholas in midtown, and Beecher's in Brooklyn.

In addition to its great location, a big part of Stillman's appeal was the size and layout of the gym. It occupied the entire second and third floors of a three-story building. The main floor of the gym was two stories high and measured 140 by 65 feet. It was dominated by two elevated boxing rings placed side by side. In front of the rings were eight rows of wooden folding chairs meant for spectators. In a corner of the gym, near the entrance, was a small lunch counter (operated by Lou Stillman's brother, Larry Ingber) where sandwiches, hot dogs, snacks, and beverages were sold. Everlast products were also for sale, as were various boxing publications. The wall adjacent to the lunch counter contained photos of famous fighters.

On the far side of the rings, against the back wall, there was a narrow space where fighters sat on benches while they waited for their turn to spar. Against the opposite wall stood a row of four phone booths. A few feet from the phones a metal stairway led to a large balcony area that overlooked the floor below. This is where the speed bags and heavy punching bags were located. There was also plenty of room for shadow boxing and floor exercises. (For many years a third boxing ring was located on this floor, but it was removed in the 1950s.)

The space underneath the balcony housed the lockers and showers, in addition to twenty wooden cubicles that were big enough for each to contain a locker and massage table. These private dressing rooms were reserved for champions and top contenders.

In an open area between the last row of spectators' chairs and the wall that separated the main floor from the dressing rooms, matchmakers, managers, promoters, and kibitzers mixed and mingled as they conducted business and exchanged gossip.

Posted on a sign at the street entrance to the gym were the names of famous boxers who were training that day. At any time one might see both active and former ring greats either training or just in for a visit. Some of the regulars included such legendary fighters as Jack Johnson, Jack Dempsey, Benny Leonard, Johnny Dundee, Tony Canzoneri, Henry Armstrong, Beau Jack, Kid Gavilan, Sandy Saddler, and Rocky Graziano.

Stillman's was open seven days a week. The busiest hours were from noon to 4 p.m. when the gym became a beehive of activity as an assortment of fighters of every size and ability, ranging from green amateurs to world champions, went through their training routines. During the 1940s gym dues were five dollars per month. Admission for spectators was 15 cents in the 1920s and 1930s, 25 cents in the 1940s, and then 50 cents in the 1950s. Sometimes as many as two hundred people would crowd into the gym to watch a famous fighter work out.

## The Best Show in Town

During boxing's heyday, an afternoon at Stillman's provided one of the greatest shows in town. For little more than the price of a cup of coffee a fan could watch some of the world's best boxers prepare for an upcoming bout. There was also the chance to converse with a past ring great who might stop by to take in the action, evaluate the latest rising star, or simply reconnect to the fight crowd.

People of every background and economic strata went to the fights. They also went to Stillman's. It was not unusual for spectators to rub shoulders with businessmen and blue-collar workers, writers and actors, gangsters and cab drivers. (For decades Stillman's was a place where rival elements of the underworld could meet under a flag of truce.)

According to Lou Stillman the most popular attractions in the history of the gym were heavyweight champion Jack Dempsey and Georges Carpentier, the debonair Frenchman who fought the "The Manassa Mauler," as Dempsey was known, for the title in 1921. But the fighter who drew the largest crowd was Primo Carnera, the six-foot-six, 270-pound Italian giant who was heavyweight champion from 1933 to 1934.[6]

"I had 1,800 people in here when Primo Carnera first came over from Italy," Stillman said. "The place is only supposed to hold 290 people. I took out all the seats and had them standing all over the place. Primo was ugly but he drew the women in."[7]

"When Carpentier was in training, the place was always crowded with Broadway chorus girls. When Carnera trained the gallery was packed with Italian women carrying their babies. I liked them better than the chorus girls, so I always let the babies in for free."[8]

Of course the world's most famous boxing gym, located in the world's greatest city, all but guaranteed that a host of "Runyonesque" characters would be on display, including, not infrequently, Damon Runyon himself. One of those characters was the ever-present Lou Stillman, who had assumed ownership of the gym in the late twenties. Lou, a quintessential New Yorker, was right out of central casting.

Described as a "big, gruff, sour-dispositioned autocrat," Lou Stillman kept everyone in line by running his gym like a drill sergeant.[9] Perched on a high stool under a big clock located near one of the rings Stillman would announce over the loudspeaker in his raspy voice which fighters were about to spar. A lot of the trainers, managers, and boxers who experienced Stillman's wrath would have liked to belt him, but they took his verbal abuse only because he held the key that opened the door to boxing's busiest and best training site. For example, the right kind of sparring is essential to a boxer's development. Due to the sheer number of boxers who regularly trained at Stillman's, a variety of sparring partners was readily available.

Although he'd never admit it, Stillman, on rare occasions, displayed a softer side. "Sure he was loud, but his heart was as big as his mouth," recalled George Palazzo, a fair lightweight boxer back in the 1920s.[10]

"Many's the time he let me wait a couple of months to pay my locker fee. He could tell when a guy had the shorts. A couple of times he slipped me a deuce when I needed it bad.

"I seen him do other things that showed he had a heart," added Palazzo. "Like with washed up fighters—some of them a little punchy. They'd come in and tell Lou they wanted to make a comeback. They'd ask if they could work out.

"Lou didn't throw them out. He'd tell them to start shadow boxing and skipping rope to get in shape. But he never let them get in the ring. Lou let them down as easy as he could."

In 1967, six years after the gym closed, and two years before his death at the age of eighty-two, Stillman was interviewed by *The Ring* magazine's Ted Carroll, who expressed surprise that Lou still wore his famous grim facial expression. "How can you change something that's been part of you for forty years?" Stillman replied. "How long do you think a man with a happy face would have lasted in my old business, running a boxing gym? Everybody called Stillman a grouch, a crab, a cranky guy who never smiled. Well that's what scared off the chiselers, moochers and deadbeats. A good-natured guy would have been played for the biggest sucker in the world."[11]

Stillman's gym appeared in two Hollywood movies: *Somebody Up There Likes Me* (1956), which depicted the life story of former middleweight champion Rocky Graziano, and *The Naked City* (1948), a film shot entirely on the streets of New York. In the Graziano biography, character actor Matt Crowley portrayed Lou Stillman and did a good job capturing the acerbic gym owner's gruff exterior.

## The Stillman's Experience

It's estimated that some 30,000 fighters and near fighters passed through Stillman's grimy but hallowed environs, including yours truly. In the fall of 1959 my father took this fourteen-year-old boxing fan to Stillman's Gym for lessons in the manly art of self-defense. Lou Stillman was no longer there, having retired a few months earlier after selling the building to a real estate syndicate. The gym remained open for two more years under the management of Irving Cohen, a prominent boxing manager.

I didn't know quite what to expect as I entered into a dimly lit hallway that led to a wide and steep staircase. As I walked up those twenty-one creaking wooden steps I thought to myself, "this is the very same staircase used by so many ring greats!" I was about to enter a world I had never seen before and could not have imagined. I was as excited as a kid going to the circus for the first time.

Arriving on the second floor (the first floor of the gym) I went through a short corridor and past a man standing by a turnstile who collected the admission fee. My attention was immediately drawn to the two full-sized elevated boxing rings. Both added a dramatic touch to the main room. In front of the rings were several rows of wooden folding chairs that by the look of them could have been the same ones that were there when the gym first opened. The walls were in need of a fresh coat of paint, and the large windows on either side of the two rings appeared not to have been cleaned in years. But all that seemed just right. This was no sterile, chrome-and-mirrored fitness salon with a slew of fancy and expensive exercise apparatus. This was a boxing gym with character and history.

Walking into Stillman's was like entering a time warp. I felt like I had suddenly found myself in an old black-and-white movie. All of my senses were engaged in taking it all in. First there was the aroma of the place—a combination of rubbing alcohol, liniment, stale cigar smoke, leather, and sweat. The place was alive with constant movement and motion. I didn't know where to look because wherever I looked there was something to watch; people walking around, fighters sparring in the two rings, others hitting the speed bags, or jumping rope, doing calisthenics, or going up and down the metal staircase that led to the second level where the punching bags were located.

A cacophony of sounds echoed throughout the gym: the rhythmic rat-a-tat-tat of the speed bags; jump ropes slapping against the hardwood floor; the thump of leather-covered fists hitting the heavy bags, and, if hit hard enough, the jangling sound of the chains that bolted them to the ceiling; fighters snorting and grunting as they shadowboxed and threw punches at imaginary opponents; trainers giving advice and instruction; someone yelling out the name of a trainer or manager who was wanted on the phone. There was a distinct rhythm to it all. It was a symphony of movement and sound that is unique to a boxing gym. And then . . . just as swiftly as it began . . . the tumult would suddenly halt as the automatic bell rang signaling the end of yet another three-minute round and the start of the one-minute rest period. Sixty seconds later the bell would ring to start another round, and it would begin all over again.

If boxing had a voice it would be the sound of Stillman's Gym on a busy afternoon.

You could spend hours at Stillman's just looking at the interesting faces of some of the characters who always showed up. I had never seen so many dented noses in one place. Half the guys standing around, whether fighters, trainers, or managers, had mugs that could have filled the cast of a *Guys and Dolls* production. To quote Norma Desmond in the classic movie *Sunset Boulevard*: "*They had faces then.*" (For whatever reasons, I have yet to see the same interesting faces in any of today's boxing gyms.)

Stillman's was a decidedly male enclave, and I would rarely see women in the gym. But I do remember seeing a woman artist sketching a boxer working out on the heavy bag. I was told it was not uncommon for artists and photographers (male and female) to visit the gym looking for interesting subjects.

Fighters were not the only people worthy of attention and respect at Stillman's. Some of the gym's teacher/trainers were celebrities in their own right. By the late 1950s many of the original retinue that were there when the gym first opened had already retired or passed on, but there were still a few left from the old days whom I was privileged to meet. These "professors of pugilism" taught the art of boxing. As Ray Arcel, the great trainer who was present at the founding of the gym (at the time of my arrival he was on hiatus from boxing), put it: "Stillman's Gymnasium was a school; it was not a gym. You went there, you learned—you learned your lessons."[12]

Fortunately, Charley Goldman, the derby-wearing gnome-like master trainer, was still there, imparting his wisdom to a new generation of boxers. Goldman, himself a veteran of some four hundred fights, was renowned for sculpting Rocky Marciano into an undefeated heavyweight champion. And little Whitey Bimstein, another famous trainer, was a constant presence in the gym, as were Freddie Brown, Chickie Ferrera, Jimmy August, Johnny Sullo, and Freddie Fierro.

On my first day in the gym I was introduced to "Hurricane" Jackson, once a top contender who fought Floyd Patterson for the heavyweight championship, and now a washed-up journeyman fighter attempting a comeback. No matter, he still rated a private dressing room.

On another memorable occasion I met Kid Norfolk, one of the greatest African American fighters to never win a title. Kid Norfolk (real name William Ward) had well over one hundred fights and was a top-ranked light heavyweight contender in the 1910s and 1920s. During his Hall of Fame career, he took on all comers, including several legendary wars with the great Harry Greb. Kid Norfolk (at the time in his midsixties) was an impressive presence. He wore a long black overcoat and had on dark glasses. Standing ramrod straight, the former ring great projected an air of dignity and pride. He also appeared to be made out of steel. I had just started taking boxing lessons at Stillman's and my trainer, a strict old-school type named Willie Grunes, encouraged me to ask Kid Norfolk any question about boxing.

I tried to think of an intelligent question and all I could come up with was "what is the most important thing in boxing?" Kid Norfolk put his left foot forward and raised his fists to affect the boxer's traditional "on guard" stance. Then, in sonorous deep tones, came the words: "Balance, son . . . balance!" It was an unforgettable moment.

Once Ingemar Johansson, the heavyweight champion of the world, made a surprise visit. Every spectator in the gym went upstairs to watch the very popular and charismatic Swede hit the heavy bag, shadowbox, and do calisthenics. I couldn't believe my luck. I was only a few feet from the heavyweight champion of the world!

I regularly worked out alongside other well-known boxers whom I often saw on the weekly nationally televised fights: Dick Tiger, Gaspar Ortega, Emile Griffith, Jorge Fernandez, Joey Archer, Rory Calhoun, Alex Miteff, Ike Chestnut, and others. Is there any other professional sport where a fan can get so close to its stars? This was the magic and allure of Stillman's, and I thank my lucky stars I was able to experience it.

## End of an Era

By the time I got to Stillman's, boxing had already begun its long gradual decline, a decline that was exacerbated by a combination of internal corruption, misuse of television, societal and demographic changes, the growing popularity of other sports, and the public's changing tastes. During the golden age, the gym's monthly membership had risen to nearly four hundred boxers. When it finally closed on December 31, 1961, only about seventy-five fighters were utilizing its facilities.

Six months later the structure that housed Stillman's and two adjoining buildings were demolished to make way for a nondescript nineteen-story apartment building. About ten years later I decided to walk into the building. In the lobby I struck up a conversation with a tenant and asked if she had ever heard of Stillman's Gym. Not surprisingly, the answer was no. I was then told she couldn't wait to move out as the building had become infested with prostitutes and pimps. I found that somewhat ironic. I wondered, was it karma? Far too many pro boxers wind up physically damaged, exploited, and broke. Yet, professional fighters are not prostitutes. They are proud, hardworking, and disciplined athletes who are courageously trying to make something of their lives in the toughest of all sports. However, when it comes to the lowlife mobsters, crooked managers and promoters who have controlled and exploited so many boxers without any concern for their health or well-being, then comparison to their like-minded pimp brethren is entirely valid.

In the late 1970s New York City gave up its position as the epicenter of the sport to the gambling hotspots of Las Vegas and Atlantic City. By that time only Madison Square Garden was presenting regularly scheduled biweekly boxing shows in its smaller 4,500-seat venue located adjacent to the main arena. A generation earlier at least a dozen small arenas (or "fight clubs" as they are known in the boxing vernacular) had operated on a weekly basis within a ten-mile radius of Times Square. Now there are none.

The glory days of New York boxing are long gone, as are the many monuments to that singular era that were so much a part of the city's culture: St. Nicholas Arena, the old Madison Square Garden on 50th Street, Dempsey's restaurant, Ridgewood Grove, Broadway Arena, Queensboro Arena, the Bronx Coliseum, Coney Island Velodrome, Eastern Parkway Arena, even the old baseball stadiums that during the summer months were the site of dozens of championship boxing matches.

If ever a building deserved to be preserved as a national historic site that building was Stillman's Gym. Sadly, there isn't even a plaque to commemorate the site of one of New York City's most historic landmarks.

The last vestige of the golden age was Sunnyside Gardens in Long Island City. The old fight club met the wrecking ball in 1977. At least someone had the good sense to put a plaque in front of the hamburger joint that now occupies the space.

Except for the occasional pay-per-view mega fight, boxing today is a fringe sport, and vastly inferior as an art form when comparing the skill level of the current champions to the best boxers of decades past. That's aside from the absurdity of having so many multiple world champions in each weight class. Over the past thirty-five years the greed and arrogance of boxing's quasi-official "sanctioning organizations," in cahoots with rapacious promoters, have all but destroyed whatever credibility the sport once possessed. When I first walked into Stillman's Gym in 1959 there were ten world champions and ten weight classes. Now there are over one hundred "champions" inhabiting seventeen weight classes.

Once upon a time everyone, even housewives and schoolchildren, knew the name of the heavyweight champion of the world. That title was the most important in all of sports. Can anyone today name the current heavyweight champion of the world? Does anyone care? I rest my case.

Even without places like Stillman's, or the hundreds of other extinct gyms and arenas that once dotted the American boxing landscape during boxing's golden age, the sport's ability to produce outstanding fighters did not suddenly come to an end. The decline of boxing's infrastructure and importance that began in the post–World War II period was more like a spinning top that slowly winds down. There were some great fighters in the 1960s, less so in the 1970s and 1980s, and perhaps one or two in the 1990s. I can't name one truly great fighter today.

Within the past twenty years boxing has deteriorated to the point where I and most of my contemporaries (in addition to many younger fans) have lost almost all interest in what has become, for all intents and purposes, a brutal burlesque of a sport. It is very difficult to support or help a sport that refuses to help itself.

From top to bottom, inside and outside of the ring, from the fighters to the fans, to the commentators, trainers, referees, managers, and commissioners, the level of ignorance is pervasive. If 95 percent of today's trainers showed up at Stillman's, they would be laughed out of the gym or assigned as bucket carriers since that low-level job would result in them doing the least damage.

Am I being too harsh? I think not. My observations are based on my particular frame of reference and perspective. To me, the glory and romance of boxing resides in its past history and I'm content to leave it at that.

I am now more aware of boxing's flaws and dangers than ever before. I realize that professional boxing has never been, and will never be, completely free of the exploitation, greed, and brutality that has marked its existence since time immemorial. It's the nature of the beast. But, in its defense, there once was a brief moment in time when the good in boxing actually outweighed the bad; when great fighters possessing extraordinary skills and seasoning fought other great fighters; when managers and trainers understood their business; when every sports fan could name the heavyweight champion of the world; when

*The Ring* magazine was still the "Bible of Boxing"; when baby-boomer sons (and even some daughters) bonded with their dads over the televised Friday Night Fight ritual. It was the time of Dempsey, Louis, Marciano, and Robinson . . . and Satchmo, Goodman, Miller, and Elvis.

It was the time of Stillman's Gym.

CHAPTER FOURTEEN

# Toots Shor

## Midcentury Icon and Monument to Sport and Booze

*Daniel A. Nathan*

### Midtown Manhattan, June 23, 1959

It was a farewell party, with plenty of food, drink, and revelry. There was also some sentimentality and several affectionate, teasing tributes. Toots Shor's famous restaurant on 51 West 51st Street was closing. Not for the night, but permanently. "With a loud gulp of nostalgia, and with the futility of spilled whisky, Toots Shor held his final black-tie party last night at his restaurant," reported the *New York Times*. "The restaurant, opened on April 30, 1940, will soon be torn down for the Zeckendorf Hotel."[1] It had been a remarkable run and place. To celebrate the saloon and its brusque but popular proprietor, three hundred sportswriters, athletes, coaches, actors, celebrities, and many others who had often partied at its circular bar and in its dining room into the wee hours of the morning came together. The tributes, wrote journalist Charles Champlin in *Life*, were "handsomely suited to the master of the affectionate slam and the endearing defamation."[2] Shor's longtime drinking buddy Jackie Gleason roasted him. Shor loved it. Sportswriter Red Smith of the *New York Herald Tribune* recollected that when Shor turned fifty years old "we all gathered here to weep great, big, slobbery tears for a fat, drunken saloonkeeper. We're doing the same tonight."[3] Shor, now fifty-six, nodded with approval. All evening long, there was laughter, backslapping, and good cheer. People must have sensed that it was the end of something special. To its credit, *Sports Illustrated* did: its July 27, 1959, cover featured twelve photographs of the event. The story in the magazine explained, "Toots Shor's was the place where you were apt to see anybody because Toots knew everybody. Most of them (well, many of them anyway) were there at the final binge in the old saloon to help him close its doors—and to instill in Mine Host enough boozy reverie to last until he can throw a door-opening affair at his new location some months hence."[4] Bigger but not better, the new Toots Shor restaurant on 52nd Street finally opened in late December 1961. It was not a success. The cultural moment had passed. The party was over.

For nearly twenty years—before, during, and after World War II—Toots Shor's restaurant on West 51st Street was a social magnet, a good-time place where people (especially successful men) in politics, business, journalism, and the entertainment and sports worlds congregated, socialized, and created a community. A cultural anthropologist at the time might have called it a quasi-public, largely homosocial space that hosted nocturnal, bacchanalian displays of hegemonic masculinity and extreme friendship. It was that, as well as a place where sports mattered. For many people at Toots Shor, sports was a *lingua franca* and a powerful social epoxy that bound them together. In its prime Toots Shor was "the country's unofficial sports headquarters," observed the writer John Bainbridge in *The Wonderful World of Toots Shor* (1951). "It is frequently referred to on the sports pages as the Toots Shor A.C."[5] Twenty-five years later, Red Smith reminisced that Toots Shor "was the mother lodge. Attendance was practically compulsory. If you wanted to see anybody, you went there, and if the guy you sought had stepped out for a moment, you could settle for Ernest Hemingway or Chief Justice Earl Warren or Yogi Berra or Paul Draper or Edward Bennett Williams or Gene Fowler or Billy Conn or Frank Sinatra or Pat O'Brien or Robert Sherwood or Jackie Gleason or Abe Attell."[6] Of course, at the center of it all was Toots Shor himself, a large, putty-faced man with small, squinty eyes, short, slicked-back hair, and an oversized personality. He could be charming and funny and he could be rude, sometimes simultaneously. Shor was "the burly, impudent, hard-working, high-spirited, sentimental proprietor of the New York restaurant that bears his name," declared Bainbridge; he also had "a great talent for making friends and enemies. Most of the people who are acquainted with Shor do not simply like him or dislike him; they love him or loathe him."[7] Either way, he was a midcentury New York icon and his restaurant was "the most famous sporting saloon this country has ever known."[8]

## Toots Shor the Man

Although he loved New York and made it his home for more than forty years, Toots Shor was not a native New Yorker. He was from a mostly Irish and Italian Catholic neighborhood in south Philadelphia.[9] Born in 1903, Bernard Shor was the son of Jewish immigrants.[10] His father, Abraham Shor, was German (of Austrian descent) and a gentle, educated, religious man. His mother, Fanny Shor (née Kaufman), was born in Russia and came to the United States when she was twelve years old.[11] Abraham Shor was in the garment business. Fanny Shor ran a cigar and candy store. "My mother ran our family," Shor reminisced.[12]

Bernard's famous sobriquet Toots, short for Tootsie, was a childhood nickname given him by an aunt, explained his sister Esther.[13] From an early age, Shor was a precocious, pugnacious, street-smart kid, whose mother encouraged him to be a fighter.[14] Sadly, his mother died in a gruesome automobile accident in 1918, when Shor was fifteen years old.[15] Five years later, his grief-stricken father committed suicide.[16]

Shor came to New York in 1930 when he was in his late twenties. He had been a n'er-do-well, then a pool hustler, and then a traveling underwear salesman.[17] Shor admitted, "I was a kid on the hustle."[18] According to his uncle, he was a bum. If he was going to be a bum, Shor thought he should be one in New York, so he hopped a bus to the city.[19] Once there, he became a bouncer for speakeasies—the 5 O'Clock Club, the Napoleon Club, and Leon and Eddie's—and was trusted and well liked by gangsters such as the notorious Owney Madden and George "Big Frenchy" De Mange.[20] They appreciated his toughness, swagger, loyalty, and discretion. Despite having a smart mouth, he knew when to keep it shut. He was also dependable, could be charming, and a lot of people liked him and enjoyed his company.

In 1936, thanks to the many connections he had made, Shor became a greeter and then the host at Billy La Hiff's Tavern on West 48th Street.[21] La Hiff's Tavern was home to Damon Runyon and a Runyonesque crowd of characters in the late 1920s and early 1930s. It was "the home-away-from-home" of New York mayor Jimmy Walker and columnists Ring Lardner, Walter Winchell, and Ed Sullivan, as well as people in show business and sundry members of the sporting crowd.[22] It was the best job Shor ever had, and it helped pave the way to his first restaurant.[23] Eventually, Shor took over the tavern for a few years, but he lost it to crippling and chronic gambling debts.

On the upside, though, a few years before he started working at the tavern, Shor married a diminutive, trim, blonde, vivacious Ziegfeld chorus girl, Marian Volk, whom her friends called Baby but whom Shor affectionately called Husky.[24] By all accounts, Shor loved and was devoted to his wife, his three children, and his many friends. He also loved booze, gambling, and sports.

It was an improbable life, to be sure. In its own way it was charmed. Toots Shor lived a kind of rough-and-tumble Horatio Alger narrative, in that as a boy he was basically a good-for-nothing running the streets. But thanks to the paternal generosity, mentoring, and protection of gangsters (such as Madden and later Frank Costello), as well as the writer-producer Mark Hellinger, who consistently encouraged his friend, Shor lived something like the American Dream. His life had many highs and lows, late nights and good times, disappointments and debt, but few regrets.

## Toots Shor the Place

In the late 1930s, Shor, like many Americans, was broke and out of work. Out of necessity, he and his wife lived with her parents. That, however, did not stop him from thinking big and looking toward the future. Shor had a vision. He wanted his own place, his own saloon. Over the years he had been to scores of bars, clubs, and restaurants, and he knew what he wanted for his own place, how he wanted it to look and feel. Shor was direct and did not like people who put on social airs. He always called himself "a saloonkeeper instead of a restaurateur."[25] His restaurant would reflect that sensibility.

As fate would have it, he caught a break in 1939. He learned that an elevated train track in Midtown was going to be razed, which would presumably increase the neighborhood's appeal and property value. Armed with that knowledge and the assistance of a real estate man, Shor "homed [*sic*] in on a desirable restaurant site, two old brownstones, 51 and 53 West 51st, opposite Radio City Music Hall."[26] Yet as Shor explained to journalist Edward Robb Ellis in a 1975 interview, "There was only one thing. I didn't have a dime."[27] Fortunately, there were some wealthy people, friends and acquaintances, among them Leo Justin, who owned motion picture theaters in New York and New Jersey, who thought Shor had something special—in a word, charisma—that could be profitable. So they lent him the money to tear down the brownstones and build a basic brick three-story restaurant. Journalist Bob Considine, Shor's friend and biographer, writes that it was a "neo-American Colonial building" and the "culmination of Toot's rugged, tumultuous, and spendthrift life."[28]

After a great deal of work (buying kitchen equipment, furnishing the restaurant, hiring staff, etc.), Toots Shor opened for business on April 30, 1940. The world little noticed. It was the same day Nazi Germany captured the Norwegian

Legendary saloonkeeper Toots Shor outside his eponymous joint in 1954. *Courtesy of Getty Images.*

village of Dombås and that Tex Carleton of the Brooklyn Dodgers pitched a no-hitter to beat the Cincinnati Reds, 3–0.[29]

Toots Shor (the restaurant) was not much to look at from the outside. It looked like a modest, almost dignified, brick house. The rectangular awning outside of the restaurant extended from the building to the curb and simply read Toots Shor. There was a revolving door. Inside, the bar was famously circular, in the middle of the room, and had red leather barstools.[30] The bartenders wore white jackets and black bowties. The drinks had large rocks of ice, were poured generously, and were served in glasses with Toots's T-S logo on the side. The bar could be boisterous and was often three deep. The dining room was well lighted and had "a vaulted ceiling and a huge brick fireplace" on the far wall and approximately forty tables for four and booths along the walls.[31] They all had white linen tablecloths. The food was also basic, "American style."[32] Shor was a meat and potatoes guy and his menu was unpretentious and the portions were plentiful.

When it opened for business, Toots Shor was but one of thousands of places to eat, drink, and be merry in New York.[33] Since Prohibition and the subsequent proliferation of speakeasies, myriad clubs and restaurants had become glamorous and popular with celebrities, politicians, businessmen (legal and illicit), athletes, and writers, among others. "Those who frequented the Stork Club and other fashionable nightclubs," notes food writer and historian Andrew F. Smith, "such as the Copacabana, El Morocco, Toots Shor's, the 21 Club, and the Latin Quarter, came to be known as 'Café Society,' a term popularized by [journalist and columnist] Lucius Beebe."[34] There were many other places, too, some of which, like the 21 Club, were relatively close to Toots Shor. Jack Dempsey's restaurant was on Broadway between 49th and 50th Streets. So there was obviously already a vibrant nightlife in New York when Toots Shor opened in 1940. For the restaurant to succeed, it needed to be distinctive. Shor knew this and thus worked hard to ensure that his joint always had plenty of "boozy bonhomie."[35]

## "The Country's Unofficial Sports Headquarters"

His whole life, Toots Shor was passionate about and loved sports. Bob Considine wrote that Shor "thought Grover Cleveland Alexander was a bigger guy than Alexander the Great; that he'd rather see Mickey Mantle belt a home run than see the 'Mona Lisa'; and that he'd rather understand Casey Stengel than the Einstein theory."[36] Sports were a part of Shor's daily social life and his identity and that of his famous saloon.

Growing up in Philadelphia, Shor played basketball and "baseball in the streets."[37] He rooted for Connie Mack's Athletics and his sister Esther sometimes took him to games at Shibe Park. "He was crazy about sports," she recalled, "all sports," much to their father's chagrin. Like many first-generation immigrant Jews, Abraham Shor thought that playing and following sports was a waste of time.[38] Worse still was gambling. To his disappointment, his son started his gambling career early, playing in neighborhood craps games. At about the same time, the young Shor became a "pool shark prodigy" of some local repute.[39] Hanging out in pool halls and on street corners, Shor ran with a rough crowd. Big, strong, and tough, Toots Shor was not afraid to fight and was good at it. Due in part to his friendship with some young Irish American pugilists, the teenage Shor considered becoming a professional prizefighter. His father disapproved, and it did not happen.[40] Later, after his father died and Shor moved to New York, his street smarts, athleticism, and willingness to mix it up served him well as a speakeasy bouncer.

During the 1930s, while working at New York speakeasies, especially Billy La Hiff's Tavern, Shor met and made friends with all manner of well-known people, including professional athletes, such as boxers and baseball players. He also got to know and become friends with many sportswriters, including Ring Lardner, Grantland Rice, and Westbrook Pegler, among others. By the time he opened his own joint, his social network was expansive and devoted. Many of his friends in the sports world became regulars at Toots Shor. Some of the journalists basically set up shop there. They traded information and gossip and drank and socialized into the night, or at least until their deadlines. Within a few years, observes writer Daniel Okrent, the restaurant "functioned as a command-and-control center that determined the nation's sense of sports."[41]

In *The Wonderful World of Toots Shor*, which was first published in the *New Yorker* as a triptych of articles in 1950, writer John Bainbridge explains, "There are some customers toward whom Shor consistently shows a measure of respect: these are athletes and sportswriters. He believes they are the salt of the earth, a naturally superior class of men."[42] His admiration for these men, which sometimes bordered on hero worship, was deep and earnest. It was rooted in his respect for talent and courage, strength and toughness. He also admired athletes who were good teammates and who enjoyed socializing (that is, drinking and talking into the night) and who did not take themselves too seriously. One of the things that contributed to the sense of belonging at Toots Shor was the ability to give and take insults. This applied to all of Shor's drinking buddies. What the cultural anthropologist Clifford Geertz said about the Balinese villagers he studied is also true of the regulars at Toots Shor: "to be teased" was "to be accepted."[43]

Shor also believed, Bainbridge reports, "that sports are the backbone of American life and that good citizenship demands a close interest in them, though he is sufficiently broadminded to make an occasional exemption."[44] What Shor meant by "good citizenship" is open to interpretation, since some of his most loyal friends and customers were gangsters, but his esteem for athletes was broadminded. He knew, liked, and appreciated "baseball players, football players, prizefighters, golfers, swimmers, tennis stars, coaches, trainers, athletic directors, sportswriters and other sports figures, including pool sharks and curling champions."[45] In this respect Shor did not discriminate, at least among sportsmen. (What he thought or how he felt about sportswomen is difficult to know, but I suspect that he did not know many of them. In general, women were not warmly welcomed at Toots Shor. It was basically a men's club.) As the bandleader Peter Duchin succinctly puts it: "He revered sportsmen."[46]

This was one reason that "members of the sporting aristocracy" never waited for a table at Toots Shor.[47] On any given night, the bar and restaurant might host Joe DiMaggio, Mickey Mantle, Billy Martin, Whitey Ford, Yogi Berra, Hank Greenberg, Willie Mays, Charlie Conerly, Frank Gifford, Jack Dempsey, Joe Louis, Rocky Marciano, Ben Hogan, Arnold Palmer, Willie Shoemaker, and countless others—not all of whom were part of the sports world, of course. Jackie Gleason and Earl Warren, Frank Sinatra and Frank Costello, Edward Bennett Williams and Ernest Hemingway were periodically there, too, mingling with one another. Yet in terms of sports, the place was often a who's who of midcentury athletic greatness. In Kristi Jacobson's excellent documentary film *Toots* (2006), Gifford remembers that Shor made athletes feel comfortable, that he protected them from overzealous and gawking fans, and that he "would bounce back and forth from table to table" to ensure that people were having a good time.[48]

For some people, Shor's hospitality and generosity extended beyond the restaurant. Shor had ready access to tickets, and he took some of his pals to all manner of New York sporting events. Shor always had ringside seats for the prizefights at Madison Square Garden, which was less than a mile away. A regular at Yankees, Giants, and Dodgers games, Shor had reserved box seats.

The great pitcher Whitey Ford saw and quietly acknowledged Shor from the mound when he played at Yankee Stadium. "He was just a great friend and a great fan," Ford recollects.[49]

For years, Shor was particularly close with the iconic if shy and discreet Joe DiMaggio. By contrast, Shor was loud and extroverted. So they seemed like an unlikely pair, an odd couple. Yet sportswriter Maury Allen notes that when the twenty-one-year-old DiMaggio joined the Yankees in 1936, Shor befriended him and "told him what the city was like."[50] He showed the young DiMaggio around town and helped make him feel comfortable in New York. "I kind of brought him out of his shell," Shor said.[51] For a time, the two men "had been inseparable."[52] When Shor opened his restaurant, DiMaggio frequently dined there. According to writer Dennis Gaffney:

> After a good game, DiMaggio would come in and eat and entertain questions from sports writers. After a bad game, DiMaggio would drive by the restaurant and send in word via the doorman to go get Toots. The two would walk up and down Fifth Avenue. "No talking, not a word said about the game or my family or anything," Shor remembered. "He just felt like going for a walk."[53]

Later, after he retired, DiMaggio sometimes brought his wife, Marilyn Monroe, with him to the restaurant. To Shor, DiMaggio was a good friend, a wonderful, humble person, and an exemplar of an athlete "who acquired class."[54] But in September 1954, the two men had a falling out. Apparently DiMaggio was upset about the filming of the famous scene in *The Seven Year Itch* (1955) in which the breeze from a passing subway car below her provocatively lifts Monroe's white skirt. He thought the scene was too revealing, undignified, and embarrassing. At Toots Shor that evening, DiMaggio confided in Shor and, as Maury Allen recalls it, "Toots trying to be his friend, he sort of sympathized with DiMaggio, and he said something kind of nasty about Marilyn."[55] Shor had inadvertently deeply insulted his friend. Angry and upset, DiMaggio left the restaurant and did not speak to Shor for twenty years. It is hard to know, but the story may be apocryphal.

Nonetheless, it was not the kind of story that would appear in the press at the time. For many of the other "members of the sporting aristocracy" at Toots Shor—the sportswriters, columnists, and editors—were respectful and discreet. They hobnobbed with Shor and the athletes, politicians, and celebrities and rarely betrayed their trust. At the same time, Toots Shor was mentioned in the newspapers almost every day. When Edward Robb Ellis asked Shor what he thought attracted celebrities to his restaurant, Shor responded, "Newspapers. Writers, writing about me all the time. I'd be in fifteen, eighteen columns every day."[56] In that pre-Internet age, when there was not much television news programming, there were eleven newspapers in New York and they were in competition with one another. They all needed content, stories, and local color. Toots Shor provided these things in abundance. He also provided a safe space for sportswriters to interact and connect with sports figures. It was mutually and personally beneficial to do so. "In those days," explained cartoonist and columnist Bill Gallo of the *Daily News*, "where we got our stuff was Toots Shor's restaurant."[57] Others agreed. In *Bury Me in an Old Press Box: The Good Life and Times of a Sportswriter* (1957), Fred Russell, native Tennessean and veteran of the *Nashville Banner*, asserted:

> I believe a writer could set up shop in Toots Shor's Restaurant on 51st Street and turn out a sprightly column every day. All he would need is a tape recorder. If I'm going to New York and want to see some friends in the sports crowd, I don't have to phone them; I know they'll be dropping into Shor's. The Football Writers Association meets there for lunch every Monday during the fall. In baseball season, it's only 12 to 15 minutes from the Polo Grounds and Yankee Stadium by subway. It's just across the street from the Associated Press offices, where many sportswriters visiting New York write their pieces. Toots uses no tricks in attracting the sports, theatrical and newspaper people into his place; I think the main lure is that he personifies that common desire of so many Americans to know sports celebrities intimately.[58]

Russell, Grantland Rice's protégé, was correct. Because of Toots Shor, the man and the place, millions of Americans could glean some sense of their sporting heroes as men, away from the fields of play. This was part of the place's allure, which Shor certainly cultivated. "Places like Shor's had a huge attraction," writer Pete Hamill asserted, "they were part of the imagination of people who had never walked into them. They knew they existed the way they knew that the Statue of Liberty existed. They were ornaments of the city."[59]

Beyond that, because New York and its news media had a disproportionate and influential place in and effect on the wider culture, the city seemed to be the center of the American sports world. (It especially seemed that way to New Yorkers.) And since so many members of that sports world congregated and socialized at Toots Shor, it became something like the nation's sports hub, a good-time place where narratives were crafted, images were burnished, and cultural values were on display and championed.

That is, until Toots Shor (who often had financial woes) was finally made a lucrative offer he could not refuse and the place closed its doors in 1959. Before it did, however, when many of his pals had gathered in June to say farewell to the restaurant, Shor was moved to say:

> This saloon isn't built of steel and bricks. . . . It is built of wonderful memories. This isn't a building being torn down, it is me! When I sold this place, I only sold the steel and bricks because the memories were worth ten times of what I was paid for and nobody has enough money to buy the spirit of this place.[60]

The restaurant was razed in August.[61] It was a watershed moment for Toots Shor, and it signified the end of an era in New York cultural and sports history.

## "A Legend among Legends"

What happened next is primarily a story of decline, rooted in decades of dissipation.

After Toots Shor closed his restaurant on 51st Street—he sold the lease for an impressive $1.5 million—he celebrated with his family and friends. Shor and his wife went on a lengthy and expensive European tour, during which they visited London, Paris, and Rome, where Shor met Pope John XXIII.[62] Shor spent his money freely, almost as if he were in a hurry to get rid of it. Much of it was spent on his friends. Before long he was close to broke, again.

Undeterred by his finances, Shor opened another eponymously named restaurant in December 1961. It was at 33 West 52nd Street (two doors down from the 21 Club) and was much bigger than the original Toots Shor. According to Donald I. Rogers of the *Herald Tribune*: "Affable, amiable, gross and sometimes grotesque, but always lovable and loved, Toots Shor has opened himself a new gin mill and eatery . . . with money borrowed from the Teamster's Union Pension Fund. He has built what is said to be the finest-equipped restaurant in the city."[63] Despite a great deal of hype, it was not a successful venture. For one thing, the new place was too big to be profitable. It never drew enough people to cover its expenses. That was partly because it lacked the intimacy and spirit of its predecessor. It was also because by the 1960s the culture and its nightlife were changing dramatically. Some of the old Toots Shor clientele had passed away. Some had moved to the expanding suburbs, which can be partially explained by the fact that New York was experiencing financial and social distress (increased poverty and crime, some of it drug related) and in some places blight. In these contexts, to many people Toots Shor the man and the place seemed passé, relics from a previous cultural moment. After many difficult years, the 52nd Street Toots Shor restaurant closed in 1971 due to crippling debt and thousands of dollars in unpaid taxes.[64]

In October 1972, Shor tried one last time. He opened a smaller place on East 54th Street. "The décor was the same," reported Dave Anderson of the *New York Times*, "but the atmosphere was not."[65] The place failed in less than a year. Then, for financial reasons, he sold the rights to his name and his services as a host to a new chain of so-called Toots Shor restaurants that were owned and operated by the Riese family (which owned or controlled over 250 restaurants at the time).[66] They were poor imitations of the original.

Eventually, Toots Shor's body began to fail. The years of hard, incessant drinking had taken a toll on him. To make matters worse, he was hospitalized with cancer.

Toots Shor died in late January 1977. He was seventy-three years old.

Over five hundred people attended his funeral, among them sportsmen and athletes such as Mel Allen, Eddie Arcaro, Billy Conn, Charley Conerly, Frank Gifford, Monte Irvin, Ralph Kiner, Bowie Kuhn, Wellington Mara, Kyle Rote, Pete Rozelle, and Horace Stoneham.[67] At his funeral service, rabbi Ronald B. Sobel remarked, "A city is most authentically reflected in its people. In a very unique manner, Toots Shor for several decades was the mirror of a special excitement and quality that set New York apart from all other cities. He was as a magnet around which flowed many of the special streams of New York's greatness. He was, in his life, a legend among legends."[68] His longtime pal Red Smith, the bespectacled dean of American sportswriters and a Toots Shor regular, wrote: "It is comforting to believe that Toots himself got a hero's welcome last Sunday midnight when he stepped out of here to join his old gang. So many of them were waiting for him—Granny Rice, Frank Graham, Bill Corum, Bob Considine, Mark Hellinger, Gene Fowler, Harry Truman, Bob Hannegan, General Rosy O'Donnell. They had gone ahead of him and left him desperately lonesome."[69] In New York or the great beyond, Toots Shor always kept interesting company and had plenty of friends.

Of course, he also contributed significantly to the vibrancy of midcentury New York's social life and sports world. In his own way, writes Bob Considine, Shor helped make New York in the 1940s and 1950s an interesting, great city; he did so by endowing "at least a portion of it with his own patented robust style."[70] As the years pass, it is more and more difficult to know that—to know that Shor was "a legend among legends," a midcentury icon, someone who added to the city's rich history.

Still, Toots Shor marked the culture. Alexander Mackendrick's film noir *Sweet Smell of Success* (1957), for instance, takes us inside of Toots Shor's restaurant, right past the famous circular bar, as the narrative follows the ambitious publicist Sidney Falco (Tony Curtis) on his quest to find the unscrupulous, arrogant gossip columnist J. J. Hunsecker (Burt Lancaster).

The prolific and successful painter and sketch artist Leroy Neiman immortalized Toots Shor, the place and the man. His painting *Toots Shor Bar* (1969) is a wild, multihued, kinetic portrait of the circular bar, its raucous patrons, and Shor, who looms large in the background. "Neiman injected an element of voyeurism into his work," writer Christopher Sharp correctly asserts, "a seductive invitation to belly up to the bar and sit elbow to elbow with Frank Sinatra in the wee small hours, to be slapped on the back and called 'Crumb Bum' by Toots Shor."[71] By contrast, Neiman's *Toots Shor as the Babe* (1976) is a relatively simple sketch done in marker that depicts Shor, tall and confident, holding a bottle of booze upside down, as if it were a baseball bat, patiently waiting for a pitch to hit.[72]

Less than a year after Shor died, on November 30, 1977, New York City officially honored him with a bronze plaque at 51 West 51st Street. The plaque reads: "The Original Site Of Toots Shor's Restaurant." Underneath, in slightly smaller letters, it declares: "Where the 'crumb bums' who played sports and the 'crumb bums' who wrote about them got together with those who rooted for them and read them, especially Toots." Reporting on the unveiling ceremony, Red Smith noted, "Plaques and statues around New York commemorate many great men—Edgar Allen Poe, poet and drinker; Edwin Booth, actor; George M. Cohan, songwriter-playwright-actor; Diamond Jim Brady, horseplayer; Father Duffy, priest. This is the first to salute a saloonkeeper."[73] The plaque was National League president Charles "Chub" Feeney's idea, and the event was well attended, despite the poor weather. "In a raw and penetrating chill reminiscent of World Series weather," Smith added, "Toots's friends huddled in overcoats" and listened to baseball commissioner Bowie Kuhn explain:

"The plaque is meant to tell you on behalf of all of us in sports how much we all loved Toots."[74] The plaque endures, even as memories fade.

A final example of Toots Shor's cultural endurance. Don DeLillo's 800-plus page mega-novel *Underworld* (1998), which *New York Times* critic Michiko Kakutani calls a "masterpiece," begins with 35,000 fans watching the famous October 3, 1951, baseball game between the Giants and the Dodgers at the Polo Grounds.[75] Among those in attendance were Jackie Gleason, Frank Sinatra, Toots Shor, and (somewhat oddly) J. Edgar Hoover.[76] DeLillo's Toots Shor is brilliantly rendered. A "big lumbering man," he has "meatcutter's hands" and "a face like a traffic accident."[77] The narrator continues, "You look at Toots and see a speakeasy vet, dense of body, with slicked-back hair and a set of chinky [*sic*] eyes that summon up a warning in a hurry. This is an ex-bouncer who throws innocent people out of his club when he is drinking."[78] Acknowledging Shor's networking skills and ability to hold his liquor, the narrator concedes, "And it's true about Toots, he knows everybody worth knowing and can drink even Gleason into the carpeting. And when he clamps a sympathetic paw on your shoulder you feel he is some provident force come to guide you out of old despond."[79] When the impossible happens and the Giants miraculously win the pennant, DeLillo's Shor says to Sinatra: "We just won unbelievable, they're ripping up the joint, I don't know whether to laugh, shit, or go blind." To which Sinatra replies: "I'm rooting for number one or number three."[80] The historical Toots Shor, I am confident, would have loved the repartee and irreverence, and being remembered, but certainly not as much as he loved being at his original 51st Street saloon with Sinatra, Gleason, and the rest of his crumb bum drinking buddies, where they would tell stories, laugh, tease one another, and talk about sports all night and into the morning.

Toots Shor, the man and the joint, and the era in which they thrived, are sometimes romanticized. That has not been my intention. Shor was a brash, every so often crude man, "outgoing and often as erratic as a rocket."[81] He sometimes insulted people, bruised their feelings, and made bad, self-injurious decisions. He could also be kind, generous, and sentimental. Similarly, his restaurant was not some idyllic, egalitarian space. It was, after all, a highly gendered space, which one could argue produced and reproduced white male privilege.[82] At the same time, Toots Shor's restaurant, "a rendezvous that served for two decades as a monument to sport and booze," was a dynamic setting where interesting, accomplished people from the sports world and other domains came together and created a synergistic cultural buzz that resonated far beyond 51st Street.[83] As for Toots Shor the man, his friend, the esteemed broadcast journalist Edward R. Murrow, declared in 1955: "Shor is many things to many people. He has been identified as a piece of genuine Americana. And a friend to the world at large. And he has also been described as phony as a three-dollar bill and exactly the kind of guy he'd throw out of his own place."[84] All true. Although he was singular, an American original, Shor did not mean one thing. He was instead Whitmanesque in that he was large and contained and entertained multitudes.

# Notes

## Introduction

1. *New York Times*, October 20, 1977, and February 5, 1978. When it came time to decide which team's uniform his Hall of Fame plaque would show him wearing, Jackson did not hesitate in choosing the Yankees over the three other clubs for whom he had played, including the Oakland Athletics, winners of three consecutive world titles in 1972, 1973, and 1974.

2. The New York Giants and Brooklyn Dodgers, although not matching the Yankees' record of success, were dominant teams in the National League for significant periods. The Giants, under their legendary manager John McGraw, won ten pennants in the twenty-one years from 1904 to 1924, and then three in the 1930s and two in the 1950s before departing for San Francisco. The Dodgers, who left the same year for Los Angeles, won six pennants between 1947 and 1956, losing tie-breaking postseason playoffs in 1946 and 1951. They lost the 1950 pennant in the last game of the season.

3. Arthur Daley, "Sports: All Big League," *New York Times Sunday Magazine*, February 1, 1953, 56.

4. Joseph Durso, *Madison Square Garden: 100 Years of History* (New York: Simon and Schuster, 1979), 202; Russell Sullivan, *Rocky Marciano: The Rock of His Times* (Urbana: University of Illinois Press, 2002), 98; John Kieran, *The American Sporting Scene* (New York: Macmillan, 1941), 192.

5. Stephen H. Norwood, "'American Jewish Muscle': Forging a New Masculinity in the Streets and in the Ring, 1890–1940," *Modern Judaism* 29 (May 2009): 186–87. Heywood Broun wrote in the *New York World-Telegram* after Louis defeated Schmeling: "One hundred years from now some historian may theorize . . . that the decline of Nazi prestige began with a left hook delivered by a former unskilled automotive worker [Joe Louis] . . . [who] exploded the Nordic myth with a bombing glove." Chris Mead, *Champion–Joe Louis: Black Hero in White America* (New York: Charles Scribner's Sons, 1985), 159.

6. David Margolick, *Beyond Glory: Joe Louis vs. Max Schmeling, and a World on the Brink* (New York: Alfred A. Knopf, 2005), 7.

7. Eliot Asinof, *Eight Men Out: The Black Sox and the 1919 World Series* (New York: Henry Holt, 1963), 19, 34–35.

8. *New York Times*, April 20, 1949, and September 22, 2010; Henry D. Fetter, *Taking on the Yankees: Winning and Losing in the Business of Baseball, 1903–2003* (New York: W. W. Norton, 2003), 187.

9. Lee Allen, *Cooperstown Corner: Columns from the Sporting News* (Cleveland, OH: Society for American Baseball Research, n.d.), 3.

10. *New York Times*, March 14, 1971.

11. Jules Tygiel, *Past Time: Baseball as History* (New York: Oxford University Press, 2000), 25–28; Michael Isenberg, *John L. Sullivan and His America* (Urbana: University of Illinois Press, 1988), 92–94 .

12. Elliott J. Gorn, *The Manly Art: Bare-Knuckle Prize Fighting in America* (Ithaca, NY: Cornell University Press, 1986), 222, 242.

13. Ted Vincent, *The Rise and Fall of American Sport: Mudville's Revenge* (Lincoln: University of Nebraska Press, 1981), 59–60.

14. The *Times* sportswriters who won Pulitzers were Arthur Daley (1956), Red Smith (1976), Ira Berkow (2001), and John Branch (2013).

15. Ira Berkow, *Red: A Biography of Red Smith* (New York: Times Books, 1986), 91, 93, 148; Jerome Holtzman, *No Cheering in the Press Box* (New York: Henry Holt, 1995 [1973]), 243–45. In *Across the River and into the Trees*, a character "poured another glass of Valpolicella, and then started to read the Paris edition of the *New York Herald Tribune*. I ought to take the pills, he thought. But the hell with the pills. . . . He was reading Red Smith, and he liked him very much." Berkow, *Red*, 148.

16. Berkow, Red, 93; Fred Russell, *Bury Me in an Old Press Box: Good Times and Life of a Sportswriter* (New York: A. S. Barnes, 1957), 223.

17. *New York Herald Tribune*, June 8, 1948.

18. Red Smith, obituary of Jesse Abramson, *New York Times*, June 12, 1979; Roger Kahn, *The Boys of Summer* (New York: Harper, 1988 [1971]), 70, 73. Kahn called Woodward "the most gloriously talented sports editor in the United States." Abramson wrote for the *New York Herald Tribune* from 1924 until the newspaper's demise in 1966.

19. Stephen H. Norwood, "American Jewish Men in Sports" in *Encyclopedia of American Jewish History*, Vol. 2, ed. Stephen H. Norwood and Eunice G. Pollack (Santa Barbara, CA: ABC-CLIO, 2008), 521.

20. Randy Roberts and James Olson, *Winning Is the Only Thing: Sports in America since 1945* (Baltimore: Johns Hopkins University Press, 1989), 95–96; Willie Pep with Robert Sacci, *Friday's Heroes: Willie Pep Remembers* (Bloomington, IN: AuthorHouse, 2008), 9–10; *New York Times*, March 17, 1960, February 19, 1964, August 8, 1964, and September 21, 1964.

21. *New York Times*, June 11 and 27, 1959, and June 19, 21, and 22, 1960. Patterson knocked out Johansson in a third title encounter in Miami in 1961.

22. *Chicago Tribune*, December 30, 1963.

23. *Los Angeles Times*, September 28, 1988; Red Barber and Robert Creamer, *Rhubarb in the Catbird Seat* (Lincoln: University of Nebraska Press, 1968), 12.

24. Bruce Markusen, "Pop Culture and the Pastime: Baseball and the Twilight Zone," *The Hardball Times*, www.thehardball times.com. Serling's short story began mournfully: "There is a large, extremely decrepit stadium overgrown by weeds and high grass that is called, whenever it is referred to . . . Tebbet's Field and it lies in a borough of New York known as Brooklyn. Many years ago it . . . hous[ed] a ball club known as the Brooklyn Dodgers. . . . Tebbet's Field today houses nothing but memories [and] a few ghosts. . . . This was one helluva place to play in its day." Rod Serling, *Stories from the Twilight Zone* (New York: Bantam, 1960), 1.

25. *Los Angeles Times*, September 28, 1988.

26. *Washington Post*, August 12, 1958.

27. On baseball's emergence, early development, and professionalization, see George B. Kirsch, *The Creation of American Team Sports: Baseball and Cricket, 1838–72* (Urbana: University of Illinois Press, 1989); Warren Goldstein, *Playing for Keeps: A History of Early Baseball* (Ithaca, NY: Cornell University Press, 1989); Harold Seymour, *Baseball: The Early Years* (New York: Oxford University Press, 1960); and Melvin Adelman, *A Sporting Time:*

*New York City and the Rise of Modern Athletics, 1820–1870* (Urbana: University of Illinois Press, 1986), chapters 6 and 7.

28. *New York Times,* June 15, 1870.

29. Steven A. Riess, *City Games: The Evolution of American Urban Society and the Rise of Sports* (Urbana: University of Illinois Press, 1989), 56; Michael Oriard, *Reading Football: How the Popular Press Created an American Spectacle* (Chapel Hill: University of North Carolina Press, 1993), 90, 95–97, 101, 121.

30. *New York Times,* November 29, 1889.

31. *New York Times,* November 27, 1891.

32. *New York Times,* November 22, 1896.

33. *New York Tribune,* November 22, 1896. The *Tribune* noted in 1894 that in the Tenderloin district "rowdyism by the students [in New York for the game] . . . usually prevails at night after the big game." The city posted special policemen "at the theaters and other places of amusement where the students usually congregate." *New York Tribune,* December 1, 1894.

34. Reed Harris, *King Football* (New York: Vanguard Press, 1932), 35–37, 41–42; Mark F. Bernstein, *Football: The Ivy League Origins of an American Obsession* (Philadelphia: University of Pennsylvania Press, 2001), 153. On Columbia's stunning upset of Stanford in the 1934 Rose Bowl, see John Kieran, *The American Sporting Scene* (New York: Macmillan, 1941), 175–86. Kieran, the *New York Times*'s first columnist with a by-line, who wrote "The Sports of the Times" from 1927 to 1943, stated in 1941: "Having watched hundreds of big football games in a quarter of a century of eager observation, I here confess that the greatest thrill came from the playing of a game almost three thousand miles away": the 1934 Columbia-Stanford Rose Bowl. *American Sporting Scene,* 175.

35. Harris, *King Football,* 32–33.

36. Wells Twombly, *Shake Down the Thunder! The Official Biography* (Radnor, PA: Chilton, 1974), 158, 162; David Maraniss, *When Pride Still Mattered: A Life of Vince Lombardi* (New York: Simon and Schuster, 1999), 31, 49.

37. *New York Times,* November 15, 1931, November 29, 1935, November 27, 1936.

38. Murray Sperber, *Shake Down the Thunder: The Creation of Notre Dame Football* (New York: Henry Holt, 1993), 146, 164–66, 178–79, 383, 432; *New York Times,* February 11, 1956.

39. Charles Fountain, *Sportswriter: The Life and Times of Grantland Rice* (New York: Oxford University Press, 1993), 3.

40. *New York Times,* December 7, 1925; John M. Carroll, *Red Grange and the Rise of Modern Football* (Urbana: University of Illinois Press, 1999), 118; Robert W. Peterson, *Pigskin: The Early Years of Pro Football* (New York: Oxford University Press, 1997). Peterson noted that at this time in the larger cities, "crowds of 15,000 were considered good" for a pro football game. Peterson, *Pigskin,* 83, 89–90.

41. *New York Times,* December 8, 1925; *Chicago Tribune,* December 10, 1925.

42. Jerry Izenberg, *Rozelle: A Biography* (Lincoln: University of Nebraska Press, 2014), 51, 56.

43. Riess, *City Games,* 107–8; Robert Peterson, *Cages to Jumpshots: Pro Basketball's Early Years* (New York: Oxford University Press, 1990), 3, 69, 101.

44. Obituary of Marty Glickman, *New York Times,* January 4, 2001; Norwood, "American Jewish Men in Sports," Norwood and Pollack, eds., *Encyclopedia of American Jewish History,* vol. 2, 522; Jack Kerouac, *On the Road* (New York: Penguin, 1957), 250.

45. Peterson, *Cages to Jumpshots,* 108–9.

46. *New York Times*, February 18, 1935, June 25, 1970, and October 6, 1974; Roger Kahn, *A Flame of Pure Fire: Jack Dempsey and the Roaring 20s* (New York: Harcourt Brace, 1999), 431–32. Randy Roberts noted that tourists visited Jack Dempsey's Restaurant "as if on a pilgrimage." Randy Roberts, *Jack Dempsey: The Manassa Mauler* (New York: Grove Press, 1980 [1979]), 270.

47. *New York Times*, December 6 and 7, 1934, and November 14, 1956. Leone's Restaurant began in 1906 as a "small cellar bistro" run by Gene Leone, his three brothers, and their mother, who did the cooking. In 1959 Gene Leone sold the restaurant to a chain. It closed in 1994. *New York Times*, May 30, 1959, January 12, 1994.

48. *New York Times*, June 23, 1946, May 13, 1959, June 2, 1963, April 29, 1968, May 14, 1972, June 13, 1984, June 24, 1994. The Spalding sporting goods company discontinued the spaldeen in 1980. *New York Times*, May 5, 1985.

## 1. The Yankees and Dodgers

1. The rivalry is riveted in the memory of New Yorkers, especially baby boomers. See, e.g., Peter Golenbock, *An Oral History of the Brooklyn Dodgers* (New York: G. P. Putnam's Sons, 1984); Harvey Frommer, *New York City Baseball: The Last Golden Age: 1947–1957* (New York: Atheneum, 1985); Carl Prince, *Brooklyn's Dodgers* (New York: Oxford University Press, 1996); Henry D. Fetter, *Taking on the Yankees: Winning and Losing in the Business of Baseball, 1903–2003* (New York: W. W. Norton, 2003); and David G. Surdam, *The Postwar Yankees: Baseball's Golden Age Revisited* (Lincoln: University of Nebraska Press, 2008). For biographies, Jules Tygiel, *Baseball's Great Experiment: Jackie Robinson and His Legacy* (New York: Vintage, 1983); Arnold Rampersad, *Jackie Robinson: A Biography* (New York: Knopf, 1997); Richard Ben Cramer, *Joe DiMaggio: The Hero's Life* (New York: Simon and Schuster, 2001); Jane Leavy, *Sandy Koufax: A Lefty's Legacy* (New York: HarperCollins, 2002); Jane Leavy, *The Last Boy: Mickey Mantle and the End of America's Childhood* (New York: Harper Perennial, 2011); Neil Lanctot, *Campy: The Two Lives of Roy Campanella* (New York: Simon and Schuster, 2011); William C. Kashatus, *Jackie and Campy: The Untold Story of Their Rocky Relationship and the Breaking of Baseball's Color Line* (Lincoln: University of Nebraska Press, 2014). On management, see, e.g., Robert W. Creamer, *Stengel: His Life and Times* (New York: Simon and Schuster, 1984); Lee Lowenfish, *Branch Rickey: Baseball's Ferocious Gentleman* (Lincoln: University of Nebraska Press, 2007); Andy McCue, *Mover and Shaker: Walter O'Malley, the Dodgers and Baseball's Westward Expansion* (Lincoln: University of Nebraska Press, 2014).

2. Paul Dickson, *The New Dickson Baseball Dictionary* (New York: Harcourt, Brace, and Company, 1999), 85.

3. "Is Brooklyn Still in the League?" (1934). *Big Apple*, May 19, 2005, http://www.barrypopik.com/index.php/new_york_city/entry/is_brooklyn_still_in_the_league_1934 (accessed April 21, 2015).

4. The Dodgers best attendance years as a percentage of total NL attendance were in 1939, 1940, and 1941 (20.30 percent, 22.23 percent, and 25.43 percent). Computed from data in http://www.baseball-reference.com/teams/LAD/attend.shtml. On the march, see Peter Marquis, "Brooklyn et 'Ses' Dodgers: Base-ball et Construction des Identités Urbaines aux États-Unis, une Sociohistoire (1883–1957)" (PhD diss., École des Hautes Études en Sciences Sociales, 2009) ("Brooklyn and Its Dodgers. A Sociocultural History of Baseball and the Making of Urban Identities in the United States"), 390.

5. The Yankees were not always a great draw, coming in fourth in the 1900s and fifth in the 1910s, a poor performance for the biggest city in the American League.

6. There were four morning papers (*Daily Mirror, Daily News, Herald Tribune,* and the *Times*); three afternoon papers (*Journal-American, World-Telegram and Sun,* and the *Post*); and three regional (*Brooklyn Eagle, Long Island Post,* and *Newsday*). On comparing the morning and afternoon coverage, see Bryan Curtis, "No Chattering in the Press Box: The Lost Tribe of Sportswriters Known as the Chipmunks," *Grantland,* May 3, 2012, http://grantland.com/features/larry-merchant-leonard-shecter-chipmunks-sportswriting-clan (accessed February 22, 2016). See also George Vecsey, "The Media: My America," in *The Glory Days: New York Baseball, 1947–1957,* ed. John Thorn (New York: Collins, 2007), 77–78, 84 n. 89.

7. Richard Ziegler, "Dick Young," in *Twentieth-Century American Sportswriters: Gale Dictionary of Literary Biography,* 171, ed. Richard Orondeker (Detroit: Gale Group, 1996), 356–64.

8. On Rosenthal and antisemitism, see Richard Orondeker, "Harold Rosenthal," in *American Sportswriters and Writers on Sport,* ed. Orondeker, 240–50; Larry Ruttman, *American Jews and America's Game: Voices of a Growing Legacy in Baseball* (Lincoln: University of Nebraska Press, 2013), 121–22.

9. For Gross's obituary, see *New York Times,* May 10, 1973, 48; Jane Gross, "A Baseball Education under the Sun," *New York Times,* March 23, 2013, http://www.nytimes.com/2013/03/24/sports/baseball/a-baseball-education-under-the-sun.html?_r=0 (accessed February 22, 2016). On Drebinger, see obituary in *New York Times,* October 24, 1979, A29; on Lang, *New York Times,* January 26, 2007, C11; and on Koppett, *New York Times,* June 24, 2003, A28. On the chipmunk journalists, see Curtis, "No Chattering in the Press Box."

10. Golenbock, *An Oral History of the Brooklyn Dodgers,* 44–45. See also Raymond Schuck, "Dodging the Past: The Brooklyn Dodgers as Public Memory" (PhD diss., Arizona State University, 2006), who argues that scholars have overdone the mythic elements of the Dodgers and their Brooklyn fans. On the other hand, anthropologist Frederick Roberts argues that the mythic history of the team as representing the golden age of Brooklyn served to bring Brooklynites together. See Frederick Roberts, "A Myth Grows in Brooklyn: Urban Death, Resurrection, and the Brooklyn Dodgers," *Baseball History* 2 (1987): 4–26, and "Dem Bums Become the Boys of Summer: From Comic Caricatures to Sacred Icons of the National Pastime," *American Jewish History* 83 (1995): 51–63.

11. *New York Times,* December 22, 1978, B6; Prince, *Brooklyn's Dodgers,* 105; Schuck, "Dodging the Past," 85–141; David Q. Voigt, *American Baseball,* Vol. 3, *From Postwar Expansion to the Electronic Age* (University Park: Pennsylvania State University Press, 1983), 98.

12. Prince, *Brooklyn's Dodgers,* 104; Elliot Willensky, *When Brooklyn Was the World, 1920–1957* (New York: Harmony Books, 1986), 11; Lowenfish, *Branch Rickey,* 214 (quote). In the early 1960s, some students at Stuyvesant High School in lower Manhattan vigorously asserted that their mothers had never been to "the city."

13. Ron Briley, "Where Have You Gone William Bendix?" in Briley, *Class at Bat, Gender on Deck and Race in the Hole: A Line-Up of Essays on Twentieth Century Culture and America's Game* (Jefferson, NC: McFarland, 2003), 40.

14. Marquis, "Brooklyn et 'Ses' Dodgers," 397; Joseph Dorinson, "Brooklyn: The Elusive Image," *Long Island Historical Journal* 1 (March 1989): 128–35. Doris Kearns Goodwin told Ken Burns, "The idea that Brooklyn felt a stepchild to New York City, and that somehow the Dodgers, the Bums, were stepchilds [*sic*] too, that were going to show the hoity-toity New Yorkers that we were really better than them, defined who Brooklyn was." See Ken Burns and Lynn Novick, *Baseball* (PBS, 1994).

15. William Marshall, *Baseball's Pivotal Era, 1945–1951* (Lexington: University of Kentucky Press, 1999), 205.

16. *New York Times*, February 12, 1943, 26.

17. Marquis, "Brooklyn et 'Ses' Dodgers," 389; Marshall, *Baseball's Pivotal Era*, 173; Elli Wohlgelernter, "Interview: Calvin R. Abrams and May Abrams," *American Jewish History* 83 (March 1995): 119. On Powell, see his interview in Stephen M. Samtur and Martin A. Jackson, *The Bronx: Lost, Found, and Remembered, 1935–1975* (New York: Back in the Bronx, 1999), 193. When schoolboy Judd Hirsch from the Bronx was visiting in Brooklyn, his buddy's friends would stop him in the schoolyard and ask him "'You a Dodger Fan?' And I'd say, 'Yes.' It was a great cover." Samtur and Jackson, *The Bronx*, 170. On radios and the making of a sports community, see Tony Silva, *Baseball over the Air: The National Pastime on the Radio and in the Imagination* (Jefferson, NC: McFarland, 2007), 129–45.

18. Correspondence of Stephen Norwood, Eunice Pollack, Lawrence W. Boies, Steven Gietschier, Lyle Spatz, Joseph Dorinson, and John Burbridge. On Shapiro and West, see their interviews in Arlene Alda, *Just Kids from the Bronx: Telling It the Way It Was: An Oral History* (New York: Henry Holt, 2015), 51–52. For a critical view of Dodger fans, see "Jimmy Cannon Says," *Newsday*, September 21, 1954, 53.

19. The Dodgers charged $3 for loge and lower box seats; $2.50 for upper stand box seats; $1.25 and $1.75 for reserved. They changed the configuration for Sundays and night games, reducing the number of general admission seats by 48 percent. See Michael J. Haupert, "Economic History of Baseball." https://eh.net/encyclopedia/the-economic-history-of-major-league-baseball (accessed August 20, 2015).

20. Marquis, "Brooklyn et 'Ses' Dodgers," 389, 541–43. Another study found that 30 percent of actual attendees were women. Marquis's data indicated that spectators were heavily Italians (40 percent) and either British or Germans (30 percent), but likely underestimated the Jewish presence since they comprised one-third of the borough's population. Marquis recognized that since Jews comprised 33.6 percent of the borough's population, their presence in his sample of fans seemed skewed. On the Jewish population of Brooklyn, see Morris Horowitz and Lawrence J. Kaplan, *The Jewish Population of the New York Area, 1900–1975* (New York: 1959), 22; and Ilana Abramovitch and Seán Galvin, eds., *Jews of Brooklyn* (Hanover, NH: Brandeis University Press, 2002), 346. The importance of supporting the Dodgers and Americanization is discussed in Schuck, "Dodging the Past," 171, exemplified by the memories of an immigrant rabbi in Pete Hamill, *Snow in August* (New York: Warner Books, 1997), 237.

21. Tom Clavin and Danny Peary, *Gil Hodges* (New York: New American Library, 2012), 108 (quote), 155.

22. Harvey Frommer, *New York City Baseball: The Last Golden Age, 1947–1957* (New York: Atheneum, 1985), 35–36; For the Heagney interview, see John G. Zinn and Paul G. Zinn, eds., *Ebbets Field: Essays and Memories of Brooklyn's Historic Ballpark, 1913–1960* (Jefferson, NC: McFarland, 2013), 194–95.

23. Steven A. Riess, *Touching Base: Professional Baseball and American Culture in the Progressive Era*, rev. ed. (Urbana: University of Illinois Press, 1999), 31, 36, 38, 448; Samtur and Jackson, *The Bronx*, 193.

24. Harold Rosenthal, "Giants' Poll Brings More Parking, Earlier Arc Play," *Sporting News*, March 2, 1955, 8.

25. Herbert Kupferberg, "What Makes a Giant Fan?" *New York Herald Tribune*, June 19, 1948, SM7; *New York Times*, February 27, 2001, B7; Arnold Hano, *A Day in the Bleachers* (New

York: Da Capo, 1982), 33; Samtur and Jackson, *The Bronx*, 193 (Powell quote). My thanks to Jonathan Rand and Robert Zimmer for comments on Giant fans.

26. Megan Roby, "The Push and Pull Dynamics of White Flight: A Study of the Bronx between 1950 and 1980," *Bronx County Historical Society Journal* 45 (March 2008): 35, 50; Gary D. Hermalyn and Lloyd Ultan, "Bronx," in Kenneth T. Jackson, ed., *The Encyclopedia of New York City* (New Haven, CT: Yale University Press, 1991), 145; Evelyn Diaz Gonzalez, *The Bronx* (New York: Columbia University Press, 2014); Lloyd Ultan and Gary Hermalyn, *The Bronx: It Was Only Yesterday, 1935–1965* (New York: Bronx County Historical Society, 1992), 16, 18. For the Jewish population, see Jonathan Mark, "For the Bronx, It's Desolation Row," July 10, 2003, http://www.thejewishweek.com/news/new-york/bronx-its-desolation-row (accessed February 15, 2016). Marty Abramowitz, president of Jewish Major Leaguers, Inc., remembers he was one of the few people he knew in Brooklyn who rooted for the Yankees because he liked winning. See Ruttman, *American Jews and America's Game*, 52. My thanks to Barton Inkeles and Jeffrey Gurock for their comments on Yankee fandom.

27. Harold Rosenthal, "'49 Series Win Weiss' Big Moment," *Sporting News*, February 8, 1956, 13–14. A 1955 poll of spectators at a Baltimore Orioles game reported that most spectators were middle class, and that 95 percent had at least a high school diploma. Nearly 80 percent got to the game by car, and just 12.5 percent came by bus or trolley. The majority was white collar (56 percent), less than one-fourth was skilled or unskilled, and about 8 percent were retired or unemployed. Fewer than 4 percent were housewives. Baltimore Baseball Club, *Survey* (Baltimore: Baltimore Baseball Club, 1954), cited in Surdam, *Postwar Yankees*, 97.

28. Al Laney, "Friendly Series Spirit Supplants Intensity of Play-Offs in N.L.," *New York Herald Tribune*, October 5, 1951, 22. From 1940 to 1958 (just after the Giants left) there was shuttle service between the Polo Grounds and Yankee Stadium over what had been the 9th Avenue elevated IRT to 167th Street on the Jerome-Woodlawn el section of the IRT Lexington Avenue subway over the Putnam Bridge. The B line currently connects the two stations. "The 9th Avenue Elevated-Polo Grounds Shuttle," http://www.nycsubway.org/wiki/The_9th_Avenue_Elevated-Polo_Grounds_Shuttle#Polo_Grounds_Shuttle_-_Walking_Tour (accessed February 13, 2016); "Remnants of the Ninth Avenue El," http://forgotten-ny.com/1999/12/remnants-of-the-ninth-avenue-el-when-is-a-subway-not-a-subway-when-its-an-el (accessed February 16, 2016); Ultan and Hermalyn, *The Bronx*, 16.

29. For an example of the Yankee fan's sense of self-satisfaction, see Bob Cooke, "Decline of the Yankee Fan," *New York Herald Tribune*, May 11, 1952, B5. A box with six seats cost $900, which meant $2.25 a game (seat cost individually $3). Many were bought by gamblers, though the plan was mainly to sell to banks. In 1950 the Yankees took in $850,000 in advance sales of box seats. Surdam, *The Postwar Yankees*, 61–62.

30. Fetter, *Taking on the Yankees*, 200. General admission was raised to $1.25 in 1955. "1950–1959 Grandstand Rain Check Ticket Stub Dating Guide," http://keymancollectibles.com/tickets/1950sgrandstanddatingguide.htm (accessed September 2, 2015).

31. On Italian Americans and baseball, see Lawrence Baldassaro, *Beyond DiMaggio: Italian Americans in Baseball* (Lincoln: University of Nebraska Press, 2011); on the social functions of sport, see Gerald R. Gems, *Sport and the Shaping of Italian American Identity*. For Hirsch and Kranepool, see Samtur and Jackson, *The Bronx*, 170, 186.

32. McCue, *Mover and Shaker*, 56.

33. Marquis, "Brooklyn et 'Ses' Dodgers," 176, 391, 392 (quote); *Brooklyn Daily Eagle*, August 14, 1951, 1–2.

34. Peter Marquis, "Penser Baseball: Formes et Enjeux de l'action Caritative des Dodgers de Brooklyn en Faveur de la Jeunesse Locale (1913–1957)," *Transatlantica* [Online], 2 | 2011, posted December 21, 2011. http://transatlantica.revues.org/5439 (accessed July 26, 2014); Prince, *Brooklyn's Dodgers*, 130–33. Similar charity work was also supported by the Yankees for the Bronx, Westchester, and Manhattan. See Golenbock, *Bums*, 476.

35. Bill Borst, *Baseball through a Knothole—A St. Louis History* (St. Louis: Krank Press, 1980), 38–39; Marquis, "Brooklyn et 'Ses' Dodgers," 444–47. The DKHC's officers were mainly educators, industrialists, judges, politicians, and representatives of the church, police, and army. On juvenile delinquency in the 1950s, see James B. Gilbert, *A Cycle of Outrage: America's Reaction to the Juvenile Delinquent in the 1950s* (New York: Oxford University Press, 1986).

36. *Brooklyn Eagle*, February 28, 1947, 1–5; Larry Moffi, *The Conscience of the Game: Baseball's Commissioners from Landis to Selig* (Lincoln: University of Nebraska Press, 2006), 126; William H. Marshall Jr., "A. B. Chandler as Baseball Commissioner, 1945–1951: An Overview," *The Register of the Kentucky Historical Society* 83 (Autumn 1984): 377.

37. On the process of integration, see Tygiel, *Baseball's Great Experiment*; Mark Armour and Daniel Levitt, "Branch Rickey," https://pursuitofpennants.wordpress.com/2015/02/13/1-branch-rickey/ (accessed June 3, 2015); Roger Kahn, *Memories of Summer: When Baseball Was an Art, and Writing about It a Game* (New York: Hyperion, 1997), 80; Schuck, "Dodging the Past," 141–53, and 154–68 on white privilege. On Lena Horne's fears for Robinson, see Prince, *Brooklyn's Dodgers*, 19. The standard biography is Rampersad, *Jackie Robinson*. The main autobiography is Jackie Robinson, *I Never Had It Made* (New York: Putnam, 1972). The best film is Thomas Toll, prod., *42*, Warner Brothers, 2013. The impact of JR being traded in 1956 is well depicted in Gary David Goldberg, prod., "Where Have You Gone, Jackie Robinson?" December 11, 1991, *Brooklyn Bridge*, Ubu Productions. On the Robinson tale compared to the Exodus story, see Steven Riess, cited in Tygiel, Baseball's *Great Experiment*, 345.

38. Fetter, *Taking on the Yankees*, 188.

39. Prince, *Brooklyn's Dodgers*, 23–44. On Rickey's relations with the Negro Leagues, see Brad Snyder, *Beyond the Shadow of the Senators: The Untold Story of the Homestead Grays and the Integration of Baseball* (Chicago: Contemporary Books, 2003), 218–19, 231.

40. Ronald A. Smith, "The Paul Robeson–Jackie Robinson Saga and a Political Collision," *Journal of Sport History* 6 (1979): 5–27.

41. Rickey to Roscoe Hobbs, November 29, 1944, in Branch Rickey Papers, Library of Congress, in McCue, *Mover and Shaker*, 46–47; Steven A. Riess, "Sports and the American Jew: An Introduction," in Riess, ed., *Sports and the American Jew*, 55.

42. On Pitler, see Kahn, *The Boys of Summer*, 110. On the eight Jewish Dodgers prior to 1947, see Burton A. Boxerman and Benita W. Boxerman, *Jews and Baseball:* Volume 1, *Entering the American Mainstream, 1871–1948* (Jefferson, NC: McFarland, 2007), 153–64. On Abrams's streak, see *New York Times*, May 26, 1951, 25. "Cal Abrams Day on July 12 Was Staged without Cal Getting into the Game," *Brooklyn Eagle*, July 13, 1951, 12. On the Abrams family and antisemitism, see Wohlgelernter, "Interview with Calvin R. Abrams and May Abrams," 114–16, 119–22; Stephen H. Norwood and Harold Brackman, "Going to Bat for Jackie Robinson: The Jewish Role in Breaking Baseball's Color Line," *Journal of Sport History* 26 (1999): 129; Harvey Araton, "A Dodger Who Faced Barriers, Too," *New York Times*, May 1, 1997, 31. On Koufax and antisemitism, see Jane Leavy, *Sandy Koufax*, 72–73, 187. On antisemitism in baseball, see also Norwood and Brackman, "Going to Bat for Jackie Robinson," 128–29, 131;

Steven A. Riess, "From Pike to Greene, with Greenberg in Between: Jewish Americans and the National Pastime," in *The American Game: Baseball and Ethnicity*, ed. Lawrence Baldassaro and Richard A. Johnson (Carbondale: Southern Illinois University, 2002), 118, 122–23, 125–27, 131, 133; Riess, "Sports and the American Jew," 40–45; Frederic C. Jaher, "Anti-Semitism in American Athletics," *Shofar: An Interdisciplinary Journal of Jewish Studies* 20 (Fall 2001): 68–70. Koufax pitched just 100 innings in 1955 and 1956, and 104 in 1957. Star pitcher Ralph Branca only found out late in life that his mother was Jewish. Joshua Prager, "For Branca, an Asterisk of a Different Kind," *New York Times*, August 14, 2011, D1.

43. Rob Neyer, "Who's the Greatest Jewish Yankee of Them All?" *SB*Nation* http://www.sbnation.com/2012/12/13/3763116/kevin-youkilis-contract-jewish-new-york-yankees (accessed May 3, 2015); Rob Neyer, *Rob Neyer's Big Book of Baseball Legends: The Truth, the Lies, and Everything Else* (New York: Simon and Schuster, 2008), 170. The first Jewish Yankees were infielder Phil Cooney (one game in 1905) and Guy Zinn (1911–1912). The Yankees tried unsuccessfully to purchase AL batting champion Buddy Myer after the 1935 season for over $100,000. See Boxerman and Boxerman, *Jews and Baseball*, 97. Myer was elected to the International Jewish Sports Hall of Fame, but was not Jewish. His father's family had converted to Christianity in a previous generation. See Warren Corbett, "Buddy Myer," https://sabr.org/bioproj/person/ce6e3ebb (accessed September 19, 2017). On the Yankee recruitment of Greenberg, see Jonathan Eig, *Luckiest Man: The Life and Death of Lou Gehrig* (New York: Simon and Schuster, 2005), 133–34.

44. Andrew Zimbalist, *Baseball and Billions: A Probing Look inside the Big Business of Our National Pastime* (New York: Basic Books, 1992), 52; Fetter, *Taking on the Yankees*, 201–3; Jerome Krase and Charles LaCerra, *Ethnicity and Machine Politics* (Lanham, MD: University Press of America, 1991), 135.

45. The Dodgers' share of NL attendance peaked in 1939, 1940, and 1941 (20.30, 22.23, and 25.43 percent). See US Congress, House, Judiciary Committee, *Organized Baseball: Hearings before the Subcommittee on Study of Monopoly Power*, 82nd Cong., 1st sess., 1951, serial 1, part 6 (Washington, DC: Government Printing Office, 1952), 1617–18.

46. US, Congress, House, Judiciary Committee, *Organized Baseball: Hearings before the Subcommittee on Study of Monopoly Power, 82nd Cong., 1st sess., 1951, serial 1, part 6* (Washington, DC: Government Printing Office, 1952), 1617–18. On the Dodgers' share of Giants attendance in 1953, see Harold Rosenthal, "Fans Helping Selves by Poll," *Sporting News*, November 25, 1953, 12; Harold Rosenthal, "Polo Grounds Survey Shows Only Few Want Durocher Out," *New York Herald Tribune*, November 3, 1953, 24; Damon Rice, *Seasons Past* (New York: Prager, 1976), 418. On Robinson's effect on attendance, see Henry D. Fetter, "Robinson in 1947: Measuring an Uncertain Impact," in *Jackie Robinson: Race, Sports and the American Dream*, ed. Joseph Dorinson and Joram Warmund (Armonk, NY: M. E. Sharpe, 1998), 183–92.

47. Scott Lindholm, "Major League Attendance Trends Past, Present, and Future." *SB Nation.* http://www.beyondtheboxscore.com/2014/2/10/5390172/major-league-attendance-trends-1950-2013 (accessed April 21, 2015).

48. Leonard Koppett, *Koppett's Concise History of Major League Baseball* (Philadelphia: Temple University Press, 1998); Chris Jaffe, *Evaluating Baseball's Managers: A History and Analysis of Performance in the Major Leagues, 1876–2008* (Jefferson, NC: McFarland, 2009); Michael Lewis, *Moneyball: The Art of Winning an Unfair Game* (New York: W. W. Norton, 2011).

49. Lowenfish, *Branch Rickey*, 345–46; McCue, *Mover and Shaker*, 12–25, 44–52.

50. McCue, *Mover and Shaker*, 71. Another study put the cost of Vero Beach at $250,000. In 1951, 15 percent of all major leaguers had played for teams in Rickey's farm systems in St. Louis or Brooklyn. See Marshall, *Baseball's Pivotal Year*, 206, 207, 253–54.

51. Tygiel, *Baseball's Great Experiment*, 47–208; Lowenfish, *Branch Rickey*, 349–84; Arnold Rampersad, *Jackie Robinson: A Biography* (New York: Random House, 1999), 121–87; On MacPhail and integration, see Tygiel, *Baseball's Great Experiment*, 82–86; and Larry MacPhail, "Plan to American League on Discouraging Integration of Baseball," in Steven A. Riess, ed., *Major Problems in American Sport History*, 2nd. ed. (Stamford, CT: Cengage, 2015), 380–81.

52. Lowenfish, *Branch Rickey*, 345–46; McCue, *Mover and Shaker*, 12–25, 44–52.

53. Mark Armour and Daniel Levitt, "#7-Buzzie Bavasi," https://pursuitofpennants.wordpress.com/2015/02/05/7-buzzie-bavasi/ (accessed June 3, 2015).

54. "Ebbets Field," http://www.ballparksofbaseball.com/past/EbbetsField.htm#sthash.AUzGoKEr.dpuf (accessed April 22, 2015); McCue, *Mover and Shaker*, 122. Bavasi said O'Malley wasn't a racist, but was concerned with growing poverty in Brooklyn. McCue, *Mover and Shaker*, 72. See also McCue, "Walter O'Malley," http://sabr.org/bioproj/person/94652b33 (accessed April 28, 2015).

55. Dennis Soh, "What Does Sabermetrics Say about How Important a Baseball Manager Is?" http://www.quora.com/What-does-sabermetrics-say-about-how-important-a-baseball-manager-is (accessed June 9, 2015); Jim McLennan, "Evaluating Baseball Managers—a Chat with Chris Jaffe," http://www.azsnakepit.com/2010/1/22/1201672/evaluating-baseball-managers-a (accessed June 9, 2015); Jaffe, *Evaluating Baseball's Managers.*

56. Jeffrey Marlett, "Leo Durocher," http://sabr.org/bioproj/person/35d925c7; Rob Edelman, "Burt Shotton," http://sabr.org/bioproj/person/97735d30 (accessed June 8, 2015); Steven Booth, "The Story of Kindly Old Burt Shotton," February 4, 2011, http://www.hardballtimes.com/the-story-of-kindly-old-burt-shotton (accessed February 11, 2016). Shotton was the last manager to not appear in a uniform. See Tim Marchman, "Tall Catchers, Managers in Uniform, Pitchers Batting 9th, and Other Bad Ideas in Baseball," *Wall Street Journal*, April 16, 2009, D10.

57. Bill Johnson, "Walter Alston," http://sabr.org/bioproj/person/cfc65169 (accessed June 9, 2015).

58. Ralph Berger, "Larry MacPhail," http://sabr.org/bioproj/person/1b708d47 (accessed April 4, 2015); Don Warfield, *The Roaring Redhead: Larry MacPhail, Baseball's Great Innovator* (South Bend, IN: Diamond Communications, 1987); Lyle Bridges, *Bridging Two Dynasties: The 1947 New York Yankees* (Lincoln: University of Nebraska Paperback, 2013); Daniel R. Levitt and Mark Armour, "Del Webb," http://sabr.org/bioproj/person/db1a9611; Daniel R. Levitt and Mark Armour, "Dan Topping," http://sabr.org/bioproj/person/f12c897a (accessed April 5, 2015).

59. Sullivan points out that the outcome of Johnson's dealings was that it produced $6 million for him, nearly the entire cost of the deal. Neil J. Sullivan, *The Dodgers Move West* (New York: Oxford University Press, 1987), 83–85. For a photograph of the parking lots by the ballpark, see Ultan and Hermalyn, *The Bronx*, 142.

60. Dan Levitt, "#5—George Weiss" https://pursuitofpennants.wordpress.com/2015/02/09/5-george-weiss/ (accessed June 3, 2015); Daniel R Levitt, "George Weiss," http://sabr.org/bioproj/person/56e50416 (accessed August 1, 2015).

61. Surdam, *Postwar Yankees*, 69–70. Weiss got a five-year, $60,000 contract after the 1951 season, *New York Times*, October 31, 1951, 35.

62. Kahn, *Boys of Summer*, 164. Kahn modified the language of the quote in his more recent book. See Roger Kahn, *The Era: 1947–1957, When the Yankees, the Giants, and the Dodgers Ruled the World* (Lincoln: University of Nebraska Press, 2002), 45n. See also Tygiel, *Baseball's Great Experiment*, 292.

63. Tygiel, *Baseball's Great Experiment*, 296–98. Surdam, *Postwar Yankees*, 187. Some supporters of the Yankees would later claim that the failure to bring up Power was because the team had another very good prospect in Bill Skowron, who seemed more "Yankee material." He joined the team in 1954, hit over .300 his first four straight years, and was an All-Star from 1957 to 1961. On Howard, see Mitchell Nathanson, *A People's History of Baseball* (Urbana: University of Illinois Press, 2012), 105 (quote).

64. Bill Bishop, "Casey Stengel," http://sabr.org/bioproj/person/bd6a83d8 (accessed June 9, 2015). Harris eventually managed twenty-nine years in the majors, retiring in 1956.

65. Robert W. Creamer, *Stengel: His Life and Times* (New York: Simon and Schuster, 1984); Steven Goldman, *Forging Genius: The Making of Casey Stengel* (Washington, DC: Potomac Books, 2000); Michael Shapiro, *Bottom of the Ninth: Branch Rickey, Casey Stengel, and the Daring Scheme to Save Baseball from Itself* (New York: Times Book, 2009). Player rotation goes back to 1887 when the Indianapolis Hoosiers switched center fielders depending on who was pitching. See Bill James, *The New Bill James Historical Baseball Abstract* (New York: Simon and Schuster, 2003), 117. On Stallings's use of a rotation, see Bryan Soderholm-Difatte, "The 1914 Stallings Platoon: Assessing Execution, Impact, and Strategic Philosophy," *Baseball Research Journal* 43 (Fall 2014). http://sabr.org/research/1914-stallings-platoon-assessing-execution-impact-and-strategic-philosophy (accessed February 11, 2016).

66. US Congress, House, Judiciary Committee, *Organized Baseball: Hearings before the Subcommittee on Study of Monopoly Power*, 82nd Cong., 1st sess., 1951, serial 1, part 6 (Washington, DC: Government Printing Office, 1952), 1599, 1615, 1636 (hereafter, *Organized Baseball*); US Senate, *Organized Professional Team Sports, Hearings before the Subcommittee on Antitrust and Monopoly of the Committee on the Judiciary* (Washington, DC: Government Printing Office, 1958), 799 (hereafter, *OPTS*, 1958). The movies had a higher profit margin than baseball from 1941 to 1943, but baseball went ahead from 1944 through 1949. Zimbalist, *Baseball and Billions*, 62, 68. Franchises sold for an average of $673,000 in the 1930s, but twenty years later were going for $1,563,000. On the value of an average franchise, see Haupert, "Economic History of Baseball."

67. *Organized Baseball*, 1599, 1615, 1636; Robert F. Burk, *Much More Than a Game: Players, Owners and the National Game* (Chapel Hill: University of North Carolina Press, 2001), 109; Haupert, "Economic History of Major League Baseball," 9; computed from US Senate, Committee on the Judiciary, *Organized Professional Team Sports, Hearings before the Subcommittee on Antitrust and Monopoly of the Committee on the Judiciary*, 85th Cong., 2nd Sess. (Washington, DC: Government Printing Office, 1957), 353 (hereafter, *OPTS*, 1957).

68. Burk, *Much More Than a Game*, 107, 109–12; Haupert, "Economic History of Major League Baseball."

69. *Sporting News*, November 14, 1951, 7. For other tables, see Steven A. Riess, "The Profits of Major League Baseball, 1900 to 1956," in *Baseball in America and America in Baseball*, ed. Donald G. Kyle and Robert B. Fairbanks (College Station: Texas A&M University Press, 2008), 88–142. The Dodgers regularly declared dividends from 1923 through 1932, and again in 1943. See *Organized Baseball*, 1601; *OPTS*, 1957, 352–53.

70. The Boston Braves lost $459,099 in 1952. *OPTS*, 1957, 353.

71. The Yankees in 1955 had a huge net income of $802,653, but also paid an enormous tax bill of $680,801, probably a record in that era. *OPTS*, 1957, 362.

72. McCue, *Mover and Shaker*, 74. McCue did not cite a bonus directly based on player sales or attendance.

73. *Organized Baseball*, 1591–92, 1600–1601, 1608; *New York Times*, November 8, 1951; Steven Gietschier, "The Los Angeles Dodgers," in *The Encyclopedia of Major League Baseball*, ed. Steven A. Riess (Westport, CT: Greenwood Press, 2006), 181–217; John Helyar, *Lords of the Realm: The Real History of Baseball* (New York: Ballantine Books, 1994), 47; Lowenfish, *Branch Rickey*, 455–58. McCue states that the Rickey Papers indicate losses of at least $560,244.94, and as high as $700,000. McCue, *Mover and Shaker*, 73.

74. *Organized Baseball*, 1611; Surdam, *Postwar Yankees*, 64, 320–23.

75. *Organized Baseball*, 1610–11; *OPTS*, 1958, 803. There was an insignificant relationship between team rank in ticket revenue and concession sales. R = 0.02381.

76. James M. Sheehan, "Baseball Clubs as Big Business," *New York Times*, June 9, 1957, 12E-1. Sheehan actually claimed that total revenues came to $2,450,000, but that was not the sum of his individual estimates.

77. *Organized Baseball*, 1608; Surdam, *Postwar Yankees*, 322–24.

78. Surdam, *Postwar Yankees*, 322, 324; computed from "Condensed Profit and Loss Statements, American League, 1946," in *Organized Baseball*, 1604.

79. Warfield, *Roaring Redhead*, 162. On MacPhail's report to baseball that criticized integration, see *Organized Baseball*, 484–85; Snyder, *Beyond the Shadows of the Senators*, 232. In 1964 the Yankees were sold for $13.2 million to CBS. Zimbalist, *Baseball and Billions*, 68. On TV, see Haupert, "Economic History of Major League Baseball."

80. David J. Halberstam, *Sports on New York Radio: A Play-by-Play History* (Lincolnwood, IL: Masters Press, 1999), 246–47; James R. Walker, *Crack of the Bat: A History of Baseball on the Radio* (Lincoln: University of Nebraska Press, 2015), 134–35, 166–67, 173; Stuart Shea, *Baseball Broadcasting from 1920 to the Present* (Phoenix, AZ: Society for American Baseball Research, 2015), 47; Curt Smith, *Voices of Summer: Ranking Baseball's 101 All-Time Announcers* (New York: Carroll & Graf, 2005), 39; "Radio," in Johnathan F. Light, *The Cultural Encyclopedia of Baseball*, 2nd ed. (Jefferson, NC: McFarland, 2005), 767. The Yankees suspended broadcasting for the 1941 season because they could not find a sponsor.

81. Curt Smith, *The Voice: Mel Allen's Untold Story* (Guilford, CT: Lyons Press, 2007), 19–96; Stephen Borelli, *How About That: The Life of Mel Allen* (Champaign, IL: Sports Publishing, 2005), 32–66; Walker, *Crack of the Bat*, 173.

82. The Dodgers management held Barber in such regard that he was the first person other than the team directors to learn about the plan to integrate baseball. He was uncomfortable with the idea, and almost resigned, but his wife advised him to stay the course. Red became an ardent supporter of Jackie once he saw him play and stand up to abusive opposing players and fans. Halberstam, *Sports on New York Radio*, 230–31, 239; Red Barber and Robert Creamer, *Rhubarb in the Catbird Seat* (Garden City, NY: Doubleday, 1968), 267–68; Red Barber, *1947: When All Hell Broke Loose in Baseball* (New York: Doubleday, 1982), 269; Warren Corbett, "Red Barber," http://sabr.org/bioproj/person/5d514087 (accessed July 15, 2015).

83. McCue, *Mover and Shaker*, 55; Walker and Bellamy Jr., *Center Field Shot*, 122, 124–25.

84. Walker and Bellamy Jr., *Center Field Shot*, 21, 24, 28, 31, 36, 68, 70; *New York Times*, October 5, 1947, X11–7, February 20, 1951, 33. The Giants were also sponsored by manly products, notably Chesterfield cigarettes and Knickerbocker beer.

85. Corbett, "Red Barber;" Golenbock, *Bums*, 394–95; Walker and Bellamy Jr., *History of Baseball on Television*, 31; Harvey Frommer, *New York City Baseball: The Last Golden Age, 1947–1957* (New York: Macmillan, 1980), 76; "Television History—The First 75 Years," http://www.tvhistory.tv/tv-prices.htm (accessed August 17, 2015).

86. Fetter, *Taking on the Yankees*, 231, 418n44; *Organized Baseball*, 1608–9; *OPTS*, 1957, 354–56, 800–801, 2046–47; Michael Shapiro, *The Last Good Season: Brooklyn, the Dodgers and Their Final Pennant Race Together* (New York: Doubleday, 2003), 131.

87. *Organized Baseball*, 1608–9; *OPTS*, 1957, 354–56; 2046–47; *OPTS*, 1958, 801–2.

88. *OPTS*, 1957, 354–63.

89. Sheehan, "Baseball Clubs as Big Business."

90. Sheehan, "Baseball Clubs as Big Business." In 1949 the Dodgers spent $44,900 on scouting. See McCue, *Mover and Shaker*, 69.

91. *Organized Baseball*, 1611. Another way of looking at this is the declining percentage of salaries related to GOI. Thus in 1929, salaries were 31.2 percent of GOI; 1933, 44.2; 1939, 30.2 percent; 1943, 29.6 percent; 1950, 21.6 percent; and 1956, 17.8 percent. *OPTS*, 1958, 800.

92. Edward Burns, "Burocrats Supply Mind Food for Baseball Figure Filberts," *Chicago Tribune*, October 28, 1951, A2; *Brooklyn Daily Eagle*, October 23, 1951, 14. The *New York Times* cited its data as of July 1, 1950, as reported to the Cellar Committee. See *New York Times*, October 23, 1951, 36–5; *Sporting News*, October 24, 1951, 8.

93. *OPTS*, 1958, 795–97.

94. For Reese's salary in 1949, see McCue, *Mover and Shaker*, 379n4. Other data drawn from http://www.baseball-almanac.com/teamstats/roster.php?y=1947&t=BRO to http://www.baseball-almanac.com/teamstats/roster.php? y=1956&t=BRO (accessed May 17, 2015); Michael J. Haupert, "MLB's Annual Salary Leaders, 1874–2012," http://sabr.org/research/mlbs-annual-salary-leaders-1874-2012 (accessed July 27, 2015).

95. "Baseball Almanac: New York Yankees Roster," http://www.baseball-almanac.com/teamstats/roster.php?y=1947&t=NYA_1947...1956, (accessed May 17, 2015); Michael J. Haupert, "MLB's Annual Salary Leaders, 1874–2012."

96. "Baseball's 100 Greatest Players by the *Sporting News* (1998)," http://www.baseball-almanac.com/legendary/lisn100.shtml (accessed May 15, 2016). The definitive source for player statistics is http://www.baseball-reference.com.

97. Biographers Jane Leavy and Allan Barra, writer Sheldon Hirsch, and sportscaster Bob Costas all argue that Mantle's statistics, as adjusted by sabermetrics, made him the superior player over the short run. See Leavy, *Last Boy*, 418–20; Allan Barra, *Mickey and Willie: Mantle and Mays, the Parallel Lives of Baseball's Golden Age* (New York: Crown Archetype, 2013); Sheldon Hirsch, "In Hindsight, Mantle Better Than Mays," February 11, 2014, http://www.realclearsports.com/articles/2014/02/11/in_hindsight_mantle_better_than_mays.html#.VzyVsvkrLIU; Harold Friend, "Branch Rickey Helped Mickey Mantle Become Better Than Willie Mays," May 13, 2001, http://bleacherreport.com/articles/699788-branch-rickey-helped-mickey-mantle-become-better-than-willie-mays. For an opposing view, see Rob Neyer, "In Willie's Time, He Was No. 1," *ESPN Baseball*, http://static.espn.go.com/mlb/columns/neyer_rob/1191263.html (accessed May 18, 2016). My thanks to Randy Roberts for reminding me of Snider's home field advantage.

98. Kahn, *The Era*, 253–55.

99. *New York Times*, August 9, 1957, 1. Brooklyn major leaguers had actually played in Queens in the late nineteenth century. In 1886 the Brooklyn Grays of the American

Association played their Sunday games at Ridgewood Park in Queens, and also played forty-nine games there between 1887 and 1889. The team, renamed the Bridegrooms in 1888, joined the National League in 1890, replaced in the AA by the Brooklyn Gladiators, who played twenty-eight games at the Queens site. On the use of Ridgewood by Dodger teams, see http://www.covehurst.net/ddyte/brooklyn/ridgewood.html; "Wallace's Ridgewood Park." Retrosheet.org (accessed February 12, 2016). On the other hand, when the New York (football) Giants, denizens of the Polo Grounds and Yankee Stadium, moved out of state to New Jersey in 1976 to East Rutherford, they never became the "New Jersey Giants," and their current helmets today carry the "NY" logo.

100. Steven A. Riess, "Historical Perspectives on Sports and Public Policy," in Wilbur C. Rich, ed., *The Economics and Politics of Sports Facilities* (Westport, CT: Quorum Books, 2000), 27–29; Sullivan, *Dodgers Move West*, 47–57, 120–33; Golenbock, *Bums*, 448. For the planning of a potential new field, see Benjamin D. Lisle, *Modern Coliseum: Stadiums and American Culture* (Philadelphia: University of Pennsylvania Press, 2017), 41–58, 73–78. On the debate over the role of Moses, see Henry Fetter, "Revising the Revisionists: Walter O'Malley, Robert Moses, and the End of the Brooklyn Dodgers," *New York History* 89 (Winter 2008): 54–74. The share of the city's cost for the downtown project was estimated at $40 million. Fetter, "Revising the Revisionists," 63, 66–73.

101. Riess, "Historical Perspectives," in Rich, *Economics and Politics of Sports Facilities*, 24–32.

102. Sullivan, *Dodgers Move West*, 18.

103. Leavy, *Last Boy*; "Rare 1952 Mickey Mantle Rookie Card Sells for Record $525,000," http://espn.go.com/mlb/story/_/id/14341441/rare-1952-topps-mickey-mantle-rookie-card-sells-auction-record-525000 (accessed May 17, 2016).

104. "Family and Television, 1950s," Marilyn J. Coleman and Lawrence H. Ganong, eds., *The Social History of the American Family: An Encyclopedia* (Thousand Oaks, CA: Safe, 2014), 1338. For critiques of American family life in the 1950s, see Stephanie Coontz, *The Way We Never Were: American Families and the Nostalgia Trap* (New York: Basic Books, 1992); and Elaine Tyler May, *Homeward Bound: American Families in the Cold War Era* (New York: Basic Books, 1988).

## 2. The Team That Time Forgot

1. Hilda reverted to her prior Dodger loyalties after a few years but remained neutral when the Dodgers played the Giants. Bob Cooke, "Price of Perilous Pennant Race," *New York Herald Tribune*, October 10, 1949; Louis Effrat "Whatever Hilda Wants Hilda Gets in Brooklyn," *New York Times*, September 3, 1955; Carl E. Prince, *Brooklyn's Dodgers* (New York: Oxford University Press, 1996), 89.

2. Robert Shaplen, "The Nine Lives of Leo Durocher," *Sports Illustrated*, June 6, 1955, 34.

3. Murray Kempton, "Willie Mays (October 5, 1962)," in *America Comes of Middle Age* (Boston: Little, Brown, 1963), 379.

4. Tallulah Bankhead, "Why I Love the Giants," *New York Times Magazine*, June 29, 1947.

5. Don Ross, "Tallulah in Fine Form for Broadway," *New York Herald Tribune*, September 12, 1954.

6. Bankhead, "Why I Love the Giants," 28.

7. She was followed by Tallulah Bankhead in 1953. Harold Rosenthal, "Tallulah Bankhead Tells Writers How to Manage a Baseball Team," *New York Herald Tribune*, February 2, 1953.

8. *New York Times*, April 20, 1952.

9. For the cover, *Sports Illustrated*, April 11, 1955; for the letters, *Sports Illustrated*, April 25, 1955, 74.

10. Arnold Hano, *A Day in the Bleachers* (New York: Thomas Y. Crowell Company, 1955).

11. Elizabeth Pollet, ed., *Portrait of Delmore: Journals and Notes of Delmore Schwartz: 1939–1959* (New York: Farrar Straus Giroux, 1986) ("Schwartz Journals"), 56 (April 18, 1942).

12. Schwartz Journals, 372 (February 24, 1951).

13. Schwartz Journals, 494–95 (July 5–11, 1954).

14. Schwartz Journals, 410 (June 4, 1952). Additional entries regarding the Giants appear on pp. 53, 315, 385.

15. Lee Lowenfish, "Two Cheers for Horace Stoneham," in *The Glory Days of New York Baseball 1947–1957*, ed. John Thorn (New York: Collins, 2007), 73.

16. Willie Mays, Monte Irvin, Hank Thompson, and Ray Noble for the Giants, Jackie Robinson and Don Newcombe for the Dodgers.

17. Steve Treder, "A Legacy of What-ifs: Horace Stoneham and the Integration of the Giants," *Nine* (Spring 2002): 74

18. Roger Angell, "The Companions of the Game," in *Five Seasons* (New York: Popular Library, 1978), 275.

19. Robert F. Garratt, "Horace Stoneham and the Breaking of Baseball's Second Color Barrier," *Nine* 22, no. 2 (Spring 2014): 42–53.

20. Schwartz to James Laughlin, February 8, 1952, in Robert Phillips, ed., *Letters of Delmore Schwartz* (Princeton, NJ: Ontario Review Press, 1984), 262.

21. New York Times, July 5, 1950; New York Herald Tribune, July 8, 1950.

22. David H. Lippman, "The Shot's Long Shadow—50 Years Later," in *The Team That Time Won't Forget: The 1951 New York Giants*, ed. Bill Nowlin and C. Paul Rogers III (Phoenix: SABR, 2015), Kindle location12369.

23. Vic Ziegel, "A Stairway to Heaven: Once, Giants Walked Here," *New York Daily News*, August 10, 2000. I thank Bob Gruber for bringing this article to my attention.

24. Ziegel, "A Stairway to Heaven."

25. Treder, "A Legacy of What-ifs: Horace Stoneham and the Integration of the Giants," 71.

26. "Major League Most Memorable Moments" at http://mlb.mlb.com/mlb/events/memorable_moments/mlb_memorable_moments.jsp (accessed July 14, 2016).

27. See Joshua Prager, "Inside Baseball: Giants' 1951 Comeback, the Sport's Greatest, Wasn't All It Seemed," *Wall Street Journal*, January 31, 1951, and *The Echoing Green* (New York: Pantheon, 2006); Dave Anderson, "A Fastball, a Swing and Forever," *New York Times*, October 1, 2001; Stan Jacoby, "The Numbers Say It Ain't So, Bobby," *New York Times*, March 4, 2001. The claim about Giant sign stealing had surfaced in 1962 but had not gained traction, perhaps because it came from an anonymous source. "Thomson Denies Secret Signal Led to Pennant-Winning Homer," *New York Times*, March 24, 1962.

28. Hano, *A Day in the Bleachers*; Roger Kahn, "A Day in the Season," *New York Times Book Review*, May 5, 1985.

29. Steve Kelman, "New York Accents, New York Baseball and Presidential Politics" at https://fcw.com/blogs/lectern/2016/06/kelman-ny-state-of-mind.aspx (accessed June 16, 2016).

30. Victor Mather, "Where Ott and Orr Fit Best: 15 Across, or Maybe 7 Down," *New York Times*, May 23, 2015.

31. Jonathan Mahler, "Mythic Fields Where Giants and Dodgers Made Miracles," *New York Times*, March 30, 2001.

32. The very name of the society is itself a marker of the team's fate in the halls of memory. Once upon a time they were *the* "New York Giants"; it was their gridiron namesake who required a qualifier: i.e., the "New York *Football* Giants" as sportscaster Marty Glickman used to refer to them.

33. Quoted in Sandomir, "Say Hey . . . ," *New York Times*, April 14, 2008.

34. Quoted in *San Francisco Chronicle*, May 29, 1957.

35. O'Malley statements in *New York Times*, August 17, 1955, August 20, 1955.

36. See Henry D. Fetter, *Taking on the Yankees: Winning and Losing in the Business of Baseball* (New York: W. W. Norton & Company, 2003), 246–53; Henry D. Fetter "Revising the Revisionists: Walter O'Malley, Robert Moses and the End of the Brooklyn Dodgers," *New York History* (Winter 2008): 55–74.

37. See US House of Representatives, *Hearings before the Antitrust Subcommittee of the Committee on the Judiciary, Organized Professional Team Sports*, 85thCong., 2d sess., (Washington, DC: Government Printing Office, 1957), 356, 1929–30, 2046–47.

38. Norman Nevard, "The Reluctant Drag-In," *Baseball Digest* (August 1957), 29–30.

39. Stoneham testimony in Organized Professional Team Sports, 1943–44.

40. For Stoneham's comments, see *Sporting News*, July 6, 1955, February 8, 1956; Roscoe McGowen, "Baseball Giants' Shift to Stadium Due Eventually, but Not in 1956," *New York Times*, November 26, 1955; John Drebinger, "Whither the Giants?" *New York Times*, July 25, 1956.

41. *New York Times*, August 20, 1955.

42. Fetter, *Taking on the Yankees*, 406.

43. Louis Effrat, "Talk of Giants Moving to Coast Idle Gossip, Stoneham Asserts," *New York Times*, November 16, 1954.

44. *New York Times*, February 23, 1957.

45. Arthur Daley in *New York Times*, February 9, 1956; John Lardner in *New York Times Magazine*, February 26, 1956.

46. Robert Creamer, "Alas, Poor Giants," *Sports Illustrated*, May 20, 1957, 32.

47. Jay Weiner, *Stadium Games: Fifty Years of Big League Greed and Bush League Boondoggles* (Minneapolis: University of Minnesota Press, 2000), 10–11.

48. Weiner, *Stadium Games*, 7.

49. Weiner, *Stadium Games*, 25, quoting Stoneham in *Minneapolis Tribune*, May 20, 1956.

50. O'Malley File Memorandum re Giants, Los Angeles, etc., March 23, 1957, available at the Walter O'Malley Official Website, walteromalley.com.

51. O'Malley's March 23, 1957, memorandum recorded Stoneham as offering $50,000 in compensation but did not record O'Malley's acceptance of that offer.

52. *New York Herald Tribune*, May 11, 1957.

53. Robert Murphy, *After Many a Summer: The Passing of the Giants and Dodgers and a Golden Age in New York Baseball* (New York: Sterling, 2009); Robert Murphy, "The Real Villain of New York Baseball," *New York Times*, June 24, 2007.

54. Weiner, *Stadium Games*, 27–28.

55. Weiner, *Stadium Games*, 17–18.

56. A stadium in the New York City borough of Queens for the New York Giants would not pose the rather spurious objection voiced by O'Malley that "they are not the Brooklyn

Dodgers . . . if they are not in Brooklyn. . . . If the Dodgers have to get out of Brooklyn, whether it is 5 miles or 5000 miles, they are no longer the Brooklyn Dodgers." O'Malley's 1957 congressional testimony quoted in Fetter, *Taking on the Yankees*, 253. The stadium would be built and would become the home of the New York Mets in 1964.

57. Nevard, "The Reluctant Drag-In," 29–30.

58. *New York Herald Tribune*, May 12, 1957.

59. *San Francisco Chronicle*, May 9, 1957.

60. Gerald Holland, "A Visit with the Artful Dodger," *Saturday Evening Post*, July 13, 1968, 57.

61. For the text of the letter of intent, see *Sporting News*, August 28, 1957.

62. "Q. You're in a room with O'Malley, Hitler and Stalin and have a gun with three bullets. What do you do? A. Shoot O'Malley three times."

63. *New York Times*, August 20, 1957.

64. Including documents on the negotiations between the Dodgers and New York City in the Robert F. Wagner Jr. Papers, New York City Municipal Archives, the Robert Moses Papers at the New York Public Library, and online at the "Walter O'Malley Official Website (walteromalley.com) established by the O'Malley family. Whatever Walter O'Malley's sins against Brooklyn may have been, the website is a major contribution to the study of Dodger history to which all researchers are properly indebted. By contrast, a recent history of the San Francisco Giants is devoid of any such archival materials in its introductory account of the team's move. Robert F. Garratt, *Home Team: The Turbulent History of the San Francisco Giants* (Lincoln: University of Nebraska Press, 2017).

65. A. J. P. Taylor, *The Origins of the Second World War* (London: Penguin Books, 1964), 38.

66. For an overview of the debate, see Fetter, "Revising the Revisionists," 55–77. For the major discussions of the move, see (in chronological order), Neil Sullivan, *The Dodgers Move West* (New York: Oxford University Press, 1985); ESPN Home Video, "The Last Trolley: A Tale of Two Cities" (1996); Michael Shapiro, *The Last Good Season* (New York: Doubleday, 2003); Fetter, *Taking on the Yankees*; HBO, "The Brooklyn Dodgers: The Ghosts of Flatbush" (2007); Michael D'Antonio, *Forever Blue* (New York: Riverhead Books, 2009); Murphy, *After Many a Summer*; Andy McCue, *Mover and Shaker: Walter O'Malley, the Dodgers and Baseball's Westward Expansion* (Lincoln: University of Nebraska Press, 2014).

67. *New York Times*, August 20, 1957. Mrs. McGraw did make her peace with the new reality in time to attend the team's 1958 opener in San Francisco. See newsreel footage at https://www.youtube.com/watch?v=CmJhdJDQWfl (accessed September 19, 2017).

68. Maurice Halbwachs, *The Collective Memory*, trans. Francis J. Ditter Jr. and Vida Yazdi-Ditter (New York: Harper Colophon Books, 1980), 69, 80.

69. Henry D. Fetter, "Ten Days in August," *National Pastime* (2008): 63–67.

70. Milton Gross, *New York Post*, June 15, 1956.

71. By comparison, when the Giants won the 1962 pennant, they were already led by their third manager in San Francisco.

72. Angell, "Farewell My Giants," 164.

73. Kempton, "Willie Mays," 379.

74. Roger Angell, "Two Strikes on the Image," [October 1964] *The Summer Game* (New York: Popular Library), 108.

75. On Candlestick Park, see Allan Temko, *No Way to Build a Ballpark and Other Irreverent Essays on Architecture* (San Francisco: Chronicle Books, 1993), 219.

76. Orlando Cepeda with Herb Fagan, *Baby Bull: From Hardball to Hard Time and Back*, (Dallas: Taylor Trade Publishing, 1998), 57. Cepeda received 18,701 votes to Mays's 11,510.

77. Quoted in David Plaut, *Chasing October: The Dodgers-Giants Pennant Race of 1962* (South Bend, IN: Diamond Communications, 1994), 133.

78. Halbwachs, *The Collective Memory*, 43.

79. "The Top 100 Sports Books of All Time," *Sports Illustrated*, December 16, 2002. The books on the Dodgers were Roger Kahn's *Boys of Summer* and Jules Tygiel's *Baseball's Great Experiment*; those on the Giants were Gordon H. Fleming, *The Unforgettable Season* (the 1908 pennant race), and Eric Rolfe Greenberg, *The Celebrant* (a novel featuring Christy Mathewson).

80. "The Weakness of Giants," *Wall Street Journal*, August 21, 1957.

81. *Sporting News*, September 29, 1954.

82. Frank Graham, *The New York Giants* (New York: G. P. Putnam's Sons, 1952), 8–9.

83. *New York Herald Tribune*, August 20, 1957.

84. Roger Angell, "Farewell, My Giants!" *Holiday* (May 1958), 82.

85. Joseph Durso, *The Days of Mr. McGraw* (Englewood Cliffs, NJ: Prentice-Hall, 1969), 175.

86. *New York Times*, April 6, 1974.

87. John Drebinger, "Whither the Giants?" *New York Times*, July 25, 1956.

88. On "Take Me Out to the Ball Game," see Fetter, *Taking on the Yankees*, 59; on the "hot dog," see Ken Belson, "Forget Spicy Tuna Rolls; Most Fans Still Just Want a Dog," *New York Times*, July 12, 2010.

89. Schwartz, "Memoirs . . . ," in *The Ego is Always at the Wheel: Bagatelles by Delmore Schwartz*, ed. Robert Phillips (New York: New Directions, 1985), 115–36.

90. Bankhead, "Why I Love the Giants."

91. See, "Demographic History of New York City" at https://en.wikipedia.org/wiki/Demographic_history_of_New_York_City#Manhattan (accessed August 15, 2016).

92. For the sharp decline in the Irish and German components of the city's population between 1900 and 1960, see Nathan Glazer and Daniel Patrick Moynihan, *Beyond the Melting Pot* (Cambridge, MA: MIT Press, 1963), 318.

93. Glazer and Moynihan, *Beyond the Melting Pot*, 217.

94. Discussion of Dodger fandom has been especially prone to sentimental effusions about the team's progressive and socially conscious supporters. Caution should be exercised about making such claims: Julius and Ethel Rosenberg may have rooted for the Dodgers, but Communist Party leader Earl Browder was a Yankee fan. Julius and Ethel Rosenberg, *Death House Letters of Ethel and Julius Rosenberg* (New York: Jero Publishing Company, 1953), 67, 109; James G. Ryan, *Earl Browder: The Failure of American Communism* (Urbana: University of Illinois Press, 1997), 145.

95. Carl E. Prince, *Brooklyn's Dodgers* (New York: Oxford University Press, 1996); Peter Marquis, "Brooklyn et 'ses' Dodgers. Baseball et construction des identités urbaines aux Etats-Unis (1883–1957)" (Thèse de doctorat en histoire et civilisation, École des hautes études en sciences sociales, Paris, 2009).

96. Dan Riley, ed., *The Dodgers Reader* (Mariner Books, 1992); Dan Riley, ed., *The Yankees Reader* (Mariner Books, 1991).

97. See, inter alia, Peter Golenbock, *Dynasty: The New York Yankees, 1949–1964* (Englewood Cliffs, NJ: Prentice-Hall, 1975); *Bums: An Oral History of the Brooklyn Dodgers* (New York: Putnam, 1984).

98. Richard Sandomir, "Say Hey, Giants Fans Are Wistful Too," *New York Times*, April 14, 2008.

99. Roger Kahn, *Memories of Summer* (New York: Hyperion, 1987), 60.
100. Roger Kahn, *The Boys of Summer* (New York: Harper & Row, 1972), 197.
101. *Aethlon* 16, no. 2 (Spring 1999): 161–62.
102. In 1972, football outpolled baseball as the favorite sport by 36 percent to 21 percent. See *The Gallup Poll 1972–1977* (Wilmington, DE: Scholarly Resources, 1978), 2. By 2008, only 10 percent of those polled chose baseball as their favorite sport compared to 41 percent for football. See *The Gallup Poll: Public Opinion 2008* (Lanham, MD: Rowman & Littlefield, 2009), 445.
103. Roger Kahn, *The Era* (New York: Ticknor & Fields, 1993), 2.
104. Aleida Assmann, "Canon to Archive," in *The Collective Memory Reader*, ed. Jeffrey K. Olick, Vered Vinitzky-Seroussi, and Daniel Levy (New York: Oxford University Press, 2011), 334.
105. Ziegel, "A Stairway to Heaven."
106. Or perhaps not. A few seasons later Kahn did cover the Giants, something which Kahn did not mention in *The Boys of Summer*, but that only led to a run-in with Durocher and Kahn's exit from daily reporting. Roger Kahn, *Into My Own* (New York: Thomas Dunne Books, 2006), 50, 120. And Kahn recalled what longtime *Herald Tribune* sports editor Stanley Woodward once wrote: "For some strange reason baseball writers develop a great attachment to the Brooklyn club if long exposed. . . . The transpontine madness seems to affect all baseball writers, no matter how sensible they outwardly seem. You must watch a Brooklyn writer for symptoms and, before they become virulent, shift him to the Yankees or tennis or golf." Kahn, *Into My Own*, 38.

## 3. The New York Giants and Cold War Manhood

1. *Washington Post*, January 1, 1957; *Los Angeles Times*, December 31, 1956; *New York Herald Tribune*, December 31, 1956.
2. *New York Times*, December 31, 1956, and January 2, 1957; *Los Angeles Times*, December 31, 1956; *Chicago Defender*, January 2, 1957. On Conerly's war record, see Frank Gifford with Harry Waters, *The Whole Ten Yards* (New York: Random House, 1993), 103.
3. *New York Times*, December 17 and 18, 1956; *Los Angeles Times*, December 17, 1956; Bob Braunwart and Bob Carroll, "The Mugging of Bobby Layne," *Coffin Corner* 2, no. 12 (1980).
4. *New York Herald Tribune*, December 31, 1956; *New York Times*, December 31, 1956; *Chicago Tribune*, December 31, 1956.
5. *New York Times*, January 1, 1955; *Washington Post*, March 1, 1959; *Los Angeles Times*, November 28, 1961.
6. *Los Angeles Times*, October 29, 1958; *Washington Post*, April 6, 1953.
7. Andy Robustelli with Jack Clary, *Once a Giant, Always . . . My Two Lives with the New York Giants* (Boston: Quinlan Press, 1987), 25.
8. David Riesman with Reuel Denny, "Football in America: A Study in Culture Diffusion," in *Individualism Reconsidered and Other Essays*, ed. David Riesman (New York: Free Press, 1954), 255.
9. "Savagery on Sunday," *Life*, October 24, 1955, 133.
10. Jane Tompkins, *West of Everything: The Inner Life of Westerns* (New York: Oxford University Press, 1992), 4–6, 28. Tompkins notes that "in 1959 there were no fewer than thirty-five Westerns running concurrently on television, and out of the top ten programs, eight were Westerns." Y. A. Tittle recalled when he was New York's quarterback during the

early 1960s, he and several other Giants would assemble every Saturday evening before a home game to watch the hit western *Gunsmoke* on television. Y. A. Tittle, *I Pass!* (New York: Franklin Watts, 1964), 276.

11. Dave Klein, *The New York Giants: Yesterday, Today, Tomorrow* (Chicago: Henry Regnery, 1973), 99; Richard Slotkin, *Gunfighter Nation: The Myth of the Frontier in Twentieth-Century America* (New York: HarperCollins, 1992), 474. The musical score from the western film *The Magnificent Seven* (1960) provided the backdrop for the Marlboro television commercials, and identified the cigarette's smokers with frontier manhood.

12. Gifford, *The Whole Ten Yards*, 104–5. Gifford stated that "occasionally [Conerly would] surrender a whole sentence." In westerns, articulate conversation and lengthy sentences are feminine traits. Obituary of Cliff Livingston in "For the Record," *Sports Illustrated*, April 5, 2010.

13. *New York Times*, September 19, 1959. The *Times* reported that many Baton Rouge women rushed home from a pregame parade "to check their ensembles" for the next day's "big event." It quoted the Baton Rouge society magazine's editor, who reported that "as usual" many of the women attending the college football game "will be wearing cocktail dresses and Walter Florell hats."

14. Tittle quoted in Ken Safarowic and Eli Kowalski, eds., *Concrete Charlie: An Oral History of Philadelphia's Greatest Football Legend, Chuck Bednarik* (Philadelphia: Sports Challenge Network, 2009), 100; Bednarik quote as told to Dick Schaap, "Who Says Pros Can't Play 60 Minutes?" *Saturday Evening Post*, November 25, 1961, 54; Parker quoted by *Chicago Tribune*, December 18, 1956.

15. "Confessions of a Dirty Football Player," *Sport*, December 1955, 10.

16. Jimmy Brown with Myron Cope, *Off My Chest* (Garden City, NY: Doubleday, 1964), 213–15. Brown noted that he was not the only one whom the Giants defense badly roughed up in what he called "that New York rumble." Ten of the Browns were unable to practice for the Eagles game, and three had to sit it out.

17. *New York Times*, November 14, 1954; Daley in *New York Times*, December 18, 1962; "Charlie Conerly: The Old Pro Grows Older," *Look*, December 6, 1960, 48. Y. A. Tittle even drew upon images of war and death in describing the Giants kicking game. He recalled that Don Chandler's late fourth quarter punt against Cleveland that ensured New York the tie it needed to clinch the Eastern division title in 1961 "sounded like a cannon shot." The punt traveled sixty-four yards and pinned the Browns on their own seven-yard line "out of reach" of scoring. Tittle remarked that Chandler had put "the Browns in a hole [that] was more like a grave." They were dead and buried: "They couldn't dig their way out either." Tittle, *I Pass!* 214; *New York Times*, December 18, 1961.

18. Al Stump, "All Van Brocklin Can Do Is Pass," *Sport*, December 1953, 73; *Washington Post*, January 1, 1962.

19. David Maraniss, *When Pride Still Mattered: A Life of Vince Lombardi* (New York: Simon and Schuster, 1999), 151, 170.

20. On Greasy Neale's defensive contribution and Philadelphia's "Suicide Seven," see Stephen H. Norwood, "The Philadelphia Eagles, the Crisis of Post–World War II Masculinity, and the Rise of Pro Football, 1946–1960," in *Philly Sports: Teams, Games, and Athletes From Rocky's Town*, ed. Ryan A. Swanson and David K. Wiggins (Fayetteville: University of Arkansas Press, 2016), 71–80.

21. *New York Times*, January 3, 1982. On how anger affects the play of offensive and defensive linemen, see comments of Ken Mendenhall, Baltimore Colts center for ten years, in

Stephen H. Norwood, *Real Football: Conversations on America's Game* (Jackson: University Press of Mississippi, 2004), 369–70.

22. Bob Carroll, *When the Grass Was Real* (New York: Simon and Schuster, 1993), 11.

23. Sarfarowic and Kowalski, *Concrete Charlie*, 101.

24. Tittle quoted in Safarowic and Kowalski, eds., *Concrete Charlie*, 100; Carroll, *When the Grass Was Real*, 117; Huff quotes from Sam Huff with Leonard Shapiro, *Tough Stuff: The Man in the Middle* (New York: St. Martin's Press, 1988), 111–12; 114; Jack Newcombe, "Is Sam Huff's World Really That Violent?" *Sport*, December 1960, 61, 68.

25. Robert O'Brien, "The Brutal Art of Red-Dogging," *Sport*, October 1960, 184.

26. Gifford, *The Whole Ten Yards*, 81, 86; Marty Glickman, interview by Stephen Steiner, March and April 1979, Oral History Collection, Dorot Jewish Division, New York Public Library.

27. Frederick Exley, *A Fan's Notes* (New York: Random House, 1968), 131; Robustelli, *Once a Giant, Always*, 38.

28. Gifford, *The Whole Ten Yards*, 82, 84; Perian Conerly, *Backseat Quarterback* (Garden City, NY: Doubleday, 1963), 18, 79. The Giants did not even use a flankerback until 1955. Frank Gifford, *Gifford on Courage* (New York: M. Evans, 1976), 140.

29. Mark F. Bernstein, *Football: The Ivy League Origins of an American Obsession* (Philadelphia: University of Pennsylvania Press, 2001), 152; *New York Times*, March 11, 1953, December 16, 1954, and January 28, 1956; Robustelli, *Once a Giant, Always*, 38; Maraniss, *When Pride Still Mattered*, 162–63.

30. Huff, *Tough Stuff*, 63; Gifford, *The Whole Ten Yards*, 67, 72, 83; *New York Times*, November 4, 1956; *New York Herald Tribune*, October 11, 1961; Joe King, "The Gifted Mr. Gifford," *Sport*, January 1956, 44, 75.

31. Leonard Shecter, "Johnny Sample: 'I'll Break Them in Half if I Have To,'" *Sport*, January 1967, 31; Exley, *A Fan's Notes*, 231; Gifford, *The Whole Ten Yards*, 73, 83, 214; *New York Times*, June 26, 1958; *Washington Post*, October 7, 1958; *New York Herald Tribune*, October 11, 1961.

32. Benny Friedman, "I Could Play Football—and I'm 48!" *Sport*, December 1953, 10, 78; Red Smith in *New York Herald Tribune*, December 27, 1960.

33. *Life's* "Savagery on Sunday" article quoted veteran Detroit Lions tackle Bob Miller, who stated: "It's no secret that star pro passers are a bad insurance risk. They get hit even after they get rid of the ball" 133.

34. Douglas A. Noverr and Lawrence E. Ziewacz, *The Games They Played: Sports in American History, 1865–1980* (Chicago: Nelson-Hall, 1983), 212.

35. "The Old Pro Grows Older," 52; Gifford, *The Whole Ten Yards*, 103; Conerly, *Backseat Quarterback*, 171.

36. Robustelli, *Once a Giant, Always*, 49–50.

37. *New York Herald Tribune*, October 19, 1962; Obituary of Roosevelt Brown, *New York Times*, June 11, 2004; Don Smith, "Roosevelt Brown," *Coffin Corner* 6, no. 4 (1984); W. N. Wallace, "Left Tackle," *New York Times Sunday Magazine*, November 8, 1964, 138, 144, 149; Braunwart and Carroll, "The Mugging of Bobby Layne." Other members of the Giants offensive line were also very highly regarded. Center Ray Wietecha, who played with the Giants from 1953 to 1962, was a four-time NFL All-Pro. Jack Stroud, who played guard for the Giants from 1951 to 1963, was a three-time All-Pro.

38. *New York Times*, November 13, 1963.

39. *New York Times*, December 17, 1950; Huff quoted in *New York Times*, November 20, 1977; Robustelli, *Once a Giant, Always*, 62–63. The Browns had crushed the defending NFL champions, the Philadelphia Eagles, 35–10 in the 1950 season opener.

40. *Chicago Tribune,* December 15 and 16, 1958; *Washington Post,* December 15 and 16, 1958; *Cleveland Plain-Dealer,* December 15, 1958; *New York Times,* December 15, 1958, and November 20, 1977.

41. Maraniss, *When Pride Still Mattered,* 184.

42. *Cleveland Plain-Dealer,* December 22, 1958; *Chicago Defender,* December 22, 1958; *Los Angeles Times,* December 22, 1958.

43. *Cleveland Plain-Dealer,* December 22, 1958; Paul Brown with Jack Clary, *PB: The Paul Brown Story* (New York: Atheneum, 1979), 255.

44. *Washington Post,* December 22, 1958; *Chicago Defender,* December 22, 1958.

45. *Chicago Tribune,* December 23, 1958.

46. Tom Landry with Gregg Lewis, *Tom Landry: An Autobiography* (New York: HarperCollins, 1990), 109; *Chicago Tribune,* December 28, 1958; *Washington Post,* December 25, 1958; *New York Times,* November 10, 1958.

47. *New York Times,* December 16, 1998, and December 29, 1958.

48. Klein, *New York Giants,* 178.

49. *New York Times,* December 29 and 30, 1958.

50. *New York Times,* December 29, 1958, December 10, 1993, and December 16, 1998; *Chicago Tribune,* December 29, 1958; Tex Maule, "Sudden Death at Yankee Stadium," in *The Fireside Book of Football,* ed. Jack Newcombe (New York: Simon and Schuster, 1964), 188–90.

51. Jerry Izenberg, *Rozelle: A Biography* (Lincoln: University of Nebraska Press, 2014), 56; *New York Times,* December 29, 1958.

52. Landry, *Tom Landry,* 109–10; *Gifford, The Whole Ten Yards,* 207, 210. On the lack of interest in pro football players at Toots Shor's in the period around 1949–1950, see David Halberstam, *Summer of '49* (New York: Avon, 1989), 128–29.

53. *New York Herald Tribune,* December 28, 1959.

54. *Chicago Tribune,* December 27, 1959; Jimmie G. Purvis, "Tribute to Charlie Conerly," *Coffin Corner* 18, no. 6 (1996).

55. *Washington Post,* December 26, 1959; *New York Times,* December 24 and 25, 1959.

56. *Chicago Tribune,* December 27, 1959; *New York Herald Tribune,* December 21, 1958.

57. *New York Herald Tribune,* December 28, 1959; *New York Times,* December 28, 1959.

58. *Los Angeles Times,* December 28, 1958.

59. Steve Gelman, "The Conquests of Chuck Bednarik," *Sport,* July 1961, 90.

60. Exley, *A Fan's Notes,* 347–48; Arthur Daley statement in *New York Times,* February 13, 1961, and November 22, 1960; Klein, *New York Giants,* 213–14; Jack McCallum with Chuck Bednarik, *Last of the Sixty-Minute Men* (Englewood Cliffs, NJ: Prentice-Hall, 1977), 162.

61. *New York Times,* November 22, 1960, and February 13, 1961; Gelman, "Conquests," 90.

62. *Chicago Tribune,* December 27, 1963.

63. Fred Russell, "Just Call Him Y. A.," *Sport,* December 1947, 92–93; Hugh McElhenny, "Y. A. Tittle as I Know Him," *Sport,* October 1964, 97.

64. Larry Klein, "Del Shofner: Pro Football's Iceman," *Sport,* December 1963, 15, 74.

65. Myron Cope, "Allie Sherman: The Most Unlikely Coach," *Sport,* January 1964, 56–57; Marty Glickman with Stan Isaacs, *The Fastest Kid on the Block* (Syracuse: Syracuse University Press, 1996), 123; Obituary of Allie Sherman, *New York Times,* January 5, 2015.

66. *New York Times,* December 31, 1961, and January 1, 1962; *Washington Post,* January 1 and 2, 1962.

67. *New York Times,* October 29 and 30, 1962; *Washington Post,* October 29, 1962. Daley and Mara quotes from *New York Times,* October 30, 1962. Daley mentioned that on the same day

as the Giants-Redskins contest, the Bears and Lions had locked horns in a low-scoring game in which neither team scored a touchdown. The defenses were so dominant that the game was "virtually a throwback to Neanderthal days."

68. Klein, *New York Giants*, 229.

69. *New York Times*, December 31, 1962; Klein, *New York Giants*, 229. *Sports Illustrated* reporter Tex Maule described Taylor "hobbl[ing] painfully out of the shower" after the game, and "speaking with difficulty because of his cut-up tongue and mouth." Tex Maule, "The Packers, Yes!" *Sports Illustrated*, January 7, 1963, 14. Taylor commented to the *Washington Post* a month after the championship game that he was still feeling the aches and pains. *Washington Post*, January 30, 1963. Y. A. Tittle recalled that the "Giants defense gave Taylor the treatment on every play. Three or four of them hit him every time he came through or around the line. They . . . flattened him on the frozen ground." Taylor would return to the Packers huddle "holding his insides together." Tittle had never seen "a back take such a beating." Taylor fumbled three times. Y. A. Tittle with Kristine Setting Clark, *Nothing Comes Easy* (Chicago: Triumph Books, 2009), 193.

70. *Chicago Tribune*, December 31, 1962.

71. *Washington Post*, January 30, 1963; *Los Angeles Times*, January 9 and May 15, 1963; *New York Times*, September 1, 1963.

72. Jack Ziegler, "1963 NFL Championship Game: Irresistible Force vs. Immovable Object," *Coffin Corner* 10, no. 6 (1988); *Chicago Tribune*, December 20, 1963; *New York Herald Tribune*, December 18 and 22, 1963.

73. *Chicago Tribune*, December 21 and 30, 1963; *New York Herald Tribune*, December 18, 1963.

74. Klein, *New York Giants*, 233; Tittle, *Nothing Comes Easy*, 196–97.

75. *New York Herald Tribune*, December 30, 1963; Robustelli, *Once a Giant, Always*, 111; Klein, *New York Giants*, 233.

76. Ziegler, "1963 NFL Championship Game;" *New York Times*, December 30, 1963; *Chicago Tribune*, December 30, 1963; Bob Carroll, "Papa Bear's Season," *Coffin Corner* 10, no. 1 (1990).

77. *Chicago Tribune*, December 30, 1963; *New York Herald Tribune*, December 30, 1963.

78. William Phillips, "A Season in the Stands," *Commentary*, July 1969, 67.

79. Michael Shapiro, "Fallen Giant," *Smithsonian* 37 (February 2007): 14; Obituary of Morris Berman, *New York Times*, June 21, 2002; Klein, *New York Giants*, 235.

80. Phillips, "A Season in the Stands," 66.

81. When Quaker Oats in 1951 offered Cleveland's star flanker Dub Jones $500 to appear in a newspaper or magazine ad endorsing its product after he scored six touchdowns in a game, Jones thought "that was out of this world." It was so unusual for a football player to receive even a small sum of money to endorse a product that Jones felt he needed to ask Coach Paul Brown's permission to accept it. Norwood, *Real Football*, 40.

82. Gifford, *The Whole Ten Yards*, 207; Exley, *A Fan's Notes*, 131–32.

83. George Plimpton, *Paper Lion* (New York: Harper & Row, 1965), 281. The Lions considered Detroit, by contrast, "a dog town."

## 4. Joe Namath

1. Dave Anderson, "Making It," *New York Times*, February 1, 1969; Arthur Daley, "The Expendable," *New York Times*, December 22, 1965; John Devaney, "Can Football Live without

Namath (& Vice-Versa)?" *Sport*, July 1972; John Devaney, "Joe Namath's Good Days and Bad," *Sport*, November 1967; Paul Zimmerman, "What His Teammates Think of Joe Namath," *Sport*, December 1970; Milton Gross, "Joe Namath Likes Girls," *The Sun*, July 27, 1965; Jim O'Brien, "The Poor Man's Joe Namath," *Sport*, August 1973; Dave Anderson, "The Creator of a Sport Megalopolis," *New York Times*, November 23, 1991; Lawrence Linderman, "*Playboy*'s Candid Conversation with the Superswinger QB Joe Namath," *Playboy*, December 1969.

2. Robert H. Boyle, "Show-Biz Sonny and His Quest for Stars," *Sports Illustrated*, July 19, 1965; Jimmy Breslin, "Namath All Night Long," *New York Magazine*, April 7, 1969; Alan Goldstein, "Joe Namath: Fact or Fiction?" *Baltimore Sun*, January 6, 1969; Devaney, "Can Football Live without Namath?"; Devaney, "Joe Namath's Good Days and Bad"; Larry Fox, "Joe Namath: His Troubles and Triumphs," *Sport*, June 1966.

3. Boyle, "Show-Biz Sonny and His Quest for Stars."

4. Boyle, "Show-Biz Sonny and His Quest for Stars"; "Joe Namath and the Jet-Propelled Offense," *Time*, October 16, 1972.

5. John Lake, "Two for the Football Show: The Swinger and the Square," *New York Times*, November 5, 1967; Dan Jenkins, "The Sweet Life of Swinging Joe," *Sports Illustrated*, October 17, 1966; Devaney, "Joe Namath's Good Days and Bad"; Dave Anderson, "The Passing Show," *New York Times*, November 3, 1968; "Joe Namath and the Jet-Propelled Offense"; Tony Kornheiser, "Off Broadway Joe: The Song and Dance of a Playboy Nearing Middle Age," *Inside Sports*, July 1981.

6. "Joe Namath and the Jet-Propelled Offense"; Devaney, "Can Football Live without Namath?"

7. Goldstein, "Joe Namath: Fact or Fiction?"; Lake, "Two for the Football Show"; Kornheiser, "Off Broadway Joe"; Devaney, "Can Football Live without Namath?"; Bill Bruns, "Different Strokes for a Different Joe," *Sport*, November 1977.

8. Linderman, "*Playboy*'s Candid Conversation with the Superswinger QB Joe Namath"; James Reston, "Joe Namath, the New Anti-Hero," *New York Times*, August 21, 1970; Jenkins, "The Sweet Life of Swinging Joe"; "Joe Namath and the Jet-Propelled Offense"; Bruns, "Different Strokes for a Different Joe"; CBS Morning Interview with Joe Namath 45 Years after Super Bowl III, www.youtube.com/watch?v=jgFoHmyLcA.

9. Devaney, "Can Football Live without Namath?"; Breslin, "Namath All Night Long"; Anderson, "Making It"; Dave Anderson, "The Special People," *New York Times*, June 27, 1969; Kay Gilman, "Sports Sex Symbols," *Los Angeles Times*, August 18, 1974; "Joe Namath and the Jet-Propelled Offense"; Jenkins, "The Sweet Life of Swinging Joe"; Gross, "Joe Namath Likes Girls"; Lake, "Two for the Football Show"; "Schoolgirl Squeals Cap Namath's Day," *Washington Post*, January 23, 1969.

10. Gilman, "Sports Sex Symbols"; Bruns, "Different Strokes for a Different Joe"; Kristin McMurran, "Game Time to Prime Time," *People Magazine*, September 25, 1978.

11. James Reston, "Joe Namath, the New Anti-Hero," *New York Times*, August 21, 1970; Lake, "Two for the Football Show"; Linderman, "*Playboy*'s Candid Conversation with the Superswinger QB Joe Namath."

12. Linderman, "*Playboy*'s Candid Conversation with the Superswinger QB"; Kornheiser, "Off Broadway Joe"; Gilman, "Sports Sex Symbols."

13. Linderman, "*Playboy*'s Candid Conversation with the Superswinger QB"; Breslin, "Namath All Night Long."

14. Joe Willie Namath (w/Dick Schaap), "The Truth According to Joe," *Baltimore Sun*, November 16, 1969; Linderman, "*Playboy*'s Candid Conversation with the Superswinger QB";

Bill Mathis and Al Hirshberg, "The Joe Namath I Know," *Esquire,* September 1968; Lake, "Two for the Football Show"; Devaney, "Joe Namath's Good Days and Bad"; Kornheiser, "Off Broadway Joe."

15. David Riesman with Reuel Denney, "Football in America: A Study in Culture Diffusion," in David Riesman, *Individualism Reconsidered* (New York: Free Press, 1954), 242–57; Gilman, "Sports Sex Symbols"; Joseph Durso, "For Star Athletes, NY Is at the End of the Rainbow," *New York Times,* August 29, 1975.

16. Adam Gopnik, "The Unbeautiful Game," *New Yorker,* January 8, 2007; Benjamin G. Rader, *American Sports: From the Age of Folk Games to the Age of Televised Sports,* 2nd ed. (Englewood Cliffs, NJ: Prentice-Hall, 1990), 263.

17. Breslin, "Namath All Night Long"; "Joe Namath and the Jet-Propelled Offense"; Jenkins, "The Sweet Life of Swinging Joe"; Linderman, "*Playboy*'s Candid Conversation with the Superswinger QB."

18. Breslin, "Namath All Night Long"; Jenkins, "The Sweet Life of Swinging Joe"; Linderman, "*Playboy*'s Candid Conversation with the Superswinger QB"; Kornheiser, "Off Broadway Joe."

19. Judy Klemsrud, "The Penthouse of Joe Namath: First There's the Llama Rug . . ." *New York Times,* December 12, 1967; Linderman, "*Playboy*'s Candid Conversation with the Superswinger QB"; Jenkins, "The Sweet Life of Swinging Joe"; Devaney, "Joe Namath's Good Days and Bad"; "Joe Namath and the Jet-Propelled Offense"; Mathis and Hirshberg, "The Joe Namath I Know"; David Shaw, "Sports Heroes and the Cult of Winning," *Los Angeles Times,* September 10, 1972; Lake, "Two for the Football Show."

20. Gilman, "Sports Sex Symbols"; J. Anthony Lukas, "The 'Alternative Life-Style' of Playboys and Playmates: Playboy's Empire: From Hotels and Movies to Tie Clips, Putters and Pillows," *New York Times,* June 11, 1972; Ron Cassie, "Bunny Tales," *Baltimore* [Magazine], August 2014.

21. Joe Namath, as told to Larry King, "Aftermath: The Joe Namath I Know," *Esquire,* December 1968, 108–14; Joseph Durso, "For Star Athletes, New York Is at the End of the Rainbow," *New York Times,* August 29, 1975; Dick Schaap, "With Joe Namath," *Sport,* November 1975.

22. Everett Mattlin, "When Joe Namath Takes to Fur . . . ," *Chicago Tribune,* September 23, 1968; Edwin Shrake, "A Champagne Party for Joe and Weeb," *Sports Illustrated,* December 9, 1968.

23. Mattlin, "When Joe Namath Takes to Fur . . ."

24. "Texas Prep Coach Says Long Hair Sign of Sissy," *Los Angeles Times,* May 22, 1973; Red Smith, "Intellectual View of God's Haircut," *New York Times,* November 16, 1973; Nicholas von Hoffman, "Broadway Joe—A Lifestyle," *Washington Post, Times Herald,* June 13, 1969; Robert Lipsyte, "Hair," *New York Times,* November 11, 1968; Shrake, "A Champagne Party for Joe and Weeb."

25. John Devaney, "The War for Joe Namath's Body," *Sport,* January 1970; Namath, as told to Larry King, "Aftermath: The Joe Namath I Know"; Gross, "Joe Namath Likes Girls"; Linderman, "*Playboy*'s Candid Conversation with the Superswinger QB"; Lipsyte, "Hair"; "Hirsute Namath Powers Jets toward AFL Title," *Baltimore Sun,* November 26, 1968.

26. Dwight Chapin, "Long Hair for Athletes Now Rule Rather Than Exception," *Los Angeles Times, Washington Post, Times Herald,* January 30, 1972; John Bloom, "Joe Namath and Super Bowl III: An Interpretation of Style," *Journal of Sport History* (Spring 1968): 70; Arnold Hano, "The Pro-Football Player Is a-Changin'," *Sport,* August 1970.

27. Chapin, "Long Hair for Athletes Now Rule"; Lipsyte, "Hair"; Smith, "Intellectual View of God's Haircut."

28. Anderson, "Making It"; Linderman, "*Playboy*'s Candid Conversation with the Superswinger QB"; Hano, "The Pro-Football Player Is a-Changin'"; Devaney, "Can Football Live without Namath?"; Lipsyte, "Hair"; "Hirsute Namath Powers Jets toward AFL Title"; "40 Years Later, Old Jets Relive Super Bowl III," *New York Times*, September 5, 2008.

29. See, for example, "Linda LeClair Presents Defense," *Columbia Spectator*, April 17, 1968.

30. Reston, "Joe Namath, the New Anti-Hero"; Lake, "Two for the Football Show: The Swinger and the Square"; Linderman, "*Playboy*'s Candid Conversation with the Superswinger QB"; Anderson, "The Special People"; Dave Anderson, "The Quarterback," *New York Times*, June 8, 1969; Mike Rathet, "Joe Namath Questions Himself after Al Atkinson Says He Resigned from Football Because of Controversial Quarterback," *Gettysburg Times*, August 6, 1970; Zimmerman, "What His Teammates Think of Joe Namath"; Robert Lipsyte, "Changing Seasons," *New York Times*, August 10, 1970.

31. Reston, "Joe Namath, the New Anti-Hero"; Hano, "The Pro-Football Player Is a-Changin'"; J. D. Salinger, *Catcher in the Rye* (Boston: Little, Brown, 1991 [1951]); Shaw, "Sports Heroes and the Cult of Winning"; William Gildea, "Athletes Striking Out as Models of Virtue," *Washington Post*, March 14, 1971.

32. Shaw, "Sports Heroes and the Cult of Winning"; Devaney, "Can Football Live without Namath?"; Mathis and Hirshberg, "The Joe Namath I Know"; Anderson, "The Quarterback."

33. Shaw, "Sports Heroes and the Cult of Winning"; Hano, "The Pro-Football Player Is a-Changin'"; Mark Kriegel, *Namath: A Biography* (New York: Penguin, 2004), 256–57, 263.

34. Kriegel, *Namath*, 256, 258, 262; Anderson, "The Quarterback."

35. Kriegel, *Namath*, 221, 257, 267–68, 270; "40 Years Later, Old Jets Relive Super Bowl III."

36. Kriegel, *Namath*, 259, 262, 266–67; "Broadway Joe: A Football Legend," www.youtube.com/watch?v=jgFoSHmxLcA.

37. Kriegel, *Namath*, 261, 273, 277–79; Dave Brady, "Jets Shock Colts in Super Bowl, 16–7," *Washington Post*, January 13, 1969; "Broadway Joe: A Football Legend"; Reston, "Joe Namath, the New Anti-Hero"; Shaw, "Sports Heroes and the Cult of Winning."

38. "Football's Super Star: Joseph William Namath," *New York Times*, January 13, 1969; Kriegel, *Namath*, 267; Anderson, "Making It"; Breslin, "Namath All Night Long"; "Schoolgirl Squeals Cap Namath's Day"; Tex Maule, "Say It's So, Joe," *Sports Illustrated*, January 20, 1969.

39. Goldstein, "Joe Namath: Fact or Fiction?"; Linderman, "*Playboy*'s Candid Conversation with the Superswinger QB"; Namath, as told to Larry King, "Aftermath: The Joe Namath I Know"; Dave Anderson, "Namath: A Most-Wanted Fella," *New York Times*, May 30, 1971; "Joe Namath and the Jet-Propelled Offense"; Devaney, "The War for Joe Namath's Body."

40. "Joe Namath and the Jet-Propelled Offense"; Boyle, "Show-Biz Sonny and His Quest for Stars"; Devaney, "Can Football Live without Namath?"; Breslin, "Namath All Night Long"; Frank Joseph DiRoma, "Joe Namath," Pennsylvania Center for the Book, Spring 2007, http://pabook2.libraries.psu.edu/palitmap/bios/Namath__Joe.html; Anderson, "The Passing Show."

41. "Joe Namath and the Jet-Propelled Offense"; Jenkins, "The Sweet Life of Swinging Joe"; Devaney, "The War for Joe Namath's Body."

42. "Joe Namath and the Jet-Propelled Offense"; Jenkins, "The Sweet Life of Swinging Joe"; Linderman, "*Playboy*'s Candid Conversation with the Superswinger QB"; Lake, "Two for the Football Show."

43. DiRoma, "Joe Namath"; Devaney, "Joe Namath's Good Days and Bad"; Anderson, "The Passing Show"; Linderman, "*Playboy*'s Candid Conversation with the Superswinger QB."

44. Zimmerman, "What His Teammates Think of Joe Namath"; Rathet, "Joe Namath Questions Himself after Al Atkinson Says He Resigned from Football Because of Controversial Quarterback"; "Joe Namath and the Jet-Propelled Offense."

45. "Joe Namath and the Jet-Propelled Offense"; Namath, as told to Larry King, "Aftermath: The Joe Namath I Know"; Linderman, "*Playboy*'s Candid Conversation with the Superswinger QB"; Dave Anderson, "Namath Is Not a Boxer or a Golfer," *New York Times*, November 25, 1975; Lake, "Two for the Football Show"; Anderson, "The Passing Show"; Gopnik, "The Unbeautiful Game."

46. Devaney, "Joe Namath's Good Days and Bad"; Fox, "Joe Namath: His Troubles and Triumphs"; Devaney, "Can Football Live without Namath?"; "Joe Namath and the Jet-Propelled Offense"; Linderman, "*Playboy*'s Candid Conversation with the Superswinger QB."

47. Linderman, "*Playboy*'s Candid Conversation with the Superswinger QB"; Devaney, "Joe Namath's Good Days and Bad"; Lake, "Two for the Football Show"; Dave Anderson, "Courage of Convictions Could Throw Namath for $5-Million Loss," *New York Times*, June 7, 1969.

48. Devaney, "The War for Joe Namath's Body"; Linderman, "*Playboy*'s Candid Conversation with the Superswinger QB"; Zimmerman, "What His Teammates Think of Joe Namath."

49. Devaney, "The War for Joe Namath's Body."

50. Devaney, "Can Football Live without Namath?"; Namath, as told to Larry King, "Aftermath: The Joe Namath I Know"; Kornheiser, "Off Broadway Joe."

51. Hano, "The Pro-Football Player Is a-Changin'"; Linderman, "*Playboy*'s Candid Conversation with the Superswinger QB"; Anderson, "Namath Is Not a Boxer or a Golfer."

52. Jimmy Breslin, "For Namath, Frustration . . . & Blackberry Brandy," *Sport*, March 1977; Kornheiser, "Off Broadway Joe."

53. Breslin, "For Namath, Frustration . . . & Blackberry Brandy."

54. Bruns, "Different Strokes for a Different Joe"; Anderson, "Namath Is Not a Boxer or a Golfer"; Mike Foss, "Joe Namath Played for the Rams Once Upon a Time," *USA Today*, May 6, 2013; Don Pierson, "Bears Put It all Together, Whip Rams," *Chicago Tribune*, October 11, 1977; McMurran, "Game Time to Prime Time."

55. John Devaney, "Joe Namath: the $400,000 Challenge," *Sport*, August 1965; T. S. Eliot, *The Complete Poems and Plays* (London, UK: Faber & Faber, 2004); Kornheiser, "Off Broadway Joe"; CBS Morning Interview with Joe Namath 45 Years after Super Bowl III; Foss, "Joe Namath Played for the Rams Once Upon a Time"; McMurran, "Game Time to Prime Time"; Bruns, "Different Strokes for a Different Joe"; Gopnik, "The Unbeautiful Game."

## 5. From Basket Ball to Hoop Heroics

1. Pete Axthelm, *The City Game: Basketball in New York* (New York: Harper's Magazine Press, 1970), ix.

2. Axthelm, *The City Game*, xi.

3. See Bernice Larson Webb, *The Basketball Man: James Naismith* (Lawrence: University Press of Kansas, 1973), 68–69.

4. *Newsweek*, December 4, 1950.

5. Much has been written on the 1951 point-shaving scandal. For example, see Neil D. Isaacs, *All the Moves: A History of College Basketball* (Philadelphia: Lippincott, 1975), chapter 13, "The Serpent in the Garden," 102–8; Stanley Cohen, *The Game They Played* (New York: Carroll and Graf, 1977); and Charley Rosen, *Scandals of '51* (New York: Seven Stories, 1978).

6. Leonard Lewin and Dick Young, "How Gamblers Move In," *True*, April 1945. Reprinted in Irving T. Marsh and Edward Ehre, eds., *Best Sports Stories of 1945* (New York: J. P. Dutton, 1946), 161–70.

7. Quoted in Sherman White, "The Basketball Fix Ruined My Life," *Sport*, July 1951, 76.

8. "Lineup for Today's Game" photo and caption appeared in the *New York Journal-American*, February 20, 1951, 1.

9. "Drive, Drive, Drive!" *Newsweek*, 76–78.

10. Quoted in Rosen, *Scandals*, 61.

11. Rosen, *Scandals*, 64.

12. "City Orders Investigation," *New York Journal-American*, November 20, 1951, 1, 6.

13. "Drive, Drive, Drive!" 76.

14. See John Russell, *Honey Russell: Between Games, between Halves* (Washington, DC: Dryad Press, 1986), 13.

15. "Gambler Gets 8 Years: Judge Blasts Coaches," *New York Journal-American*, November 19, 1951, 1, 23, 28.

16. White, "The Basketball Fix Ruined My Life," 76.

17. Cohen, *The Game They Played*, 214–15.

18. On LIU's involvement in and reaction to the scandal, see Dennis Gildea, *Hoop Crazy: The Lives of Clair Bee and Chip Hilton* (Fayetteville: University of Arkansas Press, 2013).

19. Paul Gould, "St. John's May Quit Garden, Build Gym," *Brooklyn Eagle*, March 3, 1951, 3.

20. "Big Drop in NIT Gate Reflects Fix Scandal," *New York Journal-American*, March 15, 1951, 23.

21. Bob Russell, "Gone but Not Forgotten," *Dell Sports Basketball, 1957–58*, 23.

22. See Larry Cheek, "McGuire's Miracle," *Dell Sports Basketball*, 26–29. See a profile of Kearns in the same magazine, 47. To this day, the 1957 North Carolina team is referred to in Chapel Hill as "four Catholics and a Jew," a point made in an unpublished paper by Joel Schronz presented at the Sport Literature Association conference, College of the Rockies, Canmore, British Columbia, 2014.

23. Albert J. Figone, Cheating the Spread: Gamblers, Point Shavers, and Game Fixers in College Football and Basketball (Urbana: University of Illinois Press, 2012), 108.

24. See Jeremiah Tax, "The Facts about the Fixes," *Sports Illustrated*, March 27, 1961, 18–19.

25. Connie Hawkins's fascinating story has been told by David Wolf in *Foul* (New York: Warner, 1972).

26. The most thorough treatment of Jack Molinas's life is Charley Rosen, *The Wizard of Odds* (New York: Seven Stories Press, 2001). Neil D. Isaacs has a fine novel based on Molinas, *The Great Molinas* (Washington, DC: Drinan Press, 2010,), a reprint of his 1992 novel.

27. See the NIT official program cover for the 1941 tournament.

28. "Basket Ball and Its Success," *New York Times*, November 12, 1893, 10. On newspaper coverage of the Princeton-Yale football game, see Michael Oriard, *Reading Football: How the Popular Press Created an American Spectacle* (Chapel Hill: University of North Carolina Press, 1993), 57–120.

29. "Basket Ball and Its Success," 10.

30. "Basket Ball and Its Success," 10.

31. Webb, The Basketball Man, 70.

32. Steven A. Riess, *City Games: The Evolution of American Urban Society and the Rise of Sports* (Urbana: University of Illinois Press, 1989), 107.

33. Quoted in Riess, *City Games*, 107.

34. Riess, *Sport in Industrial America, 1850–1920* (Wheeling, IL: Harlan, 1995), 19.

35. See Paula Lupkin, *Manhood Factories: YMCA Architecture and the Making of Modern Urban Culture* (Minneapolis: University of Minnesota Press, 2009), especially chapter 2, "Inventing the YMCA Building." A diagram for the interior of YMCA buildings appears on 55; a reference to gym use in New York City appears on 60.

36. "Basket Ball and Its Success," 10.

37. See Webb, *The Basketball Man*, 139–40.

38. See Riess, *City Games*, 107–8. Nat Holman learned the game in the University Settlement house. See Rosen, *Scandals*, 13.

39. Rosen, *Scandals*, 13–14.

40. Peter C. Bjarkman, *Hoopla: A Century of College Basketball* (Indianapolis, IN: Masters Press, 1996), 29.

41. Rosen, *Scandals*, 16.

42. Rosen, *Scandals*, 15.

43. "Renaissance Seeking 78th Victory in Row," *Washington Post*, March 27, 1933, 10.

44. See Ron Thomas, *They Cleared the Lane: The NBA's Black Pioneers* (Lincoln: University of Nebraska Press, 2002), 8; and Susan J. Rayl, "Holding Court: The Real Renaissance Contribution of John Isaacs," *Journal of Sport History* 38, no. 1 (Spring 2011): 7.

45. Rayl, "Holding Court," 7.

46. Quoted in Thomas, *They Cleared the Lane*, 7.

47. The best source for the history of the Harlem Rens is Rayl, "The New York Renaissance Professional Basketball Team" (Unpublished dissertation, Penn State University, 1996).

48. Rayl, "Holding Court," 7–8.

49. Robert W. Peterson, *Cages to Jump Shots: Pro Basketball's Early Years* (New York: Oxford University Press, 1990), 100.

50. Rayl, "Holding Court," 7. Also see Ron Fimrite, "Sam Lacy: Black Crusader," *Sports Illustrated*, October 29, 1990, 90–94; and Sam Lacy and Moses J. Newson, *Fighting for Fairness: The Life Story of Hall of Fame Sportswriter Sam Lacy* (Centreville, MD: Tidewater, 1999).

51. See Gildea, *Hoop Crazy*, 106–7.

52. John D. McCallum, *College Basketball, U.S.A.* (New York: Stein and Day, 1978), 47–48.

53. An excellent source for a full discussion of the 1936 Olympic basketball trials and the Berlin Games is Rich Hughes, *Netting Out Basketball, 1936* (Victoria, BC, Canada: Friesen, 2011).

54. Gildea, *Hoop Crazy*, 87.

55. Lynne Kramer quoted in Michael Weinreb, "A Team That Chose Principles over Gold Medals," *www.ESPN.com*, April 14, 2009.

56. Roger Kahn, "Success and Ned Irish," *Sports Illustrated*, March 27, 1961, 39.

57. Kahn, "Success and Ned Irish," 42.

58. See Kahn, "Success and Ned Irish," 40.

59. Isaacs, *All the Moves*, 78.

60. For a short account of some of the basketball writers luncheons, see Gildea, *Hoop Crazy*, 4–8.

61. See Gildea, *Hoop Crazy*, 103.

62. See Walter Byers, *Unsportsmanlike Conduct: Exploiting College Athletes* (Ann Arbor: University of Michigan Press), 92–95.

63. Isaacs, *All the Moves*, 112.

64. Stanley Frank, quoted in Gildea, *Hoop Crazy*, 95.

65. Nat Holman quoted in Sandy Padwe, *Basketball's Hall of Fame* (Englewood Cliffs, NJ: Prentice-Hall, 1970), 36.

66. Angelo Luisetti, quoted in Padwe, *Basketball's Hall of Fame*, 37.

67. Kareem Abdul-Jabbar, quoted in Vincent M. Mallozzi, *Asphalt Gods: An Oral History of the Rucker Tournament* (New York: Doubleday, 2003), 94.

68. Quoted in John Matthew Smith, *The Sons of Westwood: John Wooden, UCLA, and the Dynasty That Changed College Basketball* (Urbana: University of Illinois Press, 2012), 67.

69. Abdul-Jabbar quoted in Mallozzi, *Asphalt Gods*, 98.

70. Howie Evans quoted in Jarrod Jonsrud, "Harlem's Unsung Hero: The Life and Legacy of Holcombe Rucker," *Journal of Sport History* 38, no. 1 (Spring 2011): 26.

71. Jonsrud, "Harlem's Unsung Hero: The Life and Legacy of Holcombe Rucker," 29.

72. Mallozzi, *Asphalt Gods*, 13–14.

73. Earl Manigault quoted in Mallozzi, *Asphalt Gods*, 101.

74. Earl Manigault quoted in Mallozzi, *Asphalt Gods*, 94.

75. Mallozzi's *Asphalt Gods* is an excellent and thoroughly researched account of the Rucker League and the less mainstream side of New York City basketball in general.

76. Mallozzi, *Asphalt Gods*, 14–17.

77. Lou Carnesecca, quoted in Mazzolli, *Asphalt Gods*, 144–45. For Kirkland's story, see Mallozzi, *Asphalt Gods*, 121–31. For a list of the all-time top players in the Rucker League, see "Elite 24: Rucker Park Legends," at www.ESPN.com (accessed March 7, 2016).

78. Kahn, "Success and Ned Irish," 29.

79. Harvey Araton, *When the Garden Was Eden* (New York: HarperCollins, 2011), 143.

80. Walt Frazier, quoted in Araton, *When the Garden Was Eden*, 144.

81. See Araton, *When the Garden Was Eden*, 147–50.

82. Spike Lee, quoted in Araton, *When the Garden Was Eden*, 165.

83. Pete Hamill, *Tabloid City* (New York: Back Bay Books, 2012), 216.

84. Joanne Lannin, *A History of Basketball for Girls and Women: From Bloomers to Big Leagues* (Minneapolis, MN: Lerner Sports, 2000), 77–78.

85. Lannin, *A History of Basketball for Girls and Women*, 78.

86. Lena Williams, "Women's Basketball Draws 11,969 Fans at the Garden," *New York Times*, February 23, 1975, S1.

87. Lannin, *A History of Basketball for Girls and Women*, 120.

88. Williams, "Women's Basketball Draws 11,969 Fans at the Garden," S1.

89. Donna Chait Orender, quoted in Araton, "A First at the Garden Earns an Encore," *New York Times*, January 3, 2015, D1.

90. Marianne Crawford Stanley, quoted in Araton, "A First at the Garden Earns an Encore," D1.

91. Nancy Lieberman, quoted in Araton, "A First at the Garden Earns an Encore," D1.

92. See Murray Sperber, *Beer and Circus: How Big-time College Sports Is Crippling Undergraduate Education* (New York: Henry Holt, 2000), 36–38.

93. See the entry on Lou Carnesecca at www.Redstormsports.com (accessed March 13, 2016).

94. Sam Goldaper, "Nat Holman Is Dead at 98; Led CCNY Champions," *New York Times*, February 13, 1995, B7.

## 6. The New York City Marathon

1. Neil Amdur, "A Bystander's Guide for Getting the Most Out of the New York Marathon," *New York Times,* October 21, 1977.

2. *TCS New York City Marathon 2015 Media Guide,* 40–41. Full disclosure: I was one of those 50,740 runners in 2013. In exchange for raising monies for the Women's Sports Foundation, I was able to secure an invitation to participate in the event. As part of the WSF's weekend activities (they had a team of five runners, including myself), we had a prerace dinner the night before the event, and a postrace breakfast on Monday with Kathrine Switzer, who despite my plodding pace, congratulated me on my finish. Switzer remains an enthusiastic supporter of women in marathon events, as well as women in sport.

3. "200 Will Compete in City Marathon," *New York Times,* September 6, 1970. In this article, the newspaper states 126 entries. However, subsequent NYRR sources repeatedly use 127 in their materials, which I cite for consistency.

4. Al Harvin, "Husband-Wife Teams Entered in Marathon Run Here Today," New York Times, September 13, 1970.

5. Al Harvin, "Fireman Is First to Finish in Marathon," *New York Times,* September 14, 1970.

6. At this point in time, the small club operated "out of people's apartments" (see http://www.nyrr.org/about-us/nyrr-hall-of-fame/fred-lebow).

7. Ron Rubin, *Anything for a T-Shirt: Fred Lebow and the New York City Marathon, the World's Greatest Footrace* (Syracuse, NY: Syracuse University Press, 2004), 18. At this point in time, there were few regularly held marathon events in the United States. The long-heralded Boston Marathon was an annual event, as was the nearby Yonkers Marathon. However, other than those two annual races, the distance was largely neglected (in part because of the necessary training, as well as the hosting logistics). For more on the development of the marathon event, see Pamela L. Cooper, *The American Marathon* (Syracuse, NY: Syracuse University Press, 1999). Cooper, in chapter 3, examines the earliest marathons and road races in New York in the first decade of the twentieth century.

8. George Hirsch, "On the Run: Fred Lebow's Great Race," *New York Times,* November 7, 2010.

9. Gerald Eskenazi, "In New York's Marathon, They Also Run Who Only Sit and Wait," *New York Times,* October 2, 1972, 39, 48.

10. Cooper, *The American Marathon,* 158. Cooper's chapter 9 is titled, "Women, Marathon, and Corporation," in which she explains the development of women in marathon running, including in New York City.

11. Again, Cooper is helpful in explaining the growth of the mini-marathon and its relationship to the growth of women in long-distance running. See Cooper, *The American Marathon,* chapter 9, 157–75.

12. "Bronx Internist Is Victor in Fifth City Marathon," *New York Times,* September 30, 1974. For Switzer's recollections of the early New York marathons, see her *Marathon Women: Running the Race to Revolutionize Women's Sports* (Cambridge, MA: Da Capo Press, 2007). Switzer worked with Lebow and the NYRR on public relations for these events.

13. Rubin, Anything for a T-Shirt, 31.

14. Pamela L. Cooper, "The 'Visible Hand' on the Footrace: Fred Lebow and the Marketing of the Marathon," *Journal of Sport History* 19, no. 3 (1992): 244–56; especially see pages 249–50. Also see Lena Williams, "Marathon Women Ready," *New York Times,*

September 28, 1975; Steve Cady, "Women Marathon Runners Are Racing to Equality with Men," *New York Times*, September 29, 1975.

15. "City Marathon, Oct. 24, Will Span 5 Boroughs," *New York Times*, June 22, 1976.

16. "City Marathon, Oct. 24, Will Span 5 Boroughs," *New York Times*, June 22, 1976.

17. George Hirsch, "On the Run: Fred Lebow's Great Race." Also see Cooper, "The 'Visible Hand' on the Footrace," 250–51, 254, for more on the five-borough logistics, as well as the inclusion of Shorter and Rodgers.

18. Neil Amdur, "New York's First Citywide Marathon Draws Some of World's Top Runners," *New York Times*, October 25, 1976.

19. Amby Burfoot, "The History of the Marathon, 1976–Present," *Sports Medicine* 37 (4–5, 2007): 284–87.

20. Neil Amdur, "New York's First Citywide Marathon Draws Some of World's Top Runners," 31, 36. Also see "Route of Today's Marathon and Where to View It," *New York Times*, October 24, 1976; Neil Amdur, "Politicians Jump Marathon Gun," *New York Times*, September 17, 1976.

21. Cooper, The American Marathon, 131.

22. Cooper, *The American Marathon*, 141. Cooper also explains the growth of marathon running, what she refers to as the "gentrification of the marathon," in *The American Marathon*, 122–38.

23. Neil Amdur, "The Loneliness of Tom Fleming," *New York Times*, October 23, 1977. Also see Neil Amdur, "From Marathon Runs to Football, Handicapped Are Entering Sports," *New York Times*, October 31, 1977; Neil Amdur, "New York's 2d Five-Borough Marathon: Several Stars and a Cast of Thousands," *New York Times*, October 23, 1977; Neil Amdur, "A Bystander's Guide for Getting the Most Out of the New York Marathon," *New York Times*, October 21, 1977; Amdur includes a discussion of the logistics of the five-borough event. Also see "5,000 Run Next Sunday in Five-Borough Marathon," *New York Times*, October 16, 1977. For a first-person account of running the event in 1977, see Peter Wood, "Seeing New York on the Run," *New York Times*, October 7, 1979.

24. Glenn Fowler, "New Yorkers Take Marathon in Stride," *New York Times*, October 22, 1979; "Error Enlarges City Marathon," *New York Times*, September 16, 1980; Glenn Fowler, "Koch, a Jogger, Hails Marathon," *New York Times*, June 12, 1979; Neil Amdur, "Heat Is the Hot Item in Marathon Today," *New York Times*, October 21, 1979; George Vecsey, "12,622 Winners," *New York Times*, October 28, 1980; Frank Litsky, "Marathon Victors Are Toasted," *New York Times*, October 28, 1980; Neil Amdur, "The Streets of New York Get New Marathon King," *New York Times*, October 27, 1980; "A Diary of New York's Marathon Festival," *New York Times*, October 26, 1980; Tom Lederer, "A Runner Sees Time Gaining on Him," *New York Times*, October 21, 1979.

25. Liz Robbins, *A Race Like No Other: 26.2 Miles through the Streets of New York* (New York: Harper, 2009), 11.

26. See Appendix C AADT Values for Select Toll Facilities, *2008 Traffic Data Report for New York State*, New York State Department of Transportation, https://www.dot.ny.gov/divisions/engineering/technical-services/hds-respository/Traffic%20Data%20Report%202008.pdf (accessed April 11, 2016).

27. Amdur, "A Bystander's Guide for Getting the Most Out of the New York Marathon."

28. Robbins, A Race Like No Other, 29.

29. Grete Waitz and Gloria Averbuch, *Run Your First Marathon: Everything You Need to Know to Reach the Finish Line*, 2nd ed. (New York: Skyhorse Publishing, 2010), 2.

30. Toby Tanser, *The Essential Guide to Running the New York City Marathon* (New York: Berkley Publishing Group, 2003), 100.

31. Amdur, "A Bystander's Guide for Getting the Most Out of the New York Marathon."

32. *TCS New York City Marathon 2015 Media Guide*, 7. This is from the mayor's welcome letter to marathon participants.

33. Joe Cody, "The View from Williamsburg," *New York Running News Special Marathon Issue* (October 1982), 24.

34. For a discussion of Lebow's inclusion of Williamsburg, see Rubin, *Anything for a T-Shirt*, 39.

35. Fowler, "New Yorkers Take Marathon in Stride."

36. Neil Amdur, "Rodgers Beats 11,532 in Marathon as Waitz Makes Record Run," *New York Times*, October 22, 1979.

37. For more on women in the marathon event, see chapter 10 in Cooper, *The American Marathon*.

38. Cooper, *The American Marathon*, 155. Some of the discussions around money and the marathon were very public; for example, see Fred Lebow, "Let Road Runners Get Financial Rewards," *New York Times*, October 19, 1980; "Big Purse Offered Marathon," *New York Times*, September 5, 1980.

39. Jane Gross, "Inside the World of Big-Time Fred Lebow," *New York Times*, October 28, 1984, http://www.nytimes.com/1984/10/28/sports/inside-the-world-of-big-time-fred-lebow.html. Cooper discusses the appearance fees in *The American Marathon*, 137–38.

40. Moran, "Koch Bends on the Marathon."

41. Malcolm Moran, "Koch Bends on the Marathon," *New York Times*, October 17, 1984, http://www.nytimes.com/1984/10/17/sports/koch-bends-on-the-marathon.html. Also see Cooper, "The 'Visible Hand' on the Footrace," 250–51.

42. Peter Alfano, "New York Marathon to Use Drug Tests," *New York Times*, October 17, 1986, http://www.nytimes.com/1986/10/17/sports/new-york-marathon-to-use-drug-tests.html.

43. Gross, "Inside the World of Big-Time Fred Lebow."

44. Kenny Moore, "All around the Town," *Sports Illustrated*, October 30, 1978, 28.

45. Tanser, *The Essential Guide to Running the New York City Marathon*, ix.

46. Tanser, *The Essential Guide to Running the New York City Marathon*, xi.

47. Peter Alfano, "Limit Considered for Marathon Field," *New York Times*, November 4, 1986, http://www.nytimes.com/1986/11/04/sports/limit-considered-for-marathon-field.html.

48. Tim Huebsch, "Dave Obelkevich successfully completes his 40th New York City Marathon," *Canadian Running Magazine*, November 3, 2015, http://runningmagazine.ca/dave-obelkevich-successfully-completes-his-40th-new-york-city-marathon/.

49. The year prior, 9,250 runners gained entry out of 77,087 lottery entrants.

50. "Guaranteed Entry for 2016," *TCS New York City Marathon*, http://www.tcsnycmarathon.org/plan-your-race/getting-in/guaranteed-entry-for-2016.

51. William C. Rhoden, "Illness Doesn't Alter Essence of Lebow," *New York Times*, July 29, 1990. http://www.nytimes.com/1990/07/29/sports/track-and-field-illness-doesn-t-alter-essence-of-lebow.html.

52. "Sloan-Kettering Gets $652,173 from Runners," *New York Times*, May 12, 1992, http://www.nytimes.com/1992/05/12/sports/sports-people-marathon-sloan-kettering-gets-652173-from-runners.html.

53. George Vecsey, "Fred and Grete Win All of New York City," *New York Times*, November 2, 1992, http://www.nytimes.com/1992/11/02/sports/new-york-city-marathon-sports-times-fred-grete-win-all-new-york-city.html.

54. George Hirsch, "On the Run: Fred Lebow's Great Race," *New York Times*, November 7, 2010, http://query.nytimes.com/gst/fullpage.html?res=950DEED61738F934A35752C1A966 9D8B63.

55. Lisa W. Foderado, "Arriving at the Finish Line, Days before the Race," *New York Times*, November 1, 2011, A24.

56. George Vecsey, "Lebow Won His Personal Marathon," *New York Times*, October 10, 1994, http://www.nytimes.com/1994/10/10/sports/sports-of-the-times-lebow-won-his-personal-marathon.html.

57. Michael Janofsky, "Fred Lebow Is Dead at 62; Founded New York Marathon," *New York Times*, October 10, 1994, http://www.nytimes.com/1994/10/10/obituaries/fred-lebow-is-dead-at-62-founded-new-york-marathon.html.

58. Janofsky, "Fred Lebow Is Dead at 62."

59. Vecsey, "Lebow Won His Personal Marathon." Grete Waitz died of cancer in 2011. For more on her untimely death, see Frank Litsky, "Waitz and Lebow, a Friendship for the Ages," *New York Times*, April 19, 2011, http://marathon.blogs.nytimes.com/2011/04/19/waitz-and-lebow-a-friendship-for-the-ages/.

60. Joyce Purnick, "A Long Run, but He Broke the Tape," *New York Times*, November 11, 2004, http://www.nytimes.com/2004/11/11/nyregion/a-long-run-but-he-broke-the-red-tape.html?_r=0.

61. Lisa W. Foderado, "Arriving at the Finish Line, Days before the Race," A24. For more on the statue, see "Central Park: Fred Lebow Statue," *Official Website of the New York City Department of Parks and Recreation*, http://www.nycgovparks.org/parks/central-park/highlights/11248.

62. George Hirsch, "On the Run: Fred Lebow's Great Race," *New York Times*, November 7, 2010, http://query.nytimes.com/gst/fullpage.html?res=950DEED61738F934A35752C1A966 9D8B63.

63. These details are from the *TCS New York City Marathon 2015 Media Guide*.

64. http://www.nycgovparks.org/parks/central-park/highlights/11248.

## 7. "This Isn't the Sixth Race. This Is the Belmont"

1. John Scheinman, "Five Myths about the Triple Crown," *Washington Post*, May 30, 2014.

2. Eric Hobsbawm, "Introduction: Inventing Traditions," in *The Invention of Tradition*, ed. Hobsbawm and Terence Ranger (Cambridge: Cambridge University Press, 1983).

3. Joe H. Palmer, "Views of the Turf," *New York Herald Tribune*, May 31, 1948. At the time of Palmer's death in the fall of 1952, Arthur Daley of the *New York Times* said, "As a writer, he was in a class by himself." Red Smith wrote, "Joe Palmer wrote better than anybody else in the world whose stuff appeared in newspapers." See the condolences collected by the *Blood-Horse* in its edition of November 15, 1952, at page 1052.

4. References to the Derby, the Preakness, and the Belmont as the "Triple Crown" first appeared in print in the 1920s but did not command widespread recognition until the next decade, spurred by Gallant Fox's sweep of the three races in 1930. See Bennett Liebman, "The Naming of the Triple Crown," July 8, 2015, at https://saratogainstitute.wordpress.com/2015

/07/08/the-naming-of-the-triple-crown-2/. As a result, the horse now recognized as the first winner of the "Triple Crown"—Sir Barton in 1919—earned an honor that was only bestowed in retrospect.

5. Red Smith, "Races You Can See? What Next?" *New York Times,* March 10, 1976.

6. Joe Palmer, "Views of the Turf," *New York Herald Tribune,* November 8, 1949; Arthur Daley quoted in Peter Eisenstadt, *Rochdale Village: Robert Moses, 6,000 Families, and New York City's Great Experiment in Integrated Housing* (Ithaca, NY: Cornell University Press, 2010), 52. The Rochdale Village housing complex was built on the site of Jamaica Racetrack after the track was closed (in 1959) and demolished.

7. Joe H. Palmer, "Views of the Turf," *New York Herald Tribune,* May 31, 1948.

8. John Gunther, *Inside U.S.A.* (New York: Harper & Brothers, 1947), 649. The 1948 Broadway musical revue "Inside U.S.A.," based loosely on the book, set a song "Blue Grass" at Churchill Downs.

9. Smith, "Races You Can See? What Next?"

10. Joe H. Palmer, "Citation Wins Belmont Stakes and Triple Turf Crown, *New York Herald Tribune,* June 13, 1948.

11. Bill Lauder Jr., "'We'll Never Boo You, Eddie,' Happy Fans Promise Arcaro," *New York Herald Tribune,* June 13, 1948.

12. Red Smith, "Views of Sport," *New York Herald Tribune,* June 13, 1948.

13. *New York Times,* November 1, 1952.

14. James Roach, "Counterpoint, 5–1, Defeats Battlefield by 4 Lengths," *New York Times,* June 17, 1951.

15. Red Smith, "Views of Sports," *New York Herald Tribune,* June 17, 1951.

16. Smith, "Views of Sports."

17. Art Kennedy, "Turf Talk," *Newsday,* June 7, 1952.

18. Red Smith, "Views of Sport," *New York Herald Tribune,* June 12, 1955.

19. Bennett Liebman, "May 1, 1954: New York Brings Back Turf Racing," November 23, 2009, available at http://ssrn.com/abstract=1512182. "Derby Cast-offs in Swift Stakes," *Newsday,* May 1, 1954. The "turf" is a descriptive term covering all thoroughbred races. It can specifically refer to races conducted on grass, as opposed to dirt, tracks. Grass courses have always been in general use in Europe but were rarely used in the United States until the second half of the last century.

20. Bert Broome, "Whip, Spurs and Blinkers," *American Turf Monthly,* June 1956, 23.

21. Whitney Tower, "The First Dream Track," *Sports Illustrated,* July 16, 1956, 12.

22. Eisenstadt, *Rochdale Village,* 53–55.

23. Rud Rennie, "Greater N.Y. Group Opens New Era in Racing Today," *New York Herald Tribune.* October 5, 1955, B4.

24. "Jazz Age, Career Boy Entered," *Associated Press, Washington Post,* June 10, 1956.

25. "Musical Trimmings Added for Saturday's Belmont," *Associated Press, Troy Times Record,* June 14, 1956.

26. "Musical Trimmings Added for Saturday's Belmont."

27. "Musical Trimmings Added for Saturday's Belmont." James Caesar Petrillo was the prominent leader of the American Federation of Musicians.

28. Red Smith, "Defend Yourself at All Times," *New York Herald Tribune,* June 13, 1956. To the same effect, see also Lou O'Neill, "Beat Needles and Take the $," *Long Island Star-Journal,* June 14, 1956. "The only preparation we know of is that the band will play 'The Sidewalks of New York' and it will be piped over the loud-speakers."

29. Len Tracy, "The 88th Belmont," *Thoroughbred Record*, June 23, 1956, 23.

30. "This Week's Races," *Blood-Horse*, June 23, 1956, 1329.

31. James Roach, "Favorite Nips Career Boy by Neck in $119,650 Test," *New York Times*, June 17, 1956.

32. Whitney Tower, "And Still Champ," *Sports Illustrated*, June 25, 1956, 34–37.

33. Al Buck, "Needles Earned Vacation at Jersey Shore," *New York Post*, June 18, 1956; Roach, "Favorite Nips Career Boy."

34. Tracy, "88th Belmont," 23.

35. Harold Phelps Stokes, "Cheer Al Smith to 'Sidewalks of New York,'" *New York Post*, July 1, 1920.

36. "Ten Candidates Are Named in Day of Demonstration," *Baltimore Sun*, July 1, 1920.

37. When Al Smith learned in 1933 that James W. Blake, who wrote the lyrics for "Sidewalks of New York," was destitute, he took action to ensure that the man responsible for his campaign song "would never be in want." "'Al' Smith Rose from Slums to Win Worldwide Esteem," *Washington Post*, October 5, 1944.

38. https://en.wikipedia.org/wiki/The_Sidewalks_of_New_York.

39. "Folk Song Censors Stir a Kentuckian's Wrath," *Associated Press, Chicago Tribune*, August 2, 1957.

40. Jamie Malanowski, "Maryland, My Maryland," *New York Times Opinionator*, May 1, 2011. http://opinionator.blogs.nytimes.com/2011/05/01/maryland-my-maryland/.

41. Colleen Glenney Boggs, "A War of Words," *New York Times Blogs*, October 2, 2012.

42. John Wagner, "O'Malley, Who's Pushed for Retiring the Confederate Flag in S.C., Governed a State with Its Own Civil War Controversy," *Washington Post Blogs*, June 23, 2015.

43. Pamela K. Brodowsky and Tom Philbin (in cooperation with Churchill Downs, Inc.), *Two Minutes to Glory: The Official History of the Kentucky Derby* (New York: HarperCollins, 2007), 11–12.

44. James C. Nicholson, *The Kentucky Derby* (Lexington: University of Kentucky Press, 2012), 63–64, citing the *Louisville Courier-Journal*, May 8, 1921. The *Cincinnati Enquirer* reported that "My Old Kentucky Home" was played after the victory of Alan-A-Dale in the 1902 Derby. The then popular song, "She Was Bred in Old Kentucky," was played before the horses went to post. "Son of a Famous Sire, Alan-A-Dale Repeats the Victory of Halma," *Cincinnati Enquirer*, May 4, 1902.

45. Nicholson, *The Kentucky Derby*, 63–64; "Gallant Fox Wins Derby," *New York Times*, May 18, 1930, appears to be that newspaper's earliest report of the song being played to accompany the post parade at the Derby.

46. Nicholson, *The Kentucky Derby*, 63 -64, citing Henry McLemore, "Roman Soldier and Whiskolo Follow In," *Milwaukee Journal*, May 5, 1935.

47. Frank Graham, "Setting the Pace," *New York Sun*, March 18, 1939.

48. The acerbic Westbrook Pegler described the playing of the song as follows in 1929: "Just before the horses went to the post for the Preakness, half a dozen beefy red-faced characters who looked as though they had not been born but written by Charles Dickens, got up on a little platform under the judges' stand and unsheathed six of the deadliest silver cornets that ever punished any set of acoustics. After a few premonitory grunts, the boys gathered their bugles in a most disheartening rendition of 'Maryland, My Maryland' the anthem of the Free State." Westbrook Pegler, "Dr. Freeland—Wins the Hike—Home to Oats," *Washington Post*, May 11, 1929. In 1927, the song was played to accompany the governor of Maryland as he

entered the steward's stand at Pimlico. W. J. Macbeth, "H. P. Whitney's Bostonian Wins Rich Preakness," *New York Herald Tribune*, May 10, 1927.

49. Tower, "And Still Champ."

50. "The Belmont? Oh Sure That's the Seventh Race," *New York Times*, June 6, 1965.

51. The Belmont Stakes was run at nearby Aqueduct Race Track between 1963 and 1967 while Belmont Park was being renovated.

52. "The Belmont? Oh Sure That's the Seventh Race," *New York Times*, June 6, 1965.

53. Stan Isaacs, "Why the Belmont Is a Great Race," *Newsday*, June 3, 1979. Traditionally, the Belmont Stakes was run as the next to last race on the day's schedule and its move from sixth to seventh to eighth race reflected the increase in the number of races over the years on the day it was run.

54. Isaacs, "Why the Belmont Is a Great Race."

55. William Grimes, "Belmont Awaits Its Annual Return to Glory," *New York Times*, June 9, 2011; Lester Rodney, "We Started Covering the Ponies . . . and Why," *Daily Worker*, October 11, 1947.

56. Stanley Levey, "Racing Now Virtual King of Sports, Topping Baseball in Gate Appeal," *New York Times*, April 30, 1953. Ebbets Field attendance on April 15, 1947, when Robinson "broke the color line" was 26,623; attendance that day at Jamaica Race Track, 27,306—and this was a weekday afternoon, mind you.

57. Palmer, "Views of the Turf," May 31, 1948.

58. For the attendance records on which Figure 1 is based, see Table of Attendance at Major New York Horse Races 1946–2016. The authors thank Robert J. Fetter for preparing Figure 1.

59. Grimes, "Belmont Awaits Its Annual Return to Glory."

60. Liebman, "Learning from the 1960s," July 22, 2005.

61. Quoted in Henry D. Fetter, "Why No One Goes to the Racetrack Anymore," *Atlantic Online*, December 15, 2010, at http://www.theatlantic.com/entertainment/archive/2010/12/whynoonegoestotheracetrackanymore/68016/ (accessed September 29, 2016).

62. See Liebman, "Learning from the 1960s," July 22, 2005.

63. Isaacs, "Why the Belmont Is a Great Race."

64. Cindy Pierson Dulay, "Belmont Stakes Traditions," http://horseracing.about.com/od/belmontstakes/ss/aabeltraditions.htm#step4 (accessed September 29, 2016).

65. Ed Fountaine, "Jay-Z's 'Empire' Vanquishes Old Blue Eyes," *New York Post*, June 5, 2010.

66. Richard Rosenblatt, "Sinatra's Voice Returns to Belmont Stakes," June 4, 2011, Associated Press, http://archive.boston.com/ae/music/articles/2011/06/04/sinatras_voice_returns_to_belmont_stakes/ (accessed September 29, 2016).

67. See Bennett Liebman, "Ending the Triple Crown Curse," June 10, 2008, http://therail.blogs.nytimes.com/2008/06/10/endingthetriplecrowncurse/ (accessed September 29, 2016), and Henry D. Fetter, "The Curse of the Belmont Stakes," *Atlantic Online*, June 7, 2014. Only quibblers pointed out that no horse had completed a Triple Crown by winning the Belmont in the eighteen years before "Sidewalks" had been replaced in 1997. John Scheinman, "Five Myths about the Triple Crown," *Washington Post*, May 30, 2014; see the response to Scheinman in Henry D. Fetter, "The Curse of the Belmont Stakes," June 7, 2014, *Atlantic Online* at http://www.theatlantic.com/entertainment/archive/2014/06/thecurseofthebelmontstakes/372358/ (accessed September 29, 2016).

68. Grimes, "Belmont Awaits Its Return to Glory."

69. Grimes, "Belmont Awaits Its Return to Glory."

70. In 2012, I'll Have Another, the winner of the Kentucky Derby and Preakness, was scratched the day before the Belmont and did not run, but that came about after most people had made their plans to attend the race. The crowd for the 2016 Belmont, which did not feature a Triple Crown possibility, was announced at 60,114.

## 8. New York City's First Ballparks

1. Steven Riess, *City Games: The Evolution of American Urban Society and the Rise of Sports* (Urbana: University of Illinois Press, 1989), 9.

2. Melvin Adelman, *A Sporting Time: New York City and the Rise of Modern Athletics* (Urbana: University of Illinois Press, 1990); Stephen Hardy, *How Boston Played* (Boston, MA: Northeastern University Press, 1982).

3. Frank Litsky, "Now Pittsfield Lays Claim to Baseball's Origins," *New York Times*, May 12, 2004, D6.

4. Fox Butterfield, "Cooperstown? Hoboken? Try New York City," *New York Times*, October 4, 1990, B14.

5. Michael Benson, *Ballparks of North America: A Comprehensive Historical Reference to Baseball Grounds, Yards, and Stadiums, 1845 to Present* (Jefferson, NC: McFarland, 1989), 250.

6. Benson, *Ballparks of North America*, 252.

7. For more thorough analysis of how class was a factor in nineteenth-century organized sport, see Steven A. Riess, *Sport in Industrial America, 1850–1920* (Wheeling, IL: Harlan Davidson, 1995), 6–8.

8. Glenn Stout, *The Dodgers: 120 Years of Dodger's Baseball* (New York: Houghton Mifflin, 2004), 13.

9. George B. Kirsch, *The Creation of American Team Sports: Baseball and Cricket, 1838–1872* (Urbana: University of Illinois Press, 1989), 95.

10. Stephen Guschov, *The Red Stockings of Cincinnati: Base Ball's First All-Professional Team and Its 1869 and 1870 Seasons* (Jefferson, NC: McFarland, 1998).

11. John B. Manbeck, "Brooklyn," in *The Encyclopedia of New York State*, ed. Peter Eisenstadt and Laura-Eve Moss (Syracuse, NY: Syracuse University Press, 2005), 218–22; Edwin G. Burrows, "New York City," in *The Encyclopedia of New York State*, ed. Eisenstadt and Moss, 1062–77.

12. John Thorn, *Baseball in the Garden of Eden: The Secret History of the Early Game* (New York: Simon and Schuster, 2012), 116–17.

13. "The Great Baseball Match at the Fashion Course—Brooklyn Beaten," *New York Times*, July 21, 1858, 5.

14. "A Noted Pick-Pocket Arrested," *New York Times*, July 21, 1858, 5.

15. "The Great Baseball Match on the Fashion Race-Course—Long Island," *New York Times*, August 18, 1858, 5.

16. "Sporting Intelligence—The Base Ball Match at the Fashion Race Course," *New York Times*, September 7, 1858, 5.

17. "Base Ball: Brooklyn Nine vs. New York Nine—New York Victorious," *New York Times*, September 11, 1858, 1. "Fashion Base Ball Match," *Brooklyn Daily Eagle*, September 10, 1858, 3.

18. Adelman, *A Sporting Time*, 126.

19. John B. Manbeck, "Brooklyn," in *The Encyclopedia of New York State*, ed. Eisenstadt and Moss, 218–22.

20. Charles W. Cheape, *Moving the Masses: Urban Public Transit in New York, Boston, and Philadelphia, 1880–1912* (Cambridge, MA: Harvard University Press, 1980), 25. Note: because transit options were privately owned and managed, the fee charged to patrons could vary, but five cents was a common benchmark for the time.

21. Christopher G. Bates and Sarah Teetzel, "Technology," in *Sports in America: From Colonial Times to the Twenty-First Century*, vol. 3, ed. Steven Riess (London, UK: Routledge, 2015), 882.

22. Michael Gershman, *Diamonds: The Evolution of the Ballpark* (New York: Houghton Mifflin, 1993), 12–13.

23. "The Union Pond," *Brooklyn Daily Eagle*, December 8, 1862, 2.

24. "The Rutledge Club and the New Grounds," *Brooklyn Daily Eagle*, April 10, 1862, 2.

25. John B. Manbeck, "Brooklyn," in *The Encyclopedia of New York State*, ed. Eisenstadt and Moss, 219.

26. "Out Door Sports: Inauguration of the Union Base Ball and Cricket Grounds," *Brooklyn Daily Eagle*, May 16, 1862, 2.

27. Benson, *Ballparks of North America*, 52–53.

28. "The Atlantics Still Champions: Overwhelming Defeat of the Athletics," *Brooklyn Daily Eagle*, September 17, 1862, 2.

29. "Sports and Pastimes—Base Ball," *Brooklyn Daily Eagle*, July 13, 1867, 2.

30. Stout, *The Dodgers*, 14.

31. Richard Miller and Gregory Rhodes, "The Life and Times of Old Cincinnati Ballparks," *Queen City Heritage* (Summer 1988): 25–41.

32. Noel Hynd, *The Giants of the Polo Grounds: The Glorious Times of Baseball's New York Giants* (New York: Doubleday, 1988), 22–24.

33. Gershman, *Diamonds*, 40–41.

34. Gershman, *Diamonds*, 42–43.

35. Benson, *Ballparks of North America*, 255.

36. Benson, *Ballparks of North America*, 256.

37. Stew Thornley, *Land of the Giants: New York's Polo Grounds* (Philadelphia, PA: Temple University Press, 2000), 41–43.

38. Thornley, *Land of the Giants*, 45.

39. Robert Trumpbour, *The New Cathedrals: Politics and Media in the History of Stadium Construction* (Syracuse, NY: Syracuse University Press, 2007), 12–13.

40. Hynd, *The Giants of the Polo Grounds*, 61.

41. Thornley, *Land of the Giants*, 46–47.

42. Hynd, *The Giants of the Polo Grounds*, 68–69.

43. Thornley, *Land of the Giants*, 48.

44. Hynd, *The Giants of the Polo Grounds*, 75.

45. Hynd, *The Giants of the Polo Grounds*, 74.

46. Benson, *Ballparks of North America*, 59.

47. William F. McNeil, *The Dodgers Encyclopedia*, 2nd ed. (Champaign, IL: Sports Publishing, 2003), 133.

48. Benson, *Ballparks of North America*, 61.

49. Mark Amour and Daniel Levitt, *Paths to Glory: How Great Baseball Teams Got That Way* (Washington, DC: Potomac Books, 2004), 10–12.

50. Benson, *Ballparks of North America*, 61.

51. "Many of the Superbas Would Like a Change," *Pittsburgh Press*, January 10, 1905, 12.

52. Benson, *Ballparks of North America*, 61–62.

53. Warren Wilbert, *The Arrival of the American League: Ban Johnson and the 1901 Challenge to the National League Monopoly* (Jefferson, NC: McFarland, 2007), 6.

54. Richard Scheinin, *Field of Screams: The Dark Underside of America's National Pastime* (New York: W. W. Norton, 1994), 80–83.

55. Benson, *Ballparks of North America*, 264.

56. Steven A. Riess, *Touching Base: Professional Baseball and American Culture in the Progressive Era* (Urbana: University of Illinois Press, 1999), 109.

57. Ray Istorico, *Greatness in Waiting: An Illustrated History of the Early New York Yankees, 1903–1919* (Jefferson, NC: McFarland, 2008), 7.

58. Riess, *Touching Base*, 110.

59. Benson, *Ballparks of North America*, 265.

60. Marty Appel, *Pinstripe Empire: The New York Yankees from before the Babe to after the Boss* (New York: Bloomsbury, 2012), 19–20.

61. "Baseball's Big Crowd: Auspicious Opening of American League Grounds in This City," *New York Times*, May 1, 1903, 7.

62. Benson, *Ballparks of North America*, 266.

63. "Will Make Money: Highlanders Not a Financial Frost," *Sporting News*, September 26, 1903, 5.

64. Benson, *Ballparks of North America*, 265.

65. Benson, *Ballparks of North America*, 258.

66. "Polo Grounds Go Up in Flames," *New York Tribune*, April 14, 1911, 1.

67. Trumpbour, *The New Cathedrals*, 336.

68. "Crandall Comes to Giants Rescue," *New York Times*, April 16, 1911, Sporting Section, 1.

69. Gershman, *Diamonds*, 53.

70. Trumpbour, *The New Cathedrals*, 19.

71. Riess, *Touching Base*, 116.

72. Thornley, *Land of the Giants*, 65.

73. Thornley, *Land of the Giants*, 65.

74. Thornley, *Land of the Giants*, 66.

75. James S. Hirsch, *Willie Mays: The Life, the Legend* (New York: Scribner, 2010), 101.

76. Glenn Stout, *Fenway, 1912: The Birth of a Ballpark, a Championship Season, and Fenway's Remarkable First Year* (New York: Houghton Mifflin Harcourt, 2011), 234.

77. Bob McGee, *The Greatest Ballpark Ever Built: Ebbets Field and the Story of the Brooklyn Dodgers* (New Brunswick, NJ: Rivergate Books, 2005), 43–47.

78. McGee, *The Greatest Ballpark Ever Built*, 47.

79. Benson, *Ballparks of North America*, 63.

80. McNeil, *The Dodgers Encyclopedia*, 6.

81. Benson, *Ballparks of North America*, 64–65.

## 9. Municipal Golf in New York City since the 1960s

1. Douglas Martin, "The Urban Golfer," *New York Times*, June 11, 1995, CY14.

2. For the public parks movement, see Steven A. Riess, *City Games: The Evolution of American Society and the Rise of Sports* (Urbana: University of Illinois Press, 1989), 41–46, 128–32. For Boston, see Stephen Hardy, *How Boston Played: Sport, Recreation, and Community, 1865–1915* (Boston: Northeastern University Press, 1982), chap. 2

3. Thomas Bendelow, "Municipal Golf," *American City* 15 (July 1916): 1.

4. Bendelow, "Municipal Golf," 5–6.

5. *New York Sun,* May 5, 1895; H. B. Martin, *Fifty Years of American Golf* (New York: Dodd, Mead, 1936), 222–23; *New York Times,* April 21, 1896, 3; *Spirit of the Times,* November 21, 1896, 587, December 5, 1896, 637.

6. "Tourney Open at Van Cortlandt Park, Oldest City Course in the U.S.," *New York Times,* July 7, 1974, 154.

7. Newspaper clipping, 1896, scrapbook of Frank Crane, U.S.G.A. library; *New York Times,* August 17, 1899, 6.

8. "Public Golf Courses," *New York Times,* August 17, 1899, 6.

9. "Golfers Eager to Play," *New York Times,* March 26, 1899, 25.

10. *New York Times,* March 8, 1900, 10.

11. H. B. Martin, *Fifty Years of American Golf* (New York: Dodd, Mead, 1936), 87.

12. William Garrot Brown, "Golf," *Atlantic Monthly* 89 (June 1902): 735.

13. *New York Times,* March 12, 1899, 8, March 26, 1899, 15, December 24, 1899, 10, March 6, 1900, 13, March 11, 1900, 20, March 18, 1900, 10, May 1, 1900, 10, January 13, 1901, 19, October 13, 1913, 8, April 12, 1914, sec. 5, 3, April 16, 1914, 7; Jerome D. Travers and Grantland Rice, *The Winning Shot* (Garden City, NY: Doubleday, Page Co., 1915), 203–6.

14. *New York Times,* December 20, 1922, 26.

15. Peter Levine, "'Our Crowd' at Play: The Elite Jewish Country Club in the 1920s," as quoted in Steven A. Riess, ed., *Sports and the American Jew* (Syracuse, NY: Syracuse University Press, 1998), 168.

16. Riess, *Sports and the American Jew,* 169.

17. Riess, *Sports and the American Jew,* 175.

18. Bill White, "In and around New York," *Chicago Defender,* December 24, 1921, 10.

19. Calvin H. Sinnette, *Forbidden Fairways: African Americans and the Game of Golf* (Chelsea, MI: Sleeping Bear Press, 1998), 55.

20. A. B. Britton, "Taking Mental Hazard out of City Golf," *New York Times,* June 2, 1935, SM11.

21. "The Disgrace of Gotham's Public Courses," *Golf Illustrated* 40 (January 1934): 13; "Quick Action," *Golf Illustrated* 41 (April 1934): 9.

22. "Bobby Jones Advises WPA on Building and Improving 600 Municipal Golf Links," *New York Times,* April 26, 1936, 1; William P. Richardson, "Jones Pays Visit to WPA Courses," *New York Times,* May 1, 1936, 29.

23. "Golf for Crises," *New York Times,* May 3, 1936, E8.

24. John A. Brennan, "Million Rounds Yearly, Aim of New York Public Golf," *Golfdom* 23 (May 1949): 41, 44, 46; "Pros Help New York Police Build Big Golf League," *Golfdom* 22 (July 1948): 33, 36, 76; Larry Robinson, "Golf in Gotham," *Golf Digest* 4 (August 1953): 36–39; *New York Times,* December 31, 1944, 28

25. "City Plan to Fill Marsh Is Opposed," *New York Times,* December 14, 1948, 31; "City Wildlife Safe in Old Homestead," *New York Times,* December 11, 1948, 17.

26. "President Calls Golf, Fishing, Shooting Beneficial as Mild Exercise in Outdoors," *New York Times,* October 16, 1958, 18.

27. "President Urges Golf," *New York Times,* June 9, 1960, 24.

28. Barry Gottehrer, "The Widening World of TV Golf," *Golf* 5 (April 1963): 59.

29. Paul Gardner, "How Viewers Rate Golf on Television," *Golf Digest* 14 (June 1963): 38.

30. Gardner, "How Viewers Rate Golf on Television," 41.

31. Gardner, "How Viewers Rate Golf on Television," 45.

32. Lincoln A. Werden, "A New Deal on an Old Golf Course," *New York Times,* April 3, 1966, 3.

33. "Long Gray Lines Find Way to Tee," *New York Times,* April 3, 1966, S1.

34. Dave Eisenberg, "A Course Built on Garbage," *Golf Digest* 14 (August 1963): 53.

35. Interviews with Steven Schlossman and Robert Weintraub, December 19, 2014, February 13, 2015.

36. Interviews with Steven Schlossman and Robert Weintraub, December 19, 2014, February 13, 2015.

37. Lee Dembart, "City Weighing Sale of Golf Courses as Way to Help Close Budget Gap," *New York Times,* December 28, 1978, B1; "A Tale of Two Cities," *Golf Digest* 32 (March 1986): 39–41.

38. David Owen, "No Sleep Till Brooklyn," GolfDigest.com, July 2013, 142.

39. Robert Carney, "Take My Golf Course, Please," *Golf Digest* 37 (March 1986): 39–41.

40. Carney, "Take My Golf Course, Please," 41–42; Paul Hughes, "American Golf Scores on OC, National Scene," *Orange County Business Journal* 18 (September 11, 1995): 20; Kent Hansen Wadsworth, "Strike It Niche!: Municipal Golf Courses," *Journal of Property* 61 (May/June 1996): 18.

41. Bob Casey, "Opening Day at Dyker Beach," *Golf Digest* 17 (May 1966): 39.

42. Larry Sheehan, "Playing Dyker Beach with Laverne and Shirley—and Tom," *Golf Digest* 29 (June 1978): 173–74.

43. Greg Midland, "Concrete Jungle, But an Oasis Is Never Far Away," *New York Times,* July 16, 2012, D7.

44. Douglas Martin, "Chelsea Piers, Where Grown-Ups Play, Too," *New York Times,* August 4, 2000, E31.

45. William Barry Furlong, "It's a Three-Billion Dollar Business," *New York Times,* June 5, 1966, 266.

46. Furlong, "It's a Three-Billion Dollar Business," 96.

47. Furlong, "It's a Three-Billion Dollar Business," 96.

48. Douglas Martin, "The Urban Golfer," *New York Times,* June 11, 1995, CY1.

49. Laura Seigle and Mike Claffey, "Body Found Hanged in Bx," *New York Daily News,* August 29, 1999, 53.

50. Thomas J. Lueck, "In Convention Protest, Vandals Spray Paint Bronx Golf Course," *New York Times,* August 28, 2004, B6.

51. Bob Casey, "Opening Day at Dyker Beach," *Golf Digest* 17 (May 1966): 39; Douglas Martin, "The Urban Golfer," *New York Times,* June 11, 1995, CY1, 14; *Golf Digest* 52 (July 2001): 23.

52. Greg Midland, "Concrete Jungle, But an Oasis Is Never Far Away," *New York Times,* July 16, 2012, D7; Andrew Boryga, "After 7-Year Makeover, Bronx Links of Legend Try to Reclaim the Past," *New York Times,* April 28, 2014, A18.

53. Ray Rivera, "Plan for Trump to Run a Bronx Golf Course Has Critics," *New York Times,* January 10, 2012, A18.

54. Jennifer Bleyer, "For a Diamond in the Rough, Patience Wears Thin," *New York Times,* November 26, 2006, CY1; John Paul Newport, "Course Grows in the Bronx," *Wall Street Journal,* October 3, 2009: W5; Rivera, "Plan for Trump to Run a Bronx Golf Course Has Critics," A18.

55. Ginia Bellafante, ". . . 18 Holes in the Head," *New York Times,* September 30, 2012, CT1; Bradley Klein, *Wide Open Fairways* (Lincoln: University of Nebraska Press, 2013), 135–36, 145.

56. Bellafante, "... 18 Holes in the Head," CT5.

57. David Owen, "A Plea for Pushcarts: Going Old School Is What Trump's New Place Needs," *GolfDigest.com*, September 2015, 66.

58. David Owen, "Playing out of the Snow," *New Yorker*, March 28, 2005, 26–32; Corey Kilgannon, "Brooklyn Golfers Ignore Impossibility of Playing," *New York Times*, January 12, 2004, B4.

59. Al Barkow, "Lee—The People's Pro," *Golf* 14 (September 1971): 25.

60. Barkow, "Lee—The People's Pro," 25.

61. Barkow, "Lee—The People's Pro," 75.

62. Corey Kilgannon, "Korean Word for Golf? There's a Place in Queens You're Sure to Hear It," *New York Times*, June 20, 2005, B4.

63. Frank Lisky, "Municipal Courses Open Today," *New York Times*, April 1, 1967, 23; see also Pete McDaniel, *Uneven Lies: The Heroic Story of African-Americans in Golf* (Greenwich, CT: American Golfer, 2000).

64. Farrell Evans, "Too Few Good Men," *Golfing Magazine* 53 (March 2011): 116.

65. Quoted in Rhonda Glenn, *The Illustrated History of Women's Golf* (Dallas, TX: Taylor Publishing Company, 1991), 26.

66. Marcia Chambers, *The Unplayable Lie* (New York: Pocket Books, 1995), 130–31.

67. Chambers, *The Unplayable Lie*, 131–32.

68. Chambers, *The Unplayable Lie*, 136–37.

69. Chambers, *The Unplayable Lie*, 137.

70. Chambers, *The Unplayable Lie*, 140.

71. Lincoln A. Werden, "City Names First Woman Golf Pro," *New York Times*, April 18, 1971, S4.

72. Richard Singer and Forrest Richardson, "8 Tips: Put the Swing Back in Your Game for Improving Municipal Golf Facilities," *Parks and Recreation* 44 (January 2009): 23–27, 10; Lisa W. Foderaro, "Luxury Public Golf, Run by Trump, Opens on Former Dump," *New York Times*, April 1, 2015.

## 10. During the Heyday of Jewish Sports in Gotham

1. On the history of Jewish participation in sports throughout the ages and the rationale for such activity, see Jeffrey S. Gurock, *Judaism's Encounter with American Sports* (Bloomington: Indiana University Press, 2005), chapters 1 and 2. Alan Bodner, *When Boxing Was a Jewish Sport* (Westport, CT: Praeger, 1997), 177–78, and Jewsinsports.com. On Nordau's attitude, see *Max Nordau to His People: A Summons and a Challenge* (New York: Scopus, 1941), 88. On the connection of sports to socialist movements among Jews, see Jack Jacobs, "Jewish Workers' Sports Movements in Interwar Poland; Shtern and Morgenshtern in Comparative Perspective, "in *Jews, Sport and the Rites of Citizenship*, ed. Jack Kugelmass (Urbana: University of Illinois Press, 2007), 115.

2. See Peter Levine, *From Ellis Island to Ebbets Field: Sport and the American Jewish Experience* (New York: Oxford University Press, 1992), 27.

3. A. L. Shands, "The Cheder on the Hill: Some Notes on C.C.N.Y," *Menorah Journal* (March 1929): 263–69. On the negative reference to Jews at the college, see Jeffrey S. Gurock, *Jews in Gotham: New York Jews in a Changing City, 1920–2010* (New York: New York University Press, 2012), 46. There is a difference of opinion among contemporary observers and scholars

as to the proportion of Jews at CCNY during the early twentieth century. Shands, writing in 1929, said that "the student body . . . is conservatively 85 percent Jewish" ("The Cheder on the Hill," 264). Selma Berrol argued that "the proportion of Russian and Polish names [in the *Alumni Register*] increased from less than 1% in 1883 to 11% in 1923, but German Jewish names outnumbered all others throughout the period." To be sure, some of these so-called German names might have been ethnically and linguistically of Polish Jewish ancestry. She also notes that the graduating classes were very small in the early decades of the twentieth century and that "not until the thirties were [there] very large classes, which were overwhelmingly Jewish and about 50% of Russian and Polish origin." See Selma Berrol, "Education and Economic Mobility: The Jewish Experience in New York City, 1880–1920," *American Jewish Historical Quarterly* (March 1976): 262. Irving Howe, however, placed the proportion of the East European Jews at CCNY as of 1903 at the still small college at more than 75 percent and that the graduating class of 1910 had 90 Jewish students out of a class of 110. See Irving Howe, *The World of Our Fathers: The Journey of the East European Jews to America and the Life They Found and Made* (New York: Random House, 1976), 281. Howe's numbers seem to have been derived from S. Willis Rudy, *The College of the City of New York: A History, 1847–1957* (New York: City College Press, 1949), 292–93. On the percentages of Jews at Columbia and discriminatory policies, see Marcia Graham Synott, *The Half-Opened Door: Discrimination and Admissions at Harvard, Yale and Princeton,* 1900–1970 (Westport, CT: Greenwood, 1979), 158, 195.

4. See Stanley Frank, *The Jew in Sport* (New York: Miles, 1936), 49–50, noted in Levine, *From Ellis Island to Ebbets Field*, 27.

5. Rudy, *The College of the City of New York*, 35, 78, 95, 100, 174–76, 184, 189–92.

6. Rudy, The College of the City of New York, 189.

7. On the importance of sports at American universities in the last half of the nineteenth century and beyond, see E. Digby Baltzell, *The Protestant Establishment: Aristocracy and Caste in America* (New York: Random House, 1964), 129–30; Edwin E. Slosson, *Great American Universities* (Chicago: University of Chicago Press, 1910), 47; John R. Thelin, *Games Colleges Play: Scandal and Reform in Intercollegiate Athletics* (Baltimore: Johns Hopkins University Press, 1994), 19–20. Gerald R. Gems, *For Pride, Profit and Patriarchy: Football and the Incorporation of American Cultural Values* (Lanham, MD: Scarecrow Press, 2000), 20; See also, Dan A. Oren, *Joining the Club: A History of Jews and Yale* (New Haven, CT: Yale University Press, 1985), 43, 66.

8. Rudy, *The College of the City of New York*, 191. On the two CCNY players in the Yale-Princeton game, see *College Mercury*, December 4, 1896, 69.

9. Rudy, *The College of the City of New York*, 251–52, 264, 289, 296, 324, 329.

10. For the mission of settlement houses and Jews among other immigrants, see David Nasaw, *Children of the City: At Work and at Play* (Garden City, NY: Anchor Press/Doubleday, 1985). On the public school and the Jews, see Stephan Brumberg, *Going to America, Going to School: The Jewish Immigrant Public School Encounter in Turn-of-the-Century New York* (New York: Praeger, 1986). On how these Jewish students were perceived by faculty, see Rudy, *The College of the City of New York*, 293.

11. Team rosters do not identify the religious background of the players who competed. Here I am relying on Jewish-sounding names as an indicator of ethnicity. Still, many of the stars on the team have been identified as Jews in the various compendia and encyclopedias of Jewish athletes. Accordingly, it may be noted that year by year between 1925 and 1940, the percentage of Jewish players who were awarded a varsity letter was never less than two-thirds of

those recognized. These tentative statistics were derived from the names that appeared yearly in the college yearbook, *Microcosm* (1925–1940).

12. On the beginnings of college basketball, see Neil D. Isaacs, *All the Right Moves: A History of College Basketball* (New York: Harper and Row, 1994), 39–46. On the bonding experience for CCNY students at their home games, see Rudy, *The College of the City of New York*, 297.

13. The statistics on the won-loss records of CCNY teams are derived from the files of the school's athletic department that are maintained at the CCNY Archives. Particularly in the early years of the twentieth century, the game-by-game scores were not always available in the school's yearbooks or newspaper. This lacuna is true for all sports at CCNY. Thanks are due to Professor Sydney Van Nort, college archivist, and her assistant for making these records and other important sources available.

14. Sam Goldaper, "Nat Holman Is Dead at 98, Led C.C.N.Y. Champions," *New York Times*, February 13, 1995, on-line edition. On the criticism of CCNY fans by their own student newspaper, see Arieh Sclar, "A Sport at Which Jews Excel: Jewish Basketball in American Society" (Unpublished diss., Stony Brook University, 2008), 68. On the importance of these games to students, see Meyer Liben, "CCNY: A Memoir," in *City in the Center: A Collection of Writings by CCNY Alumni and Faculty*, ed. Betty Rizzo and Barry Wallenstein (New York: City College of New York, 1983), 50.

15. Shands, "The Cheder on the Hill," 267; Liben, "CCNY," 50.

16. For a strong sense, through interviews with CCNY alumni and others in New York, of what the 1950 triumph meant to the college, see "City Dump: The Story of the 1951 CCNY Basketball Scandal," George Roy and Steven Hillard Stern, directors [HBO, 1998].

17. On the multiplicity of "minor" sports and their significance at CCNY, see, for example, "Award Insignia to 55 Athletes," *Campus*, April 23, 1921, 1. On the mix of general and sports news in this newspaper, see *Campus*, December 9, 1921, 1.

18. Arthur Taft, "125 Years of Sports at City College," *City College Alumnus*, June 1973, 11–12. See also "President Favors Varsity Football," *Campus*, November 29. 1921, 1.

19. Stan Frank, "Sport Sparks," *Campus*, October 24, 1928, 4; "College Eleven Hailed as Best in Grid Annals," *Campus*, October 24, 1928, 1; *Microcosm* (1929): 194; Shands, "The Cheder on the Hill," 268. On Frank Merriwell, see "Frank Merriwell," web.stanford.edu.

20. "Morris R. Cohen Discusses Jews' Thinking Traits," *Campus*, November 9, 1928, 1. See also, on page 1 the lineups for the Norwich game.

21. Shands, "The Cheder on the Hill," 268.

22. "Great Hall Meeting Climaxes 'Boycott Olympics' Campaign," *Campus*, October 18, 1935, 1; "5,000 Students to Mobilize in Peace Assembly Today," *Campus*, November 8, 1935, 1.

23. "Conclusions to Be Drawn," *Campus*, February 25, 1931, 2; "S.C. Charter Day Boycott Cuts Attendance to 1,000," *Campus*, May 10, 1935, 1. On the athletes' support of ROTC and the administration, see Rudy, *The College of the City of New York*, 419; see also on this issue, 5. "More Suspended in City College Row," *New York Times*, June 3, 1933, 15, and "186 Awards Made at City College," *New York Times*, June 3, 1933, 9.

24. "Enter Mr. Brundage," *Campus*, October 29, 1935, 2; "Boycott the Olympics," *Campus*, October 11, 1935, 2; "Yale and the Olympics," *Campus*, November 8, 1935, 2; "Campus Launches Drive to Boycott '36 Olympics," *Campus*, October 9, 1935, 1.

25. On the problems Glickman and Stoller faced in Berlin, see Peter Levine, "'My Father and I: We Didn't Get Our Medals': Marty Glickman's American Jewish Odyssey," *American Jewish History* (March 1989): 399–424. For the CCAA position, see *Microcosm* (1936): 140.

On President Robinson's stance, see "'Boycott Olympics' Petitions to Circulate through College," *Campus*, October 11, 1935, 1.

26. "Olympics Fencing Aspirant Berlin-Bound if Selected," *Campus*, December 6, 1935, 1; "Olympics to Be Played with Guns Says Fencing Coach Joseph Vince," *Campus*, December 10, 1935, 3.

27. Richard Goldstein, "Henry Wittenberg, Champion Wrestler, Dies at 91," *New York Times*, March 9, 2010, on-line edition. See also, "Henry Wittenberg Wins Olympic Title," *Campus*, September 20, 1948, 7.

28. Edward Shapiro, "The Shame of the City: CCNY Basketball, 1950–51," in *Jews, Sports and the Rites of Citizenship*, ed. Jack Kugelmaas (Urbana: University of Illinois Press, 2007), 175, 184–85, 187, 189–91. For memoirs of what the scandal meant to students as Jews, see Avery Corman's recollections in "City Dump."

29. Shapiro, "The Shame of the City: CCNY Basketball, 1950–51," 187; the schedule of games during these seasons was compiled from the records of the CCNY athletics department. See also, "Cagers to Fly West in February on Unprecedented Trip to Coast," *Campus*, January 5, 1949, 4. On the CCNY-Yeshiva game, see "Cagers Bow to Yeshiva in First League Game," *Campus*, December 11, 1959, 4.

30. On the growth of Yeshiva's program, see Gurock, *Judaism's Encounter with American Sports*, 120–23. On recruitment successes by McGuire, see J. Samuel Walker, *ACC Basketball: The Story of the Rivalries, Traditions and Scandals of the Atlantic Coast Conference* (Chapel Hill: University of North Carolina Press, 2011), 106–7.

31. Bob Jacobson, "Only Six Lettermen return to Booters: 42-Game Undefeated Streak on Line," *Campus*, September 21, 1959, 4.

32. For a roster of the 1957 team, see *Observation Post*, October 29, 1957, 4. On Solney's story, see Artie Alexander, "Solney to Replace Departed Sund: Defenseman Slated for Scoring Role," *Observation Post*, November 21, 1958, 4.

33. Ralph Dannheiser, "Meet the Fall Coaches," *Observation Post*, December 5, 1957, 8; Jerry Eskanazi, "Sweat, Hard Work, Makes a Champ," *Observation Post*, September 17, 1957, 2. Phone interview with Gerald Eskanazi, September 27, 2015.

34. "The Spirit," *Campus*, November 4, 1959; "How about It?" *Observation Post*, October 8, 1957, 2.

35. Jerry Eskenazi, "Center Ballroom Packed for Soccer Team Rally," *Observation Post*, October 25, 1957; interview with Gerald Eskenazi.

36. Bob Jacobson, "Booters Score with 27 Seconds Left to Top Williams, 1–0 in NCAA Opener," *Campus*, November 24, 1959, 1; "Recognition," *Campus*, November 24, 1959, 4. See also *Microcosm* (1961): 105.

37. For statistics on Jewish enrollment at CCNY in the early 1960s, see Alfred Jospe, *Jewish Students and Student Services at American Universities* (Washington, DC: B'nai B'rith Hillel Foundation, 1963), 6, 7, 14. The statistics on Jewish players on CCNY varsities was derived from *Microcosm* (1968): 120, 128, 133. The statistics on Jewish members of the school's athletic Hall of Fame were derived from the posting on ccnyalumnivarsityassociation.com.

38. For an overview of the improvement of Jewish status in America after World War II, see Edward Shapiro, *A Time for Healing: American Jewry since World War II* (Baltimore: Johns Hopkins University Press, 1992), 28–42.

39. For a comprehensive examination of changed admissions policies at one elite university in the 1950s–1960s in part in response to the Cold War, see Oren, *Joining the Club*, 173–209.

40. On CCNY's pride in its roster of Nobel Laureates, see CCNY Alumni Association, "Nobel Laureates," http://ccnyalumni.org.

41. William Yardley, "Art Heyman, Star at Duke, Dies at 71," *New York Times*, August 20, 2012, on-line edition. For a listing of All-Americans, see basketball-reference.com.

42. "CCNY Basketball: Caesar at the Rubicon," *Campus*, November 25, 1969, 1; Larry Brooks, "Is There a Fork in the Road?" *Campus*, February 4, 1970, 8.

## 11. Italians and Sport in New York City

1. Gerald R. Gems, Linda J. Borish, and Gertrud Pfister, *Sports in American History: From Colonization to Globalization* (Champaign, IL: Human Kinetics, 2008), 157–58.

2. Spencer M. Di Scala, *Italy: From Revolution to Republic, 1870 to the Present* (Boulder, CO: Westview Press, 1995); M. I. Finley, Denis Mack Smith, and Christopher Duggan, *A History of Sicily* (New York: Elisabeth Sifton, 1987); Gerald R. Gems, *Sport and the Shaping of Italian American Identity* (Syracuse, NY: Syracuse University Press, 2013), 3–4, 7–10. Marx cited in Raymond A. Belliotti, *Seeking Identity: Individualism versus Community in an Ethnic Context* (Lawrence: University Press of Kansas, 1995), 30.

3. Belliotti, *Seeking Identity*, 30.

4. Maria Laurino, *The Italian Americans: A History* (New York: W. W. Norton, 2015), 49.

5. Frances M. Malpezzi and William M. Clements, *Italian-American Folklore* (Little Rock: August House, 1992), 30–31; David R. Roediger, *Working toward Whiteness: How America's Immigrants Became White: The Strange Journey from Ellis Island to the Suburbs* (New York: Basic Books, 2005), 35.

6. *Boston Globe*, June 7, 1903, cited in Lawrence Baldassaro and Richard A. Johnson, eds., *The American Game: Baseball and Ethnicity* (Carbondale: Southern Illinois University Press, 2002), 96–7.

7. Roediger, *Working toward Whiteness*, 77; A. V. Margavio and Jerome J. Salomone, *Bread and Respect: The Italians of Louisiana* (Gretna, LA; Pelican Publishing, 2002), 100.

8. Gems, Borish, and Pfister, *Sports in American History*, 180–81.

9. Gems, *Sport and the Shaping of Italian American Identity*, 22, 32–34, 235.

10. *New York Times*, November 18, 1908, 7.

11. *New York Times*, November 26, 1908, 1, November 28, 1908, 6, December 7, 1908, 10; *Chicago Tribune*, November 26, 1908, 14.

12. Gems, *Sport and the Shaping of Italian American Identity*, 35–37; Matthew P. Llewellyn, "Viva Italia! Viva Italia! Dorando Pietri and the North American Professional Marathon Craze, 1908–10," *International Journal of the History of Sport* 25, no. 6 (2008): 710–36.

13. Gems, *Sport and the Shaping of Italian American Identity*, 37–38; *Janesville (WI) Daily Gazette*, August 8, 1912, 3; *Waterloo (IA) Times-Tribune*, July 30, 1912, 2.

14. Johnny Dundee file, International Boxing Hall of Fame, Canastota, New York.

15. Frankie Genaro file, International Boxing Hall of Fame, Canastota, New York.

16. Willie Garoni file, Baseball Hall of Fame, Cooperstown, New York; Gems, *Sport and the Shaping of Italian American Identity*, 47.

17. Gems, *Sport and the Shaping of Italian American Identity*, 47–49; Ira Berkow, "The Extraordinary Life and Times of Ping Bodie," in *Reaching for the Stars: A Celebration of Italian Americans in Major League Baseball*, ed. Larry Freundlich (New York: Ballantine Books, 2003), 49–64.

18. Gems, *Sport and the Shaping of Italian American Identity,* 82, 129; Fred Glueckstein, "Tony Lazzeri," sabr.org/bioproj/person/1b3c1790 (accessed January 15, 2015); Lawrence Baldassaro, *Beyond DiMaggio: Italian Americans in Baseball* (Lincoln: University of Nebraska Press, 2011), 70 (quote).

19. Tara Krieger, "Frankie Crosetti," sabr.org/bioproj/person/460d26a7 (accessed January 15, 2015).

20. Barb Mantegani, "Tony Cuccinello," sabr.org/bioproj/personal/be5d770b (accessed January 15, 2015).

21. Warren Corbett, "Gus Mancuso," sabr.org/bioproj/person/32dfe3a5 (accessed January 15, 2015).

22. "Frank Klaus Sees Firpo in Action," *New York Times,* September 2, 1923, 18 (quote). See *Uniontown (PA) Morning Herald,* July 16, 1923, 6; and *Oakland Tribune,* September 14, 1923, 34, for similar denigratory examples.

23. This composite description is obtained from Henry L. Farrell, "Dempsey Retains Championship in Great Battle," *Wisconsin State Journal* (September 15, 1932); "Dempsey Retains Title in Ferocious Ring Battle," *Cumberland (MD) Evening Times,* September 15, 1923, 3; "Jack Dempsey Retains Title in Cave-Man Battle with Firpo," *Alton (IL) Evening Telegraph,* September 15, 1923, 6.

24. "Firpo Had the Title within His Grasp," *New York Times,* September 15, 1923, 1 (quote). See Sis Sutherland, "Latin Lacks Ring Wit to Cope with Yank, the Experienced," *Chicago Tribune,* September 15, 1923, 11.

25. Gems, *Sport and the Shaping of Italian American Identity,* 121–22; John Kieran and Arthur Daley, *The Story of the Olympic Games: 776 B.C. to 1960 A.D.* [*sic*] (Philadelphia: J. B. Lippincott, 1961), 123–24 (quote).

26. Gems, *Sport and the Shaping of Italian American Identity,* 90–92, 99–100, 146; Joseph S. Page, *Primo Carnera: The Life and Career of the Heavyweight Boxing Champion* (Jefferson, NC: McFarland, 2011); www.boxrec.com/list_bouts.php?human_id=12086&cat=boxer (accessed January 17, 2015).

27. Noel F. Busch, "Joe DiMaggio: Baseball's Most Sensational Big League Star Starts What Should Be His Best Year So Far," *Life,* May 1, 1939, 62–69 (quotes); Baldassaro and Johnson, *The American Game,* 111, on DiMaggio's debut.

28. Baldassaro, *Beyond DiMaggio,* 226.

29. Baldassaro, *Beyond DiMaggio,* 228.

30. William M. Simons, "Joe DiMaggio and the Ideal of American Masculinity," in *The Cooperstown Symposium on Baseball and American Culture, 1999,* ed. Peter M. Rutkoff (Jefferson, NC: McFarland, 2000), 227–44.

31. Stephen Fox, *The Unknown Internment: An Oral History of the Relocation of Italian Americans during World War II* (Boston: Twayne, 1990).

32. Richard C. Crepeau, SPORTHIST@pdomain.uwindsor.ca.

33. Graziano file, International Boxing Hall of Fame; Thomas Hauser and Stephen Brunt, eds., *The Italian Stallions: Heroes of Boxing's Glory Days* (Toronto: Sport Media Publishing, 2003), 75–113.

34. LaMotta file, International Boxing Hall of Fame; http://officialjakelamotta.com/fight-record (accessed January 17, 2015); Barney Nagler, "The Story of a Champion," in Hauser and Brunt, *The Italian Stallions,* 115–35.

35. http://boxrec.com/media/index.php?title=Human:10923 (accessed January 18, 2015); Gerald R. Gems, *Boxing: A Concise History of the Sweet Science* (Lanham, MD: Rowman and

Littlefield, 2014), 41, 167, 170, 227; Joe Bruno, *Penthouse* clipping, LaMotta file, International Boxing Hall of Fame (quote).

36. http://boxrec.com/media/index.php?title=Human:10923 (accessed January 18, 2015); Gems, *Sport and the Shaping of Italian American Identity*, 153–54, 158–59; Mike Rathet, "I Said 'No' to the Mafia," *Boxing Scene*, clipping, 30–34, 30 (quote) in Giardello file, International Boxing Hall of Fame.

37. Mitchell cited in Michael Oriard, *King Football: Sport and Spectacle in the Golden Age of Radio and Newsreels, Magazines, and the Weekly and Daily Press* (Chapel Hill: University of North Carolina Press, 2001), 256.

38. http ://www.hickoksports.com/biograph/littlelou.shtml.

39. http://vincelombardi.com/ (accessed January 27, 2015); Michael O'Brien, *Vince: A Personal Biography of Vince Lombardi* (New York: William Morrow, 1987), 25, 30; David Maraniss, *When Pride Still Mattered: A Life of Vince Lombardi* (New York: Simon and Schuster, 1999), 146–99.

40. Maraniss, *When Pride Still Mattered*, portrays Lombardi as treating his team as a family, while often neglecting his own.

41. Gems, *Sport and the Shaping of Italian American Identity*, 191–92.

42. Sue Ter Mat, "After Years of Waiting, Gene Melchiorre Finally in High School's Hall of Fame," *Chicago Tribune*, January 16, 2012 (accessed January 25, 2014).

43. Gems, *Sport and the Shaping of Italian American Identity*, 180–217.

## 12. Jewish Institutions and Women's Sport

I am thankful for support received from the Burnham-MacMillan History Endowment Grant, Western Michigan University, for facilitating travel to archives for research for this project. I also am appreciative of the grant for the Support for Faculty Scholars Award, Office of the Vice President for Research, Western Michigan University, for travel for research. I thank the archivists and librarians who assisted me with access to the archival collections.

1. B. A. Loeb, "The Temple of the Body: How the Hebrew Institute Is Laboring to Make Jews Physically Fit," *Sentinel*, May 1, 1914; Jacob M. Loeb Collection, Chicago Hebrew Institute (hereafter cited as CHI); Jacob Marcus Rader Center of the American Jewish Archives, Cincinnati, OH (AJA); see "The Jew as an Athlete," *American Hebrew* 101 (May 11, 1917): 101.

2. C. Baum, P. Hyman, and S. Michel, *The Jewish Woman in America* (New York: Plume Books, 1977), 190, 199–200, 214–15, 223.

3. Riv-Ellen Prell, "Rage and Representation: Jewish Gender Stereotypes in American Culture," in *American Jewish Women's History: A Reader*, ed. Pamela S. Nadell (New York: New York University Press, 2003), 238, 248.

4. Steven A. Riess, "Anti-Semitism and Sport in Central Europe and the United States, c. 1870–1932," in *Jews in the Gym: Judaism, Sports, and Athletics*, ed. Leonard Greenspoon, vol. 23, Studies in Jewish Civilization (West Lafayette, IN: Purdue University Press 2012), 97–98.

5. Riess, "Anti-Semitism and Sport," 102.

6. "The JWB Story of Health and Physical Education," Box 6, Winkler, Oliver, Health and Physical Education, 1, National Jewish Welfare Board Records, I-337 (hereafter JWB), American Jewish Historical Society, New York, NY and Boston, MA (hereafter AJHS).

7. See such studies as Annette R. Hofmann, ed., *Turnen and Sport: Transatlantic Transfers* (New York: Waxman Muenster, 2004), and Hofmann, "Lady *Turners* in the United States:

German American Identity, Gender Concerns, and *Turnerism*," *Journal of Sport History* 27, no. 3 (Fall 2000): 383–404; see Gerald R. Gems, "Sports and Identity in Chicago," in *Sports in Chicago*, ed. Elliott J. Gorn (Urbana: University of Illinois Press, 2008), 1–18, and Gems, *Windy City Wars: Labor, Leisure, and Sport in the Making of Chicago* (Lanham, MD: Scarecrow Press, 1997).

8. Linda J. Borish, "'Athletic Activities of Various Kinds': Physical Health and Sport Programs for Jewish American Women," *Journal of Sport History* 26, no. 2 (Summer 1992): 241.

9. Benjamin G. Rader, "The Quest for Subcommunities and the Rise of American Sport," *American Quarterly* 29 (Fall 1977): 355–69; see Linda J. Borish for discussion about historical issues and the place of Jewish women in American sport history in "Jewish American Women and Sport, 1880–1940s: An Historical Overview and Perspectives," in *Sport and Physical Education in the History of the Jewish Nation*, ed. George Eisen, Haim Kaufman, and Manfred Laemmer, Selected Papers from an International Seminar Held on the Occasion of the 16th Maccabiah, 12–15, 2001 Wingate Institute, Israel (Netanya, Israel: Wingate Institute, 2003), 56–69.

10. On Jewish immigration to America in the Progressive Era, see Gerald Sorin, *A Time for Building: The Third Migration, 1880–1920*, vol. 3, of The Jewish People in America, ed. Henry L. Feingold (Baltimore: Johns Hopkins University Press, 1995), 62–63, and Naomi W. Cohen, *Encounter with Emancipation: The German Jews in the United States, 1830–1914* (Philadelphia: Jewish Publication Society, 1984). For the immigration of Jewish women in America, selected works include Hyman, *Gender and Assimilation in Modern Jewish History* (Seattle: University of Washington Press, 1995); Rudolf Glanz, *The Jewish Woman in America: Two Immigrant Generations, 1820–1929*, vols. 1 and 2 (n.p. 1976); Hasia R. Diner, *A Time for Gathering: The Second Migration, 1820–1880*, vol. 2, of The Jewish People in America, ed. Henry L. Feingold; Barbara A. Schrier, *Becoming American Women: Clothing and the Jewish Immigrant Experience, 1880–1920* (Chicago: Chicago Historical Society, 1994); Andrew R. Heinze, *Adapting to Abundance: Jewish Immigrants, Mass Consumption, and the Search for American Identity* (New York: Columbia University Press, 1990); Elizabeth Ewen, *Immigrant Women in the Land of Dollars: Life and Culture on the Lower East Side, 1890–1925* (New York: Monthly Review Books, 1985).

11. Donna Gabaccia, *From the Other Side: Women, Gender and Immigrant Life in the US, 1820–1920* (Bloomington: Indiana University Press, 1994), xi.

12. See M. R. Nelson, "Basketball as Cultural Capital: The Original Celtics in Early Twentieth-Century New York City," in *Sporting Nationalisms: Identity, Ethnicity, Immigration and Assimilation*, ed. M. Cronin and D. Mayall (London: Frank Cass, 1998), 74. This collection of essays focuses on men in sport and issues of ethnicity in various countries. For a discussion of other works focusing on Jewish men and sport history, see for example, Steven A. Riess, ed., *Sports and the American Jew* (Syracuse, NY: Syracuse University Press, 1998); Jeffery S. Gurock, *Judaism's Encounter with American Sports* (Bloomington: Indiana University Press, 2005); *Beyond Stereotypes: American Jews and Sports*, University of Southern California Casden Institute for the Study of the Jewish Role in America Life, Annual Review, Volume 12. Editors, Bruce Zuckerman, Ari F. Sclar (guest editor), and Lisa Ansell (West Lafayette, IN: Purdue University Press, 2014).

13. Linda J. Borish, "Jewish Sportswomen," in *Jews and American Popular Culture*, vol. 3, Sports, Leisure, and Lifestyle, ed. Paul Buhle (Westport, CT: Praeger, 2006), 73.

14. Borish, "Jewish Sportswomen," 73–74.

15. "Hebrew Technical School for Girls," *American Hebrew* 83 (October 2, 1908): 537.

16. Borish, "Jewish Sportswomen," 74.

17. Borish, "Jewish Sportswomen," 74.

18. "Training for Womanhood. An Institution on the East Side That Lives Up to Its Ideals," *American Hebrew* 106 (November 28, 1919): 43–44.

19. "Adolph Lewisohn Heads H.T.S.G. Famous Philanthropist Accepts Post Held for 25 Years by the Late Nathanial Myers," *American Hebrew* 96 (November 4, 1921): 109, 669.

20. Quoted in Linda J. Borish, "Jewish American Women, Jewish Organizations, and Sports, 1880–1940," in *Sports and the American Jew*, ed. Steven A. Riess (Syracuse, NY: Syracuse University Press, 1998), 109.

21. Borish, "Jewish American Women, Jewish Organizations, and Sports, 1880–1940," 109–10.

22. Information on the St. Louis Educational Alliance may be found, for example, in Linda J. Borish, "Place, Identity, Physical Culture and Sport for Women in Jewish Americanization Organizations," in STADION: *Internationale Zeitschrift für Geschichte des Sports/International Journal of the History of Sport/ Revue International d' Histoire du Sport* 35 (2009): 87–108.

23. Charles S. Bernheimer, "Jewish Americanization Agencies," *American Jewish Year Book*, 5682, vol. 23, October 3, 1921–September 22, 1922 (Philadelphia: Jewish Publication Society of America, 1921), 105–6; for information on the important role of the Baron de Hirsch Fund, see Samuel Joseph, *History of the Baron de Hirsch Fund: The Americanization of the Jewish Immigrant* (Philadelphia: Jewish Publication Society of America, 1935); Gerald Sorin, *A Time for Building: The Third Migration, 1880–1920*, vol. 3, of The Jewish People in America, ed. Henry L. Feingold, 44, 49, 60, and Naomi W. Cohen, *Encounter with Emancipation: The German Jews in the United States, 1830–1914* (Philadelphia: Jewish Publication Society, 1984).

24. *New York World*, April 25, 1897, Box 3, Baroness de Hirsch—Correspondence, Clippings, Biographical Information, 1896–1899, Baron de Hirsch Fund Records, I-80.

25. Bernheimer, "Jewish Americanization Agencies," 249; Nancy B. Sinkoff, "Educating for 'Proper' Jewish Womanhood: A Case Study in Domesticity and Vocational Training, 1897–1926," *American Jewish History* 77 (June 1988): 576–77; quote from Baroness Clara De Hirsch in 1896 letter to Oscar Straus, in Sinkoff, "Educating for 'Proper' Jewish Womanhood," 576.

26. "Home for Working Girls," *New York World*, April 25, 1897; "The Clara De Hirsch Home," *New York Times*, May 23, 1899, Box 3, Baroness de Hirsch—Correspondence, Clippings, Biographical Information, 1896–1899, Baron de Hirsch Fund Records, I-80, AJHS.

27. "The Clara de Hirsch Home," Box 3, Baroness de Hirsch—Correspondence, Clippings, Biographical Information, 1896–1899, Baron de Hirsch Fund Records, I-80, AJHS.

28. "The Clara de Hirsch Home," Box 3, Baroness de Hirsch—Correspondence, Clippings, Biographical Information, 1896–1899, Baron de Hirsch Fund Records, I-80, AJHS.

29. Sorin, "A Time for Building," 89; Charlotte Baum, Paula Hyman, and Sonya Michel, *The Jewish Woman in America* (New York: Plume Books, 1977), 169; for information about some of the Jewish settlements and organizations advocating physical health and sport for Jewish women and girls, see Borish, "Jewish American Women, Jewish Organizations, and Sports, 1880–1940," 105–31, and Borish, "'Athletic Activities of Various Kinds,'" 240–70; for a history of the National Council of Jewish Women and its founding, see Faith Rogow, "Gone to Another Meeting: The National Council of Jewish Women, 1893–1993," in *American Jewish Women's History: A Reader*, ed. Pamela S. Nadell (New York: New York University Press, 2003), 64–74, and Jonathan D. Sarna, "A Great Awakening: The Transformation That Shaped Twentieth-Century American Judaism," in *American Jewish Women's History*, 55–56.

30. Rose Summerfield, *Report of the Directress,* The Clara de Hirsch Home for Working Girls, 1901, 46, Clara de Hirsch Home for Working Girls Papers, 92nd Street Young Men's-Young Women's Hebrew Association Archives, New York, NY (hereafter as 92nd St. YM-YWHA Archives); Mrs. Oscar S. Straus, *Report of the President,* The Clara de Hirsch Home for Working Girls, 1900–1901, 32–32; Clara de Hirsch Home for Working Girls materials, Dorot Jewish Division, New York Public Library, New York, NY (hereafter as NYPL).

31. Report of the Clara de Hirsch Home, 1914, 23, Dorot Jewish Division, NYPL; Sinkoff, "Educating for 'Proper' Jewish Womanhood," 591–92.

32. Report June 10, 1910, Viola Eckstein, Assistant Superintendent, Clara de Hirsch Home for Working Girls, 1–2, Clara de Hirsch Home for Working Girls Papers, 92nd St. YM-YWHA Archives.

33. Clara de Hirsch Home, Minutes, October 1911; Rose Summerfield, Report March 1916, Clara de Hirsch Home, 1, 5, Clara de Hirsch Home for Working Girls Papers, 92nd Street YM-YWHA Archives; see Sinkoff's "Educating for 'Proper' Jewish Womanhood" for information on other classes and concerns about the girls' activities at the Clara de Hirsch Home.

34. Rose Summerfield, Report November 1919, Clara de Hirsch Home, 1; Report June–July–August 1922, 1–2, Clara de Hirsch Home for Working Girls Papers, 92nd St. YM-YWHA Archives.

35. Rose Summerfield, Report November 1920, Clara de Hirsch Home, 1; Report April 1924, 1; Bessie B. Spanner, Report November 1925, 1, Clara de Hirsch Home for Working Girls Papers, 92nd St. YM-YWHA Archives. For information on the sports offered at the YWHA's Ray Hill Camp, see Borish, "Jewish American Women, Jewish Organizations, and Sports, 1880-1940," 123–25.

36. Bessie N. Rothschild, transcription of interview, March 25, 1986, the William E. Wiener Oral History Library of the American Jewish Committee, 1, 3–4, Dorot Jewish Division, NYPL.

37. Bessie N. Rothschild, transcription of interview, March 25, 1986, the William E. Wiener Oral History Library of the American Jewish Committee, 9–10, 12, 23, Dorot Jewish Division, NYPL; *Building Character for 75 Years, 1874–1949: Published on the Occasion of the 75th Anniversary of the Young Men's & Young Women's Hebrew Association,* (New York: Young Men's & Young Women's Hebrew Association, 1949), 15–16, 21, and *Addendum 1949–1964, Young Men's and Young Women's Hebrew Association,* Lexington Avenue at 92nd Street, New York City, 7–8, 92nd Street YM-YWHA Archives.

38. Young Women's Hebrew Association, *Fifth Annual Report of the President,* February 1908, 2, 12, YWHA Records, 92nd Street YM-YWHA Archives; Unterberg, "The Y.W.H.A.," 59.

39. Young Women's Hebrew Association, "Class Report," January1–February 1, 1911, YWHA Records, 92nd Street YM-YWHA Archives. See Linda J. Borish, "'An interest in Physical Well-Being among the Feminine Membership': Sporting Activities for Women at Young Men's and Young Women's Hebrew Associations," *American Jewish History* 87 (March 1999):; see also D. Kaufman, *Shul with a Pool: The "Synagogue-Center" in American Jewish History* (Hanover: University Press of New England, 1999), for information about the philosophy of YMHA-YWHAs and this early YWHA in New York City.

40. Young Women's Hebrew Association, *Fifth Annual Report of the President,* February 1908, 2, 12; Unterberg, "The Y.W.H.A.," 59.

41. Young Women's Hebrew Association, *Twentieth Anniversary Luncheon and Annual Meeting,* February 28, 1922, 5; Young Women's Hebrew Association, *Twenty-Fifth Anniversary,*

*1902–1927; Twenty-Fourth Annual Report, January 1927*, 16–17; "New Home for Girls' Club," *New York Times*, April 26, 1914, YWHA Records, 92nd Street YM-YWHA Archives; "Unterberg, Bella," *Who's Who in American Jewry, 1926* (New York, 1927), 624; "Unterberg, Mrs. Israel," *The American Jewish Year Book*, 5697 (1936–37), 38: 436.

42. *Building Character for 75 Years*, 21, 22

43. Unterberg, "The Y.W.H.A.," 57, 59. Mrs. Israel Unterberg not only served as president of the New York City YWHA but also was chairman of the Women's Work Committee of the Council of the Young Men's Hebrew Kindred Associations and provided advice to various Jewish communities about extending the work of the Young Women's Hebrew Association. For general discussion about the mission of the Young Women's Hebrew Association and the YWHA programs, see David Kaufman, "Young Women's Hebrew Association," in *Jewish Women in America: A Historical Encyclopedia*, vol. 2, ed. Paula E. Hyman and Deborah Dash Moore (New York: Routledge, 1997), 1536–40. Kaufman, *Shul with a Pool*, explores the religious and communal activities in some YM-YWHAs although he provides little information about the physical education and sport activities for Jewish women, and Benjamin Rabinowitz, *The Young Men's Hebrew Association, 1854-1913* (New York, 1948), presents the history of the YWHA and some ladies auxiliaries.

44. *Building Character for 75 Years*, 21, 22.

45. "New Home for Girls' Club," 92nd Street YM-YWHA Archives; see also Frances Kahn, "Live a Little Longer," *Kol Alamoth* 1 (June 1915): 10, YWHA Records, 92nd Street YM-YWHA Archives.

46. Young Women's Hebrew Association, *Thirteenth Annual Report*, February 1916, 12, 13; "New Home for Girls' Club," YWHA Records, 92nd Street YM-YWHA Archives; "Second Triennial Convention, Conference: Girls' and Women's Work," *Publications of the Council of YMH and Kindred Associations*, November 1916, and see *Building Character for 75 Years*. For information on the various YM and YWHAs and the athletic facilities and sport and physical education programs for Jewish women, see Borish, "'An Interest in Physical Well-Being among the Feminine Membership,'" 61–93; Borish, "Women, Sports, and American Jewish Identity in the Late Nineteenth and Early Twentieth Centuries," in *With God on Their Side: Sport in the Service of Religion*, ed. Tara Magdalinksi and Timothy J. L. Chandler (London: Routledge, 2002), 71–98. On the YMHA movement and also some of the early YWHA affiliations, see Rabinowitz, *The Young Men's Hebrew Association*, and Riess, *Sports and the American Jew*.

47. Quoted in Borish, "Jewish Sportswomen," 85–86.

48. "Cornerstone of New Building to Be Laid October 25th at 2:00 P.M.," *The Y Journal* 8 (October 23, 1925): 4, Box 1, Young Men's and Young Women's Hebrew Association, St. Louis, MO, Collection, 1924–1953, I-419, AJHS; "Physical Department Increases Its Facilities," *The Y Journal, Silver Jubilee, 1927–1952* (May 16, 1952): 10, Philadelphia Jewish Archives Center, The Balch Institute for Ethnic Studies, Philadelphia, PA.

49. Young Women's Hebrew Association, Thirteenth Annual Report, February 1916, 12–13; Twenty-Fifth Anniversary, 1902–1927: Twenty-Fourth Annual Report, January 1927, 22; Young Women's Hebrew Association Bulletin of Classes, ca. 1920s, Printed Materials, YWHA Records, 92nd Street YM-YWHA Archives; see Borish for a discussion of some of the development of this New York City YWHA and other YWHAs, "'An Interest in Physical Well-Being among the Feminine Membership,'" 61–93; for other Jewish organizations promoting Jewish identity for Jewish women and girls in sport and some of the high-level American Jewish women athletes see, too, Borish, "Women, Sport and American Jewish Identity in the Late Nineteenth and Early Twentieth Centuries," in *With God on Their Side: Sport in the*

*Service of Religion*, ed. Tara Magdalinksi and Timothy J. L. Chandler (London: Routledge Press, 2002), 71–98.

50. Young Women's Hebrew Association, *Bulletin of Classes, 1916–1917*, 92nd Street YM-YWHA Archives; "Conference: Girls' and Women's Work," *Second Triennial Convention, Council of Y.M.H. and Kindred Associations*, Publications of the Council of Y.M.H. and Kindred Associations, Document No. 3 (November 1916), 10.

51. "New Home for Girls' Club," 92nd Street YM-YWHA Archives.

52. "Hows and Whys of Big Burg's Y's. 110th Street Y.W.H.A. Has Most Comprehensive Physical Education System of Type in Entire Country," *New York Post*, January 17, 1936, Newspaper Clippings, YWHA Records, 92nd Street YM-YWHA Archives.

53. Young Women's Hebrew Association, Thirteenth Annual Report, 36–37; The Story of Six Years' Work of the Young Women's Hebrew Association 1919 through 1924, February 1924, 21, 92nd Street YM-YWHA Archives.

54. Young Women's Hebrew Association, Thirteenth Annual Report, February 1916, 12–3; Twenty-Fifth Anniversary, 1902–1927: Twenty-Fourth Annual Report, January 1927, 22; Young Women's Hebrew Association Bulletin of Classes, ca. 1920s, Printed Materials, YWHA Records, 92nd Street YM-YWHA Archives; Linda J. Borish, "Young Women's Hebrew Association," *Encyclopedia of Ethnicity and Sports in the United States*, ed. George B. Kirsch et al. (Westport, CT, 2000), 502–4.

55. Young Women's Hebrew Association, Thirteenth Annual Report, 36–37; The Story of Six Years' Work of the Young Women's Hebrew Association 1919 through 1924 (February 1924), 21, YWHA Records, 92nd Street YM-YWHA Archives.

56. Young Women's Hebrew Association, The Story of Six Years' Work of the Young Women's Hebrew Association 1919 through 1924, 21, 92nd Street YM-YWHA Archives.

57. Young Women's Hebrew Association, *Bulletin of Classes, 1916–1917*; YWHA Scrapbooks, 1920s, 1923, and 1930s, YWHA Records, 92nd Street YM-YWHA Archives. On the popularity of the Annette Kellerman swimming suit, see "Annette Swings Back . . ." *Daily Telegraph*, February 8, 1975, 5; Shirley Elizabeth Hill, "The Bikini, Where Less Is More," *Reader's Digest*, August 1987; Benjamin G. Rader, *American Sports: From the Age of Folk Games to the Age of Televised Sports* (Englewood Cliffs, NJ, 1996), 127.

58. On Charlotte Epstein, see Linda J. Borish, "'The Cradle of American Champions, Women Champions . . . Swim Champions': Charlotte Epstein, Gender and Jewish Identity, and the Physical Emancipation of Women in Aquatic Sports," *International Journal of the History of Sport* 21, no. 2 (March 2004): 197–235.

59. "Heights Girl, Leader of 'Mermaids,' Praise Home News Campaign for Swimming Pool," ca. 1917, W.S.A. Scrapbook, 1915–17; "A Brief History of the Women's Swimming Association of N.Y.," Charlotte Epstein File, Women's Swimming Association Archives, International Swimming Hall of Fame, The Henning Library, Ft. Lauderdale, Fla. (hereafter WSA Archives, ISHOF).

60. Linda J. Borish, telephone interview with Aileen Riggin Soule about Charlotte Epstein, June 1995; "A Word of Thanks," *W.S.A. News* (March 1921): 1; "Program of the National Championship Meet, Women's Swimming Association of New York at the Young Women's Hebrew Association, March 13, 1920," WSA Archives, ISHOF; see National Swimming Championship Flyer and Entry Form 1923, YWHA Scrapbook, 92nd Street YM-YWHA Archives. On Charlotte Epstein see Linda J. Borish, "Charlotte Epstein," in *Jewish Women in America: An Historical Encyclopedia*, ed. Paula E. Hyman and Deborah Dash Moore (New York: Routledge, 1997), 380–82, and Paula D. Welch and Harold A. Lerch, "The Women's

Swimming Association Launches America into Swimming Supremacy," *The Olympian* (March 1979): 14–16.

61. Borish, telephone interview with Aileen Riggin Soule about Charlotte Epstein, June 1995; "Teams Notes," *W.S.A. News* 4 (January 1924): 5, in WSA Archives, ISHOF; see also National Swimming Championship Flyer and Entry Form 1923, YWHA Scrapbook, 92nd Street YM-YWHA Archives.

62. Linda J. Borish, "Jewish Women in the American Gym: Basketball, Ethnicity and Gender in the Early Twentieth Century," in *Jews in the Gym: Judaism, Sports, and Athletics*, ed. Leonard Greenspoon, vol. 23, Studies in Jewish Civilization (West Lafayette, IN: Purdue University Press 2012), 213–37.

63. Peter Levine, *Ellis Island to Ebbets Field: Sport and the American Jewish Experience* (New York: Oxford University Press, 1992), 27.

64. Levine, *Ellis Island to Ebbets Field*, 35.

65. See Borish, "Jewish Sportswomen" and "Jewish American Women, Jewish Organizations, and Sports, 1880–1940"; on Berenson's career, see Ralph Melnick, *Senda Berenson: The Unlikely Founder of Women's Basketball* (Amherst: University of Massachusetts Press, 2007).

66. Young Women's Hebrew Association, Printed Materials of Class Activities, February 1934, 92nd Street YM-YWHA Archives.

67. Young Women's Hebrew Association, *Twenty-Fifth Anniversary Young Women's Hebrew Association, New York City, January 1927*, 22, 92nd Street YM-YWHA Archives; see "Personalities in Sports," *American Hebrew* 115 (June 6, 1924): 126.

68. Young Women's Hebrew Association, Twentieth Anniversary Luncheon and Annual Meeting Young Women's Hebrew Association, February 28, 1922 (New York, 1922) 5, 92nd Street YM-YWHA Archives.

## 13. Boxing in Olde New York

1. Michael B. Katz and Mark J. Stern, "Poverty in Twentieth-Century America," Working Paper No. 7, November 2007, 6.

2. Steven A. Riess, *City Games: The Evolution of American Urban Society and the Rise of Sports* (Urbana: University of Illinois Press, 1989), 116.

3. Mike Silver, *The Arc of Boxing: The Rise and Decline of the Sweet Science* (Jefferson, NC: McFarland, 2008), 26.

4. Silver, *The Arc of Boxing*, 35.

5. Ronald K. Fried, *Corner Men: Great Boxing Trainers* (New York: Four Walls Eight Windows, 1991), 43.

6. Lawrence S. Ritter, *East Side West Side: Tales of New York Sporting Life, 1910–1960* (Kansas City: Total Sports, 1998), 183.

7. Murray Rose, "Farewell to Stillman's," *Boxing Illustrated & Wrestling News* (October 1961), p. 21.

8. Ritter, *East Side West Side*, 183.

9. Ritter, *East Side West Side*, 182.

10. Rose, *Boxing Illustrated*, 20.

11. Fried, *Corner Men*, 52.

12. Fried, *Corner Men*, 32.

## 14. Toots Shor

I need to thank Skidmore College for its support of this chapter and Stephen Norwood, Greg Pfitzer, and Susan Taylor for their patience and good counsel.

1. "300 Faithful Cry in Beer for Shor's," *New York Times*, June 24, 1959, 33.
2. Charles Champlin, "A Laugh and a Tear for Toots," *Life*, July 6, 1959, 84.
3. Quoted in Champlin, "A Laugh and a Tear for Toots," 84, 87.
4. "They All Went To Toots's," *Sports Illustrated*, July 27, 1959, 32.
5. John Bainbridge, *The Wonderful World of Toots Shor* (Boston: Houghton Mifflin, 1951), 14.
6. Red Smith, "World's Greatest Saloonkeeper," *New York Times*, December 24, 1976, 13.
7. Bainbridge, *The Wonderful World of Toots Shor*, 1.
8. "They All Went To Toots's," 32.
9. Bob Considine, *Toots* (New York: Meredith Press, 1969), 1, 4.
10. Considine, *Toots*, 1, 4.
11. Considine, *Toots*, 4.
12. Quoted in Considine, *Toots*, 5.
13. *Toots*, DVD, directed by Kristi Jacobson (2006, Catalyst Films).
14. Considine, *Toots*, 5.
15. Considine, *Toots*, 8.
16. Considine, *Toots*, 12.
17. Considine, *Toots*, 15.
18. *Toots*.
19. Considine, *Toots*, 17.
20. Red Smith, "Toots Shor and Off-Track Betting," *Atlanta Constitution*, February 15, 1975, 2C.
21. Considine, *Toots*, 42.
22. Considine, *Toots*, 42.
23. Considine, *Toots*, 42.
24. Considine, *Toots*, 36.
25. Bainbridge, *The Wonderful World of Toots Shor*, 73.
26. Considine, *Toots*, 47.
27. Quoted in *Toots*.
28. Considine, *Toots*, 53.
29. See *New York Times*, May 1, 1940, 1, 33.
30. Bainbridge, *The Wonderful World of Toots Shor*, 41.
31. Bainbridge, *The Wonderful World of Toots Shor*, 40–41.
32. Bainbridge, *The Wonderful World of Toots Shor*, 41.
33. Bainbridge, *The Wonderful World of Toots Shor*, 45.
34. Andrew F. Smith, "Stork Club," in *Savoring Gotham: A Food Lover's Companion to New York City*, ed. Andrew F. Smith (New York: Oxford University Press, 2015), 570.
35. Jody Rosen, "A Pal to Stars, Mobsters and Other Crumb Bums," *New York Times*, September 17, 2007, E6.
36. Considine, *Toots*, 199.
37. Considine, *Toots*, 6.
38. Quoted in Considine, Toots, 6. See Irving Howe, *World of Our Fathers: The Journey of the East European Jews to America and the Life They Found and Made* (New York: Simon and Schuster, 1983 [1976]), 182.

39. Considine, *Toots*, 4.

40. Considine, *Toots*, 10–11.

41. Daniel Okrent, "Introduction," in *American Pastimes: The Very Best of Red Smith*, ed. Daniel Okrent (New York: Library of America, 2013), xxi.

42. Bainbridge, *The Wonderful World of Toots Shor*, 13.

43. Clifford Geertz, "Deep Play: Notes on the Balinese Cockfight," *Daedalus* 101 (Winter 1972): 4.

44. Bainbridge, *The Wonderful World of Toots Shor*, 13.

45. Bainbridge, *The Wonderful World of Toots Shor*, 14.

46. Quoted in *Toots*.

47. Bainbridge, *The Wonderful World of Toots Shor*, 15.

48. Quoted in *Toots*.

49. Quoted in *Toots*.

50. Quoted in *Toots*.

51. Quoted in Considine, *Toots*, 174.

52. Considine, *Toots*, 173.

53. Dennis Gaffney, "Bernard 'Toots' Shor," http://www.pbs.org/wgbh/amex/dimaggio/peopleevents/pande05.html (accessed February 22, 2017).

54. Bainbridge, *The Wonderful World of Toots Shor*, 76.

55. Quoted in *Toots*.

56. Quoted in *Toots*.

57. Quoted in *Toots*.

58. Fred Russell, *Bury Me in an Old Press Box: The Good Life and Times of a Sportswriter* (New York: A. S. Barnes and Company, 1957), 223.

59. Quoted in *Toots*.

60. Quoted in Considine, *Toots*, 118.

61. "Shor Razes Cafe," *New York Times*, August 5, 1959, 31.

62. *Toots*.

63. Quoted in Considine, *Toots*, 188.

64. Alfred E. Clark, "Tax Lien Forced Toots Shor's to Close," *New York Times*, April 3, 1971, 33.

65. Dave Anderson, "Toots Shor, 73, 'Saloonkeeper' and Host, Dies," *New York Times*, January 24, 1977, 1, 26.

66. Pamela G. Hollie, "The Family That Feeds New York," *New York Times*, October 30, 1983, F4.

67. Joseph Durso, "500 Attend Service for Toots Shor," *New York Times*, January 27, 1977, 38.

68. Quoted in Durso, "500 Attend Service for Toots Shor," 38.

69. Red Smith, "Toots's Guys Were Waiting for Him," *New York Times*, January 26, 1977, 17.

70. Considine, *Toots*, 202.

71. Christopher Sharp, "Golden Brush: Playboy Illustrator LeRoy Neiman," August 12, 2012, http://www.ivy-style.com/golden-brush-playboy-illustrator-leroy-neiman.html (accessed February 27, 2017).

72. Leroy Neiman, *All Told: My Art and Life among Athletes, Playboys, Bunnies, and Provocateurs* (Guilford, CT: Lyons Press, 2012), 276, 277.

73. Red Smith, "Tribute to a Saloonkeeper," *New York Times*, December 1, 1977, 53.

74. Quoted in Smith, "Tribute to a Saloonkeeper."

75. Michiko Kakutani, "A Prescient Novel Retains Its Power," *New York Times*, July 15, 2011, C25.

76. Ray Robinson, *The Home Run Heard 'Round the World* (Mineola, NY: Dover Publications, 2011), 241.

77. Don DeLillo, *Underworld* (New York: Scribner, 1998), 18, 699.

78. DeLillo, *Underworld*, 18.

79. DeLillo, *Underworld*, 29.

80. DeLillo, *Underworld*, 46.

81. Considine, *Toots*, 1.

82. See Daphne Spain, *Gendered Spaces* (Chapel Hill: University of North Carolina Press, 1992).

83. "They All Went to Toots's," 32.

84. Quoted in *Toots*.

# Contributors

**Stephen H. Norwood** (PhD, Columbia University) is professor of history at the University of Oklahoma. He is the author of five books, most recently *Antisemitism and the American Far Left* (2013) and *The Third Reich in the Ivory Tower: Complicity and Conflict on American Campuses* (2009), which was a Finalist for the National Jewish Book Award for Holocaust Studies. His book *Labor's Flaming Youth* won the Herbert G. Gutman Award for American Social History. Norwood coedited (with Eunice G. Pollack) the prize-winning two-volume *Encyclopedia of American Jewish History* (2008). He has published numerous scholarly articles in American social, labor, sport, gender, Jewish, and African American history. His sport history publications include *Real Football: Conversations on America's Game* and articles in several anthologies, *Journal of Sport History,* and *Modern Judaism.* He was co-winner of the Macmillan/SABR Award in Baseball History.

**Linda J. Borish** is associate professor in the History Department and Gender and Women's Studies Department at Western Michigan University. She is the lead editor of *The Routledge History of American Sport* (2017) and coauthor of *Sports in American History: From Colonization to Globalization* (2017). She has published chapters in numerous books, including *Sports in Chicago; Sports and the American Jew; Jews in the Gym: Judaism, Sports, and Athletics; A Companion to American Sport History.* Her scholarly articles have been published in the *Journal of Sport History,* the *International Journal of the History of Sport, Rethinking History: The Journal of Theory and Practice, American Jewish History,* and others. Borish is executive producer/historian of *Jewish Women in American Sport: Settlement Houses to the Olympics,* a documentary film (2007), and is a research associate of the Hadassah-Brandeis Institute, Brandeis University.

**Henry D. Fetter** is the author of *Taking on the Yankees: Winning and Losing in the Business of Baseball.* His writing has appeared in the *New York Times, Wall Street Journal, Times Literary Supplement, New York History, Journal of Sport History, National Pastime,* and *Transatlantica,* the Atlantic Online and History News Network. He is a recipient of the Kerr History Prize from the New York

State Historical Society and the McFarland-SABR Baseball Research Award from the Society for American Baseball Research. He is a graduate of Harvard Law School, has practiced business and entertainment litigation in Los Angeles, and also holds degrees in history from Harvard College and the University of California, Berkeley.

**Gerald R. Gems** is a professor of kinesiology at North Central College in Naperville, Illinois. He is the past president of the North American Society for Sport History, the current vice president of the International Society for the History of Physical Education and Sport, a Fulbright Scholar, and winner of the international Routledge Award for scholarship. He is the author/editor of nineteen books.

**Dennis Gildea**, a former sportswriter, is a professor of communications at Springfield College, the birthplace of basketball. In addition to articles on sport and sport media, he is the author of *Hoop Crazy: The Lives of Clair Bee and Chip Hilton.*

**Jeffrey S. Gurock** is the Libby M. Klaperman Professor of Jewish History at Yeshiva University.

**George B. Kirsch** is emeritus professor of History at Manhattan College. His most recent books are *Six Guys from Hackensack: Coming of Age in the Real New Jersey* (2012); *Golf in America* (2009); *Baseball in Blue and Gray: The National Pastime during the Civil War* (2003; 2007); and *The Creation of American Team Sports: Baseball and Cricket, 1838–72* (1989; 2007). He is also the author of many scholarly articles and book reviews and a few magazine articles.

**Bennett Liebman** is a government lawyer in residence and an adjunct professor of law at Albany Law School. He previously served as the executive director of Albany Law School's Government Law Center and as the deputy secretary to the New York State Governor for Gaming and Racing. He is the author of numerous articles on horse racing, gambling, government ethics, and New York State history. He has served as a columnist for the *Daily Racing Form* and *Hoof Beats,* and as a regular contributor to the *New York Times* Rail Blog. In 2012, he was the recipient of the New York State Bar Association's award for excellence in public service.

**Daniel A. Nathan** is professor and chair of American Studies at Skidmore College, the author of the award-winning *Saying It's So: A Cultural History of the Black Sox Scandal* (2003), and the editor of *Rooting for the Home Team: Sport, Community and Identity* (2013) and *Baltimore Sports: Stories from Charm City* (2016). He is past president of the North American Society for Sport History and the recipient of several honors, including a National Endowment for the Humanities Fellowship and a Fulbright Fellowship.

**Eunice G. Pollack** (PhD, Columbia University) is a professor of history and Jewish Studies at the University of North Texas. Recent publications include *Racializing Antisemitism: Black Militants, Jews, and Israel, 1950–Present* (2013); "From a Pariah People to a Pariah State" and "Foundation Myths of Anti-Zionism" in Eunice G. Pollack, ed., *From Antisemitism to Anti-Zionism: The Past and Present of a Lethal Ideology* (2017); "African Americans and the Legitimization of Antisemitism on the Campus" in Eunice G. Pollack, ed., *Antisemitism on the Campus: Past & Present* (2011). She is the editor of the series Antisemitism in America (Academic Studies Press) and coeditor (with Stephen H. Norwood) of the prize-winning two-volume *Encyclopedia of American Jewish History* (2008).

**Steven A. Riess** is a Bernard Brommel Research Professor, emeritus, at Northeastern Illinois University. The former editor of the *Journal of Sport History*, he is the author of several books including *Sports in Industrial America* (2nd ed.); *The Sport of Kings and the Kings of Crime; Horse Racing, Politics, and Crime in New York, 1865–1913; Touching Base: Professional Baseball and American Culture in the Progressive Era*, rev. ed.; and *City Games: The Evolution of American Society and the Rise of Sports.*

**Mike Silver** is a boxing historian. He is the author of *The Arc of Boxing: The Rise and Decline of the Sweet Science* (2008) and *Stars in the Ring: Jewish Champions in the Golden Age of Boxing: A Photographic History* (2016). Silver is a former inspector with the New York State Athletic Commission and has served as historical consultant and on-air commentator for nineteen televised boxing documentaries. In 2004 he was curator at the National Museum of American Jewish History for the exhibit, "Sting Like a Maccabee: The Golden Age of the American Jewish Boxer." He currently serves as an advisor to the Hank Kaplan Boxing Archives at Brooklyn College and is a member of the International Boxing Research Organization. His website is mikesilverboxing.com.

**Maureen M. Smith** is a professor in the Department of Kinesiology and Health Science at California State University, Sacramento, where she teaches sport history and sociology of sport. Smith is the coauthor (with Rita Liberti) of *(Re)Presenting Wilma Rudolph* (2015), the North American Society for Sport History Book Award winner in 2016. Smith coedited (with Liberti) *San Francisco Bay Area Sports: Golden Gate Athletics, Recreation, and Community* (2017).

**Robert C. Trumpbour** is associate professor of communications at Pennsylvania State University, Altoona College. He is coauthor of *The Eighth Wonder of the World: The Life of Houston's Iconic Astrodome* and author of *The New Cathedrals: Politics and Media in the History of Stadium Construction.* He is coeditor of *The Rise of Stadiums in the Modern United States: Cathedrals of Sport.* He has taught at Pennsylvania State University, Southern Illinois University, Saint Francis University, and Western Illinois University. Prior to teaching, he worked in various capacities at CBS in New York for the television and radio networks.

# Index